The Reader

A STUDY OF FORM AND CONTENT

William O. S. **SUTHERLAND, Jr.**

Robert L. **MONTGOMERY, Jr.**

University
of
Texas

The Reader

A STUDY OF FORM AND CONTENT

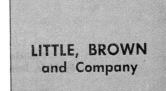

LITTLE, BROWN
and Company

BOSTON · TORONTO

Published simultaneously in Canada
by Little, Brown & Company (Canada) Limited

PRINTED IN THE UNITED STATES OF AMERICA

Preface

GOOD WRITING AND INTELLIGENT READING are clearly connected; both depend upon an awareness of the uses of language for the expression of thought.

This is a "reader" designed to provide a systematic analysis of words and their uses, through this an understanding of the basic principles of effective writing and reading, and some knowledge of how to apply these principles to the varied problems of composition. The approach is cumulative but each of the three main parts has a distinct emphasis: Part I directs attention to words as a primary element in the study of style; Part II stresses larger contexts of statement and paragraph; Part III considers the structure of the whole composition. Each part is prefaced by an explanation of the rhetorical matters to be developed and by special illustrative readings.

Within each part the separate readings are grouped under specific subjects, each of which may thus be explored in some depth and studied from different points of view. The attempt, then, is to exploit the advantages of arranging readings so as to preserve the importance of subject matter without subordinating essential principles of rhetoric. Further, the aim has been to illustrate better the different kinds of exposition through the choice of subjects that are neither too broad nor too narrow. Through this approach the connection between analytical reading and effective writing can be applied with the greatest advantage.

Commentary, questions, and topics for written and oral discussion follow every essay and underscore the book's dual purpose: to aid the reading and writing of prose. Two appendices to the anthology give suggestions for systematic, intelligent reading and for planning a written theme. Finally, there is an index of examples from the readings illustrating the rhetorical principles covered in the several introductions. The index also lists authors and titles, for convenience.

The readings, their arrangement, and the apparatus thus offer the basis of a directed course in reading and composition which may be as flexible as the instructor wishes. No class, probably, will want to digest all the readings; nor is it necessary to follow the essays in the sequence in which they are given. Instead the effort has been to supply a text that will accommodate courses at various levels, using various approaches to the study of prose.

We gratefully acknowledge assistance and advice in the preparation of the manuscript from the following people: Miss Dorothy Rattey and Mr. Samuel Van Diver of the University of Texas; Professor Richard Beal of Boston University; Professor William F. Belcher of North Texas State College; Professor George Creel of Sacramento State College; and Professor J. D. Thomas of The Rice Institute. Finally, we salute our wives for their patience and their willingness to help with many of the less exciting tasks connected with the making of a book.

W. O. S. S., Jr.
R. L. M., Jr.

Austin, Texas

Contents

PART ONE

Words

Words have meaning only as they are used, and they are used in context — in statements, paragraphs, whole compositions — to move and inform readers. To study words is to study both the writer's motive or purpose and the effect he intends to attain. With these aims in mind we must consider various levels of context, but we cannot consider them all at once. Furthermore, individual words create context, and for that reason we begin by concentrating on their function more or less as individual words in four general areas: *persuasion, information, definition,* and *figurative language.* Each of these terms describes different, though related, general purposes that writers have in using words, and at the same time each describes a general effect that writers hope to achieve. It is also possible to put the matter in another way: persuasion, information, definition, and figurative language are all types of meaning. Meaning is by no means limited to the dictionary; rather it is a process that involves both the writer who uses words and the audience that reads them. And the audience, any audience, has acquired certain preconceptions about words. It has given them certain meanings out of its own experience, and the writer must make sure that the audience's meanings do not conflict with his own and spoil his purpose.

Persuasive words: When Shakespeare has Marc Antony ask the Roman audience for the loan of their ears, he establishes the classic persuasive situation. Antony sets about provoking a complete shift in public opinion, and he succeeds. There is no great difficulty in understanding the orator's purpose in such a case: he wishes people to believe or act in a certain way and uses words to play upon their emotions, drawing their sympathies, fears, antagonisms, and self-interest toward the goal he has in mind.

In a broader sense, however, all uses of language are in some way persuasive. Persuasion may not be directly aimed at action, but it always seeks to get people to think or feel in a particular way. The informative writer, who wants his audience to know or understand something, is in reality persuading them, although persuasion of the more obvious kind may be very far from his intention. Or, a writer may try to convince by "letting the facts speak for themselves," by flattering his readers that they are quite capable of drawing their own conclusions, by appearing not to persuade at all. His language then is apt to be unemotional and restrained in its use of connotation.

Not all writers are being persuasive all the time, of course, and it is important for the reader to distinguish just which words have a directly persuasive purpose and which have some other aim. Language that is basically persuasive will make use of the nuances of meaning and emotional overtones that all words have, and these nuances and overtones are matters of individual use as well as of custom and convention. The experienced writer knows how to recognize these variations in the effects of language and he knows how to control them for his own purposes. In other words, he is aware of how words are affected by context and he is aware of what preconceptions readers have about the meanings of specific words.

Since most writers expect their readers to know other uses of their words, inexperienced readers often do not get the full impact of a piece of writing. The most demanding authors expect their readers to recognize words or phrases from some other writer and then see how the later use is like or unlike the original. The most popular of these allusions are to such well known writings as the Bible or the plays of Shakespeare. The inexperienced person is certainly at a disadvantage here. Take, for example, a statement of Prime Minister Chamberlain of England which was at one time widely quoted. Upon his return from his meeting with Hitler, at which he agreed to the detachment of Sudetanland from Czechoslovakia, he announced: "I have brought peace in our time." This statement is understandable at face value. It meant a good deal more, however, to members of the Anglican church in England, for "peace in our time" are words from liturgical responses that members of the established church had made again and again: "Give us peace in our time, O Lord." The implications of Chamberlain's remarks go far beyond the face value of the words. In effect he is announcing that he has brought the answer to men's prayers. Further, he has given to his diplomatic accomplishment an overtone of religious mission. Chamberlain puts himself on the side of the angels, always a favorable position to defend. The phrase "peace in our time" took on a different flavor when it became apparent that Chamberlain's negotiations had spectacularly failed to achieve their ends. The phrase then became an ironic, sometimes sarcastic, way of referring to the precarious relation between Germany and her enemies just before World War II.

Most writers depend on their readers' knowledge of the general use of a word rather than on a particular allusion, and most readers are entirely capable of appreciating the impact of this sort of writing. The important point with this kind of emotive language is for the reader to be aware that he is dealing with persuasive words. The word "crusade," for example, has so many favorable associations that it has understandably been used to describe drives of a crass, commercial nature as well as more high-minded activities. Though such labeling is obviously a misuse of the word, it is just as obviously profitable. Calling a "customer" by the grandiose term "patron" is a more innocent activity, but it is predicated on the same principle.

The emotive values that words carry may be collective or highly individual, universal and permanent or very temporary. "Knight-errant" is a word that suggests high adventure, noble quests, and chivalrous conduct. Its associations are evident to all and have been for many years. The word "saint" is usually favorable, too. Lost to the modern reader are the bitterly ironic overtones that it had three hundred years ago when used to describe a Calvinist who thought himself already chosen for salvation.

To repeat, words can express emotions and attitudes variably and they do so quite apart from whatever dictionary definitions they have. This expression becomes especially intense in politics, religion, or in other activities that are concerned with human values or that cause men to take sides and differ violently and deeply. The persuasive use of language is one of the main weapons of the propagandist, and most men are propagandists for the things they believe in.

The characteristics of words can best be directed by the writer (1) who has a thorough knowledge of the indirect effects of language and (2) who can manipulate context to avoid ambiguity and unintended meanings. Experience in reading and writing is the best way to learn these things, but in the absence of experience alert and careful thought makes a good substitute.

Writers on the arts deal with one of the great areas in which human values mingle and are expressed by solid realities, and such writers would normally be expected to use words with high emotive values. In the essay that follows, Frank Lloyd Wright has his say in words that are meant to inform, stimulate, enrage, and amuse. Study the particular uses of words and contexts that seem to serve these purposes. You must decide for yourself if Wright is successful.

FRANK LLOYD WRIGHT SPEAKS UP

Frank Lloyd Wright

From "Frank Lloyd Wright Speaks Up," House Beautiful, July, 1953. Reprinted by permission of the editors.

THE "International Style" is neither international nor a style. Essentially it is totalitarianism, an old totalitarian cult made new by organized publicity.

2   The "International Style" is nothing but the old architecture of the box with its face lifted.

3   Any box is more a coffin for the human spirit than an inspiration. The

box dominates, constricts, and constrains the individual into something made fit only for collectivism. Its champions now declare dictatorially that the old box is *it*. This is their great gift to the word — their "style."

4   So many university professors, museum authorities, magazine editors, feature writers, and critics seem to be trying hard to give notoriety to a group of architects imported, by a curious twist of fate, from the German Bauhaus to the New York Museum of Modern Art.

5   These Bauhaus architects ran from political totalitarianism in Germany to what is now made by specious promotion to seem their own totalitarianism in art here in America.

6   It is being more accidental than creative to mistake a disciplined sterility for austerity, mistake the plainness of bones or a barn door for simplicity (knowing nothing of *real* simplicity — the innate grace and significance of a wild flower). This is the mistake their promoters seem to make.

7   In their dubious champions, there is no sense of the depth called the third dimension. They operate on only two. Among these puppets of promotion, façades again become of uppermost importance. These façades all add up to the same thing — a cliché for tyros, teachers, and sycophants who crook the little finger and talk esthetics. Or by duped educators grasping something easy to teach, and approved as a foreign cult.

8   Sterilization is again mistaken for refinement. Provincial apostles of refinement name it "Classic," stupidly comparing it to frozen Greek classicism as though the ancient sterilization were a high virtue. But the cause of great architecture, the great truth of building beautiful buildings beautifully according to the nature of architecture, is travestied by this superficial mimicry, that always seems to follow in the wake of great ideas.

9   The classic or camouflaged old post-and-lintel box is still practiced in the glassed-in cage or the glass-walled dwelling, both approved by these publicists and this latest procession of callow-professionals, now baptized (by whom?) "International." But this latest form of glassification is no true revolt, no actual dissidence. This affection [*sic*] is for free Americans no more than the petty pretenses of small men.

10   Old Man Box merely *looks* different when glassified, that's all. The more the box is glassed, the more it becomes evident as the box. No new ideas whatever are involved as might easily be demonstrated by intelligent reference to the origin of their drawing-board façades. The old sham front has had its face lifted; the only change is merely one of outward appearance. It is a change of face, not of heart.

11   There are fresh ideas to be brought to life, if you learn to labor for them and are willing to work for them and wait. You must tire, as I do, of seeing these original forms merely renamed. All we have received from "internationalism," aside from the dropped coping, is merely: "Make the walls *all* glass, boys."

12   And what do we get now? The same old box, only you now really look

inside and through the box and see that it is more of a box than ever. Thereby the tenant, as well as the poverty-stricken imagination of the architect, is mercilessly exposed.

13   The nature of the freedom prophesied by the Declaration of Independence originally made by our nation is antipathetic to an international level either of style or of life. That "style" would be the communistic shadow descending over our own tradition, disgracing the great individualities that gave us our traditions in all their bewildering and wonderful fascination, color, and variety. Individuality is still beloved and prophesied by our nation. Never would we consent to be embalmed alive — to become prisoners of a style!

14   Organic or truly American architecture emerged from the confusion of the sudden awakening of architecture as a new idea 60 years ago. The *strength* of the *philosophy* of a free, intrinsic, or organic architecture is that it loves and cherishes these infinitely individual, human traditions of the Great Tradition.

15   Because of our increased techniques organic architecture could easily afford *all* nations new means of realization, on their own soil, along lines of character and development already peculiar to themselves. Whatever is really modern in architecture should, in this new view of reality, intensify the individualities of all nations, not strip them of the charm of their innate distinctions.

Commentary and questions

1. Language used suggestively and persuasively may be misleading, either because the writer lacks authority over his words or because he seems to be using language definitively when he is not. This selection has a very large number of statements that look like definitions: "International Style," "totalitarianism," "sterility," and "organic" — all of them key words. The validity of Wright's remarks depends in part upon what they mean.

2. For the most part Wright's terms are used for their connotations. We are told that the International Style was imported by a group of German architects, that it has something to do with box-shaped buildings, that it is connected with totalitarian political philosophy, and that it is alien to American culture. Some of these statements are factual, some evaluative. If we compare their definitive function with Allport's definition of prejudice (p. 23), there is clearly a great difference in the particularity of the definitions. We have no doubt what Allport means; Wright leaves several important questions to inference.

3. For example, what distinguishes the International Style besides its preference for box-shaped structures? When was the style imported? Precisely how does it differ from "organic" American architecture? The answers to these questions may be suggested by connotation and context, but they are not explicit.

4. On the other hand, we do not have to conclude that because he avoids definitive completeness Wright does not know what he is doing. He may assume that a majority of educated readers know what the International Style is, that it was developed in Germany in the early part of this century and transplanted to the United States by Walter Gropius and Mies Van der Rohe, and that Wright's own buildings are familiar enough to point the contrast between "organic" American architectural style and the International kind. Assuming all this knowledge in his readers, Wright seems to concern himself with persuading them that one style is better than the other. Thus, his most important words strike the reader in a suggestive, rather than a definitive, way.

"Totalitarianism" is something Americans automatically dislike, and its mere association with "International Style" tends to make the latter suspect. Similarly "box" is placed in unpleasant surroundings. It exists side by side with "old sham front," it is called "the same old box," and it is associated with "sterility." Analyze the connotative possibilities of "sterility."

5. "Organic" keeps company with "beautiful," "fresh new ideas," "freedom," and the Declaration of Independence. What are the specific connections between the concepts behind these terms? Are these concepts clear? What are the author's grounds for asking us to disapprove of Bauhaus architecture?

Topics for discussion and writing

I. What are the various ways in which words can be used persuasively? What conditions are necessary for such a use?

II. Choose half a dozen words that seem to you to have rich suggestive possibilities either for yourself or for others. List the effects these words are likely to have and consider the possible reasons for such effects. (It is not difficult, for example, to see why the mention of the Declaration of Independence is likely to arouse the feelings of Americans.) On the basis of your investigation write a theme discussing the emotive value of words.

III. Reread the excerpt from Wright and select several important words not treated in the commentary. Write a theme analyzing their connotations, the context Wright gives them, and the apparent purpose he has in using them as he does.

IV. Choose a short article or editorial in a newspaper or magazine and write a theme analyzing its use of persuasive language.

Informative words: Informative writing tries to convey information, either facts or ideas, in clear, precise, unemotional terms. Just how clear, how precise, and how unemotional a writer manages to be depends in large part upon the words he selects to describe physical things and to indicate concepts. Because of the way we learn language, we tend to use words in the same context in which we hear them. The word "sweat" conveys its information admirably, but convention rules that it is inappropriate in some contexts. Like most of the words with which we deal it is emotive as well as informative.

Not many words can be called either exclusively one or the other. Words like "Aryan," or "philosopher's stone," though they may refer to special human beliefs, have no verifiable reality behind them. What they profess to describe does not exist. Names of most complex chemical compounds (except DDT and TNT, for example), many names in a neutral context, might be purely informative. But most words that stand for any sort of real concept lie somewhere in between. Not that a word must have persuasive overtones inherently — a word may be informative in one context, then in another take on strong overtones of emotion or persuasion. The plebeian but respectable "sauerkraut" of 1914 became intolerable by 1918 to patriotic Americans. After the war, "liberty cabbage" became ridiculous, and "sauerkraut" once again seemed unaffected and natural. The dish hadn't changed; the emotional climate had. A man would be disturbed if someone said he were not a gentleman, but few men would call themselves one publicly. Some words don't depend on context at all. "Stock-market crash" carries more than information in any context, as do words like "free loader," "schlemiel," and "sucker." Still other words may become charged with emotion not by context or inherently, but in contrast to what the writer might have written. Love letters are always read this way.

The informative writer tries to handle words precisely and unemotionally. He is more inclined to let the material do its own persuading, but he is not necessarily limited to a recitation of facts. His material may include exposition, analysis, and description; it may recite a series of events, explain a scientific process, analyze an idea, describe an object, or give instructions. His ideal is to keep every word clear and unambiguous, though the indirect methods of persuasion can never be entirely avoided — even if the author wishes to. However, the informative author prefers to use these methods to illuminate more than persuade.

Informative clarity also results from a very careful handling of abstract phrases. Words need not always be used quite so concretely as George Orwell insists (see pp. 43-49), but abstractions that promote confused, unnecessarily ambiguous meanings are a common and avoidable offense. People who bandy about such phrases as "our rightful place among nations," "our way of life," or "developing individual initiative through group effort," may or may not have a definite concept behind what they say. Most readers can work out *a* meaning for these vaguenesses. But informative writing misses the mark unless the reader can work out *the* meaning and understand with some exactness what the writer intends.

Clarity and preciseness are not always easy to achieve, even when the author is trying conscientiously. Some areas of human experience so involve our emotions, our prejudices, and our subjective, preconceived opinions that to write objectively about them may take considerable self-examination. The following selection by Aristotle deals with one of these areas — politics. He deals with politics dispassionately and analytically, attempting to describe rather than pass judgment. This intended objectivity is clear from his careful methods of classification and definition. Even in translation, the detached, straightforward manner of the writing is strikingly evident.

THE FORMS OF GOVERNMENT   Aristotle

From The Politics *of Aristotle,*
translated by Benjamin Jowett.
Oxford at the Clarendon Press,
1923. Reprinted by permission.

HAVING determined these questions, we have next to consider whether there is only one form of government or many, and if many, what they are, and how many, and what are the differences between them.

2   A constitution is the arrangement of magistracies in a state, especially of the highest of all. The government is everywhere sovereign in the state, and the constitution is in fact the government. For example, in democracies the people are supreme, but in oligarchies, the few; and, therefore, we say that these two forms of government also are different: and so in other cases.

3   First, let us consider what is the purpose of a state, and how many forms of government there are by which human society is regulated. We have already said, in the first part of this treatise, when discussing household management and the rule of a master, that man is by nature a political animal. And therefore, men, even when they do not require one another's help, desire to live together; not but that they are also brought together by their common interests in proportion as they severally attain to any measure of well-being. This is certainly the chief end, both of individuals and of states. And also for the sake of mere life (in which there is possibly some noble element so long as the evils of existence do not greatly overbalance the good) mankind meet together and maintain the political community. And we all see that men cling to life even at the cost of enduring great misfortune, seeming to find in life a natural sweetness and happiness.

4   There is no difficulty in distinguishing the various kinds of authority; they have been often defined already in discussions outside the school. The rule of a master, although the slave by nature and the master by nature have

in reality the same interests, is nevertheless exercised primarily with a view to the interest of the master, but accidentally considers the slave, since, if the slave perish, the rule of the master perishes with him. On the other hand, the government of a wife and children and of a household, which we have called household management, is exercised in the first instance for the good of the governed or for the common good of both parties, but essentially for the good of the governed, as we see to be the case in medicine, gymnastic, and the arts in general, which are only accidentally concerned with the good of the artists themselves. For there is no reason why the trainer may not sometimes practise gymnastics, and the helmsman is always one of the crew. The trainer or the helmsman considers the good of those committed to his care. But, when he is one of the persons taken care of, he accidentally participates in the advantage, for the helmsman is also a sailor, and the trainer becomes one of those in training. And so in politics: when the state is framed upon the principle of equality and likeness, the citizens think that they ought to hold office by turns. Formerly, as is natural, every one would take his turn of service; and then again, somebody else would look after his interest, just as he, while in office, had looked after theirs. But nowadays, for the sake of the advantage which is to be gained from the public revenues and from office, men want to be always in office. One might imagine that the rulers, being sickly, were only kept in health while they continued in office; in that case we may be sure that they would be hunting after places. The conclusion is evident: that governments which have a regard to the common interest are constituted in accordance with strict principles of justice, and are therefore true forms; but those which regard only the interest of the rulers are all defective and perverted forms, for they are despotic, whereas a state is a community of freemen.

5   Having determined these points, we have next to consider how many forms of government there are, and what they are; and in the first place what are the true forms, for when they are determined the perversions of them will at once be apparent. The words constitution and government have the same meaning, and the government, which is the supreme authority in states, must be in the hands of one, or of a few, or of the many. The true forms of government, therefore, are those in which the one, or the few, or the many, govern with a view to the common interest; but governments which rule with a view to the private interest, whether of the one, or of the few, or of the many, are perversions. For the members of a state, if they are truly citizens, ought to participate in its advantages. Or forms of government in which one rules, we call that which regards the common interests, kingship or royalty; that in which more than one, but not many, rule, aristocracy; and it is so called, either because the rulers are the best men, or because they have at heart the best interests of the state and of the citizens. But when the citizens at large administer the state for the common interest, the government is called by the generic name — a constitution. And there is a reason

for this use of language. One man or a few may excel in virtue; but as the number increases it becomes more difficult for them to attain perfection in every kind of virtue, though they may in military virtue, for this is found in the masses. Hence in a constitutional government the fighting-men have the supreme power, and those who possess arms are the citizens.

6   Of the above-mentioned forms, the perversions are as follows: — of royalty, tyranny; of aristocracy, oligarchy; of constitutional government, democracy. For tyranny is a kind of monarchy which has in view the interest of the monarch only; oligarchy has in view the interest of the wealthy; democracy, of the needy: none of them the common good of all.

7   But there are difficulties about these forms of goverment, and it will therefore be necessary to state a little more at length the nature of each of them. For he who would make a philosophical study of the various sciences, and does not regard practice only, ought not to overlook or omit anything, but to set forth the truth in every particular. Tyranny, as I was saying, is monarchy exercising the rule of a master over the political society; oligarchy is when men of property have the government in their hands; democracy, the opposite, when the indigent, and not the men of property, are the rulers. And here arises the first of our difficulties, and it relates to the distinction just drawn. For democracy is said to be the government of the many. But what if the many are men of property and have the power in their hands? In like manner oligarchy is said to be the government of the few; but what if the poor are fewer than the rich, and have the power in their hands because they are stronger? In these cases the distinction which we have drawn between these different forms of government would no longer hold good.

8   Suppose, once more, that we add wealth to the few and poverty to the many, and name the governments accordingly — an oligarchy is said to be that in which the few and the wealthy, and a democracy that in which the many and the poor are the rulers — there will still be a difficulty. For, if the only forms of government are the ones already mentioned, how shall we describe those other governments also just mentioned by us, in which the rich are the more numerous and the poor are the fewer, and both govern in their respective states?

9   The argument seems to show that, whether in oligarchies or in democracies, the number of the governing body, whether the greater number, as in a democracy, or the smaller number, as in an oligarchy, is an accident due to the fact that the rich everywhere are few, and the poor numerous. But if so, there is a misapprehension of the causes of the difference between them. For the real difference between democracy and oligarchy is poverty and wealth. Wherever men rule by reason of their wealth, whether they be few or many, that is an oligarchy, and where the poor rule, that is a democracy. But as a fact the rich are few and the poor many; for few are well-to-do, whereas freedom is enjoyed by all, and wealth and freedom are the grounds on which the oligarchical and democratical parties respectively claim power in the state.

¹⁰ Let us begin by considering the common definitions of oligarchy and democracy, and what is justice oligarchical and democratical. For all men cling to justice of some kind, but their conceptions are imperfect and they do not express the whole idea. For example, justice is thought by them to be, and is, equality, not, however, for all, but only for equals. And inequality is thought to be, and is, justice; neither is this for all, but only for unequals. When the persons are omitted, then men judge erroneously. The reason is that they are passing judgement on themselves, and most people are bad judges in their own case. And whereas justice implies a relation to persons as well as to things, and a just distribution, as I have already said in the *Ethics*, implies the same ratio between the persons and between the things, they agree about the equality of the things, but dispute about the equality of the persons, chiefly for the reason which I have just given — because they are bad judges in their own affairs; and secondly, because both the parties to the argument are speaking of a limited and partial justice, but imagine themselves to be speaking of absolute justice. For the one party, if they are unequal in one respect, for example wealth, consider themselves to be unequal in all; and the other party, if they are equal in one respect, for example free birth, consider themselves to be equal in all. But they leave out the capital point. For if men met and associated out of regard to wealth only, their share in the state would be proportioned to their property, and the oligarchical doctrine would then seem to carry the day. It would not be just that he who paid one mina should have the same share of a hundred minae, whether of the principal or of the profits, as he who paid the remaining ninety-nine. But a state exists for the sake of a good life, and not for the sake of life only: if life only were the object, slaves and brute animals might form a state, but they cannot, for they have no share in happiness or in a life of free choice. Nor does a state exist for the sake of alliance and security from injustice, nor yet for the sake of exchange and mutual intercourse; for then the Tyrrhenians and the Carthaginians, and all who have commercial treaties with one another, would be the citizens of one state. True, they have agreements about imports, and engagements that they will do no wrong to one another, and written articles of alliance. But there are no magistracies common to the contracting parties who will enforce their engagements; different states have each their own magistracies. Nor does one state take care that the citizens of the other are such as they ought to be, nor see that those who come under the terms of the treaty do no wrong or wickedness at all, but only that they do no injustice to one another. Whereas, those who care for good government take into consideration virtue and vice in states. Whence it may be further inferred that virtue must be the care of a state which is truly so called, and not merely enjoys the name: for without this end the community becomes a mere alliance which differs only in place from alliances of which the members live apart; and law is only a convention, "a surety to one another of justice," as the sophist Lycophron says, and has no real power to make the citizens good and just.

11   This is obvious; for suppose distinct places, such as Corinth and Megara, to be brought together so that their walls touched, still they would not be one city, not even if the citizens had the right to intermarry, which is one of the rights peculiarly characteristic of states. Again, if men dwelt at a distance from one another, but not so far off as to have no intercourse, and there were laws among them that they should not wrong each other in their exchanges, neither would this be a state. Let us suppose that one man is a carpenter, another a husbandman, another a shoemaker, and so on, and that their number is ten thousand: nevertheless, if they have nothing in common but exchange, alliance, and the like, that would not constitute a state. Why is this? Surely not because they are at a distance from one another: for even supposing that such a community were to meet in one place, but that each man had a house of his own, which was in a manner his state, and that they made alliance with one another, but only against evil-doers; still an accurate thinker would not deem this to be a state, if their intercourse with one another was of the same character after as before their union. It is clear then that a state is not a mere society, having a common place, established for the prevention of mutual crime and for the sake of exchange. These are conditions without which a state cannot exist; but all of them together do not constitute a state, which is a community of families and aggregations of families in well-being, for the sake of a perfect and self-sufficing life. Such a community can only be established among those who live in the same place and intermarry. Hence arise in cities family connections, brotherhoods, common sacrifices, amusements which draw men together. But these are created by friendship, for the will to live together is friendship. The end of the state is the good life, and these are the means towards it. And the state is the union of families and villages in a perfect and self-sufficing life, by which we mean a happy and honorable life.

12   Our conclusion, then, is that political society exists for the sake of noble actions, and not of mere companionship. Hence they who contribute most to such a society have a greater share in it than those who have the same or a greater freedom or nobility of birth but are inferior to them in political virtue; or than those who exceed them in wealth but are surpassed by them in virtue.

13   From what has been said it will be clearly seen that all the partisans of different forms of government speak of a part of justice only.

Commentary and questions

1. Our major concern in this selection is the study of the informative function of its language. As a piece of writing, it is actually more than informative; it is also persuasive, for Aristotle is trying to convince us that his version of the ideal political community is the correct one. You may want to re-examine Aristotle at a later time when you take up the strategy of argument.

2. *Paragraphs 1-4* outline the context in which Aristotle's information will be relevant: the purpose of the exercise of authority generally and, more specifically, of government. The informative task of Aristotle's language is chiefly to make distinctions between types of state or government. He is in effect classifying governments on the basis of definitions of common terms: royalty, tyranny; aristocracy, oligarchy; constitution, democracy.

3. *Paragraph 3:* Aristotle organizes these terms according to their role as descriptive of good and bad versions of the same types of government. Having brought up the issue of value, Aristotle would seem to be departing from strictly informative writing. But notice that he is not trying to make his readers dislike the "perversions" of each type of government; rather he wants them to recognize the grounds for calling certain forms of political community perverted.

   Therefore, his main effort is to establish accurate and unequivocal meanings for each term. Accuracy or precision of meaning is relative and shifting, however. In paragraph 3, where Aristotle lists the premises for his discussion, he uses the words "well-being," "sweetness," and "happiness." These are rather broad terms, and he does not go into detail about them. He seems to assume that we understand what he means by them, although we might well quarrel about whether a man were happy or not in a specific situation. But such a quarrel would perhaps be irrelevant here. The point to note is that he distinguishes "well-being" from "mere life" and that "sweetness" and "happiness" are qualities that are inherent in living in spite of the possible necessity of "enduring great misfortune."

   The provisional and limited exactness of these terms reminds us that words are precise only in relation to other words and in relation to the author's purpose in writing. It is enough for Aristotle to use the terms we have just talked about in a very general way because he wishes to distinguish them only from their exact opposites, the absence of well-being, a point of view that finds existence basically repugnant, and unhappiness.

4. *Paragraph 3* uses several words that might, in another context, strike us as highly charged with emotion and bias: "rule," "master," and "slave." Our own political experience teaches us that these words may suggest conditions that we consider morally wrong. The American Revolution and the Civil War still make it difficult for us to use such words objectively. But for Aristotle the term "slave" carries no emotional reverberations. Slavery was an accepted and unquestioned institution in ancient Greece and he seems to use the word almost casually as we might use "chair" or "sidewalk," or "electorate."

5. *Paragraph 3* is also important because it demonstrates rather neatly the importance of working definitions as a basis for discussion. Aristotle must distinguish sharply between his basic political terms in order to pursue his treatment of correct and incorrect forms of government in paragraphs 5, 6, and 7. In these sections we can see an increasing effort toward precision of language, especially in the appearance of contrasts: "poverty" and "wealth," "the many" and "the few."

6. *Paragraph* 8 extends the process of definition, considering "oligarchy" and "democracy" in relation to "justice." What does "justice" seem to mean to Aristotle? Is his meaning precise enough? Examine the terms "good life" and "life," "alliance," "virtue," "vice," "community," and "convention." Aristotle makes no great effort to define these words explicitly. Are they nevertheless used accurately?

Topics for discussion and writing

I. The word "state" in paragraph 10 is crucial, and by this time it has acquired a special and precise meaning in Aristotle's use of it. Can you describe and analyze that meaning?

II. Turn to the excerpt from Darwin's *Origin of Species* (pp. 386-394). Select the words most clearly indicating that Darwin's purpose is informative.

III. Write a theme explaining the context within which the important words in a newspaper article are informative. In the article you have chosen, what principles make the effect of the diction nonpersuasive?

IV. Write a theme explaining how you would discuss a controversial issue in politics or religion informatively. How would you try to avoid rousing the emotions of your audience, especially if you knew that they were ready to take sides on the issue?

V. Re-examine the excerpt from Aristotle's *Politics*. What words would be difficult to use in a neutral, nonemotive way if Aristotle were writing for a modern audience?

Definition in use: "What meaning does this word have in this context?" This is the basic question that all good readers must constantly answer. The question is necessary because one word may have many meanings, and the reader must know what meaning the author intends in each particular context. Since words are mere counters they can be shifted about by any speaker or writer. If they are shifted too freely — without previous notice — communication breaks down. A symbol works only so long as everyone agrees in general on what it symbolizes.

Most readers recognize an obvious breakdown when they come to an unfamiliar word. Consequently they think of vocabulary problems as large, unwieldy words that they have never seen before or as familiar words used in an unfamiliar sense. Actually, though most familiar, this is the simplest vocabulary difficulty, largely because the situation is so obvious. It is simplest, too, because learning new words or new meanings for old words is one of our easiest and most common intellectual accomplishments. Even a child can do it.

In fact, the child's way is ultimately the only way. The child listens and imitates. He works out the definition in use. Almost all our words are learned this way, though we are not usually conscious of the process. Take the word "counters" in the first paragraph. The reader who does not know what concept it stands for can work it out from the context. Counters can be shifted about. The word "mere" indicates that they have little intrinsic value. The parallel to the word "symbol" indicates they stand for something beyond themselves. The context further indicates that everyone understands that these counters have value only as long as everyone agrees they have value. Considering similar words, obviously this is not the same counter over which children buy candy. There may, however, be some relation to the word "accounts" and to such lines as "the king was in his counting house counting out his money."

This analysis has not lead to an actual definition of "counters"; it has provided the element of the word that is important in the context. The fact that a counter may be an object used in reckoning or in games (poker chips, for example) is irrelevant here, but it may be important in another context. Not having a full definition of a word is not necessarily an indication the user does not understand it. Many people use words all their lives without knowing the full definition. They know only one element of the word, but, of course, that is enough. "I'll throw in my 'lot' with him." Not everyone who says this can say something informative about the word "lot," but there is no ambiguity in the word. The user understands as much as he needs to know for his purpose.

Unfamiliar words such as "counters" may take time, but they are not a serious source of misreading. The words that cause the most difficulty are those the reader has seen and used all his life. The author used them in one sense; the reader takes them in another. No word "has" meaning. Every word is "given" meaning. Confusion arises because even when two speakers are using a word in divergent ways, there is usually a common element of meaning that obscures the divergence. The question "Do you like music?" can be answered *yes* or *no* or *I don't know* depending upon whether "music" means classical music, jazz, "The Stars and Stripes Forever," or just bongo drums. But it can be answered. Nor is the dictionary of much help to the reader, for the common element of meaning is the very thing the dictionary makers have tried to extract from numerous uses of the word. This common element we call the *denotation* of the word. The dictionary omits, as it must, the particular application of each word — the *connotation*. Although the dictionary is a necessity for words the reader does not know, it cannot give the nuances of meaning which the careful reader should have. The denotation of a word is actually an incomplete definition. The reader's problem is to work out connotation as well. The context itself is the best place to determine the full meaning.

There is no easy method to determine exact meaning. In some cases it cannot be determined. But assuming that the author is doing his best to inform accurately, there are a few things any reader can do to increase the accuracy of his reading:

(1) Certain kinds of material bring out the worst in all readers and should be read with an awareness of the reader's and the writer's limitations. Any material the reader has strong preconceptions about is open to misinterpretation. Most of us are very likely to twist or misread the language of an article whose subject, conclusion, or author we don't like. We are just as likely to read our own concepts into an author who seems to be defending our side of an argument. Violent emotions have a way of suspending the rational process.

(2) Perhaps it is unnecessary to say that we ought to draw conclusions about unfamiliar material with especial care. The danger here is oversimplification. Psychology seems to be a subject with which most readers are least cautious. "Oedipus complex," "inferiority complex," and "will to power" are often used by people who seem to have overheard them.

(3) In working out an author's meaning for a difficult word, as many uses of the word as can be found ought to be examined. Although the author's use may be eccentric, it is usually consistent. The more examples consulted, the more accurate the definition is likely to be.

(4) Especially difficult words and phrases often yield to paraphrase. The paraphrase ought, of course, to be made up of words whose meanings are unambiguous to the reader.

(5) A concept can often be clarified by comparing or contrasting it to others that are similar but slightly different. This is a useful means of analysis which the author himself may employ.

(6) Some kinds of words cause difficulty consistently; others seldom do. Words that stand for physical things are usually clear. The physical thing, if it doesn't change, holds the word for it. Lack of physical definiteness may mean that the concept can change while the word remains the same. The words "Karl Marx" are not at all troublesome to most readers. Those words stand for one man. The word "Marxism," however, puts everyone on guard. Here is a word that stands for an intellectual concept, is used by many writers, and often occurs in an emotional context. One of the marks of a good writer is careful handling of abstract words.

(7) Words that express human values or that stand for things people regard as valuable are especially liable to misconstruction. "Patriot" may be a word used of a hero or a scoundrel. "Home," "mother," and "flag" are traditionally misused by politicians.

(8) Finally, every reader ought to be alert for words that are meaningless, for the concept for which a word ostensibly stands may not really exist. Because the language contains the word "ghost," the reader should not assume there is any reality behind the symbol. As long as men have talked, they have invented names for things that did not exist. The language of superstition is an empty monument to man's irrational assumption that a name means reality.

AMERICANISM   Edmund Wilson

From A Piece of My Mind *by Edmund Wilson. Reprinted by permission of Farrar, Straus and Cudahy Company.*

IT IS curious to trace the vicissitudes of the term *Americanism.* The first quotation given in the *Dictionary of Americanisms* published by Chicago University is from a letter of Jefferson's of 1797: "The parties here in debate continually charged each other . . . with being governed by an attachment to this or that of the belligerent nations, rather than the dictates of reason and pure Americanism." This is Americanism in the sense defined by Webster (1906) as "a love of America and preference of her interest." In Jefferson's time, of course, it meant the interests of the revolted colonists. But by the fifties of the following century, the word *Americanism* was to take on a new political meaning. It was used by the American or Know Nothing party to designate its own policy — already mentioned above — of combating the Roman Catholicism of German and Irish immigrants and of debarring persons of foreign birth from exercising political rights till they had lived here twenty-one years. It is in this sense that Lincoln uses it when, in a letter of May 15, 1858, he speaks of the chances of the Republican party: "I think our prospects gradually, and steadily, grow better; though we are not clear out of the woods by a great deal. There is still some effort to make trouble out of 'Americanism.' " This meaning was soon to lapse with the demise of the Know Nothing party. But the word was to be revived, with quite different implications, by Theodore Roosevelt in the nineties. The first use of it in Roosevelt's correspondence is in a letter of December 8, 1888, to Thomas R. Lounsbury, congratulating him on his *Life of Cooper:* "As a very sincere American myself, I feel like thanking you for the genuine Americanism of your book; which is quite as much displayed in its criticisms as in its praises."

Here he is speaking merely of an American point of view; but by the time he writes to William Archer in 1899 (August 31), he is giving the word a meaning of his own: "I have exactly the feeling about Americanism you describe. Most important of all is it for this country to treat an American on his worth as a man, and to disregard absolutely whether he be of English, German, Irish or any other nation; whether he be of Catholic or Protestant faith." . . . This is Roosevelt at his best. He has changed the Know Nothings' emphasis: instead of wanting to exclude the immigrant, he wishes to take him in and to propose a common ideal of disinterested public service. He is to talk, from the nineties on, a good deal about Americanism, and to give the word a general currency. He is eventually to make it stand for the whole of his political philosophy. Here is his definition in a letter to S. Stanwood Menken of January 10, 1917: "Americanism means many things. It means equality of rights and therefore equality of duty and of obligation. It means service to our common country. It means loyalty to one flag, to our flag, the flag of all of us. It means on the part of each of us respect for the rights of the rest of us. It means that all of us guarantee the rights of each of us. It means free education, genuinely representative government, freedom of speech and thought, equality before the law for all men, genuine political and religious freedom, and the democratizing of industry so as to give at least a measurable quality of opportunity for all, and so as to place before us, as our ideal in all industries where this ideal is possible of attainment, the system of coöperative ownership and management, in order that the tool-users may, so far as possible, become the tool-owners. Everything is un-American that tends either to government by a plutocracy or government by a mob. To divide along the lines of section or caste or creed is un-American. All privileges based on wealth, and all enmity to honest men merely because they are wealthy, are un-American — both of them equally so. Americanism means the virtues of courage, honor, justice, truth, sincerity, and hardihood — the virtues that made America." The last letter included in his published correspondence — written on January 3, 1919, three days before his death, to be read at a benefit concert of the American Defense Society — has, however, an emphasis that is somewhat different. This was written at the end of the first world war, in the era — referred to above — of the mass deportation of radicals. The old chief in retirement had by this time passed into an apoplectic phase in which he was convinced, for example, that the International Workers of the World were necessarily a criminal organization and that labor leaders were guilty, as a matter of course, of the crimes of which, in that moment of hysteria, they were lavishly being accused. "There must be no sagging back," writes Roosevelt, "in the fight for Americanism merely because the war is over. . . . There can be no divided allegiance here. . . . Any man who says he is an American, but something else also, isn't an American at all. We have room for but one flag, the American flag, and this excludes the red flag which symbolizes all wars against liberty and civilization just as much as it excludes any foreign flag of a nation to which we are hostile." This is the fear of the foreigner again. It was rampant after Roosevelt's death, and anyone with a non-Anglo-Saxon name who ventured to complain about anything or to propose a social reform was likely to be told at once that if he didn't like it here in the United States, he ought to go back where he came from. By this time, the very term "Americanism" had become a black-mailing menace. One remembers reading in the New York *Tribune* of March 3, 1920, that the younger Theodore Roosevelt, chairman of the American Legion's "Americanism Commission," had called a meeting "at which it was decided to thoroughly Americanize all war veterans, then to utilize them in the work of making good citizens of the foreign-born of the State." It may not be true that "Americanism" — like Dr. Johnson's "patriotism" — is invariably "the last refuge of a scoundrel"; but it has been made to serve some very bad causes, and is now a word to avoid.

Commentary and questions

1. Edmund Wilson works on the assumption that a single word may have many meanings. Each meaning is determined by examining the context in which it occurs.

What does Wilson mean by the word "vicissitudes" in the first sentence? Why does he use this word rather than "definitions"?

2. What is the advantage of arranging the definitions chronologically?

3. Why is the term "Americanism" one that might be expected to demonstrate rather drastic changes in meaning from time to time and from person to person?

4. What methods does Wilson use to make explicit what he thinks the various uses of "Americanism" means?

5. What is the advantage of using Theodore Roosevelt to show more than one meaning of the term "Americanism"?

6. What does Wilson mean when he says that "Americanism" is "now a word to avoid"? Does current use of the term support Wilson in his conclusion?

7. Look up the word "Americanism" in the dictionary. How is the definition you find there useful? What does Wilson show that the dictionary does not?

8. Would you say that the word "patriotism" ought also to be avoided? Give your reasons.

Explicit definition: Most readers and writers are not nearly so concerned with absolute or explicit definition as they are with definition in use. Usually we want to know what the word "love" means in a particular context rather than what all the related meanings for the word are. There have been many intelligent and perceptive discussions of poetry by critics who cannot define the word "poetry" with any sort of clarity or precision. Biologists can use the word "life" without having to draw the line that divides inert matter from living material. There are, however, occasions on which it is necessary to understand what a word means in as full a sense as can be determined.

(1) Whenever a term, or concept, is itself the matter for discussion an understanding of what the term entails may be necessary for any discussion to be valid. A psychologist who discusses "love" or "fear" must make clear what those terms comprehend. "Mind," "soul," "instinct" are terms about which there is so much disagreement and varying opinion that anyone who undertook to examine them would be required to make clear what he meant and did not mean by the words.

(2) Whenever a term is used as a basis for logical development of thought it should be defined. "Freedom" may be one of the bases for the "democratic way of life," but the latter term cannot be made clear and meaningful unless "freedom" has earlier been given a precise and limited definition.

(3) The full meaning of a word is important when examining our own thinking. The man interested in the ethics of his actions will ask himself whether the terms "bribe," "gift," "little present," "Christmas present," "baksheesh," and "a little something to make the wheels turn faster" do or do not refer to the same concept. A man who asks himself whether he is prejudiced must ask himself what "prejudice" is.

Definition as used here, the explanation of the concept for which a term stands, has restricted uses. Often it is an irrelevant operation. The philosophers who asked for the meaning of "justice," "courage," and similar words were distracted by the notion that the understanding of words was a value in itself. Such an operation is meaningful only as its end is meaningful.

The basic assumption in explicit definition is that the word itself is nothing; the concept for which the word stands is everything. The task, then, is to delineate the concept for which the word stands. The method of delineating may have five different steps:

(1) Find occurrences of the concept. The word "concept" is used deliberately here because examples of "fear" may or may not be concealed behind words like "prudence" and "caution." Occurrences of the concept means examples of specific actions or of uses that are a part of the concept to be explained.

(2) The crucial part of the definition is to make a generalization about the occurrences. What is common to all the occurrences and relative to the concept must be expressed in words. The expression of the generalization is important. The generalization should avoid the common fallacies of definitions.

(3) Find occurrences of concepts that are *not* the one under discussion but are similar in some way to it.

(4) Make a statement or statements limiting the concept. "Caution" may or may not have the elements of "fear." A statement of the part of "caution" that is not "fear" is a limitation upon the concept "fear." One of the supreme examples of definition is the Internal Revenue Service's attempt to define "taxable income." Statements of what is not taxable are quite as necessary as statements of what is taxable.

(5) Clarification may be the last step. Though often not included as a part of definition, clarification can be a valuable and desirable adjunct. Synonyms should be included under clarification rather than under definition itself. Examples should also be included if they are selected as typical or representative.

The following essay defining prejudice is an example of a difficult problem met and solved. The author knows that almost any casual reader of his title, "The Nature of Prejudice," will understand what the book is about. But that is not enough. Before he begins his detailed analysis of case histories he wants his reader to know exactly what material he considers relevant and exactly what material he considers irrelevant. His definition leaves no doubt in the reader's mind.

WHAT IS THE PROBLEM? Gordon W. Allport

From Gordon W. Allport, The Nature of Prejudice, *Addison-Wesley Publishing Company, Reading, Mass., 1954.*

For myself, earth-bound and fettered to the scene of my activities, I confess that I do feel the differences of mankind, national and individual. . . . I am, in plainer words, a bundle of prejudices — made up of likings and dislikings — the veriest thrall to sympathies, apathies, antipathies.

CHARLES LAMB

IN Rhodesia a white truck driver passed a group of idle natives and muttered, "They're lazy brutes." A few hours later he saw natives heaving two-hundred pound sacks of grain onto a truck, singing in rhythm to their work. "Savages," he grumbled. "What do you expect?"

2   In one of the West Indies it was customary at one time for natives to hold their noses conspicuously whenever they passed an American on the street. And in England, during the war, it was said, "The only trouble with the Yanks is that they are over-paid, over-sexed, and over here."

3   Polish people often called the Ukrainians "reptiles" to express their contempt for a group they regarded as ungrateful, revengeful, wily, and treacherous. At the same time Germans called their neighbors to the east "Polish cattle." The Poles retaliated with "Prussian swine" — a jibe at the presumed uncouthness and lack of honor of the Germans.

4   In South Africa, the English, it is said, are against the Afrikaner; both are against the Jews; all three are opposed to the Indians; while all four conspire against the native black.

5   In Boston, a dignitary of the Roman Catholic Church was driving along a lonesome road on the outskirts of the city. Seeing a small Negro boy trudging along, the dignitary told his chauffeur to stop and give the boy a lift. Seated together in the back of the limousine, the cleric, to make conversation, asked, "Little Boy, are you a Catholic?" Wide-eyed with alarm, the boy replied, "No sir, it's bad enough being colored without being one of those things."

6   Pressed to tell what Chinese people really think of Americans, a Chinese student reluctantly replied, "Well, we think they are the best of the foreign devils." This incident occurred before the Communist revolution in China. Today's youth in China are trained to think of Americans as the *worst* of the foreign devils.

7   In Hungary, the saying is, "An anti-Semite is a person who hates the Jews more than is absolutely necessary."

8   No corner of the world is free from group scorn. Being fettered to our respective cultures, we, like Charles Lamb, are bundles of prejudice.

Two Cases

9   An anthropologist in his middle thirties had two young children, Susan and Tom. His work required him to live for a year with a tribe of American Indians in the home of a hospitable Indian family. He insisted, however, that his own family live in a community of white people several miles distant from the Indian reservation. Seldom would he allow Tom and Susan to come to the tribal village, though they pleaded for the privilege. And on rare occasions when they made the visit, he sternly refused to allow them to play with the friendly Indian children.

10   Some people, including a few of the Indians, complained that the anthropologist was untrue to the code of his profession — that he was displaying race prejudice.

11   The truth is otherwise. This scientist knew that tuberculosis was rife in

the tribal village, and that four of the children in the household where he lived had already died of the disease. The probability of infection for his own children, if they came much in contact with the natives, was high. His better judgment told him that he should not take the risk. In this case, his ethnic avoidance was based on rational and realistic grounds. There was no feeling of antagonism involved. The anthropologist had no generally negative attitude toward the Indians. In fact he liked them very much.

12   Since this case fails to illustrate what we mean by racial or ethnic prejudice, let us turn to another.

13   In the early summer season two Toronto newspapers carried between them holiday advertisements from approximately 100 different resorts. A Canadian social scientist, S. L. Wax, undertook an interesting experiment.[1] To each of these hotels and resorts he wrote two letters, mailing them at the same time, and asking for room reservations for exactly the same dates. One letter he signed with the name "Mr. Greenberg," the other with the name "Mr. Lockwood." Here are the results:

   To "Mr. Greenberg":
      52 percent of the resorts replied;
      36 percent offered him accommodations.
   To "Mr. Lockwood":
      95 percent of the resorts replied;
      93 percent offered him accommodations.

Thus, nearly all of the resorts in question welcomed Mr. Lockwood as a correspondent and as a guest; but nearly half of them failed to give Mr. Greenberg the courtesy of a reply, and only slightly more than a third were willing to receive him as a guest.

14   None of the hotels knew "Mr. Lockwood" or "Mr. Greenberg." For all they knew "Mr. Greenberg" might be a quiet, orderly gentleman, and "Mr. Lockwood" rowdy and drunk. The decision was obviously made not on the merits of the individual, but on "Mr. Greenberg's" supposed membership in a group.

15   Unlike our first case, this incident contains the two essential ingredients of ethnic prejudice. (1) There is definite hostility and rejection. The majority of the hotels wanted nothing to do with "Mr. Greenberg." (2) The basis of the rejection was categorical. "Mr. Greenberg" was not evaluated as an individual. Rather, he was condemned on the basis of his presumed group membership.

16   A close reasoner might at this point ask the question: What basic difference exists between the cases of the anthropologist and the hotels in the matter of "categorical rejection"? Did not the anthropologist reason from the high probability of infection that it would be safer not to risk contact between his children and the Indians? And did not the hotelkeepers reason

---

[1] See references at end of the selection.

from a high probability that Mr. Greenberg's ethnic membership would in fact bring them an undesirable guest? The anthropologist knew that tubercular contagion was rampant; did not the innkeepers know that "Jewish vices" were rampant and not to be risked?

¹⁷   This question is legitimate. If the innkeepers were basing their rejection on facts (more accurately, on a high probability that a given Jew will have undesirable traits), their action would be as rational and defensible as the anthropologist's. But we can be sure that such is not the case.

¹⁸   Some managers may never have had any unpleasant experiences with Jewish guests — a situation that seems likely in view of the fact that in many cases Jewish guests had never been admitted to the hotels. Or, if they have had such experiences, they have not kept a record of their frequency in comparison with objectionable non-Jewish guests. Certainly they have not consulted scientific studies concerning the relative frequency of desirable and undesirable traits in Jews and non-Jews. If they sought such evidence, they would, as we shall learn in Chapter 6, find no support for their policy of rejection.

¹⁹   It is, of course, possible that the manager himself was free from personal prejudice, but, if so, he was reflecting the anti-Semitism of his gentile guests. In either event our point is made.

Definition

²⁰   The word *prejudice,* derived from the Latin noun *praejudicium,* has, like most words, undergone a change of meaning since classical times. There are three stages in the transformation.²

(1) To the ancients, *praejudicium* meant a *precedent* — a judgment based on previous decisions and experiences.

(2) Later, the term, in English, acquired the meaning of a judgment formed before due examination and consideration of the facts — a premature or hasty judgment.

(3) Finally the term acquired also its present emotional flavor of favorableness or unfavorableness that accompanies such a prior and unsupported judgment.

²¹   Perhaps the briefest of all definitions of prejudice is: *thinking ill of others without sufficient warrant.*³ This crisp phrasing contains the two essential ingredients of all definitions — reference to unfounded judgment and to a feeling-tone. It is, however, too brief for complete clarity.

²²   In the first place, it refers only to *negative* prejudice. People may be prejudiced in favor of others; they may think *well* of them without sufficient warrant. The wording offered by the New English Dictionary recognizes positive as well as negative prejudice:

> A *feeling, favorable or unfavorable, toward a person or thing, prior to, or not based on, actual experience.*

While it is important to bear in mind that biases may be *pro* as well as *con*, it is none the less true that *ethnic* prejudice is mostly negative. A group of students was asked to describe their attitudes toward ethnic groups. No suggestion was made that might lead them toward negative reports. Even so, they reported eight times as many antagonistic attitudes as favorable attitudes. In this volume, accordingly, we shall be concerned chiefly with prejudice *against,* not with prejudice *in favor of,* ethnic groups.

23   The phrase "thinking ill of others" is obviously an elliptical expression that must be understood to include feelings of scorn or dislike, of fear and aversion, as well as various forms of antipathetic conduct: such as talking against people, discriminating against them, or attacking them with violence.

24   Similarly, we need to expand the phrase "without sufficient warrant." A judgment is unwarranted whenever it lacks basis in fact. A wit defined prejudice as "being down on something you're not up on."

25   It is not easy to say how much fact is required in order to justify a judgment. A prejudiced person will almost certainly claim that he has sufficient warrant for his views. He will tell of bitter experiences he has had with refugees, Catholics, or Orientals. But, in most cases, it is evident that his facts are scanty and strained. He resorts to a selective sorting of his own few memories, mixes them up with hearsay, and overgeneralizes. No one can possibly know *all* refugees, Catholics, or Orientals. Hence any negative judgment of these groups *as a whole* is, strictly speaking, an instance of thinking ill without sufficient warrant.

26   Sometimes, the ill-thinker has no first-hand experience on which to base his judgment. A few years ago most Americans thought exceedingly ill of Turks — but very few had ever seen a Turk nor did they know any person who had seen one. Their warrant lay exclusively in what they had heard of the Armenian massacres and of the legendary crusades. On such evidence they presumed to condemn all members of a nation.

27   Ordinarily, prejudice manifests itself in dealing with individual members of rejected groups. But in avoiding a Negro neighbor, or in answering "Mr. Greenberg's" application for a room, we frame our action to accord with our categorical generalization of the group as a whole. We pay little or no attention to individual differences, and overlook the important fact that Negro X, our neighbor, is not Negro Y, whom we dislike for good and sufficient reason; that Mr. Greenberg, who may be a fine gentleman, is not Mr. Bloom, whom we have good reason to dislike.

28   So common is this process that we might define prejudice as:

> an avertive or hostile attitude toward a person who belongs to a group, simply because he belongs to that group, and is therefore presumed to have the objectionable qualities ascribed to the group.

This definition stresses the fact that while ethnic prejudice in daily life is ordinarily a matter of dealing with individual people it also entails an unwarranted idea concerning a group as a whole.

²⁹   We can never hope to draw a hard and fast line between "sufficient" and "insufficient" warrant. For this reason we cannot always be sure whether we are dealing with a case of prejudice or nonprejudice. Yet no one will deny that often we form judgments on the basis of scant, even nonexistent, probabilities.

³⁰   *Overcategorization* is perhaps the commonest trick of the human mind. Given a thimbleful of facts we rush to make generalizations as large as a tub. One young boy developed the idea that all Norwegians were giants because he was impressed by the gigantic stature of Ymir in the saga, and for years was fearful lest he meet a living Norwegian. A certain man happened to know three Englishmen personally and proceeded to declare that the whole English race had the common attributes that he observed in these three.

³¹   There is a natural basis for this tendency. Life is so short, and the demands upon us for practical adjustments so great, that we cannot let our ignorance detain us in our daily transactions. We have to decide whether objects are good or bad by classes. We cannot weigh each object in the world by itself. Rough and ready rubrics, however coarse and broad, have to suffice.

³²   Not every overblown generalization is a prejudice. Some are simply *misconceptions,* wherein we organize wrong information. One child had the idea that all people living in Minneapolis were "monopolists." And from his father he had learned that monopolists were evil folk. When in later years he discovered the confusion, his dislike of dwellers in Minneapolis vanished.

³³   Here we have the test to help us distinguish between ordinary errors of prejudgment and prejudice. If a person is capable of rectifying his erroneous judgments in the light of new evidence he is not prejudiced. *Prejudgments become prejudices only if they are not reversible when exposed to new knowledge.* A prejudice, unlike a simple misconception, is actively resistant to all evidence that would unseat it. We tend to grow emotional when a prejudice is threatened with contradiction. Thus the difference between ordinary prejudgments and prejudice is that one can discuss and rectify a prejudgment without emotional resistance.

³⁴   Taking these various considerations into account, we may now attempt a final definition of negative ethnic prejudice — one that will serve us throughout this book. Each phrase in the definition represents a considerable condensation of the points we have been discussing:

> Ethnic prejudice is an antipathy based upon a faulty and inflexible generalization. It may be felt or expressed. It may be directed toward a group as a whole, or toward an individual because he is a member of that group.

The net effect of prejudice, thus defined, is to place the object of prejudice at some disadvantage not merited by his own misconduct.

Is Prejudice a Value Concept?

35   Some authors have introduced an additional ingredient into their definitions of prejudice. They claim that attitudes are prejudiced only if they violate some important norms or values accepted in a culture.[4, 5] They insist that prejudice is only that type of prejudgment that is ethically disapproved in a society.

36   If we use the term in this sense we should have to say that the older caste system in India — which is now breaking down — involved no prejudice. It was simply a convenient stratification in the social structure, acceptable to nearly all citizens because it clarified the division of labor and defined social prerogatives. It was for centuries acceptable even to the untouchables because the religious doctrine of reincarnation made the arrangement seem entirely just. An untouchable was ostracized because in previous existences he failed to merit promotions to a higher caste or to a supermortal existence. He now has his just deserts and likewise an opportunity through an obedient and spiritually directed life to win advancement in future reincarnations. Assuming that this account of a happy caste system really marked Hindu society at one time, was there then no question of prejudice?

37   Or take the Ghetto system. Through long stretches of history Jews have been segregated in certain residential zones, sometimes with a chain around the region. Only inside were they allowed to move freely. The method had the merit of preventing unpleasant conflict, and the Jew, knowing his place, could plan his life with a certain definiteness and comfort. It could be argued that his lot was much more secure and predictable than in the modern world. There were periods in history when neither the Jew nor gentile felt particularly outraged by the system. Was prejudice then absent?

38   Even today, in certain states, a *modus vivendi* has been worked out between white and colored people. A ritual of relations is established, and most people abide unthinkingly by the realities of social structure. Since they merely follow the folkways they deny that they are prejudiced. The Negro simply knows his place, and white people know theirs. Shall we then say, as some writers have, that prejudice exists only when actions are *more* condescending, *more* negative, than the accepted culture itself prescribes? Is prejudice to be regarded merely as deviance from common pratice? [6]

39   What shall we say about this line of argument? It has impressed some critics so much that they hold the whole problem of prejudice to be nothing more than a value-judgment invented by "liberal intellectuals."

40   These critics, it would seem, confuse two separate and distinct problems. Prejudice in the simple psychological sense of negative, overgeneralized judgment exists just as surely in caste societies, slave societies, or countries believing in witchcraft as in ethically more sensitive societies. The second problem — whether prejudice is or is not attended by a sense of moral outrage — is a separate issue altogether.

41   There is not the slightest justification for confusing the objective facts

of prejudice with cultural or ethical judgment of these facts. The unpleasant flavor of a word should not mislead us into believing that it stands only for a value-judgment. Take the word *epidemic*. It suggests something disagreeable. No doubt Pasteur, the great conqueror of epidemics, hated them. But his value-judgment did not affect in the slightest degree the objective facts with which he dealt so successfully. *Syphilis* is a term flavored with opprobrium in our culture. But the emotional tinge has no bearing whatever upon the operations of the spirochete within the human frame.

42   Some cultures, like our own, abjure prejudice; some do not; but the fundamental psychological analysis of prejudice is the same whether we are talking about Hindus, Navahos, the Greeks of antiquity, or Middletown, U.S.A. Whenever a negative attitude toward persons is sustained by a spurious overgeneralization we encounter the syndrome of prejudice. It is not essential that people deplore this syndrome. It has existed in all ages in every country. It constitutes a bona fide psychological problem. The degree of moral indignation engendered is irrelevant.

Functional Significance

43   Certain definitions of prejudice include one additional ingredient. The following is an example:

> Prejudice is a pattern of hostility in interpersonal relations which is directed against an entire group, or against its individual members; it fulfills a specific irrational function for its bearer.[7]

The final phrase of this definition implies that negative attitudes are not prejudices unless they serve a private, self-gratifying purpose for the person who has them.

44   It will become abundantly clear in later chapters that much prejudice is indeed fashioned and sustained by self-gratifying considerations. In most cases prejudice seems to have some "functional significance" for the bearer. Yet this is not always the case. Much prejudice is a matter of blind conformity with prevailing folkways. Some of it, as Chapter 17 will show, has no important relation to the life-economy of the individual. For this reason it seems unwise to insist that the "irrational function" of prejudice be included in our basic definition.

Attitudes and Beliefs

45   We have said that an adequate definition of prejudice contains two essential ingredients. There must be an *attitude* of favor or disfavor; and it must be related to an overgeneralized (and therefore erroneous) *belief*. Prejudiced statements sometimes express the attitudinal factor, sometimes the belief factor. In the following series the first item expresses attitude, the second, belief:

I can't abide Negroes.
Negroes are smelly.

I wouldn't live in an apartment house with Jews.
There are a few exceptions, but in general all Jews are pretty much alike.

I don't want Japanese-Americans in my town.
Japanese-Americans are sly and tricky.

46   Is it important to distinguish between the attitudinal and belief aspects of prejudice? For some purposes, no. When we find one, we usually find the other. Without some generalized beliefs concerning a group as a whole, a hostile attitude could not long be sustained. In modern researches it turns out that people who express a high degree of antagonistic attitudes on a test for prejudice, also show that they believe to a high degree that the groups they are prejudiced against have a large number of objectionable qualities.[8]
47   But for some purposes it is useful to distinguish attitude from belief. For example, we shall see in Chapter 30 that certain programs designed to reduce prejudice succeed in altering beliefs but not in changing attitudes. Beliefs, to some extent, can be rationally attacked and altered. Usually, however, they have the slippery propensity of accommodating themselves somehow to the negative attitude which is much harder to change. The following dialogue illustrates the point:

Mr. X: The trouble with the Jews is that they only take care of their own group.
Mr. Y: But the record of the Community Chest campaign shows that they give more generously, in proportion to their numbers, to the general charities of the community, than do non-Jews.
Mr. X: That shows they are always trying to buy favor and intrude into Christian affairs. They think of nothing but money; that is why there are so many Jewish bankers.
Mr. Y: But a recent study shows that the percentage of Jews in the banking business is negligible, far smaller than the percentage of non-Jews.
Mr. X: That's just it; they don't go in for respectable business; they are only in the movie business or run night clubs.

Thus the belief system has a way of slithering around to justify the more permanent attitude. The process is one of *rationalization* — of the accommodation of beliefs to attitudes.
48   It is well to keep these two aspects of prejudice in mind, for in our subsequent discussions we shall have occasion to make use of the distinction. But wherever the term *prejudice* is used without specifying these aspects, the reader may assume that both attitude and belief are intended.

Acting Out Prejudice

⁴⁹   What people actually do in relation to groups they dislike is not always directly related to what they think or feel about them. Two employers, for example, may dislike Jews to an equal degree. One may keep his feelings to himself and may hire Jews on the same basis as any workers — perhaps because he wants to gain goodwill for his factory or store in the Jewish community. The other may translate his dislike into his employment policy, and refuse to hire Jews. Both men are prejudiced, but only one of them practices *discrimination*.

⁵⁰   It is true that any negative attitude tends somehow, somewhere, to express itself in action. Few people keep their antipathies entirely to themselves. The more intense the attitude, the more likely it is to result in vigorously hostile action.

⁵¹   We may venture to distinguish certain degrees of negative action from the least energetic to the most.

1. *Antilocution.* Most people who have prejudices talk about them. With like-minded friends, occasionally with strangers, they may express their antagonism freely. But many people never go beyond this mild degree of antipathetic action.

2. *Avoidance.* If the prejudice is more intense, it leads the individual to avoid members of the disliked group, even perhaps at the cost of considerable inconvenience. In this case, the bearer of prejudice does not directly inflict harm upon the group he dislikes. He takes the burden of accommodation and withdrawal entirely upon himself.

3. *Discrimination.* Here the prejudiced person makes detrimental distinctions of an active sort. He undertakes to exclude all members of the group in question from certain types of employment, from residential housing, political rights, educational or recreational opportunities, churches, hospitals, or from some other social privileges. Segregation is an institutionalized form of discrimination, enforced legally or by common custom.⁹

4. *Physical attack.* Under conditions of heightened emotion prejudice may lead to acts of violence or semiviolence. An unwanted Negro family may be forcibly ejected from a neighborhood, or so severely threatened that it leaves in fear. Gravestones in Jewish cemeteries may be desecrated. The Northside's Italian gang may lie in wait for the Southside's Irish gang.

5. *Extermination.* Lynchings, pogroms, massacres, and the Hitlerian program of genocide mark the ultimate degree of violent expression of prejudice.

⁵²   This five-point scale is not mathematically constructed, but it serves to call attention to the enormous range of activities that may issue from prejudiced attitudes and beliefs. While many people would never move from anti-

locution to avoidance; or from avoidance to active discrimination, or higher on the scale, still it is true that activity on one level makes transition to a more intense level easier. It was Hitler's antilocution that led Germans to avoid their Jewish neighbors and erstwhile friends. This preparation made it easier to enact the Nürnberg laws of discrimination which, in turn, made the subsequent burning of synagogues and street attacks upon Jews seem natural. The final step in the macabre progression was the ovens at Auschwitz. [53] From the point of view of social consequences much "polite prejudice" is harmless enough — being confined to idle chatter. But unfortunately, the fateful progression is, in this century, growing in frequency. And as the peoples of the earth grow ever more interdependent, they can tolerate less well the mounting friction.

NOTES AND REFERENCES

1. S. L. Wax. A survey of restrictive advertising and discrimination by summer resorts in the Province of Ontario. Canadian Jewish Congress: *Information and comment,* 1948, 7, 10-13.

2. Cf. *A New English Dictionary.* (Sir James A. H. Murray, Ed.) Oxford: Clarendon Press, 1909, Vol. VII, Pt. II, 1275.

3. This definition is derived from the Thomistic moralists who regard prejudice as "rash judgment." The author is indebted to the Rev. J. H. Fichter, S.J., for calling this treatment to his attention. The definition is more fully discussed by the Rev. John LaFarge, S.J., in *The Race Question and the Negro,* New York: Longmans, Green, 1945, 174 ff.

4. Cf. R. M. Williams, Jr. The reduction of intergroup tensions. New York: *Social Science Research Council,* 1947, Bulletin 57, 37.

5. H. S. Dyer. The usability of the concept of "Prejudice." *Psychometrika,* 1945, 10, 219-224.

6. The following definition is written from this relativistic point of view: "A prejudice is a generalized anti-attitude, and/or an anti-action toward any distinct category or group of people, when either the attitude or the action or both are judged by the community in which they are found to be less favorable to the given people than the normally accepted standard of that community." P. Black and R. D. Atkins. Conformity versus prejudice as exemplified in white-Negro relations in the South: some methodological considerations. *Journal of Psychology,* 1950, 30, 109-121.

7. N. W. Ackerman and Marie Jahoda. *Anti-Semitism and Emotional Disorder.* New York: Harper, 1950, 4.

8. Not all scales for measuring prejudice include items that reflect both attitudes and beliefs. Those that do so report correlations between the two types of items of the order of .80. Cf. Babette Samelson. *The patterning of attitudes and beliefs regarding the American Negro.* (Unpublished.) Radcliffe College Library, 1945. Also, A. Rose, *Studies in reduction of prejudice.* (Mimeograph.) Chicago: American Council on Race Relations, 1947, 11-14.

9. Aware of the world-wide problem of discrimination, the Commission on Human Rights of the United Nations has prepared a thorough analysis of *The main types and causes of discrimination.* United Nations Publications, 1949, XIV, 3.

Commentary and questions

1. *Paragraphs 1-8:* The introductory section has selected anecdotes that should be called clarification. They are chosen for their illustrative value, and each is ironic, perhaps amusing in a sardonic way. At first glance, the second anecdote may not seem ironic, but when the reader understands that it is an illustration of prejudice *against* Americans whereas

the essay concerns prejudice *by* Americans, the paragraph takes on the same ironic complexion as the others.

2. *Paragraphs 9-19:* The second section, "Two Cases," is further clarification, but here the illustrations are chosen on a different principle. The author is beginning to discriminate between what prejudice is and is not. Note that the positive illustration is longer than the negative, and that Allport even meets possible objections to his interpretation of the Lockwood-Greenberg letters. The net effect of using illustrations before the general definition is to encourage the reader to think along with the author.

3. *Paragraphs 20-34:* The section "Definition" takes the crucial step of proposing the general definition. The etymology of "prejudice" must be regarded as clarification, since past meanings do not necessarily affect current usage. Allport's use of the dictionary points up its inadequacy for handling the problem of explicit definition.

Step 1 in the process of explicit definition appears in his use of examples: he observes various occurrences of the word "prejudice." His general definition exhibits step 2. His distinction between ordinary errors of judgment and prejudice illustrates step 3, what prejudice is not; and the illustrations he gives manifest his collection of occurrences outlining the limits of prejudice (step 4). His use of illustrations, some of which are evidence gathered as a result of steps 1, 3, and 4, shows his use of clarification (step 5). Note that the final statement of the general definition at the end of this section mentions two elements common to all the illustrations and relevant to the concept of prejudice. These two elements are later identified as "attitude" and "belief."

4. The next two sections "Is Prejudice a Value Concept?" (*paragraphs 35-42*) and "Functional Significance" (*paragraphs 43-44*) are devoted to a denial that these two issues limit the definition of "prejudice."

5. "Acting Out Prejudice" (*paragraphs 49-58*) is designed to show how prejudice is displayed rather than what it is. This section is also devoted to defining, however, for Allport must analyze his five degrees of intenseness. These words may have had no meaning (antilocution) to the reader before Allport gave them definitions, or different meanings. ("Discrimination" may well have been used previously to describe all the first four degrees of intenseness.)

The justness of Allport's limitations of his term and the completeness of his definition can be judged only if the reader is himself willing to examine numerous occurrences of the concept, though some definitions can be attacked on purely logical grounds.

Topics for discussion and writing

I. Assume that you have decided to explain the concept "desire." List words other than "desire" that you would expect to harbor at least part of this concept. What words harbor concepts that you might want to distinguish from love?

II. Give a one-sentence exposition of at least three different concepts that go by the word "desire." Do these overlap with one another? Do all three overlap?

III. Courses in psychology often discuss the concept of "fear." Write an essay explaining the three or four chief difficulties you see in defining the word "fear."

IV. A midwestern university recently announced that it had acquired its millionth book. What are the problems of definition in counting the "books" in a library?

V. What are the problems of definition in words like "phlogiston," "powers of darkness," "spontaneous generation," "witch," "tired blood," "magic," and "unicorn." Are there concepts behind these words? Which of these words probably cause the least trouble? Which the most?

VI. Under what circumstances would it be important to define the word "poetry"? Under what circumstances would a definition be irrelevant?

VII. Write a paragraph explaining briefly the concept behind the word "socialism" when it is used as a technical term by economists.

Write a paragraph explaining briefly the concept or concepts behind the word "socialism" when it is used to attack a political opponent.

Is there overlapping between these concepts? What are the problems faced in writing each paragraph? Why are the problems somewhat different for the two paragraphs?

Figurative language: Not all ideas can be expressed directly; not all subjects can be accurately rendered without the help of metaphor, simile, or less frequent types of figurative expression. We "see" ideas, "change" our minds, and "fall" for "outlandish" schemes. We have a habit of shifting words from their original designations and applying them to new situations, and this shift eventually results in figures of speech. After a time no one thinks about the description of a bed as having four legs, a head, and a foot. Such language is no longer felt as metaphorical, but essentially it is. Figurative language is fundamental.

Metaphor is by far the most common type of figurative language, and it is the type we shall be primarily concerned with here. A metaphor is essentially a comparison. We can call it a simile deprived of "like," but this is not enough because the real purpose of metaphor goes beyond the simple making of a comparison. Instead the comparison becomes the basis for talking about something or someone in terms more accurate and vivid than are otherwise possible. We describe and criticize music, painting, sculpture, and literature in terms of other things usually because that is the only way we can talk about them. "Harsh" was originally and still is used to describe the reactions of our five senses to concrete things, but it is also useful for talking about a writer's style or a quality of emotion. When this happens, the word has been transferred from its original designation to the realm of emotions and impressions, and if we try to find a substitute for a painter's "warm" use of color or a man's "hot" anger, it is likely that we will choose other metaphors.

Metaphors that no longer have any impact may have a bad effect on both writers and readers. The word "blood," for example, abuses most of the people who use it. "There's bad blood in that family" is a metaphor. One man shot his sweetheart and his first cousin was a horse thief. The implication of the metaphor is that these criminal tendencies are inherited, when there is little if any responsible scientific evidence that such tendencies can be passed through the genes. But the metaphor does more than that — it also implies that criminal tendencies may well be rampant in other members of the family who have otherwise shown no evidence of unfortunate behavior. Stated nonmetaphorically the notion is weak. Since the man who shot his sweetheart and the man who stole the horse have a common grandfather, it is certain (so the argument runs) that they have acted this way through some sort of physiologically inherited characteristic. It is most likely that other members of the family have also inherited this characteristic and thus may well be criminals. The logic is wrong, but the metaphor transcends logic. "Lower" class and "upper" class are metaphors that help fix as well as express our opinions of men and women. Many a man has found that "to be let in on the ground floor" means to take a low-paying job in a small firm that may or may not grow. Metaphors affect our thinking and acting though we may never know it.

Fresh, conscious metaphor can be used to make a sudden, striking revelation to the reader. It can clarify and persuade in a way that mere logic can never imitate. Although it can be one of a writer's most useful devices, it is often ignored or, even worse, used with thoughtless ineptitude. Metaphor, which is used here to include simile, has its basis in a supposed likeness between two things, or actions, or ideas, which are usually thought of as unlike. Ideally it is used both to inform and to persuade. Always there are two parts: the *subject,* the main topic of discussion, the thing to be illuminated, and the *substitute,* the part that by being like the subject in some way illuminates it. Take, for example, the headline often used to describe a situation in parliamentary countries: "Government Topples." "Topples" is a metaphor which implies an adverse vote followed by the resignation of the cabinet. The vote and resignation are the subject. "Topples" is the substitute. In this case there is actually an intermediate metaphor. The cabinet members are going from a "high" position to a "low" position, a figure that makes the idea of toppling appropriate. The metaphor works because it refers to the essential fact of the situation, the vote and resignation; it relates at an essential point, the sudden fall; and it conveys a feeling about what has happened, that it is a sudden disaster. It is also good in that the word "topples" carries with it the notion of unsteadiness before the fall. It is not, however, a metaphor that would recommend itself to most writers because it is common enough to have lost its ability to startle or surprise.

A bad metaphor is one that is inexact or relates to some unessential point, one that is shopworn or hackneyed from overuse, or one that points up a similarity not appropriate to the subject or the context. In most contexts it would be inappropriate to compare a cynical, evil business tycoon to a scrubbed baby because he happened to have a bald head and a pink face. Chances are such a metaphor would not point up anything aside from a likeness. Assuming that the essential matter is the man's cynicism or wickedness, his appearance is irrelevant unless it somehow comments on these. Metaphors that have been used again and again lose their effectiveness because they no longer call attention to themselves. "Henpecked husband" has become a vague phrase rather than a meaningful metaphor. Repeated use in different contexts may also mean loss of exactness as well as loss of freshness.

A metaphor should not be thought of as a stylistic device but as a legitimate and effective way of clarifying a concept. If it were only a way of making language vivid and arresting, any metaphorical statement could be put into nonmetaphorical language without loss of meaning. But this is not possible. Such a relationship can never be expressed adequately. Take, for example, a metaphor found in one of the selections that follow. George Orwell remarks: "This kind of writing is not universal, and *outcrops* of simplicity will occur here and there in the worst-written page." "Outcrops" is a clear metaphor, and all the more prominent in that it exists in a passage essentially nonmetaphorical. More important, it carries the essence of Orwell's idea. "Outcrops" comes most immediately from geology and describes the way certain kinds of rock emerge in the midst of a type of rock or soil more typical of the surface. Thus Orwell transmits the idea that stylistic simplicity exists somewhat sparsely and almost by accident in the midst of more general and characteristic badness of style. The metaphor makes it possible to apprehend this idea suddenly and completely. The selection from Koestler's "Anatomy of Snobbery" (following) also has this quality.

A precise sense of what a metaphor is intended to do and what it actually does is crucial for the careful reader. Strict attention to what the writer is doing enables the reader to test a metaphorical statement for clarity, exactness, and consistency of thought. The appropriateness of the metaphor can be judged by asking whether the element compared is significant and whether the metaphor itself touches on only one point of comparison or whether it rests on several, as Orwell's "outcrops" does.

George Orwell's "Politics and the English Language" (following) is complete and accurate enough in its discussion of the abuse of language that little need be said here. But it is important to remember that most inadequacies of style which cannot be traced to bad language habits can be traced to slovenly, careless thinking. Inexactness, vagueness, or ambiguity in definition or in using words tentatively mean that the writer has failed to think his ideas through carefully and failed as well to consider what effect his words may have. In a similar way, the writer whose words connote what is inappropriate to his discussion or who uses stale metaphors, clichés, or jargon has stopped thinking for himself.

Cliché and jargon need special mention because they are so widespread. The cliché, usually the sort of worn-out metaphor Orwell mentions, conveys a meaning, but one that is usually ambiguous. It is itself a substitute for words that could convey a more precise meaning. It properly belongs to the spoken language, where ambiguity or vagueness may be eliminated by gesture, tone of voice, or repetition. The cliché is a short cut and is used so often in conversation because it is easier and takes less time than a careful explanation would. The speaker is not pressed to make his meaning immediately clear. If he fails the first time he can tell by the listener's response. The writer does not have the same liberty of improvisation, for most readers object to unnecessary repetition.

Jargon is language that grows out of the habits of expression of a particular group, often professional. Doctors, social scientists, scholars, newspapermen, and bureaucrats all have their own jargon, and very often it is confusing to the nonspecialist. One of the reasons that jargon exists is that professional people must talk to and write for each other in precise and accurate ways which might not be served by the ambiguities and varied meanings of everyday language. Here jargon is necessary. When doctors communicate with one another the words "cold" or "fever" may be inaccurate to describe the particular ailment in question.

Unfortunately all professional groups also must communicate with the rest of us and in doing so they frequently let their jargons take the place of simpler, more readily understood language. An experienced bureaucrat can take a very simple idea and initiate it, take it under advisement, finalize it, and finally implement it. A sociologist may talk about peer-group integration when he means that people fit in with others like themselves. Jargon may sometimes use fewer words than nonjargon, but it is not for that reason any clearer. And sometimes even within a professional group jargon is a mask for confused, sloppy thought or deliberate lying. George Orwell cites some grotesque but common examples of these in the selection that follows.

Sooner or later a good many words and phrases that begin as jargon become common figures of speech, for language is in a constant state of change. The trick is to recognize jargon when it is jargon and to see whether or not other words will do the job.

THE ANATOMY OF SNOBBERY   Arthur Koestler

From "The Anatomy of Snobbery," The Anchor Review, No. 1, Doubleday Anchor Books. Reprinted by permission of the author and editor.

WE CAN add to our knowledge and experience, but we cannot subtract from it. When Picasso decides to disregard the laws of perspective, that means that he has passed through and beyond a certain technique — unlike the Egyptian painter, who has never acquired it. Evolution is an irreversible process; the culture of a period might apparently point into the same direction as an earlier one, but it does so from a different turn of the spiral. A modern primitive is different from a primitive primitive; contemporary classicism is different from any classical classicism; only the mentally insane are able to amputate part of their past.

2   And yet when we contemplate works of the past, we must perform just such a process of mental subtraction, by attuning our minds to the climate and experience of the period. In order to appreciate them, we must enter into their spirit, by forgetting our modern experience and all that we have learnt since that Homeric epic or Byzantine mosaic was created. We must descend into the past, making our mind a blank; and as we do so, we unconsciously condescend. We close our eyes to crudities of technique, naiveties of perception, prevailing superstitions, limitations of knowledge, factual errors. We make allowances. A little honest introspection will always reveal the element of condescension contained in our admiration for the classics; and part of our enjoyment when listening to the voices of the past is derived from this half-consciously patronizing attitude — "how clever of them to know that at their age." We feel that we have descended a turn of the spiral; we are looking up in awe and wonder at Dante's dreadful Paradise, but at the same time we seem to be bending down, with a tender, antiquarian stoop.

3   This legitimate kind of aesthetic double-think degenerates into snobbery at the point where the frame of reference becomes more important than the

picture, when the thrill derived from the gesture of bending over the past
dominates the aesthetic experience. The result is a widespread confusion
of critical judgment — overestimation of the dead and belittlement of the
living, indiscriminate reverence for anything that is "classical," "antique,"
"primitive," or simply old. In its extreme form this tendency prompts people
to have their wall brackets and picture frames artificially dirtied to lend
them the patina of age; so let us call it the "patina snobbery."

4   The process that leads to these distortions of judgment is basically the
same as outlined before: the projection of one scale of values to a psychologically related but objectively alien field of experience. The essence of
snobbery is to assess value according to a wrong type of scale; the snob is
always trying to measure beauty with a thermometer or weight with a clock.

Commentary and questions

1. *Paragraph 1:* This is a fine example of quiet, unobtrusive metaphor.
But those Koestler uses are deliberate. "Add" and "subtract," "passed
through and beyond," "point in the same direction," and "turn in the
spiral," and "amputate" form a pattern in which the metaphors are increasingly noticeable and sharp. As Koestler moves from the first sentence to the last, he moves from a relatively neutral, unemotional fashion
of speech to one suggesting violence. This is effective for impressing the
reader that what he has to say is crucial and should be attended to.

But something else happens in this paragraph. There are at least
three fairly clear concepts in the metaphors and all of them are developed and clarified by the order in which the metaphors appear. Addition and subtraction imply a process of accumulation, "pass through and
beyond" are concepts of motion and time (note that both of these figures
are used in reference to knowledge, experience, and artistic technique).
In other words they establish the contexts in which Koestler will talk
about human attitudes toward art. The context is first very broad, taking
in general knowledge and experience; then it is narrowed to the notion
of changing technique in art as a progressive development. Next, because
Koestler is aware that cultures widely different in time may nevertheless
have likenesses, he moves to the metaphor of direction, which also qualifies and sharpens the idea of motion in time established earlier. But because he wants to tell us that cultural similarities and differences exist
side by side and must be viewed within the contexts of time and evolutionary change, he finally resorts to two other metaphors, the spiral and
amputation. The spiral very efficiently renders the notion that two cultures may be broadly similar but that being separated in time, one having developed beyond the other, they are also different. Finally, the
arresting metaphor "amputate" reminds us that past culture or experience cannot be obliterated; thus the notion of evolution, which has already been called "an irreversible process," is reinforced.

The analysis of this paragraph shows that metaphor can be used
both to supplement more direct statement, to make statement somewhat

less quickly and more impressively than direct means might do, and to organize the pattern, the order by which concepts are developed.

2. *Paragraph 2:* Here Koestler reverses his field and says, in effect, that what he has already established as impossible is precisely what we do when we appreciate the art of the past. Here he resorts again to a metaphor of motion, this time centering mainly on the processes of ascent and descent, developing the latter into a pun involving "condescend." The pun is crucial to the distinctions the author is trying to make in this paragraph. How does it assist them? Precisely what attitude is Koestler trying to describe? Does the reappearance of the spiral metaphor help?

This commentary deliberately omits discussion of other metaphors in the selection. Find them and analyze their function in the passage. Pay attention to their consistency with one another, and try to decide whether they merely color statements already made directly or convey ideas by themselves. Are there any mixed metaphors in the passage?

POLITICS AND THE
ENGLISH LANGUAGE

George Orwell

From Shooting an Elephant and Other Essays, *by George Orwell, copyright 1945, 1946, 1949, 1950 by Sonia Brownell Orwell. Reprinted by permission of Harcourt, Brace and Company, Inc. Canadian rights granted by Secker and Warburg, London.*

MOST people who bother with the matter at all would admit that the English language is in a bad way, but it is generally assumed that we cannot by conscious action do anything about it. Our civilization is decadent and our language — so the argument runs — must inevitably share in the general collapse. It follows that any struggle against the abuse of language is a sentimental archaism, like preferring candles to electric light or hansom cabs to aeroplanes. Underneath this lies the half-conscious belief that language is a natural growth and not an instrument which we shape for our own purposes.

2 Now, it is clear that the decline of a language must ultimately have political and economic causes: it is not due simply to the bad influence of this or that individual writer. But an effect can become a cause, reinforcing the original cause and producing the same effect in an intensified form, and so on indefinitely. A man may take to drink because he feels himself to be a failure, and then fail all the more completely because he drinks. It is rather the same thing that is happening to the English language. It becomes ugly and inaccurate because our thoughts are foolish, but the slovenliness of our language makes it easier for us to have foolish thoughts. The point is that the process is reversible. Modern English, especially written English, is full

of bad habits which spread by imitation and which can be avoided if one is willing to take the necessary trouble. If one gets rid of these habits one can think more clearly, and to think clearly is a necessary first step towards political regeneration: so that the fight against bad English is not frivolous and is not the exclusive concern of professional writers. I will come back to this presently, and I hope that by that time the meaning of what I have said here will have become clearer. Meanwhile, here are five specimens of the English language as it is now habitually written.

³   These five passages have not been picked out because they are especially bad — I could have quoted far worse if I had chosen — but because they illustrate various of the mental vices from which we now suffer. They are a little below the average, but are fairly representative samples. I number them so that I can refer back to them when necessary:

> (1) I am not, indeed, sure whether it is not true to say that the Milton who once seemed not unlike a seventeenth-century Shelley had not become, out of an experience ever more bitter in each year, more alien [*sic*] to the founder of that Jesuit sect which nothing could induce him to tolerate.
>
> Professor Harold Laski
(Essay in *Freedom of Expression*).

> (2) Above all, we cannot play ducks and drakes with a native battery of idioms which prescribes such egregious collocations of vocables as the Basic *put up with* for *tolerate* or *put at a loss* for *bewilder*.
>
> Professor Lancelot Hogben (*Interglossa*).

> (3) On the one side we have the free personality: by definition it is not neurotic, for it has neither conflict nor dream. Its desires, such as they are, are transparent, for they are just what institutional approval keeps in the forefront of consciousness; another institutional pattern would alter their number and intensity; there is little in them that is natural, irreducible, or culturally dangerous. But *on the other side,* the social bond itself is nothing but the mutual reflection of these self-secure integrities. Recall the definition of love. Is not this the very picture of a small academic? Where is there a place in this hall of mirrors for either personality or fraternity?
>
> Essay on psychology in *Politics* (New York).

> (4) All the "best people" from the gentlemen's clubs, and all the frantic fascist captains, united in common hatred of Socialism and bestial horror of the rising tide of the mass revolutionary movement, have turned to acts of provocation, to foul incendiarism, to medieval legends of poisoned wells, to legalize their own destruction of proletarian organizations, and rouse the agitated petty-bourgeoisie to chauvinistic fervor on behalf of the fight against the revolutionary way out of the crisis.
>
> Communist pamphlet.

> (5) If a new spirit is to be infused into this old country, there is one thorny and contentious reform which must be tackled, and that is the

humanization and galvanization of the B.B.C. Timidity here will bespeak canker and atrophy of the soul. The heart of Britain may be sound and of strong beat, for instance, but the British lion's roar at present is like that of Bottom in Shakespeare's *Midsummer Night's Dream* — as gentle as any sucking dove. A virile new Britain cannot continue indefinitely to be traduced in the eyes, or rather ears, of the world by the effete languors of Langham Place, brazenly masquerading as "standard English." When the Voice of Britain is heard at nine o'clock, better far and infinitely less ludicrous to hear aitches honestly dropped than the present priggish, inflated, inhibited, school-ma'amish arch braying of blameless bashful mewing maidens!

Letter in *Tribune*.

4   Each of these passages has faults of its own, but, quite apart from avoidable ugliness, two qualities are common to all of them. The first is staleness of imagery; the other is lack of precision. The writer either has a meaning and cannot express it, or he inadvertently says something else, or he is almost indifferent as to whether his words mean anything or not. This mixture of vagueness and sheer incompetence is the most marked characteristic of modern English prose, and especially of any kind of political writing. As soon as certain topics are raised, the concrete melts into the abstract and no one seems able to think of turns of speech that are not hackneyed: prose consists less and less of *words* chosen for the sake of their meaning, and more and more of *phrases* tacked together like the sections of a prefabricated henhouse. I list below, with notes and examples, various of the tricks by means of which the work of prose-construction is habitually dodged:

5   *Dying metaphors.* A newly invented metaphor assists thought by evoking a visual image, while on the other hand a metaphor which is technically "dead" (e.g. *iron resolution*) has in effect reverted to being an ordinary word and can generally be used without loss of vividness. But in between these two classes there is a huge dump of worn-out metaphors which have lost all evocative power and are merely used because they save people the trouble of inventing phrases for themselves. Examples are: *Ring the changes on, take up the cudgels for, toe the line, ride roughshod over, stand shoulder to shoulder with, play into the hands of, no axe to grind, grist to the mill, fishing in troubled waters, on the order of the day, Achilles' heel, swan song, hotbed.* Many of these are used without knowledge of their meaning (what is a "rift," for instance?), and incompatible metaphors are frequently mixed, a sure sign that the writer is not interested in what he is saying. Some metaphors now current have been twisted out of their original meaning without those who use them even being aware of the fact. For example, *toe the line* is sometimes written *tow the line.* Another example is *the hammer and the anvil,* now always used with the implication that the anvil gets the worst of it. In real life it is always the anvil that breaks the hammer, never the other way about: a writer who stopped to think what he was saying would be aware of this, and would avoid perverting the original phrase.

6   *Operators* or *verbal false limbs*. These save the trouble of picking out appropriate verbs and nouns, and at the same time pad each sentence with extra syllables which give it an appearance of symmetry. Characteristic phrases are *render inoperative, militate against, make contact with, be subjected to, give rise to, give grounds for, have the effect of, play a leading part (role) in, make itself felt, take effect, exhibit a tendency to, serve the purpose of, etc., etc.* The keynote is the elimination of simple verbs. Instead of being a single word, such as *break, stop, spoil, mend, kill*, a verb becomes a *phrase*, made up of a noun or adjective tacked on to some general-purposes verb such as *prove, serve, form, play, render*. In addition, the passive voice is wherever possible used in preference to the active, and noun constructions are used instead of gerunds (*by examination of* instead of *by examining*). The range of verbs is further cut down by means of the *-ize* and *de-* formations, and the banal statements are given an appearance of profundity by means of the *not un-* formation. Simple conjunctions and prepositions are replaced by such phrases as *with respect to, having regard to, the fact that, by dint of, in view of, in the interests of, on the hypothesis that;* and the ends of sentences are saved by anticlimax by such resounding common-places as *greatly to be desired, cannot be left out of account, a development to be expected in the near future, deserving of serious consideration, brought to a satisfactory conclusion,* and so on and so forth.

7   *Pretentious diction*. Words like *phenomenon, element, individual* (as noun), *objective, categorical, effective, virtual, basic, primary, promote, constitute, exhibit, exploit, utilize, eliminate, liquidate,* are used to dress up simple statement and give an air of scientific impartiality to biased judgments. Adjectives like *epoch-making, epic, historic, unforgettable, triumphant, age-old, inevitable, inexorable, veritable,* are used to dignify the sordid processes of international politics, while writing that aims at glorifying war usually takes on an archaic color, its characteristic words being: *realm, throne, chariot, mailed fist, trident, sword, shield, buckler, banner, jackboot, clarion.* Foreign words and expressions such as *cul de sac, ancien régime, deus ex machina, mutatis mutandis, status quo, gleichschaltung, weltanschauung,* are used to give an air of culture and elegance. Except for the useful abbreviations *i.e., e.g.,* and *etc.,* there is no real need for any of the hundreds of foreign phrases now current in English. Bad writers, and especially scientific, political and sociological writers, are nearly always haunted by the notion that Latin or Greek words are grander than Saxon ones, and unnecessary words like *expedite, ameliorate, predict, extraneous, deracinated, clandestine, subaqueous* and hundreds of others constantly gain ground from their Anglo-Saxon opposite numbers.[1] The jargon peculiar to Marxist writing (*hyena, hangman,*

---

[1] An interesting illustration of this is the way in which the English flower names which were in use till very recently are being ousted by Greek ones, *snapdragon* becoming *antirrhinum, forget-me-not* becoming *myosotis,* etc. It is hard to see any practical reason for this change of fashion: it is probably due to an instinctive turning-away from the more homely word and a vague feeling that the Greek word is scientific.

cannibal, petty bourgeois, these gentry, lacquey, flunkey, mad dog, White Guard, etc.) consists largely of words and phrases translated from Russian, German or French; but the normal way of coining a new word is to use a Latin or Greek root with the appropriate affix and, where necessary, the size formation. It is often easier to make up words of this kind (*deregionalize, impermissible, extramarital, nonfragmentary* and so forth) than to think up the English words that will cover one's meaning. The result, in general, is an increase in slovenliness and vagueness.

8   *Meaningless words.* In certain kinds of writing, particularly in art criticism and literary criticism, it is normal to come across long passages which are almost completely lacking in meaning.[2] Words like *romantic, plastic, values, human, dead, sentimental, natural, vitality,* as used in art criticism, are strictly meaningless, in the sense that they not only do not point to any discoverable object, but are hardly ever expected to do so by the reader. When one critic writes, "The outstanding feature of Mr. X's work is its living quality," while another writes, "The immediately striking thing about Mr. X's work is its peculiar deadness," the reader accepts this as a simple difference of opinion. If words like *black* and *white* were involved, instead of the jargon words *dead* and *living,* he would see at once that language was being used in an improper way. Many political words are similarly abused. The word *Fascism* has now no meaning except in so far as it signifies "something not desirable." The words *democracy, socialism, freedom, patriotic, realistic, justice,* have each of them several different meanings which cannot be reconciled with one another. In the case of a word like *democracy,* not only is there no agreed definition, but the attempt to make one is resisted from all sides. It is almost universally felt that when we call a country democratic we are praising it: consequently the defenders of every kind of régime claim that it is a democracy, and fear that they might have to stop using the word if it were tied down to any one meaning. Words of this kind are often used in a consciously dishonest way. That is, the person who uses them has his own private definition, but allows his hearer to think he means something quite different. Statements like *Marshal Pétain was a true patriot, The Soviet Press is the freest in the world, The Catholic Church is opposed to persecution,* are almost always made with intent to deceive. Other words used in variable meanings, in most cases more or less dishonestly, are: *class, totalitarian, science, progressive, reactionary, bourgeois, equality.*

9   Now that I have made this catalogue of swindles and perversions, let me give another example of the kind of writing that they lead to. This time it must of its nature be an imaginary one. I am going to translate a passage

---

[2] Example: "Comfort's catholicity of perception and image, strangely Whitmanesque in range, almost the exact opposite in aesthetic compulsion, continues to evoke that trembling atmospheric accumulative hinting at a cruel, an inexorably serene timelessness. . . . Wrey Gardiner scores by aiming at simple bull's-eyes with precision. Only they are not so simple, and through this contented sadness runs more than the surface bittersweet of resignation." (Poetry Quarterly.)

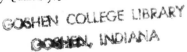

of good English into modern English of the worst sort. Here is a well-known verse from *Ecclesiastes:*

"I returned and saw under the sun, that the race is not to the swift, nor the battle to the strong, neither yet bread to the wise, nor yet riches to men of understanding, nor yet favour to men of skill; but time and chance happeneth to them all."

10   Here it is in modern English:

"Objective consideration of contemporary phenomena compels the conclusion that success or failure in competitive activities exhibits no tendency to be commensurate with innate capacity, but that a considerable element of the unpredictable must invariably be taken into account."

11   This is a parody, but not a very gross one. Exhibit (3), above, for instance, contains several patches of the same kind of English. It will be seen that I have not made a full translation. The beginning and ending of the sentence follow the original meaning fairly closely, but in the middle the concrete illustrations — race, battle, bread — dissolve into the vague phrase "success or failure in competitive activities." This had to be so, because no modern writer of the kind I am discussing — no one capable of using phrases like "objective consideration of contemporary phenomena" — would ever tabulate his thoughts in that precise and detailed way. The whole tendency of modern prose is away from concreteness. Now analyze these two sentences a little more closely. The first contains forty-nine words but only sixty syllables, and all its words are those of everyday life. The second contains thirty-eight words of ninety syllables: eighteen of its words are from Latin roots, and one from Greek. The first sentence contains six vivid images, and only one phrase ("time and chance") that could be called vague. The second contains not a single fresh, arresting phrase, and in spite of its ninety syllables it gives only a shortened version of the meaning contained in the first. Yet without a doubt it is the second kind of sentence that is gaining ground in modern English. I do not want to exaggerate. This kind of writing is not yet universal, and outcrops of simplicity will occur here and there in the worst-written page. Still, if you or I were told to write a few lines on the uncertainty of human fortunes, we should probably come much nearer to my imaginary sentence than to the one from *Ecclesiastes.*

12   As I have tried to show, modern writing at its worst does not consist in picking out words for the sake of their meaning and inventing images in order to make the meaning clearer. It consists in gumming together long strips of words which have already been set in order by someone else, and making the results presentable by sheer humbug. The attraction of this way of writing is that it is easy. It is easier — even quicker, once you have the habit — to say *In my opinion it is not an unjustifiable assumption that* than to say *I think.* If you use ready-made phrases, you not only don't have to hunt about for words; you also don't have to bother with the rhythms of your sentences, since these phrases are generally so arranged as to be more

or less euphonious. When you are composing in a hurry — when you are dictating to a stenographer, for instance, or making a public speech — it is natural to fall into a pretentious, Latinized style. Tags like *a consideration which we should do well to bear in mind* or *a conclusion to which all of us would readily assent* will save many a sentence from coming down with a bump. By using stale metaphors, similes and idioms, you save much mental effort, at the cost of leaving your meaning vague, not only for your reader but for yourself. This is the significance of mixed metaphors. The sole aim of a metaphor is to call up a visual image. When these images clash — as in *the Fascist octopus has sung its swan song, the jackboot is thrown into the melting pot* — it can be taken as certain that the writer is not seeing a mental image of the objects he is naming; in other words he is not really thinking. Look again at the examples I gave at the beginning of this essay. Professor Laski (1) uses five negatives in fifty-three words. One of these is superfluous, making nonsense of the whole passage, and in addition there is the slip *alien* for akin, making further nonsense, and several avoidable pieces of clumsiness which increase the general vagueness. Professor Hogben (2) plays ducks and drakes with a battery which is able to write prescriptions, and, while disapproving of the everyday phrase *put up with,* is unwilling to look *egregious* up in the dictionary and see what it means; (3), if one takes an uncharitable attitude towards it, is simply meaningless: probably one could work out its intended meaning by reading the whole of the article in which it occurs. In (4), the writer knows more or less what he wants to say, but an accumulation of stale phrases chokes him like tea leaves blocking a sink. In (5), words and meaning have almost parted company. People who write in this manner usually have a general emotional meaning — they dislike one thing and want to express solidarity with another — but they are not interested in the detail of what they are saying. A scrupulous writer, in every sentence that he writes, will ask himself at least four questions, thus: What am I trying to say? What words will express it? What image or idiom will make it clearer? Is this image fresh enough to have an effect? And he will probably ask himself two more: Could I put it more shortly? Have I said anything that is avoidably ugly? But you are not obliged to go to all this trouble. You can shirk it by simply throwing your mind open and letting the ready-made phrases come crowding in. They will construct your sentences for you — even think your thoughts for you, to a certain extent — and at need they will perform the important service of partially concealing your meaning even from yourself. It is at this point that the special connection between politics and the debasement of language becomes clear.

13   In our time it is broadly true that political writing is bad writing. Where it is not true, it will generally be found that the writer is some kind of rebel, expressing his private opinions and not a "party line." Orthodoxy, of whatever color, seems to demand a lifeless, imitative style. The political dialects to be found in pamphlets, leading articles, manifestoes, White Papers and the

speeches of under-secretaries do, of course, vary from party to party, but they are all alike in that one almost never finds in them a fresh, vivid, home-made turn of speech. When one watches some tired hack on the platform mechanically repeating the familiar phrases — *bestial atrocities, iron heel, bloodstained tyranny, free peoples of the world, stand shoulder to shoulder* — one often has a curious feeling that one is not watching a live human being but some kind of dummy: a feeling which suddenly becomes stronger at moments when the light catches the speaker's spectacles and turns them into blank discs which seem to have no eyes behind them. And this is not altogether fanciful. A speaker who uses that kind of phraseology has gone some distance towards turning himself into a machine. The appropriate noises are coming out of his larynx, but his brain is not involved as it would be if he were choosing his words for himself. If the speech he is making is one that he is accustomed to make over and over again, he may be almost unconscious of what he is saying, as one is when one utters the responses in church. And this reduced state of consciousness, if not indispensable, is at any rate favorable to political conformity.

14   In our time, political speech and writing are largely the defence of the indefensible. Things like the continuance of British rule in India, the Russian purges and deportations, the dropping of the atom bombs on Japan, can indeed be defended, but only by arguments which are too brutal for most people to face, and which do not square with the professed aims of political parties. Thus political language has to consist largely of euphemism, question-begging and sheer cloudy vagueness. Defenceless villages are bombarded from the air, the inhabitants driven out into the countryside, the cattle machine-gunned, the huts set on fire with incendiary bullets: this is called *pacification*. Millions of peasants are robbed of their farms and sent trudging along the roads with no more than they can carry: this is called *transfer of population* or *rectification of frontiers*. People are imprisoned for years without trial, or shot in the back of the neck or sent to die of scurvy in Arctic lumber camps: this is called *elimination of unreliable elements*. Such phraseology is needed if one wants to name things without calling up mental pictures of them. Consider for instance some comfortable English professor defending Russian totalitarianism. He cannot say outright, "I believe in killing off your opponents when you can get good results by doing so." Probably, therefore, he will say something like this:

15·   "While freely conceding that the Soviet régime exhibits certain features which the humanitarian may be inclined to deplore, we must, I think, agree that a certain curtailment of the right to political opposition is an unavoidable concomitant of transitional periods, and that the rigors which the Russian people have been called upon to undergo have been amply justified in the sphere of concrete achievement."

16   The inflated style is itself a kind of euphemism. A mass of Latin words falls upon the facts like soft snow, blurring the outlines and covering up all the details. The great enemy of clear language is insincerity. When there is

a gap between one's real and one's declared aims, one turns as it were instinctively to long words and exhausted idioms, like a cuttlefish squirting out
ink. In our age there is no such thing as "keeping out of politics." All issues
are political issues, and politics itself is a mass of lies, evasions, folly, hatred
and schizophrenia. When the general atmosphere is bad, language must
suffer. I should expect to find — this is a guess which I have not sufficient
knowledge to verify — that the German, Russian and Italian languages have
all deteriorated in the last ten or fifteen years, as a result of dictatorship.

¹⁷   But if thought corrupts language, language can also corrupt thought. A
bad usage can spread by tradition and imitation, even among people who
should and do know better. The debased language that I have been discussing is in some ways very convenient. Phrases like *a not unjustifiable as-*
sumption, leaves much to be desired, would serve no good purpose, a con-
sideration which we should do well to bear in mind, are a continuous
temptation, a packet of aspirins always at one's elbow. Look back through
this essay, and for certain you will find that I have again and again committed the very faults I am protesting against. By this morning's post I have
received a pamphlet dealing with conditions in Germany. The author tells
me that he "felt impelled" to write it. I open it at random, and here is almost
the first sentence that I see: "[The Allies] have an opportunity not only of
achieving a radical transformation of Germany's social and political structure in such a way as to avoid a nationalistic reaction in Germany itself, but
at the same time of laying the foundations of a co-operative and unified
Europe." You see, he "feels impelled" to write — feels, presumably, that he
has something new to say — and yet his words, like cavalry horses answering
the bugle, group themselves automatically into the familiar dreary pattern.
This invasion of one's mind by ready-made phrases (*lay the foundations,*
achieve a radical transformation) can only be prevented if one is constantly
on guard against them, and every such phrase anesthetizes a portion of one's
brain.

¹⁸   I said earlier that the decadence of our language is probably curable.
Those who deny this would argue, if they produced an argument at all, that
language merely reflects existing social conditions, and that we cannot influence its development by any direct tinkering with words and constructions.
So far as the general tone or spirit of a language goes, this may be true, but
it is not true in detail. Silly words and expressions have often disappeared,
not through any evolutionary process but owing to the conscious action of
a minority. Two recent examples were *explore every avenue* and *leave no*
stone unturned, which were killed by the jeers of a few journalists. There is
a long list of flyblown metaphors which could similarly be got rid of if
enough people would interest themselves in the job; and it should also be
possible to laugh the *not un-* formation out of existence,[3] to reduce the
amount of Latin and Greek in the average sentence, to drive out foreign

[3] One can cure oneself of the *not un-* formation by memorizing this sentence: *A not*
unblack dog was chasing a not unsmall rabbit across a not ungreen field.

phrases and strayed scientific words, and, in general, to make pretentiousness unfashionable. But all these are minor points. The defence of the English language implies more than this, and perhaps it is best to start by saying what it does *not* imply.

19   To begin with it has nothing to do with archaism, with the salvaging of obsolete words and turns of speech, or with the setting up of a "standard English" which must never be departed from. On the contrary, it is especially concerned with the scrapping of every word or idiom which has outworn its usefulness. It has nothing to do with correct grammar and syntax, which are of no importance so long as one makes one's meaning clear, or with the avoidance of Americanisms, or with having what is called a "good prose style." On the other hand it is not concerned with fake simplicity and the attempt to make written English colloquial. Nor does it even imply in every case preferring the Saxon word to the Latin one, though it does imply using the fewest and shortest words that will cover one's meaning. What is above all needed is to let the meaning choose the word, and not the other way about. In prose, the worst thing one can do with words is to surrender to them. When you think of a concrete object, you think wordlessly, and then, if you want to describe the thing you have been visualizing you probably hunt about till you find the exact words that seem to fit it. When you think of something abstract you are more inclined to use words from the start, and unless you make a conscious effort to prevent it, the existing dialect will come rushing in and do the job for you, at the expense of blurring or even changing your meaning. Probably it is better to put off using words as long as possible and get one's meaning as clear as one can through pictures or sensations. Afterwards one can choose — not simply *accept* — the phrases that will best cover the meaning, and then switch round and decide what impression one's words are likely to make on another person. This last effort of the mind cuts out all stale or mixed images, all prefabricated phrases, needless repetitions, and humbug and vagueness generally. But one can often be in doubt about the effect of a word or a phrase, and one needs rules that one can rely on when instinct fails. I think the following rules will cover most cases:

(i) Never use a metaphor, simile or other figure of speech which you are used to seeing in print.

(ii) Never use a long word where a short one will do.

(iii) If it is possible to cut a word out, always cut it out.

(iv) Never use the passive where you can use the active.

(v) Never use a foreign phrase, a scientific word or a jargon word if you can think of an everyday English equivalent.

(vi) Break any of these rules sooner than say anything outright barbarous.

These rules sound elementary, and so they are, but they demand a deep change of attitude in anyone who has grown used to writing in the style now fashionable. One could keep all of them and still write bad English, but one could not write the kind of stuff that I quoted in those five specimens at the beginning of this article.

20 I have not here been considering the literary use of language, but merely language as an instrument for expressing and not for concealing or preventing thought. Stuart Chase and others have come near to claiming that all abstract words are meaningless, and have used this as a pretext for advocating a kind of political quietism. Since you don't know what Fascism is, how can you struggle against Fascism? One need not swallow such absurdities as this, but one ought to recognize that the present political chaos is connected with the decay of language, and that one can probably bring about some improvement by starting at the verbal end. If you simplify your English, you are freed from the worst follies of orthodoxy. You cannot speak any of the necessary dialects, and when you make a stupid remark its stupidity will be obvious, even to yourself. Political language — and with variations this is true of all political parties, from Conservatives to Anarchists — is designed to make lies sound truthful and murder respectable, and to give an appearance of solidity to pure wind. One cannot change this all in a moment, but one can at least change one's own habits, and from time to time one can even, if one jeers loudly enough, send some worn-out and useless phrase — some *jackboot, Achilles' heel, hotbed, melting pot, acid test, veritable inferno* or other lump of verbal refuse — into the dustbin where it belongs.

Commentary

For the most part, the preceding essay is self-explanatory, but a few matters need mention. The first is Orwell's justification for his strong criticism of the weaknesses of contemporary English and American prose style. It is a justification in the name of politics, which was for Orwell the most crucial area of human activity.

This political bias nevertheless does not seem to interfere with the justness of Orwell's remarks; they are just as valid without it, for the accurate and independent use of language depends on clear thinking and a willingness to tell the truth.

Nor is a failure to tell the truth in writing simply a matter of dishonesty. More often, perhaps, it is a willingness to accept the stale phrase (and with it the stale thought). So the cliché, the polysyllables of jargon, the sloppy use of negatives, weak passive constructions, and meaningless phrases crowd in upon the expression of the inattentive, thoughtless writer.

Since Orwell himself lists and catalogues what he considers the major faults of prose style and their causes and cures, no further mention seems necessary here. But it might be instructive to do two things:

(1) Try to find examples in the essay of the faults most abhorrent to Orwell.

(2) Orwell makes a great deal of stale, visually weak metaphor as

a symptom of bad writing. He himself uses metaphorical language frequently and deliberately. Test his usage against his own rules and against what is said about metaphor in the previous examples (pp. 35-38).

Topics for discussion and writing

Examine the following paragraphs. Point out the metaphors, comment on what they are intended to accomplish and on their freshness, appropriateness, and significance.

"The inadequacy of our institutions only intensifies the tribute that society levies from man: it but exacerbates the moral crisis. The rise of totalitarianism, in other words, signifies more than an internal crisis for democratic man. There is a Hitler, a Stalin in every breast." (*From A. M. Schlesinger, Jr., "Freedom: A Fighting Faith," p. 470.*)

"We teach the past, we see farther backward into time than any race before us, but we stop at the present, or, at best, we project far into the future idealized versions of ourselves. All that long way behind us we see, perhaps inevitably, through human eyes alone. We see ourselves as the culmination and the end, and if we do indeed consider our passing, we think that sunlight will go with us and the earth be dark. We are the end. For us continents rose and fell, for us the waters and the air were mastered, for us the great living web has pulsated and grown more intricate." (*From Loren Eiseley, "The Snout," p. 372.*)

"The God that holds you over the pit of hell, much as one holds a spider, or some loathsome insect over the fire, abhors you, and is dreadfully provoked: his wrath towards you burns like fire; he looks upon you as worthy of nothing else, but to be cast into the fire; he is of purer eyes than to bear to have you in his sight; you are ten thousand times more abominable in his eyes, than the most hateful venomous serpent is in ours. You have offended him infinitely more than ever a stubborn rebel did his prince; and yet it is nothing but his hand that holds you from falling into the fire every moment. It is to be ascribed to nothing else, that you did not go to hell the last night; that you was suffered to awake again in this world, after you closed your eyes to sleep. And there is no other reason to be given, why you have not dropped into hell since you arose in the morning, but that God's hand has held you up. There is no other reason to be given why you have not gone to hell, since you have sat here in the house of God, provoking his pure eyes by your sinful wicked manner of attending his solemn worship. Yea, there is nothing else that is to be given as a reason why you do not this very moment drop down into hell." (*From Jonathan Edwards, "Sinners in the Hands of an Angry God."*)

"Wo to thee, De Launay, in such an hour, if thou canst not, taking some one firm decision, *rule* circumstances! Soft speeches will not serve; hard grapeshot is questionable; but hovering between the two is *unques-*

tionable. Ever wilder swells the tide of men; their infinite hum waxing ever louder, into imprecations, perhaps into crackle of stray musketry, — which latter, on walls nine feet thick, cannot do execution. The Outer Drawbridge has been lowered for Thuriot; new *deputation of citizens* (it is the third, and noisiest of all) penetrates that way into the Outer Court: soft speeches producing no clearance of these, De Launay gives fire; pulls up his Drawbridge. A slight sputter; — which has *kindled* the too combustible chaos; made it a roaring fire-chaos! Burst forth Insurrection, at sight of its own blood (for there were deaths by that sputter of fire), into endless rolling explosion of musketry, distraction, execration; — and over head, from the Fortress, let one great gun, with its grapeshot, go booming, to show what we *could* do. The Bastille is besieged!" (*From Thomas Carlyle,* The French Revolution, *p. 320.*)

The subject matter of education: WHAT THE

SCHOOL IS and THE SUBJECT MATTER OF EDUCATION, John Dewey · THE
ORGANIZATION CHILDREN, William H. Whyte, Jr. · AIMLESSNESS IN EDUCATION,
Arthur E. Bestor, Jr. · THOUGHTS ON TEACHERS AND SCHOOLS, David Riesman

WHAT the public schools should teach is a topic on which
most people have an opinion, whether informed or uninformed. Although an
intellectual problem, it arouses strong emotions. Dewey's essay defines what
he thinks the school is and describes what it ought to teach. Whyte describes
what a modern school is like. Bestor then gives his opinion of the modern
school with strong views of the way it ought to be changed. Riesman, whose
essay shows familiarity with Dewey, Whyte, and Bestor, is sympathetic to
Bestor's complaints and yet resembles Dewey in recognizing the function of
the school as a social institution.

In a broad sense all four authors are engaged in persuasion. Each has
a point of view he wishes the reader to accept. But their language takes a
variety of persuasive forms. Dewey urges his case enthusiastically and appeals to the social feelings of a democratic audience, but at the same time
his arguments are founded on specific concepts. Whyte's account of the Park
Forest school system is a case study, reflecting the attitudes of the people he
has interviewed. Yet he too takes a position and employs the tools of persuasion. The reader should especially note his use of paraphrase. Bestor, the
critic of current educational practices, uses the language of attack, but behind his criticism lie clear positive concepts of his own. And like Dewey he
appeals to a set of social attitudes in his audience. Riesman is the most detached of the four writers. His language is cooler and more deliberate, revealing an attempt at precision in the expression of his ideas. Nonetheless his
essay, too, tries to persuade.

54

WHAT THE SCHOOL IS and THE SUBJECT MATTER OF EDUCATION

John Dewey

From My Pedagogic Creed, *1897.*

What the School Is: I BELIEVE THAT

1 — the school is primarily a social institution. Education being a social process, the school is simply that form of community life in which all those agencies are concentrated that will be most effective in bringing the child to share in the inherited resources of the race, and to use his own powers for social ends.

2 — education, therefore, is a process of living and not a preparation for future living.

3 — the school must represent present life — life as real and vital to the child as that which he carries on in the home, in the neighborhood, or on the playground.

4 — that education which does not occur through forms of life, forms that are worth living for their own sake, is always a poor substitute for the genuine reality, and tends to cramp and to deaden.

5 — the school, as an institution, should simplify existing social life; should reduce it, as it were, to an embryonic form. Existing life is so complex that the child cannot be brought into contact with it without either confusion or distraction; he is either overwhelmed by the multiplicity of activities which are going on, so that he loses his own power of orderly reaction, or he is so stimulated by these various activities that his powers are prematurely called into play and he becomes either unduly specialized or else disintegrated.

6 — as such simplified social life, the school life should grow gradually out of the home life; that it should take up and continue the activities with which the child is already familiar in the home.

7 — it should exhibit these activities to the child, and reproduce them in such ways that the child will gradually learn the meaning of them, and be capable of playing his own part in relation to them.

8 — this is a psychological necessity, because it is the only way of securing continuity in the child's growth, the only way of giving a background of past experience to the new ideas given in school.

9 — it is also a social necessity because the home is the form of social life in which the child has been nurtured and in connection with which he has had his moral training. It is the business of the school to deepen and extend his sense of the values bound up in his home life.

10 — much of present education fails because it neglects this fundamental principle of the school as a form of community life. It conceives the school

as a place where certain information is to be given, where certain lessons are to be learned, or where certain habits are to be formed. The value of these is conceived as lying largely in the remote future; the child must do these things for the sake of something else he is to do; they are mere preparations. As a result they do not become a part of the life experience of the child and so are not truly educative.

11   — the moral education centers upon this conception of the school as a mode of social life, that the best and deepest moral training is precisely that which one gets through having to enter into proper relations with others in a unity of work and thought. The present educational systems, so far as they destroy or neglect this unity, render it difficult or impossible to get any genuine, regular moral training.

12   — the child should be stimulated and controlled in his work through the life of the community.

13   — under existing conditions far too much of the stimulus and control proceeds from the teacher, because of neglect of the idea of the school as a form of social life.

14   — the teacher's place and work in the school is to be interpreted from this same basis. The teacher is not in the school to impose certain ideas or to form certain habits in the child, but is there as a member of the community to select the influences which shall affect the child and to assist him in properly responding to these influences.

15   — the discipline of the school should proceed from the life of the school as a whole and not directly from the teacher.

16   — the teacher's business is simply to determine, on the basis of larger experience and riper wisdom, how the discipline of life shall come to the child.

17   — all questions of the grading of the child and his promotion should be determined by reference to the same standard. Examinations are of use only so far as they test the child's fitness for social life and reveal the place in which he can be of the most service and where he can receive the most help.

The Subject Matter of Education: I BELIEVE THAT

1   — the social life of the child is the basis of concentration, or correlation, in all his training or growth. The social life gives the unconscious unity and the background of all his efforts and of all his attainments.

2   — the subject matter of the school curriculum should mark a gradual differentiation out of the primitive unconscious unity of social life.

3   — we violate the child's nature and render difficult the best ethical results by introducing the child too abruptly to a number of special studies, of reading, writing, geography, etc., out of relation to this social life.

4   — the true center of correlation on the school subjects is not science, nor literature, nor history, nor geography, but the child's own social activities.

5   — education cannot be unified in the study of science, or so-called nature study, because apart from human activity, nature itself is not a unity; nature in itself is a number of diverse objects in space and time, and to attempt to make it the center of work by itself is to introduce a principle of radiation rather than one of concentration.

6   — literature is the reflex expression and interpretation of social experience; that hence it must follow upon and not precede such experience. It, therefore, cannot be made the basis, although it may be made the summary, of unification.

7   — once more that history is of educative value in so far as it presents phases of social life and growth. It must be controlled by reference to social life. When taken simply as history it is thrown into the distant past and becomes dead and inert. Taken as the record of man's social life and progress it becomes full of meaning. I believe, however, that it cannot be so taken excepting as the child is also introduced directly into social life.

8   — the primary basis of education is in the child's powers at work along the same general constructive lines as those which have brought civilization into being.

9   — the only way to make the child conscious of his social heritage is to enable him to perform those fundamental types of activity which make civilization what it is.

10   — in the so-called expressive or constructive activities as the center of correlation.

11   — this gives the standard for the place of cooking, sewing, manual training, etc., in the school.

12   — they are not special studies which are to be introduced over and above a lot of others in the way of relaxation or relief, or as additional accomplishments. I believe rather that they represent, as types, fundamental forms of social activity; and that it is possible and desirable that the child's introduction into the more formal subjects of the curriculum be through the medium of these activities.

13   — the study of science is educational in so far as it brings out the materials and processes which make social life what it is.

14   — one of the greatest difficulties in the present teaching of science is that the material is presented in purely objective form, or is treated as a new peculiar kind of experience which the child can add to that which he has already had. In reality, science is of value because it gives the ability to interpret and control the experience already had. It should be introduced, not as so much new subject-matter, but as showing the factors already in-

volved in previous experience and as furnishing tools by which that experience can be more easily and effectively regulated.

15 — at present we lose much of the value of literature and language studies because of our elimination of the social element. Language is almost always treated in the books of pedagogy simply as the expression of thought. It is true that language is a logical instrument, but it is fundamentally and primarily a social instrument. Language is the device for communication; it is the tool through which one individual comes to share the ideas and feelings of others. When treated simply as a way of getting individual information, or as a means of showing off what one has learned, it loses its social motive and end.

16 — there is, therefore, no succession of studies in the ideal school curriculum. If education is life, all life has, from the outset, a scientific aspect, an aspect of art and culture, and an aspect of communication. It cannot, therefore, be true that the proper studies for one grade are mere reading and writing, and that at a later grade, reading, or literature, or science, may be introduced. The progress is not in the succession of studies, but in the development of new attitudes towards, and new interests in, experience.

17 — education must be conceived as a continuing reconstruction of experience; that the process and the goal of education are one and the same things.

18 — to set up any end outside of education, as furnishing its goal and standard, is to deprive the educational process of much of its meaning, and tends to make us rely upon false and external stimuli in dealing with the child.

Commentary and questions

What the School Is

1. *Paragraph 1:* The word "social" recurs frequently in this little pamphlet. What does Dewey mean by "social"? Has he, in making it a key word, also charged it with emotional overtones?

When he describes the school as a "social institution," which word conveys most of his feeling and thought? Since all institutions are social, is it a tautology to use the word "social"? Is it ever brought into contrast with another concept? Does the word "social" convey a value as well as information?

When Dewey says "the school is simply that form of community life," why does he use the word "simply"?

At the end of the first paragraph, compare "social ends" with your definition of "social." Is it the same concept? Give one or two examples of what you think he means by "social ends." Are your illustrations helpful or harmful to the community? Do you think Dewey intends this same sort of value? Why do you think so?

2. *Paragraphs 3 and 4:* In the paragraph that begins "the school must represent present life," what does the word "represent" mean? Does the entire sentence mean that the child should do the same things in school that he does in the home, in the neighborhood, or on the playground? Does the next paragraph help interpret this one? Can you give illustrations of forms of life that are worth living for their own sake?

3. *Paragraph 5:* Write a paraphrase of the paragraph that begins "the school, as an institution . . . ." When Dewey uses the word "child" in this section, what minimum age would you assign to the child? Do you think a child of that age could become unduly specialized? In what sense could a child become unduly specialized? What maximum age would you assign to this child? Do you think that existing life is so complex that a child of this age cannot be brought into contact with it? Does such a child come into contact with existing life outside school? Does he lose his powers of orderly reaction, by your own observations?

4. *Paragraph 14:* Dewey says in this paragraph that the teacher is not to impose certain ideas or to form certain habits in the child but "to select the influences which shall affect the child and to assist him in properly responding to these influences." Is there a difference between imposing certain ideas and selecting the influences that affect a child? Is there a difference between forming certain habits and assisting him to respond properly?

The Subject Matter of Education

5. *Paragraph 4:* What does Dewey mean by "true center of correlation"? Why does he say "true center" rather than merely "center"?

6. *Paragraph 5:* Explain how "apart from human activity, nature itself is not a unity." Is this a reason for not unifying education around nature? What is a "principle of radiation"? Does Dewey think it good or bad? Do you know why it is good or bad?

7. *Paragraph 6:* How adequate is Dewey's definition of literature? Assuming that he is correct, can you conclude from this that literature necessarily follows upon the experience? At what point should readers be given murder mysteries? (The definition of "such experiences" becomes a crux in answering this question.)

8. *Paragraph 8:* Compare "primary basis of education" with the "true center of correlation" of paragraph 4. Are you able to cite examples of "the same general constructive lines as those which have brought civilization into being."

9. *Paragraph 11:* How are cooking, sewing, and manual training both ends and means? Are they, as Dewey implies, social activities of children?

10. *Paragraph 13:* Explain "what it is" in the excerpt "the materials and processes which make social life what it is."

Topics for discussion and writing

I. Write a unified essay explaining Dewey's concept of what a school is. Be sure your thesis sentence expresses Dewey's underlying notion.

II. Write an essay showing whether or not Dewey would be satisfied with the high school you attended.

III. Write a paraphrase of the first and second paragraphs of "The Subject Matter of Education."

IV. Write a short essay developing three reasons why Dewey would oppose a curriculum of reading, writing, and arithmetic in elementary school.

V. Write a short essay explaining Dewey's ideas of the relation of the school to the home and community.

VI. Is there a necessary distinction between language as the expression of thought and language as a social instrument? The phrase "a means of showing off what one has learned" indicates Dewey is saying what he does not believe in as well as what he does believe in. Write an essay in which you build up from evidence in these two articles characteristics of the system of education Dewey is against.

THE ORGANIZATION CHILDREN

William H. Whyte, Jr.

Copyright 1956, by William H. Whyte, Jr. Reprinted by permission of Simon and Schuster, Inc.

THE organization man's emphasis on the group, I have been maintaining, is not a temporary phenomenon dictated by external necessity; it is a response to what he feels is a moral imperative, and more and more he is openly articulating it. I have looked at the church in this perspective; now I would like to turn to the schools. Like the churches they had to be built from scratch, and in building them the young parents had to declare themselves. Their children will be transients too, and the pressures of the organization life ahead for them will be, if anything, more intense. What, then, should be emphasized? In helping shape the curriculum, parents are at once giving a guide and revealing themselves.

2   The Park Foresters threw themselves into the job of creating a school system with tremendous energy. With few precedents to go on and virtually no industrial tax base, they have developed a system which includes a spankingly attractive high school, six cheerful elementary schools, and several more a-building. Educators all over the country have been lavish in their praise. In 1954 the high school was selected as one of the five winners

in the "All-America Schools" contest of the National Municipal League, and other awards for the school have been streaming in.

3   They have both profited and suffered from an unusual turnover problem. The leadership of the school boards, for example, is constantly turning over. The first elementary-school superintendent, Robert Anderson, and the young chemist who headed the school board could never be sure from one month to the next just who would be working with them. While they were there, board members worked devotedly. Just about the time one became saturated in the school problems, it seemed, his company would transfer him, and the break in continuity persists to this day.

4   Teachers have also been a worry. There is a high turnover of younger teachers in any community, but Park Forest is at an especial disadvantage in this matter. There aren't any bachelors around. (Of some 5,000 males in 1954 only one was unmarried, and he has since left.) Several court units have been set aside for unmarried girl teachers, but this kind of sorority life doesn't jibe with the community, or with the girls, and the rate of departure has been heavy.

5   More important, the children move too. The impact is as severe on the teachers as on the children themselves, for the teachers are thereby robbed of a good bit of the feeling of achievement they get from watching the children develop. As Anderson put it: "In any school you have to put a six-months' investment in a child before the two of you can start functioning right — you have to test them, get the parents involved, get the kids settled down in a group. We do this all right — but then what happens? They move, and you have to start all over again."

6   The children, however, have proved to be highly adaptable material, and the teachers who have had experience in traditional communities are quick to note how much more socially responsive the children of transients are than others. "Social maturity comes faster here for children like this," explains one teacher. "The adjustment to the group doesn't seem to involve so many problems for them. I have noticed that they seem to get the feeling that nobody is the boss — there is a feeling of complete co-operation. Partly this comes from early exposure to court play."

7   Like their parents, in short, the children already have a high degree of social skill, and the environment itself will further intensify this in them. This being the case, it could be argued, there is no necessity for the school to duplicate, and thus they are all the more free to concentrate on the other, more inward, aspects. But neither the parents nor the schools feel this way. From the beginning the curriculum has borne down very heavily on the pragmatic and the social, and the concept of adjustment has been dominant.

8   The first superintendent left, with a well-earned sigh of relief, to be a professor at the Harvard Graduate School of Education. What curriculum changes have ensued, however, have not been major. Anderson's successor, Superintendent Gerald Smith, has talked of introducing the "Fourth R, Re-

sponsibility," but this seems largely another way of describing the established policy. The disciplining vehicle, Smith explains, is the group. The teacher strives not to discipline the child directly but to influence all the children's attitudes so that as a group they recognize correct behavior. If a child falls out of line, he does not have to be subjected to authoritarian strictures of elders; he senses the disapproval of the group and, in that way, the school believes, learns to discipline himself as much as possible.

9   The child who tends to be withdrawn is given special attention. "Johnny wasn't doing so well at school," one mother told me. "The teacher explained to me that he was doing fine on his lessons but that his social adjustment was not as good as it might be. He would pick just one or two friends to play with, and sometimes he was happy to remain by himself." There are many such instances, and, save for a few odd parents, most are grateful that the schools work so hard to offset tendencies to introversion and other suburban abnormalities.

10   Park Forest schools are not extreme in this respect, and most Park Foresters are anxious that the curriculum be recognized as middle of the road. But they do agree that there is a noticeably permissive atmosphere. They point out, for example, that the schools follow a method by which the student group is encouraged to take a strong hand in the planning of what they are to be taught. The children are not exactly put in charge, but the teacher makes a point of asking them what it is they would like to know about a particular subject, rather than unilaterally giving them what she thinks they ought to learn. As Superintendent Smith explained it: "If the topic under discussion is India, the children are asked what they would like to know about that country. Queries might range from elephants to the mysteries of bathing in the Ganges. By the time juvenile curiosities are satisfied, the children have a reasonable knowledge of India's terrain, vegetation, animal life, religions, caste systems, and politics."

11   The schools are similarly flexible in grading. To use fixed standards of performance, the authorities feel, would strait-jacket the child. As a consequence, the primaries, as in many other schools, are ungraded, and in later classes formal reports of the A-B-C-D-F or percentage type have been discarded. "It is obviously impossible," curriculum consultant Lucille Thimblin explains, "for a teacher to reduce the many-sided aspects of a pupil's development to an accurate numerical value." Under the old method, she says, a bright pupil who has made little effort might get the highest mark while another child who works hard might fail to get a respectable mark. The school could get around this by simply using the two terms "satisfactory" and "unsatisfactory" and this would be helpful, Mrs. Thimblin points out, in that "this type of report does reduce the competition for scholastic leadership." Unfortunately, however, while it would make for better adjustment, "it is very likely also to reduce some pupils' incentive to do better work." The solution: a check list to supplement parent-teacher conferences. In this

the student's academic progress is rated on the basis of his individual capabilities rather than against an arbitrary norm. He is also rated in terms of his social group and whether or not he meets the standards attainable for every member of the group.

12   There are a few parental misgivings about the elementary schools. As far as discipline is concerned, parents sometimes wonder if perhaps the school isn't a bit too permissive. Occasionally parents talk of sending their children to Park Forest's parochial school so they would "get some discipline"; they rarely get around to trying, but they still sigh aloud over the elementary schools' laxness. Even parents who are satisfied with the children's behavior are sometimes critical, for though not many may think their own children lack discipline, they are very sure that everybody else's children do. Habitual is the complaint of their "freshness." ("The kids here call everybody by their first names. If one of my neighbors' children ever came up and called me Mrs. George, I think I would drop dead from surprise.") As a few Park Foresters take pains to note, however, parents are somewhat unreasonable about this; whatever their faults, harsh parental discipline is not one of them, and they cannot fairly ask the schools to do what they won't.

13   There is always a controversy of some kind going on over the elementary schools, but it is more on administration and taxes than matters scholastic.[1] On the whole, it seems clear, the parents are very well satisfied with the curriculum. At Park Forest, a PTA committee proudly agreed, learning is a "painless process." "The teacher and the pupils plan together," the committee's report went on, "and everyone has a conscious feeling of belonging — as an individual and as a group participant. . . . Everything they learn is related to something they've experienced in their everyday life or through TV, radio, movies, or on the playground." A few parents are still not altogether adjusted to the absence of primary grades, but this criticism usually comes from people who arrived from a town with a more traditional school, and in time evaporates. Similarly, though some feel there is a slighting of fundamentals, all are impressed with the reports from Park Forest alumni that their children are doing very well academically in their new communi-

---

[1] A notable fracas was over the schools' use of tests to screen kindergarten applicants. Parents whose children flunked were outraged, and when Superintendent Smith's contract came up for renewal in early 1956 many parents were on hand to protest. The board voted to retain Smith but the proceedings were unusually acrimonious — even for Park Forest. From the Park Forest *Reporter*, February 2: "An unruly crowd of nearly 180 jammed the Sauk Trail multi-purpose room to hear the verdict . . . rules of order were violated left and right as spectators voiced opinions . . . [board member] Glassner's prepared speech was two-pronged and included a tabulated 'score' of Smith's administrative successes and failures . . . even more bitter was his indictment of his fellow board members during which he accused former President Albertz of breach of faith . . . Joseph Egan's immediate criticism was of the 'betrayal' of private conversations held with members of the board and employees of the school district." Participation, as I noted earlier, has not died out at Park Forest.

ties because of their Park Forest schooling. If they had to choose, further-more, most Park Foresters would hate to see the schools discard the em-phasis on practical, contemporary problems. "Janet is studying marketing," one parent told me, "and she's only in the sixth grade. She's studying ads and discounts — things I didn't get until college. These kids are certainly getting a broad view of things."

14   It is in the high school, however, that the new suburbia's philosophy gets its most significant expression. The philosophy is by no means unique to Park Forest. High-school superintendent Eric Baber speaks very much like many superintendents elsewhere, and his writings do not show un-orthodoxy but, rather, a deep grasp of contemporary educational literature. What makes Park Forest's high school unique is that, where in traditional communities what has been called the "life adjustment" curriculum has been introduced a bit at a time, at Park Forest it has been the foundation. The new $1,600,000 "learning laboratory" is not only one of the most modern in the country; in spirit as well as brick it is the embodiment of the suburban temper.

15   Five years ago, when the school was still in the planning stage, Baber told parents that the trouble with U.S. education is that it is concentrated far too much on the intellectual aspect of education. Even teachers' colleges, he observed sadly, still require plane geometry for admission. Except for a small coterie, he asked, of what value to most people are the traditional academic disciplines? "The so-called 'bright student' is often one of the dumbest or least apt when he gets away from his textbooks and memory work," Baber told a teachers' workshop. "This is evidenced by the fact that many $20,000-to-$100,000-a-year jobs in business, sales, sports, radio . . . are held by persons with I.Q.s of less than ninety."

16   Baber is not actually against intelligence. He believes it should be channeled toward real-life, vocational needs more than to the academic requirements of the colleges. Since Park Forest, unlike many towns, is pre-dominantly college-educated, most students will be going on to college anyway; thus the "two-school," vocational versus academic problems might not seem particularly pertinent. A large share of the school plant neverthe-less was designed with great attention to the vocational, and so was the curriculum.

17   Of the total of seventy subjects originally offered, only one half were in traditional academic subjects — and the latter, furthermore, were by no means ivory tower. Of seven offerings in English available to juniors and seniors, the one devoted to grammar, rhetoric, and composition was a one-semester "refresher course . . . for students who feel the need for additional preparation." Of more appeal to teenagers would be the full-year courses in journalism and in speech (for which, in the "communication laboratory," facilities are available for practical things like radio and TV debating).

¹⁸   The seventy formal subject offerings by no means exhausted the life-adjustment curriculum. Baber felt that the schools must assume more responsibility for the *total* growth of the child. Conceivably, this could be left to other agencies — to the family, or the church, or society itself, for example. Nevertheless, through such media as courses in family group living (twelfth-grade elective) and "doing" sessions in actual situations, the school tackled it. "Ours is an age of group action," Baber says.²

¹⁹   Partly because so many parents are college-educated, Park Forest would not seem to be ideal soil for the full development of the life-adjustment curriculum. When the curriculum was first being planned several years ago, a questionnaire was sent to parents, and somewhat to Baber's surprise, over half of the parents checked French, Spanish — and Latin, of all things — as desirable electives. Most, furthermore, showed a disinterest in vocational courses of the craft type.

²⁰   As elsewhere, of course, colleges have also been a stumbling block. Most colleges, Baber regrets, still require specified academic credits for admission, and this has been a brake on further enrichment. Core courses like Unified Studies offer some flexibility: if a student lacks a credit in English, for example, Unified Studies can be translated as English; if he needs history credit, as history. But this only mitigates, and like many another educator, Baber feels that the colleges continue to lag behind secondary education in acceptance of modern trends.

²¹   Another cloud has developed. While the school board and the majority of parents have been well satisfied with the school, what is usually referred to as a "vocal minority" has materialized. In 1955 a special curriculum advisory committee was formed. The laymen, each under the impression that he might be a lone dissenter, were surprised to find that they shared the same misgivings. After a survey they drew up quite a caustic report, the gist of which was that while Baber deserved tribute for the formidable job he had done, much too large a share of the school's energies were devoted to what was essentially extracurricular. The ideal of education might be Mark Hopkins on one end of a log and a student on the other, the initial report tartly observed, but it isn't Mark Hopkins and an administrative assistant and a guidance counselor and a psychologist and a curriculum consultant in between.

² Lest I seem to be applying the word *vocational* unfairly, let me note that Dr. Baber is equable about it. From a letter to the writer from Dr. Baber: "In general, I believe you have given a reasonably accurate description of the high-school situation. The frequent use of the word *vocational* as applied to our educational program is acceptable if broadly defined as useful or functional. . . . We emphasize *general education* and the development of understandings, skills, and critical thinking directly related to current problems of social living. If I were to attempt to define the bases of our educational program I believe it would be in terms of three fundamental concepts: (1) the philosophy of experimentalism, compromised somewhat by the pressures of tradition, (2) an organismic (or Gestalt) psychology, and (3) democratic educational leadership."

22   The final report was somewhat more tempered, but its conclusions were inescapably combative. "We believe in hard work per se, and, therefore, until educators discover some harder work, we believe in such courses as Latin and algebra as 'disciplines.' We do not believe that all knowledge must have an immediate or even, indeed, an eventual 'use.' . . . There is a tendency to design courses of study so that students will not be able to fail. This is completely unrealistic so far as life is concerned. Real life includes failures as well as success, and failure *can be* a challenge to make greater efforts to succeed."

23   Because the critics have been responsible ones, their work has had some effect. Baber has taken it all in good humor and while he still feels there are things more important than academic studies and memory learning, the pamphlets the school has been lately turning out could easily mislead the bystander into thinking the school has slipped back into medievalism. ("There are no substitutes for subject-matter information," one pamphlet declares.) The school points to the larger number of students in academic courses than in vocational ones, albeit with repressed enthusiasm; it also speaks of its increasing interest in the gifted student and the desire to accelerate such students by special classes.

24   Justifiably, Baber also points with pride to his strong academic teaching staff. The challenge of teaching in a new community like Park Forest has attracted an unusually able group, and on statistics alone the school is well over-average in the number of M.S.s and Ph.D.s. In view of the salaries they are paid, indeed, they would seem a good bit better than the taxpayers deserve. Their average salary, $4,500, is less than the income of the lowest-salaried junior executives who enter the community, and where the latter can expect to double their salaries in ten or fifteen years, the teachers will be lucky to inch up a hundred or so a year. As was pointedly observed in the biographical sketches recently printed in the papers of the teachers, a majority perform outside work to make ends meet.[3]

25   Essentially, however, the school has been kept to the original vision, and little of the emphasis on the practical has been sacrificed. "Family Living," for example, has been built into one of the key offerings, and the school is

[3] While the taxpayers have displayed parsimony in this matter, the schools themselves are partly to blame. Events indicate that if the school administrators were a little less fascinated with physical facilities, they would have an easier time getting better salaries for the teachers. While the cement was still cooling on the new $1,600,000 school, Baber and his board went to the voters with a request for an additional $1,250,000 bond issue for a five-year package of additional construction. The voters balked. Baber's estimates of the high-school population needs have been consistently high, for he has tended to project the elementary-school figures without taking sufficient account of the peculiar nature of Park Forest's turnover. In balking at the bond issue, unfortunately, the taxpayers rather heedlessly turned down a companion request for an educational levy increase that would up salaries. Eventually, after two unsuccessful tries and some scolding from its friends, the school got the bond issue by scaling it down to $450,000. In so doing, however, it also had to scale down the levy increase for salaries, which, as a result, continue to be lower than the Park Forest average.

proud that boys as well as girls take it. ("All aspects of family group life are open to study. Units of study include money management, everyday social relationships, care of the sick, nutrition and food management, clothing and housing the family, and preparation for marriage. Home and community resources are used. The accent is on 'shared responsibility' in building a successful, happy home.") The testing program is extensive. In addition to a battery of achievement tests, such as the Iowa tests, and intelligence tests, the school has given students the Kuder Vocational Preference Record, the Bell Adjustment Inventory, and the California Personal Adjustment Test.

26   Part of the concentration in the academic column of the curriculum is due to the large number of students enrolled in Unified Studies, and for this reason some of the laymen feel that they still have plenty of work cut out for them. They are not yet satisfied as to what the studies unify. Here is part of a description written by the school for a local paper:

> *How can I improve my study habits? Is going steady a good idea? How can I pick a career? Why does Park Forest call its governing body a board of trustees, when Chicago Heights has a mayor and aldermen? Why does my family expect so much of me?*
> *If you stepped into a Unified Studies classroom at Rich High you might hear students discussing any one of these or other problems of a personal, group, or community nature. You might find John Scott, Village Manager, or Colonel Plavsic, Director of Public Safety, discussing the government of Park Forest or the problem of juvenile delinquency.*

27   If laymen cavil, the school can count on the moral support of professional educators elsewhere. The school's way of reporting grades is a case in point. Some parents are disturbed because the reports seem to give as much weight to "co-operating with the group" as they do to academic marks. (Grades on examinations are only one of sixteen sub-grades.) Precisely because of this weighting, however, the Park Forest report system has been cited as one of the most advanced in the country by Dr. Ruth Strang of Teachers College, Columbia.

28   Dr. Strang is well aware of the difficulties a school's concern with total growth can provoke from some parents. "If the parents' philosophy is one that emphasizes rugged individualism and competition," she says, with scarcely concealed disapproval, "a report that emphasizes development as a co-operative social person may not have much meaning for the parent." But such a report can also help educate parents. Criticism notwithstanding, Dr. Strang argues, the reports should clearly reflect the underlying philosophy of the school — and in this respect, certainly, Park Forest parents have no cause for complaint.[4]

---

[4] As this book was going to press, the school board announced, with what appeared genuine regret, that Baber was going to accept the very excellent post of head of the Waukegan, Illinois, high-school system and oversee its ambitious expansion program. To fill his shoes the board secured Dr. Robert G. Andree, previously head of the Brookline, Massachusetts, high school. It is clear, however, that the majority of the citizens do not expect, or want, any basic changes in school philosophy.

29   It is possible, if not very probable, that there will be shifts in the future. Significantly, the few critics are from what is regarded as the progressive element in Park Forest, and they are poles apart from the right-wing re-actionaries who have muddied the issue in some communities. But they re-main very much a minority, and at present writing it must be concluded that the philosophy of the elementary and high schools is a fair reflection of the community. If any debate has developed, it is because Baber has been so eminently fair in making his position explicit.

30   The majority do not see any basic philosophic differences. Differences of degree, yes — they don't want the school to be *too* progressive, *too* practical — but on the basic concept of social utility they have no argument to make. If one wishes to quarrel with the philosophy, he must address him-self to the people themselves. The educators may be in the vanguard, but they are going with, not against, the grain of their society.

31   For what is it that the parents want most emphasized by the school? At Park Forest they were asked just such a question, and when they wrote the answer in their own words, one note was found more often than any other. The primary job of the high school, they wrote, should be to teach students how to be citizens and how to get along with other people.

Commentary and questions

1. This is an informative essay in which the author uses words to convey information as well as an attitude. Most of the emotive words are intro-duced by direct or indirect quotation. Note that the author indicates, by spacing, six parts of "The Organization Children."

2. *Paragraphs 1-4:* Whyte moves at the outset from buildings to board members to teachers to students. His reporting is factual, but how exact is his report? Is he trying to give you material to draw your own conclu-sion or is he presenting a conclusion? In paragraph 4, select the words that are exactly informative, those that give more general information, and those that tend toward persuasion.

3. *Paragraph 5:* What does the metaphor "investment" indicate about the superintendent's thinking? Why is it significant that he should say "get the kids settled down in a group" rather than "get the kids settled down"?

4. *Paragraph 6:* From the context of this paragraph what do you think the speaker meant by "adjustment to the group"? What other use of the word "court" gives you an understanding of the phrase "court play"?

5. *Paragraph 7:* What do you understand by "other, more inward, as-pects"?

6. *Paragraph 8:* The word "discipline" occurs in one form or another three times. Does it mean the same thing in each instance? Would you say that "authoritarian strictures" could be expressed by the word "dis-

cipline"? Why does Whyte use the phrase "authoritarian strictures"? Are these Whyte's words or Gerald Smith's?

7. *Paragraph 9:* You see the sense in which "social adjustment" is frequently used in this essay. Why do you think Whyte included the last sentence of the quotation? Do the "odd parents" and "suburban abnormalities" of the next sentence indicate Whyte's own attitude?

8. *Paragraph 11:* Why does Whyte pick up "strait jacket" from the authorities in order to present their side of the case in their own language? Do you think this accounts for Whyte's language in other places? Does this ever show an attitude on Whyte's part?

9. *Paragraph 13:* Why does Whyte use quotation marks when he reports that the committee called learning a "painless process"? Also Whyte quotes one parent on Janet's studying marketing. The phrase "broad view of things" is vague and indefinite. Why does Whyte include it even though it could have been omitted? Is the quotation included because it is a statement about Janet or because it is an indirect statement about the speaker? Why did Whyte put it at the end of this section?

10. *Paragraph 16:* In the sentence "Baber is not actually against intelligence," what does the word "actually" do in the sentence? Is the sentence the same without it?

11. *Paragraph 19:* In all but the last sentence of this paragraph, the phrase "of all things" could express the attitude of Whyte or of Baber. From the context, whose attitude would you say it is?

12. *Paragraph 21:* The word "cloud" is a metaphor. What does it imply?

13. *Paragraph 23:* How do "good humor," "medievalism," and the coupling of "academic studies and memory learning" show Baber's evaluation of his critics and their ideas?

14. *Paragraph 29:* How does the "progressive element" differ from the "right-wing reactionaries"? What does he mean by "muddied the issue"?

15. *Paragraph 31:* Whyte could have put the last sentence of the essay in the first paragraph in order to let his readers know immediately what to expect. Was he wise in developing his exposition the way he did? What is the advantage he exploits? Why does Whyte think the high school rather than elementary school the place where "the new suburbia's philosophy gets its most significant expression"? Show that the outline of the essay helps Whyte maintain a fairly objective presentation of his topic.

Topics for discussion and writing

I. Write an essay showing whether or not the schools in Park Forest exemplify Dewey's ideas of what the school is and what it ought to teach.

II. Using Whyte's last sentence as a thesis sentence, write an essay showing what the high school in Park Forest is like.

III. Write an essay showing how Whyte's use of quotations illuminates the people quoted and their basic attitudes toward education as well as the particular matter under discussion.

IV. Baber is quoted as saying: "Ours is an age of group action." Write an essay showing how the schools of Park Forest illustrate this statement.

V. In paragraphs 14-18 Whyte presents Baber's own ideas by direct and indirect quotation. Write an essay to show how Whyte is able to use the indirect quotations to intrude his own opinions.

AIMLESSNESS IN EDUCATION   Arthur E. Bestor, Jr.

*From "Aimlessness in Educa-
tion," by Arthur E. Bestor, Jr.*
Scientific Monthly, *Vol. 75 (August, 1952). Reprinted by permission of* Scientific Monthly.

"IF A nation expects to be ignorant and free," said Jefferson, ". . . it expects what never was and never will be." Americans have taken this dictum to heart. No belief is more firmly held in the United States than belief in education. But belief is not enough. We must understand education as well as believe in it. The thing that counts, after all, is not the number of schoolrooms we have, but what goes on in them. And if we really believe that education is vital to our safety, then we need to know exactly what kind of schooling constitutes genuine education, and what kind is merely a gaudy show.

2   Education, first of all, is the opposite of ignorance. Jefferson makes this clear. The phrases he uses elsewhere as synonyms of education indicate the positive meaning he attaches to the concept. The kind of schooling that is vital to a democratic society is the kind that results in the "spread of information" and the "diffusion of knowledge"; the kind that regards "science . . . (as) more important in a republican than in any other government"; the kind that recognizes that "the general mind must be strengthened by education"; the kind that aims to make the people "enlightened" and to "inform their discretion." [1] These are the ends that the schools must serve if a free people are to remain free. These, be it noted, are intellectual ends. Genuine education, in short, is intellectual training.

3   The nation depends upon its schools and colleges to furnish this intellectual training to its citizenry as a whole. Society has no other institution upon which it can rely in the matter. If schools and colleges do not emphasize rigorous intellectual training, there will be none. This is not true of the other services that educational institutions may incidentally render. It is

[1] Padover, S. K., Ed. *Thomas Jefferson on Democracy.* New York: Penguin Books, 89, 149, 87, 90, 118, 90 (1946).

well for the schools to pay attention to public health, for example, but if they are unable to do so, the health of our citizens will not go uncared for. The medical profession and the existing welfare agencies remain unimpaired. But if the schools neglect their central purpose of intellectual training, the loss to society is an irreparable one.

4   The loss is catastrophic whether or not the students concerned go on into college; in point of fact, the situation is more dangerously irreparable if they do not. College preparation, in other words, is not the matter at issue. A command of written English, mathematics, science, history, and the other disciplines in which we find high school graduates so often deficient, is vital for many things besides advanced study. Throughout history these intellectual disciplines have been rightly considered fundamental to education for practical life and for citizenship. Every vocation has grown more complicated in the modern world. The artisan of an earlier century might make his way in the world even though he were illiterate and all but unlearned in elementary arithmetic. Today even the simplest trades require more than this. The responsibilities of citizenship, too, are more complex than ever before. Intelligent citizenship does not mean merely a simple faith in American democracy. It calls for a thorough knowledge of political principles and institutions, of history, and of economics. It demands a clear understanding of the various sciences, for the intelligent citizen must help decide public policy on such complex matters as atomic energy. Above all, intelligent citizenship requires an ability to read, to understand, and to test the logic of arguments far more complicated than any that have hitherto been addressed to the public at large.

5   The economic and political life of a democratic state depends upon how successfully its educational system keeps pace with the increasingly heavy intellectual demands of modern life. Our civilization requires of every man and woman a variety of complex skills which rest upon the power to read, write, and calculate, and upon sound knowledge of science, history, economics, and other fundamental disciplines.

6   The concept of education that I have just stated is *not* guiding the American public schools today. It is a concept which professors of education have repudiated, and which they caricature at every opportunity. According to a recent article by a professor of education, the scientists and scholars on university faculties

> . . . visualize the mind as a sort of cold storage warehouse, which is empty at birth. The process of learning consists in hanging on the walls of the warehouse chunks of fact and information. . . . The chunks hang there in the same condition in which they were first stored until some day the student needs one or more of them; then he can go into the warehouse, unhook the right chunk, and use it for some mature purpose which he could not have conceived in the immature condition of his mind when he first acquired the material. . . . The conception that new learn-

ings become part of the learner through their digestion and assimilation into other previously acquired material is quite foreign to this idea of learning.[2]

7   I assume that incompetents can be found who perform thus. I doubt if anyone can be found who believes thus, and I am certain that I have never met anyone who would defend, nor read a single sentence that seriously propounded, such a doctrine.

8   The caricature in itself is unimportant. What is important is the fact that American educators are deliberately and consciously cutting the public schools loose from the disciplines of science and scholarship, because they think that what they are repudiating is the theory described in this quotation. Unfortunately, what they are casting away is something utterly different from this. The liberal disciplines are not chunks of frozen fact. They are not facts at all. They are the powerful tools and engines by which a man discovers and handles facts. Without the scientific and scholarly disciplines he is helpless in the presence of facts. With them he can command facts and make them serve his varied purposes. With them he can even transcend facts and deal as a rational man with the great questions of purpose and meaning.

9   Consider how the disciplines of science and learning came into being. The world is first known to us — and was to mankind — as a great tangle of confused perceptions. Before man can deal with it at all, he must differentiate one experience from another and he must discover relationships among them: similarity and diversity, cause and effect, and the like. Gradually he discovers that one kind of relationship can best be investigated in one way (by controlled experiment, it may be), and another in another way (by the critical study of written records or of fossil remains, perhaps). Thus the separate disciplines were born, not out of arbitrary invention but out of evolving experience. Trial and error, prolonged over centuries, has resulted in the perfecting of these tools of investigation. The methods can be systematized and taught, hence the intellectual power that mankind has accumulated throughout its entire history can be passed on to successive generations. Thereby each generation is enabled to master the new environment and the new conditions of life that surround it. This ability to solve new problems by using the accumulated intellectual power of the race is mankind's most precious possession. To transmit this power of disciplined thinking is the primary and inescapable responsibility of an educational system.

10   That present-day professional educators are seeking to evade this primary responsibility is the grave charge which members of the learned professions are making. The evidence is to be found in the educators' own widely publicized statements of educational aim. One carefully analyzed

[2] Reeder, E. H. The Quarrel between Professors of Academic Subjects and Professors of Education: Analysis. *Am. Assoc. Univ. Professors Bull.* 37, 514 (Autumn 1951).

example is better than a score of quotations at random. Let us therefore look carefully at the curricular revision that is going on in the high schools of Illinois, remembering that similar movements are afoot in practically every one of the forty-eight states.

11   The Illinois Secondary School Curriculum Program is sponsored by the state superintendent of public instruction and has as its director the associate dean of the College of Education of the University of Illinois. Over the past five years it has conducted a series of studies, one of which — a so-called Follow-Up Study — will concern us here. This study makes use of a group of widely circulated questionnaires, all based upon a central document entitled *Problems of High School Youth,* prepared by a professor of education. Fifty-five problems are listed,[3] and the questions are essentially rephrasing of these items. The answers, it is said, will "afford a measure, at the level of informed opinion, of the performance of the school." And these, in turn, "will be helpful in 'engineering' an improved, broadly based consensus regarding what the local high school should be doing for its students."[4]

12   The first thing that strikes one on reading the list is the grotesque disproportion between the different problems presented. Trivia are elaborated beyond all reason, and substantial matters are lumped together in a very small number of separate items, thus reducing them to relative insignificance in the whole. Among the fifty-five points are these: "the problem of improving one's personal appearance," "the problem of selecting a 'family dentist' and acquiring the habit of visiting him systematically," "the problem of developing one or more 'making things,' 'making it go,' or 'tinkering' hobbies," and "the problem of developing and maintaining wholesome boy-girl relationships." Not a whit more weight or emphasis is placed upon the following, each of which constitutes but a single point among the fifty-five: "the problem of acquiring the ability to study and help solve economic, social, and political problems," and "the problem of making one's self a well-informed and sensitive 'citizen of the world.'"

13   Needless to say, the scholarly and scientific disciplines have no place among these "real-life problems." Arithmetic has sometimes been considered of practical importance, but, although "athletic games," "camping," "collecting art objects, etc.," and "doing parlor stunts" are mentioned by name, each in a separate item of the list of fifty-five, not one of the branches of mathematics is even hinted at. The word "science" occurs nowhere in the list, nor any term synonymous with it or descriptive of its various branches. That history and foreign languages are absent, even by remotest

---

[3] Illinois Secondary School Curriculum Program. Bull. No. 11, *How to Conduct the Follow-Up Study,* 30 (Aug. 1950). The printed text lists only 55 problems, but all the accompanying statements speak of "56 real-life problems" (*ibid.,* 11). The unexpressed 56th problem — insoluble, perhaps — is doubtless that of summing up correctly the following figures: $6+10+5+3+12+7+4+8$.

[4] ———. Bull. No. 13, 15, 14.

implication, goes without saying. The final item on the list is "the problem of securing adequate preparation for successful college work. . . ." One can imagine that this will prove the most difficult problem of all.

14   The intermingling of the trivial and the important in these lists and questionnaires is not an accident but a symptom. It is not enough to say that "neither the order in which needs are given nor the amount of space devoted to each need is indicative of the relative significance of the different needs." [5] The arrangement of items in a list like this, and the attention devoted to each, do have a meaning — a very profound meaning. The order and emphasis of a man's writing are just as truly a part of what he says to his reader as any of his particular assertions. And what the list of *Problems of High School Youth* says to the reader is that order, balance, discrimination, and a sense of values are matters of no consequence whatever to the pedagogues who are remaking the curricula of our public schools.

15   Men who cannot compile a simple list without revealing their mental limitations do not inspire confidence that they will know how to accomplish even the saner of their objectives. Take, for example, "the problem of acquiring the ability to study and help solve economic, social, and political problems." The question for the educator is not *whether* the school should do anything in the matter, but *how*. The traditional curriculum offered a clear-cut answer: through careful and systematic study of history, political science, philosophy, economics, sociology, and the other relevant disciplines. The aim was to cultivate sound judgment based upon critical thinking and thorough knowledge. To the new pedagogical medicine man, however, all this is sheer pedantry, just as bacteriology is so much learned nonsense to the happy faith healer.

16   Political, economic, and social problems that have taxed the intelligence of the best-educated men from antiquity to the present are to be solved, so the educator blithely assures us, through a "common learnings course" in the high school, wherein "materials from science, literature, history, mathematics, industrial education, homemaking, business education, art, music, and all other areas of the curriculum would be included." [6] And from the *Problems of High School Youth* we are acquainted with the exquisite sense of order and proportion that a professional educator brings to the task of organizing a set of problems rationally and effectively. We must not detain him to ask for proof that his short cut to wisdom will actually produce it. After all, he has fifty-four other problems to wrestle with, and he must hasten on to the next — "the problem of acquiring the ability to select and enjoy good motion pictures," perhaps, or "the problem of acquiring the social skills of dancing, playing party games, doing parlor stunts, etc."

17   If men and women prefer the latter things to intellectual training, the

[5] ———. Bull. No. 1, 10.
[6] *Ibid.*, 35.

educator will argue, should they not have them? The question is really irrelevant, for the questionnaires do not provide, and cannot provide, one iota of evidence that the public is making any such choice. The most damning part of the whole study is that the questionnaires it uses are patently dishonest. They purport to ask parents, citizens, teachers, and pupils what they "think is the job of the secondary school." [7] But the persons questioned are not permitted to give the slightest indication that they believe the job of the secondary school is to give intellectual training. In the entire battery of questionnaires there is not a single blank that one can check in order to express the view that the public schools should offer sound training in mathematics, in natural science, in grammar and composition, in foreign languages, or in history. The citizen may respond in the negative to every question implying the substitution of frivolous aims, but he cannot indicate in any manner whatever the kind of positive program he would favor. The questionnaires are so rigged that the results are predetermined from the beginning. However overwhelming the public sentiment in favor of disciplined intellectual training may be, the professor of education who constructed the questionnaires has taken care that this sentiment shall not appear anywhere in the answers.

18 The Follow-Up Study is not an attempt to ascertain public opinion; it is obviously designed to manufacture the appearance of public support for curricular changes that the professional educators have determined upon in advance. This purpose comes out stark and clear in the official statements explaining the questionnaires: "Given the American tradition of the local lay-control of public education, it is both necessary and desirable that a community (patrons, pupils, teachers) consensus be engineered in understanding support of the necessary changes before they are made." [8] I find difficulty in following some of the involved syntax of this sentence, but I have no difficulty whatever in grasping the significance of a "consensus" that is to be "engineered." We approach here the real meaning of what educators euphemistically describe as "democracy in education." It is the democracy of the "engineered" consensus.

19 The lighthearted prospectus of these curriculum engineers contains this exhortation: "There are many ways of getting under way in a program of curriculum revision. The important thing is that we need to pry ourselves loose from the present situation. Maybe one lever will do the prying loose; perhaps, it may require several. . . . Pick your lever(s) and let's get

---

[7] ———. Bull. No. 11, 33.

[8] *Ibid.*, 10 (italics omitted). Note also the following statements: "The central purpose underlying the use of this questionnaire is precisely that of securing factual evidence which can be used to persuade a larger proportion of the pupils, teachers, and school patrons of the necessity of thus functionalizing the high school curriculum" (p. 13); repeated almost verbatim on p. 27: "If, on the other hand, such a consensus [in favor of a "real-life" curriculum] does not exist [in the answers to a given questionnaire], it is apparent that the data afforded by the other questionnaires . . . will afford the basis for engendering the requisite consensus" (p. 28).

started." [9] (The metaphor is apt. The kind of lever that one uses for prying things loose is sold in hardware stores under the name of wrecking-bar.)

20   Pry loose from what? The answer is implicit in the entire program. The secondary school curriculum must be pried loose from the established disciplines of science and scholarship. The public school must be pried loose from its relationship to institutions of higher learning. College entrance requirements are a thorn in the side of the public school directorate, for they give some support, feeble though it may be, to intellectual training in the secondary schools. The Illinois Curriculum Program is ready to deal with this menace to "real-life" education. It recommends "that the colleges adopt admission policies which do not specify the courses the students are to take in high school." College entrance requirements in the basic intellectual disciplines of "English, foreign language, mathematics, science, and social studies" are "particularly limiting for smaller schools." These, alas, cannot afford to offer both the fundamental courses that scientists, scholars, and citizens believe in, and also the gilded fripperies after which the new pedagogues hanker. The lever for prying the schools loose from all intellectual requirements has at last been found. It is the new guiding principle that the Curriculum Program advances: "Since the high school carries the responsibility for educating all youth, it, and not the college or university, has the responsibility of specifying the content of the high school curriculum." [10]

21   Uncontrolled discretion will at last be vested in up-to-date school administrators like the author of the following remarks, which were addressed to the National Association of Secondary-School Principals and published in its official proceedings:

> Through the years we've built a sort of halo around reading, writing, and arithmetic. We've said they were for everybody . . . rich and poor, brilliant and not-so-mentally endowed, ones who liked them and those who failed to go for them. Teacher has said that these were something "everyone should learn." The principal has remarked, "All educated people know how to write, spell, and read." When some child declared a dislike for a sacred subject, he was warned that, if he failed to master it, he would grow up to be a so-and-so.
>
> The Three R's for All Children, and All Children for the Three R's! That was it.
>
> We've made some progress in getting rid of that slogan. But every now and then some mother with a Phi Beta Kappa award or some employer who has hired a girl who can't spell stirs up a fuss about the schools . . . and ground is lost. . . .
>
> When we come to the realization that not every child has to read, figure, write and spell . . . that many of them either cannot or will not

9 ————. Bull. No. 1, 25.
10 ————. Bull. No. 9, 14, 5, 13.

master these chores . . . then we shall be on the road to improving the junior high curriculum.

Between this day and that a lot of selling must take place. But it's coming. We shall some day accept the thought that it is just as illogical to assume that every boy must be able to read as it is that each one must be able to perform on a violin, that it is no more reasonable to require that each girl shall spell well than it is that each one shall bake a good cherry pie. . . .

When adults finally realize that fact, everyone will be happier . . . and schools will be nicer places in which to live. . . .

If and when we are able to convince a few folks that mastery of reading, writing, and arithmetic is not the one road leading to happy, successful living, the next step is to cut down the amount of time and attention devoted to these areas in general junior high-school courses. . . .

One junior high in the East has, after long and careful study, accepted the fact that some twenty per cent of their students will not be up to standard in reading . . . and they are doing other things for these boys and girls. That's straight thinking. Contrast that with the junior high which says, "Every student must know the multiplication tables before graduation."

Such a requirement attaches more importance to those tables than I'm willing to accord them.[11]

22   There are even more pernicious strongholds of intellectualism than the junior high schools. But the professional educators, undaunted, are preparing to reduce them. Colleges and universities still resist, but blueprints have at least been made of future institutions of higher learning after the educators shall have purged them. There has been at least one dress rehearsal in Michigan, described in a volume entitled *A College Curriculum Based on Functional Needs of Students.* Here is an enthusiastic report of the work in college mathematics:

> Originally there was no time set aside for instruction in mathematics except a small amount for remedial work on the simple, everyday uses of addition, subtraction, division, multiplication, and other fundamental operations. With the development of other fields of instruction certain abilities became necessary: ability to interpret and make graphs, profiles, charts, and tables; ability to interpret test scores; understanding of cer-

11 Lauchner, A. H. How Can the Junior High School Curriculum Be Improved? *Bull. Natl. Assoc. Secondary-School Principals,* 35 (177), 299 (Mar. 1951). In reprinting this passage I have made and indicated a few omissions at the end of paragraphs. The three dots that occasionally occur in the middle of sentences, however, are not marks of ellipsis but are the author's substitutes for traditional punctuation. Mr. Lauchner, at the time of reading this paper, was principal of the Thornburn Junior High School in Urbana, seat of the University of Illinois. Although his remarks were fully reported in the local newspapers, and have subsequently been cited several times, no member of the faculty of the College of Education of the university has publicly expressed an adverse opinion of them.

tain statistical terms; ability to use the other skills necessary to the general curriculum. . . . This has led to the setting-aside of two hours each week throughout the Freshman year when the student can go to the mathematics laboratory to work, under the supervision of an instructor, on his own inadequacies in the field.[12]

23   This program was doubtless adequate to accomplish the ends of higher education as these educators conceived them, for in their comprehensive list of the "functional needs" that a college education should serve appears the following high objective: "Ability to read long numbers and to 'round them off.' " [13]

24   Professional educators are fond of talking about the complexity of modern problems. They speak oracularly of "education for the atomic age." And *this* is how they propose to train citizens to cope with the vast technical questions that are posed by science, by an intricate industrial system, and by international anarchy. After nine full years of formal schooling a student need not be expected to read his native language or to know the multiplication table. And in college he is doing well if he can "read long numbers and . . . 'round them off.' " . . .

25   When Americans, a century or so ago, committed themselves to the ideal of universal democratic education, they were not thinking in terms of the trivia that fascinate present-day educators. They did not intend, by making education universal, to debase and destroy it. They were not seeking to water down the great tradition of disciplined and liberal study. They were undertaking the heroic task of raising an entire nation to the highest attainable level of intellectual competence. Liberal education, they believed, was not and should not be the exclusive prerogative of the aristocratic few. Even the humblest man, whatever his trade, was capable of a liberal education. In a democracy he was entitled to it. His intellectual horizon should not be limited, as it had been for the lower classes in times gone by, to his occupation and to the routine details of his everyday life. He should receive training for his occupation, true. But far more important than that, he should be given an opportunity to develop his mind to the fullest extent possible. He should be given command of the intellectual resources that had once been the badge — and one of the principal bulwarks — of aristocracy. His mind furnished with the knowledge and disciplined to the strength that had made the old ruling classes great and powerful, the American freeman would be in a position to rule himself. And the civilization he built would be a humane and magnificent civilization because it offered to every man not only equality before the law, not only the right to vote and to work, but, most precious of all, the opportunity to develop through liberal education his own highest qualities of manhood.

26   Let us never be satisfied with less.

[12] Heaton, K. L., and Koopman, G. R. *A College Curriculum Based on Functional Needs of Students.* Chicago: Univ. Chicago Press, 64 (1936). This volume reports an actual experiment involving the Central State Teachers College at Mount Pleasant, Mich.
[13] *Ibid.*, 148.

Commentary and questions

1. *Paragraph 1:* Does Bestor expect his readers to apply the word "ignorant" to the products of our schools? How does Jefferson intend the word to be understood? How does Bestor expect it to be applied in this context? What does Bestor mean by the word "belief"? How does his use of the word "understand" help you to define "belief"? Why does he use the term "genuine education" instead of simply "education"?

2. *Paragraph 2:* What is the meaning of "intellectual"? In this and the following paragraph the phrase "intellectual training" is repeated four times. Why is it repeated so often? Where does Bestor help you define it?

3. *Paragraphs 3-4:* In the last sentence of paragraph 3 and the first sentence of paragraph 4 occur the words "irreparable," "catastrophic," "dangerously irreparable." How emotive are these words? What words are emphasized in paragraph 4? What advantage does Bestor gain from repetition?

4. *Paragraph 5:* How many times are the words "intellectual" and "intelligent" used in the first five paragraphs? What is the effect of using these words after the question in paragraph 1? Write a paragraph giving Bestor's idea of the proper concept of education.

5. *Paragraph 6:* Why is the word "repudiated" stronger than words like "disagreed with" or "refused to accept"? What does it imply that the other words do not?

How does the word "caricature" prepare you for the quotation that follows? The quotation contains an extended analogy which is obviously meant to be persuasive. If the original author thought this analogy would bring readers to his side, why does Bestor quote it?

6. *Paragraph 8:* What does the word "disciplines" mean? Comment on the informative-persuasive qualities of "cutting loose," "casting away," "chunks of frozen fact," "powerful tools and engines," "discover and handle," "helpless in the presence of," "command facts," "make them serve," and "transcend," all of which appear in paragraph 8. What sort of impressions are these intended to create in the reader?

7. *Paragraph 9:* Bestor uses the phrase "power of disciplined thinking." Has he defined "disciplined"? Why does he use the metaphor "power"? Compare it to other words he might have used, words like "ability" or "skill."

8. *Paragraph 11:* In the footnote Bestor calls the math problem "insoluble." What is the effect of making you add up the figures?

9. *Paragraph 12:* Comment on "grotesque," "trivia," and "lumped." After looking at the problems quoted in the latter part of the paragraph, do you think these words are undue exaggerations?

10. *Paragraph 13:* Why does Bestor quote "real-life problems"? Comment on other uses of quotation marks in this essay.

11. *Paragraph 15:* Point out the terms that indicate disapproval. What impression does Bestor want you to have of professional educators? Has he prepared you for such terms previously?

12. *Paragraph 16:* How many problems has Bestor quoted? Do you think this is probably a fair sampling? Are the ones quoted enough without any others?

13. *Paragraph 20:* Bestor repeats the names of disciplines like natural science, grammar and composition, foreign languages, and history instead of calling them the intellectual curriculum or traditional curriculum as he often might. Why does he repeat the names of the individual disciplines so often?

14. *Paragraph 21:* How does the author of the quotation get his "folksy" approach? Examine his metaphors. Why is Bestor willing to give such a long quotation from someone on the other side? Pick out the clichés of this speaker.

15. *Paragraph 22:* Comment on "pernicious strongholds of intellectualism," "undaunted," "purged," and "dress rehearsal." Bestor uses the term "professional educator" in paragraphs 10, 16, 18, and 22. How does he expect his readers to characterize a "professional educator"?

16. *Paragraphs 23-24:* The phrase "round them off" occurs. What does it mean? Why does Bestor repeat it? In paragraph 24, what is the difference between "nine years of formal schooling" and "nine full years of formal schooling"?

Topics for discussion and writing

I. A good deal of the effect of this essay can be traced to the contrast between two concepts of education. Are the basic tenets of each presented systematically? Is either identified by a word or phrase consistently? What is the effect of either identifying or not identifying each concept in this way?

II. Write a theme explaining Bestor's concept of what the school ought to do. Can you find a good thesis sentence in Bestor's article?

III. Contrast Bestor's concept of genuine education with the concept he opposes. Develop the opposition concept out of the evidence Bestor offers.

IV. Write a long paragraph explaining what Bestor means by intellectual training.

V. Write a theme comparing the educational concepts of John Dewey with those of Arthur Bestor.

VI. Write a theme in which you maintain that the educational concepts attacked by Bestor either are or are not those developed by John Dewey.

VII. Write a theme in which you show either (a) what Arthur Bestor would think of the schools in Park Forest, or (b) what the superintendent of the Park Forest High School would think of Arthur Bestor's educational concept.

THOUGHTS ON TEACHERS AND SCHOOLS

David Riesman

From "Thoughts on Teachers and Schools," The Anchor Review, *No. 1. Reprinted by permission of the author and editor.*

PROGRESSIVE education in its initial American formulation (between about 1900 and 1925) was the product of highly intellectual teachers. These were men and women of marked individuality, talent, and enthusiasm, who became aware of the emotional shallowness and the rote learning of the traditional schools, and sought to found new schools which would not only encourage the arts, the education of the emotions, and group co-operativeness, but which would do an even better intellectual job because more individualized and more closely geared to the child's developing pattern of motivations. These pioneers (being in this like other reformers whose plans have to some degree miscarried) could take for granted their own cultivation and belief in learning, as well as their own zeal, and they could go on from that foundation to try to give the children in their care — as most of us want to give our own children — the things they had missed in their own schooling. I have myself interviewed children and observed classes at several progressive private schools, and I can testify that at their best they turn out interesting and interested children, some of whom their parents and later teachers may find glib and unruly, but not stuffy or deceitful. For many children from narrow or emotionally frozen families, such a school provides an opportunity to thaw out in a milieu at once therapeutic and stimulating.

2   As I have remarked, the doctrinal tenets of such schools have filtered into many public schools with very mixed results. The filtering has not only been "downward" from the superior institutions (such as Teachers College at Columbia) to the junior colleges which have called themselves "teachers colleges" in the hinterland. There has also been a movement "upwards" from the nursery school model, where miracles appear to be accomplished by teachers unable to fall back on the drill of reading or writing in dealing with these preliterate tribes of fours, fives, and sixes: this demonstration of a happy school group, devoted to not much else than its being "happy" and being a "group," has influenced many primary and even high school teachers. It would not have done so to the same degree if the diffusion of progressive (and nursery model) education had not coincided with the growing emphasis on social skills in the community at large — an emphasis itself in part the product of the same social developments which freed millions to

attend school and other millions to teach, transport, and feed them. As our society becomes more play-oriented and less work-oriented, more willing to admit personal sensitivity and warmth to the roster of prime virtues, more concerned with the mood of the group and perhaps less with the achievements of the individual, those goals which the original progressive educators wanted to add to traditional purposes tend in many public (and indeed some private) schools to become the only goals — goals, indeed, no longer so essential for the schools to aim at, since parents and the mass media, among many other social forces, are already active in securing them.

3   Listen, for instance, to a Massachusetts bread salesman describing to an interviewer what he hopes for in the high school education of one of his sons (and explaining incidentally why he is not sending the young man to college, though he is intelligent enough and the family could afford it):

> I tried to tell him where he isn't going to be a doctor or lawyer or anything like that, I told him he should learn English and learn to meet people. Then he could go out and sell something worthwhile where a sale would amount to something for him. . . . I took typing, shorthand, bookkeeping and we had Latin, French, geometry. We had everything. But anything I would know then I've forgotten now. . . . I don't think a high school diploma is important. I mean only in so far as you might apply for a job and if you can say, "I have a diploma," it might help get the job . . .

Or listen (as recorded by William Whyte, Jr.) to a parent in Park Forest, a suburb of Chicago:

> Janet is studying marketing and she's only in the sixth grade. She's studying ads and discounts, things I didn't get until college. The children are certainly getting a broad view of things.

Implicit in the attitude of both these parents is the belief that the school should prepare children for adult life by imitating that life; indeed, the same "child-centered" schools that would fear maladjustment through advancing an intellectually precocious child beyond his social age-mates often do their best to anticipate in the schoolroom the adult "here and now" of buying and selling, of parliamentary procedure and civic responsibility.

4   In this situation, as I have indicated, some of our teachers are fighting a losing battle in defense of the traditional intellectual values and the classical curriculum. But others (including many school superintendents) have turned necessity into virtue and favor the sort of programs that the parents I have just quoted would themselves like to see installed. Thus, Eric Baber, the high school superintendent in Park Forest, tells his teachers and parents that American education is still "far too much concentrated on the intellectual aspect of education." As he said in a teachers workshop:

> The so-called "bright student" is often one of the dumbest or least apt when he gets away from his textbooks and memory work. This is evi-

denced by the fact that many $20,000 to $100,000-a-year jobs in business, sales, sports, radio . . . are held by persons with I.Q.'s of less than
ninety.

Baber is very proud of the "communication laboratory" his modern school
plant includes; as he says, "ours is an age of group action," and one in which
the children "must have actual experiences in solving problems that have
meaning for *them*." No less explicit is the principal of a junior high school
in Urbana, Illinois, speaking to a meeting of the National Association of Secondary-School Principals:

> Through the years we've built a sort of halo around reading, writing and
> arithmetic. . . . The Three R's for All Children and All Children for the
> Three R's! That was it. We've made some progress in getting rid of that
> slogan. But every now and then some mother with a Phi Beta Kappa
> award or some employer who has hired a girl who can't spell stirs up a
> fuss about the schools . . . and the ground is lost. . . . When we come
> to the realization that not every child has to read, figure, write, and
> spell . . . that many of them either cannot or will not master these
> chores . . . then we shall be on the road to improving the junior high
> curriculum. Between this day and that a lot of selling must take place.
> But it's coming. We shall some day accept the thought that it is just as
> illogical to assume that every boy must be able to read as it is that each
> one must be able to perform on a violin, that it is no more reasonable to
> require that each girl shall spell well than it is that each one shall bake a
> good cherry pie. . . .
>
> When adults finally realize that fact, everyone will be happier . . .
> and schools will be nicer places in which to live. . . .

5   This official may well be convinced that he is heretical and ahead of his
time for, after all, he does come from the same university town as does
Arthur Bestor (Professor of History at the University of Illinois) whose *Educational Wastelands* quotes this gem. This book is one of the least intem-
perate of a number of recent slashing attacks on just these self-styled "progressive" tendencies in secondary school teaching, some of which blame all
attenuation of standards on John Dewey. We professors and intellectuals are
generally inclined to trace tendencies we do not like to the ideas of other
intellectuals, and this may in the long run be legitimate, but I do feel that
Bestor exaggerates the autonomous role of the schools, and hence of their
mentors, in fostering a mindless pragmatism and vocationalism which they
often simply absorb from their constituencies.

6   Indeed, so strong are these constituencies that teachers and school officials are today frequently harassed beyond endurance by outsiders who have
more prestige or power than they and who therefore feel free to intervene.
The result is that it is hard for many in the school system to distinguish between a Barzun or a Bestor (or a Riesman) who has made some effort to
understand their problems from within, and that horde of uninformed and

usually reactionary "taxpayer" critics of "new-fangled" notions in the schools. The latter are apt to urge that what was good enough for grandpappy is good enough for his descendants. Since the grandchildren will face stiffer competition in terms of formal educational credentials, this penny-pinching view (sometimes abetted by local commerce and industry) simply kicks away a ladder to mobility which the new generation needs if it is to keep step with the rising educational and living standards of the country as a whole. In contrast, my own view is that grandpappy's education was not good enough for him in a day when artistic and empathic skills were seldom transmitted, but it does have certain redeeming virtues which only become evident when the rest of the society has caught up with an outlook that was rare at the turn of the century. In other words, I feel that schools can perform something of a *counter-cyclical* (or "governor") function; within the limits of their weakness, they can fall back on older traditions with very contemporary purposes in mind.

7   When faced with such a plea coming from a university campus, the school teacher — beleaguered, as I have said, with a multiplicity of special pleading — is apt to appear to turn a deaf ear and to use a diplomatic tongue. She knows that males are apt to be abstract, idealistic, and impractical — and patronizing. There is also the awareness that university professors, like other people, often have vested interests of their own, in discipline and in their "disciplines," to protect. Yet the very democratizing tendencies we have been discussing, which have had such unanticipated regressive consequences, compel teachers and school personnel generally to be accessible. It is hard for them to be other than defensive toward criticism, or, like all professionals faced with troublesome clients, duplicitous in finding the semantics by which all comers can be fended off.

8   Still, would these teachers be so vulnerable to the many competing demands now made upon them if these demands did not awaken echoes within them of unsolved problems in their own lives?

9   In interviews with Kansas City high school teachers, the poignant note comes up again and again of a self-confessed adolescent shyness. They feel this was bad, that they should have been "more outgoing" (perhaps they would have found a husband); some indicated that in becoming teachers they had conquered their shyness. In their relations with other teachers, they have established a coterie that they missed in school (and one that protects them to some extent from the unflattering public image of the unmarried school teacher). More important, they want very much to appear vivacious, warm, and outgoing in class. (One could make an interesting comparison here with current models of appropriate behavior in social workers and clergymen.) They want very much to be liked by the children, as well as by their colleagues, and they are perhaps more aware than before whether or not they are liked, especially as the children, good little communicators that they are, include among their social skills the ability to exploit the teachers' need for approval.

10 Is it true, then, that the cultivated and intellectual teacher has lost her role as a model for other teachers? Not completely. Quite a few, whatever their superintendents might sometimes prefer, do not wish to be merely "outgoing." There is the case of one high school drama teacher, the daughter of a very cosmopolitan newspaper editor; after a divorce she returned to the city of her birth and started teaching school there (political pull, of the sort now waning, helped her get a certificate). This teacher, well-traveled and sophisticated, has a remarkable gift for exciting her pupils' interest in the theatre; she is proud of "graduates on Broadway and in Hollywood." But her fellow-teachers have grave misgivings about her. They complain that she cares "too much about the drama" and "too little about the children." They complain that her productions demand too much time and effort, that the children who get so enthusiastic about putting on plays have little time for other subjects and for sociability, and they feel that the plays should involve a greater number of the children in their production, even at the cost of making the performances less professional. It would be more democratic, they say, to "give everybody a chance," and the drama, like other activities, is seen as one more way to encourage group participation rather than as a way to encourage vocations in the theatre. (The new school principal, a younger man who believes that the duty of the school is to "cultivate the total personality" of the child, has made life difficult for the drama teacher. What he wants is a good working-team of teachers, not stars on the Broadway firmament . . . nor excessive demands on the school auditorium.) I suspect, however, that these teachers would be less critical of their colleague, less articulate about her allegedly disproportionate preoccupation with the theatre, if they did not themselves in some degree aspire to cosmopolitan ways. In taking on responsibility for the child's social and emotional development, they have not wholly relinquished the older responsibility for "culture"; and it is their very ambivalence about partially contending models of school teaching that makes them so angry with those teachers, holdovers from an earlier day, who represent not only unequivocally high and secure social status but also the not entirely downgraded status of intellectual discipline and urbanity.

11 And it is equally true that a great many, if not all, of the "old-fashioned" teachers have been influenced and even upset by the newer pressures for a more democratic school system — democratic in its attention to the less scholarly (i.e. the non-college-preparatory) group, and to the standards set by the children and their parents. Here is an elderly English teacher at a high school which once was proud of its high academic demands (it had been modeled on the "Latin schools" of New England):

> Mr. —— believed so thoroughly in education as I really believe in it, yet I realize that it can't go on. I mean you can't go on pounding classical education into everybody's head as long as you are going to have everybody going to the same school. . . . Mr. ——, I am sure, felt that there were a lot of people who couldn't learn. . . . But he never relaxed

what he thought were necessary standards . . . and if they couldn't make it they couldn't make it and that was all. . . . The older teachers who grew up with that were hard put — they like Mr. —— [the new principal], it's hard for anyone not to like him, but they just think everything is going to pot. . . . I think what he is trying to do is win over the student body to the idea that school administrators and school teachers aren't off there in another world. And then once he has their cooperation to let them make some of the rules and regulations they will be willing to abide by. . . . There have been so many educators and educators that have the theory that reading and writing and arithmetic are sort of overrated; that you must teach people how to be people. . . .

It is plain from such interviews that few teachers are so case-hardened as not to feel some ambivalance concerning the "battle of the books."

12   This conflict also emerges clearly in a series of group discussions with public school teachers in Chicago and Milwaukee which my colleague, Hedda Bolgar, a clinical psychologist, has been conducting. She finds that once the initial defensiveness of teachers against inquisitiveness is overcome, teachers are very eager to talk to an understanding outsider about their inner aims and external conflicts. Underneath a protective coating of cynicism and careerism these teachers frequently harbor a most grandiose and self-defeating expectation of omnicompetence in the classroom. They expect themselves to respond sympathetically to individual problem-children, even psychotic ones that would baffle an experienced psychologist. Partly aware of current mental-health emphases, they can no longer simply reject a child as "a troublemaker," or if they do they will feel guilty about it. In other words, the teachers have been exposed enough to psychiatric currents of thought to learn that children's aggressive behavior has to be explained and cannot be simply reacted to with counteraggression, but they do not often have sufficient knowledge to accept their own aggression.

13   Overtly, they may resist the expectation that there is no child they cannot handle, no child to whose needs they cannot minister while preventing it from dominating the group; they may say to one another, "Who does the School Board think we are, parking such little bastards with us?" Overtly, they may think they have done their job if they "keep the kids out of a messy home five hours a day," and they may, as we know, punish a teacher who does too much for the children, who is too enthusiastic — who is a scab or rate-buster in setting too high standards of performance. But underneath they seem to be demanding of themselves that they achieve therapeutic or motherly relations with all the children. Just because they no longer think of themselves as teachers of a subject but rather as teachers of an age-grade, they are at once tempted and betrayed by an ideal of omnicompetence. Though they are in fact in the position of the Old Woman Who Lived in a Shoe, they somehow accept the inner responsibility for making up in their own persons for all the deficiencies in the community. They feel badly if

"their" children break windows or go to jail or drop out, no matter what the objective situation — much as many mothers feel.

14   I suggest that the cynicism with which many teachers talk among themselves is thus in part a defense against a still unextinguished (if often unconscious) ideal image of themselves as unruffled magnanimous individuals, at once motherly and wholly competent. If it were not for this, the teachers as a close-knit colleguial group could cope somewhat better than they do with well-meant interferences by social workers, psychiatrists, superintendents, and educators, who directly and indirectly reinforce this extravagant image of what the teacher should be, pushing it always further from the traditional conception of the teacher as a subject-matter specialist, which is to say, a person of limited competence.

15   When it is pointed out to them that they are not, after all, psychiatrists and cannot expect themselves to cure problem-children, but only at best not to harm them, they react first with anger at the threat to their ideal of omnicompetence, but eventually with relief. And there is some evidence that they become better, less harassed teachers when they can fully realize that their function is limited — primarily, to teach a subject — and that they cannot as individuals compensate for all the ways in which our social organization now puts children in school because it doesn't want them in the labor force, or on the street corner, or because it has no other place for the disturbed child at the moment.

16   This relinquishment of claims, however, is easier said than done. What is a teacher to do when, as happened the other day in a Chicago elementary school, a lonely Negro girl comes to her to complain of the fact that she has "no friends in school," and that her mother will not allow her to make friends by inviting any children to her home? Is the teacher to send this twelve-year-old child back to her hopeless English lesson? What is the teacher to do as she watches a twelve-year-old boy, son of Jewish immigrant parents, develop an increasing contempt for children who have not raced through as many encyclopedias as he has in amassing an armory of unrelated facts with which, in quiz-kid style, he goes into battle? Is she to wait until the school, which needs a new building (though in general our school buildings are the cathedrals of our time) and more teachers, gets around to appointing a school psychologist? She would have to be more unequivocally devoted to learning for its own sake than are most of my university colleagues in order to be able to resist the appeal to her motherly, or clinical, sympathies. The result is that she pays less attention to the balanced and potentially gifted child who, she rationalizes, can look after himself.

17   In this situation, where the schools and the teachers cannot possibly meet all the demands they put on themselves, I think it would be helpful to develop a systematic theory of education as *counter-cyclical*. Just as Keynesian economics would have the government and the banks save in a time

of inflation and spend in a time of depression, so teachers, in selecting among the expectations held out to them, have some modest opportunities to oppose "life" in its momentary excesses. A generation or so ago teachers were far-sighted in being preoccupied with social skills, and in those many too many areas where underprivileged children still lack access to those skills, it remains important to emphasize them. In fact, to return to our theme at the beginning of the article, where the community continues to be production-minded, the schools can afford to emphasize the gentler arts of social and personal understanding; even today, the country is undoubtedly overplentifully supplied with sadistic teachers who employ their subject-matter superiorities to torment children in the Victorian manner. Increasingly, however, such settings would appear to be waning in frequency and impact; as the community becomes more consumption-minded, and as the out-of-school context helps cultivate the children's social skills, humaneness as such in the schools may on occasion be given a slightly lower priority and an emphasis on the teacher's own production-mindedness — whether with respect to French, football, or mathematics — is likely to be more beneficial and less traumatic. For in the middle-class homes of today children are listened to — they are no longer seen and not heard. The home is itself a "communication laboratory," at least in the middle class. Children can and do use the movies, TV, comics, and magazines like *Seventeen,* as well as each other's example, to learn proper social behavior, especially since they no longer have to do many chores around the house. No one should sneer at the children's social proficiencies: if one compares American young people with their counterparts a generation ago (or in Europe today) one is struck by their poise, their understanding of themselves, each other, and adults; they can often handle touchy questions with a tact and facility our diplomats might well envy. As in the comic strip *Penny,* it is often the adults, not the adolescents, who are the awkward ones. But this very discrepancy, as I have observed, leads both parents and teachers, often conscious of their own childhood inadequacies and gaucheries, to give many children what amounts to postgraduate education in sociability when what they need, for the most part, is something very different. What they need, I suggest, is protection for those long-term intellectual and humanistic interests that are momentarily under severe pressure from so many sides.[1]

[1] Counter-cyclical thinking and practice, as is evident, requires that such generalizations be perennially re-examined for accuracy and scope. My own views represent, *inter alia,* the animated revival of classical and humanistic concerns in the universities and among many businessmen. The "great books," the liberal arts, and similar activities have had the benefit of some energetic polemicists, often quite unafraid to be vulgar in attacking what they deem vulgar in secondary education and vocationalism generally. Sometimes this approach shades over into a new obscurantism which attacks the schools for any interest in the psychology of the learning process, treats John Dewey with condescending unfairness, and insists that there is only one donnish curriculum for everybody. In view of the speed with which, thanks to a resonant communications net, fashions in America change, such incipient cycles must not be overlooked even while one focuses on major national developments.

18 From this perspective, progressive education was undoubtedly a counter-cyclical force a generation ago (as it still is in many "backward" areas and for many individual children). It put pressure on conservative and conventional parents, and on their children. It involved the family in a dialectic which, if at times confusing, was frequently productive for all members — for the parents who strove to "keep up," and for the children who strove to understand and even sympathize with parents. Today, in many more prosperous suburbs, it is these children who presently are parents, and whose children are in turn attending schools that are no longer bucking the tide, are no longer experimental. No strong disagreements within the family, no tensions between family and school now require creative resolution. Yet the relaxed adjustment achieved in this way, while in some respects an undeniable advance over earlier miseries, means in terms of the life cycle less variety and less challenge.

19 This implies that, in many schools, where warm and outgoing teachers are present in sufficient number, effort should be directed to seeing that the children have contact with at least one teacher who cares profoundly about a subject matter like Latin or music which is at first sight remote from the concerns of everyday life. To be sure, such a teacher need not be indifferent to children. She may well come to be particularly attached to those pupils who are attached to her subject (as in Mary McCarthy's recent personal memoir). Such a person can do something to set up a competing model to the mediocrity that results from turning a school entirely over to teachers who have been shy and want to be personable and who hence care too much whether the children respond pleasantly to them and to each other; these are the teachers who have entered the profession to escape the farm or the working class and who come to be captivated by the paraphernalia of professionalism, such as "teacher talk" about classrom skills and audio-visual aids. If schools were to eliminate the difficult or eccentric teachers who present alternative models of good teaching, they would indeed become like life in 1955, only more so.

20 For truly high aims, whether they be occupational, personal, or intellectual, tend to contradict life as it is lived in any given place and time. Schools in the past, more by accident and even ignorance than design, have opened vistas to such aims (for at least a minority) by their very *un-lifelike* character. A student who, through a devoted teacher, could learn to live with Cicero or Mercutio, Joan of Arc or Jane Austen, might well succeed in discovering forms of existence transcending the observable in home or playground: transcending both the bread salesman and the idea salesman.

21 If children, tough and adaptable creatures that they are, can stand being confronted with a wider gamut of personal models than most public schools now make available, all I have said so far would imply that teachers — a group who reach a plateau of grown-upness early and stay on it long — are much less hardy and cannot be asked to face the personal consequences of

counter-cyclical behavior. Indeed, in writing as I do I have the ironical mis-
giving that I, too, may only be adding to expectations for omnicompetence
which, as I have contended, are already unrealistic. Just as I would not expect a banker who believed a depression was coming, and who had read
Keynes, to invest his personal fortune as a way of increasing purchasing
power, so I do not expect individual teachers to carry the whole system on
their backs while beginning a counter-cyclical revolution. Still, I want to
encourage some of them to give up trying to be psychiatrists, mothers, and
moralists, to give up making citizens, democrats, and tolerant children.
Could they not be persuaded to concentrate more than many now feel justified in doing on their roles as teachers of specific subjects? This is, after all,
a job no one else is assigned or trained to do.

²²   I am not arguing that the entire responsibility for counter-cyclical cultural activity must be borne by the secondary schools. The universities, the
media, and the other makers of taste and opinion have a similar responsibility. Nor am I contending for a simple "middle way" between extremes,
which can be discovered by a metaphorical thermostat or servo-mechanism.
We lack at present the most elementary indices for telling, let us say, that
the coming generation will possess "enough" social skills but not enough
musical or mathematical ones.² I am arguing that, for the foreseeable future,
no agency with any leeway should make it its business to imitate "life" or
to be "realistic" in the Philistine sense of that term, but rather that it should
make a good guess as to where "life" is leading, and then proceed to criticize
and correct it. Since in most quarters the dangers of intellectual arrogance
are fast passing, school officials might make it a matter of professional pride
to be as unpopular (short of dismissal) with the community as they can. It
would help educate parents as well as children if a few principals and superintendents supported their teachers against any pressures for lowering of
standards and insisted on high competence in subject matter in as many

² For the same reason, the Keynesian analogy is possibly misleading. It may suggest that
it is as easy to institute counter-cyclical measures in the education industry as in commerce and finance. We have no similar indices of prosperity and depression; and education is a lifelong, omnipresent affair, responsibility for which is neither centralized nor
assigned. Even Keynesian balancing can conceal complex choices among general alternatives; thus, a Schumpeter might defend cycles as stimuli to innovation and creativity, and
fear the equilibrium achieved by governmental stabilizers and shock absorbers. The
choices in the case of the schools are even less concealed.

I realize that counter-cyclical action inevitably defends a good deal in the status
quo that has little on its face to recommend it (although it is at the same time an experiment on behalf of an indeterminate future). These difficulties in the policy are so
great that, let me repeat, I am not adding to teachers' burdens the further one of judging society and the school in order to make profound counter-cyclical judgments.
I am asking that school officials, critics, and controllers make such judgments at the
very outset when they set curricula and select personnel. However, teachers themselves
may take comfort from counter-cyclical thinking in the many instances where they feel
uneasy about their preoccupation with subject matter, or less than fully committed to
classroom group dynamics. Counter-cyclical considerations can be for them a protection against certain fashions, and a defense for views which, in other contexts, might
properly be attacked as out of date or unduly rigid.

appointees as possible. This will occasionally involve them in defending and befriending someone like our drama teacher; eccentric as such teachers are apt to be in their devotion to a subject, they may not be quite the best "team players" in the teacher colleague-group.

23   Paradoxically, it is in a non-academic area that this is already standard practice. I refer to the sports coach, who is ordinarily expected to get his pupils to do their best (even, sometimes, at shocking cost to body and soul). In this field, "democracy" means a free way for talent and not, save in a few schools which are hostile to competition as such, that everyone must proceed at a medium pace, or be elected rather than selected for the team.[3] Many of us — forgetting that before the days of organized sports our schools and colleges were locales of barely controlled roistering — tend to look down on the coach, though he may today be a better teacher than many of his colleagues by virtue of his more unequivocal aims: The excellence of his pupils is the answer to his prayers. Even while we moderate his zeal, we might use it as a model for teachers of painting and poetry, some of whom should unquestionably concern themselves with children's self-expression, but others with giving even the less gifted children the valuable sense that there are cultural continuities and standards of excellence.

[3] Since writing the foregoing, I have come across an instance in a private school where the girls' basketball team was elected — to the dismay of new girls not popular enough to be chosen and of those who preferred spending the scarce time in the gym actually playing rather than voting.

Commentary and questions

1. *Paragraph 1:* This paragraph explains what the pioneers of progressive education in America were trying to do. Point out the words that indicate Riesman's feeling toward his topic. What do you think he intends by the phrases "encourage the arts," "education of the emotions," and "group co-operativeness"? What is the "child's developing pattern of motivations"? Compare this paragraph to the selection by John Dewey.

2. *Paragraph 2:* Explain why Riesman uses quotation marks as he does. What does the metaphor "filter" imply about the ways these ideas reached "teachers colleges" and the accuracy of the information once it had arrived? What is "the growing emphasis on social skills in the community at large"? Explain "play-oriented" and "work-oriented."

3. *Paragraph 3:* In the bread-salesman's statement, point out the words and phrases that are vague and indefinite or have, apparently, no concept at all behind them. The quotation on Janet has appeared before. Did you analyze "broad view of things"? How exactly does a person go about "studying ads and discounts"? Would the phrase have the same meaning when applied to a sixth-grade student as it would applied to a college student?

Riesman mentions the assumption "that the school should prepare children for adult life by imitating that life." Dewey says that education should "occur through forms of life, forms that are worth living for their own sake." Later he says that "school life should grow gradually out of home life." Is there a difference in Dewey's statements and in the assumptions Riesman sees in the parents he quotes? At the end of the paragraph, could there be significance in the three particulars Riesman uses — buying and selling, parliamentary procedure, and civic responsibility?

4. *Paragraph 4:* Does the phrase "turned necessity into virtue" indicate an attitude toward men like Eric Baber? How does Baber's quoted remark favor the sort of program that the bread-salesman favored? Is the "fact" that "many" high-paying jobs in "business, sales, sports, and radio" are held by persons with I.Q.'s of "less than ninety" evidence that the "so-called 'bright student'" is one of the "dumbest" or "least apt" when he "gets away from his textbooks and memory work"?

5. *Paragraph 8:* Riesman here begins a section analyzing the teachers and their values. Does he show that such an analysis is germane to his topic?

6. *Paragraph 9:* Explain why the words "communicators" and "social skills" are ironic and amusing.

7. *Paragraph 11:* Comment on the words and phrases that seem vague or trite.

8. *Paragraph 17:* "Counter-cyclical" means against the cycle. Before you can understand the term fully you must understand what cycle Riesman is talking about and what goes against it. This is a key paragraph in Riesman's argument. Examine the connotations of his words carefully. Note especially his attempt to avoid categoric statements and extreme positions.

9. *Paragraph 19:* In the first sentence explain the advantage Riesman gains in using the phrase "at least one teacher" instead of "teachers." What other phrase or phrases in the paragraph seem to be selected for the same end?

10. *Paragraph 20:* Explain the use of the word "contradict." Give an example of "forms of existence transcending the observable." Why is it appropriate to link the bread salesman and idea salesman together?

11. *Paragraph 21:* Comment on the effect gained by the juxtaposition of "psychiatrists, mothers, and moralists." Comment similarly on "citizens, democrats, and tolerant children."

12. *Paragraph 22:* What does this paragraph add to Riesman's argument? Explain his use of the term "realistic." What does he mean by "unpopular"?

13. *Paragraph 23:* Explain the two meanings of "democracy." Why is the coach a "better teacher"? Explain how the terms of the last sentence summarize the two sides of the educational debate.

Topics for discussion and writing

I. Write a theme explaining Riesman's counter-cyclical theory and showing how it might be applied in a high school.

II. Write a theme in which you argue that Riesman is or is not fair to the educators and their critics. Use the articles by Dewey, Whyte, and Bestor as the sources for your information.

III. Compare the positions of Riesman and Bestor on the advisability of changing the present dominant educational policy and on the reasons for this change.

IV. Write a theme explaining as fully as you can what Riesman thinks of John Dewey's ideas.

V. Write a theme explaining why Riesman uses quotation marks the way he does and comment on their effectiveness. Use examples.

VI. Write a theme comparing the ideas of Dewey, Bestor, and Riesman on the functions of the schools.

VII. You have now read three essays in which Dewey's ideas are somehow fundamental. How accurately and fairly do Baber, Bestor, and Riesman interpret Dewey?

The rebel: WHAT IS A REBEL? Albert Camus · BORIS SAVINKOV, Winston Churchill · LEON TROTSKY, ALIAS BRONSTEIN, Winston Churchill · SIGNIFICANT GESTURE, Malcolm Cowley · CIVIL DISOBEDIENCE, Henry David Thoreau

CAMUS, Churchill, and Thoreau are, in many respects, very different writers, both in the stylistic techniques they use and in the approaches they offer to a single topic — the study of man, or men, in sharp conflict with their surroundings. Camus, one of the more influential and thoughtful contemporary French novelists, regards the rebel as a type that has grown increasingly important in twentieth-century society. In defining the rebel, he defines rebellion, the act, the motives and conditions that prompt it, and the things that make it distinct from other acts of a similar kind. Churchill, on the other hand, has no carefully worked out philosophical point of view. He is interested in two individuals, and he judges them according to personal and specific moral standards. Thoreau is also highly personal, but in another way. He himself is the rebel; the government, indeed all government, his antagonist. And he writes with a strong sense of the unpopularity of his views. Indeed, today his understanding of the individual conscience as a kind of supreme court in human affairs will seem stranger than it would have in the mid-nineteenth century, but Thoreau's is merely the extension of an individualism which Americans sometimes like to claim for themselves.

Of the three writers, Camus and Churchill are the most obviously systematic, the one following an openly explicit strategy of definition, the other openly persuasive and descriptive. This need not mean that Thoreau is a random thinker, but his strategy is less obvious, more roundabout, and the reader must examine carefully the assumptions behind his statements and his use of particular words.

Cowley's brief experience as a rebel is less momentous than those related by Churchill, and he implicitly rejects the brand of philosophical sanction of

94

rebellion defined by Camus. Nevertheless, the incident he narrates makes clear not only his own attitude, both during and after the event, but also attempts to suggest the quality of rebellion in a whole, and by now famous, generation of artists and intellectuals. These were the expatriates and icono-clasts of the twenties, the people Gertrude Stein called "a lost generation." Cowley's piece has the advantage and interest of being a personal report.

WHAT IS A REBEL? Albert Camus

Reprinted from the Vintage Books Edition of The Rebel *by Albert Camus, translated by Anthony Bower, by special arrangement with Alfred A. Knopf, Inc. Copyright 1956 by Alfred A. Knopf, Inc.*

WHAT is a rebel? A man who says no, but whose refusal does not imply a renunciation. He is also a man who says yes, from the moment he makes his first gesture of rebellion. A slave who has taken orders all his life suddenly decides that he cannot obey some new command. What does he mean by saying "no"?

2   He means, for example, that "this has been going on too long," "up to this point yes, beyond it no," " you are going too far," or, again, "there is a limit beyond which you shall not go." In other words, his no affirms the existence of a borderline. The same concept is to be found in the rebel's feeling that the other person "is exaggerating," that he is exerting his authority beyond a limit where he begins to infringe on the rights of others. Thus the movement of rebellion is founded simultaneously on the categorical rejection of an intrusion that is considered intolerable and on the confused conviction of an absolute right which, in the rebel's mind, is more precisely the impression that he "has the right to . . ." Rebellion cannot exist without the feeling that, somewhere and somehow, one is right. It is in this way that the rebel slave says yes and no simultaneously. He affirms that there are limits and also that he suspects — and wishes to preserve — the existence of certain things on this side of the borderline. He demonstrates, with obstinacy, that there is something in him which "is worth while . . ." and which must be taken into consideration. In a certain way, he confronts an order of things which oppresses him with the insistence on a kind of right not to be oppressed beyond the limit that he can tolerate.

3   In every act of rebellion, the rebel simultaneously experiences a feeling of revulsion at the infringement of his rights and a complete and spontaneous loyalty to certain aspects of himself. Thus he implicitly brings into play a standard of values so far from being gratuitous that he is prepared to support

it no matter what the risks. Up to this point he has at least remained silent and has abandoned himself to the form of despair in which a condition is accepted even though it is considered unjust. To remain silent is to give the impression that one has no opinions, that one wants nothing, and in certain cases it really amounts to wanting nothing. Despair, like the absurd, has opinions and desires about everything in general and nothing in particular. Silence expresses this attitude very well. But from the moment that the rebel finds his voice — even though he says nothing but "no" — he begins to desire and to judge. The rebel, in the etymological sense, does a complete turnabout. He acted under the lash of his master's whip. Suddenly he turns and faces him. He opposes what is preferable to what is not. Not every value entails rebellion, but every act of rebellion tacitly invokes a value. Or is it really a question of values?

4   Awareness, no matter how confused it may be, develops from every act of rebellion: the sudden, dazzling perception that there is something in man with which he can identify himself, even if only for a moment. Up to now this identification was never really experienced. Before he rebelled, the slave accepted all the demands made upon him. Very often he even took orders, without reacting against them, which were far more conducive to insurrection than the one at which he balks. He accepted them patiently, though he may have protested inwardly, but in that he remained silent he was more concerned with his own immediate interests than as yet aware of his own rights. But with loss of patience — with impatience — a reaction begins which can extend to everything that he previously accepted, and which is almost always retroactive. The very moment the slave refuses to obey the humiliating orders of his master, he simultaneously rejects the condition of slavery. The act of rebellion carries him far beyond the point he had reached by simply refusing. He exceeds the bounds that he fixed for his antagonist, and now demands to be treated as an equal. What was at first the man's obstinate resistance now becomes the whole man, who is identified with and summed up in this resistance. The part of himself that he wanted to be respected he proceeds to place above everything else and proclaims it preferable to everything, even to life itself. It becomes for him the supreme good. Having up to now been willing to compromise, the slave suddenly adopts ("because this is how it must be . . .") an attitude of All or Nothing. With rebellion, awareness is born.

5   But we can see that the knowledge gained is, at the same time, of an "all" that is still rather obscure and of a "nothing" that proclaims the possibility of sacrificing the rebel to this "All." The rebel himself wants to be "all" — to identify himself completely with this good of which he has suddenly become aware and by which he wants to be personally recognized and acknowledged — or "nothing"; in other words, to be completely destroyed by the force that dominates him. As a last resort, he is willing to accept the final defeat, which is death, rather than be deprived of the per-

sonal sacrament that he would call, for example, freedom. Better to die on one's feet than to live on one's knees.

6   Values, according to good authorities, "most often represent a transition from facts to rights, from what is desired to what is desirable (usually through the intermediary of what is generally considered desirable)." [1] The transition from facts to rights is manifest, as we have seen, in rebellion. So is the transition from "this must be" to "this is how I should like things to be," and even more so, perhaps, the idea of the sublimation of the individual in a henceforth universal good. The sudden appearance of the concept of "All or Nothing" demonstrates that rebellion, contrary to current opinion, and though it springs from everything that is most strictly individualistic in man, questions the very idea of the individual. If the individual, in fact, accepts death and happens to die as a consequence of his act of rebellion, he demonstrates by doing so that he is willing to sacrifice himself for the sake of a common good which he considers more important than his own destiny. If he prefers the risk of death to the negation of the rights that he defends, it is because he considers these rights more important than himself. Therefore he is acting in the name of certain values which are still indeterminate but which he feels are common to himself and to all men. We see that the affirmation implicit in every act of rebellion is extended to something that transcends the individual in so far as it withdraws him from his supposed solitude and provides him with a reason to act. But it is already worth noting that this concept of values as pre-existent to any kind of action contradicts the purely historical philosophies, in which values are acquired (if they are ever acquired) after the action has been completed. Analysis of rebellion leads at least to the suspicion that, contrary to the postulates of contemporary thought, a human nature does exist, as the Greeks believed. Why rebel if there is nothing permanent in oneself worth preserving? It is for the sake of everyone in the world that the slave asserts himself when he comes to the conclusion that a command has infringed on something in him which does not belong to him alone, but which is common ground where all men — even the man who insults and oppresses him — have a natural community.[2]

7   Two observations will support this argument. First, we can see that an act of rebellion is not, essentially, an egoistic act. Of course, it can have egoistic motives. But one can rebel equally well against lies as against oppression. Moreover, the rebel — once he has accepted the motives and at the moment of his greatest impetus — preserves nothing in that he risks everything. He demands respect for himself, of course, but only in so far as he identifies himself with a natural community.

8   Then we note that rebellion does not arise only, and necessarily, among the oppressed, but that it can also be caused by the mere spectacle of op-

---

[1] Lalande: *Vocabulaire philosophique.*
[2] The community of victims is the same as that which unites victim and executioner. But the executioner does not know this.

pression of which someone else is the victim. In such cases there is a feeling of identification with another individual. And it must be pointed out that this is not a question of psychological identification — a mere subterfuge by which the individual imagines that it is he himself who has been offended. On the contrary, it can often happen that we cannot bear to see offenses done to others which we ourselves have accepted without rebelling. The suicides of the Russian terrorists in Siberia as a protest against their comrades' being whipped is a case in point. Nor is it a question of the feeling of a community of interests. Injustices done to men whom we consider enemies can, actually, be profoundly repugnant to us. There is only identification of one's destiny with that of others and a choice of sides. Therefore the individual is not, in himself alone, the embodiment of the values he wishes to defend. It needs all humanity, at least, to comprise them. When he rebels, a man identifies himself with other men and so surpasses himself, and from this point of view human solidarity is metaphysical. But for the moment we are only talking of the kind of solidarity that is born in chains.

9   It would be possible for us to define the positive aspect of the values implicit in every act of rebellion by comparing them with a completely negative concept like that of resentment as defined by Scheler. Rebellion is, in fact, much more than pursuit of a claim, in the strongest sense of the word. Resentment is very well defined by Scheler as an autointoxication — the evil secretion, in a sealed vessel, of prolonged impotence. Rebellion, on the contrary, breaks the seal and allows the whole being to come into play. It liberates stagnant waters and turns them into a raging torrent. Scheler himself emphasizes the passive aspect of resentment and remarks on the prominent place it occupies in the psychology of women who are dedicated to desire and possession. The fountainhead of rebellion, on the contrary, is the principle of superabundant activity and energy. Scheler is also right in saying that resentment is always highly colored by envy. But one envies what one does not have, while the rebel's aim is to defend what he is. He does not merely claim some good that he does not possess or of which he was deprived. His aim is to claim recognition for something which he has and which has already been recognized by him, in almost every case, as more important than anything of which he could be envious. Rebellion is not realistic. According to Scheler, resentment always turns into either unscrupulous ambition or bitterness, depending on whether it is implanted in a strong person or a weak one. But in both cases it is a question of wanting to be something other than what one is. Resentment is always resentment against oneself. The rebel, on the contrary, from his very first step, refuses to allow anyone to touch what he is. He is fighting for the integrity of one part of his being. He does not try, primarily, to conquer, but simply to impose.

10   Finally, it would seem that resentment takes delight, in advance, in the

pain that it would like the object of its envy to feel. Nietzsche and Scheler are right in seeing an excellent example of this in the passage where Tertullian informs his readers that one of the greatest sources of happiness among the blessed will be the spectacle of the Roman emperors consumed in the fires of hell. This kind of happiness is also experienced by the decent people who go to watch executions. The rebel, on the contrary, limits himself, as a matter of principle, to refusing to be humiliated without asking that others should be. He will even accept pain provided his integrity is respected.

11   It is therefore hard to understand why Scheler completely identifies the spirit of rebellion with resentment. His criticism of the resentment to be found in humanitarianism (which he treats as the non-Christian form of love for mankind) could perhaps be applied to certain indeterminate forms of humanitarian idealism, or to the techniques of terror. But it rings false in relation to man's rebellion against his condition — the movement that enlists the individual in the defense of a dignity common to all men. Scheler wants to demonstrate that humanitarian feelings are always accompanied by a hatred of the world. Humanity is loved in general in order to avoid having to love anybody in particular. This is correct, in some cases, and it is easier to understand Scheler when we realize that for him humanitarianism is represented by Bentham and Rousseau. But man's love for man can be born of other things than a mathematical calculation of the resultant rewards or a theoretical confidence in human nature. In face of the utilitarians, and of Émile's preceptor, there is, for example, the kind of logic, embodied by Dostoievsky in Ivan Karamazov, which progresses from an act of rebellion to metaphysical insurrection. Scheler is aware of this and sums up the concept in the following manner: "There is not enough love in the world to squander it on anything but human beings." Even if this proposition were true, the appalling despair that it implies would merit anything but contempt. In fact, it misunderstands the tortured character of Karamazov's rebellion. Ivan's drama, on the contrary, arises from the fact that there is too much love without an object. This love finding no outlet and God being denied, it is then decided to lavish it on human beings as a generous act of complicity.

12   Nevertheless, in the act of rebellion as we have envisaged it up to now, an abstract ideal is not chosen through lack of feeling and in pursuit of a sterile demand. We insist that the part of man which cannot be reduced to mere ideas should be taken into consideration — the passionate side of his nature that serves no other purpose than to be part of the act of living. Does this imply that no rebellion is motivated by resentment? No, and we know it only too well in this age of malice. But we must consider the idea of rebellion in its widest sense on pain of betraying it; and in its widest sense rebellion goes far beyond resentment. When Heathcliff, in *Wuthering Heights*, says that he puts his love above God and would willingly go to hell in order

to be reunited with the woman he loves, he is prompted not only by youth and humiliation but by the consuming experience of a whole lifetime. The same emotion causes Eckart, in a surprising fit of heresy, to say that he prefers hell with Jesus to heaven without Him. This is the very essence of love. Contrary to Scheler, it would therefore be impossible to overemphasize the passionate affirmation that underlies the act of rebellion and distinguishes it from resentment. Rebellion, though apparently negative, since it creates nothing, is profoundly positive in that it reveals the part of man which must always be defended.

13   But, to sum up, are not rebellion and the values that it implies relative? Reasons for rebellion do seem to change, in fact, with periods and civilizations. It is obvious that a Hindu pariah, an Inca warrior, a primitive native of central Africa, and a member of one of the first Christian communities had not at all the same ideas about rebellion. We could even assert, with considerable assurance, that the idea of rebellion has no meaning in these particular cases. However, a Greek slave, a serf, a *condottiere* of the Renaissance, a Parisian bourgeois during the Regency, a Russian intellectual at the beginning of the twentieth century, and a contemporary worker would undoubtedly agree that rebellion is legitimate, even if they differed about the reasons for it. In other words, the problem of rebellion seems to assume a precise meaning only within the confines of Western thought. It is possible to be even more explicit by remarking, like Scheler, that the spirit of rebellion finds few means of expression in societies where inequalities are very great (the Hindu caste system) or, again, in those where there is absolute equality (certain primitive societies). The spirit of rebellion can exist only in a society where a theoretical equality conceals great factual inequalities. The problem of rebellion, therefore, has no meaning except within our own Western society. One might be tempted to affirm that it is relative to the development of individualism if the preceding remarks had not put us on our guard against this conclusion.

14   On the basis of the evidence, the only conclusion that can be drawn from Scheler's remark is that, thanks to the theory of political freedom, there is, in the very heart of our society, an increasing awareness in man of the idea of man and, thanks to the application of this theory of freedom, a corresponding dissatisfaction. Actual freedom has not increased in proportion to man's awareness of it. We can only deduce from this observation that rebellion is the act of an educated man who is aware of his own rights. But there is nothing which justifies us in saying that it is only a question of individual rights. Because of the sense of solidarity we have already pointed out, it would rather seem that what is at stake is humanity's gradually increasing self-awareness as it pursues its course. In fact, for the Inca and the pariah the problem never arises, because for them it had been solved by a tradition, even before they had had time to raise it — the answer being that

tradition is sacred. If in a world where things are held sacred the problem of rebellion does not arise, it is because no real problems are to be found in such a world, all the answers having been given simultaneously. Metaphysic is replaced by myth. There are no more questions, only eternal answers and commentaries, which may be metaphysical. But before man accepts the sacred world and in order that he should be able to accept it — or before he escapes from it and in order that he should be able to escape from it — there is always a period of soul-searching and rebellion. The rebel is a man who is on the point of accepting or rejecting the sacred and determined on laying claim to a human situation in which all the answers are human — in other words, formulated in reasonable terms. From this moment every question, every word, is an act of rebellion while in the sacred world every word is an act of grace. It would be possible to demonstrate in this manner that only two possible worlds can exist for the human mind: the sacred (or, to speak in Christian terms, the world of grace[3]) and the world of rebellion. The disappearance of one is equivalent to the appearance of the other, despite the fact that this appearance can take place in disconcerting forms. There again we rediscover the *All or Nothing*. The present interest of the problem of rebellion only springs from the fact that nowadays whole societies have wanted to discard the sacred. We live in an unsacrosanct moment in history. Insurrection is certainly not the sum total of human experience. But history today, with all its storm and strife, compels us to say that rebellion is one of the essential dimensions of man. It is our historic reality. Unless we choose to ignore reality, we must find our values in it. Is it possible to find a rule of conduct outside the realm of religion and its absolute values? That is the question raised by rebellion.

15   We have already noted the confused values that are called into play by incipient rebellion. Now we must inquire if these values are to be found again in contemporary forms of rebellious thought and action, and if they are, we must specify their content. But, before going any farther, let us note that the basis of these values is rebellion itself. Man's solidarity is founded upon rebellion, and rebellion, in its turn, can only find its justification in this solidarity. We have, then, the right to say that any rebellion which claims the right to deny or destroy this solidarity loses simultaneously its right to be called rebellion and becomes in reality an acquiescence in murder. In the same way, this solidarity, except in so far as religion is concerned, comes to life only on the level of rebellion. And so the real drama of revolutionary thought is announced. In order to exist, man must rebel, but rebellion must respect the limit it discovers in itself — a limit where minds meet and, in meeting, begin to exist. Rebellious thought, therefore, cannot dispense with

3 There is, of course, an act of metaphysical rebellion at the beginning of Christianity, but the resurrection of Christ and the annunciation of the kingdom of heaven interpreted as a promise of eternal life are the answers that render it futile.

memory: it is a perpetual state of tension. In studying its actions and its results, we shall have to say, each time, whether it remains faithful to its first
noble promise or if, through indolence or folly, it forgets its original purpose
and plunges into a mire of tyranny or servitude.

16   Meanwhile, we can sum up the initial progress that the spirit of rebellion provokes in a mind that is originally imbued with the absurdity and
apparent sterility of the world. In absurdist experience, suffering is individual. But from the moment when a movement of rebellion begins, suffering is seen as a collective experience. Therefore the first progressive step for
a mind overwhelmed by the strangeness of things is to realize that this
feeling of strangeness is shared with all men and that human reality, in its
entirety, suffers from the distance which separates it from the rest of the
universe. The malady experienced by a single man becomes a mass plague.
In our daily trials rebellion plays the same role as does the *"cogito"* in the
realm of thought: it is the first piece of evidence. But this evidence lures the
individual from his solitude. It founds its first value on the whole human
race. I rebel — therefore we exist.

Commentary and questions

In his definition Camus discusses no individuals. He is more concerned
to provide an abstract category into which individual rebels can be put
or from which others may be excluded. The tone of this selection from
his study is, on the whole, objective and informative, but it needs to be
tested. Does he ever use emotive, highly colored language? How important is metaphor in his style? How factual are the examples and evidence
he employs? And most important, on what grounds does he deny some
types of individual his label, "The Rebel"? The answer to that question
will help decide precisely what kind of definition the author has made.

1. *Paragraph 2:* Examine the phrase "confused conviction of absolute
rights." Is Camus passing adverse judgment? What conditions does he
establish here which are necessary to his full portrait of the rebel? What
does "absolute right" mean in this context?

2. *Paragraphs 2-3:* According to Camus, the rebel says "yes" and "no"
at the same time. Paraphrase Camus' explanation of this point.

3. *Paragraph 3:* What is the meaning of "gratuitous"? Why must the
rebel move from a state of obedience to rebellion? Does this seriously
limit the author's understanding of rebellion or does it clarify his position?

4. *Paragraph 7:* Camus takes pains to tell us that rebellion is not an
"egoistic" act. Why should he point this out? What does the word mean
as used here? What is its opposite? What connotative values does "egoistic" have in this context? How does Camus show that he is aware of
them? In the same paragraph, what is a "natural community"?

5. Slavery is an important illustration of the conditions for rebellion. As
an example, is it too broad, too narrow, or apt for the purposes of such
a definition as this?

6. How explicit is Camus' distinction between "rebellion" and "resentment"? What different concepts do the two terms imply? To what extent do they reflect similar concepts of human behavior and attitude? Is Camus trying to get us to approve of rebellion and disapprove of resentment?

7. *Paragraph 13:* "The spirit of rebellion can exist only in a society where a theoretical equality conceals great factual inequalities." How does this statement limit the definition of a rebel? Has Camus established a sound basis for making it? Explain. Can you cite examples that support *and* confute this statement?

Topics for discussion and writing

I. How many of the conditions for an explicit, working definition does Camus satisfy? (See pp. 21-23.) Which of them are essential to his definition?

II. Compare this selection to Edmund Wilson's definition of "Americanism" (pp. 19-21). What differences do you notice in their purposes? Which is the most objective and complete? Which is the more "loaded" term today, "Americanism" or "rebel"? If one is easier to use dispassionately and disinterestedly, does this difference have anything to do with the different strategies of each writer?

III. Write a definition of "togetherness" as it is used today. Does it have more than one common use? What connotations must you be alert for? How should these be controlled in your definition? Do the same for "scientific."

IV. Explain the senses in which Camus uses these abstract, general terms: "despair," "the absurd" (paragraph 3), "values" (3), "resentment" (9), "integrity of one part of his being" (9), "age of malice" (12), "solidarity" (15).

BORIS SAVINKOV   Winston Churchill

From Great Contemporaries *by Sir Winston S. Churchill. Copyright 1937. Reprinted by permission of G. P. Putnam's Sons. Permission rights outside the United States granted by Odhams Press, Ltd.*

"How do you get on with Savinkov?" I asked M. de Sazonov when we met in Paris in the summer of 1919.

2   The Czar's former Foreign Minister made a deprecating gesture with his hands.

3   "He is an assassin. I am astonished to be working with him. But what is

one to do? He is a man most competent, full of resource and resolution. No one is so good."

4   The old gentleman, gray with years, stricken with grief for his country, a war-broken exile striving amid the celebrations of victory to represent the ghost of Imperial Russia, shook his head sadly and gazed upon the apartment with eyes of inexpressible weariness.

5   "Savinkov. Ah, I did not expect we should work together."

*   *   *

6   Later on it was my duty to see this strange and sinister man myself. The "Big Five" had just decided to support Koltchak, and Boris Savinkov was his accredited agent. I had never seen a Russian Nihilist except on the stage, and my first impression was that he was singularly well cast for the part. Small in stature; moving as little as possible, and that noiselessly and with deliberation; remarkable gray-green eyes in a face of almost deathly pallor; speaking in a calm, low, even voice, almost a monotone; innumerable cigarettes. His manner was at once confidential and dignified; a ready and ceremonious address, with a frozen, but not a freezing, composure; and through all the sense of an unusual personality, of veiled power in strong restraint. As one looked more closely into this countenance and watched its movement and expression, its force and attraction became evident. His features were agreeable; but though still only in the forties, his face was so lined and crow's-footed that the skin looked in places — and particularly round the eyes — as if it were crinkled parchment. From these impenetrable eyes there flowed a steady regard. The quality of this regard was detached and impersonal, and it seemed to me laden with doom and fate. But then I knew who he was, and what his life had been.

7   Boris Savinkov's whole life had been spent in conspiracy. Without religion as the Churches teach it; without morals as men prescribe them; without home or country; without wife or child, or kith or kin; without friend; without fear; hunter and hunted; implacable, unconquerable, alone. Yet he had found his consolation. His being was organized upon a theme. His life was devoted to a cause. That cause was the freedom of the Russian people. In that cause there was nothing he would not dare or endure. He had not even the stimulus of fanaticism. He was that extraordinary product — a Terrorist for moderate aims. A reasonable and enlightened policy — the Parliamentary system of England, the land tenure of France, freedom, toleration and good will — to be achieved whenever necessary by dynamite at the risk of death. No disguise could baffle his clear-cut perceptions. The forms of government might be revolutionized; the top might become the bottom and the bottom the top; the meaning of words, the association of ideas, the roles of individuals, the semblance of things might be changed out of all recognition without deceiving him. His instinct was sure; his course was unchanging. However winds might veer or currents shift, he always knew the

port for which he was making; he always steered by the same star, and that star was red.

8 During the first part of his life he waged war, often single-handed, against the Russian Imperial Crown. During the latter part of his life, also often single-handed, he fought the Bolshevik Revolution. The Czar and Lenin seemed to him the same thing expressed in different terms, the same tyranny in different trappings, the same barrier in the path of Russian freedom. Against that barrier of bayonets, police, spies, gaolers and executioners he strove unceasingly. A hard fate, an inescapable destiny, a fearful doom! All would have been spared him had he been born in Britain, in France, in the United States, in Scandinavia, in Switzerland. A hundred happy careers lay open. But born in Russia with such a mind and such a will, his life was a torment rising in crescendo to a death in torture. Amid these miseries, perils and crimes he displayed the wisdom of a statesman, the qualities of a commander, the courage of a hero, and the endurance of a martyr.

❀   ❀   ❀

9 In his novel, *The Pale Horse,* written under an assumed name, Savinkov has described with brutal candor the part he played in the murders of M. de Plehve and the Grand Duke Serge. He depicts with an accuracy that cannot be doubted the methods, the daily life, the psychological state and the hair-raising adventures of a small group of men and women, of whom he was the leader, working together for half a year in mortal pursuit of a High Personage. From the moment when, posing as a British subject with a passport signed by Lord Lansdowne in his pocket and "three kilograms of dynamite under the table," he arrives in the town of N., till the murder of "the Governor" who is blown to pieces in the street, and the death, execution or suicide of three out of his four companions, all is laid bare. Most instructive of all is the account given by implication of the relations of the actual Terrorists with the Nihilist Central Committee who lay deep and secure in the underworld of the great cities of Europe and the United States.

10 "M. le Ministre," he said to me, "I know them well, Lenin and Trotsky. For years we worked hand in hand for the liberation of Russia. Now they have enslaved her worse than ever."

11 Between Savinkov's first forlorn war against the Czar and his second against Lenin there was a brief but remarkable interlude. The outbreak of the Great War struck Savinkov and his fellow revolutionary, Bourtzev, in exactly the same way. They saw in the cause of the Allies a movement towards freedom and democracy. Savinkov's heart beat in sympathy with the liberal nations of the West, and his ardent Russian patriotism, put to the test, sundered him from the cold Semitic internationalists with whom he had been so long associated. Even under the Czar, Bourtzev was invited back to Russia, and threw himself into the task of national defense. Savinkov re-

turned with the Revolution. In June, 1917, he was appointed by Kerensky, then Minister for War, to the post of Political Commissar of the 7th Army on the Galician front. The troops were in mutiny. The death penalty had been abolished. German and Austrian agents had spread the poison of Bolshevism through the whole Command. Several regiments had murdered their officers. Discipline and organization were gone. Equipment and munitions had long been lacking. Meanwhile the enemy battered ceaselessly on the crumbling front.

12   Here was the opportunity for his qualities. No sincere revolutionary could impugn his blood-dyed credentials of Nihilism. No loyal officer could doubt his passion for victory. And when it came to political philosophy and the interminable arguments with which the Russians beguiled the road to ruin, there lived no more accomplished student or devastating critic of Karl Marx than the newly-appointed Commissar. Alone, though not unarmed, he visited regiments who had just killed their officers, and brought them back to their duty. On one occasion he is reported to have shot with his own hand the delegates from a Bolshevik Soldiers' Council who were seducing a hitherto loyal unit. Meanwhile his organizing gifts amid a thousand difficulties repaired the administrative structure. In a month he had put a new heart into the discouraged Army Commander and his staff, and had so far redisciplined the Army as to enable it to take the offensive and win a notable action at Brzezany early in July.

13   Kerensky, becoming aware of Savinkov's good work, having himself seen evidence of it on a visit to the 7th Army front, appointed him forthwith Chief Commissar for the Army Group of the South Western front, then commanded by General Gutor. Savinkov had no sooner reached the scene than the front was broken by the Germans at Tarnopol (July 16-19, 1917). The military disaster was followed by wholesale desertions to the enemy, mutinies, massacres of officers and widespread revolt among the civil population. At the instance of Savinkov, Gutor was replaced on the 20th July by General Kornilov. We now approach one of the great mischances of Russian history. In Kornilov Savinkov believed that he had found the man who was to be the complement to his own character, a simple, obstinate soldier, popular among officers and men, with rigid views upon discipline, with no class prejudices, a sincere love of Russia and a knowledge of how to carry through schemes propounded by others. The time had come for a strong and ruthless hand, preferably corporate, if the Army was to be steadied and the country saved. Together with Kornilov, who in all Army matters shared his views, Savinkov demanded the reimposition of the death penalty for cowardice, desertion or espionage, both behind the line and among the fighting troops. Kerensky thus had at his disposal at this most fateful moment in Russian destinies both the political and the military man of action whom the crisis demanded; and both these men were heart and soul together. Here already at the summit of power was the triumvirate that could even at the eleventh

hour have saved Russia from the awful fate which impended, which could have gained at a stroke both Russian victory and Russian freedom. Those who united could have retrieved all were in the event destroyed separately.

✦   ✦   ✦

14   Space does not allow me to unravel the melancholy tangle of ill luck and cunning devices by which Kornilov was separated from Kerensky, and Savinkov rendered powerless to prevent the breach. For a time all marched in the right direction. Kornilov became Commander-in-Chief of all the Russian armies, and Savinkov Deputy Minister of War. Here with one hand upon the vain, doctrinaire, but none the less forceful and well-meaning head of the Government, and the other on the loyal bull-dog soldier, Savinkov seemed to be the appointed agent of Russian salvation. A little more time, a little more help, a little more confidence, a few more honest men, the blessing of Providence and a rather better telephone service — all would have been well! But the tides of chaos mounted swiftly, the German artillery thundered on the front, and the Bolshevik infection spread behind the lines. Profound and adroit intrigues divided the doubting Kerensky from the headstrong Kornilov. On September 9 the General claimed by a *coup d'état* dictatorial powers and was arrested at Kerensky's orders. Savinkov, although exonerated after an inquiry of all complicity in the attempt and placed in full command of Petrograd during the crisis, became the target of the extremist element and was driven to resign. Loyal to Kerensky, loyal to Kornilov, loyal above all to Russia, he lost the control of affairs at the very moment when his was the only hand that could have averted the impending ruin.

15   The Bolshevik revolution of October followed. Kerensky and his supine Government vanished from the scene. Savinkov, eluding his foes, joined General Alexiev on the Don and drew the sword against the new tyranny. This desperate and ultimately vain struggle occupied the rest of his life. He became the official representative of the Russian cause in Europe, first to Alexiev, then to Koltchak, and lastly to Denikin. Responsible for all the relations with the Allies and with the not less important Baltic and Border States which formed at that time the "Sanitary Cordon" of the west, the ex-Nihilist displayed every capacity whether for command or intrigue. Finally, when in 1919 resistance on the soil of Russia was beaten down and the new armies raised in her defense shattered or destroyed, Savinkov on Polish territory formed armies of his own. This last feat was little short of miraculous. Without funds, staff or equipment, with only his old friend Pilsudski as protector, with an authority among the anti-Bolshevik Russians always doubtful and disputed, he nevertheless had by September, 1920, collected 30,000 officers and men and formed them into two organized corps. This last effort, prodigious as it had been, was also doomed to failure. The consolidation of the Bolshevik power, the increasing inclination of the Great Powers to make arrangements with the successful despotism, the pressure of events upon the

small Border States, the internal dissensions of his poverty-stricken army, dissipated the last vestiges of strength. Forced to quit Poland, Savinkov continued the fight from Prague. All hopes of invading Russia with an armed power having vanished, he organized the widespread guerrilla of the Green Guards — a sort of Robin Hood warfare — throughout broad areas of Soviet territory. Gradually, with every circumstance of ruthless terrorism and butchery, all resistance to the Bolsheviks in Russia was stamped out, and the vast populations from the Pacific to Poland and from Archangel to Afghanistan congealed into the long night of another glacial period.

16   It was a little before the final failure that I saw him for the last time. Mr. Lloyd George sought information on the Russian situation, and I was authorized to bring Savinkov to Chequers. We motored there together. The scene upon arrival must have been a novel experience for Savinkov. It was Sunday. The Prime Minister was entertaining several leading Free Church divines, and was himself surrounded by a band of Welsh singers who had traveled from their native Principality to do him choral honors. For several hours they sang Welsh hymns in the most beautiful manner. Afterwards we had our talk. I recall only one of its episodes. The Prime Minister argued that revolutions like diseases run a regular course, that the worst was already over in Russia, that the Bolshevik leaders confronted with the responsibilities of actual government would quit their Communistic theories or that they would quarrel among themselves and fall like Robespierre and St. Just, that others weaker or more moderate would succeed them, and that by successive convulsions a more tolerable regime would be established.

17   "Mr. Prime Minister," said Savinkov in his formal way, "you will permit me the honor of observing that after the fall of the Roman Empire there ensued The Dark Ages."

                    *   *   *

18   In the end the Bolshevik revenge was complete. After two years of subterranean negotiations they lured him back to Russia. Krassin was at one time the intermediary, but there were others. The trap was carefully baited. All resistance by arms, it was said, was now impossible. But within the Bolshevik Government itself the elements of sanity needed only the aid of such a man as Savinkov. The Government could be reconstructed not on a Bolshevik but on a Social-Revolutionary basis. Names and formulas might be kept for a time in order to mask a profound shifting of the balances. "Why not help us to save ourselves?" whispered seductive voices. In June, 1924, Kamenev and Trotsky definitely invited him to return. The past would be condoned, a mock trial would be staged followed by an acquittal and high employment. "Then we shall all be together as in the old days, and break the Communist tyranny as we have broken the Czar." It seems incredible that with his knowledge of these men and of what he had done against them, Savinkov should have entered the trap. Perhaps it was this very knowledge

that betrayed him. He thought he knew their mentality, and trusted to the perverted code of honor of conspirators. It is even possible that truth was mingled with falsehood in their snares. Anyhow they got him.

19 Physical torture was not applied. For their arch-enemy they had reserved more ingenious and refinied cruelties. Later events have made us familiar with these, and their effect in extorting confessions. Tormented in his prison cell with false hopes and shifting promises, squeezed by the most subtle pressures, he was at length induced to write his notorious letter of recantation and to proclaim the Bolshevik Government as the liberator of the world. Thus shamed before history, branded by his friends as a Judas, he could feel each week the rigors of his confinement sensibly increasing; and his final appeal to Djerjinski was answered only by mockery. Whether he was quietly shot in prison or committed suicide in his despair, is uncertain and unimportant. They had destroyed him body and soul. They had reduced his life's efforts to meaningless grimace, had made him insult his cause, and had fouled his memory forever. Yet when all is said and done, and with all the stains and tarnishes there be, few men tried more, gave more, dared more and suffered more for the Russian people.

Commentary and questions

This and the essay on Trotsky (following) are typical of Churchill's flamboyant, often compelling style. The idiom and rhythm are oratorical and might well suit the kind of public speech for which he is famous. But it is more important to understand the purposes such a style serves. Churchill, unlike Camus, is less interested in analysis and precise definition than in creating vivid impressions of a personality. Like Camus' essay, Churchill's are carefully planned and their diction attempts to produce a specific series of responses in his readers.

1. What is the effect of the conversation that opens the essay? What particular quality does Churchill want to convey? Does he later develop the quality hinted at here?

2. *Paragraph 6:* What is the effect of the description of Savinkov's appearance? What concept of the man's character does it suggest?

3. *Paragraph 7:* Examine the phrase, "His being was organized upon a theme." What does it mean? Does it indicate Churchill's attitude toward Savinkov? Does the organization of the essay reflect this idea? What words suggest Savinkov's isolation from the common run of men?

4. *Paragraph 8:* Why does Churchill use the words "fate," "destiny," and "doom"?

5. *Paragraph 8:* Churchill suggests that Savinkov might have had a different career in another country. Does this notion imply that there are permanently valuable traits in Savinkov's character? Does it affect the reader's attitude toward Savinkov in any way?

Do later supporting incidents justify the emotive words in the last two sentences of paragraph 8?

6. *Paragraphs 11-12:* Study the phrases "heart beat in sympathy with," "cold Semitic internationalists," "blood-dyed credentials of Nihilism," "beguiled the road to ruin." Describe their connotative effects. Are they clichés? Find similar phrases elsewhere in the essay and analyze them.

7. *Paragraph 13:* Churchill makes the generalization that Savinkov and others might have saved Russia. Does he offer any effective evidence for this assertion?

8. Note the final sentence in the essay, "Few men tried more, gave more, dared more, and suffered more for the Russian people." Is it accurate? Does Churchill intend it to be a sober conclusion based upon facts he has established in the body of the essay?

Topics for discussion and writing

I. Write an essay demonstrating whether or not Savinkov, as revealed by this portrait, satisfies Camus' criteria for a rebel.

II. Does Churchill's obvious admiration for Savinkov seem to interfere with his judgment of the man? Does Churchill report anything about Savinkov that might be interpreted differently?

III. The effect of Churchill's discussion depends to some extent upon the creation of an exaggerated emotional atmosphere for the reader. Write an essay explaining how Churchill tries to influence or organize the reader's response. What particularly important words does he use for this purpose? What widespread public convictions does he make use of?

IV. How much metaphorical language do you find in this essay? How effective is it, and according to what standards of metaphorical usage is it managed?

V. Write a theme describing the qualities and activities of Savinkov of which Churchill approves. From this, deduce what moral values Churchill himself seems to hold. Make whatever modification the text requires.

LEON TROTSKY, ALIAS BRONSTEIN

Winston Churchill

From Great Contemporaries *by Sir Winston S. Churchill. Copyright 1937. Reprinted by permission of G. P. Putnam's Sons. Permission rights outside the United States granted by Odhams Press, Ltd.*

WHEN the usurper and tyrant is reduced to literary controversy, when the Communist instead of bombs produces effusions for the capitalist Press, when the refugee War Lord fights his battles over again, and the discharged executioner becomes chatty and garrulous at his fireside, we may rejoice in the signs that better days are come. I have before me an article that Leon Trotsky *alias* Bronstein has recently contributed to *John o' London's Weekly* in which he deals with my descriptions of Lenin, with the Allied Intervention in Russia, with Lord Birkenhead and other suggestive topics. He has written this article from his exile in Turkey while supplicating England, France and Germany to admit him to the civilizations it has been — and still is — the object of his life to destroy. Russia — his own Red Russia — the Russia he had framed and fashioned to his heart's desire regardless of suffering, all his daring, all his writing, all his harangues, all his atrocities, all his achievements, have led only to this — that another "comrade," his subordinate in revolutionary rank, his inferior in wit, though not perhaps in crime, rules in his stead, while he, the once triumphant Trotsky whose frown meted death to thousands, sits disconsolate — a skin of malice stranded for a time on the shores of the Black Sea and now washed up in the Gulf of Mexico.

2   But he must have been a difficult man to please. He did not like the Czar, so he murdered him and his family. He did not like the Imperial Government, so he blew it up. He did not like the Liberalism of Guchkov and Miliukov, so he overthrew them. He could not endure the Social Revolutionary moderation of Kerensky and Savinkov, so he seized their places. And when at last the Communist regime for which he had striven with might and main was established throughout the whole of Russia, when the Dictatorship of the Proletariat was supreme, when the New Order of Society had passed from visions into reality, when the hateful culture and traditions of the individualist period had been eradicated, when the Secret Police had become the servants of the Third International, when in a word his Utopia had been achieved, he was still discontented. He still fumed, growled, snarled, bit and plotted. He had raised the poor against the rich. He had raised the penniless against the poor. He had raised the criminal against the penniless. All had fallen out as he had willed. But nevertheless the vices of human society required, it seemed, new scourgings. In the deepest depth he sought with desperate energy for a deeper. But — poor wretch — he had reached rock-bottom. Nothing lower than the Communist criminal class could be found. In vain he turned his gaze upon the wild beasts. The apes could not appreciate his eloquence. He could not mobilize the wolves, whose numbers had so notably increased during his administration. So the criminals he had installed stood together, and put him outside.

3   Hence these chatty newspaper articles. Hence these ululations from the Bosphorus. Hence these entreaties to be allowed to visit the British Museum and study its documents, or to drink the waters of Malvern for his rheumatism, or of Nauheim for his heart, or of Homburg for his gout, or of some other place for some other complaint. Hence these broodings in Turkish

shades pierced by the searching eye of Mustafa Kemal. Hence these exits from France, from Scandinavia. Hence this last refuge in Mexico.

4   It is astonishing that a man of Trotsky's intelligence should not be able to understand the well-marked dislike of civilized governments for the leading exponents of Communism. He writes as if it were due to mere narrow-minded prejudice against new ideas and rival political theories. But Communism is not only a creed. It is a plan of campaign. A Communist is not only the holder of certain opinions; he is the pledged adept of a well-thought-out means of enforcing them. The anatomy of discontent and revolution has been studied in every phase and aspect, and a veritable drill book prepared in a scientific spirit for subverting all existing institutions. The method of enforcement is as much a part of the Communist faith as the doctrine itself. At first the time-honored principles of Liberalism and Democracy are invoked to shelter the infant organism. Free speech, the right of public meeting, every form of lawful political agitation and constitutional right are paraded and asserted. Alliance is sought with every popular movement towards the left.

5   The creation of a mild Liberal or Socialist regime in some period of convulsion is the first milestone. But no sooner has this been created than it is to be overthrown. Woes and scarcity resulting from confusion must be exploited. Collisions, if possible attended with bloodshed, are to be arranged between the agents of the New Government and the working people. Martyrs are to be manufactured. An apologetic attitude in the rulers should be turned to profit. Pacific propaganda may be made the mask of hatreds never before manifested among men. No faith need be, indeed may be, kept with non-Communists. Every act of good will, of tolerance, of conciliation, of mercy, of magnanimity on the part of Governments or Statesmen is to be utilized for their ruin. Then when the time is ripe and the moment opportune, every form of lethal violence from mob revolt to private assassination must be used without stint or compunction. The citadel will be stormed under the banners of Liberty and Democracy; and once the apparatus of power is in the hands of the Brotherhood, all opposition, all contrary opinions must be extinguished by death. Democracy is but a tool to be used and afterwards broken; Liberty but a sentimental folly unworthy of the logician. The absolute rule of a self-chosen priesthood according to the dogmas it has learned by rote is to be imposed upon mankind without mitigation progressively forever. All this, set out in prosy textbooks, written also in blood in the history of several powerful nations, is the Communist's faith and purpose. To be forewarned should be to be forearmed!

6   I wrote this passage nearly seven years ago: but is it not an exact account of the Communist plot which has plunged Spain into the present hideous welter against the desires of the overwhelming majority of Spaniards on both sides?

7   It is probable that Trotsky never comprehended the Marxian creed: but

of its drill-book he was the incomparable master. He possessed in his nature all the qualities requisite for the art of civic destruction — the organizing command of a Carnot, the cold detached intelligence of a Machiavelli, the mob oratory of a Cleon, the ferocity of Jack the Ripper, the toughness of Titus Oates. No trace of compassion, no sense of human kinship, no apprehension of the spiritual, weakened his high and tireless capacity for action. Like the cancer bacillus he grew, he fed, he tortured, he slew in fulfillment of his nature. He found a wife who shared the Communist faith. She worked and plotted at his side. She shared his first exile to Siberia in the days of the Czar. She bore him children. She aided his escape. He deserted her. He found another kindred mind in a girl of good family who had been expelled from a school at Kharkov for persuading the pupils to refuse to attend prayers and to read Communist literature instead of the Bible. By her he had another family. As one of his biographers (Max Eastman) puts it: "If you have a perfectly legal mind, she is not Trotsky's wife, for Trotsky never divorced Alexandra Ivovna Sokolovski, who still uses the name of Bronstein." Of his mother he writes in cold and chilling terms. His father — old Bronstein — died of typhus in 1920 at the age of 83. The triumphs of his son brought no comfort to this honest hard-working and believing Jew. Persecuted by the Reds because he was a bourgeois; by the Whites because he was Trotsky's father, and deserted by his son, he was left to sink or swim in the Russian deluge, and swam on steadfastly to the end. What else was there for him to do?

8   Yet in Trotsky, in this being so removed from the ordinary affections and sentiments of human nature, so uplifted, shall we say, above the common herd, so superbly fitted to his task, there was an element of weakness especially serious from the Communist point of view. Trotsky was ambitious, and ambitious in quite a common worldly way. All the collectivism in the world could not rid him of an egoism which amounted to a disease, and to a fatal disease. He must not only ruin the State, he must rule the ruins thereafter. Every system of government of which he was not the head or almost the head was odious to him. The Dictatorship of the Proletariat to him meant that he was to be obeyed without question. He was to do the dictating on behalf of the proletariat. "The toiling masses," the "Councils of Workmen, Peasants and Soldiers," the gospel and revelation of Karl Marx, the Federal Union of Socialist Soviet Republics, etc., to him were all spelt in one word: Trotsky. This led to trouble. Comrades became jealous. They became suspicious. At the head of the Russian Army, which he reconstructed amid indescribable difficulties and perils, Trotsky stood very near the vacant throne of the Romanovs.

9   The Communist formulas he had used with devastating effect upon others, were now no impediment to him. He discarded them as readily as he had discarded his wife, or his father, or his name. The Army must be remade; victory must be won; and Trotsky must do it and Trotsky profit

from it. To what other purpose should revolutions be made? He used his exceptional prowess to the full. The officers and soldiers of the new model army were fed, clothed and treated better than anyone else in Russia. Officers of the old Czarist regime were wheedled back in thousands. "To the devil with politics — let us save Russia." The salute was reintroduced. The badges of rank and privilege were restored. The authority of commanders was re-established. The higher command found themselves treated by this Communist upstart with a deference they had never experienced from the Ministers of the Czar. The abandonment by the Allies of the Russian Loyalist cause crowned these measures with a victory easy but complete. In 1922 so great was the appreciation among the military for Trotsky's personal attitude and system that he might well have been made Dictator of Russia by the armed forces, but for one fatal obstacle.

10   He was a Jew. He was still a Jew. Nothing could get over that. Hard fortune when you have deserted your family, repudiated your race, spat upon the religion of your fathers, and lapped Jew and Gentile in a common malignity, to be baulked of so great a prize for so narrow-minded a reason! Such intolerance, such pettiness, such bigotry were hard indeed to bear. And this disaster carried in its train a greater. In the wake of disappointment loomed catastrophe.

11   For meanwhile the comrades had not been idle. They too had heard the talk of the officers. They too saw the possibilities of a Russian Army reconstituted from its old elements. While Lenin lived the danger seemed remote. Lenin indeed regarded Trotsky as his political heir. He sought to protect him. But in 1924 Lenin died: and Trotsky, still busy with his army, still enjoying the day-to-day work of administering his department, still hailed with the acclamations which had last resounded for Nicholas II, turned to find a hard and toughly-wrought opposition organized against him.

12   Stalin, the Georgian, was a kind of General Secretary to the governing instrument. He managed the caucus and manipulated the innumerable committees. He gathered the wires together with patience and pulled them in accordance with a clearly-perceived design. When Trotsky advanced hopefully, confidently indeed, to accept the succession to Lenin, the party machine was found to be working in a different direction. In the purely political arena of Communist activities Trotsky was speedily outmaneuvered. He was accused on the strength of some of his voluminous writings of "Anti-Leninism." He does not seem to have understood that Lenin had replaced God in the Communist mind. He remained for some time under the impression that any such desirable substitution had been effected by Trotsky. He admitted his heresy and eagerly explained to the soldiers and workers the very cogent reasons which had led him to it. His declarations were received with blank dismay. The Ogpu was set in motion. Officers known to be under an obligation to Trotsky were removed from their appointments. After a period of silent tension he was advised to take a holiday. This holiday after some interruptions still continues.

13 Stalin used his success to build a greater. The Politbureau, without the spell of Lenin, or the force of Trotsky, was in its turn purged of its remaining elements of strength. The politicians who had made the Revolution were dismissed and chastened and reduced to impotence by the party manager. The caucus swallowed the Cabinet, and with Stalin at its head became the present Government of Russia. Trotsky was marooned by the very mutineers he had led so hardily to seize the ship.

14 What will be his place in history? For all its horrors, a glittering light plays over the scenes and actors of the French Revolution. The careers and personalities of Robespierre, of Danton, even of Marat, gleam luridly across a century. But the dull, squalid figures of the Russian Bolsheviks are not redeemed in interest even by the magnitude of their crimes. All form and emphasis is lost in a vast process of Asiatic liquefaction. Even the slaughter of millions and the misery of scores of millions will not attract future generations to their uncouth lineaments and outlandish names. And now most of them have paid the penalty of their crimes. They have emerged from the prison-cells of the Cheka, to make their strange unnatural confessions to the world. They have met the death in secret to which they had consigned so many better and braver men.

15 But Trotsky survives. He lingers on the stage. He has forgotten his efforts, which Lenin restrained, to continue the War against Germany rather than submit to the conditions of Brest-Litovsk. He has forgotten his own career as a War Lord and the opportunist remaker of the Russian Army. In misfortune he has returned to Bolshevik Orthodoxy. Once again he has become the exponent of the purest sect of Communism. Around his name gather the new extremists and doctrinaires of world-revolution. Upon him is turned the full blast of Soviet malignity. The same vile propaganda which he used with so much ruthlessness upon the old regime, is now concentrated upon himself by his sole-surviving former comrade. All Russia from Poland to China, from the North Pole to the Himalayas, is taught to regard him as the supreme miscreant seeking in some way or other to add new chains to the workers, and bring the Nazi invader into their midst. The name of Lenin, the doctrine of Karl Marx, are invoked against him at the moment when he frantically endeavors to exploit them. Russia is regaining strength as the virulence of Communism abates in her blood. The process may be cruel, but it is not morbid. It is a need of self-preservation which impels the Soviet Government to extrude Trotsky and his fresh-distilled poisons. In vain he screams his protests against a hurricane of lies; in vain he denounces the bureaucratic tyranny of which he would so blithely be the head; in vain he strives to rally the underworld of Europe to the overthrow of the Russian Army he was once proud to animate. Russia has done with him, and done with him forever.

16 He will perhaps have leisure to contemplate his handiwork. No one could wish him a better punishment than that his life should be prolonged, and that his keen intelligence and restless spirit should corrode each other

in impotence and stultification. Indeed we may foresee a day when his theories, exploded by their application, will have ceased even to be irritating to the active, hopeful world outside, and when the wide tolerance which follows from a sense of security, will allow him to creep back, discredited and extinct, to the European and American haunts, where so many of his early years were spent. It may be that in these future years, he will find as little comfort in the work which he has done, as his father found in the son he had begotten.

Commentary and questions

1. *Paragraph 1:* Why does Churchill use the phrase *"alias* Bronstein"? (Bronstein was Trotsky's real name.) Examine the phrase, "inferior in wit, though not perhaps in crime." It refers to Stalin. How does such an irony influence the reader's response?

2. *Paragraph 2:* "He did not like the Czar, so he murdered him and his family." Churchill here is deliberately illogical. Is there any truth in the statement? "He still fumed, growled, snarled, bit and plotted." To what would the first four words ordinarily apply? What impression do they create? What is the force of "plotted" in the sequence? What concepts lie behind this use of language?

3. *Paragraph 4:* Note the abrupt change in tone from the previous three paragraphs. What is the purpose of this shift? What words make it possible and why?

Explain Churchill's distinction between Communism as a "creed" and as "a plan of campaign."

4. *Paragraph 7:* What bearing does Churchill's account of Trotsky's treatment of his family have on the purpose of the essay? Why is it used here? How has he prepared for the quotation from Trotsky's biography?

5. *Paragraphs 8-10:* Describe the impression of Trotsky's personality and motives. How does the kind of language Churchill uses assist this impression?

Describe the point of view from which the statements in paragraphs 9-10 are made.

Topics for discussion and writing

I. What is the purpose of this essay? Why did Churchill include Trotsky among his great contemporaries?

II. In spite of Churchill's personal opinion of the man, does his portrait of Trotsky satisfy any of the major conditions in Camus's definition of the rebel?

III. Might Trotsky fit Camus' description of resentful disobedience? Write a theme comparing the portraits of Savinkov and Trotsky in this respect.

IV. Broadly speaking irony is a technique of pointing up the unexpected or incongruous. What we would like to happen does not; what we expected does not come to pass; we discover unsuspected weaknesses in great men. Such events and perceptions can be called ironic, and Churchill makes liberal use of irony in this essay. Describe this use: point out good examples and explain their effects.

V. Pick three of four key words and discuss their use throughout the essay. How does Churchill make them count in putting across his point of view?

VI. What underlying moral assumptions on Churchill's part does his disapproval of Trotsky reveal? Write a paper explaining why Churchill approves of Savinkov but disapproves of Trotsky.

VII. Go through the essay and note Churchill's use of metaphor. Write an essay in which you show how Churchill's metaphoric language is a part of his denunciation of Trotsky.

SIGNIFICANT GESTURE   Malcolm Cowley

From Exile's Return *by Malcolm Cowley. Copyright 1934, 1951 by Malcolm Cowley. Reprinted by permission of The Viking Press, Inc.*

DURING the last three weeks before sailing for America, I wrote no letters. I was much too excited to write letters; I had never, in fact, spent prouder, busier or more amusing days. I was being arrested and tried for punching a café proprietor in the jaw.

2   He deserved to be punched, though not especially by me; I had no personal grudge against him. His café, the Rotonde, had long been patronized by revolutionists of every nation. Lenin used to sit there, I was told; and proletarian revolts were still being planned, over coffee in the evening, by quiet men who paid no attention to the hilarious arguments of Swedish and Rumanian artists at the surrounding tables. The proprietor — whose name I forget — used to listen unobtrusively. It was believed, on more or less convincing evidence, that he was a paid informer. It was said that he had betrayed several anarchists to the French police. Moreover, it was known that he had insulted American girls, treating them with the cold brutality that French café proprietors reserve for prostitutes. He was a thoroughly disagreeable character and should, we felt, be called to account.

3   We were at the Dôme, ten or twelve of us packed together at a table in the midst of the crowd that swirled in the Boulevard Montparnasse. It was July 14, 1923, the national holiday. Chinese lanterns hung in rows among the trees; bands played at every corner; everywhere people were

dancing in the streets. Paris, deserted for the summer by its aristocrats, bankers and politicians, forgetting its hordes of tourists, was given over to a vast plebeian carnival, a general madness in which we had eagerly joined. Now, tired of dancing, we sipped our drinks and talked in loud voices to make ourselves heard above the music, the rattle of saucers, the shuffle of feet along the sidewalk. I was trying, with my two hands on the table, to imitate the ridiculous efforts of Tristan Tzara to hop a moving train. "Let's go over," said Laurence Vail, tossing back his long yellow hair from his forehead, "and assault the proprietor of the Rotonde."

4   "Let's," I said.

5   We crossed the street together, some of the girls in bright evening gowns and some in tweeds, Louis Aragon slim and dignified in a dinner jacket, Laurence bareheaded and wearing a raincoat which he never removed in the course of the hot starlit night, myself coatless, dressed in a workman's blue shirt, worn trousers and rope-soled shoes. Delayed and separated by the crowd on the pavement, we made our way singly into the bar, which I was the last to enter. Aragon, in periodic sentences pronounced in a beautifully modulated voice, was expressing his opinion of all stool pigeons — *mouchards* — and was asking why such a wholly contemptible character as the proprietor of the Rotonde presumed to solicit the patronage of respectable people. The waiters, smelling a fight, were forming a wall of shirt fronts around their employer. Laurence Vail pushed through the wall; he made an angry speech in such rapid French that I could catch only a few phrases, all of them insults. The proprietor backed away; his eyes shifted uneasily; his face was a dirty white behind his black mustache. Harold Loeb, looking on, was a pair of spectacles, a chin, a jutting pipe and an embarrassed smile.

6   I was angry at my friends, who were allowing the situation to resolve into a series of useless gestures; but even more I was seized with a physical revulsion for the proprietor, with his look of a dog caught stealing chickens and trying to sneak off. Pushing past the waiters, I struck him a glancing blow in the jaw. Then, before I could strike again, I was caught up in an excited crowd and forced to the door.

7   Five minutes later our band had once more assembled on the terrace of the Dôme. I had forgotten the affair already: nothing remained but a vague exhilaration and the desire for further activity. I was obsessed with the idea that we should *changer de quartier:* that instead of spending the rest of the night in Montparnasse, we should visit other sections of Paris. Though no one else seemed enthusiastic, I managed by force of argument to assemble five hesitant couples, and the ten of us went strolling southeastward along the Boulevard Montparnasse.

8   On reaching the first café we stopped for a drink of beer and a waltz under the chestnut trees. One couple decided to return to the Dôme. Eight of us walked on to another café, where, after a bock, two other couples be-

came deserters. "Let's change our quarter," I said once more. At the next café, Bob Coates consulted his companion. "We're going back to the Dôme," he said. Two of us walked on sadly. We caught sight of Montrouge — more Chinese lanterns and wailing accordions and workmen dancing with shop-girls in the streets — then we too returned to Montparnasse.

9   It was long after midnight, but the streets were as crowded as before and I was eager for adventure. At the Dôme I met Tristan Tzara, seized him by the arm and insisted that we go for a stroll. We argued the question whether the Dada movement could be revived. Under the chestnut trees we met a high-brown woman dressed in barbaric clothes; she was thought to be a princes from Senegal. I addressed her extravagant compliments in English and French; Tzara added others in French, German and his three words of Rumanian. "Go 'way, white boys," she said in a Harlem voice. We turned back, passing the crowded terrace of the Rotonde. The proprietor was standing there with his arms folded. At the sight of him a fresh rage surged over me.

10   *"Quel salaud!"* I roared for the benefit of his six hundred customers. *"Ah, quel petit mouchard!"*

11   Then we crossed the street once more toward the Dôme, slowly. But when I reached the middle of the tracks I felt each of my arms seized by a little blue policeman. "Come along with us," they said. And they marched me toward the station house, while Tzara rushed off to get the identification papers left behind in my coat. The crowds disappeared behind us; we were alone — I and the two *flics* and the proprietor of the Rotonde.

12   One of the two policemen was determined to amuse himself. "You're lucky," he said, "to be arrested in Paris. If you were arrested by those brutal policemen of New York, they would cuff you on the ear — like this," he snarled, cuffing me on the ear, "but in Paris we pat you gently on the shoulder."

13   I knew I was in trouble. I said nothing and walked peacefully beside him.

14   "Ah, the police of Paris are incomparably gentle. If you were arrested in New York, they would crack you in the jaw — like this," he said, cracking me in the jaw, "but here we do nothing; we take you with us calmly."

15   He rubbed his hands, then thrust his face toward mine. His breath stank of brandy.

16   "You like the police of Paris, *hein?*"

17   "Assuredly," I answered. The proprietor of the Rotonde walked on beside us, letting his red tongue play over the ends of his mustache. The other *flic* said nothing.

18   "I won't punch you in the nose like the New York policemen," said the drunken man, punching me in the nose. "I will merely ask you to walk on in front of me. . . . Walk in front of me, pig!"

19   I walked in front of him, looking back suspiciously under my armpit.

His hand was on his holster, loosening the flap. I had read about people shot "while trying to escape" and began walking so very slowly that he had to kick me in the heels to urge me up the steps of the police station. When we stood at the desk before the sergeant, he charged me with an unprovoked assault on the proprietor of the Rotonde — and also with forcibly resisting an officer. "Why," he said, "he kicked me in the shins, leaving a scar. Look here!"

20   He rolled up his trouser leg, showing a scratch half an inch long. It was useless for me to object that my rope-soled shoes wouldn't have scratched a baby. Police courts in France, like police courts everywhere, operate on the theory that a policeman's word is always to be taken against that of an accused criminal.

21   Things looked black for me until my friends arrived — Laurence and Louis and Jacques Rigaut and my wife — bearing with them my identification papers and a supply of money. Consulting together, we agreed that the drunken policeman must be bribed, and bribed he was: in the general confusion he was bribed twice over. He received in all a hundred and thirty francs, at least four times as much as was necessary. Standing pigeon-toed before the sergeant at the desk and wearing an air of bashful benevolence, he announced that I was a pretty good fellow after all, even though I had kicked him in the shins. He wished to withdraw the charge of resisting an officer.

22   My prospects brightened perceptibly. Everyone agreed that the false charge was the more serious of the two. For merely punching a stool-pigeon, the heaviest sentence I could receive would be a month in jail. Perhaps I would escape with a week.

23   A preliminary hearing was held on the following evening, after a night in jail and a day spent vainly trying to sleep between visits from the police and telephone calls from anxious friends. I stopped at the Dôme to collect my witnesses; fortunately there was a party that evening and they were easy to find. They consisted of nine young ladies in evening gowns. None of them had been present at the scene in the Rotonde the night before, but that didn't matter: all of them testified in halting French that I hadn't been present either; the whole affair was an imposition on a writer known for his serious character; it was a hoax invented by a café proprietor who was a pig and very impolite to American young women.

24   The examining magistrate was impressed. He confided later to André Salmon that the proprietor of the Rotonde had only his waiters to support the story he told, whereas I had nine witnesses, all of them very respectable people, *des gens très bien*. That helped Salmon to get me out of the scrape, although he also brought his own influence to bear. He was a poet and novelist who was also a star reporter and covered all the important murder trials for *Le Matin*. Since magistrates liked to be on good terms with him,

he managed to have my trial postponed from day to day and finally abandoned.

25   But the most amusing feature of the affair, and my justification for dealing with it at length, was the effect it produced on my French acquaintances. They looked at me with an admiration I could not understand, even when I reflected that French writers rarely came to blows and that they placed a high value on my unusual action. Years later I realized that by punching a café proprietor in the jaw I had performed an act to which all their favorite catchwords could be applied. First of all, I had acted for reasons of public morality; bearing no private grudge against my victim, I had been *disinterested*. I had committed an *indiscretion*, acted with *violence* and *disdain* for the law, performed an *arbitrary* and *significant gesture*, uttered a *manifesto;* in their opinion I had shown *courage*. . . . For the first time in my life I became a public character. I was entertained at dinners and cocktail parties, interviewed for the newspapers, asked to contribute to reviews published by the Dadaists in Amsterdam, Brussels, Lyon and Belgrade. My stories were translated into Hungarian and German. A party of Russian writers then visiting Paris returned to Moscow with several of my poems, to be printed in their own magazines.

26   The poems were not at all revolutionary in tone, but they dealt with a subject that, in those briefly liberal days of the New Economic Policy in Russia, had been arousing the enthusiasm of Soviet writers. They were poems about America, poems that spoke of movies and skyscrapers and machines, dwelling upon them with all the nostalgia derived from two long years of exile. I, too, was enthuiastic over America; I had learned from a distance to admire its picturesque qualities. And I was returning to New York with a set of values that bore no relation to American life, with convictions that could not fail to be misunderstood in a country where Dada was hardly a name, and moral judgments on literary matters were thought to be in questionable taste — in a city where writers had only three justifications for their acts: they did them to make money, or to get their name in the papers, or because they were drunk.

Commentary and questions

1. *Paragraph 1:* Note the combination of "prouder," "busier," and "more amusing" with "I was being tried for punching a café proprietor in the jaw." The short paragraph has a distinct tone. Describe it. Does it persist through the entire account? If it is modified, how and where is it modified?

2. *Paragraph 2:* As Cowley builds up his case against the proprietor he slips in the observation that "proletarian revolts were being planned . . . by quiet men." How does this affect the atmosphere described in the paragraph? How does it suggest the significance of the scene?

3. *Paragraph 3:* Describe the means Cowley uses to identify and evaluate himself and his friends. How do they relate to the surroundings and background?

4. *Paragraph 5:* Is there anything significant about the way the group is dressed?

5. *Paragraph 6:* What does the phrase "series of useless gestures" suggest about the author's friends? Why are they useless?

6. *Paragraphs 6-9:* What do the events described here contribute to Cowley's general thesis?

7. *Paragraphs 11-24:* Cowley narrates his arrest and release, which are central in his account. What is his purpose here? Is he trying to attract the reader's sympathy for himself, indict the French administration of justice, or hint that his gesture was not worth the consequences?

8. *Paragraphs 23-24:* Cowley's witnesses are "very respectable people." What does the turn of events described here suggest about the value of Cowley's "gesture"?

9. *Paragraph 25:* Note the phrases in italics. Why does Cowley have them printed this way? Recall his own feelings which prompted his assault on the café proprietor and then his brief fame. What is Cowley's own attitude as he writes of these events? How do the italicized terms help us understand that attitude?

Topics for discussion and writing

I. In the final paragraph Cowley says that he acquired "a set of values that bore no relation to American life." Evidently some of these values are touched upon in the essay. Write a theme describing what you think they are and suggesting why they are irrelevant to American life.

II. Cowley's act is not rebellion against someone or something he had previously obeyed. In other respects does he qualify as a rebel according to Camus' standards?

III. Cowley's style is largely narrative and his approach to the significance of what he narrates is indirect. Describe this style in some detail. What specific indirect techniques do you find? Which are most important?

IV. Describe in detail Cowley's attitude toward his friends. How is it made clear?

V. It is possible that the word "significant" in the title is used ironically. If this is true, how does Cowley establish its irony?

VI. According to Cowley's point of view, would Thoreau's defiance of civil authority be a useless gesture? Write a theme explaining your answer.

CIVIL DISOBEDIENCE   Henry David Thoreau

First published in 1849.

I HEARTILY accept the motto, — "That government is best which governs least"; and I should like to see it acted up to more rapidly and systematically. Carried out, it finally amounts to this, which also I believe, — "That government is best which governs not at all"; and when men are prepared for it, that will be the kind of government which they will have. Government is at best but an expedient; but most governments are usually, and all governments are sometimes, inexpedient. The objections which have been brought against a standing army, and they are many and weighty, and deserve to prevail, may also at last be brought against a standing government. The standing army is only an arm of the standing government. The government itself, which is only the mode which the people have chosen to execute their will, is equally liable to be abused and perverted before the people can act through it. Witness the present Mexican war, the work of comparatively a few individuals using the standing government as their tool; for, in the outset, the people would not have consented to this measure.

2   This American government, — what is it but a tradition, though a recent one, endeavoring to transmit itself unimpaired to posterity, but each instant losing some of its integrity? It has not the vitality and force of a single living man; for a single man can bend it to his will. It is a sort of wooden gun to the people themselves. But it is not the less necessary for this; for the people must have some complicated machinery or other, and hear its din, to satisfy that idea of government which they have. Governments show thus how successfully men can be imposed on, even impose on themselves, for their own advantage. It is excellent, we must all allow. Yet this government never of itself furthered any enterprise, but by the alacrity with which it got out of its way. *It* does not keep the country free. *It* does not settle the West. *It* does not educate. The character inherent in the American people has done all that has been accomplished; and it would have done somewhat more, if the government had not sometimes got in its way. For government is an expedient by which men would fain succeed in letting one another alone; and, as has been said, when it is most expedient, the governed are most let alone by it. Trade and commerce, if they were not made of India-rubber, would never manage to bounce over the obstacles which legislators are continually putting in their way; and, if one were to judge these men wholly by the effects of their actions and not partly by their intentions, they would deserve to be classed and punished with those mischievous persons who put obstructions on the railroads.

3   But, to speak practically and as a citizen, unlike those who call themselves no-government men, I ask for, not at once no government, but *at once* a better government. Let every man make known what kind of government would command his respect, and that will be one step toward obtaining it.

⁴   After all, the practical reason why, when the power is once in the hands of the people, a majority are permitted, and for a long period continue, to rule is not because they are most likely to be in the right, nor because this seems fairest to the minority, but because they are physically the strongest. But a government in which the majority rule in all cases cannot be based on justice, even as far as men understand it. Can there not be a government in which majorities do not virtually decide right and wrong, but conscience? — in which majorities decide only those questions to which the rule of expediency is applicable? Must the citizen ever for a moment, or in the least degree, resign his conscience to the legislator? Why has every man a conscience, then? I think that we should be men first, and subjects afterward. It is not desirable to cultivate a respect for the law, so much as for the right. The only obligation which I have a right to assume is to do at any time what I think right. It is truly enough said, that a corporation has no conscience; but a corporation of conscientious men is a corporation *with* a conscience. Law never made men a whit more just; and, by means of their respect for it, even the well-disposed are daily made the agents of injustice. A common and natural result of an undue respect for law is, that you may see a file of soldiers, colonel, captain, corporal, privates, powder-monkeys, and all, marching in admirable order over hill and dale to the wars, against their wills, ay, against their common sense and consciences, which makes it very steep marching indeed, and produces a palpitation of the heart. They have no doubt that it is a damnable business in which they are concerned; they are all peaceably inclined. Now, what are they? Men at all? or small movable forts and magazines, at the service of some unscrupulous man in power? Visit the Navy-Yard, and behold a marine, such a man as an American government can make, or such as it can make a man with its black arts, — a mere shadow and reminiscence of humanity, a man laid out alive and standing, and already, as one may say, buried under arms with funeral accompaniments, though it may be, —

> "Not a drum was heard, not a funeral note,
>   As his corse to the rampart we hurried;
> Not a soldier discharged his farewell shot
>   O'er the grave where our hero we buried."

⁵   The mass of men serve the state thus, not as men mainly, but as machines, with their bodies. They are the standing army, and the militia, jailors, constables, posse comitatus, etc. In most cases there is no free exercise whatever of the judgment or of the moral sense; but they put themselves on a level with wood and earth and stones; and wooden men can perhaps be manufactured that will serve the purpose as well. Such command no more respect than men of straw or a lump of dirt. They have the same sort of worth only as horses and dogs. Yet such as these even are commonly esteemed good citizens. Others — as most legislators, politicians, lawyers,

ministers, and office-holders — serve the state chiefly with their heads; and, as they rarely make any moral distinctions, they are as likely to serve the Devil, without *intending* it, as God. A very few, as heroes, patriots, martyrs, reformers in the great sense, and *men*, serve the state with their consciences also, and so necessarily resist it for the most part; and they are commonly treated as enemies by it. A wise man will only be useful as a man, and will not submit to be "clay," and "stop a hole to keep the wind away," but leave that office to his dust at least: —

> "I am too high-born to be propertied,
> To be a secondary at control,
> Or useful serving-man and instrument
> To any sovereign state throughout the world."

6   He who gives himself entirely to his fellow-men appears to them useless and selfish; but he who gives himself partially to them is pronounced a benefactor and philanthropist.

7   How does it become a man to behave toward this American government to-day? I answer, that he cannot without disgrace be associated with it. I cannot for an instant recognize that political organization as *my* government which is the *slave's* government also.

8   All men recognize the right of revolution; that is, the right to refuse allegiance to, and to resist, the government, when its tyranny or its inefficiency are great and unendurable. But almost all say that such is not the case now. But such was the case, they think, in the Revolution of '75. If one were to tell me that this was a bad government because it taxed certain foreign commodities brought to its ports, it is most probable that I should not make an ado about it, for I can do without them. All machines have their friction; and possibly this does enough good to counterbalance the evil. At any rate, it is a great evil to make a stir about it. But when the friction comes to have its machine, and oppression and robbery are organized, I say, let us not have such a machine any longer. In other words, when a sixth of the population of a nation which has undertaken to be the refuge of liberty are slaves, and a whole country is unjustly overrun and conquered by a foreign army, and subjected to military law, I think that it is not too soon for honest men to rebel and revolutionize. What makes this duty the more urgent is the fact that the country so overrun is not our own, but ours is the invading army. . . .

9   Practically speaking, the opponents to a reform in Massachusetts are not a hundred thousand politicians at the South, but a hundred thousand merchants and farmers here, who are more interested in commerce and agriculture than they are in humanity, and are not prepared to do justice to the slave and to Mexico, *cost what it may*. I quarrel not with far-off foes, but with those who, near at home, coöperate with, and do the bidding of, those far away, and without whom the latter would be harmless. We are accus-

tomed to say, that the mass of men are unprepared; but improvement is slow, because the few are not materially wiser or better than the many. It is not so important that many should be as good as you, as that there be some absolute goodness somewhere; for that will leaven the whole lump. There are thousands who are *in opinion* opposed to slavery and to the war, who yet in effect do nothing to put an end to them; who, esteeming themselves children of Washington and Franklin, sit down with their hands in their pockets, and say that they know not what to do, and do nothing; who even postpone the question of freedom to the question of free-trade, and quietly read the prices-current along with the latest advices from Mexico, after dinner, and, it may be, fall asleep over them both. What is the price-current of an honest man and patriot to-day? They hesitate, and they regret, and sometimes they petition; but they do nothing in earnest and with effect. They will wait, well disposed, for others to remedy the evil, that they may no longer have it to regret. At most, they give only a cheap vote, and a feeble countenance and Godspeed, to the right, as it goes by them. There are nine hundred and ninety-nine patrons of virtue to one virtuous man. But it is easier to deal with the real possessor of a thing than with the temporary guardian of it. . . .

10   I hear of a convention to be held at Baltimore, or elsewhere, for the selection of a candidate for the Presidency, made up chiefly of editors, and men who are politicians by profession; but I think, what is it to any independent, intelligent, and respectable man what decision they may come to? Shall we not have the advantage of his wisdom and honesty, nevertheless? Can we not count upon some independent votes? Are there not many individuals in the country who do not attend conventions? But no: I find that the respectable man, so called, has immediately drifted from his position, and despairs of his country, when his country has more reason to despair of him. He forthwith adopts one of the candidates thus selected as the only *available* one, thus proving that he is himself *available* for any purposes of the demagogue. His vote is of no more worth than that of any unprincipled foreigner or hireling native, who may have been bought. O for a man who is a *man*, and, as my neighbor says, has a bone in his back which you cannot pass your hand through! Our statistics are at fault: The population has been returned too large. How many *men* are there to a square thousand miles in this country? Hardly one. Does not America offer any inducement for men to settle here? The American has dwindled into an Odd Fellow, — one who may be known by the development of his organ of gregariousness, and a manifest lack of intellect and cheerful self-reliance; whose first and chief concern, on coming into the world, is to see that the Almshouses are in good repair; and, before yet he has lawfully donned the virile garb, to collect a fund for the support of the widows and orphans that may be; who, in short, ventures to live only by the aid of the Mutual Insurance company, which has promised to bury him decently.

¹¹ It is not a man's duty, as a matter of course, to devote himself to the eradication of any, even the most enormous wrong; he may still properly have other concerns to engage him; but it is his duty, at least, to wash his hands of it, and, if he gives it no thought longer, not to give it practically his support. If I devote myself to other pursuits and contemplations, I must first see, at least, that I do not pursue them sitting upon another man's shoulders. I must get off him first, that he may pursue his contemplations too. See what gross inconsistency is tolerated. I have heard some of my townsmen say, "I should like to have them order me out to help put down an insurrection of the slaves, or to march to Mexico; — see if I would go"; and yet these very men have each, directly by their allegiance, and so indirectly, at least, by their money, furnished a substitute. The soldier is applauded who refuses to serve in an unjust war by those who do not refuse to sustain the unjust government which makes the war; is applauded by those whose own act and authority he disregards and sets at naught; as if the state were penitent to that degree that it hired one to scourge it while it sinned, but not to that degree that it left off sinning for a moment. Thus, under the name of Order and Civil Government, we are all made at last to pay homage to and support our own meanness. After the first blush of sin comes its indifference; and from immoral it becomes, as it were, *un*moral, and not quite unnecessary to that life which we have made.

¹² The broadest and most prevalent error requires the most disinterested virtue to sustain it. The slight reproach to which the virtue of patriotism is commonly liable, the noble are most likely to incur. Those who, while they disapprove of the character and measures of a government, yield to it their allegiance and support are undoubtedly its most conscientious supporters, and so frequently the most serious obstacles to reform. Some are petitioning the state to dissolve the Union, to disregard the requisitions of the President. Why do they not dissolve it themselves, — the union between themselves and the state, — and refuse to pay their quota into its treasury? Do not they stand in the same relation to the state that the state does to the Union? And have not the same reasons prevented the state from resisting the Union which have prevented them from resisting the state?

¹³ How can a man be satisfied to entertain an opinion merely, and enjoy *it*? Is there any enjoyment in it, if his opinion is that he is aggrieved? If you are cheated out of a single dollar by your neighbor, you do not rest satisfied with knowing that you are cheated, or with saying that you are cheated, or even with petitioning him to pay you your due; but you take effectual steps at once to obtain the full amount, and see that you are never cheated again. Action from principle, the perception and the performance of right, changes things and relations; it is essentially revolutionary, and does not consist wholly with anything which was. It not only divides states and churches, it divides families; ay, it divides the *individual*, separating the diabolical in him from the divine.

¹⁴ Unjust laws exist: shall we be content to obey them, or shall we endeavor to amend them, and obey them until we have succeeded, or shall we transgress them at once? Men generally, under such a government as this, think that they ought to wait until they have persuaded the majority to alter them. They think that, if they should resist, the remedy would be worse than the evil. But it is the fault of the government itself that the remedy *is* worse than the evil. *It* makes it worse. Why is it not more apt to anticipate and provide for reform? Why does it not cherish its wise minority? Why does it cry and resist before it is hurt? Why does it not encourage its citizens to be on the alert to point out its faults and *do* better than it would have them? Why does it always crucify Christ, and excommunicate Copernicus and Luther, and pronounce Washington and Franklin rebels? . . . .

¹⁵ I meet this American government, or its representative, the state government, directly, and face to face, once a year — no more — in the person of its tax-gatherer; this is the only mode in which a man situated as I am necessarily meets it; and it then says distinctly, Recognize me; and the simplest, most effectual, and, in the present posture of affairs, the indispensablest mode of treating with it on this head, of expressing your little satisfaction with and love for it, is to deny it then. My civil neighbor, the tax-gatherer, is the very man I have to deal with, — for it is, after all, with men and not with parchment that I quarrel, — and he has voluntarily chosen to be an agent of the government. How shall he ever know well what he is and does as an officer of the government, or as a man, until he is obliged to consider whether he shall treat me, his neighbor, for whom he has respect, as a neighbor and well-disposed man, or as a maniac and disturber of the peace, and see if he can get over this obstruction to his neighborliness without a ruder and more impetuous thought or speech corresponding with his action. I know this well, that if one thousand, if one hundred, if ten men whom I could name, — if ten *honest* men only, — ay, if *one* HONEST man, in this State of Massachusetts, *ceasing to hold slaves,* were actually to withdraw from this copartnership, and be locked up in the county jail therefor, it would be the abolition of slavery in America. For it matters not how small the beginning may seem to be: what is once well done is done forever. But we love better to talk about it: that we say is our mission. Reform keeps many scores of newspapers in its service, but not one man. If my esteemed neighbor, the State's ambassador, who will devote his days to the settlement of the question of human rights in the Council Chamber, instead of being threatened with the prisons of Carolina, were to sit down the prisoner of Massachusetts, that State which is so anxious to foist the sin of slavery upon her sister, — though at present she can discover only an act of inhospitality to be the ground of a quarrel with her, — the Legislature would not wholly waive the subject the following winter.

¹⁶ Under a government which imprisons any unjustly, the true place for a just man is also a prison. The proper place to-day, the only place which

Massachusetts has provided for her freer and less desponding spirits, is in her prisons, to be put out and locked out of the State by her own act, as they have already put themselves out by their principles. It is there that the fugitive slave, and the Mexican prisoner on parole, and the Indian come to plead the wrongs of his race should find them; on that separate, but more free and honorable ground, where the State places those who are not *with* her, but *against* her, — the only house in a slave State in which a free man can abide with honor. If any think that their influence would be lost there, and their voices no longer afflict the ear of the State, that they would not be as an enemy within its walls, they do not know by how much truth is stronger than error, nor how much more eloquently and effectively he can combat injustice who has experienced a little in his own person. Cast your whole vote, not a strip of paper merely, but your whole influence. A minority is powerless while it conforms to the majority; it is not even a minority then; but it is irresistible when it clogs by its whole weight. If the alternative is to keep all just men in prison, or give up war and slavery, the State will not hesitate which to choose. If a thousand men were not to pay their tax-bills this year, that would not be a violent and bloody measure, as it would be to pay them, and enable the State to commit violence and shed innocent blood. This is, in fact, the definition of a peaceable revolution, if any such is possible. If the tax-gatherer, or any other public officer, asks me, as one has done, "But what shall I do?" my answer is, "If you really wish to do anything, resign your office." When the subject has refused allegiance, and the officer has resigned his office, then the revolution is accomplished. But even suppose blood should flow. Is there not a sort of blood shed when the conscience is wounded? Through this wound a man's real manhood and immortality flow out, and he bleeds to an everlasting death. I see this blood flowing now. . . .

[17]   I have paid no poll-tax for six years. I was put into a jail once on this account, for one night; and, as I stood considering the walls of solid stone, two or three feet thick, the door of wood and iron, a foot thick, and the iron grating which strained the light, I could not help being struck with the foolishness of that institution which treated me as if I were mere flesh and blood and bones, to be locked up. I wondered that it should have concluded at length that this was the best use it could put me to, and had never thought to avail itself of my services in some way. I saw that, if there was a wall of stone between me and my townsmen, there was a still more difficult one to climb or break through before they could get to be as free as I was. I did not for a moment feel confined, and the walls seemed a great waste of stone and mortar. I felt as if I alone of all my townsmen had paid my tax. They plainly did not know how to treat me, but behaved like persons who are un-derbred. In every threat and in every compliment there was a blunder; for they thought that my chief desire was to stand the other side of that stone wall. I could not but smile to see how industriously they locked the door on my meditations, which followed them out again without let or hindrance,

and *they* were really all that was dangerous. As they could not reach me, they had resolved to punish my body; just as boys, if they cannot come at some person against whom they have a spite, will abuse his dog. I saw that the State was half-witted, that it was timid as a lone woman with her silver spoons, and that it did not know its friends from its foes, and I lost all my remaining respect for it, and pitied it.

18   Thus the State never intentionally confronts a man's sense, intellectual or moral, but only his body, his senses. It is not armed with superior wit or honesty, but with superior physical strength. I was not born to be forced. I will breathe after my own fashion. Let us see who is the strongest. What force has a multitude? They only can force me who obey a higher law than I. They force me to become like themselves. I do not hear of *men* being *forced* to live this way or that by masses of men. What sort of life were that to live? When I meet a government which says to me, "Your money or your life," why should I be in haste to give it my money? It may be in a great strait, and not know what to do: I cannot help that. It must help itself; do as I do. It is not worth the while to snivel about it. I am not responsible for the successful working of the machinery of society. I am not the son of the engineer. I perceive that, when an acorn and a chestnut fall side by side, the one does not remain inert to make way for the other, but both obey their own laws, and spring and grow and flourish as best they can, till one, perchance, overshadows and destroys the other. If a plant cannot live according to its nature, it dies; and so a man. . . .

Commentary and questions

1. *Paragraph 1:* Thoreau begins with a broad, challenging generalization: "That government is best which governs least." How does this serve as the unifying idea for the paragraph? What is the effect of equating "standing army" and "standing government"? Examine the connotations of "standing." What is the effect of contrasting "an expedient" with "inexpedient"?

2. *Paragraph 2:* How does Thoreau use the term "government"? Examine the figurative language. What is implied in each figure or metaphor?

3. *Paragraph 4:* How are the words "justice," "right and wrong," "conscience," and "law" related to Thoreau's concept of government? How precise are their meanings? In what sense are these emotional terms?

4. *Paragraph 5:* Examine the individual figures. What common effect do they have?

5. *Paragraph 8:* Is "All machines have their friction" a consistent figure? Is the extension of it, "when the friction comes to have its machine" a consistent figure? Is it effective?

6. *Paragraph 9:* Explain the distinction between opinion and action.

7. *Paragraph 10:* The word "man" reappears in italics. Has it gained any further meaning since paragraph 4?

8. *Paragraph 12:* Thoreau writes: "The broadest and most prevalent error requires the most disinterested virtue to sustain it." Explain why the modification "most disinterested" is essential to this notion.

9. *Paragraphs 15-18:* Does Thoreau's account of his tax difficulties effectively bear out his views on the proper exercise of individual conscience?

Topics for discussion and writing

I. Write a theme explaining Thoreau's concept of government.

II. Write a paper analyzing some phase of Thoreau's use of figurative language.

III. Do you think Thoreau wants no government at all, as he says in the first paragraph? Explain.

IV. Would Thoreau's arguments against the power of government have any practical bearing today?

V. Write a theme explaining whether or not Thoreau is a rebel according to Camus' definition.

VI. Thoreau depends for part of his effect on aphorisms, short pithy sayings. Analyze his use of these striking remarks. You might consider their occurrence, their relation to his main point, and the extent to which they are developed and elaborated.

Automation: WHAT IS AUTOMATION? Jack Rogers · THE STOCK

EXCHANGE, John Diebold · AN AUTOMATIC MACHINE TOOL, William Pease ·
MACHINES AND MAN, Wassily Leontief

WHAT is automation? How does it work? What will its
consequences be? These are the questions most often asked about this
new concept of industrial process, and these are the questions taken up in
this section. From a formal point of view, these questions require for answers
a definition, a process (two in this case), and finally a projection or hypothesis. Each of these is a type of writing common whenever an explanation
is being made. In its particular application, automation can arouse great
enthusiasm and deep resentment. In the examples that follow, however,
three of the authors attempt to use informative rather than persuasive words;
the fourth, John Diebold, expresses a persuasive enthusiasm for reforming
the stock exchange.

Two examples of process are given in order that the two most popular
forms could be presented. The description of the automatic machine tool by
William Pease discloses an author who has something new and interesting
to say and wants to explain it as clearly and completely as he can. A machine
tool is a metal turning and cutting machine used to produce anything from
a round rod to an airplane propeller. With an operator in control, on an
intricate job the machine can cut only one plane at a time. Under automation
it can make multi-plane cuts, thereby saving an incredible amount of time.
This may be an exciting fact, but it is the process, not the excitement that
Pease tries to convey. Diebold, on the other hand, though he doesn't have
something to sell, does have an enthusiastic, emotional interest in persuading his reader that the stock exchange is a "glaring anachronism."

132

WHAT IS AUTOMATION?   Jack Rogers

From Automation. *Reprinted by
permission of the Regents of the
University of California and the
Institute of Industrial Relations.*

FEW newly coined words have attained wide usage as rapidly as "automation" has. Five years ago it would have been hard to find anyone who had heard it; today it would be hard to find anyone who has not. Yet misunderstanding and controversy continue to surround it.

2   For some, mention of automation conjures up an image of a world of robots in which humans do no work. For others, automation suggests the intricate engineering problems of self-regulating systems. To many, automation is practically synonymous with mechanization in industry. For most, however, the term is a vague one having something to do with electronics and automatic production. Just what it all means for the man in the street is not too clear.

3   Predictions of the consequences of automation are sharply contrasting. It has been said that most of industry ultimately will be involved and that we are in the midst of a Second Industrial Revolution. It also has been said that only a fraction of industry ever will be affected and that no discontinuous development worthy of being called a revolution is in prospect. Alarmist articles warning of sweeping technological unemployment have been answered by debunking articles with the theme that automation will create new employment opportunities. What automation will do to or for jobs, workers, unions, companies, industries, and consumers has been foretold with an abundance of disagreement. One thing is plain, unless we understand what automation is and is not, we are in a poor position to evaluate its effects. In order to gain this understanding, we must spend some time in becoming acquainted with the concepts and terminology of automation.

4   Short stretches of what is to follow will be tough going for the reader who is not used to technical language. We will try to be as uncomplicated as we can, however, and explain what may be unfamiliar terms as they crop up. Those who are interested mostly in automation's effects and either know how it works or don't particularly care to find out in detail may skim until they reach Chapter III.

1. MECHANIZATION AND AUTOMATIC PRODUCTION

5   Before we can begin to discuss the subject in even a preliminary way, we must define it. As we go on, we can refine our tentative statement as necessary. The following definition will remain valid even when special meanings are given to parts of it later:

6   *Automation refers to the design, manufacture, and use of automatic equipment for industrial or other processes.* The word itself is a compression of the awkward word "automatization" and apparently was invented independently by John Diebold, the author of *Automation: The Advent of the*

Automatic Factory, and by D. S. Harder, a Ford Motor Company executive. If "automation" is to behave like other words, "to automate" must mean "to make automatic" and "automation" must mean "the process of making automatic," the reference being to industrial processes primarily.

7   What automation actually means, as a word then, depends on the meaning given to "automatic." Here is where the trouble starts. The dictionary tells us that automatic means having the power of self-motion, self-regulation, or self-action. Most of the machines used in industry today have some properties of self-action, so why should we need a new word to describe an old fact? Those who use the word must have more in mind.

8   Let us set out from familiar ground. One of the major trends of industrial development since the opening of the nineteenth century has been progressive mechanization, the substitution of mechanical and electrical devices for human functions in the performance of work. Today lifting and carrying operations are done by cranes, fork-trucks, and conveyors instead of by men's backs, arms, and legs; fabricating operations such as cutting, melting, sewing, nailing, grinding, and other processes which change the form or state of materials are performed with the aid of powered equipment; refining, sorting, counting, inspecting — in fact almost every conceivable kind of manufacturing step — is performed by or with the aid of machines. Most of the industrial equipment in use currently, however, requires operator surveillance and control. Men must feed material to machines, watch their operation, and regulate their actions.

9   Mechanization has transferred man's "muscle functions" to machines. The embodiment of man's "sensor functions" and "mental functions" in equipment has been of less importance. Properties of self-action have been built into machines mainly by providing for repetitive activation as in the firing sequence of the cylinder of a gasoline engine, the alternating polarities of rotor and stator in an electric motor, or the cam-directed successive indexing of tools in a screw machine. Production equipment commonly is classified as manually operated semi-automatic, or automatic depending on whether an operator must control throughout every cycle, load and unload work during each cycle, or tend the equipment only intermittently. Manually operated equipment, however, may be self-acting to a degree (for example, a pneumatic hammer or portable electric drill and semi-automatic equipment may complete unattended a cycle consisting of several individual operations.

10   Development of equipment which is to some degree automatic always has been part and parcel of mechanization in industry. For this reason it is sometimes asserted that automation is really nothing new or that the word serves mainly to describe production systems in which materials and parts are handled in and out of machines automatically in contrast to those in which this feature is absent. In recent years, the linking up of special purpose machines by conveyors and other work handling devices to form assemblages

called "transfer machines" has permitted performance of long sequences of metalworking operations without operator intervention. In substance, this advance amounts to incorporation of the "line production layout" long familiar in mass-production industries into the equipment itself, with work stations consisting of machines alone instead of men and machines. A plant in which every operation on a product was performed without human intervention as it moved automatically from station to station would be a true "push-button" factory. This condition now is approached closely in some of the component manufacturing plants of the automobile industry. Automatic production of this type has been labeled "Detroit automation."

11   A closer look at the kind of automatic production just described reveals that it is automatic in a strictly limited sense. The machines which compose such a system are set to perform one sequence of operations and one only. The dimensions to be held in fabricating the parts determine the position of the individual machine elements and their tool settings. An elaborate system of limit switches and interconnected stops or gates assures that only one piece is in position at a station at a time and that the way is clear before a piece is advanced. Inspection operations also are built into the line's equipment so faulty pieces can be sidetracked mechanically. Controls which signal the need for replacement when tools begin to wear past permissible tolerances are included. For a *fixed sequence of fixed operations* the whole complex functions automatically so long as none of the pre-selected conditions are violated. The process, however, is not self-regulating in the sense that what is happening in it can alter it. Operation is on an all-or-none basis: output either is completely satisfactory or there is no output.

12   Highly automatic machines of the fixed sequence-fixed operation type of manufacture of standardized articles exist in many branches of industry and account for a large share of all industrial production. Although they typically represent large equipment investments, they reduce unit cost of output as compared to methods of production using less specialized equipment and relying more heavily on manual operations. Their superiority lies principally in high output rates and uniform quality which are characteristic of mechanized production. A listing of specific examples of equipment for this type of production easily could run to hundreds of pages and include such varied items as knitting machines, rolling-mills, paper-making machines, glass bottle molders, can sealers, strip ovens for bakeries, bag fillers, carpet looms, rotary printing presses, barrel rolls, screw machines, mechanical stokers, plastic molding presses, and die casting machines.

13   If automation consisted only of extension of the principles of mechanization in designing, making, and using equipment for production to put greater power at the command of the worker, reduce manual effort, permit operation at higher speeds and more continuously, and integrate individual machine operations into larger units, it would be worthy of attention as a significant industrial development. Automation, however, is more than mecha-

nization in the view of many authorities. In important respects it is a "jump"
in technological progress and not just a gradual acceleration. The reason
is that full automation is the application of the theory of automatic control
in technical innovations to make possible full automatic production with
self-regulation as well as self-action. It contemplates the wholesale reproduction of the sensory and mental functions of human operators in production systems which go far beyond the fixed sequence-fixed operation variety
of automatic production.

2. feedback and automatic control

14   A simple concept, and an old one, is the keystone of all methods and
devices for automatic control. Whether called control through feedback,
closed-loop control, or something else, the unifying principle is the same:
what happens in a process may be used to affect the process to achieve a
desired result. When there are physical cause and effect relationships in a
system, the effects can be made to serve as modifying causes by proper
translation. As is true of many fundamental concepts, it is not the statement
of the idea that is impressive but the implications of it. Potentially, practically any physical process controllable by man can be made to control
itself. A process which cannot be controlled satisfactorily by man may be
made self-controlling. Since a factory basically is just a location where a
number of processes take place to change materials from one form to another, the idea of a workerless factory is no different in kind than the idea
of a self-regulating machine, though more grandiose.

15   We have used the words "process," "system," and "control" so far in an
abstract way. The notion of control through feedback becomes much clearer
in example. Imagine a "system" consisting of a wood stove, a pot of soup,
and a housewife. The "process" is the heating of the soup. "Control" of the
process consists of getting the soup to the proper temperature without its
boiling over. Taking the system as a whole, the temperature of the soup is
the condition to be controlled, the housewife is both the means of judging
the condition and doing something to control it, and the stove is the energy
source for the process.

16   There are several ways in which the control may function. The housewife may look at the soup, smell it, or taste it. In any case the state of the
soup is compared to the desired state and some action taken. If it is getting
too hot, the pot may be pushed to the back of the stove or the damper closed.
If it is not hot enough, more wood may be fed to the fire or the damper
opened. The process continues until the soup is to be served with the housewife acting as its regulator in a loop which runs from soup to housewife to
stove and back to soup again.

17   Obviously this is not an automatic control system even though information concerning the state of the soup is "fed back" and results in alteration
of the process. Technically it is an open-loop control system into which an
operator's functions must be inserted when it is to function.

18   If we substitute an electric heating unit for the wood stove, we can "close the loop" by replacing the housewife's observations and actions with a temperature monitoring and regulating device. The control device will permit current to flow to the heating unit so long as the soup temperature is below that set and shut off the current when the set temperature is exceeded. The soup will be brought to the desired temperature and held within a few degrees of it. Our new arrangement, in which the process guides itself by altering its own state as necessary, is closed-loop automatic control.

19   For satisfactory automatic control it is necessary that (1) the process be one which can be controlled by changes in a regulating device (e.g., a valve, a brake, or a variable resistance), (2) the variable to be controlled be measurable, and (3) the measurement and resulting regulation take place fast enough to keep the controlled variable near the desired value. If there are appreciable time lags in the system, as between measurement and change in the regulating device or between change in the regulating device and change in the variable, the system may oscillate in undesirable fashion. Depending on the relation between the process and the means of control, the value of the variable may fluctuate above and below the desired value during correction of a change and these fluctuations may die out, be sustained, or increase.

20   Oscillation in a control system may be illustrated, in the case of the housewife and her soup pot, by assuming that she wants the soup at serving temperature at a given hour, but has difficulty adjusting the fire and the position of the pot to bring about this result. Opening the damper and pulling the pot over the fire bring a too rapid increase in heat. Closing the damper and pushing the pot to the back of the stove to prevent boiling causes the soup to cool too much. Theoretically, by standing at the stove and making corrections fast enough, she can bring the soup to just the right temperature. If she has other things to do, however, each time she gets around to the soup she may find it has cooled too much or has begun to boil.

21   Most automatic control systems have a somewhat similar problem, caused by time lag between determination of the need for a correction and the start of the correction process, on the one hand, and over or under correction on the other. The problem is met in various ways. For example, monitoring devices are made more or less sensitive to increase or decrease the strength or frequency of feedback, high speed communicating means are employed to shorten time lags, or secondary feedback loops are used to introduce corrections to the corrections. Leaving out the refinements which are necessary to secure exactly the control behavior desired, the typical elements of a control system are those shown in the diagram [p. 138].

22   Beginning at the lower right-hand corner of the diagram we have the sensing element, any device that measures some characteristic of the process and emits signals representing the measurements. Apparatus for amplifying the signals may follow the sensing element in the feedback loop. Next comes the comparison element which is designed to compare the signal it

DIAGRAM OF AN AUTOMATIC CONTROL SYSTEM

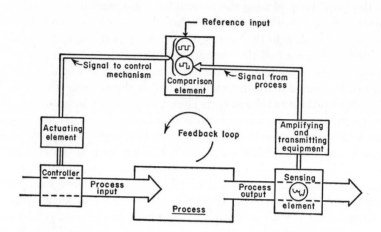

receives to a signal fed into it as a so-called "reference input." This comparison is made for the purpose of detecting deviation of the feedback value from the desired value represented by the reference input. A deviation causes the comparison element to originate a signal which when conveyed along the loop will operate an actuating element. The actuating element, in turn, governs the operation of whatever mechanism is used to vary the process characteristic — in this case a controller which varies the process input and thereby the process output which is being controlled.

23   If we compare a system for automatic control to control based on the actions of an operator, we see that the judgment of a human being is replaced in automatic control by what amounts to decision-making equipment. It is true that the decisions must be reduced to very simple terms, such as plus or minus, that the built-in criteria are inflexible, that a separate control loop is needed for each characteristic to be controlled, and that characteristics which cannot be measured cannot be handled. Nevertheless, in a crude sense the system "reasons" — at least well enough for it to substitute for some routine mental process. As a necessary adjunct the system has some sensory function which is the equivalent of a human sense. In short, an automatic control system observes, communicates internally, decides, and acts.

24   If automation has to do in large part with the application of automatic control in which functions corresponding to physical, sensory, and mental functions of an operator are embodied in equipment, our original definition should be revised:

> *Automation refers to the design, manufacture, and use of automatic equipment and self-regulating systems for industrial or other mechanized processes.*

For purposes of this definition, any process performed with powered equipment is said to be mechanized; automatic equipment is that which normally does not require control by an operator but which need not be self-regulating; self-regulating systems are those which employ feedback for control. Whenever the necessity for operator control of a mechanized process is eliminated, we have automation according to our definition. Although this is a somewhat broader statement than the technically-minded may like, it takes account of the fact that the word automation has been and probably will continue to be used loosely to refer mainly to elimination of operator control functions.

3. THE IMPORTANCE OF INFORMATION HANDLING

25   Automatic control, and hence automation, depends more on the handling of information than any other single factor. We have seen already that any closed-loop control system functions by feeding back information about a process to govern it. A self-guided missile, for example, must have some way of ascertaining where it is at all times if it is to make course corrections automatically and hit its target; position information is essential to its operation. An automatic process controller for a chemical reaction functions by interpreting information about the state of the reaction and initiating actions which hold within prescribed limits such variables as concentration, temperature, pressure, or other quantities which determine the yield of the reaction. An automated tin-plate mill relies on the continuous generation and interpretation of information concerning the gauge of the steel strip to regulate roll pressure and tension for production of strip of uniform thickness.

26   Automation may be regarded as the process of arranging for one kind of machine to run another kind. Machines of the first kind have as their function the handling of information. The function of the second kind is transformation of materials or performance of useful functions. Machines which handle information commonly are called "computers," because computation thus far has been the principal task assigned to these electronic instruments. Electronic computers operate with closed-loop control and constitute "systems" in themselves. If clerical or computational routines are viewed as "processes," automatic production of numerical results from data is parallel to automatic production of goods from materials. Business and industry may employ automation in office work, in manufacturing, or in both, for numerical results can be translated into actuating signals for process control.

27   It is possible to conceive of a single, large, fully automatic computing and production unit which would eliminate the manifold tasks of recording and analysis of information which now accompany the planning and direction of business activities and tie together all routine management processes and production activities. Input information would consist of criteria to be satisfied by the plant's operation and data including prices, sales quantities, and material qualities. Operation of the plant would be adjusted automatically toward an optimum with every change in external and internal

conditions. Needless to say, the instrumentation of such a manufacturing unit would be intricate and expensive. No manufacturing unit of this description exists now, but technology probably is now far enough along to allow its development if it were justified economically. Exactly how far away the day may be when automation equipment becomes sufficiently simple, reliable, and cheap to bring integrated, fully automated production on the scene no one can say.

4. THE MEANING OF AUTOMATION

28   The problem of definition should not be allowed to obscure the implications of automation. Any major change in the rate or the nature of mechanization — the replacement of men by machines — is bound to have far reaching effects. Whether or not automation comprises only automatic production accomplished through feedback control, the fact remains that an upsurge in technological change is in process. As a direct consequence, the rate and scope of replacement of human functions in industry is climbing. Human information handling functions which in the past have been more resistant to the incursion of the machine than energy providing functions are beginning to be supplanted on a significant scale. In the popular view, this is automation.

29   The real meaning of automation lies less in the machines involved than in what the machines will do. The possibility of substantial change in the relation between men and machines brings with it the possibility of change in conditions of work, occupations, and the structure of enterprise. Automation means technical change and technical change always has meant economic and social change. After we have looked in the next chapter at some of the ways automatic control is being put to work, we will consider what the results may be as automation matures.

Commentary and questions

1. The discussion of explicit definition (pp. 21-23) lists five steps that a writer framing a definition might go through: (1) Find occurrences of the concept, (2) make a generalization about the occurrences, (3) look for somewhat similar yet different concepts, (4) make a statement limiting the original concept, and (5) clarify, especially by examples.

The fact that Rogers is giving a preliminary definition indicates his approach may well be to seem to discover the definition as the reader does. This technique only seems casual. It requires as careful preparation as any other. Note, for example, the logical order of the successive stages of definition. What are they?

2. *Paragraph 6:* How satisfactory is the preliminary definition? Does it indicate Rogers is thinking in terms of defining words or defining concepts?

3. *Paragraphs 8-13:* Which of the five steps toward definition appear here? Why are they useful at this point?

4. *Paragraphs 14-24:* These deal with feedback. Why does this discussion come after mechanization? This section contains a definition within a definition. What is the principle means used to define "feedback"? How helpful is the analogical diagram? What is its advantage, if any, over the example of soup tasting?

5. *Paragraph 24:* Compare Rogers' definition to that given in the first sentence of paragraph 26. Is one better than the other? Why?

6. In the last paragraph Rogers speaks of the "real meaning of automation." How has he changed the meaning of "meaning"? Why does he?

Topics for discussion and writing

I. Write an essay in which you contrast an automated process with a mechanized or automatic process. Let your contrast bring out the essential differences.

II. Discuss Rogers' use of informative as opposed to persuasive words. How does the impersonal point of view contribute to the objective nature of the essay?

III. Write an essay in which you discuss the problems to be faced in defining "mechanization," or "remote control," or "automatic factory."

THE STOCK EXCHANGE   John Diebold

From John Diebold, Automation. *Copyright 1952, D. Van Nostrand Company, Inc., Princeton, New Jersey.*

We often become so accustomed to doing things in a certain way that we no longer question the basic purposes of our actions. This happens in all areas of human endeavor. As time goes on, we are likely to decorate obsolete processes with new gadgets and then deceive ourselves into thinking that we have made improvements. The world is rife with examples, but none is more typical than the New York Stock Exchange.

2   Characterized as the nerve center of American industry, the exchange is really a glaring anachronism. On the floor of the exchange as in the ancient market places, the traders stand at their posts and offer wares — not stone jugs, but stocks and bonds. Hundreds of men swarm over the paper-strewn floor. Messengers dart to and fro with scribbled bits of paper. The glitter of a few modern devices such as the high-speed ticker tape (which records what has happened but does not participate in the action) is so blinding that we never question the basic process.

3   How can the exchange be automatized? A faster ticker tape? Walkie-talkie radios from office to floor broker? Conveyor belts for handling the papers? These all sound workable, but they amount to no more than adding

gadgets to the existing process. These gadgets may be useful in saving manpower, but they represent no basic improvement in the process itself. What is called for is something completely different from the exchange floor as it exists today.

4   We start by thinking of basic functions. The basic function of the exchange floor is to provide a means for interchange of information concerning the sale, and purchase of stocks and bonds.

5   Can this function be performed automatically? Computers are designed primarily to receive, manipulate, and communicate information. They provide a means for eliminating the exchange floor altogether.

6   Today, after receiving a customer's order, a broker relays it to a representative on the exchange floor by telephone or messenger. The "floor broker" completes the transaction by finding another floor broker interested in his offer. Information about the transaction is relayed back to the brokerage office as well as to the ticker tape machine operators.

7   With an electronic stock exchange the broker, instead of calling his man on the exchange floor, would put the order into a machine in his office. This could be accomplished by a process as simple as dialing. The office machine would be connected electrically with a central computing mechanism that would keep records of the market in each stock on magnetized drums. These are similar in principle to magnetic tape recorders except that a coded electronic impulse rather than a voice is recorded. Orders to buy and sell at various prices would be stored as received and executed in sequence of receipt as the market fluctuates. Dials for each stock would indicate on the machine in the broker's office the price of the last sale, the bid and asked prices, and the quantity being offered.

8   The memory unit of the computer would contain an up-to-the-second record of all orders to buy and sell stock for each company whose shares are traded on the exchange. As information can be added to or deleted from the memory unit as a regular part of the machine's operation, a complete set of orders for future trading can be recorded magnetically. This is the function now performed with ink and paper by the broker who keeps tally of orders that are to be executed at prices other than those prevailing at the time they are placed.

9   If an order to buy U.S. Steel at 45 is received and if Steel is selling above 45, the order is entered by the broker and is recorded by the magnetic "memory," coded as to the purchaser and the time. When someone offers Steel at 45, the transaction is automatically consummated, provided that the investor did not change his mind in the interim and that other orders to buy at 45 were not entered previously. Information about this sale is transmitted simultaneously to the brokerage office selling the stock, the brokerage office buying the stock, the "last sale" dials of all machines in the offices of member firms, and it is also automatically reported on the ticker tape — which never gets behind the market. From there on, all brokerage activity

that normally takes place continues as it does today. The firms could clear the transactions through the Stock Exchange Clearing Corporation — or this could be done continuously by machine for record purposes. But as stock certificates would have to be physically transferred and changed, an automatic clearing device would seem to add little to an electronic exchange.

10   Rather than making the whole process automatic, the best answer seems to lie, as it so often does, some place between the present system and a fully automatic one. Replacement of the exchange floor is entirely practical both technically and economically. Mechanization of the brokerage office and the clearing house is of dubious value.

11   The proposed stock exchange would produce no change in relations between investor and broker. Automatic quoting of prices, although technologically possible, would not be introduced because the customer's call to the broker is too often a request for advice and comment along with a request for quotations. The process of buying and selling stock with an electronic exchange would perhaps be a bit faster, but the execution of orders is rapid enough at present. For the investor, things would remain just as they are today. But the electronic stock exchange would alter the relationship between brokerage office and floor representative by eliminating both the representative and the floor.

12   The machine we describe can be built today by any of a number of capable manufacturers. Despite the fact that the cost of electronic equipment is high, a stock exchange computer could produce savings of such magnitude that the entire outlay could be recouped within two years, even allowing for reduced brokerage commissions.

13   No new invention is needed to build an automatic stock exchange. The problems are not technical. Rather, they are partly a lack of knowledge by financial people of what is technologically possible and partly too great a preoccupation with present practices to allow basic rethinking of the functions of the Exchange. The former difficulty, lack of knowledge, can be overcome in rather short order; the solution to the second problem is not so simple. "Mechanization" has thus far taken the form of new gadgets — faster tickers, flashing lights, and photoelectric cells — rather than replacement of the whole antiquated mechanism of the exchange floor.

14   But if all of this is really possible and economical, why hasn't someone built such a machine? There is no clearcut answer. A great many practical innovations are never adopted. In the present case two separate groups of people, stock brokers and engineers, are involved. Neither is particularly aware of the problems of the other. In fact, the present operation of the Stock Exchange is scarcely considered by the brokers to be a problem.

15   Management consultants frequently encounter such management "blind spots" about the existence of certain problems. Recognizing that a problem exists many times seems to be harder than solving it. It is in large measure because the stock exchange floor is not perceived to be a comparatively

antiquated and inefficient operation that steps have not been taken to re-think and automatize it.

AN AUTOMATIC
MACHINE TOOL

William Pease

From "An Automatic Machine Tool," Scientific American *(September, 1952). Reprinted by permission of* Scientific American.

THE M.I.T. system combines digital and analogue processes under feedback control to govern a milling machine whose cutting tool moves in three planes relative to the work piece. In this case the "model" of the object to be fabricated is supplied to the machine in the form of a perforated paper tape similar to that used in teletype systems. For a typical operation, 10 feet of tape will keep the machine busy for an hour.

2   The components of the M.I.T. system are grouped into two major assemblies. The first of these, called the "machine," comprises the milling machine itself, the three servo-mechanisms employed to operate its moving parts, and the instruments required to measure the relative positions of these parts. The second assembly, called the "director," contains all the data-handling equipment needed to interpret the information on the tape and to pass it on as operating commands to the machine. The director contains three major elements — a data-input system, a data-interpreting system and a set of three decoding servo-mechanisms.

3   The purpose of the data-input system is to take the original instructions off the tape and feed them into the interpretive and command elements of the director. It consists of a reader, whose metal fingers scan the tape and report the presence or absence of holes by electrical signals, and a set of six relay registers (two for each of the basic machine motions) which store and transmit this information in numerical form. The registers are supplied in pairs, so that while one of them is in control of the machine, the other can receive information from the tape. At the end of each operating interval, command is transferred instantaneously from one register to the other.

4   The data-interpreting system picks up the numerical instructions stored in the registers and transmits them as pulse instructions to the decoding servo-mechanisms. These pulses are generated by an electronic oscillator, the "clock," which acts as the master time reference for the entire system. By means of a series of flip-flop switches, and in accordance with the instructions stored in the registers, these pulses are sent on to each of the three decoding servo-mechanisms.

5   Up to this point in the process, information has been handled in digital form. The three servo-mechanisms now convert the instructions to the ana-

logue form required by the machine tool. Pulses from the data-interpreting system are translated into the rotation of a shaft — one degree of rotation for each pulse. The shafts are connected to synchro transmitters which are themselves connected to the drive servo-mechanisms of the machine. A feedback circuit, inserted at this point in the director, makes certain that the conversion from digital to analogue information has been accurately carried out. It works as follows:

6   The mechanical element of each decoding servo-mechanism consists of the shaft connected to the synchro transmitter, a unit called a "coder" and a small two-phase induction servo-motor with appropriate gearing. The coder generates a feedback signal in the form of one electrical pulse for each degree of shaft rotation. The number of these feedback pulses is then compared with the number of pulses emanating from the data-interpreting system by a device called a "summing register." If the two counts agree, the summing register is at zero; if they do not agree, an electric voltage is generated and the two-phase servo-motor rotates the shaft to bring the count to zero. Thus a feedback path makes certain that the output shaft position faithfully corresponds with the series of command pulses from the frequency divider. Information, coded first on tape, converted to digital and then to analogue form, is now transmitted to the working elements of the machine.

7   Each motion of the machine is accomplished by a lead screw driven by a hydraulic servo-mechanism. The motor converts electrical commands received from the decoding mechanisms into the mechanical motions of the machine. Feedback is again introduced at the point of actual cutting to make certain that each element moves according to the instructions of its own decoding mechanism. A standard synchro receiver is coupled to each of the moving elements of the mill in such a way that each .0005 inch of tool travel causes the shaft of the synchro receiver to rotate one degree. The feedback signal derived from this shaft position is compared with the shaft position of the synchro transmitter at the decoding mechanism. Any difference of position between the two shafts appears as an alternating-current voltage which controls the speed of the hydraulic transmission. Thus the machine element follows continuously the rotations of the synchro transmitter in the ratio of .0005 inch of linear travel to each degree of rotation.

8   How are the instructions for the machine's job put on the tape? The desired path of the cutting tool over the work is reduced to incremental straight-line segments; the segments are specified by numbers, and these are then translated into a code which can be punched on the tape.

9   The cutting path and the speed at which the work is to be fed to the machine are based on a number of factors: the amount of stock to be removed, the sequence of the machining operations, the setup of the work on the machine, spindle speeds, and so on. After the human operator determines the locus of the cutter center which will produce the desired cutting path, he divides the locus into a series of straight-line segments. They should be as long as possible without differing from the ideal tool-center locus by more than the machining tolerance. The dimensions of each straight-line segment are then resolved into components parallel to each of the three directions of motion of the machine. For each straight-line segment, a time for execution is chosen to produce the desired feed rate. All this — the cutter motions and the time — is tabulated in a predetermined order to form a single set of control instructions. A separate set of instructions is made for each segment, in the order in which they will be used by the machine. The instructions, translated into patterns of holes, are punched in the paper tape by a special typewriter keyboard.

10   By inserting a new reel of tape for each job to be performed, the milling machine can be converted from one manufacturing task to the next with little more effort than is required to change a phonograph record. And for every job that a given machine has ever performed, there is left a permanent record, in the shape of a tape containing full instructions. Another great advantage of the machine is that it produces continuously; unlike a machine tool run by a human operator, it does not need to be stopped for periodic measurements and adjustments.

11   The performance of this M.I.T. model shows that fully automatic machine tools are not only possible but are certain to be developed in practicable form. It is surely startling (how much more startling it would have been to Maudslay and the other pioneers!) to think of versatile machine tools which will perform any kind of work without the guidance of a human hand. The possible economic effects of such machines, on many industries besides metal-cutting, are beyond prediction. Automatized general-purpose machine tools, combined with high-production special-purpose tools, would make possible the automatic metals-fabricating factory. Nor are we restricted to metals. With digital machines in control we can conceive of factories which will process, assemble and finish any article of manufacture.

12   It is unlikely that the automatic factory will appear suddenly. Like the machine tool itself, it will just grow by steps until eventually it is here.

Commentary and questions

The Stock Exchange

1. *Paragraphs 1-2:* What words are emotive? Are they at the same time informative? Do the paragraphs mislead? What would be Diebold's alternative?

2. *Paragraph 4:* In stating the basic function of the exchange, Diebold restricts himself to only one activity of the exchange. Does he retain a narrative form for the process?

3. *Paragraphs 6-9:* In the before-and-after comparisons, list the advantages Diebold sees in using computers rather than the present system. You must go beyond paragraph 9 to find all the advantages.

4. In the last three paragraphs, what hints as to the purpose of this article does Diebold's language give?

An Automatic Machine Tool

1. In an analogue process the machine imitates the physical situation. A cash register is an analogue computer. In the digital process information is converted to digits or units. An electronic computer is based upon the digital principle; it counts rather than measures.

2. Most process descriptions follow a narrative structure. How is that structure modified in Pease's explanation?

3. In each paragraph note the words that are used in a special sense or that seem to be peculiar to engineering. Do they represent difficulties in definition?

4. Are any paragraphs harder to follow than others? If so, analyze why this is so. Is it a matter of organization? These questions seem to imply that the difficulty arises because of the reader or the writer. Is it necessarily one or the other? A particular piece of writing may be "hard" for one audience because it is not directed toward them.

Topics for discussion and writing

I. Compare the language of Diebold and Pease. What conclusions concerning audience and purpose do your findings suggest?

II. An author writing up a process is usually concerned with one of two things, though sometimes both. He usually wants either to show what happens to a "product," or to show the way in which the agents of the process, whether men or machines, operate. Select a process with which you are familiar. Write it up twice, the first time to show the changes that take place in the thing being processed, the second time to show how the agents of the process operate.

III. Describe a process with which you are familiar.

IV. Select a familiar process that is open to improvement. Write a paper in which you explain the present process and your suggestions for improvement.

MACHINES AND MAN   Wassily Leontief

From Scientific American (*September, 1952*). *Reprinted by permission of* Scientific American *and the author.*

APPROXIMATELY 500 years ago the study of nature ceased to be solely a servant of philosophy and became a patron of applied arts and a source of practical invention. The economic development of the Western world has since proceeded at an ever-increasing pace; waves of technological change, driven by the surge of scientific discoveries, have followed one another in accelerated succession. The developmental lag between pure science and engineering application has progressively shortened. It took nearly 100 years for the steam engine to establish itself as part and parcel of the industrial scene, but electric power took less than 50 years and the internal combustion engine only 30. The vacuum tube was in almost every American home within 15 years of its invention, and the numerous progeny of Dr. Baekeland's synthetic plastics matured before we learned to pronounce "polyisobutylene." At the turn of the 20th century it was said that "applied science is pure science 20 years later"; today the interval is much shorter — often only five years and sometimes but one or two.

2   From the engineering standpoint the era of automatic control has begun. Some of the fully automatic "factories of the future" are already on paper; they can be described and studied. Engineering, however, is only the first step; what automatic technology will mean to our economic system and our society is still decidedly a thing of the future. In judging its probable impact all we have to go by is tenuous analogy with past experience and theoretical deductions from our very limited information on the new techniques. And it is no help that some of the crucial facts and figures are veiled in secrecy.

3   Important new inventions are traditionally held to presage the dawn of a new era; they also mark the twilight of an old. For some observers they contain promise; for others, fear. James Hargreaves constructed the first practical multiple spindle machine in 1767, and one year later a mob of spinners invaded his mill and destroyed the new equipment. The economists of the time (the golden age of "classical economics" was about to begin) came to the defense of the machines. They explained to labor that the loss of jobs in spinning would be compensated by new employment in machine-building. And for the next hundred years England did indeed prosper. Its labor force expanded both in textiles and in textile machinery, and wage rates by the end of the 19th century were at least three times as high as at its beginning.

4   But the men-*v.*-machines controversy blazed on. Karl Marx made of "technological unemployment" the cornerstone of his theory of capitalist exploitation. The conscientious John Stuart Mill came to the conclusion that, while the introduction of machinery might — in most cases would — benefit labor, it would not necessarily do so always. The answer depended on the circumstances of the case. And today that is still the only reasonable point of view one can maintain.

5   We are hardly in a position to reduce to detailed computation the effects that automatic technology will have on employment, production or our national standard of living. Aside from the paucity of our information on this new development, our understanding of the structural properties of our

Dollars in billions

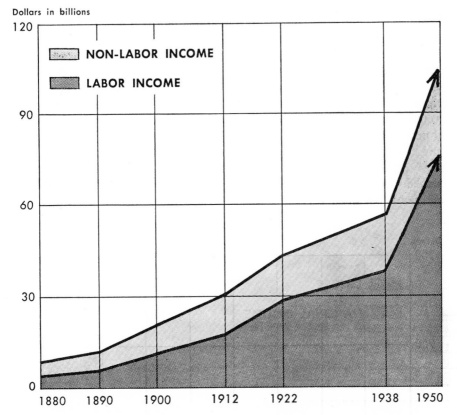

| | | | | | | |

TOTAL NATIONAL INCOME of the U. S., measured in terms of 1940 prices, has increased from $9.2 billion in 1880 to $160 billion in 1950. The ratio between labor income (the compensation of employees) and non-labor income (profits, interest, rent and so on) is stable, but the share for labor has increased.

economic system itself is still incomplete. We must therefore rely on reasonable conjecture.

6   The economy of a modern industrial nation — not unlike the feedback mechanisms discussed throughout this issue — must be visualized as a complicated system of interrelated processes. Each industry, each type of activity, consumes the products and services of other sectors of the economy and at the same time supplies its own products and services to them. Just as the operating properties of a servo-mechanism are determined by the technical characteristics of the measuring, communicating and controlling units of which it is composed, so the operating properties of an economy depend upon the structural characteristics of its component parts and on the way in which they are coupled together. It is not by coincidence that in

some advanced phases of his work the modern economist resorts to systems of differential equations similar to those used by the designers of self-regulating machinery.

7   The services of labor constitute one important set of inputs into the national economy. That it is the largest one is reflected in the fact that labor receives in wages some 73 per cent (in 1950) of the nation's annual net product. But labor is not the only type of input that goes into all other sectors. Certain natural resources, machinery, equipment and other kinds of productive capital feed into almost every branch of agriculture, manufacture, transportation and distribution. In the chart at the top of the preceding page, depicting the growth of our total national product since 1880, is a breakdown of the share going into salaries and wages on the one hand and into non-labor income (profits, interest, rents and so on) on the other. The

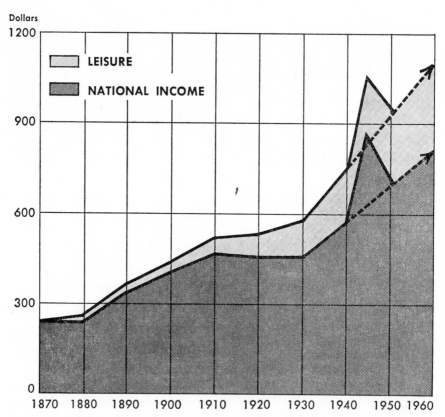

INCOME PER CAPITA, measured in terms of 1940 prices and excluding agriculture, increased from $230.60 in 1870 to $706.70 in 1950 (*bottom curve*). If 1870 hours of work had been maintained, the per capita income would be larger (*top curve*). The difference between the two curves shows increase in leisure.

ratio between these two has been generally stable, but labor's share has steadily gained. Behind these figures lie the intricate processes of our economic development, influenced by such factors as population growth, the discovery of new and the exhaustion of old natural resources, the increase in the stock of productive plant and equipment and, last but not least, a steady technological progress.

8 A better insight into the nature of that progress is given by the charts on pages 154-55. The number of man-hours required for an average unit of output has gone down steadily since 1880. In the first 30 years of that period the saving of labor seems to have been accompanied by a corresponding increase in capital investment. Between 1880 and 1912 the amount of machinery and of other so-called fixed investment per unit of output rose by 34 per cent, while the man-hour input fell 40 per cent. Then the ratio of investment to output began to drop. We introduced more efficient machinery rather than just a greater quantity of it. That it actually was more efficient can be seen from the fact that labor productivity rose apace. In 1938 a unit of output consumed only about half as many man-hours as would have been spent upon its production in 1918.

9 Such is the stage which the new technology — the technology of automatic control — has now entered. The best index we have of how far automatization has gone is the annual U. S. production of "measuring and controlling instruments." The trend of this production is outlined in the chart on page 152. After hesitation during the depression and the war years, it now rises rapidly. In part this rise mirrors the recent accelerating pace of industrial investment in general, but the chart shows that the instrument production curve is going up more steeply than that of plant investment as a whole. This gain is a measure of the progressive "instrumentation" of the U. S. economy. A breakdown of the relative progress of automatic operation in individual industries appears in the table on page 153. The chemical and machinery industries lead; next come metal processing (mainly in the smelting department) and ceramics. In interpreting this table one must take into account the fact that instrumental control is less costly for some processes than for others.

10 The estimated cost of complete instrumentation of a new modern plant to automatize it as fully as possible today ranges from 1 to 19 per cent (depending on the industry) of the total investment in process equipment. The average for all industries would be about six per cent. On this basis, if all the new plants built in 1950 had been automatized, some $600 million would have been spent for measuring and control instruments. Actually the production of such instruments in 1950 totaled only $67 million. In other words, to automatize new plants alone, to say nothing of those already built, would require nearly 10 times as great an investment in instruments as we are now making.

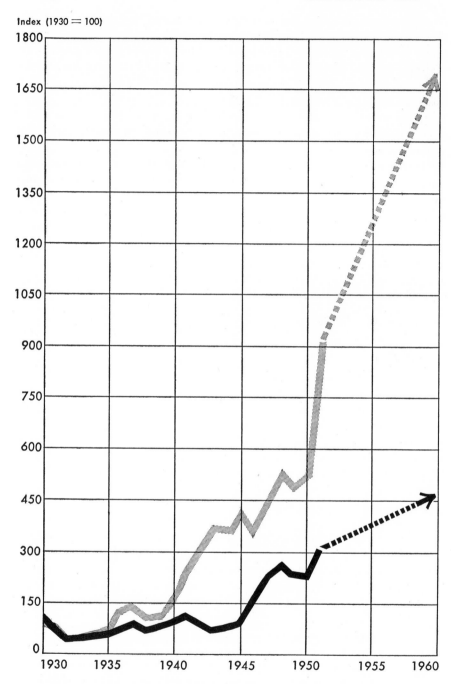

Index (1930 = 100)

SALES OF INSTRUMENTS for industrial recording and controlling purposes
have increased enormously since 1930 (*light line*) as compared with the
total U. S. expenditure for plant and equipment (*heavy line*).

11 Yet six per cent is far from a formidable figure. Furthermore, the investment in instruments would not necessarily mean a net increase in the total plant investment per unit of output. On the contrary, the smoother and better-balanced operation of self-regulating plants has already shown that they can function with less capitalization than a non-automatic plant of identical capacity. And much existing equipment can readily be converted from manual to automatic control. It therefore seems that the automatization of our industries, at least to the extent made possible by present technology, is likely to advance rapidly. The mechanization of the 19th century required heavy capital investment and proceeded slowly; the new technology, unhampered by such vast capital requirements, can be introduced at a much faster pace.

Industry	1946	1947	1948	1949	1950	1951
Ceramics	110	113	106	70	102	131
Chemicals	125	110	101	62	117	208
Foods	125	107	96	66	103	107
Machinery	107	112	119	61	105	168
Metals	113	98	106	81	134	249
Petroleum	80	90	140	86	98	132
Textiles	106	105	112	75	129	128
Utilities	72	96	122	111	147	222
Total	100	104	115	82	122	192

GROWTH OF INSTRUMENTATION in various industries is shown in this table, which lists the sales of instruments to those industries by years. The index of the table: 1946-1949 average sales of instruments = 100.

12 In transportation and agriculture, machines by now have practically eliminated the need for human muscle power. Man has all but ceased to be a lifter and mover and become primarily a starter and stopper, a setter and assembler and repairer. With the introduction of self-controlled machinery, his direct participation in the process of production will be narrowed even further. The starter and stopper will disappear first, the setter and assembler will go next. The trouble-shooter and repairman of course will keep their jobs for a long time to come; the need for them will even increase, for the delicate and complicated equipment of automatic control will require constant expert care. We shall continue to need inventors and designers, but perhaps not many even of them: the chief engineer of a large electronic equipment firm recently expressed to me his apparently well-founded hope that before long he would have circuits designed by an electronic machine, eliminating human errors.

13 All this inevitably will change the character of our labor force. The proportion of unskilled labor has already declined greatly in recent decades; it

Index (1880 = 100)

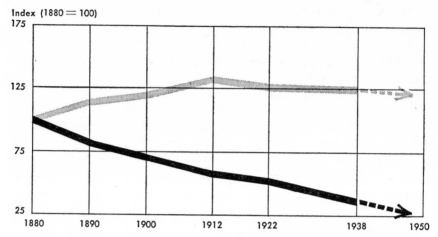

U. S. PRODUCTION has increased in efficiency. The light line plots the decreasing index of plant and equipment required to produce one unit of output; the heavy line, the man-hours required to produce one unit.

is down to less than 20 per cent. Meanwhile the numbers of the semiskilled have risen, and they now constitute over 22 per cent of the labor force. This trend has slowed down during the past decade, however. Now we shall probably see an accelerated rise in the proportion of skilled workers, clerks and professional personnel, who already make up 42 per cent of our working population.

14 In a country with a less fluid and more differentiated social structure than ours, these rapid changes in the occupational composition of the population might have brought about considerable strain. But the celebrated, and

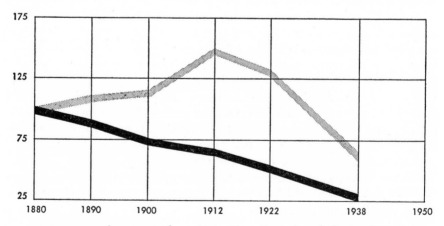

AGRICULTURE shows a similar pattern. Here the index of plant and equipment per unit of output is actually lower in 1938 than in 1880, reflecting the enormous increase in the productivity of agricultural machinery.

often criticized, uniformity of American living renders the effects of such transition almost imperceptible. For example, recent studies indicate that the family of a typical $3,000-a-year clerk spends its money in very much the same way as the family, say, of a machine-press operator with a similar income.

15   Will the machine-press operator be able to earn his $3,000 when an automatic controlling device takes over his job? The answer must depend in part on the speed with which the labor force is able to train and to retrain itself. If such upgrading were to fall behind the demand of the changing tech-

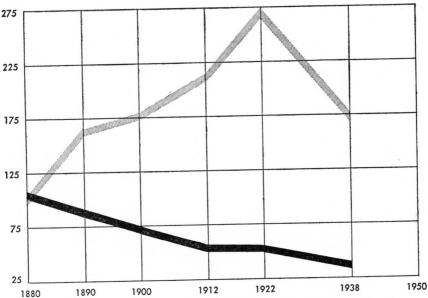

MINING AND MANUFACTURE similarly increased in productivity. Labor savings have been secured largely by expenditure on plant equipment. Increasing efficiency of plant is now reflected in declining capital cost.

nology, semiskilled and unskilled workers certainly would suffer unemployment or at least sharply reduced earning power. The experience of the last 20 years, however, has undermined the flexibility of U.S. workmen. Under the stimulus of the general American striving toward social and economic betterment, they have been quick to take to vocational training for new jobs. There has been no surplus of unskilled and semiskilled labor; indeed, wages in these fields have risen even faster than in skilled and professional work.

16   But if automatic machines largely take over our production, will there be enough jobs, skilled or otherwise, to go around? Admittedly the possibility of eventual unemployment cannot be excluded on *a priori* grounds. If the capital investment were to increase rapidly while the need for manpower dropped, the resulting rise in capital's share of the national income

could cause drastic unemployment. But as we have seen, the amount of capital needed for each unit of output has actually been reduced in recent years, and the installation of automatic machinery will further reduce it. Therefore labor should be able to maintain or improve its relative share of the national income. The danger of technological unemployment should be even smaller in the foreseeable future than it was at the end of the 19th century, when capital requirements were rising.

17   While the increase in productivity need not lead to involuntary idleness, it certainly does result in a steady reduction in the number of years and hours that an average American spends at making his living. The average work-week has been shortened from 67.2 hours in 1870 to 42.5 hours in 1950. This reflects a deliberate decision by the American people to enjoy an ever-increasing part of their rising standard of living in the form of leisure. If we had kept to the 67-hour week, we would be turning out a considerably greater amount of goods than we actually are. The difference between this hypothetical per capita output, computed on the basis of the well-known Cobb-Douglas formula, and the actual present output is indicated in the chart at the bottom of page 150. This difference represents the amount of commodities and services which the average American has chosen *not* to produce and consequently not to consume in order to enjoy shorter hours and longer vacations. The spread between the two curves has steadily increased; in other words, we have chosen to spend more and more of our ever-increasing production potential on leisure. The temporary shift to a high output of material goods during the last war only emphasizes this tendency, for we returned to the long-run trend immediately after the war. In the future, even more than in the past, the increased productivity of the American economy will be enjoyed as additional leisure.

18   Looking back, one can see that 1910 marked the real turning point in this country's economic and social development. That was the year when the last wave of immigration reached its crest; the year, also, when our rural population began to decline in absolute terms. Between 1890 and 1910 our national input of human labor had shot up from 28.3 million standard man-years to 42.5 million. Then in 1909 the model-T Ford began to roll off the first continuous production line. This great shift to mass production by machine was immediately reflected in shorter hours. In the next decade our manpower input increased by only one million man-years, and after 1920 it leveled off and remained almost constant until the early 1940s. Even at the peak of the recent war effort our total labor input, with an enormously larger population, was only 10 per cent greater than in 1910. Automatization will accelerate the operation of forces which have already shaped the development of this country for nearly half a century.

19   The new technology will probably have a much more revolutionary effect on the so-called underdeveloped countries than on the U.S. or other

old industrial nations. Shortage of capital and lack of a properly conditioned and educated labor force have been the two major obstacles to rapid industrialization of such backward areas. Now automatic production, with its relatively low capital and labor requirements per unit of output, radically changes their prospects. Instead of trying to lift the whole economy by the slow, painful methods of the past, an industrially backward country may take the dramatic shortcut of building a few large, up-to-date automatic plants. Towering up in the primitive economy like copses of tall trees on a grassy plain, they would propagate a new economic order. The oil refineries of the Near East, the integrated steel plant built after the war in Brazil, the gigantic fertilizer plant recently put into operation in India — these are examples of the new trend in underdeveloped regions of the world. How formidable the application of modern technology in a backward country may become is demonstrated by the U.S.S.R.'s recent great strides in industrialization.

20   At the outbreak of the First World War the U.S. suddenly lost its source of many indispensable chemicals in Germany. Domestic production had to be organized practically overnight. The newly created U.S. chemical industry had no force of experienced chemical craftsmen such as Germany had. The problem was solved, however, by the introduction of mechanization and automatization to a degree theretofore unknown. The American plants were run with amazingly small staffs of skilled workers. The same thing is now happening, and possibly will continue on a much larger scale, in backward countries. Advanced design, imported mostly from the U.S., will compensate at least in part for their scarcity of high-quality labor.

21   Naturally automatization, while solving some problems, will everywhere create new and possibly more difficult ones. In Western civilization the liberation from the burdens of making a living has been going on for some time, and we have been able to adjust to the new situation gradually. In the rising new countries economic efficiency may at least temporarily run far ahead of progress toward social maturity and stability. Much of the stimulus for the educational advancement of the Western nations came from economic necessity. Automatization may weaken that powerful connection. It remains to be seen whether the backward countries will find a driving force to help them develop the social, cultural and political advances necessary to help them cope with the new economic emancipation.

Commentary and questions

1. How many paragraphs make up Leontief's introduction? As an introduction, is it separate from what follows or does it, for example, establish some principle or modification that affects our understanding of what follows? Why does he call the controversy men versus machines?

2. *Paragraph 6:* What advantage does he gain from the feedback analogy?

3. *Paragraph 8:* Why are the figures on the average number of man hours per unit of output important? Is this reason stated explicitly or do you infer it?

4. *Paragraph 10:* Leontief is dealing in general terms with a large number of specific instances. He naturally hesitates to make his statements categorical. Go through this paragraph and note all the words and phrases that indicate modification.

5. *Paragraph 12:* Are the first two sentences accurate? Would the hired man on a Wisconsin dairy farm agree with Leontief? In what sense, then, are these statements true?

6. *Paragraph 13:* What do the figures 20%, 22%, and 42% mean to you? Would it surprise you if the unskilled labor force were 22%, the semi-skilled 42%, and the skilled worker, clerks and professional personnel 20%? What does this imply about statistics?

7. *Paragraph 14:* Define the words "fluid," "differentiated," "uniformity of American living," and "typical."

8. *Paragraph 15:* Explain the argument.

9. *Paragraph 18:* The last sentence is based upon the statements of the paragraph. What assumption underlies the conclusion?

10. *Paragraph 19:* Are the "new technology" of the first sentence and "modern technology" of the last sentence the same? If the U.S.S.R. is not an example of automation, why is it cited?

11. Are there two points of view to the thesis of the last paragraph?

Topics for discussion and writing

I. Write an essay discussing Leontief's selection of statistics.

II. Write a paragraph or two stating briefly the position Leontief takes in this essay.

III. Outline Leontief's essay.

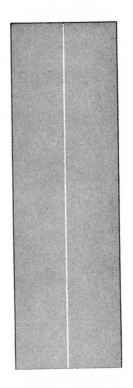

PART TWO

Statements and paragraphs

Statement: What is meant when we say we "read" an essay? To understand what it is to "read" is to understand the fundamental importance of statement.

We look at a ten-page essay, and, as we begin, the pages and paragraphs are clearly in evidence. But in the sense that the word is used here, we do not "read" pages. We don't even read paragraphs; we construct them. The basic unit of our reading is the statement.

Knowing little or nothing of the essay (except what is evident from its title), we begin with the first statement. This conveys information, attitude, or perhaps both. We read the second statement, and in one way or another it modifies the first. It may repeat the same idea as the first but give it a more complete context; it may add a related idea to the first; it may add an example of what is meant by the first. The possibilities are, of course, extensive, but as the written word moves from statement to statement, modification and change continue to take place. Thus we move from one intellectual position to another, and each of these shifts is planned by the author.

Statements are the author's means of drawing us forward through what he has to say, and it is by statement and the juxtaposition of statements that he convinces or fails to convince. In short, it is by statement that the author stands or falls. It is upon statement, too, that the reader must build his comprehension of what he reads, and although each statement is an individual matter, there are several generalizations about them that can be applied as a test of particular statements.

There are statements of fact and statements of opinion. Statements of fact are verifiable. *Ducks are migratory waterfowl. A psychiatrist must have an M.D. I can fly nonstop from New York to Los Angeles.* All these statements can be verified or tested by one means or another, and all will, it so happens, be confirmed as true. In fact, the process of verification is the same as the process of establishing the statement in the first place, for a statement of fact is, in reality, a conclusion based upon observation of one kind or another. If I say to you, "I promise to come on Thursday," you know it is a fact that I have made that promise because you have heard me. (Whether or not I *do* come on Thursday does not alter the fact that I have made a promise.) You can confidently report my promise as a fact, and your report would be a statement of fact. (Remember that we are talking about a kind of statement and not what the statement is about.)

161

But a statement of fact may also be false. *All Irishmen are lovable drunkards. The average man is twelve feet tall. Eighteen states require voters to pay a poll tax.* As far as our definition of these statements is concerned, truth or falsehood is irrelevant. We can, with access to the appropriate information, test the statements, but, true or false, they remain statements of fact.

Statements of opinion cannot be verified in this way. *An ignorant, illiterate citizenry cannot remain free.* There is no way of testing this statement empirically. *If the tariff on South African broughams is lowered, our native brougham industry will wither and die.* The conclusion is based upon a logical inference, rather than upon observation or measurement. Of course, statements of opinion may become statements of fact. Several hundred years ago the question of whether or not the moon was made of green cheese could be argued only on logical grounds. Now, by various mathematical and observational techniques, we can make the statement that it is not cheese, but we do so on different grounds. The dire predictions made at election time usually become verifiable in a few years.

Some statements offer such serious problems in vocabulary that they cannot be classified or analyzed until the reader knows what the terms actually mean. If I say, "Ty Cobb was the best hitter in baseball," I may refer to a matter of fact (lifetime average, seasons leading the league, or some other matter of record) or I may simply mean that he followed the ball, hit the ball, and judged the pitchers more skillfully than others. In the latter case my statement obviously becomes an opinion. It is a conclusion based upon my estimate of Cobb's performance, relative to the performance of other hitters, but it is not the only conclusion possible — and it is unprovable. *Speeding is the cause of most serious accidents. An atomic bomb can devastate an entire city. Man is a higher biological type than the shark.* These are statements that are provable or unprovable depending upon the definition of the terms within the statement. If everyone agrees upon the definitions of "best," "cause," "serious," "devastate," "city," "higher," "biological type," then the statements in which they appear can be classified.

The reader who can separate statements of fact from statements of opinion and who can determine whether the words of the statement are ambiguous or not is prepared to read intelligently and efficiently. He knows that statements of fact are not matters for argument. *The continent of Africa has an area of 11,600,000 square miles and a population of around 200,000,-000.* I may argue about the accuracy of the area or census. I may argue about what is included as Africa. But once I have accepted a definition of terms and a method of proof there can be no argument. The distance from Mars to the earth at any particular instant is provable no matter how poor my mathematics may be. Of course, a reader's understanding that a statement is one of fact rather than opinion does not guarantee the truth of the statement. It simply means that he knows the statement is subject to empirical test.

Unprovable statements — statements of opinion — are by nature more difficult to deal with than matters of fact, and all of them cannot be dealt with in the same way. Two different kinds are generally identified: hypothetical statements and assertions. The differences between one kind of statement and another can best be shown by illustration.

1. STATEMENT OF FACT: *Queen Victoria died in 1901.*
2. HYPOTHESIS: *Trilobites became extinct toward the end of the Paleozoic Period.*
3. ASSERTION: *Lincoln was a better president than Calvin Coolidge.*

The first statement can be verified. The second statement cannot be verified beyond all doubt; in this case the evidence is negative. (As we approach the period fossils become rarer. Finally no more are found.) The third statement is one that by its nature does not yield to observation, nor can it be tested by physical means. It is a problem of value. Even though there were general agreement that Lincoln was the better president, it remains unverifiable. (Statements of opinion can, of course, be argued well or badly, as the remarks on support [following] and the explication of the whole essay at the beginning of Part III suggest.)

There is an interrelationship among fact, hypothesis, and assertion. A statement of fact is an empirical observation based upon an empirical assumption. An hypothesis is based upon empirical conditions, but the answer is accessible only by means of logic. An assertion is a conclusion arrived at through logic but based upon assumptions that are, in part at least, evaluative or logical. Each kind of statement is distinct. At the same time there is overlapping between fact and hypothesis and between hypothesis and assertion. Each kind must be tested by a different method, a method appropriate to the assumptions behind it and the sort of proof that validates it.

Authors cannot select arbitrarily the type of statement they wish to make. This is governed by the nature of their material and by their purpose. A man writing about the origin of the American Indian will have to make hypotheses. A man reporting an experiment will deal at least partly in statements of fact. A man expounding a theory of history will deal with opinion, even though part of the raw material of his opinions will be factual. No one can avoid opinion simply because he would prefer to deal wholly in facts. The important issue for the reader to understand is that statements differ and each must be examined according to its own nature.

Support: Argumentation is the most highly categorized and extensively documented area in the field of writing, and support is probably its largest single subject. Nevertheless, the essential facts concerning support are soon told.

In the form we usually encounter it, support is a form of statement. It would not be a bad definition to say that support is a statement used to authenticate another statement. As such, it shares the same qualities that have already been seen in the section on statement.

Statements used for support must be examined in the same way and with the same care that any other statement is examined. Any attempt to do this will reveal a paradoxical condition which, since there is no term for it, we might call the recession of proof. We take a statement and demand that it be supported. Another statement is made in support. But that statement, not being self-evident, requires a statement to support it. But this statement may not be acceptable without first being proved itself.

> And smaller fleas have smaller yet to bite 'em
> And so on down ad infinitum.

This recession may continue until we reach a fact (Lake Superior is larger than Lake Michigan.) or until we reach an assumption (God exists). Properly speaking, factual statements also contain assumptions.

In our culture, factual statement is the type of support whose authenticity is most immediately accepted. Indeed, in common use the word "fact" is also used to mean "opinion." All of us have heard people "get down to the facts" when what they really got down to was opinion. They accept as "facts" vague evaluations such as *He is a better husband than she is a wife* or *Math is harder than English.*

Statement of opinion is also used for support. Socialized medicine, for example, is a subject on which there can be few facts in the United States. But the debate continues with both sides enlisting opinion and hypothesis to support their contentions. Bathing-beauty contests, livestock exhibitions, and dog shows all give prizes based on opinion, the best-in-the-show prize ranking as the purest opinion of all. Except for the beauty contests, there is often a surprising unanimity of opinion, showing that the judges started with the same assumptions and exercised similar judgment.

Negative support, or support by inference, is a third type. It looms large in our thinking, though in writing it occurs only briefly and inconspicuously. Everyone accepts the "fact" that dinosaurs are extinct. It isn't hard to answer the question "How many dinosaurs would it take to make fools of ten thousand naturalists?" We accept letters of recommendation, walk with blissful confidence on the green light, and buy the brand that our friends never have had any trouble with. We live with negative evidence because we have to. Everyone recognizes that it can have limitations. Sometimes we learn the hard way: "Don't worry — he never bites."

Support can extend beyond statement, however. Negative evidence is one kind that does. The other chief kind is cumulative evidence. How many examples of superior intelligence and application does it take to make a good student? When does a man decide the used car he bought was a lemon? No single fact by itself might suffice, yet together they may be overpowering.

The misuse of support is a matter on which much could be written, either in the more classical form of the study of fallacies or in the more recent analysis of propaganda. This approach is chiefly negative, however. Here, stated positively, are the chief matters to consider either in reading or in writing.

(1) The support ought to represent an honest presentation of the evidence. The main object of a writer or reader ought to be to find the truth, and material in which contrary evidence is intentionally suppressed is dishonest material. If the other side is better than your own, change sides.

(2) Support ought to be selected in order to give as true a picture as possible. The principle of selection will vary from piece to piece, but the author and reader ought to be conscious of the principle that was followed.

(3) Support should be valid. Here again the material must determine the test for validity. Statistical and theological arguments require different tests.

(4) Support should be directly applicable to the case. If a man is applying for a job as a steam-shovel operator, it makes no difference that at the age of three he consorted with a person who later became known as an Odd Fellow. Nor should we consider it a recommendation that a mouthwash will actually kill the dread tsetse fly.

(5) The supporting material should be free from ambiguity. Sometimes this ambiguity may result from inadequate information. This is a common failing of experimental data. Another kind of ambiguity is ambiguity in terms.

(6) Finally, a matter of cardinal importance: All statements, both those in support and those that are being supported, should contain either explicitly or by implication all necessary modifications. The sweeping statement or generality is the enemy of precise thought and expression. *Blondes are superior to brunettes. Modern art is for the birds. Degas is a better painter than Renoir. My school is a better school than your school. Crime does not pay.* All these are statements that require some sort of modification.

Generalities are popular because they oversimplify and, as some of these examples show, because they often allow the writer or speaker to make an emotional as well as intellectual affirmation.

Support is such a critical matter and, often, such an emotional matter that we should watch ourselves and our authors with great care. We ourselves will do best if we act with intelligent honesty.

(*Note:* A further discussion of support and general statement as they relate to the complete essay will be found in Part III, "The Whole Composition.")

Underlying assumptions: Most arguments are about matters of opinion. Two men may disagree about who is the taller, but usually not for long. The argument is too easy to settle. But the same two men may argue late into the night about which political party has done most for the country. There is no measure to decide that question.

Most arguments over matters of opinion are never settled. Nor is this surprising, considering the nature of disagreement on such matters. Since the arguers have different conclusions, that is the point at which they begin. One says yes, the other no. Then they begin to marshal their evidence. The evidence on each side is piled high. Most of it consists of "facts," but somehow these do not impress the man on the other side. Sometimes he scoffs, at other times claims the evidence is irrelevant, and sometimes actually admits a point has been made. On the other hand, each man presents his evidence with care. Not only does he look for what he thinks is impressive; he realizes that his opponent has certain idiosyncrasies, shall we say, that lead him to regard some trivial matters as points well made and to regard the strongest and best evidence as little more than time wasted on useless topics. The two contestants finally desist. Though neither has convinced the other, they have confirmed themselves in their old ideas most admirably.

Such an argument fails, and the point is good for analysis and exposition as well as argument, because the two debaters fail to go beyond the conclusion and the evidence. They fail to consider the underlying assumptions in both positions.

Every question and statement has assumptions behind it. We may never be consciously aware of some of them. The simple question "How tall is he?" assumes "he" is measurable, assumes the person asked can comprehend the question, has some knowledge on the subject, will regard the question with at least some degree of seriousness, and will disclose the information. If we think that the person asked may not know, one of the assumptions — that he has some knowledge on the subject — may be uppermost in our minds. Under ordinary circumstances, the assumption that the person asked is capable of answering the question is not conscious. Only if the person asked were to answer in a foreign language or an idiotic mumble would we become aware that there was even a possibility for such a false assumption.

Here is a paragraph with certain clear assumptions. It is a part of Samuel Johnson's famous dissenting opinion on Milton's poem "Lycidas."

> In this poem there is no nature, for there is no truth; there is no art, for there is nothing new. Its form is that of a pastoral: easy, vulgar, and, therefore, disgusting; whatever images it can supply are long ago exhausted; and its inherent improbability always forces dissatisfaction on the mind.

Here we can follow Johnson's reasoning because his assumptions are clear in his own mind and stated explicitly for his readers. Compare that form to one in which the assumptions remain unstated.

> In this poem there is no nature, no art. Its form, that of the pastoral, is disgusting. Its images do not satisfy. The situation it presents forces dissatisfaction on the mind.

The first version is better. The second version offers the same verdicts, but the first tells why. There are, of course, further assumptions that help us judge what Johnson has said. He thinks, for example, that truth is necessary for nature. He further thinks there can be nature in a poem; indeed, he seems to regard it as a prerequisite. On the same grounds he requires that a poem have art. We know, too, that almost any poem in the pastoral form would be unpleasing to him because he seems to regard unpleasantness as an inherent quality of the form. We could say more, but these remarks make the point that by analyzing Johnson's remarks on this one poem, we can tell a good deal about what he thought of poetry in general.

Here is another example, this from a sixteenth-century pamphlet by John Knox, *The First Blast of the Trumpet against the Monstrous Regiment of Women.*

> To promote a woman to bear rule, superiority, dominion or empire above any realm, nation, or city, is repugnant to nature, contumely to God, a thing most contrarious to revealed will and approved ordinance, and finally it is the subversion of good order, of all equity and justice.

Behind what Knox writes are a number of important assumptions that anyone inclined to argue (or agree) intelligently must consider. In the first place, Knox assumes that there is a difference between a male ruler and a female ruler. Next we consider the phrase "repugnant to nature." Before accepting this, we must assume that there is some sort of norm (however Knox would define it) and that it makes a difference if this natural situation or order is violated. If we do not accept this assumption, one part of Knox's denunciation is wasted. Next the phrase "contumely to God" calls for attention. Here Knox assumes that God cares whether there is a ruler, who the ruler is, and whether the ruler is male or female. We must further assume that God accepts the "nature" of the preceding phrase. The other parts of the paragraph can be given similar analysis. There is more to this paragraph than just women. There is Knox's basic notion of an ordered universe, and of a God who not only sees all but also takes a direct interest in what happens. We see also an acceptance of the Scriptures as the word of God and as a guide to ethical and moral conduct. Finally, we see acceptance of an ordered state, but a state whose order is related to divine order. There is not much point in arguing with Knox on his treatment of women unless we first find out what makes him think the way he does.

An examination of assumptions is often necessary to evaluate a writer's opinion on a given topic. Look at this section of William Byrd's *History of the Dividing Line* (written in Virginia in 1728 but not published in English until 1842).

> Indian Corn is of so great increase that a little Pains will Subsist a very large Family with Bread, and then they may have meat without any pains at all, by the Help of the Low Grounds, and the great Variety of Mast that grows on the High-land. The Men, for their Parts, just like the Indians, impose all the Work upon the poor Women. They make their Wives rise out of their Beds early in the Morning, at the same time that they lye and Snore, till the Sun has run one third of his course, and disperst all the unwholesome Damps. Then, after Stretching and Yawning for half an Hour, they light their Pipes, and, under the Protection of a cloud of Smoak, venture out into the open Air; tho', if it happens to be never so little cold, they quickly return Shivering into the Chimney corner. When the Weather is mild, they stand leaning with both their arms upon the corn-field fence, and gravely consider whether they had best go and take a Small Heat at the Hough: but generally find reasons to put it off till another time.
>
> Thus they loiter away their Lives, like Solomon's Sluggard, with their Arms across, and at the Winding up of the Year Scarcely have Bread to Eat.
>
> To speak the Truth, tis a thorough Aversion to Labor that makes People file off to N Carolina, where Plenty and a Warm Sun confirm them in their Disposition to Laziness for their whole Lives.

Now consider the following assumptions on Byrd's part:
  (1) What it takes to support a family.
  (2) Whether the husband and wife should share the work.
  (3) Whether the example Indians set in their treatment of their wives is admirable.
  (4) How a man should spend the day, especially whether he should work.

(5) Whether the Bible furnishes us examples to heed.

(6) How a good husbandman's books ought to stand at the end of the year.

(7) Whether people ought to move to a new location to make life easier.

The man who shares Byrd's assumptions will read his account with sympathy. The man who believes that life is made to be enjoyed and the less work the better is not likely to feel that Byrd's presentation is adequate.

Consider the following statements that are voiced so frequently that we cannot remember where we heard them first, nor indeed the last time we heard them:

He has paid his debt to society. This statement, among other things, assumes that a man who has done wrong has incurred a debt to society. It assumes that society is an entity that can be wronged, and not only can be wronged but can demand retribution. It assumes further that guilt can be atoned for. Each of these assumptions could be the basis of a long and interesting discussion.

Everyone should get out and vote. This exhortation is so thoroughly accepted that radio and television stations carry it free, an infallible sign that it is noncontroversial. It carries the interesting assumption that all the voters are wiser than 60 or 50 per cent of the voters. Since no one knows exactly which 40 or 50 per cent of the eligible voters did not go to the polls, this assumption must contain an element of faith. The exhortation also contains the assumption that the vote of the man who stayed away from the polls is of the same value as that of the man who did vote. Often, too, there seems to accompany this statement the notion that if 100 per cent of the voters participated, the results might differ from the results obtained when 50 per cent voted. This assumption is also conjectural.

I think that in college it's more important for me to learn to get along with people than it is to make high grades. This remark assumes first of all that the speaker *could* learn to get along with people and *could* make high grades. It assumes next that there is such a thing as "learning to get along with people." Finally the remark assumes that there is some sort of antithesis between learning to get along with people and making high grades. It assumes that one must of necessity limit himself to a single goal.

Topics for discussion

Examine the assumptions behind the following statements:

1. The American government is better than the Russian government.

2. We are the best educated people in history. Something like 50 per cent of our high school graduates go to college.

3. I think Ernest Hemingway is a better author than either William Faulkner or William Shakespeare.

4. The Jackson's Hole-Teton area is the most beautiful place in America.

5. One opinion is as good as another.

6. Our nation will remain strong as long as it remains free.

7. A stitch in time saves nine.

8. This is a very poor paper. I hope the next one will be better.

9. There is a little bit of good in everyone.

Topics for writing

I. Clip out a newspaper editorial and write a paper examining its basic assumptions.

II. Listen to a radio or television newscast. Write a paper showing, on the basis of that one program, the assumptions it made as to what makes news and what makes important news.

III. Write a paper showing the basic values that are assumed to be good in a drama or comedy written either for the legitimate stage or for television.

Paragraph: The paragraph is the basic unit of *developed* thought, the unit toward which statements are directed. Without it, the essay would break down in a welter of unrelated, unsupported statements of fact, hypotheses, and assertions. Used properly, it provides the means for statements to lead to something beyond themselves; it provides the tight, coherent units of thought that develop or support a central idea, the thesis of the essay.

A good paragraph is a well developed idea. More specifically, though, we can identify a good paragraph by three qualities: (1) its logical construction, (2) its use of appropriate materials for development, and (3) its fullness of development.

(1) There is no formula for constructing a paragraph. The best method of development is simply the one that conveys the thought most clearly and accurately. Nonetheless, most paragraphs tend to be like one of two different types. The first type is usually called the *paragraph of support*. Here the materials of the paragraph are devoted to the illustration, modification, or logical support of a single idea. The paragraph of support is especially valuable in making a convincing argument and in clarifying details. Writers of description, for example, find this paragraph invaluable. James Boswell illus-

trates this type in his *Life of Johnson* when he considers what incidents of a man's life a biography ought to include:

> There are many invisible circumstances, which whether we read as enquirers after natural or moral knowledge, whether we intend to enlarge our science, or increase our virtue, are more important than publick occurrences. Thus Sallust, the great master of nature, has not forgot in his account of Catiline, to remark, that his walk was now quick, and again slow, as an indication of a mind revolving with violent commotion. Thus the story of Melancthon affords a striking lecture on the value of time, by informing us, that when he made an appointment, he expected not only the hour, but the minute to be fixed, that the day might not run out in idleness of suspense; and all the plans and enterprises of De Wit are now of less importance to the world than that part of his personal character, which represents him as careful of his health, and negligent of his life.

Although this is a simple, straightforward example of the paragraph of support, it is ideal, not typical. Most writers offer us more complex structures, or paragraphs that state the topic incompletely or not at all. These may all be excellent paragraphs, for the question is not whether they conform to an ideal pattern but whether they use a development that presents the idea accurately and clearly.

The second type of development begins with one position and ends with another. It can be called the *paragraph of logical development*. The one that follows was taken from the Earl of Shaftesbury's *An Inquiry Concerning Virtue or Merit*.

> The mind, which is spectator or auditor of other minds, cannot be without its eye and ear; so as to discern proportion, distinguish sound, and scan each sentiment or thought which comes before it. It can let nothing escape its censure. It feels the soft and harsh, the agreeable and disagreeable, in the affections; and finds a foul and fair, a harmonious and dissonant, as really and truly here as in any musical numbers or in the outward forms or representations of sensible things. Nor can it withhold its admiration and ecstasy, its aversion and scorn, any more in what relates to one than to the other of these subjects. So that to deny the common and natural sense of a sublime and beautiful in things, will appear an affectation merely, to anyone who considers duly of this affair.

Most paragraphs exhibit their own peculiarities, and not all will follow these two types. Some paragraphs consist of little more than a series of assertions with only tenuous connections.

Finding the author's pattern is important because it means uncovering the way the thought in the paragraph develops. It is a mistake, however, to depend too entirely upon pattern. For example, the common notion that every paragraph has a topic sentence can be dangerously misleading to the reader who does not expect this maxim to be violated in most of the paragraphs he reads. Authors who use the paragraph of logical or narrative development usually have no topic sentence. Writers who use the support paragraph may state their topic in a truncated form, may use two or more sentences to state it, or may be conscientious enough to state their subject completely in the first sentence. Even the most conscientious, however, often state the topic in the second rather than the first sentence.

(2) The materials used in developing paragraphs are varied and overlapping, but four kinds predominate:

>   (a) Details
>   (b) Comparison and contrast
>   (c) Statements
>   (d) Examples and illustrations

There is nothing mutually exclusive in these categories. All might appear in the same paragraph.

(a) *Details* may be used for illustration or for proof. The effect they have depends upon whether they themselves are matters of fact or opinion and whether the statement they support is fact or opinion. Factual details, especially statistical details, constitute one of the most convincing methods of paragraph development. (b) *Comparison and contrast* are useful for clarifying explanations and definitions. At times they constitute the structure of the entire paragraph; at other times they function more like details. (c) *Statements* are the usual materials of a paragraph of narrative or logical development. The logically developed paragraph is often associated with difficult reading, since it may deal in rapid order with a number of difficult concepts and since each succeeding statement may be a conclusion for which the evidence is not present. (d) *Examples*, illustrations, and anecdotes are valuable methods of providing clarification.

An understanding of the limitations inherent in the use of each of the methods of development — for instance, examples cannot ordinarily furnish proof — reveals immediately whether or not an author can accomplish his ostensible purpose in a paragraph. An understanding of the materials themselves helps the reader to discriminate between the essential and the illustrative statements of a paragraph.

(3) In addition to logical construction and appropriate development, the thought of a good paragraph also shows elaboration and development adequate to the subject and the audience. A historian of art writing for an audience with a knowledge of art history might well say: "Of course, we all know that in eighteenth-century England the conversation piece became one of the most popular genres." But most audiences would need a good deal

more. They would like to know what a conversation piece is, who painted some, how they differ from formal portraits, and perhaps why they should become popular at that particular time. The reader himself has no control over the author's development, but he can decide how closely he needs to read a particular piece. A knowledgeable reader need not labor through material that illustrates points that are obvious to him. A reader who sees that he needs further examples, illustrations, or details in order to understand a paragraph fully knows either that he is dealing with a poor writer or that he is into material designed for an audience more familiar with the subject than he. The latter is a warning to him to go slow and check his conclusions carefully.

After the reader has considered construction, materials, and development, he is ready to summarize the idea that the paragraph develops. Since many writers do not include a summary statement in each paragraph, this is a task the reader himself must usually perform. In the paragraph of support, this is usually a relatively simple job. In the paragraph of narrative or logical development, the job becomes more complex. In any event, it is vastly simplified for the reader who has a knowledge of the methods, materials, and extent of paragraph development.

Commentary and questions

Ask these five questions of each of the selections below:

1. How should each statement be classified?

2. For each statement, what underlying assumptions should be considered? Are these explicit or hidden?

3. What kind of support is used? Is it necessary for the author to offer support?

4. What is the thesis of each paragraph? How much of the thesis is stated explicitly?

5. What is the pattern of the paragraph, and what materials are used for developing it?

I. The estimated cost of complete instrumentation of a new modern plant to automatize it as fully as possible today ranges from 1 to 19 per cent (depending on the industry) of the total investment in process equipment. The average for all industries would be about 6 per cent. On this basis, if all the new plants built in 1950 had been automatized, some $600 million would have been spent for measuring and control instruments. Actually the production of such instruments in 1959 totaled only $67 million. In other words, to automatize new plants alone, to say nothing of those already built, would require nearly 10 times as great an investment in instruments as we are now making. (*From Wassily Leontief, "Machines and Man," p. 151.*)

II. The third process to which we have abandoned too much humanistic education at all levels is the timid, prudential, pseudo-cultural response to the arts. In a desire to act upon the natural human capacities for sheer enjoyment, or perhaps in a higher-minded encouragement of the natural human impulse to praise beauty and goodness, the humanities have compromised too often with the process of so-called "appreciation." "Appreciation" had a meaning for an earlier day. In too many quarters it has now become the organized practice of critical insincerity. By such practices we have left off important educative uses of dislike and have brought up many young Americans in the erroneous notion that something is unalterably wrong — wrong with them personally — if they do not at once "like" Shakespeare or Mozart or Matisse. We have abandoned our search — more difficult than the seeking of scientists — for the individual student with capacities for taste and with powers of judgment: talents of some importance to humanistic education and to the future of our civilization. (*From H. H. Ransom, "The Arts of Uncertainty,"* The Texas Quarterly, *Vol. I, No. 3, 1958, p. ix. Reprinted by permission of the author and the University of Texas Press.*)

III. What I believe is mainly what has been established by plausible and impartial evidence, *e.g.*, that the square on the hypotenuse of a right triangle is equal to the squares on the other two sides, that water is composed of oxygen and hydrogen, and that man is a close cousin to the ape. Further than that I do not care to go. Is there a life after death, as so many allege, wherein the corruptible puts on incorruption and the mortal immortality? I can only answer that I do not know. My private inclination is to hope that it is not so, but that hope is only a hope, and hopes and beliefs, it seems to me, can have nothing in common. If, while the taxidermists are stuffing my integument for some fortunate museum of anatomy, a celestial catchpole summons my psyche to Heaven, I shall be very gravely disappointed, but (unless my habits of mind change radically at death) I shall accept the command as calmly as possible, and face eternity without repining.

Most of the sorrows of man, I incline to think, are caused by just such repining. Alone among the animals, he is dowered with the capacity to invent imaginary worlds, and he is always making himself unhappy by trying to move into them. Thus he underrates the world in which he actually lives, and so misses most of the fun that is in it. That world, I am convinced, could be materially improved, but even as it stands it is good enough to keep any reasonable man entertained for a lifetime.

As for me, I roll out of my couch every morning with the most agreeable expectations. In the morning paper there is always massive and exhilarating evidence that the human race, despite its ages-long effort to imitate the seraphim, is still doomed to be irrevocably human, and in my morning mail I always get soothing proof that there are men left who are even worse asses than I am. (*By H. L. Mencken, from* Living Philosophies. *Reprinted by permission of Simon and Schuster, Inc. Copyright 1931 by Simon and Schuster, Inc.*)

IV. THE LEVEL OF STEEL WAGES

Wage levels can be compared in terms of earnings or rates. The wage rate is the basic payment per hour, day or week that is guaranteed in the employment contract. It relates to a particular job or occupation. Earnings include, in addition to the basic rate, incentive payments, premiums for overtime or work on late shifts, bonuses, etc. Average earnings for an entire industry are influenced by the proportion of workers at various skill levels. These proportions vary widely among industries. Basic steel employs a relatively large proportion of workers in skilled occupations.

Measured in terms of average hourly earnings, steel wages are higher than those in most other industries. The May, 1959, average of $3.10 in the steel industry compared with $2.23 in manufacturing as a whole, $2.68 in automobiles.

Wage rates, job for job, compare more nearly with those in other high-wage industries, such as automobile production and petroleum refining. For example, the hourly rate for common labor in the steel industry is $2.13. Rates for unskilled labor paid by a number of major employers for whom information is available range from $2 to $2.47.

Many steel workers (about 60 per cent of the total) receive incentive pay which is less commonly found in most other high-wage industries. Incentives may add 10 per cent, 15 per cent, 20 per cent or more to basic rates. They are commonly associated with greater worker effort and increased production. (*Secretary of Labor James P. Mitchell's report on the statistical findings in the steel controversy. August 19, 1959.*)

V. Ignorance is the natural result of a want of knowledge. . . . Consequently, where children never go to school, it is not probable that learning will flourish. Accordingly, nothing can equal the barbarous ignorance of both the children and grown-up persons in this republican city. I happened to be at the house of a judge of one of the courts, and was astonished to find, on my giving his son, a boy of about twelve years old, a book to read, that he could not comprehend a single word! The poor mother, who was, I suppose, a little mortified on account of my being a stranger (they don't mind these things among themselves), patted the booby on the back, and assured me the poor boy was *so* bashful! Most of the justices of the peace here make their mark instead of signing their names to warrants, &c. and what is difficult to believe, many of the clerks in the banks can't write their names. I never saw a school while in Boston. There is a college, to be sure, but I was assured the professors did not quite understand English. The Rev. Cotton Mather, one of the most enlightened and popular preachers here, has written a book called the Magnalia, in which he gives a variety of witch stories, such as would be laughed at, even among the Indians, but which they all believe here, as if it were Holy Writ. The work is just come out, and affords apt illustration of the state of the human intellect on this side of the Atlantic. (*From James Kirke Paulding*, John Bull in America; or, The New Munchausen, *1825.*)

Description: Although description and words are usually most closely associated, here description is placed in the discussion of statement. Of course good description uses words sensitively and effectively. All good writing does. But a discussion of description that limits it to words fails to bring out one of its essential qualities: description does not tell what a thing is like — it shows what the author thinks it is like.

Many authors would not want to admit that there is a difference between what they see and what the thing itself is like. All we must do, however, is to compare two descriptions to see that there is a difference. An American might describe the sacred stone of Mohammedanism scientifically and calmly. A Mohammedan would describe it with reverence. Each describes only one aspect of the stone; each describes what he sees when he looks at it. Nor is it enough to say that one description is scientific and the other emotional. Both represent legitimate aspects of the stone.

Description is, then, a species of statement. It conveys information and attitude. It is limited by what the author does not know or does know and decides to leave out. It is further limited by the language the author chooses to describe what he does leave in. Description is often misleading because of the illusions of completeness and objectivity and because the reader does not realize the limitation of the author's concepts.

The following selections illustrate the handling of the same material by three different authors. All three of these men were on the same trip across the prairies and all three looked at the same prairie dogs together.

A REPUBLIC OF PRAIRIE DOGS   Washington Irving

From A Tour on the Prairies,
first published in 1835.

ON RETURNING from our expedition in quest of the young Count, I learned that a burrow, or village, as it is termed, of prairie dogs had been discovered on the level summit of a hill, about a mile from the camp. Having heard much of the habits and peculiarities of these little animals, I determined to pay a visit to the community. The prairie dog is, in fact, one of the curiosities of the Far West, about which travellers delight to tell marvellous tales, endowing him at times with something of the politic and social habits of a rational being, and giving him systems of civil government and domestic economy, almost equal to what they used to bestow upon the beaver.

2   The prairie dog is an animal of the coney kind, and about the size of a rabbit. He is of a sprightly mercurial nature; quick, sensitive, and somewhat petulant. He is very gregarious, living in large communities, sometimes of several acres in extent, where innumerable little heaps of earth show the entrances to the subterranean cells of the inhabitants, and the well beaten tracks, like lanes and streets, show their mobility and restlessness. According to the accounts given of them, they would seem to be continually full of sport, business, and public affairs; whisking about hither and thither, as if on gossiping visits to each other's houses, or congregating in the cool of the evening, or after a shower, and gambolling together in the open air. Sometimes, especially when the moon shines, they pass half the night in revelry, barking or yelping with short, quick, yet weak tones, like those of very young puppies. While in the height of their playfulness and clamour, however, should there be the least alarm, they all vanish into their cells in an instant, and the village remains blank and silent. In case they are hard pressed by their pursuers, without any hope of escape, they will assume a pugnacious air, and a most whimsical look of impotent wrath and defiance.

3   The prairie dogs are not permitted to remain sole and undisturbed inhabitants of their own homes. Owls and rattlesnakes are said to take up their abodes with them; but whether as invited guests or unwelcome intruders, is a matter of controversy. The owls are of a peculiar kind, and would seem to partake of the character of the hawk; for they are taller and more erect on their legs, more alert in their looks and rapid in their flight than ordinary owls, and do not confine their excursions to the night, but sally forth in broad day.

4   Some say that they only inhabit cells which the prairie dogs have deserted, and suffered to go to ruin, in consequence of the death in them of some relative; for they would make out this little animal to be endowed with keen sensibilities, that will not permit it to remain in the dwelling where it has witnessed the death of a friend. Other fanciful speculators represent the owl as a kind of housekeeper to the prairie dog; and, from having a note very similar, insinuate that it acts, in a manner, as family preceptor, and teaches the young litter to bark.

5   As to the rattlesnake, nothing satisfactory has been ascertained of the part he plays in this most interesting household; though he is considered as little better than a sycophant and sharper, that winds himself into the concerns of the honest, credulous little dog, and takes him in most sadly. Certain it is, if he acts as toad-eater, he occasionally solaces himself with more than

the usual perquisites of his order; as he is now and then detected with one of the younger members of the family in his maw.

6   Such are a few of the particulars that I could gather about the domestic economy of this little inhabitant of the prairies, who, with his pigmy republic, appears to be a subject of much whimsical speculation and burlesque remarks, among the hunters of the Far West.

7   It was towards evening that I set out with a companion, to visit the village in question. Unluckily, it had been invaded in the course of the day by some of the rangers, who had shot two or three of its inhabitants, and thrown the whole sensitive community in confusion. As we approached, we could perceive numbers of the inhabitants seated at the entrances of their cells, while sentinels seemed to have been posted on the outskirts, to keep a look out. At sight of us, the picket guards scampered in and gave the alarm; whereupon every inhabitant gave a short yelp, or bark, and dived into his hole, his heels twinkling in the air as if he had thrown a somerset.

8   We traversed the whole village, or republic, which covered an area of about thirty acres; but not a whisker of an inhabitant was to be seen. We probed their cells as far as the ramrods of our rifles would reach, but could unearth neither dog, nor owl, nor rattlesnake. Moving quietly to a little distance, we lay down upon the ground, and watched for a long time, silent and motionless. By and bye, a cautious old burgher would slowly put forth the end of his nose, but instantly draw it in again. Another, at a greater distance, would emerge entirely; but, catching a glance at us, would throw a somerset, and plunge back again into his hole. At length, some who resided on the opposite side of the village, taking courage from the continued stillness, would steal forth, and hurry off to a distant hole, the residence possibly of some family connexion, or gossiping friend, about whose safety they were solicitous, or with whom they wished to compare notes about the late occurrences.

9   Others, still more bold, assembled in little knots, in the streets and public places, as if to discuss the recent outrages offered to the commonwealth, and the atrocious murders of their fellow burghers.

10   We rose from the ground and moved forward, to take a nearer view of these public proceedings, when, yelp! yelp! yelp! — there was a shrill alarm passed from mouth to mouth; the meetings suddenly dispersed; feet twinkled in the air in every direction; and in an instant all had vanished into the earth.

11   The dusk of the evening put an end to our observations, but the train of whimsical comparisons produced in my brain by the moral attributes which I had heard given to these little politic animals, still continued after my return to camp; and late in the night, as I lay awake after all the camp was asleep, and heard in the stillness of the hour, a faint clamour of shrill voices from the distant village, I could not help picturing to myself the inhabitants gathered together in noisy assemblage, and windy debate, to devise plans for the public safety, and to vindicate the invaded rights and insulted dignity of the republic.

THE PRAIRIE DOGS

Charles Joseph Latrobe

From The Rambler in North America, *1836.*

As AN object of natural history, nothing diverted us more than a part of the smooth prairies near our camp, where, for the space of many acres, the surface was marked by the mounds raised by a strange little animal, vulgarly and absurdly called the prairie-dog.[1] They are a species of marmot, of small size, rarely measuring more than fifteen or twenty inches from the top of their nose to the extremity of the tail, with a large head, short ears, and longish body. Like the beaver, they appear to be republicans, living in large communities, in burrows spread under a wide extent of prairie. The sod within their territories was everywhere well-shaven and dry, and had all the appearance of being well-trodden. The opening to each burrow was seen at the top of a little flattened mound of the earth removed in making the necessary subterraneous excavations. In these they are said to live in families. They were very shy and difficult of approach for a man on foot, while at the same time a horseman could ride in among them without giving half the alarm; which was attributed to their being accustomed to the presence of the wild horses of the prairie.

It was amusing to watch their sprightly movements from a distance, and the cautious manner in which they would on ascending from their burrows, raise themselves upon their hind legs like a squirrel, and make a long neck, to see if the coast was clear. If they noticed distant danger, they uttered a sharp and singular bark, and never failed to make good their retreat. I noticed that they were very apt to fall foul of each other, and squabble and wrangle together like some of their republican neighbours more to the eastward.

Their burrows, however, serve for places of retreat to others besides themselves. The burrowing-owl, a distinct species, is frequently found in them, and the rattlesnake and badger also. Our friend Irving threw light upon this singular fact, by shrewdly surmising that these strange gentry were probably the ambassadors and plenipotentiaries of foreign powers at the seat of the Republic; and I believe you will hardly find a more plausible one.

WASHINGTON IRVING ON THE PRAIRIE

Harry Leavitt Ellsworth

From Washington Irving on the Prairie, *edited by Stanley T. Williams and Barbara D. Simison. Reprinted by permission of the American Book Company.*

— IN THE meantime Doct Holt and myself walked up the hill 3/4 of a mile to see the Republic of Prairie dogs, a very interesting settlement — these dogs

---

[1] Arctomys Ludoviciana.

are little larger than a grey squirrel — they burrough in small holes, which they excavate, making the mouth of their burrow, resemble a large ant heap. Upon the approach of strangers, they stood up on their hind legs, and barked incessantly — they occupy at this place 30 acres at least — From the shortness of the grass around this republic, I should suppose they eat that vegitable — We shot a few of them, and I eat part of one which was as good as a squirrel — they appear to live very happy and enjoy a perfect democracy — all are equal and there is no aristocracy — they may have however a sort of Greccian or Belgian king, placed over them by the allied powers of wild bea[s]ts — For on this very same ground, was found & killed a large *badger* — a *Marmot* and 2 Rattle Snakes — all these burrowed in the same field and in holes adjoining if not the same — it is said that all these Prairie dogs burrows come together under ground — this fact I doubt but that the marmout & rattle snake find it very convenient to creep into the handsome holes dug out by the Prairie dogs I have no doubt — The badger also expects the dogs to assist him — perhaps he is king —

Commentary and questions

All three of these men have seen the same village and, as Latrobe's account discloses, discussed it in terms of a republic. There is no disagreement among them, but the impressions they give are not identical.

A convenient way to examine the material is to divide it into statements of what the author has seen, statements of conclusions he has drawn from what he has seen, and statements of what he has heard. This makes an interesting approach to the descriptions of the prairie dog. Latrobe reports the observation that the animal is usually less than fifteen or twenty inches from nose to tail. He has heard that it is a marmot, and he concludes it is one of the small size. He further concludes that the head is large, the ears short, and the body longish. This is a satisfactory description for anyone who already knows what a prairie dog looks like. Probably the most helpful part of this description is the report that the animal is a marmot. A reader might, for example, think of the prairie dog as a slightly undersized woodchuck.

Ellsworth leaves a different impression. He knows that the animal is not a dog, yet his account (written for his wife) very clearly leaves the impression that it is a dog the size of a squirrel. Irving's use of the word "coney" may refer to the pika, an animal somewhat resembling a guinea pig. Using the rabbit to show the size of the prairie dog introduces further complications.

All three travelers are describing the same animals, yet three different concepts of the prairie dog clearly emerge.

Why should these three accounts begin with the same animal but end with different concepts? The explanation lies chiefly in the sort of statement that is made about the animal. If all three had put down only observed facts, they would probably have stayed much closer together. There would still have been some difference because of selection and emphasis. But observed fact is laborious to collect and tedious to relate. There are much quicker ways to describe, by analogy for instance. There are also quicker ways of transmitting the author's concept. This concept, though it may be very useful, may not be accurate and it may be misleading. The phrase "about the size of a rabbit" is useful if the reader does not transfer the rabbit's ears to the prairie dog.

Go through these three essays separating out statements of observed fact, statements of conclusion, and statements of reported fact.

Note how Irving's conclusion that the prairie dog village is like a human community so dominates his description that even his observed fact is altered to fit his fantastic conclusion.

Note the use, omission, and alteration of Ellsworth's report of having shot and eaten some of the prairie dogs. What is the effect of the different reports of this matter?

Compare the conjectures each makes concerning the rattlesnakes. What do they actually know about the snakes? Did any of them see owls? Why did Irving omit the badger? Why did the others include him? Would you say that they have sufficient evidence to assume that owls, rattlesnakes, and badgers live in prairie-dog villages?

Vagrants and sturdy beggars: THE VAGRANTS OF

WICKLOW, John M. Synge · ROAD-KIDS AND GAY-CATS, Jack London · PADDY,
George Orwell

THE MARGINAL, furtive, occasionally criminal, and nearly always savage lives dealt with in the following selections are familiar to very few people, but all three of the authors have seen them at close hand. George Orwell and Jack London lived the existence of vagrants for a time and were thus equipped to express the outlook and understand the psychology of men living as few of us would care to. Synge was an outsider, a writer interested in the glimpses of character and motive he could find in men and women whom he must have observed frequently and with some sympathy. Thus the authority of all three writers comes directly from personal observation or experience.

As one might expect, their styles are all fundamentally narrative and descriptive, and their commentary is thus limited or simply suggested by the events and personalities they depict. There are, however, important differences in the accounts. Synge is obviously attracted by the free, anarchic dignity he finds in his Irish vagrants and gypsies. London, in spite of the violence and brutality of the life that was part of his youth, treats his subject with humor and not a little bravado (the defiance of authority and moral codes is narrated perhaps a little boastfully; yet he writes of the boy who lost his legs with no show of sympathy). Of the three, Orwell is most clearly the social critic, writing of things that will stir the reader's disgust and horror, either with the men he knew, or with the conditions that forced them to live as they did. Yet with a few exceptions Orwell seems merely to narrate and to describe. His statements appear matter-of-fact, and rarely does he allow himself the degree of emotionalism or colored language used by Synge and London.

It is for their selection and presentation of details that these selections are chosen. Most of the few generalizations are about the lives of vagrants, and their support is the sense of authoritative personal observation each writer tries to bring to his subject. Therefore, the reality of the individual, narrated fact and description of character, and persuasiveness of each statement should command our attention as readers. It is especially important to notice two things: the picture of himself that each writer gives and the amount and manner of conversation he uses. Finally, the reader should observe how Synge, London, and Orwell use suggestive statement. Together these three elements of narrative style should indicate fairly accurately what we are expected to accept as true.

THE VAGRANTS OF WICKLOW John M. Synge

From The Complete Works of
John M. Synge. *Copyright 1935
by The Modern Library, Inc.
Reprinted by permission of
Random House, Inc.*

SOME features of County Wicklow, such as the position of the principal workhouses and holiday places on either side of the coach road from Arklow to Bray, have made this district a favourite with the vagrants of Ireland. A few of these people have been on the road for generations; but fairly often they seem to have merely drifted out from the ordinary people of the villages, and do not differ greatly from the class they come from. Their abundance has often been regretted; yet in one sense it is an interesting sign, for wherever the labourer of a country has preserved his vitality, and begets an occasional temperament of distinction, a certain number of vagrants are to be looked for. In the middle classes the gifted son of a family is always the poorest — usually a writer or artist with no sense for speculation — and in a family of peasants, where the average comfort is just over penury, the gifted son sinks also, and is soon a tramp on the roadside.

2   In this life, however, there are many privileges. The tramp in Ireland is little troubled by the laws, and lives in out-of-door conditions that keep him in good-humour and fine bodily health. This is so apparent, in Wicklow at least, that these men rarely seek for charity on any plea of ill-health, but ask simply, when they beg: "Would you help a poor fellow along the road?" or, "Would you give me the price of a night's lodging, for I'm after walking a great way since the sun rose?"

3   The healthiness of this life, again, often causes these people to live to a great age, though it is not always easy to test the stories that are told of their longevity. One man, however, who died not long ago, claimed to have reached one hundred and two with a show of likelihood; for several old people remember his first appearance in a certain district as a man of middle

age, about the year of the Famine, in 1847 or 1848. This man could hardly be classed with ordinary tramps, for he was married several times in different parts of the world, and reared children of whom he seemed to have forgotten, in his old age, even the names and sex. In his early life he spent thirty years at sea, where he sailed with some one he spoke of afterwards as "Il mio capitane," visiting India and Japan, and gaining odd words and intonations that gave colour to his language. When he was too old to wander in the world, he learned all the paths of Wicklow, and till the end of his life he could go the thirty miles from Dublin to the Seven Churches without, as he said, "putting out his foot on a white road, or seeing any Christian but the hares and moon." When he was over ninety he married an old woman of eighty-five. Before many days, however, they quarreled so fiercely that he beat her with his stick, and came out again on the roads. In a few hours he was arrested at her complaint, and sentenced to a month in Kilmainham. He cared nothing for the plankbed and uncomfortable diet; but he always gathered himself together, and cursed with extraordinary rage, as he told how they cut off the white hair which had grown down upon his shoulders. All his pride and his half-conscious feeling for the dignity of his age seemed to have set themselves on this long hair, which marked him out from the other people of this district; and I have often heard him say to himself, as he sat beside me under a ditch: "What use is an old man without his hair? A man has only his bloom like the trees; and what use is an old man without his white hair?"

4   Among the country people of the East of Ireland the tramps and tinkers who wander round from the West have a curious reputation for witchery and unnatural powers.

5   "There's great witchery in that country," a man said to me once, on the side of a mountain to the east of Aughavanna, in Wicklow. "There's great witchery in that country, and great knowledge of the fairies. I've had men lodging with me out of the West — men who would be walking the world looking for a bit of money — and every one of them would be talking of the wonders below in Connemara. I remember one time, a while after I was married, there was a tinker down there in the glen, and two women along with him. I brought him into my cottage to do a bit of a job, and my first child was there lying in the bed, and he covered up to his chin with the bedclothes. When the tallest of the women came in, she looked around at him, and then she says —

6   " 'That's a fine boy, God bless him.'

7   " 'How do you know it's a boy,' says my woman, " 'when it's only the head of him you see?'

8   " 'I know rightly,' says the tinker, 'and it's the first too.'

9   "Then my wife was going to slate me for bringing in people to bewitch her child, and I had to turn the lot of them out to finish the job in the lane."

10   I asked him where most of the tinkers came from that are met with in Wicklow.

11   "They come from every part," he said. "They're gallous lads for walking round through the world. One time I seen fifty of them above on the road to Rathdangan, and they all match-making and marrying themselves for the year that was to come. One man would take such a woman, and say he was going such roads and places, stopping at this fair and another fair, till he'd meet them again at such a place, when the spring was coming on. Another, maybe, would swap the woman he had with one from another man, with as much talk as if you'd be selling a cow. It's two hours I was there watching them from the bog underneath, where I was cutting turf, and the like of the crying and the kissing, and the singing and the shouting began when they went off this way and that way, you never heard in your life. Sometimes when a party would be gone a bit down over the hill, a girl would begin crying out and wanting to go back to her ma. Then the man would say: 'Black hell to your soul, you've come with me now, and you'll go the whole way.' I often seen tinkers before and since, but I never seen such a power of them as were in it that day."

12   It need hardly be said that in all tramp life plaintive and tragic elements are common, even on the surface. Some are peculiar to Wicklow. In these hills the summer passes in a few weeks from a late spring, full of odor and color, to an autumn that is premature and filled with the desolate splendor of decay; and it often happens that, in moments when one is most aware of this ceaseless fading of beauty, some incident of tramp life gives a local human intensity to the shadow of one's own mood.

13   One evening, on the high ground near the Avonbeg, I met a young tramp just as an extraordinary sunset had begun to fade, and a low white mist was rising from the bogs. He had a sort of table in his hands that he seemed to have made himself out of twisted rushes and a few branches of osier. His clothes were more than usually ragged, and I could see by his face that he was suffering from some terrible disease. When he was quite close, he held out the table.

14   "Would you give me a few pence for that thing?" he said. "I'm after working at it all day by the river, and for the love of God give me something now, the way I can get a drink and lodging for the night."

15   I felt in my pockets, and could find nothing but a shilling piece.

16   "I wouldn't wish to give you so much," I said, holding it out to him, "but it is all I have, and I don't like to give you nothing at all, and the darkness coming on. Keep the table; it's no use to me, and you'll maybe sell it for something in the morning."

17   The shilling was more than he expected, and his eyes flamed with joy.

18   "May the Almighty God preserve you and watch over you and reward you for this night," he said, "but you'll take the table; I wouldn't keep it at

all, and you after stretching out your hand with a shilling to me, and the darkness coming on."

19 He forced it into my hands so eagerly that I could not refuse it, and set off down the road with tottering steps. When he had gone a few yards, I called after him: "There's your table; take it and God speed you."

20 Then I put down his table on the ground, and set off as quickly as I was able. In a few minutes he came up with me again, holding the table in his hands, and slipped round in front of me so that I could not get away.

21 "You wouldn't refuse it," he said, "and I after working at it all day below by the river."

22 He was shaking with excitement and the exertion of overtaking me; so I took his table and let him go on his way. A quarter of a mile further on I threw it over the ditch in a desolate place, where no one was likely to find it.

23 In addition to the more genuine vagrants a number of wandering men and women are to be met with in the northern parts of the country, who walk out for ferns and flowers in bands of from four or five to a dozen. They usually set out in the evening, and sleep in some ditch or shed, coming home the next night with what they have gathered. If their sales are successful, both men and women drink heavily; so that they are always on the edge of starvation, and are miserably dressed, the women sometimes wearing nothing but an old petticoat and shawl — a scantiness of clothing that is sometimes met with also among the road-women of Kerry.

24 These people are nearly always at war with the police, and are often harshly treated. Once after a holiday, as I was walking home through a village on the border of Wicklow, I came upon several policemen, with a crowd round them, trying to force a drunken flower-woman out of the village. She did not wish to go, and threw herself down, raging and kicking, on the ground. They let her lie there for a few minutes, and then she propped herself up against the wall, scolding and storming at every one, till she became so outrageous the police renewed their attack. One of them walked up to her and hit her a sharp blow on the jaw with the back of his hand. Then two more of them seized her by the shoulders and forced her along the road for a few yards, till her clothes began to tear off with the violence of the struggle, and they let her go once more.

25 She sprang up at once when they did so.

26 "Let this be the barrack's yard, if you wish it," she cried, tearing off the rags that still clung about her. "Let this be the barrack's yard, and come on now, the lot of you."

27 Then she rushed at them with extraordinary fury; but the police, to avoid scandal, withdrew into the town, and left her to be quieted by her friends.

28 Sometimes, it is fair to add, the police are generous and good-humored. One evening, many years ago, when Whit Monday in Enniskerry was a very

different thing from what it is now, I was looking out of a window in that village, watching the police, who had been brought in for the occasion, getting ready to start for Bray. As they were standing about, a young ballad-singer came along from the Dargle, and one of the policemen, who seemed to know him, asked him why a fine, stout lad the like of him wasn't earning his bread, instead of straying on the roads.

29 Immediately the young man drew up on the spot where he was, and began shouting a loud ballad at the top of his voice. The police tried to stop him; but he went on, getting faster and faster, till he ended, swinging his head from side to side, in a furious patter, of which I seem to remember —

> Botheration
> Take the nation,
> Calculation,
> In the stable,
> Cain and Abel,
> Tower of Babel,
> And the Battle of Waterloo.

30 Then he pulled off his hat, dashed in among the police, and did not leave them till they had all given him the share of money he felt he had earned for his bread.

31 In all the circumstances of this tramp life there is a certain wildness that gives it romance and a peculiar value for those who look at life in Ireland with an eye that is aware of the arts also. In all the healthy movements of art, variations from the ordinary types of manhood are made interesting for the ordinary man, and in this way only the higher arts are universal. Beside this art, however, founded on the variations which are a condition and effect of all vigorous life, there is another art — sometimes confounded with it — founded on the freak of nature, in itself a mere sign of atavism or disease. This latter are, which is occupied with the antics of the freak, is of interest only to the variation from ordinary minds, and for this reason is never universal. To be quite plain, the tramp in real life, Hamlet and Faust in the arts, are variations; but the maniac in real life, and Des Esseintes and all his ugly crew in the arts, are freaks only.

Commentary and questions

1. *Paragraphs 1-4:* Synge introduces his subject with a number of fairly general comments about his vagrants, in contrast to the methods of London and Orwell. A possible reason for this strategy is that Synge wishes the reader to accept a somewhat surprising point of view. Notice how the first two paragraphs contrast. Is it the "privileges" of a vagrant life that most impress Synge? Paragraph 3 is a supporting paragraph. Is the old man mentioned here a convincing example of these privileges? What elements in his life are expected to demonstrate the point?

2. *Paragraphs 5-9:* The mild autobiographical element here is intended to offer Synge's authority for speaking as he does. Point out statements in which his own personality and attitude emerge.

3. *Paragraphs 10-11:* The "plaintive and tragic elements" here contrast to Synge's earlier celebration of vagrancy. What, precisely, are the sources of "tragedy" Synge mentions? Is there any inconsistency here? What is the purpose of this element of contrast?

4. *Paragraphs 12-22:* This section, giving an account of the author's meeting with the young man at sunset, is carefully detailed and narrated. How would you describe the young man's character? Does Synge present him so that issues and points of view developed earlier are illustrated here? What details strike you as most effective?

5. *Paragraphs 23-27:* Are the fern-gatherers, and in particular the drunken young woman, presented as sympathetically as the young man? Are they seen as victims of society or merely nuisances to the police? What particular statements support your conclusion?

6. *Paragraph 31:* Synge's conclusion involves two main points: he discovers in the vagrant life "a certain wildness that gives it romance" and he considers it of interest for the arts. Perhaps we may concede the former, but the latter should provoke discussion. Has Synge demonstrated his connection of "variations from the ordinary types of manhood" with the way in which the "higher arts" are universal? What do you find in the revelations of character and personality Synge attempts which might be called "universal"? How would you describe the two types of art Synge mentions here? (One of the instances he uses to make this distinction concerns Des Esseintes, the dubious and decadent hero of J. K. Huysmann's novel, *Against the Grain*. The allusion would have been more familiar fifty years ago than it is today.)

Topics for discussion and writing

I. How concerned is Synge with the moral standards of the people he describes? Does he take up in any way the ethical problems that grow out of the attitude of society toward vagrants? What similarities and differences do you find between Synge's characters and people in conventional, settled society?

II. Write a theme describing the characters Synge concentrates on and showing the particular significance each has for the essay. Is there any purpose to the order in which they appear? Does each character fit one of the generalizations Synge makes about vagrant life?

III. Synge, in his conclusion, disapproves of art "founded on the freak of nature." Are any of his characters freakish?

IV. Write an essay in which you describe some of Synge's characters from a point of view different from the one he takes.

ROAD-KIDS AND GAY-CATS   Jack London

From The Road. *Reprinted by permission of Irving Shepard.*

EVERY once in a while, in newspapers, magazines, and biographical diction-aries, I run upon sketches of my life, wherein, delicately phrased, I learn that it was in order to study sociology that I became a tramp. This is very nice and thoughtful of the biographers, but it is inaccurate. I became a tramp — well, because of the life that was in me, of the wanderlust in my blood that would not let me rest. Sociology was merely incidental; it came afterward, in the same manner that a wet skin follows a ducking. I went on "The Road" because I couldn't keep away from it; because I hadn't the price of the railroad fare in my jeans; because I was so made that I couldn't work all my life on "one same shift"; because — well, just because it was easier to than not to.

2   It happened in my own town, in Oakland, when I was sixteen. At that time I had attained a dizzy reputation in my chosen circle of adventurers, by whom I was known as the Prince of the Oyster Pirates. It is true, those immediately outside my circle, such as honest bay-sailors, longshoremen, yachtsmen, and the legal owners of the oysters, called me "tough," "hood-lum," "smoudge," "thief," "robber," and various other not nice things — all of which was complimentary and but served to increase the dizziness of the high place in which I sat. At that time I had not read "Paradise Lost," and later, when I read Milton's "Better to reign in hell than serve in heaven," I was fully convinced that great minds run in same channels.

3   It was at this time that the fortuitous concatenation of events sent me upon my first adventure on The Road. It happened that there was nothing doing in oysters just then; that at Benicia, forty miles away, I had some blankets I wanted to get; and that at Port Costa, several miles from Benicia, a stolen boat lay at anchor in charge of the constable. Now this boat was owned by a friend of mine, by name Dinny McCrea. It had been stolen and left at Port Costa by Whiskey Bob, another friend of mine. (Poor Whiskey Bob! Only last winter his body was picked up on the beach shot full of holes by nobody knows whom.) I had come down from "up river" some time be-fore, and reported to Dinny McCrea the whereabouts of his boat; and Dinny McCrea had promptly offered ten dollars to me if I should bring it down to Oakland to him.

4   Time was heavy on my hands. I sat on the dock and talked it over with Nickey the Greek, another idle oyster pirate. "Let's go," said I, and Nickey was willing. He was "broke." I possessed fifty cents and a small skiff. The former I invested and loaded into the latter in the form of crackers, canned corned beef, and a ten-cent bottle of French mustard. (We were keen on French mustard in those days.) Then, late in the afternoon, we hoisted our small spritsail and started. We sailed all night, and next morning, on the first of a glorious flood-tide, a fair wind behind us, we came booming up the Car-

quinez Straits to Port Costa. There lay the stolen boat, not twenty-five feet from the wharf. We ran alongside and doused our little spritsail. I sent Nickey forward to lift the anchor, while I began casting off the gaskets.

5   A man ran out on the wharf and hailed us. It was the constable. It suddenly came to me that I had neglected to get a written authorization from Dinny McCrea to take possession of his boat. Also, I knew that constable wanted to charge at least twenty-five dollars in fees for capturing the boat from Whiskey Bob and subsequently taking care of it. And my last fifty cents had been blown in for corned beef and French mustard, and the reward was only ten dollars anyway. I shot a glance forward to Nickey. He had the anchor up-and-down and was straining at it. "Break her out," I whispered to him, and turned and shouted back to the constable. The result was that he and I were talking at the same time, our spoken thoughts colliding in mid-air and making gibberish.

6   The constable grew more imperative, and perforce I had to listen. Nickey was heaving on the anchor till I thought he'd burst a blood-vessel. When the constable got done with his threats and warnings, I asked him who he was. The time he lost in telling me enabled Nickey to break out the anchor. I was doing some quick calculating. At the feet of the constable a ladder ran down the dock to the water, and to the ladder was moored a skiff. The oars were in it. But it was padlocked. I gambled everything on that padlock. I felt the breeze on my cheek, saw the surge of the tide, looked at the remaining gaskets that confined the sail, ran my eyes up the halyards to the blocks and knew that all was clear, and then threw off all dissimulation.

7   "In with her!" I shouted to Nickey, and sprang to the gaskets, casting them loose and thanking my stars that Whiskey Bob had tied them in square-knots instead of "grannies."

8   The constable had slid down the ladder and was fumbling with a key at the padlock. The anchor came aboard and the last gasket was loosed at the same instant that the constable freed the skiff and jumped to the oars.

9   "Peak-halyards!" I commanded my crew, at the same time swinging on to the throat-halyards. Up came the sail on the run. I belayed and ran aft to the tiller.

10   "Stretch her!" I shouted to Nickey at the peak. The constable was just reaching for our stern. A puff of wind caught us, and we shot away. It was great. If I'd had a black flag, I know I'd have run it up in triumph. The constable stood up in the skiff, and paled the glory of the day with the vividness of his language. Also, he wailed for a gun. You see, that was another gamble we had taken.

11   Anyway, we weren't stealing the boat. It wasn't the constable's. We were merely stealing his fees, which was his particular form of graft. And we weren't stealing the fees for ourselves, either; we were stealing them for my friend, Dinny McCrea.

12   Benicia was made in a few minutes, and a few minutes later my blankets

were aboard. I shifted the boat down to the far end of Steamboat Wharf, from which point of vantage we could see anybody coming after us. There was no telling. Maybe the Port Costa constable would telephone to the Benecia constable. Nickey and I held a council of war. We lay on deck in the warm sun, the fresh breeze on our cheeks, the flood-tide rippling and swirling past. It was impossible to start back to Oakland till afternoon, when the ebb would begin to run. But we figured that the constable would have an eye out on the Carquinez Straits when the ebb started, and that nothing remained for us but to wait for the following ebb, at two o'clock next morning, when we could slip by Cerberus in the darkness.

13 So we lay on deck, smoked cigarettes, and were glad that we were alive. I spat over the side and gauged the speed of the current.

14 "With this wind, we could run this flood clear to Rio Vista," I said.

15 "And it's fruit-time on the river," said Nickey.

16 "And low water on the river," said I. "It's the best time of the year to make Sacramento."

17 We sat up and looked at each other. The glorious west wind was pouring over us like wine. We both spat over the side and gauged the current. Now I contend that it was all the fault of that flood-tide and fair wind. They appealed to our sailor instinct. If it had not been for them, the whole chain of events that was to put me upon The Road would have broken down.

18 We said no word, but cast off our moorings and hoisted sail. Our adventures up the Sacramento River are no part of this narrative. We subsequently made the city of Sacramento and tied up at a wharf. The water was fine, and we spent most of our time in swimming. On the sand-bar above the railroad bridge we fell in with a bunch of boys likewise in swimming. Between swims we lay on the bank and talked. They talked differently from the fellows I had been used to herding with. It was a new vernacular. They were road-kids, and with every word they uttered the lure of The Road laid hold of me more imperiously.

19 "When I was down in Alabama," one kid would begin; or, another, "Coming up on the C. & A. from K.C."; whereat, a third kid, "On the C. & A. there ain't no steps to the 'blinds.'" And I would lie silently in the sand and listen. "It was at a little town in Ohio on the Lake Shore and Michigan Southern," a kid would start; and another, "Ever ride the Cannonball on the Wabash?"; and yet another, "Nope, but I've been on the White Mail out of Chicago." "Talk about railroadin' — wait till you hit the Pennsylvania, four tracks, no water tanks, take water on the fly, that's goin' some." "The Northern Pacific's a bad road now." "Salinas is on the 'hog,' the 'bulls' is 'horstile.'" "I got 'pinched' at El Paso, along with Moke Kid." "Talkin' of 'poke-outs,' wait till you hit the French country out of Montreal — not a word of English — you say, '*Mongee, Madame, mongee, no spika da French,*' an' rub your stomach an' look hungry, an' she gives you a slice of sow-belly an' a chunk of dry 'punk.'"

20   And I continued to lie in the sand and listen. These wanderers made my oyster-piracy look like thirty cents. A new world was calling to me in every word that was spoken — a world of rods and gunnels, blind baggages and "side-door Pullmans," "bulls" and "shacks," "floppings" and "chewin's," "pinches" and "get-aways," "strong arms" and "bindle-stiffs," "punks" and "profesh." And it all spelled Adventure. Very well; I would tackle this new world. I "lined" myself up alongside those road-kids. I was just as strong as any of them, just as quick, just as nervy, and my brain was just as good.

21   After the swim, as evening came on, they dressed and went up town. I went along. The kids began "battering" the "main-stem" for "light pieces," or in other words, begging for money on the main street. I had never begged in my life, and this was the hardest thing for me to stomach when I first went on The Road. I had absurd notions about begging. My philosophy, up to that time, was that it was finer to steal than to beg; and that robbery was finer still because the risk and the penalty were proportionately greater. As an oyster pirate I had already earned convictions at the hands of justice, which, if I had tried to serve them, would have required a thousand years in state's prison. To rob was manly; to beg was sordid and despicable. But I developed in the days to come all right, all right, till I came to look upon begging as a joyous prank, a game of wits, a nerve-exerciser.

22   That first night, however, I couldn't rise to it; and the result was that when the kids were ready to go to a restaurant and eat, I wasn't. I was broke. Meeny Kid, I think it was, gave me the price, and we all ate together. But while I ate, I meditated. The receiver, it was said, was as bad as the thief; Meeny Kid had done the begging, and I was profiting by it. I decided that the receiver was a whole lot worse than the thief, and that it shouldn't happen again. And it didn't. I turned out next day and threw my feet as well as the next one.

23   Nickey the Greek's ambition didn't run to The Road. He was not a success at throwing his feet, and he stowed away one night on a barge and went down river to San Francisco. I met him, only a week ago, at a pugilistic carnival. He has progressed. He sat in a place of honor at the ring-side. He is now a manager of prize-fighters and proud of it. In fact, in a small way, in local sportdom, he is quite a shining light.

24   "No kid is a road-kid until he has gone over 'the hill' " — such was the law of The Road I heard expounded in Sacramento. All right, I'd go over the hill and matriculate. "The hill," by the way, was the Sierra Nevadas. The whole gang was going over the hill on a jaunt, and of course I'd go along. It was French Kid's first adventure on The Road. He had just run away from his people in San Francisco. It was up to him and me to deliver the goods. In passing, I may remark that my old title of "Prince" had vanished. I had received my "monica." I was now "Sailor Kid," later to be known as " 'Frisco Kid," when I had put the Rockies between me and my native state.

25   At 10.20 P.M. the Central Pacific overland pulled out of the depot at

Sacramento for the East — that particular item of time-table is indelibly engraved on my memory. There were about a dozen in our gang, and we strung out in the darkness ahead of the train ready to take her out. All the local road-kids that we knew came down to see us off — also, to "ditch" us if they could. That was their idea of a joke, and there were only about forty of them to carry it out. Their ring-leader was a crackerjack road-kid named Bob. Sacramento was his home town, but he'd hit The Road pretty well everywhere over the whole country. He took French Kid and me aside and gave us advice something like this: "We're goin' to try an' ditch your bunch, see? Youse two are weak. The rest of the push can take care of itself. So, as soon as youse two nail a blind, deck her. An' stay on the decks till youse pass Roseville Junction, at which burg the constables are horstile, sloughin' in everybody on sight."

26   The engine whistled and the overland pulled out. There were three blinds on her — room for all of us. The dozen of us who were trying to make her out would have preferred to slip aboard quietly; but our forty friends crowded on with the most amazing and shameless publicity and advertisement. Following Bob's advice, I immediately "decked her," that is, climbed up on top of the roof of one of the mail-cars. There I lay down, my heart jumping a few extra beats, and listened to the fun. The whole train crew was forward, and the ditching went on fast and furious. After the train had run half a mile, it stopped, and the crew came forward again and ditched the survivors. I, alone, had made the train out.

27   Back at the depot, about him two or three of the push that had witnessed the accident, lay French Kid with both legs off. French Kid had slipped or stumbled — that was all, and the wheels had done the rest. Such was my initiation to The Road. It was two years afterward when I next saw French Kid and examined his "stumps." This was an act of courtesy. "Cripples" always like to have their stumps examined. One of the entertaining sights on The Road is to witness the meeting of two cripples. Their common disability is a fruitful source of conversation; and they tell how it happened, describe what they know of the amputation, pass critical judgment on their own and each other's surgeons, and wind up by withdrawing to one side, taking off bandages and wrappings, and comparing stumps.

28   But it was not until several days later, over in Nevada, when the push caught up with me, that I learned of French Kid's accident. The push itself arrived in bad condition. It had gone through a train-wreck in the snow-sheds; Happy Joe was on crutches with two mashed legs, and the rest were nursing skins and bruises.

29   In the meantime, I lay on the roof of the mail-car, trying to remember whether Roseville Junction, against which burg Bob had warned me, was the first stop or the second stop. To make sure, I delayed descending to the platform of the blind until after the second stop. And then I didn't descend. I was new to the game, and I felt safer where I was. But I never told the push

that I held down the decks the whole night, clear across the Sierras, through snow-sheds and tunnels, and down to Truckee on the other side, where I arrived at seven in the morning. Such a thing was disgraceful, and I'd have been a common laughing-stock. This is the first time I have confessed the truth about that first ride over the hill. As for the push, it decided that I was all right, and when I came back over the hill to Sacramento, I was a full-fledged road-kid.

30 Yet I had much to learn. Bob was my mentor, and he was all right. I remember one evening (it was fair-time in Sacramento, and we were knocking about and having a good time) when I lost my hat in a fight. There was I bare-headed in the street, and it was Bob to the rescue. He took me to one side from the push and told me what to do. I was a bit timid of his advice. I had just come out of jail, where I had been three days, and I knew that if the police "pinched" me again, I'd get good and "soaked." On the other hand, I couldn't show the white feather. I'd been over the hill, I was running full-fledged with the push, and it was up to me to deliver the goods. So I accepted Bob's advice, and he came along with me to see that I did it up brown.

31 We took our position on K Street, on the corner, I think, of Fifth. It was early in the evening and the street was crowded. Bob studied the head-gear of every Chinaman that passed. I used to wonder how the road-kids all managed to wear "five-dollar Stetson stiff-rims," and now I knew. They got them, the way I was going to get mine, from the Chinese. I was nervous — there were so many people about; but Bob was cool as an iceberg. Several times, when I started forward toward a Chinaman, all nerved and keyed up, Bob dragged me back. He wanted me to get a good hat, and one that fitted. Now a hat came by that was the right size but not new; and, after a dozen impossible hats, along would come one that was new but not the right size. And when one did come by that was new and the right size, the rim was too large or not large enough. My, Bob was finicky. I was so wrought up that I'd have snatched any kind of a head-covering.

32 At last came the hat, the one hat in Sacramento for me. I knew it was a winner as soon as I looked at it. I glanced at Bob. He sent a sweeping lookabout for police, then nodded his head. I lifted the hat from the Chinaman's head and pulled it down on my own. It was a perfect fit. Then I started. I heard Bob crying out, and I caught a glimpse of him blocking the irate Mongolian and tripping him up. I ran on. I turned up the next corner, and around the next. This street was not so crowded as K, and I walked along in quietude, catching my breath and congratulating myself upon my hat and my get-away.

33 And then, suddenly, around the corner at my back, came the bare-headed Chinaman. With him were a couple more Chinamen, and at their heels were half a dozen men and boys. I sprinted to the next corner, crossed the street, and rounded the following corner. I decided that I had surely played him out, and I dropped into a walk again. But around the corner at

my heels came that persistent Mongolian. It was the old story of the hare and the tortoise. He could not run so fast as I, but he stayed with it, plodding along at a shambling and deceptive trot, and wasting much good breath in noisy imprecations. He called all Sacramento to witness the dishonor that had been done him, and a goodly portion of Sacramento heard and flocked at his heels. And I ran on like the hare, and ever that persistent Mongolian, with the increasing rabble, overhauled me. But finally, when a policeman had joined his following, I let out all my links. I twisted and turned, and I swear I ran at least twenty blocks on the straight away. And I never saw that Chinaman again. The hat was a dandy, a brand-new Stetson, just out of the shop, and it was the envy of the whole push. Furthermore, it was the symbol that I had delivered the goods. I wore it for over a year.

34   Road-kids are nice little chaps — when you get them alone and they are telling you "how it happened"; but take my word for it, watch out for them when they run in pack. Then they are wolves, and like wolves they are capable of dragging down the strongest man. At such times they are not cowardly. They will fling themselves upon a man and hold on with every ounce of strength in their wiry bodies, till he is thrown and helpless. More than once have I seen them do it, and I know whereof I speak. Their motive is usually robbery. And watch out for the "strong arm." Every kid in the push I travelled with was expert at it. Even French Kid mastered it before he lost his legs.

35   I have strong upon me now a vision of what I once saw in "The Willows." The Willows was a clump of trees in a waste piece of land near the railway depot and not more than five minutes walk from the heart of Sacramento. It is night-time, and the scene is illumined by the thin light of stars. I see a husky laborer in the midst of a pack of road-kids. He is infuriated and cursing them, not a bit afraid, confident of his own strength. He weighs about one hundred and eighty pounds, and his muscles are hard; but he doesn't know what he is up against. The kids are snarling. It is not pretty. They make a rush from all sides, and he lashes out and whirls. Barber Kid is standing beside me. As the man whirls, Barber Kid leaps forward and does the trick. Into the man's back goes his knee; around the man's neck, from behind, passes his right hand, the bone of the wrist pressing against the jugular vein. Barber Kid throws his whole weight backward. It is a powerful leverage. Besides, the man's wind has been shut off. It is the strong arm.

36   The man resists, but he is already practically helpless. The road-kids are upon him from every side, clinging to arms and legs and body, and like a wolf at the throat of a moose Barber Kid hangs on and drags backward. Over the man goes, and down under the heap. Barber Kid changes the position of his own body, but never lets go. While some of the kids are "going through" the victim, others are holding his legs so that he cannot kick and thresh about. They improve the opportunity by taking off the man's shoes. As for him, he has given in. He is beaten. Also, what of the strong arm at his throat, he is short of wind. He is making ugly choking noises, and the kids

hurry. They really don't want to kill him. All is done. At a word all holds are released at once, and the kids scatter, one of them lugging the shoes — he knows where he can get half a dollar for them. The man sits up and looks about him, dazed and helpless. Even if he wanted to, bare-footed pursuit in the darkness would be hopeless. I linger a moment and watch him. He is feeling at his throat, making dry, hawking noises, and jerking his head in a quaint way as though to assure himself that the neck is not dislocated. Then I slip away to join the push, and see that man no more — though I shall always see him, sitting there in the starlight, somewhat dazed, a bit frightened, greatly dishevelled, and making quaint jerking movements of head and neck.

37   Drunken men are the especial prey of the road-kids. Robbing a drunken man they call "rolling a stiff"; and wherever they are, they are on the constant lookout for drunks. The drunk is their particular meat, as the fly is the particular meat of the spider. The rolling of a stiff is ofttimes an amusing sight, especially when the stiff is helpless and when interference is unlikely. At the first swoop the stiff's money and jewellery go. Then the kids sit around their victim in a sort of pow-wow. A kid generates a fancy for the stiff's necktie. Off it comes. Another kid is after underclothes. Off they come, and a knife quickly abbreviates arms and legs. Friendly hoboes may be called in to take the coat and trousers, which are too large for the kids. And in the end they depart, leaving beside the stiff the heap of their discarded rags.

38   Another vision comes to me. It is a dark night. My push is coming along the sidewalk in the suburbs. Ahead of us, under an electric light, a man crosses the street diagonally. There is something tentative and desultory in his walk. The kids scent the game on the instant. The man is drunk. He blunders across the opposite sidewalk and is lost in the darkness as he takes a short-cut through a vacant lot. No hunting cry is raised, but the pack flings itself forward in quick pursuit. In the middle of the vacant lot it comes upon him. But what is this? — snarling and strange forms, small and dim and menacing, are between the pack and its prey. It is another pack of road-kids, and in the hostile pause we learn that it is their meat, that they have been trailing it a dozen blocks and more and that we are butting in. But it is the world primeval. These wolves are baby wolves. (As a matter of fact, I don't think one of them was over twelve or thirteen years of age. I met some of them afterward, and learned that they had just arrived that day over the hill, and that they hailed from Denver and Salt Lake City.) Our pack flings forward. The baby wolves squeal and screech and fight like little demons. All about the drunken man rages the struggle for the possession of him. Down he goes in the thick of it, and the combat rages over his body after the fashion of the Greeks and Trojans over the body and armor of a fallen hero. Amid cries and tears and wailings the baby wolves are dispossessed, and my pack rolls the stiff. But always I remember the poor stiff and his befuddled

amazement at the abrupt eruption of battle in the vacant lot. I see him now, dim in the darkness, titubating in stupid wonder, good-naturedly essaying the rôle of peacemaker in that multitudinous scrap the significance of which he did not understand, and the really hurt expression on his face when he, unoffending he, was clutched at by many hands and dragged down in the thick of the press.

39 "Bindle-stiffs" are favorite prey of the road-kids. A bindle-stiff is a working tramp. He takes his name from the roll of blankets he carries, which is known as a "bindle." Because he does work, a bindle-stiff is expected usually to have some small change about him, and it is after that small change that the road-kids go. The best hunting-ground for bindle-stiffs is in the sheds, barns, lumber-yards, railroad-yards, etc., on the edges of a city, and the time for hunting is the night, when the bindle-stiff seeks these places to roll up in his blankets and sleep.

40 "Gay-cats" also come to grief at the hands of the road-kids. In more familiar parlance, gay-cats are short-horns, *chechaquos*, new chums, or tenderfeet. A gay-cat is a newcomer on The Road who is man-grown, or, at least, youth-grown. A boy on The Road, on the other hand, no matter how green he is, is never a gay-cat; he is a road-kid or a "punk," and if he travels with a "profesh," he is known possessively as a "prushun." I was never a prushun, for I did not take kindly to possession. I was first a road-kid and then a profesh. Because I started in young, I practically skipped my gay-cat apprenticeship. For a short period, during the time I was exchanging my 'Frisco Kid monica for that of Sailor Jack, I labored under the suspicion of being a gay-cat. But closer acquaintance on the part of those that suspected me quickly disabused their minds, and in a short time I acquired the unmistakable airs and ear-marks of the blowed-in-the-glass profesh. And be it known, here and now, that the profesh are the aristocracy of The Road. They are the lords and masters, the aggressive men, the primordial noblemen, the *blond beasts* so beloved of Nietzsche.

41 When I came back over the hill from Nevada, I found that some river pirate had stolen Dinny McCrea's boat. (A funny thing at this day is that I cannot remember what became of the skiff in which Nickey the Greek and I sailed from Oakland to Port Costa. I know that the constable didn't get it, and I know that it didn't go with us up the Sacramento River, and that is all I do know.) With the loss of Dinny McCrea's boat, I was pledged to The Road; and when I grew tired of Sacramento, I said good-by to the push (which, in its friendly way, tried to ditch me from a freight as I left town) and started on a *passear* down the valley of the San Joaquin. The Road had gripped me and would not let me go; and later, when I had voyaged to sea and done one thing and another, I returned to The Road to make longer flights, to be a "comet" and a profesh, and to plump into the bath of sociology that wet me to the skin.

Commentary and questions

1. *Paragraphs 1-22:* The technique is primarily narrative, but some paragraphs are analytical. Separate the two types. What does London suggest
his motives were for going on the road? How would you describe his
youthful set of values? Support your description by statements in the
text. What can you discover about his attitude toward his early career
at the time he was writing?

2. *Paragraphs 24-27:* What is the tone? What words signal a change to
come in paragraph 28? Is the manner of the early paragraphs preserved?

3. *Paragraphs 32-33:* What language contributes to the impression that
the theft of the Chinaman's hat was a game?

4. *Paragraphs 34-38:* In the incidents narrated here London characterizes "road-kids" as "wolves." Is the metaphor facetious or serious? London calls the incident in which a drunk is "rolled" an "amusing sight."
Does his description bear out this comment? Note the simile to a combat
between Greeks and Trojans in paragraph 38.

5. *Paragraph 41:* Is the last paragraph appropriate? Study the "literary"
or formal vocabulary in this section. What is its impact?

Topics for discussion and writing

I. Much of London's style is narrative. Discuss the ways in which he
uses narrative statement, or modifies it, to establish tone and point of
view. What variety do you find in the tone? What purposes do they
serve?

II. Write a theme comparing London's narrative technique to that of
Synge.

III. Write a theme comparing London's view of the vagrant life to that
of Synge. You might want to consider the following questions: What is
the attitude of each toward legal authority? How do they compare in
finding "romance" and "tragedy" in this life? Are they both equally interested in the personalities they describe?

IV. Make a list of the various aspects of road life that London takes up.
Where does each come in the narrative? Is there any purpose behind
their order? What stylistic techniques (types of statement, metaphor,
connotation, slang, formal language, etc.) predominate in each section?

V. Write an essay in which you explain, with supporting evidence, what
London's attitude toward the road-kids and their actions is.

PADDY

George Orwell

From Down and Out in Paris
and London. *Harcourt, Brace
and Company. Copyright 1933
by George Orwell. Canadian
rights granted by Secker and
Warburg, London.*

PADDY was my mate for about the next fortnight, and, as he was the first tramp I had known at all well, I want to give an account of him. I believe that he was a typical tramp and there are tens of thousands in England like him.

2   He was a tallish man, aged about thirty-five, with fair hair going grizzled and watery blue eyes. His features were good, but his cheeks had lanked and had that greyish, dirty in the grain look that comes of a bread and margarine diet. He was dressed, rather better than most tramps, in a tweed shooting-jacket and a pair of old evening trousers with the braid still on them. Evidently the braid figured in his mind as a lingering scrap of respectability, and he took care to sew it on again when it came loose. He was careful of his appearance altogether, and carried a razor and bootbrush that he would not sell, though he had sold his "papers" and even his pocket-knife long since. Nevertheless, one would have known him for a tramp a hundred yards away. There was something in his drifting style of walk, and the way he had of hunching his shoulders forward, essentially abject. Seeing him walk, you felt instinctively that he would sooner take a blow than give one.

3   He had been brought up in Ireland, served two years in the war, and then worked in a metal polish factory, where he had lost his job two years earlier. He was horribly ashamed of being a tramp, but he had picked up all a tramp's ways. He browsed the pavements unceasingly, never missing a cigarette end, or even an empty cigarette packet, as he used the tissue paper for rolling cigarettes. On our way into Edbury he saw a newspaper parcel on the pavement, pounced on it, and found that it contained two mutton sandwiches, rather frayed at the edges; these he insisted on my sharing. He never passed an automatic machine without giving a tug at the handle, for he said that sometimes they are out of order and will eject pennies if you tug at them. He had no stomach for crime, however. When we were in the outskirts of Romton, Paddy noticed a bottle of milk on a doorstep, evidently left there by mistake. He stopped, eyeing the bottle hungrily.

4   "Christ!" he said, "dere's good food goin' to waste. Somebody could knock dat bottle off, eh? Knock it off easy."

5   I saw that he was thinking of "knocking it off" himself. He looked up and down the street; it was a quiet residential street and there was nobody in sight. Paddy's sickly, chap-fallen face yearned over the milk. Then he turned away, saying gloomily:

"Best leave it. It don't do a man no good to steal. T'ank God, I ain't never stolen nothin' yet."

7   It was funk, bred of hunger, that kept him virtuous. With only two or three sound meals in his belly, he would have found courage to steal the milk.

8   He had two subjects of conversation, the shame and come-down of being a tramp, and the best way of getting a free meal. As we drifted through the streets he would keep up a monologue in this style, in a whimpering, self-pitying Irish voice:

9   "It's hell bein' on de road, eh? It breaks yer heart goin' into dem bloody spikes. But what's a man to do else, eh? I ain't had a good meat meal for about two months, an' me boots is getting bad, an' — Christ! How'd it be if we was to try for a cup o' tay at one o' dem convents on de way to Edbury? Most times dey're good for a cup o' tay. Ah, what'd a man do widout religion, eh? I've took cups o' tay from de convents, an' de Baptists, an' de Church of England, an' all sorts. I'm a Catholic meself. Dat's to say, I ain't been to confession for about seventeen year, but still I got me religious feelin's, y'understand. An' dem convents is always good for a cup o' tay . . ." etc. etc. He would keep this up all day, almost without stopping.

10   His ignorance was limitless and appalling. He once asked me, for instance, whether Napoleon lived before Jesus Christ or after. Another time, when I was looking into a bookshop window, he grew very perturbed because one of the books was called *Of the Imitation of Christ*. He took this for blasphemy. "What de hell do dey want to go imitatin' of *Him* for?" he demanded angrily. He could read, but he had a kind of loathing for books. On our way from Romton to Edbury I went into a public library, and, though Paddy did not want to read, I suggested that he should come in and rest his legs. But he preferred to wait on the pavement. "No," he said, "de sight of all dat bloody print makes me sick."

11   Like most tramps, he was passionately mean about matches. He had a box of matches when I met him, but I never saw him strike one, and he used to lecture me for extravagance when I struck mine. His method was to cadge a light from strangers, sometimes going without a smoke for half an hour rather than strike a match.

12   Self-pity was the clue to his character. The thought of his bad luck never seemed to leave him for an instant. He would break long silences to exclaim, apropos of nothing, "It's hell when yer clo'es begin to go up de spout, eh?" or "Dat tay in de spike ain't tay, it's piss," as though there was nothing else in the world to think about. And he had a low, worm-like envy of anyone who was better off — not of the rich, for they were beyond his social horizon, but of men in work. He pined for work as an artist pines to be famous. If he saw an old man working he would say bitterly, "Look at dat old —— keepin' able-bodied men out o' work"; or if it was a boy, "It's dem young devils what's takin' de bread out of our mouths." And all foreigners to him were "dem bloody dagoes" — for, according to his theory, foreigners were responsible for unemployment.

13 He looked at women with a mixture of longing and hatred. Young, pretty women were too much above him to enter into his ideas, but his mouth watered at prostitutes. A couple of scarlet-lipped old creatures would go past; Paddy's face would flush pale pink, and he would turn and stare hungrily after the women. "Tarts!" he would murmur, like a boy at a sweet-shop window. He told me once that he had not had to do with a woman for two years — since he had lost his job, that is — and he had forgotten that one could aim higher than prostitutes. He had the regular character of a tramp — abject, envious, a jackal's character.

14 Nevertheless, he was a good fellow, generous by nature and capable of sharing his last crust with a friend; indeed he did literally share his last crust with me more than once. He was probably capable of work too, if he had been well fed for a few months. But two years of bread and margarine had lowered his standards hopelessly. He had lived on this filthy imitation of food till his own mind and body were compounded of inferior stuff. It was malnutrition and not any native vice that had destroyed his manhood.

II

1 On the way to Edbury I told Paddy that I had a friend from whom I could be sure of getting money, and suggested going straight into London rather than face another night in the spike. But Paddy had not been in Edbury spike recently, and, tramp-like, he would not waste a night's free lodging. We arranged to go into London the next morning. I had only a halfpenny, but Paddy had two shillings, which would get us a bed each and a few cups of tea.

2 The Edbury spike did not differ much from the one at Romton. The worst feature was that all tobacco was confiscated at the gate, and we were warned that any man caught smoking would be turned out at once. Under the Vagrancy Act tramps can be prosecuted for smoking in the spike — in fact, they can be prosecuted for almost anything; but the authorities generally save the trouble of a prosecution by turning disobedient men out of doors. There was no work to do, and the cells were fairly comfortable. We slept two in a cell, "one up, one down" — that is, one on a wooden shelf and one on the floor, with straw palliasses and plenty of blankets, dirty but not verminous. The food was the same as at Romton, except that we had tea instead of cocoa. One could get extra tea in the morning, as the Tramp Major was selling it at a halfpenny a mug, illicitly no doubt. We were each given a hunk of bread and cheese to take away for our midday meal.

3 When we got into London we had eight hours to kill before the lodging-houses opened. It is curious how one does not notice things. I had been in London innumerable times, and yet till that day I had never noticed one of the worst things about London — the fact that it costs money even to sit down. In Paris, if you had no money and could not find a public bench, you would sit on the pavement. Heaven knows what sitting on the pavement

would lead to in London — prison, probably. By four we had stood five hours, and our feet seemed red-hot from the hardness of the stones. We were hungry, having eaten our ration as soon as we left the spike, and I was out of tobacco — it mattered less to Paddy, who picked up cigarette ends. We tried two churches and found them locked. Then we tried a public library, but there were no seats in it. As a last hope Paddy suggested trying a Rowton House; by the rules they would not let us in before seven, but we might slip in unnoticed. We walked up to the magnificent doorway (the Rowton Houses really are magnificent) and very casually, trying to look like regular lodgers, began to stroll in. Instantly a man lounging in the doorway, a sharp-faced fellow, evidently in some position of authority, barred the way.

4   "You men sleep 'ere last night?"

5   "No."

6   "Then —— off."

7   We obeyed, and stood two more hours on the street corner. It was unpleasant, but it taught me not to use the expression "street corner loafer," so I gained something from it.

8   At six we went to a Salvation Army shelter. We could not book beds till eight and it was not certain that there would be any vacant, but an official, who called us "Brother," let us in on the condition that we paid for two cups of tea. The main hall of the shelter was a great white-washed barn of a place, oppressively clean and bare, with no fires. Two hundred decentish, rather subdued-looking people were sitting packed on long wooden benches. One or two officers in uniform prowled up and down. On the wall were pictures of General Booth, and notices prohibiting cooking, drinking, spitting, swearing, quarreling and gambling. As a specimen of these notices, here is one that I copied word for word:

> "Any man found gambling or playing cards will be expelled and will not be admitted under any circumstances.
> "A reward will be given for information leading to the discovery of such persons.
> "The officers in charge appeal to all lodgers to assist them in keeping this hostel free from the DETESTABLE EVIL OF GAMBLING."

9   "Gambling or playing cards" is a delightful phrase.

10   To my eye these Salvation Army shelters, though clean, are far drearier than the worst of the common lodging-houses. There is such a hopelessness about some of the people there — decent, broken-down types who have pawned their collars but are still trying for office jobs. Coming to a Salvation Army shelter, where it is at least clean, is their last clutch at respectability. At the next table to me were two foreigners, dressed in rags but manifestly gentlemen. They were playing chess verbally, not even writing down the moves. One of them was blind, and I heard them say that they had been saving up for a long time to buy a board, price half a crown, but could never

manage it. Here and there were clerks out of work, pallid and moody. Among a group of them a tall, thin, deadly pale young man was talking excitedly. He thumped his fist on the table and boasted in a strange, feverish style. When the officers were out of hearing he broke out into startling blasphemies:

11 "I tell you what, boys, I'm going to get that job tomorrow. I'm not one of your bloody down-on-the-knee brigade; I can look after myself. Look at that —— notice there! 'The Lord will provide!' A bloody lot He's ever provided me with. You don't catch me trusting to the —— Lord. You leave it to me, boys. *I'm going to get that job,*" etc. etc.

12 I watched him, struck by the wild, agitated way in which he talked; he seemed hysterical, or perhaps a little drunk. An hour later I went into a small room, apart from the main hall, which was intended for reading. It had no books or papers in it, so few of the lodgers went there. As I opened the door I saw the young clerk in there all alone; he was on his knees, *praying.* Before I shut the door again I had time to see his face, and it looked agonised. Quite suddenly I realised, from the expression of his face, that he was starving.

13 The charge for beds was eightpence. Paddy and I had fivepence left, and we spent it at the "bar," where food was cheap, though not so cheap as in some common lodging-houses. The tea appeared to be made with tea *dust,* which I fancy had been given to the Salvation Army in charity, though they sold it at three-halfpence a cup. It was foul stuff. At ten o'clock an officer marched round the hall blowing a whistle. Immediately everyone stood up.

14 "What's this for?" I said to Paddy, astonished.

15 "Dat means you has to go off to bed. An' you has to look sharp about it, too."

16 Obediently as sheep, the whole two hundred men trooped off to bed, under the command of the officers.

17 The dormitory was a great attic like a barrack room, with sixty or seventy beds in it. They were clean and tolerably comfortable, but very narrow and very close together, so that one breathed straight into one's neighbour's face. Two officers slept in the room, to see that there was no smoking and no talking after lights-out. Paddy and I had scarcely a wink of sleep, for there was a man near us who had some nervous trouble, shell-shock perhaps, which made him cry out "Pip!" at irregular intervals. It was a loud, startling noise, something like the toot of a small motor-horn. You never knew when it was coming, and it was a sure preventer of sleep. It appeared that Pip, as the others called him, slept regularly in the shelter, and he must have kept ten or twenty people awake every night. He was an example of the kind of thing that prevents one from ever getting enough sleep when men are herded as they are in these lodging-houses.

18 At seven another whistle blew, and the officers went round shaking those who did not get up at once. Since then I have slept in a number of

Salvation Army shelters, and found that, though the different houses vary a little, this semi-military discipline is the same in all of them. They are certainly cheap, but they are too like workhouses for my taste. In some of them there is even a compulsory religious service once or twice a week, which the lodgers must attend or leave the house. The fact is that the Salvation Army are so in the habit of thinking themselves a charitable body that they cannot even run a lodging-house without making it stink of charity.

19   At ten I went to B.'s office and asked him to lend me a pound. He gave me two pounds and told me to come again when necessary, so that Paddy and I were free of money troubles for a week at least. We loitered the day in Trafalgar Square, looking for a friend of Paddy's who never turned up, and at night went to a lodging-house in a back alley near the Strand. The charge was elevenpence, but it was a dark, evil-smelling place, and a notorious haunt for the "nancy boys." Downstairs, in the murky kitchen, three ambiguous-looking youths in smartish blue suits were sitting on a bench apart, ignored by the other lodgers. I suppose they were "nancy boys." They looked the same type as the apache boys one sees in Paris, except that they wore no side-whiskers. In front of the fire a fully dressed man and a stark-naked man were bargaining. They were newspaper sellers. The dressed man was selling his clothes to the naked man. He said:

20   " 'Ere y'are, the best rig-out you ever 'ad. A tosheroon [half a crown] for the coat, two 'ogs for the trousers, one and a tanner for the boots, and a 'og for the cap and scarf. That's seven bob."

21   "You got a 'ope! I'll give yer one and a tanner for the coat, a 'og for the trousers, and two 'ogs for the rest. That's four and a tanner."

22   "Take the 'ole lot for five and a tanner, chum."

23   "Right y'are, off with 'em. I got to get out to sell my late edition."

24   The clothed man stripped, and in three minutes their positions were reversed; the naked man dressed, and the other kilted with a sheet of the *Daily Mail.*

25   The dormitory was dark and close, with fifteen beds in it. There was a horrible hot reek of urine, so beastly that at first one tried to breathe in small, shallow puffs, not filling one's lungs to the bottom. As I lay down in bed a man loomed out of the darkness, leant over me and began babbling in an educated, half-drunken voice:

26   "An old public school boy, what? [He had heard me say something to Paddy.] Don't meet many of the old school here. I am an old Etonian. You know — twenty years hence this weather and all that." He began to quaver out the Eton boating-song, not untunefully:

>   "Jolly boating weather,
>   And a hay harvest——"

27   "Stop that —— noise!" shouted several lodgers.

28   "Low types," said the old Etonian, "very low types. Funny sort of place for you and me, eh? Do you know what my friends say to me? They say,

'M——, you are past redemption.' Quite true, I *am* past redemption. I've come down in the world; not like these ——s here, who couldn't come down if they tried. We chaps who have come down ought to hang together a bit. Youth will be still in our faces — you know. May I offer you a drink?"

29   He produced a bottle of cherry brandy, and at the same moment lost his balance and fell heavily across my legs. Paddy, who was undressing, pulled him upright.

30   "Get back to yer bed, you silly ole ——!"

31   The old Etonian walked unsteadily to his bed and crawled under the sheets with all his clothes on, even his boots. Several times in the night I heard him murmuring, "M——, you are past redemption," as though the phrase appealed to him. In the morning he was lying asleep fully dressed, with the bottle clasped in his arms. He was a man of about fifty, with a re-fined, worn face, and, curiously enough, quite fashionably dressed. It was queer to see his good patent-leather shoes sticking out of that filthy bed. It occurred to me, too, that the cherry brandy must have cost the equivalent of a fortnight's lodging, so he could not have been seriously hard up. Perhaps he frequented common lodging-houses in search of the "nancy boys."

32   The beds were not more than two feet apart. About midnight I woke up to find that the man next to me was trying to steal the money from beneath my pillow. He was pretending to be asleep while he did it, sliding his hand under the pillow as gently as a rat. In the morning I saw that he was a hunchback, with long, apelike arms. I told Paddy about the attempted theft. He laughed and said:

33   "Christ! You got to get used to dat. Dese lodgin' houses is full o' thieves. In some houses dere's nothin' safe but to sleep wid all yer clo'es on. I seen 'em steal a wooden leg off a cripple before now. Once I see a man — fourteen stone man he was — come into a lodgin'-house wid four pound ten. He puts it under his mattress. 'Now,' he says, 'any —— dat touches dat money does it over my body,' he says. But dey done him all de same. In de mornin' he woke up on de floor. Four fellers had took his mattress by de corners an' lifted him off as light as a feather. He never saw his four pound ten again."

Commentary and questions

Section I

1. *Paragraphs 1-7:* There are examples of three kinds of material: a physical description of Paddy, his past history, and revealing incident. Each of these brings out something significant about the man. Analyze the means Orwell uses for this process. How much direct comment of his own does he make?

2. *Paragraph 9:* What is the dominant theme of Paddy's conversation? How does Orwell employ humor?

3. *Paragraphs 10-13:* Each paragraph takes up an aspect of Paddy's character. How many different stylistic techniques does Orwell use?

4. *Paragraph 14:* Does Orwell feel it necessary to mention Paddy's virtues? What does he suggest about the causes for Paddy's attitudes and behavior?

5. How many paragraphs begin with conclusive statements? Do such statements govern the selection of descriptive detail? What sort govern the selection of descriptive detail? What sort of detail may have been omitted?

Section II

6. This section describes Orwell's and Paddy's adventures in several types of lodging and shelter, the Edbury spike, a Rowton House, the Salvation Army shelter, and a cheap rooming house. Is there anything significant about the order in which these appear?

7. *Paragraph 2:* How does Orwell's description of the no-smoking rule render his attitude toward the "spike"?

8. *Paragraphs 8-10:* Orwell definitely intrudes his own commentary into the description, but it nevertheless needs the reader's interpretation. Why does he call the shelter "oppressively clean"? What is the effect of the phrase "decentish, subdued-looking people"? He notes that the rule about "gambling and playing cards" is a "delightful phrase." What is the point of the irony? Orwell describes several types of people. What does he suggest about them as a group? What is the effect of Orwell's discovery that the young man is starving? Does it in any way reveal his attitude toward organized charity?

9. *Paragraphs 13-18:* What central idea organizes this description of a night in the shelter? What techniques does Orwell use to reveal that idea?

10. *Paragraphs 19-33:* List the types of people described. What does Orwell do to influence the reader's reaction to them? What is his own attitude? Is it constant or varied? Is Paddy's account of nighttime theft merely funny?

Topics for discussion and writing

I. List the major types of statement Orwell uses. How are they used to suggest his attitude about the situations he describes? How does he attempt to provoke the reader's disgust? Is one's reaction to despise the people Orwell depicts, or does revulsion go in another direction?

II. Does Orwell's account qualify as factual, objective reporting in spite of the personal opinion he occasionally expresses?

III. Write a theme discussing Orwell's opinions of organized charity.

IV. Write a theme comparing Synge, London, and Orwell on one or more of the following points: (a) the extent to which they romanticize or "expose" vagrant life; (b) what they suggest about the causes and motives for individuals' taking to vagrancy; (c) their attitudes toward the people they portray and the attitudes they report toward the rules and laws of conventional, respectable society; (d) their methods of presenting their material.

V. Which author makes the most effective use of the technique of personal reporting? What standards do you choose by which to evaluate their technique?

VI. Write a theme discussing the use each author makes of reported conversation. Be sure to examine the context in which dialogue appears and the effect of dialogue as both evidence and atmosphere.

The Guggenheim Museum: PLAN AND PHOTOGRAPHS

· THE MODERN GALLERY, from *Architectural Forum* · GUGGENHEIM MUSEUM IN PROGRESS, from *Architectural Record* · WRIGHT VS. PAINTING, **John Canaday**

ALL these essays convey an impression of the Solomon R. Guggenheim Memorial Museum in New York.

The first two authors wrote before the museum was completed. They consider it as a building, as architecture, and their predisposition in its favor is clear from the outset. Both recognize that they are dealing with an aesthetic judgment, and neither weighs the pros and cons in an objective, logical way. Each explains what he sees that attracts him. The third author, Canaday, writes about the building as a museum, rather than the museum as a building. His different point of view leads him to a different conclusion.

All write about the building in terms of their own concepts. The comparison of the building to a chambered nautilus, a leaf, the wing of a bird, and a snail implies the notion that there is a relation between this building and nature. But this relationship exists in the mind only. The assumption of one author that the ramps spiral up and of the other that they spiral down convey concepts that also belong to the authors rather than to the building.

The difficulty, if not the impossibility, of "objective" description, the pitfalls as well as advantages of "persuasive" description, become clearer as the writers try to describe one object in both ways. The photographs and drawing are included as a controlled subject for description as well as illumination for the essays.

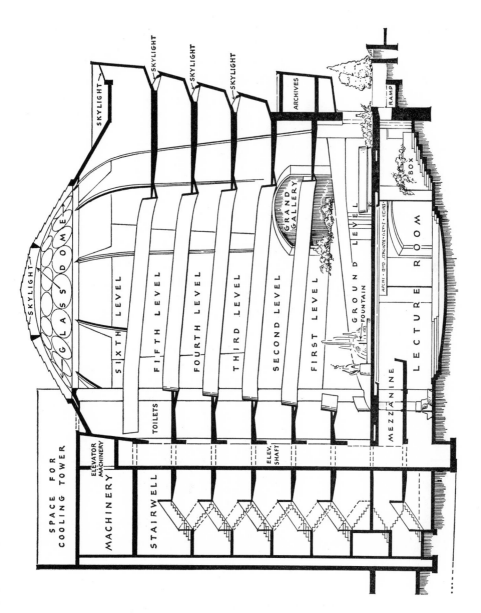

(*Redrawn from* ARCHITECTURAL RECORD)

The labels in the figure read:

SKYLIGHT
SKYLIGHT
SKYLIGHT
SKYLIGHT
SKYLIGHT
ARCHIVES
RAMP
SKYLIGHT
GLASS DOME
GRAND GALLERY
BOX
SIXTH LEVEL
FIFTH LEVEL
FOURTH LEVEL
THIRD LEVEL
SECOND LEVEL
FIRST LEVEL
GROUND LEVEL
FOUNTAIN
LECTURE ROOM
TOILETS
MEZZANINE
SPACE FOR COOLING TOWER
ELEVATOR MACHINERY
MACHINERY
STAIRWELL
ELEV. SHAFT

*A full view of the Guggenheim Museum
through the trees of Central Park*

Skylight and spiral ramp from the main floor

Typical bays of paintings

View across the gallery

THE MODERN GALLERY

THE supreme achievement of a great architect, the thing that sets him apart from lesser men for all time, is not merely his arrangement of areas for convenient use, nor the setting up of a structure that is both sound and economical: it is the creation of a space so enclosed that the very air inside seems to be alive. For a generation reared to consider the functional solution as the basic problem in architecture, this concept may seem strange to the point of heresy, yet historically it is the only one that retains validity. In every period the problems of function and structure have been solved with greater or less success, as the case may be, but it is some other quality that sets the great buildings apart from the others. St. Sophia in Istanbul contains a vast quantity of air, as does the concourse in New York's Pennsylvania Station: their difference lies in the staggering emotional impact produced by the former. Certain artists working in architecture have the ability to so arrange masses, shapes, surfaces and colors that the space enclosed comes to life and the building becomes merely a vessel. Frank Lloyd Wright is one of the very few who have had the ability to do this. Strangely enough, he is also practically the only contemporary architect known by name to the average American.

2   About a month ago Wright's model of the proposed Guggenheim museum of non-objective art, the Modern Gallery, was unveiled in New York for members of the press. It was promptly run in all of the big morning and afternoon papers, and, a few days later, in TIME, LIFE and other magazines. The building is an extraordinary building, but what comes to mind is not this so much as the curious fact of Wright's hold on the public interest. There is no other architect in the U. S. whose work and other activities have been chronicled so persistently in the press.

3   A good deal of Wright's fame began, of course, with the same kind of irrelevant, unfortunate publicity that once made a New York exhibit of Vincent Van Gogh's paintings sensationally popular: a popularity due at least as much to certain widely-publicized details of his private life as to his glowing canvases. Another architect — Stanford White — trod the same dubious path to unwanted recognition, but the parallel stops there. Wright is a genius, a great, austere figure. By comparison, Stanford White was a feckless, mildly talented college boy. Everywhere — even to a considerable extent in his own country — Wright is considered the greatest living architect, and when the history books are written again he will take on the stature of Michelangelo. And even in the face of our overwhelming indifference to architecture, Wright has periodically turned out buildings which have shocked the public into an awareness of what life might be like if all build-

ings in cities were designed at this level. Because of this shock value in his work, the name of Frank Lloyd Wright has also been news.

4   A case in point is the Imperial Hotel, which was floated on a mat of concrete in place of a conventional foundation. The design was without precedent, and in the considered opinion of top U. S. engineers, it was also without structural merit. But when the Japanese earthquake of 1925 came, almost the first news that came through was that the hotel had floated through with a minimum of damage. Practically every paper in the country carried the story — there was something akin to the tale of David and Goliath in the way Wright had faced the problem of an earthquake, brushed aside the warnings of specialists, and won — in a way, he had become a popular symbol of a universal desire.

5   This was not the first nor the last time Wright stumped the experts. There was, for instance, the case of the now-famous house for Edgar Kaufmann, near Bear Run, Pennsylvania. For Kaufmann, Wright designed a vacation house of stone, glass and concrete, a good part of which was cantilevered over water and rocks. All went well until drawings of the house went to a large steel company, which was to furnish the concrete reinforcing rods. Out of curiosity some of the company's technical people made calculations to determine whether or not the house would stand up. The figures showed that it wouldn't, and a letter accompanied by pages of engineering calculations was dispatched to Mr. Kaufmann, who very sensibly passed them on to his architect. For weeks there was no word from Wright, until one day a sealed lead box arrived, and a letter which said in effect, "I should like this box put under the cornerstone of your house when the cornerstone is laid. I want this done so that when the house is *torn down,* 2,000 years from now, people will learn what complete damn fools these engineers are!" The Kaufmann house is approaching the end of its first decade, and doing nicely.

6   Whether these stories are true in the letter or only in spirit is of no great moment — they are part of a great and growing legend which is in itself testimony to the power of Wright as a personality and as a builder. There is one story, however, which can be vouched for, as it was heard at first hand. The occasion was the one already mentioned, when Wright showed his new museum to a group of editors.

7   "This building," said Wright, patting the model as if it were a baby, "is built like a spring. You can see how the ramp, which is coiled in the shape of a true logarithmic spiral, is one continuous piece from top to bottom, integral with the outside wall and the inside balcony. When the first atomic bomb lands on New York it will not be destroyed. It may be blown a few miles up into the air, *but when it comes down it will bounce!"*

8   For most of the people present, the statement no doubt was sheer bombast and sensationalism, but basically it was true, and a new demonstration of the confidence, vitality and architectural genius which had long since made the man world-famous. The papers and magazines confined themselves

to a description taken from a press release, and such comfortably patronizing adjectives as "bizarre" and "strange." If this building is "strange," so is the chambered nautilus, the structure of a leaf, the wing of a bird. We have been so hardened to the artificial and illogical in architecture that the natural and organic is almost incomprehensible. But when the building is built, and people drive in off the street to the front door and see the great ramps swirling round and round to the dome of stainless steel and glass tubing, eight stories above them — when they ascend in the elevators to the top level through circular shafts of glass — when they stroll down an easy grade for an unbroken three-quarters of a mile without any feeling of fatigue — then they will have had their first real experience of what architecture can be like. Many will be uneasy and make jokes about it, because we are not accustomed to thinking of buildings in terms of an emotional experience. But they will come back for more, and then the name of Frank Lloyd Wright will again be news, and this time for the right reason.

Commentary and questions

1. This essay is an introduction to photographs and plans of the Guggenheim Museum. Although the museum is not mentioned in the first paragraph, explain how this paragraph predisposes the reader to an opinion.

2. *Paragraph 3:* Comparison and contrast are used here. What are the effects produced by the use of Van Gogh, White, and Michelangelo?

3. What are the examples of the Imperial Hotel and the Kaufmann house at Bear Run intended to support? Show in detail how each of the instances is developed so that it predisposes the reader emotionally as well as logically.

4. *Paragraph 6:* Comment on the statement, "Whether these stories are true in the letter or only in the spirit is of no great moment."

5. *Paragraph 8:* What does the author mean when he says that Wright's statement is basically true?

Topics for discussion and writing

I. Write an essay examining the last paragraph as an instance of persuasive writing.

II. Write an essay discussing the use of metaphor in this essay.

III. Write an essay in which you explain and defend, not necessarily limiting yourself to architecture, the statement that whether a story is true in letter or in spirit is of no great moment.

IV. Examine the photographs of the museum. (a) Write a description phrased as nearly as possible in informative, uncolored language. (b) Write an essay in which you describe the museum in both persuasive and informative language.

GUGGENHEIM MUSEUM IN PROGRESS

Reprinted from Architectural Record, *May, 1958. Copyright 1958 by F. W. Dodge Corporation with all rights reserved.*

"FOR the first time, a building has been designed which destroys everything square, rectilinear. It destroys the rectilinear frame of reference. Gravity is used to assist in presentation of the pictures [descent down the ramp]. You see paintings under the same conditions in which the artists did them [as they would rest on an easel, illuminated by a mixture of daylight and artificial light]. It provides an open road for the painter who sees beyond what is being done now. The Guggenheim Museum does not stem from the dead hand of the past — but from the living sense of the present for the past."

2 These are the words that Frank Lloyd Wright chose in telling ARCHITECTURAL RECORD the reasons for the spiral ramp in the main gallery, with domed skylight overhead, and ribboned skylight at the periphery; for the fin-shaped columns; for the several-faceted arched opening from which you look down into the grand gallery; for the semi-circular skylights in the grand gallery; for the opposing curves and sculptured windows of the lecture room ("A herald of all views that can be taken of the future of art, architecture, and religion. An advance agent of the future."); for the finned columns and tower in the Monitor building ("These shapes are the grammar of the whole museum.")

3 A tour through the Guggenheim Museum, six months ahead of completion, leaves several strong impressions. One is that it has an abundance of "Delight." Interest never flags because your eye moves from one handsome curve into another, and from one elegant space into another. (The concrete work is excellent with absolutely true curves and knife-like edges.) You know instantly that the building is Wright, and you are reminded of it by such trademarks as the frieze atop the Monitor building.

4 The ramp is widest at the top and decreases at a constant rate to its narrowest width at the first level. This prevents the ramp from having the monotony of a traditional arcade, and funnels attraction up toward the top skylight.

5 We were rather curious about how the structure of the Museum works. Some time ago Wright talked of the structure as a spring . . . the ramp coiled in a logarithmic spiral . . . one continuous piece from top to bottom. Recently he described the outer wall as a "spine" and the floor as "ribs growing inward."

6 Ordinarily, very little is said about the actual structural behavior of some of our most prominent buildings. And while the mechanics of structure deserve careful attention, they are usually subservient to the principal factors that make the building a success visually. Perhaps for this reason, the creative people in architecture are accustomed to speak of "structure" quite expressively, but their thoughts pertain to how the structure works

esthetically rather than actually, which may be a key to the way their concepts are developed.

7   Any tendency of the web-columns — the vertical members of the main gallery — to tip inward is resisted by arch action of the spiral ramp (think of the ramp as an arch in the horizontal plane).

8   The webs are rather deep on most levels. This plus the fact that they are restrained by the roof and floor may reduce their flexibility and make the portion of the ramp between webs tend to act as a flat slab, and that projecting beyond the web as a cantilever, tied by reinforcement back to the slab section, which in turn is tied to the columns.

9   In the Monitor building, advantage is taken of several phenomena: compression ring and hoop action of the floor slabs, and the buckling resistance of the cylindrical ground floor wall. A very simple analogy for the ground floor would be a covered cylindrical tank with a hole in the middle of the roof. As the roof tries to drop down, its action is to pull in the cylindrical wall, but this is resisted by the compression ring behavior of the roof slab. This analogy pertains only to the ground floor level and floor above. At the second and third level floors, the slab cantilevers out from either side of a ring beam, the largest cantilever being toward the outside. The tendency here is to pull the ring apart.

10   Directly below individual supporting columns at first floor level are brackets which transfer the load to the cylindrical wall which by virtue of its curvature resists the eccentric loading. The brackets are further aided by the flat circular plate floor slab directly above.

Commentary and questions

1. *Paragraph 1:* Explain what Wright means by his statements. What are the assumptions behind them? What does the first paragraph tell you about Wright's notion of successful architecture?

2. *Paragraph 2:* The second paragraph could have read this way: "These are the words that Frank Lloyd Wright chose in telling ARCHITECTURAL RECORD the reasons for building the museum the way he did." What does the second paragraph accomplish that this sentence does not accomplish?

3. *Paragraphs 2-4:* How do these paragraphs convey the author's conception of the building at the same time as they describe it?

Topics for discussion and writing

I. Write an essay comparing the words and statements of the first half of the essay (paragraphs 1-4) and the second half (5-10).

II. Write an essay comparing the persuasive devices in "The Modern Gallery" with this essay.

III. Write an essay discussing some of the problems faced by an author who intends to describe a building.

WRIGHT VS. PAINTING   John Canaday

From The New York Times,
*October 21, 1959. Reprinted by
permission of the author and*
The New York Times.

THE Solomon R. Guggenheim Museum, open to the public as of this afternoon, is a war between architecture and painting in which both come out
badly maimed.

2   The Pyrrhic victory belongs to the architecture, or to the shade of the
architect, the late Frank Lloyd Wright, over the museum's director, James
Johnson Sweeney, who was faced with the problem of adapting an abstract
architectural composition to its function as an exhibition gallery.

3   But Wright's snail-curl balcony, climbing in circles from ground level
to dome level around a great core of space, was an invincible opponent.

4   At so important an event as the opening of this building and the exhibition in it, graceful courtesies belong in dedicatory speeches. But a critique
of the museum must be as objective as possible, unaffected by the excitement
of the occasion or by gratitude for the philanthropy that brings an important
monument to the city to house an increasingly important collection.

5   As the big building rose at 1071 Fifth Avenue, at Eighty-eighth Street, so
many tales circulated about difficulties encountered in making it into a
usable museum, and about desperate expedients to make it so, that the whole
affair began to sound like a salvage operation. Ignoring these stories in the
light of the completed job, and leaving operational difficulties to be dealt
with behind the scenes, what does the public see?

6   There are plenty of scars to show that Mr. Sweeney has put up a game
and ingenious fight against an impossible scheme. Wright was not too fond
of painting, believing that its only legitimate function was that of an adjunct
to architecture. If he had deliberately designed an interior to annihilate
painting as an expressive art, and to reduce it to an architectural accessory,
he could not have done much better.

7   It takes effort and concentration to savor the pictures for themselves,
even though Wright's original scheme for their hanging has been modified
to their advantage.

8   Wright made a moderately ambiguous statement on the lighting he
visualized for the paintings that line the outside wall on his snail curve. (The
inside curve drops off into the vast central pit, from which one is protected
by a rather frighteningly low parapet.) Wright objected to the "constant
flood of artificial light" in which, according to opinions other than his, pictures are best displayed. He said that "the charm of any work of art, either
of painting, sculpture, or architecture, is to be seen in normal, naturally
changing light."

9   Thus on gray days, Wright believed, the pictures should go dim along
with the rest of the interior, or on bright days brighten with it, and so on, in
spite of some assistance from artificial sources.

10   Regarding pictures as part of an architectural whole, fine. Regarding pictures as something one comes to a museum to see, terrible, if the sun is not out.

11   The lighting has been redesigned to maintain a steady illumination for the benefit of the pictures.

12   The paintings project from the wall on long metal arms attached to the centers of their backs (Mr. Sweeney's idea, not Wright's), seeming to float in space, dramatically.

13   They are thus beautifully revealed, but at the expense of the total architectural harmony. They occupy their space so uncomfortably, like intruders, that their clear revelation loses much of its point. One comes again and again to the conclusion that the solution is a tragic compromise, yet that no better compromise could be found.

14   In addition, the snail-curl is a kind of strait jacket for the visitor. No wandering back and forth from one favorite picture to another. No going from room to room through convenient doors. One is inexorably led from picture to picture and from level to level along the spiral, with only an occasional lucky assist when the elevator is in the right spot.

15   Finally there is the sheer geometrical implacability of a spiral. By its slant, its occasional subtle flattenings, its odd curves and its curious junctures with partitions, the spiral creates to a small but very bothersome degree the giddiness of the fun house in amusement parks where everything is built in a skewed perspective so that one tumbles and falls.

16   Progression through the spiral makes one dizzy, not from the slow circular movement, but from the verticals that are not quite vertical, the horizontals that are not quite horizontal, the right angles that are not quite right.

17   The pictures seem to hang askew, seen from one point, and to hang askew in the opposite direction seen from another. And those seen from across the central void, looking up or down, are unpleasantly bisected, with only a top or bottom showing.

18   The new museum is frequently compared to the Pantheon in Rome, sometimes to Hagia Sophia in Istanbul, both also architectural designs of space surmounted by domes and illuminated from them. Those elaborately ornamented buildings are harmonious entities because ornament and architecture are harmonious.

19   Stripped of its pictures, existing solely as a design, Wright's building might be a third in the trio. But unfortunately the pictures disfigure the building, and the building disfigures the pictures, and in honesty, for this writer at any rate, there is no point in pretending anything else.

Commentary and questions

1. State Canaday's thesis and show how it dominates the essay.

2. In paragraphs 1-6 why is the extended metaphor of the battle effective?

3. Point out other metaphors that Canaday uses to reinforce his opinion of the building.

4. Does Canaday follow any organizing principle as he moves through the essay?

5. Examine each sentence in which Wright's name occurs. What does Canaday seem to think of Wright? (You cannot, of course, generalize beyond this essay without further evidence.)

6. Discuss Canaday's use of parallel structure, especially in making the well-turned sentence.

7. Discuss Canaday's use of unexpected words to make a point effectively.

Topics for discussion and writing

I. Behind Canaday's article are a series of assumptions about an ideal museum. What are the assumptions and how do you justify them from the text?

II. Using the three essays on the Guggenheim museum, explain how purpose helps determine organization of the essays and selection and emphasis of details.

III. The Guggenheim Museum is called a "controversial" building. What do these three essays indicate is a cause for the controversy? Why is it unlikely the controversy will be resolved?

Censorship: THE NATURE OF THE BATTLE OVER CENSORSHIP, Walter Lippmann · THE FRUSTRATE CENSOR, Bernard DeVoto · COURT DECISION ON *Ulysses,* John M. Woolsey · COURT DECISION ON *Lady Chatterley's Lover,* Frederick vanPelt Bryan

SOCRATES was condemned and executed on the grounds that his teachings corrupted the youth of Athens, and Plato proposed banishing poets from his ideal republic. Censorship is an old and continuing issue, largely involving politics, morals, and art. No one has permanently solved the problems it raises, but they continue to be debated, and censors continue their efforts to censor.

The following essays and court decisions demonstrate the variety of problems that arise when anyone considers censorship. Lippmann tries to explain the nature of censorship by pointing out its primary function, to prevent overt rebellion. DeVoto is mainly concerned to demonstrate that censorship is unworkable in any form, a position that has interesting implications. Judge Woolsey and Judge Bryan are, in a sense, less free than Lippmann and DeVoto. They had to make the practical decisions that the other two could only talk about. In effect the two judges played the role of censor, but each, as their decisions show, avoided censoring. Moreover, they were both bound by the legal definitions of obscenity; they were not entirely free to choose the grounds upon which to discuss the issues before them. Thus, the problem of workable definition is a major factor in what they write. They must make concrete application of a definition they themselves did not form.

Finally, there is the problem of the nature of the evidence one may resort to in support of an opinion about censorship. Legal authority, contemporary social habits and standards, unseconded opinion and judgment are all in play here, and they all condition the nature of the conclusions reached.

THE NATURE OF THE BATTLE
OVER CENSORSHIP

Walter Lippmann

From Walter Lippmann, Men of
Destiny. *Copyright 1927 by The
Macmillan Company and used
with the publisher's permission.*

Not long ago I was at work in my study writing, when, as was her custom,
the lady across the way burst into song. There was something about that
lady's voice which prevented the use of a human intelligence, and I called
upon the janitor to give her my compliments and then silence her. She replied
with a good deal of conviction that this was a free country and she would
sing when the spirit moved her; if I did not like it, I could retire to the
great open spaces.

2   The lady and I both love liberty, I think. But she loves her liberty
whereas I love mine. There does not seem to be a theory of liberty which
can be used to decide between us. Lord Acton, for example, was a great
historian of the problem of liberty, but as between the lady and myself, I
see no help from him when he says that "by liberty I mean the assurance
that every man shall be protected in doing what he believes his duty against
the influence of authority and majorities, custom and opinion." It was the
lady's custom to feel it her duty to practice her singing at the precise moment when I felt it my duty to write an article. The janitor never seemed
so completely convinced as I was that mine was much the higher form of
duty until he had had a chance on the day after Christmas to compare the
lady's gift with mine. Then apparently he read John Stuart Mill, learned
that "the sole end for which mankind are warranted, individuals or collec-
tively, in interfering with the liberty of action of any of their number, is self-
protection." I got protection and it cost me a box of Corona Coronas,
twenty-five dollars, and an old overcoat.

3   I am somewhat persuaded that no one has ever succeeded in defining
the area of liberty more precisely than I did in this case. The classic attempts by Milton and Mill end, if you examine them, in vagueness and
compromise. Milton, for example, would have granted freedom of opinion
to every one but the Papists and the Atheists; Mill was prepared to suppress
any one who did "evil" to "others," leaving it to the others, it would seem,
to decide what was evil. Had Milton been asked why Papists and Atheists
should be denied the freedom he asked for Dissenters, he would probably
have said that they would abuse their freedom. Mill argued that if you gave
too much liberty to some men there would be none left for other men. He
may have been right, but when you admit this to be true you have disposed
of the claim that there is a clear and universal doctrine of liberty.

4   A theory of liberty is usually stated in general terms, but in fact its real
meaning in concrete cases is derived from the nature of these cases themselves. Milton worked out his doctrine of liberty as a weapon which the
Puritans could use against the Stuarts; Mill wrote for Victorian England
during the ascendancy of the middle class, in that short interval between

the downfall of the squirearchy and before the rise of the great corporations. He addressed himself to a section of the English people which did not then contemplate the possibility of really serious divisions of opinion.

5   The history of Luther's ideas shows how closely related is a theory of liberty to the specific needs of the man who preaches it. When Luther first came into conflict with the Holy See he stood very much alone. There was at that time no Protestant Church, the German princes had not taken him up, he had not worked out a Protestant theology. At this juncture he made his famous utterance on behalf of liberty, saying that "Princes are not to be obeyed when they command submission to superstitious errors, but their aid is not to be invoked in support of the word of God." Facing a bull of excommunication, living in fear of assassination, he preached that heretics must be converted by Scripture and not by fire, otherwise the hangman would be the greatest doctor. But later when the religious revolution had won in Germany, it developed, like all revolutions, beyond anything that Luther had desired. In the name of that right of private judgment and dissent which he had proclaimed against Leo X, there arose heresies within the heresy, the sects of Zwingli and the Anabaptists, and the red jacobinism of the Peasants' War. Luther was horrified at these threats against the security of the Church he had founded. "Out of the gospel and divine truth come devilish lies," he cried, "from the blood in our body comes corruption." The devil, he said, having failed to put him down by the help of the Pope, was seeking his destruction through the preachers of treason and blood. He exhorted the nobles to crush the rebels without mercy. "If there are innocent persons among them, God will surely save and preserve them as He did with Lot and Jeremiah."

6   Lord Acton, from whom I have taken this account, says that in appealing to the sword Luther had in reality reverted to his original teaching, and that the notion of liberty, whether civil or religious, was hateful to his despotic nature and contrary to his interpretation of Scripture. It remains a fact that Luther had at one time preached the revolutionary doctrine of the right of private judgment, and that this doctrine was worked out to justify his own rebellion against Rome.

7   Heywood Broun and Margaret Leech say in their book on Anthony Comstock that "anything remotely bearing upon sex was to his mind obscene." This helps to explain Comstock, but it is quite misleading if it is meant as an account of Comstockery. This crusading is not a one-man affair, and the psychopathology of the vice crusader does not, I think, give a convincing explanation of his success in enlisting the support of the community. Obviously American society from the Civil War to the World War was not composed entirely or even largely of Anthony Comstocks. Yet for forty years the vice crusade was carried on with the consent of the community punctuated only here and there by the jeers of a minority. Comstock got his support

not because of what he believed about the uncleanness of sex but because of what he did toward suppressing those particular manifestations of sex which respectable people wished to have suppressed.

8   The patrons of his society, the public officials, the clergy, and the fathers and mothers who backed him were not much interested in, and many were no doubt embarrassed by, his idiotic assaults on September Morn and the nude classics. They were thinking of the tons of plainly indecent books and pictures he destroyed rather than the occasional masterpiece which he insulted.

9   A realistic study of censorship will show, I believe, that it is almost wholly directed against the unadjusted outsiders. It is not the idea as such which the censor attacks, whether it be heresy or radicalism or obscenity. He attacks the circulation of the idea among the classes which in his judgment are not to be trusted with the idea.

10   The censor himself may be cited as proof of this assertion that the danger is believed to be not in the idea itself but in the peculiar corruptibility of a certain part of the community. The censor exposes himself daily to every corrupting influence. I do not know, of course, what goes on in the dreams of those who compile the Index Expurgatorius, spend their days reading bolshevik pamphlets in the Department of Justice, see all the prohibited films and read all the dirty books. They may in their unconscious minds come to doubt God, insult the flag, and despise chastity. But whatever the private consequences may be, outwardly the censors remain doubly convinced of the sanctity of the institution they are protecting. No one has ever been known to decline to serve on a committee to investigate radicals on the ground that so much exposure to their doctrines would weaken his patriotism, nor on a vice commission on the ground that it would impair his morals. Anything may happen inside the censor, but what counts is that in his outward appearances after his ordeal by temptation he is more than ever a paragon of the conforming virtues. Perhaps his appetites are satisfied by an inverted indulgence, but to a clear-sighted conservative that does not really matter. The conservative is not interested in innocent thoughts. He is interested in loyal behavior.

11   Apart from certain residual tabus which have the power to cause irrational fear, the essence of censorship has always been, not to suppress subversive ideas as such, but to withhold them from those who are young or unprivileged or otherwise undependable. The purpose of censorship is to prevent overt rebellion against the state, the church, the family, and the economic system. Where there is no danger of overt action there is rarely any interference with freedom.

12   That is why there has so often been amazing freedom of opinion within an aristocratic class which at the same time sanctioned the ruthless suppression of heterodox opinion among the common people. When the Inquisition was operating most effectively against the bourgeois who had lapsed

into heresy, the princes of the Church and the nobles enjoyed the freedom of the Renaissance. There are indeed historians who point out that the Inquisition was not concerned with Jews, Mohammedans and infidels but almost entirely with Christians who had lapsed. For the evil which the Inquisition attacked was not disbelief as such but disloyalty to the Church.

13 An old Roman maxim said: *de internis non iudicat praetor,* the judge is not concerned with subjective things. Neither is the censor. He does not bother about the internal freedom of an aristocracy, the free speculation which has long been practiced within the Jesuit order, the private candor of politicians and journalists, the unimpressed realism of bankers about business men. Opinions in such a medium are free because they are safe. There is no organic disposition to run wild because the mind is free.

14 For purposes of argument the advocates of censorship will often pretend that they are worried about the intrinsic viciousness of an idea. Advocates of censorship are often muddle-headed and therefore not clear as to why they are doing what they are doing. But actions speak louder than words, and when you look at censorship as a whole it is plain that it is actually applied in proportion to the vividness, the directness, and the intelligibility of the medium which circulates the subversive idea. The moving picture is perhaps the most popular medium of expression there is; it speaks clearly to the lowest and the most immature intelligence. It is therefore forbidden to present many scenes which the theater is free to present. There are less theaters and the seats cost more. In America, at least, the theater is now largely confined to the metropolitan centers, and it is patronized by a well-to-do, comparatively mature, and sophisticated audience. It is only when a play goes into a long run and begins to be seen by the very general public, as was "The Captive," for example, that the authorities are compelled to pay much attention to protests from the guardians of morality. The scandal about "The Captive" was at bottom its success. Had it been played for a limited run in a theater attended by the sophisticated, it would not have been clubbed to death. But when "The Captive" had run four months on Broadway it had exhausted its mature audience; it was then being patronized by much simpler people, and it was from them and from those who heard from them that the demand for suppression arose and gradually became irresistible.

15 The newspapers and magazines of general circulation are much freer than the stage. They discuss regularly matters which if presented on the stage would bring out the police reserves. Men are much less moved by what they read than by what they see, and literacy is a recent and uncertain accomplishment of the human race. The proprietors of the tabloids found this out a few years ago and it has been a very profitable discovery. They have produced a new type of paper which is consciously adapted to a low and hurried intelligence. But the essence of tabloid journalism is that it caters with extreme skill to the unadjusted and unprivileged part of the

community. It offers them not rebellion but vicarious satisfaction, and therefore it is a kind of narcotic bolshevism as distinguished from the stimulant bolshevism that Lenin preached. There is some protest against the tabloids, but it is not as yet very severe, because the tabloids are in effect a substitute for rebellion rather than a cause of it. Nevertheless they are suspect because, like the moving picture, they reach the suspect classes, and one may confidently predict that if censorship is ever applied to American newspapers it will be due to some breach of the peace which is ascribed to the tabloids. Unless they turn respectable, as some of them show signs of doing, the logic of their formula will compel them to explore newer and newer excitements. They will experiment until at last they bring down upon themselves the wrath of the established community.

16 The novel is even freer than the press to-day because it is an even denser medium of expression. And in the jargon of a learned treatise a man may if he likes discuss with equanimity the advantages and disadvantages of incest among the Egyptian Pharoahs, or assassination as a method of social reform. For the practical limitations on the freedom of thought and speech are fixed by the estimate of those who have the power to suppress as to how effectively a dangerous idea is being presented to those who might be disposed to rebel.

17 Any one who with a moderately objective mind examines our own great controversies about freedom and suppression cannot fail, I think, to realize how little their avowed theory has to do with the attitude men take. The arguments which men used to justify the nullification of the Fifteenth Amendment in Georgia are now heard in Massachusetts to justify the nullification of the Eighteenth Amendment. The same corporate interests which object to regulation at home as an intolerable form of paternalism insist when they go abroad that the government shall protect them as if they were helpless children. The word "liberty" as used to-day may mean the open shop if an employer is speaking, a closed shop if a labor leader is speaking. There is no commonly accepted definition of liberty. The government of human affairs consists in finding a compromise among conflicting interests: liberty is the watchword used by an interest to justify it in doing what it would like to do, and authority is the watchword of an interest that does not wish to be interfered with by some other interest while it is doing what it wishes to do.

18 In concrete questions the verbal encounter throws little light on the issue. Suppression through some form of censorship is a means of defense, and, speaking broadly, suppression is practiced by the guardians of the state, the church, the family, and property. The support of censorship is to be found among those who feel themselves to be in harmony with the purposes of the institution that is attacked — that is to say, among officials and party workers and the classes who depend most upon the protection

of the state, among churchmen and the devout, among parents, teachers, the guardians of the young, among the elderly and the sexually settled, and also among the impotent and inhibited — all those in short whose manner of life would become confused if the particular institution were radically altered. They are the reserves of conservatism from which are mobilized the legions of defense against the irregular forces of the outsiders — the immature, the unprivileged, the unsettled, and the unadjusted, by whom rebellions are made.

19 The defenders of authority assume that a considerable part of the people, including all children, are not attached by fixed and reliable habits to the existing order. Being unattached they are impressionable, and might therefore be seduced by agitators. They do not have within themselves, inherent in their characters, that interested loyalty to things as they are which makes men immune to subversive influences. In matters of this sort we must remember that the words "right" and "wrong" mean simply friendly or hostile to the purposes of the institution in question; that is why it is said that the outsiders do not have the interest of the institution sufficiently at heart to feel instinctively the difference between right and wrong. They cannot be allowed to judge for themselves because they are without the premises of sound judgment. They are not unconsciously loyal, and their impressions have to be controlled by the insiders who are intuitively right-minded.

20 The rationalist argument for liberty, as stated for example by Mill, does not meet this powerful dogma squarely. That, it seems to me, is why the stock theories of liberty are persuasive only to the party which is in rebellion and to a few neutrals who are not vitally concerned with the quarrel. The doctrinaires of liberty base their theory on the assumption that almost all men have the ability to weigh evidence and choose reasonably. Whether almost all men have the ability or not, they certainly do not use it. They are governed by their interests as they conceive them by consulting their feelings about them. The men who ever reach a conclusion which is contrary to their bias and their convenience are too few to make any important difference in the course of events. I have taken into account the fact that some men will sacrifice their lives, their fortunes, and their reputations in the pursuit of an ideal or under the compulsion of some deep necessity of which they may not be wholly aware. The hero and the saint would not be so distinguished if their conduct were normal. For the run of men and women, who make up human society, the thing which decides their attitude in a concrete and critical issue is not evidence, argument and repartee, but whether they are attached to or repelled by the institution which is under fire.

21 The neutrally-minded person with a somewhat liberal disposition often misunderstands this conflict because it does not really touch him. He merely apprehends it as he apprehends the news that forty miners have been trapped in a mine. But your rebel knows his side of the conflict as the doomed miners know their anguish, in a way that a disinterested mind can never know it. The rebel feels his rebellion not as a plea for this or that reform but as an unbearable tension in his viscera. He must break down the cause of his frustration or jump out of his own skin. The true conservative has the same sort of organic need: his institution is to him a mainstay of his being; it exists not as an idea but in the very structure of his character, and the threat to destroy it fills him with anxiety and with fury.

22   The battles of liberty are organic conflicts between the adjusted and the unadjusted.

Commentary and questions

1. *Paragraphs 1-3:* Does Lippmann's anecdote define liberty or pose the difficulty of adequate definition?

2. *Paragraphs 4-6:* These are supporting paragraphs, using historical reference to back Lippmann's assertion that liberty has meaning only in individual cases. Show precisely how the reference to Martin Luther supports this assertion.

3. *Paragraphs 7-9:* These introduce the censor and his motives. What bearing do the first six paragraphs have on this topic?

4. *Paragraph 10:* Is this a supporting paragraph or does it mix support and assertion or conclusion? Paraphrase the crucial distinction made here.

5. *Paragraph 11:* Is Lippmann's notion that censorship tries to withhold subversive ideas from certain people consistent with his remarks about the censor's own exposure to temptation in paragraph 10? Does he use the word "subversive" in a political, social, or moral sense?

6. *Paragraph 14:* In your own words describe the nature and actions of censorship as Lippmann presents them. What sort of evidence does he have to demonstrate his analysis here and in surrounding paragraphs?

7. *Paragraphs 17-22:* Summarize Lippmann's arguments for his conclusion in the final paragraph. Explain his distinction between words and actions.

Topics for discussion and writing

I. To what extent does Lippmann see the censor as concerned with the preservation of social order?

II. What explicit connections does Lippmann make between the problem of defining liberty and the problem of censorship?

III. Would you call this essay an attempt at definition of a problem or an attempt at its solution?

IV. Is Lippmann for or against censorship? Does he indicate his position at all? Write an essay discussing this question, drawing your evidence from Lippmann's explicit and implicit ideas.

V. You may have personally witnessed examples of censorship. If so, write a theme discussing the extent to which your experience does or does not conform to Lippmann's idea that censorship is a conflict between "the adjusted and the unadjusted."

THE FRUSTRATE CENSOR   Bernard DeVoto

From Harper's Magazine, *Vol. 175 (June, 1937). Copyright 1937 by Harper and Brothers. Reprinted by permission of Mrs. DeVoto.*

WHEN the dictatorship of the proletariat has at last raised up a generation capable of creating the great society there will be no attempt to censor art, literature, and entertainment. Prophecy does not reveal whether the race will be too strong to yield to temptation or whether the capacity to be tempted at all will have been bred out of it; but one or the other reason will make censorship unnecessary. And that is just as well, for the only solution to the problem of censorship is to do away with it entirely. In these disheartening, pre-millennial stages of the unfolding plan, the censor has the most futile job in the world. In all history no effort to control literature or entertainment in the interest of morality has ever succeeded for very long. Cromwell has no sooner closed the theaters than the populace is sneaking up back alleys to attend illicit performances, and there has hardly been time to organize that service effectively before Charles II is on the throne, all London is crowding the reopened box-offices, and the plays are bawdier than they ever were before.

2   In our own time we have had twenty years of unceasing effort by the righteous to drive nudity from the stage and throughout those years nudity on the stage has steadily become more common. Twenty years ago a chorus without stockings was something of a sensation; to-day completely naked choruses are a commonplace in revues and restaurants, and the strip-tease act has spread from the burlesque and the honky-tonk to the most respectable theaters. Such organizations as the Society for the Suppression of Vice have labored just as vigorously to prohibit indecency in fiction. To-day you can buy practically any novel they have ever proceeded against in practically any bookstore, and the sole result of their labor has been to confer popular successes on a number of books which, if they had not advertised them, would have perished in remainder sales. It is only three years since a group of aghast clerics, backed by one of the most powerful church organizations in America and directly or indirectly encouraged by most other churches, undertook to purify the movies of indecency, immodesty, lubricity, salaciousness, concupiscence, violence, horror, cruelty, propaganda, levity, and a miscellany of other evils. This was no bush-league effort but a powerful campaign by powerful people, backed by a threat of mass pressure so menacing

that it scared the movie-makers into compliance with all the demands made on them. But when you enter a movie theater to-day you perceive at once that the formidable effort has accomplished exactly nothing. Quantitatively, the movies are just as cruel, indecent, lubricious, and salacious as they ever were, and qualitatively, they are more effective at it, for their technic has improved.

3   The specific problems which censorship faces in the movies are somewhat different from those it faces elsewhere, but the principles and forces that frustrate it in the movies are the same everywhere. The campaign of the bishops was defeated practically because there is no way of distinguishing between fashion and morality in entertainment, because there is no way of predicting either the course or the duration of a fashion, and because there is no way of anticipating the means by which indecency may be expressed. It was defeated socially because the public has an insatiable desire for entertainment, because there is no way of defining either morality or decency so that the public will support the definition, and because censorship is never content to accept a role which is socially acceptable but always tries to assume a further one which is not. Any of these is enough in itself to wreck a censorship, and most, if not all, of them operate when one is attempted. In sum they indicate a simple conclusion — that effective censorship of literature and entertainment is impossible.

4   The code of regulations drawn up by the latest censors (it is almost identical with earlier ones which regulated the industry) is still in effect. It is an absorbing document. It prohibits derision of ministers — and may be effective here; for though the man of God is usually a stock comic figure in the movies, he is seldom derided. It prohibits contempt of the law and representation of the methods of crime, of illegal traffic in drugs, third-degree methods, surgical operations, and various kinds of violence, cruelty, and brutality. All of these flourish quite unchecked in the movies, though morality is sometimes provided for by the right kind of ending, or violence and cruelty may be suggested rather than represented, which is far more effective. But the attempts to abate them have probably been perfunctory, for over half of the code and at least ninety-nine per cent of the censors' energy is devoted to sex. It always is. Effectively, censorship means the censorship of sex. And sex is quite uncensorable.

5   The movie censors have not been able to determine, as a practical working basis, what aspects, accessories, and treatments of sex are tolerable; they have not been able even to compose a satisfactory theory. The code is impossibly narrow and rigid. On the one hand it tries to prohibit certain specific kinds of scenes, actions, and themes. At the same time it tries to prohibit certain tones, emphases, attitudes, and colorations. It tries to prohibit the representation of certain emotions on the screen and to prevent the evocation of certain other emotions in the audience. And all its attempts

have in common the fact that they are out of touch not only with the freedom permitted other arts but also with the realities of public behavior, public taboos, and public sanctions.

6   The people who try to censor fiction have given up hope of suppressing anything except a half-dozen monosyllables. The novelist is free to write scenes in which sexual intercourse occurs, to describe any behavior that leads up to or follows it, to express all the emotions associated with passion, and to concentrate his whole work, if he chooses, on the direct or indirect motives of sex. The movies would not dream of using the monosyllables or of representing sexual intercourse on the screen. For similar values they had different technics and these rest upon the real taboos of the public, but the Production Code disregards the technics and the social realities. Its interest is not in what society taboos but in what it ought to taboo on behalf of society. "Impure love [defined as love outside the marriage relation] must not be presented as attractive or beautiful." If that commandment were to be enforced on fiction to-day the race of novelists would have to go on Relief to-morrow. Society does not forbid such treatment of "impure love" to literature — and your corner movie house testifies that it extends to the screen the freedom which the censors forbid it. Dancing which involves "movements of the breasts [or] excessive body movements while the feet are stationary" is forbidden by the Code — but the public conscience permits it in any high-school auditorium. Semi-nudity and "silhouette" are forbidden the movies — but are quite proper in newspaper advertisements, family magazines, shop-windows, and religious pageantry. And, returning to impure love, it "must not be the subject of comedy or farce or treated as material for laughter," though literature, the stage, the newspaper headlines, and the daily conversation of the Ladies' Aid are perfectly free to laugh at it as much as they please.

7   These and all the other provisions of the code are violated every day. Impure love remains a stock theme of the movies — perhaps their commonest theme, and when it is not presented as attractive and beautiful it is commonly treated as material for laughter. Suggestive dancing is a staple of the musicals and a common interlude in other films. Silhouette, semi-nudity, and even complete nudity are commonplaces; by a happy coincidence, a logical development of the plot usually requires the heroine to undress or to be surprised in the bathtub. As for the major and minor motives of sex, well, the movies are an industry where boy eventually gets girl, and their entire climate is erotic. Continually, deliberately, and unavoidably erotic. In an erotic climate you cannot escape suggestive actions, passionate emotions, and exciting scenes. You cannot, in short, deal with love unless you deal with love. No one can censor the erotic, for no one can repeal psychology; no one can censor the suggestive, for no one can predict individual response; and no one can censor the salacious, for the tones of

the voice and the expressions of the face and body are beyond legislation. Censorship has merely refined the skill of presentation and opened up new possibilities of expression and suggestion.

8   Every other form of art and entertainment has demonstrated the same principles. A censor who works within the public's taboos, confining himself to its ideas of what is fraught with harm or danger to itself, has a good chance of being sustained. Thus the traffic in smutty post cards is driven underground and the movies which are shown to stag parties could never be presented in public. But the censor who goes beyond and acts on his own ideas of what is good for the public invariably fails. As a policeman he has a chance; as an uplifter he is licked before he starts.

9   The public instinctively, or let us say by a sentiment as deep as consciousness and probably deeper, rejects the hypothesis that to witness a fictional representation on the screen is to be tempted or stimulated to action. Several years ago, when the cycle of gangster movies was at its apex, the censors demanded their suppression on the ground that they would impel children, adolescents, and weakminded adults to rob banks and kidnap millionaires. The public accepted the risk and attended the gangster films in ecstatic multitudes. We have not become a nation of criminals, the fashion has lapsed, and currently there is a cycle of movies which celebrate sweetness and light. On the theory that condemned the earlier cycle, this one should turn our children and weakminded to wholesale self-sacrifice, heroism, and austere virtue. The public seems willing to accept that risk too, and it is probably right. For no one has yet brought to the judgment bar of science any conclusive evidence that screen plays produce imitative behavior, and in the absence of evidence, the theory that they in fact reduce the psychological necessity for it is probably the better one.

10   Certainly it is the better one in regard to the censors' cherished nightmare, sex. The public seems to understand that there is a difference between fiction and reality, and to understand further that a fictional representation may have a very valuable use in place of reality. The eroticism of the screen is a release of phantasy, and the troubled mind of man gets from it a gratification of the greatest sanitary value. Many of the impulses of the Old Adam are socially unacceptable, in fact, socially impossible, and the theater permits them to be drawn off over a spillway, whereas to dam them up would be dangerous. Far from producing immoral behavior, the movies are a powerful prophylaxis against it. The classless society will unquestionably root out the Old Adam's primitive impulses to wade to the good life through murder and sexuality; but till then it is better to permit them substitute gratification on the screen than to shorten the way to action by forbidding phantasy. During the intermediary stage of the dictatorship of the proletariat, which will be logical above all else, we shall probably require the populace to attend movies of lynching and adultery on the same principle that **sends** them to the clinic for inoculation against typhoid.

11   The censors also ignore the public's rule-of-thumb distinction between virtue and rationalization. The public fervently agrees with the theories of antisepsis preached by the censors, and would probably be willing to embody them in a constitutional amendment. Yet it supports the movies that violate them. It believes that precepts should be phrased in language of the highest moral idealism, but believes that such precepts must not interfere with its freedom of action. What the movies ought to be in theory, in short, has nothing to do with what they may be in action. This verbal paradox betrays the censors, who try to make moral precepts binding on behavior. The public sees no necessary relationship, and acts as if it held that to attend immoral performances is not only psychologically sound but morally sound as well.

12   Ethical analysis of this phenomenon must be left to experts, but certain observations are open to everyone. The binding conventions, the social taboos that are the effective determinants of behavior, become more rigid and far more strict as we go down the social scale. The upper middle class is much more tolerant of unconventional — immoral — behavior than the lower middle class. But it is only in the upper half that perturbation about immoral entertainment occurs — it is there that censorship arises, and Minsky's will never be closed by an uprising in the slums. The bottom half is more conventional — more moral — in its behavior but completely receptive of salacious movies. It enforces its taboos more generally on behavior; it relaxes them more on entertainment. It acts as if entertainment had nothing to do with virtue. Maybe it is right.

13   Hence the futility of censorship. It tries to improve society instead of policing it. It tries to infuse with morality an area that society considers non-moral. It fails to distinguish between fiction and reality. It mistakes a verbalism for a psychological and ethical principle. And it is perpetually out of touch with society as it is, and so finds itself stopped by social energies which it perpetually misunderstands.

14   No one need grieve therefore. Working on the lowest common denominator of two or three hundred million people, the movies are neither corrupting society nor pandering to its evil impulses nor playing upon its weaknesses. They are merely entertaining it. Within that greater function they are serving other functions. They are lowering the potential of primitive and antisocial instincts, they are neutralizing centrifugal forces, they are supplying vicarious fulfillments to an age which, as Freud says, has to live psychologically beyond its means. The flywheel that makes them safe is the fact that society distinguishes between the imagined and the actual, between entertainment and reality, and is not afraid of temptation. There exist some people who are stimulated to involuntary action by the sight of a fire-alarm box. Society knows that such people exist but it provides asylums for them; it does not destroy the socially useful system of fire-alarms in order to remove temptation from their path. Society acts effectively to put immoral enter-

tainment on precisely the same level. The censors can neither think that clearly nor feel that acutely. That is why the censors always lose.

Commentary and questions

1. *Paragraph 1:* Examine the first sentence. The ironic prophecy leads DeVoto into the statement that censorship is virtually impossible. What is the effect of this evocation of Marxist utopianism? Should DeVoto have been more plain and direct?

How does the Cromwell illustration support DeVoto's assertion? Does it suggest that censorship is evil as well as futile? Note the position of the main thesis of the paragraph: it is preceded by one literary device and followed by another. According to conventional standards of paragraph unity DeVoto's technique is disorganized. In your opinion is the paragraph effective?

2. *Paragraph 2:* Note the statement beginning "It is only three years since. . . ." What is the effect of the long list? Is DeVoto making a strictly factual statement? Restate his opinion of censorship and what it tries to control.

3. *Paragraph 3:* Can this be reduced to a single statement of the reasons why censorship is impossible?

4. *Paragraphs 4-5:* How do these paragraphs develop: by further illustration and example, further explanation of the reasons for the failure of censorship, a shift to new premises, or all three?

5. *Paragraphs 5-6:* What concept mentioned in paragraph 5 reappears in paragraph 6? What crucial distinction is made in paragraph 6? How is it supported?

6. *Paragraph 9:* How does this paragraph present what DeVoto considers to be the basic motives of the censor?

7. *Paragraphs 10-12:* These lead up to the general conclusion in paragraph 13: "Hence the futility of censorship." What precisely are DeVoto's supporting arguments? How would you classify them: logical, factual, humorous, suggestive, assertive?

Topics for discussion and writing

I. DeVoto's argument seems to rest, at bottom, on a certain concept of human nature. How would you describe this concept?

II. Why does DeVoto concentrate on the movies to illustrate his ideas about censorship?

III. Throughout his essay DeVoto implies that the public is more intelligent than the censors. What are his grounds for this opinion? How does it serve him as argumentative ammunition? Is it an opinion with which his audience would be likely to agree?

IV. Write a short theme describing DeVoto's interpretation of the censor's motives. Is this view substantially the same as Lippmann's? If not, what are the significant points of difference?

V. Write a theme explaining DeVoto's distinction between entertainment and action. What usefulness does he see for entertainment?

VI. DeVoto frequently refers to the "suggestiveness" of the movies. What does he mean by the term? Why does he assume the primary importance of sex as the object of censorship?

COURT DECISION ON *ULYSSES*　　John M. Woolsey

United States *v.* One Book Called "Ulysses," *U.S. District Court, Southern District of New York. Decision rendered Dec. 6, 1933.*

THE motion for a decree dismissing the libel herein is granted, and, consequently, of course, the government's motion for a decree of forfeiture and destruction is denied.

2　　Accordingly a decree dismissing the libel without costs may be entered herein.

3　　I. The practice followed in this case is in accordance with the suggestion made by me in the case of *United States* v. *One Book Entitled "Contraception,"* 51 F. (2d) 525, and is as follows:

4　　After issue was joined by the filing of the claimant's answer to the libel for forfeiture against "Ulysses," a stipulation was made between the United States Attorney's office and the attorneys for the claimant providing:

1. That the book "Ulysses" should be deemed to have been annexed to and to have become part of the libel just as if it had been incorporated in its entirety therein.
2. That the parties waived their right to a trial by jury.
3. That each party agreed to move for decree in its favor.
4. That on such cross motions the Court might decide all the questions of law and fact involved and render a general finding thereon.
5. That on the decision of such motions the decree of the Court might be entered as if it were a decree after trial.

5　　It seems to me that a procedure of this kind is highly appropriate in libels such as this for the confiscation of books. It is an especially advantageous procedure in the instant case because on account of the length of "Ulysses" and the difficulty of reading it, a jury trial would have been an extremely unsatisfactory, if not an almost impossible, method of dealing with it.

6   II. I have read "Ulysses" once in its entirety and I have read those passages of which the Government particularly complains several times. In fact, for many weeks, my spare time has been devoted to the consideration of the decision which my duty would require me to make in this matter.
7   "Ulysses" is not an easy book to read or to understand. But there has been much written about it, and in order properly to approach the consideration of it it is advisable to read a number of other books which have now become its satellites. The study of "Ulysses" is, therefore, a heavy task.

8   III. The reputation of "Ulysses" in the literary world, however, warranted my taking such time as was necessary to enable me to satisfy myself as to the intent with which the book was written, for, of course, in any case where a book is claimed to be obscene it must first be determined, whether the intent with which it was written was what is called, according to the usual phrase, pornographic, — that is, written for the purpose of exploiting obscenity.
9   If the conclusion is that the book is pornographic that is the end of the inquiry and forfeiture must follow.
10   But in "Ulysses," in spite of its unusual frankness, I do not detect anywhere the leer of the sensualist. I hold, therefore, that it is not pornographic.

11   IV. In writing "Ulysses," Joyce sought to make a serious experiment in a new, if not wholly novel, literary genre. He takes persons of the lower middle class living in Dublin in 1904 and seeks not only to describe what they did on a certain day early in June of that year as they went about the City bent on their usual occupations, but also to tell what many of them thought about the while.
12   Joyce has attempted — it seems to me, with astonishing success — to show how the screen of consciousness with its ever-shifting kaleidoscopic impressions carries, as it were on a plastic palimpest, not only what is in the focus of each man's observation of the actual things about him, but also in a penumbral zone residua of past impressions, some recent and some drawn up by association from the domain of the subconscious. He shows how each of these impressions affects the life and behavior of the character which he is describing.
13   What he seeks to get is not unlike the result of a double or, if that is possible, a multiple exposure on a cinema film which would give a clear foreground with a background visible but somewhat blurred and out of focus in varying degrees.
14   To convey by words an effect which obviously lends itself more appropriately to a graphic technique, accounts, it seems to me, for much of the obscurity which meets a reader of "Ulysses." And it also explains another aspect of the book, which I have further to consider, namely, Joyce's sincerity and his honest effort to show exactly how the minds of his characters operate.

15   If Joyce did not attempt to be honest in developing the technique which he has adopted in "Ulysses" the result would be psychologically misleading and thus unfaithful to his chosen technique. Such an attitude would be artistically inexcusable.

16   It is because Joyce has been loyal to his technique and has not funked its necessary implications, but has honestly attempted to tell fully what his characters think about, that he has been the subject of so many attacks and that his purpose has been so often misunderstood and misrepresented. For his attempt sincerely and honestly to realize his objective has required him incidentally to use certain words which are generally considered dirty words and has led at times to what many think is a too poignant preoccupation with sex in the thoughts of his characters.

17   The words which are criticized as dirty are old Saxon words known to almost all men and, I venture, to many women, and are such words as would be naturally and habitually used, I believe, by the types of folk whose life, physical and mental, Joyce is seeking to describe. In respect of the recurrent emergence of the theme of sex in the minds of his characters, it must always be remembered that his locale was Celtic and his season Spring.

18   Whether or not one enjoys such a technique as Joyce uses is a matter of taste on which disagreement or argument is futile, but to subject that technique to the standards of some other technique seems to me to be little short of absurd.

19   Accordingly, I hold that "Ulysses" is a sincere and honest book and I think that the criticisms of it are entirely disposed of by its rationale.

20   V. Furthermore, "Ulysses" is an amazing *tour de force* when one considers the success which has been in the main achieved with such a difficult objective as Joyce set for himself. As I have stated, "Ulysses" is not an easy book to read. It is brilliant and dull, intelligible and obscure by turns. In many places it seems to me to be disgusting, but although it contains, as I have mentioned above, many words usually considered dirty, I have not found anything that I consider to be dirt for dirt's sake. Each word of the book contributes like a bit of mosaic to the detail of the picture which Joyce is seeking to construct for his readers.

21   If one does not wish to associate with such folk as Joyce describes, that is one's own choice. In order to avoid indirect contact with them one may not wish to read "Ulysses"; that is quite understandable. But when such a real artist in words, as Joyce undoubtedly is, seeks to draw a true picture of the lower middle class in a European city, ought it to be impossible for the American public legally to see that picture?

22   To answer this question it is not sufficient merely to find, as I have found above, that Joyce did not write "Ulysses" with what is commonly called pornographic intent, I must endeavor to apply a more objective standard to his book in order to determine its effect in the result, irrespective of the intent with which it was written.

23   VI. The statute under which the libel is filed only denounces, in so far as we are here concerned, the importation into the United States from any foreign country of "any obscene book." Section 305 of the Tariff Act of 1930, Title 19 United States Code, Section 1305. It does not marshal against books the spectrum of condemnatory adjectives found, commonly, in laws dealing with matters of this kind. I am, therefore, only required to determine whether "Ulysses" is obscene within the legal definition of that word.

24   The meaning of the word "obscene" as legally defined by the Courts is: tending to stir the sex impulses or to lead to sexually impure and lustful thoughts. *Dunlop* v. *United States,* 165 U.S. 486, 501; *United States* v. *One Book Entitled "Married Love,"* 48 F. (2d) 821, 824; *United States* v. *One Book Entitled "Contraception,"* 51 F. (2d) 525, 528; and compare *Dysart* v. *United States,* 272 U.S. 655, 657; *Swearingen* v. *United States,* 161 U.S. 446, 450; *United States* v. *Dennett,* 39 F. (2d) 564, 568 (C.C.A. 2); *People* v. *Wendling,* 258 N.Y. 451, 453.

25   Whether a particular book would tend to excite such impulses and thoughts must be tested by the Court's opinion as to its effect on a person with average sex instincts — what the French would call *l'homme moyen sensuel* — who plays, in this branch of legal inquiry, the same role of hypothetical reagent as does the "reasonable man" in the law of torts and "the man learned in the art" on questions of invention in patent law.

26   The risk involved in the use of such a reagent arises from the inherent tendency of the trier of facts, however fair he may intend to be, to make his reagent too much subservient to his own idiosyncrasies. Here, I have attempted to avoid this, if possible, and to make my reagent herein more objective than he might otherwise be, by adopting the following course:

27   After I had made my decision in regard to the aspect of "Ulysses," now under consideration, I checked my impressions with two friends of mine who in my opinion answered to the above stated requirement for my reagent.

28   These literary assessors — as I might properly describe them — were called on separately, and neither knew that I was consulting the other. They are men whose opinion on literature and on life I value most highly. They had both read "Ulysses," and, of course, were wholly unconnected with this cause.

29   Without letting either of my assessors know what my decision was, I gave to each of them the legal definition of obscene and asked each whether in his opinion "Ulysses" was obscene within that definition.

30   I was interested to find that they both agreed with my opinion: that reading "Ulysses" in its entirety, as a book must be read on such a test as this, did not tend to excite sexual impulses or lustful thoughts but that its net effect on them was only that of a somewhat tragic and very powerful commentary on the inner lives of men and women.

31   It is only with the normal person that the law is concerned. Such a test as I have described, therefore, is the only proper test of obscenity in the case

of a book like "Ulysses" which is a sincere and serious attempt to devise a new literary method for the observation and description of mankind.

32 I am quite aware that owing to some of its scenes "Ulysses" is a rather strong draught to ask some sensitive, though normal, persons to take. But my considered opinion, after long reflection, is that whilst in many places the effect of "Ulysses" on the reader undoubtedly is somewhat emetic, nowhere does it tend to be an aphrodisiac.

33 "Ulysses" may, therefore, be admitted into the United States.

Commentary and questions

1. *Paragraphs 1-5:* These concern the preliminaries of Woolsey's decision forbidding the government to block the importation of copies of James Joyce's novel *Ulysses*. Paragraph 5 is especially interesting in that it treats the conditions under which a legal decision can be made. In essence the problem of censorship is "who decides?" Here the judge decides. Would you describe the substitution of the judge for a jury a matter of convenience or the denial of the competence of a jury to pass on the issue?

2. *Paragraphs 8-10:* Woolsey states that the legal issue rests on the legal definition of obscenity (see paragraphs 23-24). Compare this definition with Woolsey's reference to "the intent with which the book was written." Is there any logical discrepancy between the two criteria? Is there an assumed connection between them?

What synonym for "pornographic" is used in paragraph 10? Is it accurate?

3. *Paragraphs 11-19:* This section deals with Woolsey's interpretation of Joyce's intent. What support does he give for that interpretation? What particular words and phrases reveal his attitude toward *Ulysses?*

4. *Paragraphs 23-25:* Why does Woolsey bring in the full legal definition of obscenity here rather than earlier? Are there any undefined terms in that definition?

5. *Paragraphs 26-30:* To what extent is Woolsey's use of two independent "literary assessors" authoritative? Does it constitute "evidence" in your understanding of the term? What, if any, alternatives might he have chosen?

Topics for discussion and writing

I. The legal definition of obscenity (paragraph 24) includes the phrase "tending to stir the sex impulses." Do this definition and the assumptions behind it concur with Lippmann's and DeVoto's understanding of obscenity (or pornography)? Is the legal definition consistent with Woolsey's own phrase "dirt for dirt's sake" in paragraph 20?

II. To what extent might the legal definition of obscenity be used to suppress or censor media of expression (literature, art, television, movies, magazines, etc.) that are normally left alone? (*Note:* This is a hypothetical question, but it involves the problem of interpreting particular forms of expression according to a broad definition and therefore tests the definition itself.)

III. Write a theme showing how Woolsey's explanation of his decision illustrates DeVoto's thesis of the "impossibility" of censorship.

IV. Write a theme debating the proposition that "obscenity" is impossible to define for the purposes of censorship.

COURT DECISION ON
LADY CHATTERLEY'S LOVER

Frederick vanPelt Bryan

From Grove Press, Inc. and Readers' Subscription, Inc. *against* Robert K. Christenberry, Individually and as Postmaster of the City of New York, *U.S. District Court, Southern District of New York. Decision rendered July 21, 1959.*

THESE two actions against the Postmaster of New York, now consolidated, arise out of the denial of the United States mails to the recently published Grove Press unexpurgated edition of "Lady Chatterley's Lover" by D. H. Lawrence.

2   Plaintiffs seek to restrain the Postmaster from enforcing a decision of the Post Office Department that the unexpurgated "Lady Chatterley's Lover," and circulars announcing its availability, are non-mailable under the statute barring obscene matter from the mails (18 U.S.C. § 1461).[1] They also seek a declaratory judgment to the effect (1) that the novel is not "obscene, lewd, lascivous, indecent or filthy" in content or character, and is not non-mailable under the statute or, in the alternative, (2) that if the novel be held to fall within the purview of the statute, the statute is to that extent invalid and violates plaintiffs' rights in contravention of the First and Fifth Amendments. . . .

I

3   The basic question here is whether the unexpurgated "Lady Chatterley's Lover" is obscene within the meaning of 18 U.S.C. § 1461, and is thus

[1] The relevant portions of § 1461 provide:
   "Every obscene, lewd, lascivious, indecent, filthy or vile article . . . and
   "Every written or printed . . . circular, . . . or notice of any kind giving information . . . where, or how, or from whom . . . any of such . . . articles . . . may be obtained . . .
   "Is declared to be nonmailable matter and shall not be conveyed in the mails or delivered from any post office or by any letter carrier."
The statute provides penalties for violation of up to five years' imprisonment and a maximum fine of $5,000 for a first offense and up to ten years' imprisonment and a maximum $10,000 fine for subsequent offenses.

excluded from the protections afforded freedom of speech and the press by the First Amendment. . . .

II

4   This unexpurgated edition of "Lady Chatterley's Lover" has never before been published either in the United States or England, though comparatively small editions were published by Lawrence himself in Italy and authorized for publication in France, and a number of pirated copies found their way to this country.

5   Grove Press is a reputable publisher with a good list which includes a number of distinguished writers and serious works. Before publishing this edition Grove consulted recognized literary critics and authorities on English literature as to the advisability of publication. All were of the view that the work was of major literary importance and should be made available to the American public.

6   No one is naive enough to think that Grove Press did not expect to profit from the book. Nevertheless the format and composition of the volume, the advertising and promotional material and the whole approach to publication, treat the book as a serious work of literature. The book is distributed through leading bookstores throughout the country. There has been no attempt by the publisher to appeal to prurience or the prurient minded.

7   The Grove edition has a preface by Archibald MacLeish, former Librarian of Congress, Pulitzer Prize winner, and one of this country's most distinguished poets and literary figures, giving his appraisal of the novel. There follows an introduction by Mark Schorer, Professor of English Literature at the University of California, a leading scholar of D. H. Lawrence and his work. The introduction is a critique of the novel against the background of Lawrence's life, work and philosophy. At the end of the novel there is a bibliographical note as to the circumstances under which it was written and first published. Thus, the novel is placed in a setting which emphasizes its literary qualities and its place as a significant work of a major English novelist.

8   Readers' Subscription has handled the book in the same vein. Its Literary Board, which was composed of Jacques Barzun, Dean of Graduate Facilities at Columbia, Lionel Trilling of the Columbia Faculty of English Literature, and the poet W. H. Auden, all distinguished critics and writers, critically appraised the book before Readers' Subscription acquired its rights. The relatively small number of Readers' Subscription subscribers is composed largely of people in academic, literary and scholarly fields. Its list of books includes works of high literary merit, including books by and about D. H. Lawrence.

9   There is nothing of "the leer of the sensualist" in the promotion or methods of distribution of this book. There is no suggestion of any attempt

to pander to the lewd and lascivious minded for profit. The facts are all to the contrary. . . .

[10] Publication of the Grove edition was a major literary event. It was greeted by editorials in leading newspapers throughout the country unanimously approving the publication and viewing with alarm possible attempts to ban the book.

[11] It was against this background that the New York Postmaster impounded the book and the Postmaster General barred it. The decision of the Postmaster General, in a brief four pages, relied on three cases, *Roth* v. *United States, supra, United States* v. *One Book Called "Ulysses,"* D.C.S.D. N.Y., 5 F. Supp. 182, aff'd, 2 Cir., 72 F.2d 705, and *Besig* v. *United States,* 9 Cir., 208 F.2d 142. While he quotes from *Roth* the Postmaster General relies principally on *Besig,* which was not reviewed by the Supreme Court. It may be noted that the Ninth Circuit relied heavily on *Besig* in *One Book, Inc.* v. *Olesen, supra,* which was summarily reversed by the Supreme Court on the authority of *Roth.*

[12] He refers to the book as "currently withheld from the mails in the United States and barred from the mails by several other major nations." His only discussion of its content is as follows:

> "The contemporary community standards are not such that this book should be allowed to be transmitted in the mails.
>
> "The book is replete with descriptions in minute detail of sexual acts engaged in or discussed by the book's principal characters. These descriptions utilize filthy, offensive and degrading words and terms. Any literary merit the book may have is far outweighed by the pornographic and smutty passages and words, so that the book, taken as a whole, is an obscene and filthy work.
>
> "I therefore see no need to modify or reverse the prior ruling of this Department and the Department of the Treasury with respect to this edition of this book."

[13] This seems to be the first time since the notable opinions of Judge Woolsey and Judge Augustus Hand in *United States* v. *One Book Called "Ulysses," supra,* in 1934 that a book of comparable literary stature has come before the federal courts charged with violating the federal obscenity statutes. That case held that James Joyce's "Ulysses" which had been seized by the Customs under Section 305 of the Tariff Act of 1930 was not obscene within the meaning of that statute. It thoroughly discussed the standards to be applied in determining this question.

[14] The essence of the *Ulysses* holding is that a work of literary merit is not obscene under federal law merely because it contains passages and language dealing with sex in a most candid and realistic fashion and uses many four-letter Anglo-Saxon words. Where a book is written with honesty and seriousness of purpose, and the portions which might be considered obscene are relevant to the theme, it is not condemned by the statute even though "it

justly may offend many." "Ulysses" contains numerous passages dealing very frankly with sex and the sex act and is free in its use of four-letter Anglo-Saxon words. Yet both Judge Woolsey in the District Court, and Judge Hand in the Court of Appeals, found that it was a sincere and honest book which was not in any sense "dirt for dirt's sake." They both concluded that "Ulysses" was a work of high literary merit, written by a gifted and serious writer, which did not have the dominant effect of promoting lust or prurience and therefore did not fall within the interdiction of the statute.

15   *Roth* v. *United States, supra,* decided by the Supreme Court in 1957, twenty-three years later, unlike the *Ulysses* case, did not deal with the application of the obscenity statutes to specific material. It laid down general tests circumscribing the area in which matter is excludable from constitutional protections because it is obscene, so as to avoid impingement on First Amendment guarantees.[2]

16   The court distilled from the prior cases (including the *Ulysses* case, which it cited with approval) the standards to be applied — "whether to the average person, applying contemporary community standards, the dominant theme of the material taken as a whole appeals to prurient interest."

17   The court saw no significant difference between this expression of the standards and those in the American Law Institute Model Penal Code to the effect that

> ". . . a thing is obscene if, considered as a whole, its predominant appeal is to prurient interest, i. e., a shameful or morbid interest in nudity, sex, or excretion, and if it goes substantially beyond customary limits of candor in description or representation of such matters. . . ."

18   These standards are not materially different from those applied in *Ulysses* to the literary work considered there. Since the *Roth* case dealt with these standards for judging obscenity in general terms and the *Ulysses* case dealt with application of such standards to a work of recognized literary stature, the two should be read together.

19   A number of factors are involved in the application of these tests.

20   As Mr. Justice Brennan pointed out in *Roth*, sex and obscenity are by no means synonymous and "[t]he portrayal of sex, e.g., in art, literature and scientific works, is not in itself sufficient reason to deny material the constitutional protection of freedom of speech and press." As he said, sex has been "a subject of absorbing interest to mankind through the ages; it is one of the vital problems of human interest and public concern." The subject may be discussed publicly and truthfully without previous restraint or fear of subsequent punishment as long as it does not fall within the narrowly circumscribed interdicted area.

21   Both cases held that, to be obscene, the dominant effect of the book

---

2 There was no question but that the material involved in *Roth* was hard core pornography and that the defendants were engaged "in the commercial exploitation of the morbid and shameful craving for materials with prurient effect." (354 U. S. p. 496.)

must be an appeal to prurient interest — that is to say, shameful or morbid interest in sex. Such a theme must so predominate as to submerge any ideas of "redeeming social importance" which the publication contains.

22 It is not the effect upon the irresponsible, the immature or the sensually minded which is controlling. The material must be judged in terms of its effect on those it is likely to reach who are conceived of as the average man of normal sensual impulses, or, as Judge Woolsey says, "what the French call l'homme moyen sensuel."

23 The material must also exceed the limits of tolerance imposed by current standards of the community with respect to freedom of expression in matters concerning sex and sex relations. Moreover, a book is not to be judged by excerpts or individual passages but must be judged as a whole.

24 All of these factors must be present before a book can be held obscene and thus outside constitutional protections.

25 Judged by these standards, "Lady Chatterley's Lover" is not obscene. The decision of the Postmaster General that it is obscene and therefore non-mailable is contrary to law and clearly erroneous. This is emphasized when the book is considered against its background and in the light of its stature as a significant work of a distinguished English novelist.

26 D. H. Lawrence is one of the most important novelists writing in the English language in this century. Whether he is, as some authorities say, the greatest English novelist since Joseph Conrad, or one of a number of major figures, makes little difference. He was a writer of great gifts and of undoubted artistic integrity.

27 The text of this edition of "Lady Chatterley's Lover" was written by Lawrence toward the close of his life and was his third version of the novel, originally called "Tenderness."

28 The book is almost as much a polemic as a novel.

29 In it Lawrence was expressing his deep and bitter dissatisfaction with what he believed were the stultifying effects of advancing industrialization and his own somewhat obscure philosophic remedy of a return to "naturalness." He attacks what he considered to be the evil effects of industrialization upon the wholesome and natural life of all classes in England. In his view this was having disastrous consequences on English society and on the English countryside. It had resulted in devitalization of the upper classes of society and debasement of the lower classes. One result, as he saw it, was the corrosion of both the emotional and physical sides of man as expressed in his sexual relationships which had become increasingly artificial and unwholesome.

30 The novel develops the contrasts and conflicts in characters under these influences.

31 The plot is relatively simple.

32 Constance Chatterley is married to a baronet, returned from the first world war paralyzed from the waist down. She is physically frustrated and

dissatisfied with the artificiality and sterility of her life and of the society in which she moves. Her husband, immersed in himself, seeks compensation for his own frustrations in the writing of superficial and brittle fiction and in the exploitation of his coal mining properties, a symbol of the creeping industrial blight. Failing to find satisfaction in an affair with a man in her husband's circle, Constance Chatterley finds herself increasingly restless and unhappy. Her husband half-heartedly urges her to have a child by another man whom he will treat as his heir. Repelled by the suggestion that she casually beget a child, she is drawn to Mellors, the gamekeeper, sprung from the working class who, having achieved a measure of spiritual and intellectual independence, is a prototype of Lawrence's natural man. They establish a deeply passionate and tender relationship which is described at length and in detail. At the conclusion she is pregnant and plans to obtain a divorce and marry the gamekeeper.

33   This plot serves as a vehicle through which Lawrence develops his basic theme of contrast between his own philosophy and the sterile and debased society which he attacks. Most of the characters are prototypes. The plot and theme are meticulously worked out with honesty and sincerity.

34   The book is replete with fine writing and with descriptive passages of rare beauty. There is no doubt of its literary merit.

35   It contains a number of passages describing sexual intercourse in great detail with complete candor and realism. Four letter Anglo-Saxon words are used with some frequency.

36   These passages and this language understandably will shock the sensitive minded. Be that as it may, these passages are relevant to the plot and to the development of the characters and of their lives as Lawrence unfolds them. The language which shocks, except in a rare instance or two, is not inconsistent with character, situation or theme.

37   Even if it be assumed that these passages and this language taken in isolation tend to arouse shameful, morbid and lustful sexual desires in the average reader, they are an integral, and to the author a necessary[3] part of the development of theme, plot and character. The dominant theme, purpose and effect of the book as a whole is not an appeal to prurience or the prurient minded. The book is not "dirt for dirt's sake." [4] Nor do these passages

---

[3] See D. H. Lawrence, "Sex, Literature, and Censorship," (Twayne Publishers, 1953) p. 89. Essay "A Propros of Lady Chatterley's Lover."

[4] As Mr. Justice Frankfurter pointed out in *Kingsley International Pictures Corp.* v. *Regents, supra,* Lawrence

"knew there was such a thing as pornography, dirt for dirt's sake, or, to be more accurate, dirt for money's sake. This is what D. H. Lawrence wrote:

    " 'But even I would censor genuine pornography, rigorously. It would not be very difficult. In the first place, genuine pornography is almost always underworld, it doesn't come into the open. In the second, you can recognize it by the insult it offers invariably, to sex, and to the human spirit.

    " 'Pornography is the attempt to insult sex, to do dirt on it. This is unpardonable. Take the very lowest instance, the picture post-card sold underhand, by the underworld,

and this language submerge the dominant theme so as to make the book obscene even if they could be considered and found to be obscene in isolation.

[38]   What the Postmaster General seems to have done is precisely what the Supreme Court in *Roth* and the courts in the *Ulysses* case said ought not to be done. He has lifted from the novel individual passages and language, found them to be obscene in isolation and therefore condemned the book as a whole. He has disregarded the dominant theme and effect of the book and has read these passages and this language as if they were separable and could be taken out of context. Thus he has "weighed" the isolated passages which he considered obscene against the remainder of the book and concluded that the work as a whole must be condemned.

[39]   Writing about sex is not in itself pornographic, as the Postmaster General recognized. Nor does the fact that sex is a major theme of a book condemn the book as obscene. Neither does the use of "four letter" words, despite the offense they may give. "Ulysses" was found not to be obscene despite long passages containing similar descriptions and language. As Judge Woolsey said there (5 F. Supp. pp. 183, 184):

> "The words which are criticized as dirty are old Saxon words known to almost all men and, I venture, to many women, and are such words as would be naturally and habitually used, I believe, by the types of folk whose life, physical and mental, Joyce is seeking to describe."

Such words "are, almost without exception of honest Anglo-Saxon ancestry and were not invented for purely scatological effect."

[40]   The tests of obscenity are not whether the book or passages from it are in bad taste or shock or offend the sensibilities of an individual, or even of a substantial segment of the community. Nor are we concerned with whether the community would approve of Constance Chatterley's morals. The statute does not purport to regulate the morals portrayed or the ideas expressed in a novel, whether or not they are contrary to the accepted moral code, nor could it constitutionally do so. *Kingsley International Pictures* v. *Regents, supra.*

[41]   Plainly "Lady Chatterley's Lover" is offensive to the Postmaster General, and I respect his personal views. As a matter of personal opinion I disagree with him for I do not personally find the book offensive.

[42]   But the personal views of neither of us are controlling here. The standards for determining what constitutes obscenity under this statute have been laid down. These standards must be objectively applied regardless of personal predilections.

[43]   There has been much discussion of the intent and purpose of Lawrence

---

in most cities. What I have seen of them have been of an ugliness to make you cry. The insult to the human body, the insult to a vital human relationship! Ugly and cheap they make the human nudity, ugly and degraded they make the sexual act, trivial and cheap and nasty.' (D. H. Lawrence, Pornography and Obscenity, p. 13.)" (Collected in Lawrence "Sex, Literature, and Censorship," *supra,* p. 69.)

in writing Lady Chatterley. It is suggested that the intent and purpose of the author has no relevance to the question as to whether his work is obscene and must be disregarded.

44 No doubt an author may write a clearly obscene book in the mistaken belief that he is serving a high moral purpose. The fact that this is the author's purpose does not redeem the book from obscenity.

45 But the sincerity and honesty of purpose of an author as expressed in the manner in which a book is written and in which his theme and ideas are developed has a great deal to do with whether it is of literary and intellectual merit. Here, as in the *Ulysses* case, there is no question about Lawrence's honesty and sincerity of purpose, artistic integrity and lack of intention to appeal to prurient interest.

46 Thus, this is an honest and sincere novel of literary merit and its dominant theme and effect, taken as a whole, is not an appeal to the prurient interest of the average reader.

47 This would seem to end the matter. However, the Postmaster General's finding that the book is non-mailable because it offends contemporary community standards bears some discussion.

48 I am unable to ascertain upon what the Postmaster General based this conclusion. The record before him indicates general acceptance of the book throughout the country and nothing was shown to the contrary. The critics were unanimous. Editorial comment by leading journals of opinion welcomed the publication and decried any attempts to ban it.

49 It is true that the editorial comment was excluded by the Judicial Officer at the hearing. But it seems to me that this was error. These expressions were relevant and material on the question of whether the book exceeded the limits of freedom of expression in matters involving sex and sex relations tolerated by the community at large in these times.

50 The contemporary standards of the community and the limits of its tolerance cannot be measured or ascertained accurately. There is no poll available to determine such questions. Surely expressions by leading newspapers, with circulations of millions, are some evidence at least as to what the limits of tolerance by present day community standards are, if we must embark upon a journey of exploration into such uncharted territory.

51 Quite apart from this, the broadening of freedom of expression and the frankness with which sex and sex relations are dealt with at the present time require no discussion. In one best selling novel after another frank descriptions of the sex act and "four-letter" words appear with frequency. These trends appear in all media of public expression, in the kind of language used and the subjects discussed in polite society, in pictures, advertisements and dress, and in other ways familiar to all. Much of what is now accepted would have shocked the community to the core a generation ago. Today such things are generally tolerated whether we approve or not.

52 I hold that, at this stage in the development of our society, this major English novel does not exceed the outer limits of the tolerance which the

community as a whole gives to writing about sex and sex relations.
53   One final word about the constitutional problem implicit here.

54   It is essential to the maintenance of a free society that the severest restrictions be placed upon restraints which may tend to prevent the dissemination of ideas. It matters not whether such ideas be expressed in political pamphlets or works of political, economic or social theory or criticism, or through artistic media. All such expressions must be freely available.

55   A work of literature published and distributed through normal channels by a reputable publisher stands on quite a different footing from hard core pornography furtively sold for the purpose of profiting by the titillation of the dirty minded. The courts have been deeply and properly concerned about the use of obscenity statutes to suppress great works of art or literature. As Judge Augustus Hand said in *Ulysses* (72 F.2d p. 708):

> ". . . The foolish judgments of Lord Eldon about one hundred years ago, proscribing the works of Byron and Southey, and the finding by the jury under a charge by Lord Denman that the publication of Shelley's 'Queen Mab' was an indictable offense are a warning to all who have to determine the limits of the field within which authors may exercise themselves."

56   To exclude this book from the mails on the grounds of obscenity would fashion a rule which could be applied to a substantial portion of the classics of our literature. Such a rule would be inimical to a free society. To interpret the obscenity statute so as to bar "Lady Chatterley's Lover" from the mails would render the statute unconstitutional in its application, in violation of the guarantees of freedom of speech and the press contained in the First Amendment.

57   It may be, as the plaintiffs urge, that if a work is found to be of literary stature, and not "hard core" pornography, it is *a fortiori* within the protections of the First Amendment. But I do not reach that question here. For I find that "Lady Chatterley's Lover" is not obscene within the meaning of 18 U.S.C. § 1461, and is entitled to the protections guaranteed to freedoms of speech and press by the First Amendment. I therefore hold that the order of the Postmaster General is illegal and void and violates plaintiffs' rights in contravention of the Constitution.

58   Defendant's motion for summary judgment is denied. Plaintiffs' cross-motions for summary judgment are granted. An order will issue permanently restraining the defendant from denying the mails to this book or to the circulars announcing its availability.

59   Settle order on notice.

Commentary and questions

1. *Paragraphs 4-10:* What is the purpose of Bryan's reference to the conditions under which *Lady Chatterley's Lover* was published?

2. *Paragraph 15, footnote 2:* This statement contrasts "hard core" pornography and works of literary merit. Is the distinction as self-evident as the text would seem to imply?

3. *Paragraphs 11-25:* This section mentions the Postmaster General's stated reasons for objecting to the novel and refers to the legal tests for obscenity. How many of these criteria does the Postmaster General use?

4. *Paragraphs 26-37:* Does Bryan's description of the novel effectively demonstrate that it is a work of literary merit? What criteria, explicit and implicit, does he use to define literary merit? How much of this section is unsupported opinion?

5. *Paragraph 44:* Compare this statement with Woolsey's remarks on James Joyce's purpose in writing *Ulysses*. Is there any contradiction?

6. *Paragraphs 45-46:* These assert Lawrence's "sincerity and honesty of purpose." Does Bryan's account of the novel make this assertion plausible? Are sincerity and honesty of purpose mentioned or implied in the legal definition of obscenity?

7. *Paragraphs 47-52:* Is Bryan's argument about the Postmaster General's assessment of "contemporary community standards" merely an unsupported difference of opinion?

8. *Paragraphs 53-56:* The remarks here seem to apply more than statutory standards to the problem of censorship. Separate the legal and nonlegal criteria mentioned here.

Topics for discussion and writing

I. List the criteria Bryan uses for judging a book obscene or not. Are they all dependent upon legal authority? If not, what other factors are involved in such a judgment?

II. Bryan refers frequently to Woolsey's decision. Is Bryan's reference to the legal tests for obscenity more or less complete than Woolsey's? Does he refer only to the strictly statutory portions of Woolsey's decision?

III. Bryan's decision rests in part upon a distinction between "hard core" pornography and serious literary productions. Write a theme explaining the grounds for this distinction and its implications.

IV. In what ways do Bryan's and Woolsey's decisions confirm Lippmann's view that censorship is concerned with overt behavior?

V. Drawing your material from the two essays and the two court decisions, write a theme discussing the role of definition of terms in censorship.

VI. Write a theme using all the material in this section and treating *one* of the following topics: (a) the role of "contemporary community standards" in censorship; (b) the problems in censoring different media of communication and expression; (c) the supposed reactions of audience and public in determining what is obscene or acceptable; (d) expediency as a criterion in determining the value of censorship; (e) censorship as an infringement upon liberty of thought and expression.

What is art? THE AESTHETIC HYPOTHESIS, Clive Bell · AN ESSAY IN AESTHETICS, Roger Fry · THE DYNAMIC IMAGE, Susanne K. Langer

THE QUESTION, "What is art?" will never admit an answer upon which everyone will agree for very long. Aestheticians are just as quarrelsome and contentious as theologians or political theorists, and the very nature of the topic, as Mrs. Langer explains, excludes it from the comfort of factual statement. In the selections that follow, we have three theorists all making statements of opinion, that is, making assertions that cannot be proven by fact.

But these statements can be tested, first, by illustration, second, by an appeal to concepts or experiences upon which most readers (in the opinion of the authors) are likely to agree, and, third, by the careful definition of terms. Bell, unlike Fry and Mrs. Langer, is unique in adding an emotional appeal, perhaps because his case is less easily demonstrated by the other means of explanation. Fry and Mrs. Langer, on the other hand, are concerned to define art in terms of experiences and sensations and emotions that are universal, or nearly so. A good many of the differences in particular statements will be seen to derive from this distinction of purpose between the authors.

Nevertheless, all of them agree in a broad sense in trying to isolate what it is that makes us call one object a work of art and another not a work of art. The reader who patiently examines the ways in which each author makes this division will be able to test the relative value of each essay, and may, incidentally, sharpen his own understanding of the particular form of art with which he is most familiar.

250

THE AESTHETIC HYPOTHESIS   Clive Bell

From Art. *Reprinted by permission of Chatto and Windus,
Ltd., and G. P. Putnam's Sons,
1958.*

It is improbable that more nonsense has been written about aesthetics than
about anything else: the literature of the subject is not large enough for
that. It is certain, however, that about no subject with which I am acquainted has so little been said that is at all to the purpose. The explanation
is discoverable. He who would elaborate a plausible theory of aesthetics
must possess two qualities — artistic sensibility and a turn for clear thinking. Without sensibility a man can have no aesthetic experience, and, obviously, theories not based on broad and deep aesthetic experience are
worthless. Only those for whom art is a constant source of passionate emotion can possess the data from which profitable theories may be deduced;
but to deduce profitable theories even from accurate data involves a certain
amount of brain-work, and, unfortunately, robust intellects and delicate sensibilities are not inseparable. As often as not, the hardest thinkers have had
no aesthetic experience whatever. I have a friend blessed with an intellect as
keen as a drill, who, though he takes an interest in aesthetics, has never
during a life of almost forty years been guilty of an aesthetic emotion. So,
having no faculty for distinguishing a work of art from a handsaw, he is apt
to rear up a pyramid of irrefragable argument on the hypothesis that a handsaw is a work of art. This defect robs his perspicuous and subtle reasoning
of much of its value; for it has ever been a maxim that faultless logic can win
but little credit for conclusions that are based on premises notoriously false.
Every cloud, however, has its silver lining, and this insensibility, though un-
lucky in that it makes my friend incapable of choosing a sound basis for his
argument, mercifully blinds him to the absurdity of his conclusions while
leaving him in full enjoyment of his masterly dialectic. People who set out
from the hypothesis that Sir Edwin Landseer was the finest painter that ever
lived will feel no uneasiness about an aesthetic which proves that Giotto was
the worst. So, my friend, when he arrives very logically at the conclusion
that a work of art should be small or round or smooth, or that to appreciate
fully a picture you should pace smartly before it or set it spinning like a top,
cannot guess why I ask him whether he has lately been to Cambridge, a
place he sometimes visits.

2   On the other hand, people who respond immediately and surely to
works of art, though, in my judgment, more enviable than men of massive
intellect but slight sensibility, are often quite as incapable of talking sense
about aesthetics. Their heads are not always very clear. They possess the
data on which any system must be based; but, generally, they want the
power that draws correct inferences from true data. Having received aesthetic emotions from works of art, they are in a position to seek out the
quality common to all that have moved them, but, in fact, they do nothing

of the sort. I do not blame them. Why should they bother to examine their feelings when for them to feel is enough? Why should they stop to think when they are not very good at thinking? Why should they hunt for a common quality in all objects that move them in a particular way when they can linger over the many delicious and peculiar charms of each as it comes? So, if they write criticism and call it aesthetics, if they imagine that they are talking about Art when they are talking about particular works of art or even about the technique of painting, if loving particular works they find tedious the consideration of art in general, perhaps they have chosen the better part. If they are not curious about the nature of their emotion, nor about the quality common to all objects that provoke it, they have my sympathy, and, as what they say is often charming and suggestive, my admiration too. Only let no one suppose that what they write and talk is aesthetics; it is criticism, or just "shop."

3   The starting-point for all systems of aesthetics must be the personal experience of a peculiar emotion. The objects that provoke this emotion we call works of art. All sensitive people agree that there is a peculiar emotion provoked by works of art. I do not mean, of course, that all works provoke the same emotion. On the contrary, every work produces a different emotion. But all these emotions are recognizably the same in kind; so far, at any rate, the best opinion is on my side. That there is a particular kind of emotion provoked by works of visual art, and that this emotion is provoked by every kind of visual art, by pictures, sculptures, buildings, pots, carvings, textiles, &c., &c., is not disputed, I think, by anyone capable of feeling it. This emotion is called the aesthetic emotion; and if we can discover some quality common and peculiar to all the objects that provoke it, we shall have solved what I take to be the central problem of aesthetics. We shall have discovered the essential quality in a work of art, the quality that distinguishes works of art from all other classes of objects.

4   For either all works of visual art have some common quality, or when we speak of "works of art" we gibber. Everyone speaks of "art," making a mental classification by which he distinguishes the class "works of art" from all other classes. What is the justification of this classification? What is the quality common and peculiar to all members of this class? Whatever it be, no doubt it is often found in company with other qualities; but they are adventitious — it is essential. There must be some one quality without which a work of art cannot exist; possessing which, in the least degree, no work is altogether worthless. What is this quality? What quality is shared by all objects that provoke our aesthetic emotions? What quality is common to Sta. Sophia and the windows at Chartres, Mexican sculpture, a Persian bowl, Chinese carpets, Giotto's frescoes at Padua, and the masterpieces of Poussin, Piero della Francesca, and Cézanne? Only one answer seems possible — significant form. In each, lines and colours combined in a particular way, certain forms and relations of forms, stir our aesthetic emotions. These relations

and combinations of lines and colours, these aesthetically moving forms, I call "Significant Form"; and "Significant Form" is the one quality common to all works of visual art.

5   At this point it may be objected that I am making aesthetics a purely subjective business, since my only data are personal experiences of a particular emotion. It will be said that the objects that provoke this emotion vary with each individual, and that therefore a system of aesthetics can have no objective validity. It must be replied that any system of aesthetics which pretends to be based on some objective truth is so palpably ridiculous as not to be worth discussing. We have no other means of recognising a work of art than our feeling for it. The objects that provoke aesthetic emotion vary with each individual. Aesthetic judgments are, as the saying goes, matters of taste; and about tastes, as everyone is proud to admit, there is no disputing. A good critic may be able to make me see in a picture that had left me cold things that I had overlooked, till at last, receiving the aesthetic emotion, I recognise it as a work of art. To be continually pointing out those parts, the sum, or rather the combination, of which unite to produce significant form, is the function of criticism. But it is useless for a critic to tell me that something is a work of art; he must make me feel it for myself. This he can do only by making me see; he must get at my emotions through my eyes. Unless he can make me see something that moves me, he cannot force my emotions. I have no right to consider anything a work of art to which I cannot react emotionally; and I have no right to look for the essential quality in anything that I have not *felt* to be a work of art. The critic can affect my aesthetic theories only by affecting my aesthetic experience. All systems of aesthetics must be based on personal experience — that is to say, they must be subjective.

6   Yet, though all aesthetic theories must be based on aesthetic judgments, and ultimately all aesthetic judgments must be matters of personal taste, it would be rash to assert that no theory of aesthetics can have general validity. For, though A, B, C, D are the works that move me, and A, D, E, F the works that move you, it may well be that x is the only quality believed by either of us to be common to all the works in his list. We may all agree about aesthetics, and yet differ about particular works of art. We may differ as to the presence or absence of the quality x. My immediate object will be to show that significant form is the only quality common and peculiar to all the works of visual art that move me; and I will ask those whose aesthetic experience does not tally with mine to see whether this quality is not also, in their judgment, common to all works that move them, and whether they can discover any other quality of which the same can be said.

7   Also at this point a query arises, irrelevant indeed, but hardly to be suppressed: "Why are we so profoundly moved by forms related in a particular way?" The question is extremely interesting, but irrelevant to aesthetics. In pure aesthetics we have only to consider our emotion and its object: for the

purposes of aesthetics we have no right, neither is there any necessity, to pry behind the object into the state of mind of him who made it. Later, I shall attempt to answer the question; for by so doing I may be able to develop my theory of the relation of art to life. I shall not, however, be under the delusion that I am rounding off my theory of aesthetics. For a discussion of aesthetics, it need be agreed only that forms arranged and combined according to certain unknown and mysterious laws do move us in a particular way, and that it is the business of an artist so to combine and arrange them that they shall move us. These moving combinations and arrangements I have called, for the sake of convenience and for a reason that will appear later, "Significant Form."

8   A third interruption has to be met.

9   "Are you forgetting about colour?" someone inquires. Certainly not; my term "significant form" included combinations of lines and of colours. The distinction between form and colour is an unreal one; you cannot conceive a colourless line or a colourless space; neither can you conceive a formless relation of colours. In a black and white drawing the spaces are all white and all are bounded by black lines; in most oil paintings the spaces are multi-coloured and so are the boundaries; you cannot imagine a boundary line without any content, or a content without a boundary line. Therefore, when I speak of significant form, I mean a combination of lines and colours (counting white and black as colours) that moves me aesthetically.

10   Some people may be surprised at my not having called this "beauty." Of course, to those who define beauty as "combinations of lines and colours that provoke aesthetic emotion," I willingly concede the right of substituting their word for mine. But most of us, however strict we may be, are apt to apply the epithet "beautiful" to objects that do not provoke that peculiar emotion produced by works of art. Everyone, I suspect, has called a butterfly or a flower beautiful. Does anyone feel the same kind of emotion for a butterfly or a flower that he feels for a cathedral or a picture? Surely, it is not what I call an aesthetic emotion that most of us feel, generally, for natural beauty. I shall suggest, later, that some people may, occasionally, see in nature what we see in art, and feel for her an aesthetic emotion; but I am satisfied that, as a rule, most people feel a very different kind of emotion for birds and flowers and the wings of butterflies from that which they feel for pictures, pots, temples and statues. Why these beautiful things do not move us as works of art move is another, and not an aesthetic, question. For our immediate purpose we have to discover only what quality is common to objects that do move us as works of art. In the last part of this chapter, when I try to answer the question — "Why are we so profoundly moved by some combinations of lines and colours?" I shall hope to offer an acceptable explanation of why we are less profoundly moved by others.

11   Since we call a quality that does not raise the characteristic aesthetic emotion "Beauty," it would be misleading to call by the same name the

quality that does. To make "beauty" the object of the aesthetic emotion, we must give to the word an over-strict and unfamiliar definition. Everyone sometimes uses "beauty" in an unaesthetic sense; most people habitually do so. To everyone, except perhaps here and there an occasional aesthete, the commonest sense of the word is unaesthetic. Of its grosser abuse, patent in our chatter about "beautiful huntin'" and "beautiful shootin'," I need not take account; it would be open to the precious to reply that they never do so abuse it. Besides, here there is no danger of confusion between the aesthetic and the non-aesthetic use; but when we speak of a beautiful woman there is. When an ordinary man speaks of a beautiful woman he certainly does not mean only that she moves him aesthetically; but when an artist calls a withered old hag beautiful he may sometimes mean what he means when he calls a battered torso beautiful. The ordinary man, if he be also a man of taste, will call the battered torso beautiful, but he will not call a withered hag beautiful because, in the matter of women, it is not to the aesthetic quality that the hag may possess, but to some other quality that he assigns the epithet. Indeed, most of us never dream of going for aesthetic emotions to human beings, from whom we ask something very different. This "something," when we find it in a young woman, we are apt to call "beauty." We live in a nice age. With the man-in-the-street "beautiful" is more often than not synonymous with "desirable"; the word does not necessarily connote any aesthetic reaction whatever, and I am tempted to believe that in the minds of many the sexual flavour of the word is stronger than the aesthetic. I have noticed a consistency in those to whom the most beautiful thing in the world is a beautiful woman, and the next most beautiful thing a picture of one. The confusion between aesthetic and sensual beauty is not in their case so great as might be supposed. Perhaps there is none; for perhaps they have never had an aesthetic emotion to confuse with their other emotions. The art that they call "beautiful" is generally closely related to the women. A beautiful picture is a photograph of a pretty girl; beautiful music, the music that provokes emotions similar to those provoked by young ladies in musical farces; and beautiful poetry, the poetry that recalls the same emotions felt, twenty years earlier, for the rector's daughter. Clearly the word "beauty" is used to connote the objects of quite distinguishable emotions, and that is a reason for not employing a term which would land me inevitably in confusions and misunderstandings with my readers.

12   On the other hand, with those who judge it more exact to call these combinations and arrangements of form that provoke our aesthetic emotions, not "significant form," but "significant relations of form," and then try to make the best of two worlds, the aesthetic and the metaphysical, by calling these relations "rhythm," I have no quarrel whatever. Having made it clear that by "significant form" I mean arrangements and combinations that move us in a particular way, I willingly join hands with those who prefer to give a different name to the same thing.

13   The hypothesis that significant form is the essential quality in a work of art has at least one merit denied to many more famous and more striking — it does help to explain things. We are all familiar with pictures that interest us and excite our admiration, but do not move us as works of art. To this class belongs what I call "Descriptive Painting" — that is, painting in which forms are used not as objects of emotion, but as means of suggesting emotion or conveying information. Portraits of psychological and historical value, topographical works, pictures that tell stories and suggest situations, illustrations of all sorts, belong to this class. That we all recognize the distinction is clear, for who has not said that such and such a drawing was excellent as illustration, but as a work of art worthless? Of course many descriptive pictures possess, amongst other qualities, formal significance, and are therefore works of art: but many more do not. They interest us; they may move us too in a hundred different ways, but they do not move us aesthetically. According to my hypothesis they are not works of art. They leave untouched our aesthetic emotions because it is not their forms but the ideas or information suggested or conveyed by their forms that affect us.

14   Few pictures are better known or liked than Frith's "Paddington Station"; certainly I should be the last to grudge it its popularity. Many a weary forty minutes have I whiled away disentangling its fascinating incidents and forging for each an imaginary past and an improbable future. But certain though it is that Frith's masterpiece, or engravings of it, have provided thousands with half-hours of curious and fanciful pleasure, it is not less certain that no one has experienced before it one half-second of aesthetic rapture — and this although the picture contains several pretty passages of colour, and is by no means badly painted. "Paddington Station" is not a work of art; it is an interesting and amusing document. In it line and colour are used to recount anecdotes, suggest ideas, and indicate the manners and customs of an age: they are not used to provoke aesthetic emotion. Forms and the relations of forms were for Frith not objects of emotion, but means of suggesting emotion and conveying ideas.

15   The ideas and information conveyed by "Paddington Station" are so amusing and so well presented that the picture has considerable value and is well worth preserving. But, with the perfection of photographic processes and of the cinematograph, pictures of this sort are becoming otiose. Who doubts that one of those *Daily Mirror* photographers in collaboration with a *Daily Mail* reporter can tell us far more about "London day by day" than any Royal Academician? For an account of manners and fashions we shall go, in future, to photographs, supported by a little bright journalism, rather than to descriptive painting. Had the imperial academicians of Nero, instead of manufacturing incredibly loathsome imitations of the antique, recorded in fresco and mosaic the manners and fashions of their day, their stuff, though artistic rubbish, would now be an historical gold-mine. If only they had been Friths instead of being Alma Tademas! But photography has

made impossible any such transmutation of modern rubbish. Therefore it must be confessed that pictures in the Frith tradition are grown superfluous; they merely waste the hours of able men who might be more profitably employed in works of a wider beneficence. Still, they are not unpleasant, which is more than can be said for that kind of descriptive painting of which "The Doctor" is the most flagrant example. Of course "The Doctor" is not a work of art. In it form is not used as an object of emotion, but as a means of suggesting emotions. This alone suffices to make it nugatory; it is worse than nugatory because the emotion it suggests is false. What it suggests is not pity and admiration but a sense of complacency in our own pitifulness and generosity. It is sentimental. Art is above morals, or, rather, all art is moral because, as I hope to show presently, works of art are immediate means to good. Once we have judged a thing a work of art, we have judged it ethically of the first importance and put it beyond the reach of the moralist. But descriptive pictures which are not works of art, and, therefore, are not necessarily means to good states of mind, are proper objects of the ethical philosopher's attention. Not being a work of art, "The Doctor" has none of the immense ethical value possessed by all objects that provoke aesthetic ecstasy; and the state of mind to which it is a means, as illustration, appears to me undesirable.

16   The works of those enterprising young men, the Italian Futurists, are notable examples of descriptive painting. Like the Royal Academicians, they use form, not to provoke aesthetic emotions, but to convey information and ideas. Indeed, the published theories of the Futurists prove that their pictures ought to have nothing whatever to do with art. Their social and political theories are respectable, but I would suggest to young Italian painters that it is possible to become a Futurist in thought and action and yet remain an artist, if one has the luck to be born one. To associate art with politics is always a mistake. Futurist pictures are descriptive because they aim at presenting in line and colour the chaos of the mind at a particular moment; their forms are not intended to promote aesthetic emotion but to convey information. These forms, by the way, whatever may be the nature of the ideas they suggest, are themselves anything but revolutionary. In such Futurist pictures as I have seen — perhaps I should except some by Severini — the drawing, whenever it becomes representative as it frequently does, is found to be in that soft and common convention brought into fashion by Besnard some thirty years ago, and much affected by Beaux-Art students ever since. As works of art, the Futurist pictures are negligible; but they are not to be judged as works of art. A good Futurist picture would succeed as a good piece of psychology succeeds; it would reveal, through line and colour, the complexities of an interesting state of mind. If Futurist pictures seem to fail, we must seek an explanation, not in a lack of artistic qualities that they never were intended to possess, but rather in the minds the states of which they are intended to reveal.

[17]   Most people who care much about art find that of the work that moves them most the greater part is what scholars call "Primitive." Of course there are bad primitives. For instance, I remember going, full of enthusiasm, to see one of the earliest Romanesque churches in Poitiers (Notre-Dame-la-Grande), and finding it as ill-proportioned, over-decorated, coarse, fat and heavy as any better class building by one of those highly civilised architects who flourished a thousand years earlier or eight hundred later. But such exceptions are rare. As a rule primitive art is good — and here again my hypothesis is helpful — for, as a rule, it is also free from descriptive qualities. In primitive art you will find no accurate representation; you will find only significant form. Yet no other art moves us so profoundly. Whether we consider Sumerian sculpture or pre-dynastic Egyptian art, or archaic Greek, or the Wei and T'ang masterpieces,[1] or those early Japanese works of which I had the luck to see a few superb examples (especially two wooden Bodhisattvas) at the Shepherd's Bush Exhibition in 1910, or whether, coming nearer home, we consider the primitive Byzantine art of the sixth century and its primitive developments amongst the Western barbarians, or, turning far afield, we consider that mysterious and majestic art that flourished in Central and South America before the coming of the white men, in every case we observe three common characteristics — absence of representation, absence of technical swagger, sublimely impressive form. Nor is it hard to discover the connection between these three. Formal significance loses itself in preoccupation with exact representation and ostentatious cunning.[2]

[18]   Naturally, it is said that if there is little representation and less saltimbancery in primitive art, that is because the primitives were unable to catch a likeness or cut intellectual capers. The contention is beside the point. There is truth in it, no doubt, though, were I a critic whose reputation depended on a power of impressing the public with a semblance of knowledge,

---

[1] The existence of the Ku K'ai-chih makes it clear that the art of this period (fifth to eighth centuries), was a typical primitive movement. To call the great vital art of the Liang, Chen, Wei, and Tang dynasties a development out of the exquisitely refined and exhausted art of the Han decadence — from which Ku K'ai-chih is a delicate straggler — is to call Romanesque sculpture a development out of Praxiteles. Between the two something has happened to refill the stream of art. What had happened in China was the spiritual and emotional revolution that followed the onset of Buddhism.

[2] This is not to say that exact representation is bad in itself. It is indifferent. A perfectly represented form may be significant, only it is fatal to sacrifice significance to representation. The quarrel between significance and illusion seems to be as old as art itself, and I have little doubt that what makes most palaeolithic art so bad is a preoccupation with exact representation. Evidently palaeolithic draughtsmen had no sense of the significance of form. Their art resembles that of the more capable and sincere Royal Academicians: it is a little higher than that of Sir Edward Poynter and a little lower than that of the late Lord Leighton. That this is no paradox let the cave-drawings of Altamira, or such works as the sketches of horses found at Bruniquel and now in the British Museum, bear witness. If the ivory head of a girl from the Grotte du Pape, Brassempouy (*Musée St. Germain*) and the ivory torso found at the same place (*Collection St. Cric*), be, indeed, palaeolithic, then there were good palaeolithic artists who created and did not imitate form. Neolithic art is, of course, a very different matter.

I should be more cautious about urging it than such people generally are. For to suppose that the Byzantine masters wanted skill, or could not have created an illusion had they wished to do so, seems to imply ignorance of the amazingly dexterous realism of the notoriously bad works of that age. Very often, I fear, the misrepresentation of the primitives must be attributed to what the critics call, "wilful distortion." Be that as it may, the point is that, either from want of skill or want of will, primitives neither create illusions, nor make display of extravagant accomplishment, but concentrate their energies on the one thing needful — the creation of form. Thus have they created the finest works of art that we possess.

19   Let no one imagine that representation is bad in itself; a realistic form may be as significant, in its place as part of the design, as an abstract. But if a representative form has value, it is as form, not as representation. The representative element in a work of art may or may not be harmful; always it is irrelevant. For, to appreciate a work of art we need bring with us nothing from life, no knowledge of its ideas and affairs, no familiarity with its emotions. Art transports us from the world of man's activity to a world of aesthetic exaltation. For a moment we are shut off from human interests; our anticipations and memories are arrested; we are lifted above the stream of life. The pure mathematician rapt in his studies knows a state of mind which I take to be similar, if not identical. He feels an emotion for his speculations which arises from no perceived relation between them and the lives of men, but springs, inhuman or super-human, from the heart of an abstract science. I wonder, sometimes, whether the appreciators of art and of mathematical solutions are not even more closely allied. Before we feel an aesthetic emotion for a combination of forms, do we not perceive intellectually the rightness and necessity of the combination? If we do, it would explain the fact that passing rapidly through a room we recognise a picture to be good, although we cannot say that it has provoked much emotion. We seem to have recognised intellectually the rightness of its forms without staying to fix our attention, and collect, as it were, their emotional significance. If this were so, it would be permissible to inquire whether it was the forms themselves or our perception of their rightness and necessity that caused aesthetic emotion. But I do not think I need linger to discuss the matter here. I have been inquiring why certain combinations of forms move us; I should not have travelled by other roads had I enquired, instead, why certain combinations are perceived to be right and necessary, and why our perception of their rightness and necessity is moving. What I have to say is this: the rapt philosopher, and he who contemplates a work of art, inhabit a world with an intense and peculiar significance of its own; that significance is unrelated to the significance of life. In this world the emotions of life find no place. It is a world with emotions of its own.

20   To appreciate a work of art we need bring with us nothing but a sense of form and colour and a knowledge of three-dimensional space. That bit of

knowledge, I admit, is essential to the appreciation of many great works, since many of the most moving forms ever created are in three dimensions. To see a cube or a rhomboid as a flat pattern is to lower its significance, and a sense of three-dimensional space is essential to the full appreciation of most architectural forms. Pictures which would be insignificant if we saw them as flat patterns are profoundly moving because, in fact, we see them as related planes. If the representation of three-dimensional space is to be called "representation," then I agree that there is one kind of representation which is not irrelevant. Also, I agree that along with our feeling for line and colour we must bring with us our knowledge of space if we are to make the most of every kind of form. Nevertheless, there are magnificent designs to an appreciation of which this knowledge is not necessary: so, though it is not irrelevant to the appreciation of some works of art it is not essential to the appreciation of all. What we must say is that the representation of three-dimensional space is neither irrelevant nor essential to all art, and that every other sort of representation is irrelevant.

21   That there is an irrelevant representative or descriptive element in many great works of art is not in the least surprising. Why it is not surprising I shall try to show elsewhere. Representation is not of necessity baneful, and highly realistic forms may be extremely significant. Very often, however, representation is a sign of weakness in an artist. A painter too feeble to create forms that provoke more than a little aesthetic emotion will try to eke that little out by suggesting the emotions of life. To evoke the emotions of life he must use representation. Thus a man will paint an execution, and, fearing to miss with his first barrel of significant form, will try to hit with his second by raising an emotion of fear or pity. But if in the artist an inclination to play upon the emotions of life is often the sign of a flickering inspiration, in the spectator a tendency to seek, behind form, the emotions of life is a sign of defective sensibility always. It means that his aesthetic emotions are weak or, at any rate, imperfect. Before a work of art people who feel little or no emotion for pure form find themselves at a loss. They are deaf men at a concert. They know that they are in the presence of something great, but they lack the power of apprehending it. They know that they ought to feel for it a tremendous emotion, but it happens that the particular kind of emotion it can raise is one that they can feel hardly or not at all. And so they read into the forms of the work those facts and ideas for which they are capable of feeling emotion, and feel for them the emotions that they can feel — the ordinary emotions of life. When confronted by a picture, instinctively they refer back its forms to the world from which they came. They treat created form as though it were imitated form, a picture as though it were a photograph. Instead of going out on the stream of art into a new world of aesthetic experience, they turn a sharp corner and come straight home to the world of human interests. For them the significance of a work of art depends on what they bring to it; no new thing is added to their lives,

only the old material is stirred. A good work of visual art carries a person who is capable of appreciating it out of life into ecstasy: to use art as a means to the emotions of life is to use a telescope for reading the news. You will notice that people who cannot feel pure aesthetic emotions remember pictures by their subjects; whereas people who can, as often as not, have no idea what the subject of a picture is. They have never noticed the representative element, and so when they discuss pictures they talk about shapes of forms and the relations and quantities of colours. Often they can tell by the quality of a single line whether or no a man is a good artist. They are concerned only with lines and colours, their relations and quantities and qualities; but from these they win an emotion more profound and far more sublime than any that can be given by the description of facts and ideas.

22   This last sentence has a very confident ring — over-confident, some may think. Perhaps I shall be able to justify it, and make my meaning clearer too, if I give an account of my own feelings about music. I am not really musical. I do not understand music well. I find musical form exceedingly difficult to apprehend, and I am sure that the profounder subtleties of harmony and rhythm more often than not escape me. The form of a musical composition must be simple indeed if I am to grasp it honestly. My opinion about music is not worth having. Yet, sometimes, at a concert, though my appreciation of the music is limited and humble, it is pure. Sometimes, though I have a poor understanding, I have a clean palate. Consequently, when I am feeling bright and clear and intent, at the beginning of a concert for instance, when something that I can grasp is being played, I get from music that pure aesthetic emotion that I get from visual art. It is less intense, and the rapture is evanescent; I understand music too ill for music to transport me far into the world of pure aesthetic ecstasy. But at moments I do appreciate music as pure musical form, as sounds combined according to the laws of a mysterious necessity, as pure art with a tremendous significance of its own and no relation whatever to the significance of life; and in those moments I lose myself in that infinitely sublime state of mind to which pure visual form transports me. How inferior is my normal state of mind at a concert. Tired or perplexed, I let slip my sense of form, my aesthetic emotion collapses, and I begin weaving into the harmonies, that I cannot grasp, the ideas of life. Incapable of feeling the austere emotions of art, I begin to read into the musical forms human emotions of terror and mystery, love and hate, and spend the minutes, pleasantly enough, in a world of turbid and inferior feeling. At such times, were the grossest pieces of onomatopoeic representation — the song of a bird, the galloping of horses, the cries of children, or the laughing of demons — to be introduced into the symphony, I should not be offended. Very likely I should be pleased; they would afford new points of departure for new trains of romantic feeling or heroic thought. I know very well what has happened. I have been using art as a means to the emotions of life and reading into it the ideas of life. I have been cutting blocks with a razor. I

have tumbled from the superb peaks of aesthetic exaltation to the snug foot-hills of warm humanity. It is a jolly country. No one need be ashamed of enjoying himself there. Only no one who has ever been on the heights can help feeling a little crestfallen in the cosy valleys. And let no one imagine, because he has made merry in the warm tilth and quaint nooks of romance, that he can even guess at the austere and thrilling raptures of those who have climbed the cold, white peaks of art.

23   About music most people are as willing to be humble as I am. If they cannot grasp musical form and win from it a pure aesthetic emotion, they confess that they understand music imperfectly or not at all. They recognise quite clearly that there is a difference between the feeling of the musician for pure music and that of the cheerful concertgoer for what music suggests. The latter enjoys his own emotions, as he has every right to do, and recog-nises their inferiority. Unfortunately, people are apt to be less modest about their powers of appreciating visual art. Everyone is inclined to believe that out of pictures, at any rate, he can get all that there is to be got; everyone is ready to cry "humbug" and "impostor" at those who say that more can be had. The good faith of people who feel pure aesthetic emotions is called in question by those who have never felt anything of the sort. It is the preva-lence of the representative element, I suppose, that makes the man in the street so sure that he knows a good picture when he sees one. For I have noticed that in matters of architecture, pottery, textiles, &c., ignorance and ineptitude are more willing to defer to the opinions of those who have been blest with peculiar sensibility. It is a pity that cultivated and intelligent men and women cannot be induced to believe that a great gift of aesthetic appre-ciation is at least as rare in visual as in musical art. A comparison of my own experience in both has enabled me to discriminate very clearly between pure and impure appreciation. Is it too much to ask that others should be as honest about their feelings for pictures as I have been about mine for music? For I am certain that most of those who visit galleries do feel very much what I feel at concerts. They have their moments of pure ecstasy; but the moments are short and unsure. Soon they fall back into the world of human interests and feel emotions, good no doubt, but inferior. I do not dream of saying that what they get from art is bad or nugatory; I say that they do not get the best that art can give. I do not say that they cannot understand art; rather I say that they cannot understand the state of mind of those who understand it best. I do not say that art means nothing or little to them; I say they miss its full significance. I do not suggest for one moment that their appreciation of art is a thing to be ashamed of; the majority of the charm-ing and intelligent people with whom I am acquainted appreciate visual art impurely; and, by the way, the appreciation of almost all great writers has been impure. But provided that there be some fraction of pure aesthetic emotion, even a mixed and minor appreciation of art is, I am sure, one of the most valuable things in the world — so valuable, indeed, that in my

giddier moments I have been tempted to believe that art might prove the world's salvation.

24 Yet, though the echoes and shadows of art enrich the life of the plains, her spirit dwells on the mountains. To him who woos, but woos impurely, she returns enriched what is brought. Like the sun, she warms the good seed in good soil and causes it to bring forth good fruit. But only to the perfect lover does she give a new strange gift — a gift beyond all price. Imperfect lovers bring to art and take away the ideas and emotions of their own age and civilisation. In twelfth-century Europe a man might have been greatly moved by a Romanesque church and found nothing in a T'ang picture. To a man of a later age, Greek sculpture meant much and Mexican nothing, for only to the former could he bring a crowd of associated ideas to be the objects of familiar emotions. But the perfect lover, he who can feel the profound significance of form, is raised above the accidents of time and place. To him the problems of archaelogy, history, and hagiography are impertinent. If the forms of a work are significant its provenance is irrelevant. Before the grandeur of those Sumerian figures in the Louvre he is carried on the same flood of emotion to the same aesthetic ecstasy as, more than four thousand years ago, the Chaldean lover was carried. It is the mark of great art that its appeal is universal and eternal.[3] Significant form stands charged with the power to provoke aesthetic emotion in anyone capable of feeling it. The ideas of men go buzz and die like gnats; men change their institutions and their customs as they change their coats; the intellectual triumphs of one age are the follies of another; only great art remains stable and unobscure. Great art remains stable and unobscure because the feelings that it awakens are independent of time and place, because its kingdom is not of this world. To those who have and hold a sense of the significance of form what does it matter whether the forms that move them were created in Paris the day before yesterday or in Babylon fifty centuries ago? The forms of art are inexhaustible; but all lead by the same road of aesthetic emotion to the same world of aesthetic ecstasy.

[3] Mr. Roger Fry permits me to make use of an interesting story that will illustrate my view. When Mr. Okakura, the Government editor of *The Temple Treasures of Japan*, first came to Europe, he found no difficulty in appreciating the pictures of those who from want of will or want of skill did not create illusions but concentrated their energies on the creation of form. He understood immediately the Byzantine masters and the French and Italian Primitives. In the Renaissance painters, on the other hand, with their descriptive preoccupations, their literary and anecdotic interests, he could see nothing but vulgarity and muddle. The universal and essential quality of art, significant form, was missing, or rather had dwindled to a shallow stream, overlaid and hidden beneath weeds, so the universal response, aesthetic emotion, was not evoked. It was not till he came on to Henri-Matisse that he again found himself in the familiar world of pure art. Similarly, sensitive Europeans who respond immediately to the significant forms of great Oriental art, are left cold by the trivial pieces of anecdote and social criticism so lovingly cherished by Chinese dilettanti. It would be easy to multiply instances did not decency forbid the laboring of so obvious a truth.

Commentary and questions

1. *Paragraphs 1-4:* These form a unit in which Bell seeks to establish a basis for his account of what art is, and by examining the structure of these paragraphs the reader can begin to test the quality of the hypothesis. The first paragraph breaks down into two closely related assertions — that there is very little relevant aesthetic theory and that a competent theorist must possess "artistic sensibility" and "a turn for clear thinking" — and one illustration, that of the friend with a good logical mind and no "artistic sensibility." The illustration does not prove the two assertions to be true; it merely suggests that they may be accurate. And notice that part of the illustration is itself an unproven assertion: We have only Bell's word for it that his friend is aesthetically insensitive.

The second paragraph continues this illustrative process, but in another direction. This time Bell asserts that many people with aesthetic sensitivity and powers of "criticism" are yet unable to theorize.

On the basis of the first two paragraphs examine the statements in paragraph 3: What is their purpose? You can also ask a substantive question: How does one identify those people capable of "artistic feeling"?

What function does the fourth paragraph perform? Does it assert, support, or both? How does Bell suggest "significant form" may be recognized?

2. *Paragraphs 5-9:* These attempt to dispose of objections to what Bell has previously argued. By what kind of statement is this refutation made? See especially paragraph 7.

3. *Paragraphs 10-11, 13-18:* Here Bell tries to distinguish "art" from other kinds of expression. What is his ground for that distinction? Does he exclude things you would normally consider "art"? Which paragraphs develop the distinction by example? What must the reader agree to in order to accept the validity of the examples as Bell uses them?

4. *Paragraphs 19-23:* These distinguish aesthetic emotion from ordinary human feelings. How does Bell try to demonstrate the notion that aesthetic feelings are not the "emotions of life" (paragraph 21)? Does he support the assertion?

5. The concluding paragraph shows a distinct alteration in the tone of its language. List the more emotive words and metaphors. In what way do they suggest that "pure" aesthetic emotion is different from the emotions of life?

Topics for discussion and writing

I. Make a list of the types of statement used by Bell. Then list the types of support he uses. How many of his most fundamental assertions receive adequate support?

II. Bell's thesis seems to rest largely on his concept of a "peculiar" aesthetic emotion. How fully does he describe this emotion? (Remember that it is virtually impossible to *prove* factually that an emotion is what we say it is. No two people will be moved in precisely the same way by any experience or sensation, and at this point the careful reader might wish to raise the question of how we agree that there are such states of being common to all of us. On the basis of such a question, one might be able to agree or disagree with Bell's assertion that there is a distinct kind of feeling provoked by art.) In what respects does he attempt to describe this emotion negatively?

III. Write a theme explaining Bell's distinction between primitive and representational art. Can you think of any example that might fit his definitions of each?

IV. Write a theme arguing the thesis that Bell is merely talking about the kind of art *he* likes.

V. Write a theme explaining Bell's theory of significant form.

AN ESSAY IN AESTHETICS Roger Fry

From Vision and Design. *Reprinted by permission of Chatto and Windus, Ltd., and Meridian Books, Inc. Meridian Edition first published September, 1956.*

A CERTAIN painter, not without some reputation at the present day, once wrote a little book on the art he practises, in which he gave a definition of that art so succinct that I take it as a point of departure for this essay.

2 "The art of painting," says that eminent authority, "is the art of imitating solid objects upon a flat surface by means of pigments." It is delightfully simple, but prompts the question — Is that all? And, if so, what a deal of unnecessary fuss has been made about it. Now, it is useless to deny that our modern writer has some very respectable authorities behind him. Plato, indeed, gave a very similar account of the affair, and himself put the question — is it then worth while? And, being scrupulously and relentlessly logical, he decided that it was not worth while, and proceeded to turn the artists out of his ideal republic. For all that, the world has continued obstinately to consider that painting was worth while, and though, indeed, it has never quite made up its mind as to what, exactly, the graphic arts did for it, it has persisted in honouring and admiring its painters.

3 Can we arrive at any conclusions as to the nature of the graphic arts, which will at all explain our feelings about them, which will at least put them into some kind of relation with the other arts, and not leave us in the extreme perplexity, engendered by any theory of mere imitation? For, I suppose, it must be admitted that if imitation is the sole purpose of the graphic arts, it is surprising that the works of such arts are ever looked upon as more than curiosities, or ingenious toys, are ever taken seriously by

grown-up people. Moreover, it will be surprising that they have no recog-
nisable affinity with other arts, such as music or architecture, in which the
imitation of actual objects is a negligible quantity.

4   To form such conclusions is the aim I have put before myself in this
essay. Even if the results are not decisive, the inquiry may lead us to a view
of the graphic arts that will not be altogether unfruitful.

5   I must begin with some elementary psychology, with a consideration of
the nature of instincts. A great many objects in the world, when presented
to our senses, put in motion a complex nervous machinery, which ends in
some instinctive appropriate action. We see a wild bull in a field; quite
without our conscious interference a nervous process goes on, which, unless
we interfere forcibly, ends in the appropriate reaction of flight. The nervous
mechanism which results in flight causes a certain state of consciousness,
which we call the emotion of fear. The whole of animal life, and a great part
of human life, is made up of these instinctive reactions to sensible objects,
and their accompanying emotions. But man has the peculiar faculty of
calling up again in his mind the echo of past experiences of this kind, of
going over it again, "in imagination" as we say. He has, therefore, the possibility of a double life; one the actual life, the other the imaginative life.
Between these two lives there is this great distinction, that in the actual life
the processes of natural selection have brought it about that the instinctive
reaction, such, for instance, as flight from danger, shall be the important part
of the whole process, and it is towards this that the man bends his whole
conscious endeavour. But in the imaginative life no such action is necessary,
and, therefore, the whole consciousness may be focussed upon the perceptive
and the emotional aspects of the experience. In this way we get, in the imaginative life, a different set of values, and a different kind of perception.

6   We can get a curious side glimpse of the nature of this imaginative life
from the cinematograph. This resembles actual life in almost every respect,
except that what the psychologists call the conative part of our reaction to
sensations, that is to say, the appropriate resultant action is cut off. If, in a
cinematograph, we see a runaway horse and cart, we do not have to think
either of getting out of the way or heroically interposing ourselves. The result is that in the first place we *see* the event much more clearly; see a
number of quite interesting but irrelevant things, which in real life could
not struggle into our consciousness, bent, as it would be, entirely upon the
problem of our appropriate reaction. I remember seeing in a cinematograph
the arrival of a train at a foreign station and the people descending from the
carriages; there was no platform, and to my intense surprise I saw several
people turn right round after reaching the ground, as though to orientate
themselves; an almost ridiculous performance, which I had never noticed in
all the many hundred occasions on which such a scene had passed before
my eyes in real life. The fact being that at a station one is never really a
spectator of events, but an actor engaged in the drama of luggage or pro-

spective seats, and one actually sees only so much as may help to the appropriate action.

7   In the second place, with regard to the visions of the cinematograph, one notices that whatever emotions are aroused by them, though they are likely to be weaker than those of ordinary life, are presented more clearly to the consciousness. If the scene presented be one of an accident, our pity and horror, though weak, since we know that no one is really hurt, are felt quite purely, since they cannot, as they would in life, pass at once into actions of assistance.

8   A somewhat similar effect to that of the cinematograph can be obtained by watching a mirror in which a street scene is reflected. If we look at the street itself we are almost sure to adjust ourselves in some way to its actual existence. We recognise an acquaintance, and wonder why he looks so dejected this morning, or become interested in a new fashion in hats — the moment we do that the spell is broken, we are reacting to life itself in however slight a degree, but, in the mirror, it is easier to abstract ourselves completely, and look upon the changing scene as a whole. It then, at once, takes on the visionary quality, and we become true spectators, not selecting what we will see, but seeing everything equally, and thereby we come to notice a number of appearances and relations of appearances, which would have escaped our notice before, owing to that perpetual economising by selection of what impressions we will assimilate, which in life we perform by unconscious processes. The frame of the mirror, then, does to some extent turn the reflected scene from one that belongs to our actual life into one that belongs rather to the imaginative life. The frame of the mirror makes its surface into a very rudimentary work of art, since it helps us to attain to the artistic vision. For that is what, as you will already have guessed, I have been coming to all this time, namely that the work of art is intimately connected with the secondary imaginative life, which all men live to a greater or less extent.

9   That the graphic arts are the expression of the imaginative life rather than a copy of actual life might be guessed from observing children. Children, if left to themselves, never, I believe, copy what they see, never, as we say, "draw from nature," but express, with a delightful freedom and sincerity, the mental images which make up their own imaginative lives.

10   Art, then, is an expression and a stimulus of this imaginative life, which is separated from actual life by the absence of responsive action. Now this responsive action implies in actual life moral responsibility. In art we have no such moral responsibility — it presents a life freed from the binding necessities of our actual existence.

11   What then is the justification for this life of the imagination which all human beings live more or less fully? To the pure moralist, who accepts nothing but ethical values, in order to be justified, it must be shown not only *not* to hinder but actually to forward right action, otherwise it is not only

useless but, since it absorbs our energies, positively harmful. To such a one two views are possible, one the Puritanical view at its narrowest, which regards the life of the imagination as no better or worse than a life of sensual pleasure, and therefore entirely reprehensible. The other view is to argue that the imaginative life does subserve morality. And this is inevitably the view taken by moralists like Ruskin, to whom the imaginative life is yet an absolute necessity. It is a view which leads to some very hard special pleading, even to a self-deception which is in itself morally undesirable.

12   But here comes in the question of religion, for religion is also an affair of the imaginative life, and, though it claims to have a direct effect upon conduct, I do not suppose that the religious person if he were wise would justify religion entirely by its effect on morality, since that, historically speaking, has not been by any means uniformly advantageous. He would probably say that the religious experience was one which corresponded to certain spiritual capacities of human nature, the exercise of which is in itself good and desirable apart from their effect upon actual life. And so, too, I think the artist might if he chose take a mystical attitude, and declare that the fullness and completeness of the imaginative life he leads may correspond to an existence more real and more important than any that we know of in mortal life.

13   And in saying that, his appeal would find a sympathetic echo in most minds, for most people would, I think, say that the pleasures derived from art were of an altogether different character and more fundamental than merely sensual pleasures, that they did exercise some faculties which are felt to belong to whatever part of us there may be which is not entirely ephemeral and material.

14   It might even be that from this point of view we should rather justify actual life by its relation to the imaginative, justify nature by its likeness to art. I mean this, that since the imaginative life comes in the course of time to represent more or less what mankind feels to be the completest expression of its own nature, the freest use of its innate capacities, the actual life may be explained and justified by its approximation here and there, however partially and inadequately, to that freer and fuller life.

15   Before leaving this question of the justification of art, let me put it in another way. The imaginative life of a people has very different levels at different times, and these levels do not always correspond with the general level of the morality of actual life. Thus in the thirteenth century we read of barbarity and cruelty which would shock even us; we may, I think, admit that our moral level, our general humanity is decidedly higher to-day, but the level of our imaginative life is incomparably lower; we are satisfied there with a grossness, a sheer barbarity and squalor which would have shocked the thirteenth century profoundly. Let us admit the moral gain gladly, but do we not also feel a loss; do we not feel that the average business man would be in every way a more admirable, more respectable being if his

imaginative life were not so squalid and incoherent? And, if we admit any loss then, there is some function in human nature other than a purely ethical one, which is worthy of exercise.

16   Now the imaginative life has its own history both in the race and in the individual. In the individual life one of the first effects of freeing experience from the necessities of appropriate responsive action is to indulge recklessly the emotion of self-aggrandisement. The day-dreams of a child are filled with extravagant romances in which he is always the invincible hero. Music — which of all the arts supplies the strongest stimulus to the imaginative life, and at the same time has the least power of controlling its direction — music, at certain stages of people's lives, has the effect merely of arousing in an almost absurd degree this egoistic elation, and Tolstoy appears to believe that this is its only possible effect. But with the teaching of experience and the growth of character the imaginative life comes to respond to other instincts and to satisfy other desires, until, indeed, it reflects the highest aspirations and the deepest aversions of which human nature is capable.

17   In dreams and when under the influence of drugs the imaginative life passes out of our own control, and in such cases its experiences may be highly undesirable, but whenever it remains under our own control it must always be on the whole a desirable life. That is not to say that it is always pleasant, for it is pretty clear that mankind is so constituted as to desire much besides pleasure, and we shall meet among the great artists, the great exponents, that is, of the imaginative life, many to whom the merely pleasant is very rarely a part of what is desirable. But this desirability of the imaginative life does distinguish it very sharply from actual life, and is the direct result of that first fundamental difference, its freedom from necessary external conditions. Art, then, is, if I am right, the chief organ of the imaginative life; it is by art that it is stimulated and controlled within us, and, as we have seen, the imaginative life is distinguished by the greater clearness of its perception, and the greater purity and freedom of its emotion.

18   First with regard to the greater clearness of perception. The needs of our actual life are so imperative, that the sense of vision becomes highly specialised in their service. With an admirable economy we learn to see only so much as is needful for our purposes; but this is in fact very little, just enough to recognise and identify each object or person; that done, they go into an entry in our mental catalogue and are no more really seen. In actual life the normal person really only reads the labels as it were on the objects around him and troubles no further. Almost all the things which are useful in any way put on more or less this cap of invisibility. It is only when an object exists in our lives for no other purpose than to be seen that we really look at it, as for instance at a China ornament or a precious stone, and towards such even the most normal person adopts to some extent the artistic attitude of pure vision abstracted from necessity.

19   Now this specialisation of vision goes so far that ordinary people have

almost no idea of what things really look like, so that oddly enough the one standard that popular criticism applies to painting, namely, whether it is like nature or not, is one which most people are, by the whole tenour of their lives, prevented from applying properly. The only things they have ever really *looked* at being other pictures; the moment an artist who has looked at nature brings to them a clear report of something definitely seen by him, they are wildly indignant at its untruth to nature. This has happened so constantly in our own time that there is no need to prove it. One instance will suffice. Monet is an artist whose chief claim to recognition lies in the fact of his astonishing power of faithfully reproducing certain aspects of nature, but his really naïve innocence and sincerity were taken by the public to be the most audacious humbug, and it required the teaching of men like Bastien-Lepage, who cleverly compromised between the truth and an accepted convention of what things looked like, to bring the world gradually round to admitting truths which a single walk in the country with purely unbiassed vision would have established beyond doubt.

20   But though this clarified sense perception which we discover in the imaginative life is of great interest, and although it plays a larger part in the graphic arts than in any other, it might perhaps be doubted whether, interesting, curious, fascinating as it is, this aspect of the imaginative life would ever by itself make art of profound importance to mankind. But it is different, I think, with the emotional aspect. We have admitted that the emotions of the imaginative are generally weaker than those of actual life. The picture of a saint being slowly flayed alive, revolting as it is, will not produce the same physical sensations of sickening disgust that a modern man would feel if he could assist at the actual event; but they have a compensating clearness of presentment to the consciousness. The more poignant emotions of actual life have, I think, a kind of numbing effect analogous to the paralysing influence of fear in some animals; but even if this experience be not generally admitted, all will admit that the need for responsive action hurries us along and prevents us from ever realising fully what the emotion is that we feel, from co-ordinating it perfectly with other states. In short, the motives we actually experience are too close to us to enable us to feel them clearly. They are in a sense unintelligible. In the imaginative life, on the contrary, we can both feel the emotion and watch it. When we are really moved at the theatre we are always both on the stage and in the auditorium.

21   Yet another point about the emotions of the imaginative life — since they require no responsive action we can give them a new valuation. In real life we must to some extent cultivate those emotions which lead to useful action, and we are bound to appraise emotions according to the resultant action. So that, for instance, the feelings of rivalry and emulation do get an encouragement which perhaps they scarcely deserve, whereas certain feelings which appear to have a high intrinsic value get almost no stimulus in actual life. For instance, those feelings to which the name of the cosmic

emotion has been somewhat unhappily given find almost no place in life, but, since they seem to belong to certain very deep springs of our nature, do become of great importance in the arts.

22   Morality, then, appreciates emotion by the standard of resultant action. Art appreciates emotion in and for itself.

23   This view of the essential importance in art of the expression of the emotions is the basis of Tolstoy's marvellously original and yet perverse and even exasperating book, "What is Art?" and I willingly confess, while disagreeing with almost all his results, how much I owe to him.

24   He gives an example of what he means by calling art the means of communicating emotions. He says, let us suppose a boy to have been pursued in the forest by a bear. If he returns to the village and merely states that he was pursued by a bear and escaped, that is ordinary language, the means of communicating facts or ideas; but if he describes his state first of heedlessness, then of sudden alarm and terror as the bear appears, and finally of relief when he gets away, and describes this so that his hearers share his emotions, then his description is a work of art.

25   Now in so far as the boy does this in order to urge the villagers to go out and kill the bear, though he may be using artistic methods, his speech is not a pure work of art; but if of a winter evening the boy relates his experience for the sake of the enjoyment of his adventure in retrospect, or better still, if he makes up the whole story for the sake of the imagined emotions, then his speech becomes a pure work of art. But Tolstoy takes the other view, and values the emotions aroused by art entirely for their reaction upon actual life, a view which he courageously maintains even when it leads him to condemn the whole of Michelangelo, Raphael and Titian, and most of Beethoven, not to mention nearly everything he himself has written, as bad or false art.

26   Such a view would, I think, give pause to any less heroic spirit. He would wonder whether mankind could have always been so radically wrong about a function that, whatever its value be, is almost universal. And in point of fact he will have to find some other word to denote what we now call art. Nor does Tolstoy's theory even carry him safely through his own book, since, in his examples of morally desirable and therefore good art, he has to admit that these are to be found, for the most part, among works of inferior quality. Here, then, is at once the tacit admission that another standard than morality is applicable. We must therefore give up the attempt to judge the work of art by its reaction on life, and consider it as an expression of emotions regarded as ends in themselves. And this brings us back to the idea we had already arrived at, of art as the expression of the imaginative life.

27   If, then, an object of any kind is created by man not for use, for its fitness to actual life, but as an object of art, an object subserving the imaginative life, what will its qualities be? It must in the first place be adapted to

that disinterested intensity of contemplation, which we have found to be the effect of cutting off the responsive action. It must be suited to that heightened power of perception which we found to result therefrom.

28   And the first quality that we demand in our sensations will be order, without which our sensations will be troubled and perplexed, and the other quality will be variety, without which they will not be fully stimulated.

29   It may be objected that many things in nature, such as flowers, possess these qualities of order and variety in a high degree, and these objects do undoubtedly stimulate and satisfy that clear disinterested contemplation which is characteristic of the æsthetic attitude. But in our reaction to a work of art there is something more — there is the consciousness of purpose, the consciousness of a peculiar relation of sympathy with the man who made this thing in order to arouse precisely the sensations we experience. And when we come to the higher works of art, where sensations are so arranged that they arouse in us deep emotions, this feeling of a special tie with the man who expressed them becomes very strong. We feel that he has expressed something which was latent in us all the time, but which we never realised, that he has revealed us to ourselves in revealing himself. And this recognition of purpose is, I believe, an essential part of the æsthetic judgment proper.

30   The perception of purposeful order and variety in an object gives us the feeling which we express by saying that it is beautiful, but when by means of sensations our emotions are aroused we demand purposeful order and variety in them also, and if this can only be brought about by the sacrifice of sensual beauty we willingly overlook its absence.

31   Thus, there is no excuse for a china pot being ugly, there is every reason why Rembrandt's and Degas' pictures should be, from the purely sensual point of view, supremely and magnificently ugly.

32   This, I think, will explain the apparent contradiction between two distinct uses of the word beauty, one for that which has sensuous charm, and one for the æsthetic approval of works of imaginative art where the objects presented to us are often of extreme ugliness. Beauty in the former sense belongs to works of art where only the perceptual aspect of the imaginative life is exercised, beauty in the second sense becomes as it were supersensual, and is concerned with the appropriateness and intensity of the emotions aroused. When these emotions are aroused in a way that satisfies fully the needs of the imaginative life we approve and delight in the sensations through which we enjoy that heightened experience because they possess purposeful order and variety in relation to those emotions.

33   One chief aspect of order in a work of art is unity; unity of some kind is necessary for our restful contemplation of the work of art as a whole, since if it lacks unity we cannot contemplate it in its entirety, but we shall pass outside it to other things necessary to complete its unity.

34   In a picture this unity is due to a balancing of the attractions of the eye about the central line of the picture. The result of this balance of attractions is that the eye rests willingly within the bounds of the picture. Dr. Denman Ross of Harvard University has made a most valuable study of the elementary considerations upon which this balance is based in his "Theory of Pure Design." He sums up his results in the formula that a composition is of value in proportion to the number of orderly connections which it displays.

35   Dr. Ross wisely restricts himself to the study of abstract and meaningless forms. The moment representation is introduced forms have an entirely new set of values. Thus a line which indicated the sudden bend of a head in a certain direction would have far more than its mere value as line in the composition because of the attraction which a marked gesture has for the eye. In almost all paintings this disturbance of the purely decorative values by reason of the representative effect takes place, and the problem becomes too complex for geometrical proof.

36   This merely decorative unity is, moreover, of very different degrees of intensity in different artists and in different periods. The necessity for a closely woven geometrical texture in the composition is much greater in heroic and monumental design than in genre pieces on a small scale.

37   It seems also probable that our appreciation of unity in pictorial design is of two kinds. We are so accustomed to consider only the unity which results from the balance of a number of attractions presented to the eye simultaneously in a framed picture that we forget the possibility of other pictorial forms.

38   In certain Chinese paintings the length is so great that we cannot take in the whole picture at once, nor are we intended to do so. Sometimes a landscape is painted upon a roll of silk so long that we can only look at it in successive segments. As we unroll it at one end and roll it up at the other we traverse wide stretches of country, tracing, perhaps, all the vicissitudes of a river from its source to the sea, and yet, when this is well done, we have received a very keen impression of pictorial unity.

39   Such a successive unity is of course familiar to us in literature and music, and it plays its part in the graphic arts. It depends upon the forms being presented to us in such a sequence that each successive element is felt to have a fundamental and harmonious relation with that which preceded it. I suggest that in looking at drawings our sense of pictorial unity is largely of this nature; we feel, if the drawing be a good one, that each modulation of the line as our eye passes along it gives order and variety to our sensations. Such a drawing may be almost entirely lacking in the geometrical balance which we are accustomed to demand in paintings, and yet have, in a remarkable degree, unity.

40   Let us now see how the artist passes from the stage of merely gratifying

our demand for sensuous order and variety to that where he arouses our emotions. I will call the various methods by which this is effected the emotional elements of design.

41   The first element is that of the rhythm of the line with which the forms are delineated.

42   The drawn line is the record of a gesture, and that gesture is modified by the artist's feeling which is thus communicated to us directly.

43   The second element is mass. When an object is so represented that we recognise it as having inertia we feel its power of resisting movement, or communicating its own movement to other bodies, and our imaginative reaction to such an image is governed by our experience of mass in actual life.

44   The third element is space. The same-sized square on two pieces of paper can be made by very simple means to appear to represent either a cube two or three inches high, or a cube of hundreds of feet, and our reaction to it is proportionately changed.

45   The fourth element is that of light and shade. Our feelings towards the same object become totally different according as we see it strongly illuminated against a black background or dark against light.

46   A fifth element is that of colour. That this has a direct emotional effect is evident from such words as gay, dull, melancholy in relation to colour.

47   I would suggest the possibility of another element, though perhaps it is only a compound of mass and space: it is that of the inclination to the eye of a plane, whether it is impending over or leaning away from us.

48   Now it will be noticed that nearly all these emotional elements of design are connected with essential conditions of our physical existence: rhythm appeals to all the sensations which accompany muscular activity; mass to all the infinite adaptations to the force of gravity which we are forced to make; the spatial judgment is equally profound and universal in its application to life; our feeling about inclined planes is connected with our necessary judgments about the conformation of the earth itself; light again, is so necessary a condition of our existence that we become intensely sensitive to changes in its intensity. Colour is the only one of our elements which is not of critical or universal importance to life, and its emotional effect is neither so deep nor so clearly determined as the others. It will be seen, then, that the graphic arts arouse emotions in us by playing upon what one may call the overtones of some of our primary physical needs. They have, indeed, this great advantage over poetry, that they can appeal more directly and immediately to the emotional accompaniments of our bare physical existence.

49   If we represent these various elements in simple diagrammatic terms, this effect upon the emotions is, it must be confessed, very weak. Rhythm of line, for instance, is incomparably weaker in its stimulus of the muscular sense than is rhythm addressed to the ear in music, and such diagrams can at best arouse only faint ghost-like echoes of emotions of differing qualities; but when these emotional elements are combined with the presentation of

natural appearances, above all with the appearance of the human body, we find that this effect is indefinitely heightened.

50 When, for instance, we look at Michelangelo's "Jeremiah," and realise the irresistible momentum his movements would have, we experience powerful sentiments of reverence and awe. Or when we look at Michelangelo's "Tondo" in the Uffizi, and find a group of figures so arranged that the planes have a sequence comparable in breadth and dignity to the mouldings of the earth mounting by clearly-felt gradations to an overtopping summit, innumerable instinctive reactions are brought into play.[1]

51 At this point the adversary (as Leonardo da Vinci calls him) is likely enough to retort, "You have abstracted from natural forms a number of so-called emotional elements which you yourself admit are very weak when stated with diagrammatic purity; you then put them back, with the help of Michelangelo, into the natural forms whence they were derived, and at once they have value, so that after all it appears that the natural forms contain these emotional elements ready made up for us, and all that art need do is to imitate Nature."

52 But, alas! Nature is heartlessly indifferent to the needs of the imaginative life; God causes His rain to fall upon the just and upon the unjust. The sun neglects to provide the appropriate limelight effect even upon a triumphant Napoleon or a dying Cæsar.[2] Assuredly we have no guarantee that in nature the emotional elements will be combined appropriately with the demands of the imaginative life, and it is, I think, the great occupation of the graphic arts to give us first of all order and variety in the sensuous plane, and then so to arrange the sensuous presentment of objects that the emotional elements are elicited with an order and appropriateness altogether beyond what Nature herself provides.

53 Let me sum up for a moment what I have said about the relation of art to Nature, which is, perhaps, the greatest stumbling-block to the understanding of the graphic arts.

54 I have admitted that there is beauty in Nature, that is to say, that certain objects constantly do, and perhaps any object may, compel us to regard it with that intense disinterested contemplation that belongs to the imaginative life, and which is impossible to the actual life of necessity and action; but that in objects created to arouse the æsthetic feeling we have an added consciousness of purpose on the part of the creator, that he made it on purpose not to be used but to be regarded and enjoyed; and that this feeling is characteristic of the æsthetic judgment proper.

---

[1] Rodin is reported to have said, "A woman, a mountain, a horse — they are all the same thing; they are made on the same principles." That is to say, their forms, when viewed with the disinterested vision of the imaginative life, have similar emotional elements.

[2] I do not forget that at the death of Tennyson the writer in the *Daily Telegraph* averred that "level beams of the setting moon streamed in upon the face of the dying bard"; but then, after all, in its way the *Daily Telegraph* is a work of art.

55   When the artist passes from pure sensations to emotions aroused by means of sensations, he uses natural forms which, in themselves, are calculated to move our emotions, and he presents these in such a manner that the forms themselves generate in us emotional states, based upon the fundamental necessities of our physical and physiological nature. The artist's attitude to natural form is, therefore, infinitely various according to the emotions he wishes to arouse. He may require for his purpose the most complete representation of a figure, he may be intensely realistic, provided that his presentment, in spite of its closeness to natural appearance, disengages clearly for us the appropriate emotional elements. Or he may give us the merest suggestion of natural forms, and rely almost entirely upon the force and intensity of the emotional elements involved in his presentment.

56   We may, then, dispense once for all with the idea of likeness to Nature, of correctness or incorrectness as a test, and consider only whether the emotional elements inherent in natural form are adequately discovered, unless, indeed, the emotional idea depends at any point upon likeness, or completeness of representation.

Commentary and questions

1. *Paragraphs 1-4:* This unit is an introduction that seeks to justify the existence of art and mankind's interest in it by objecting to its definition as imitation. Fry does not define imitation. Is a definition implicit in the context?

2. *Paragraphs 5-10:* The first stage of Fry's exposition of his theory falls here. Broadly speaking these paragraphs are a series of related assertions: that we have an imaginative life, that it permits us to *see* certain actions and events more clearly if they are presented in a certain medium (as in motion pictures), that the emotions aroused by these sensations are felt more clearly, that "life" which is seen as in the frame of a mirror is viewed more sharply and detachedly, and that the graphic arts are an expression of "imaginative life." Like Clive Bell, Fry relies on assertion as the basis of his argument. Also like Bell, he illustrates his assertions. Are the illustrations the same kind as Bell's? Do we agree more readily to Fry's examples of the bull, the "cinematograph," the mirror, than we do to Bell's friend who has no aesthetic sensibility or to the pictures Bell cites as examples of representation? If so, why?

    Notice also that Fry's assertions are linked so that they tend to define each other. What assumption must be agreed upon to make the first two assertions valid?

3. *Paragraphs 11-15:* Analyze these paragraphs, discussing the types of statement, their relationships to each other, and the relationship of this stage of the argument to the previous stage.

4. *Paragraphs 16-22:* These develop the concept that morality and art evaluate emotions by different standards. Examine each paragraph to see

if it is built upon the spelling out of distinctions between morality and art. Does Fry use analogy in any place? If so, what is its effect?

5. *Paragraphs 23-26:* How does Fry further develop his distinction between morality and art? To what extent does he agree with Tolstoy?

6. *Paragraphs 27-39:* Fry considers various aspects of the "quality" of art. What major elements does he isolate? How does he illustrate them and in which paragraphs? Are his explanations based entirely on qualities inherent in art objects? See paragraph 29.

7. *Paragraphs 40-56:* These constitute the final stage of the essay, but this unit may be broken down. First Fry discusses the particular elements in the graphic arts which provoke human emotions. Notice that paragraphs 41-47 are all relatively short. Why? Paragraph 48 connects the six elements Fry has chosen with "essential conditions of our physical existence." Are these essential conditions fact, or are they merely assertions? Does Fry explain all the connections between art and physical existence with equal explicitness?

Paragraphs 49-50 are an attempt to show the basis in art for our interest and response to it. Is this stage of the argument consistent with Fry's rejection of "imitation" as a definition of art? See paragraphs 1-4, and paragraphs 55-56.

Topics for discussion and writing

I. Make an outline or paraphrase of the main sections of Fry's essay. Include the illustrations and examples he uses to support his argument identifying each type of support. This exercise should be a useful introduction to Part III of this anthology.

II. How many types of paragraph can you identify? Which are the most essential to Fry's purpose?

III. Examine the following key words in their contexts: "imaginative life," "morality," "emotion," "order" (or "unity"), "beauty." How is each defined? How are they paraphrased or restated by Fry?

IV. Both Fry and Bell discuss the graphic arts with respect to the emotions they produce. Write a theme comparing the two authors on this point. Does each understand the same concept in using the word "emotion"? Does each identify emotions with equal clarity? Does each have the same basic concept of good and bad art? Does each react in the same way to representational or imitative art? Is Fry's "imaginative life" essentially the same thing as Bell's "aesthetic emotion"?

V. Write a theme explaining and comparing Bell's and Fry's understanding of form in the graphic arts.

THE DYNAMIC IMAGE   Susanne K. Langer

*Reprinted with the permission
of Charles Scribner's Sons from*
Problems of Art *by Susanne K.
Langer. Copyright, 1957, Susanne K. Langer.*

ONCE upon a time a student, paging through a college catalogue, asked me
in evident bewilderment: "What is 'philosophy of art'? How in the world
can art be philosophical?"

2   Art is not philosophical at all; philosophy and art are two different
things. But there is nothing one cannot philosophize about — that is, there
is nothing that does not offer some philosophical problems. Art, in particular,
presents hosts of them. Artists do not generally moot such matters explicitly,
though they often have fairly good working notions of a philosophical sort
— notions that only have to be put into the right words to answer our questions, or at least to move them along toward their answers.

3   What, exactly, is a philosophical question?

4   A philosophical question is always a demand for the *meaning* of what
we are saying. This makes it different from a scientific question, which is a
question of fact; in a question of fact, we take for granted that we know
what we mean — that is, what we are talking about. If one asks: "How far
from here is the sun?" the answer is a statement of fact, "About ninety million miles." We assume that we know what we mean by "the sun" and by
"miles" and "being so-and-so far from here." Even if the answer is wrong —
if it fails to state a fact, as it would if you answered "twenty thousand miles"
— we still know what we are talking about. We take some measurements
and find out which answer is true. But suppose one asks: "What is space?"
"What is meant by 'here'?" "What is meant by 'the distance' from here to
somewhere else?" The answer is not found by taking measurements or by
making experiments or in any way discovering facts. The answer can only
be found by thinking — reflecting on what we mean. This is sometimes
simple; we analyze our meanings and define each word. But more often we
find that we have no clear concepts at all, and the fuzzy ones we have
conflict with each other so that as soon as we analyze them, i.e., make them
clear, we find them contradictory, senseless, or fantastic. Then logical analysis does not help us; what we need then is the more difficult, but also more
interesting part of philosophy, the part that cannot be taught by any rule —
logical construction. We have to figure out a meaning for our statements, a
way to think about the things that interest us. Science is not possible unless
we can attach some meaning to "distance" and "point" and "space" and "ve-
locity," and other such familiar but really quite slippery words. To establish
those fundamental meanings is philosophical work; and the philosophy of
modern science is one of the most brilliant intellectual works of our time.

5   The philosophy of art is not so well developed, but it is full of life and
ferment just now. Both professional philosophers and intellectually gifted
artists are asking questions about the meaning of "art," of "expression," of

"artistic truth," "form," "reality," and dozens of other words that they hear and use, but find — to their surprise — they cannot define, because when they analyze what they mean it is not anything coherent and tenable.

6   The construction of a coherent theory — a set of connected ideas about some whole subject — begins with the solution of a central problem; that is, with the establishing of a key concept. There is no way of knowing, by any general rule, what constitutes a central problem; it is not always the most general or the most fundamental one you can raise. But the best sign that you have broached a central philosophical issue is that in solving it you raise new interesting questions. The concept you construct has *implications*, and by implication builds up further ideas, that illuminate other concepts of the whole subject, to answer other questions, sometimes before you even ask them. A key concept solves more problems than it was designed for.

7   In philosophy of art, one of the most interesting problems — one that proves to be really central — is the meaning of that much-used word, "creation." Why do we say an artist creates a work? He does not create oil pigments or canvas, or the structure of tonal vibrations, or words of a language if he is a poet, or, in the case of a dancer, his body and its mobility. He finds all these things and uses them, as a cook uses eggs and flour and so forth to make a cake, or a manufacturer uses wool to make thread, and thread to make socks. It is only in a mood of humor or extravagance that we speak of the cake Mother "created." But when it comes to works of art, we earnestly call them creations. This raises the philosophical question: What do we mean by that word? What is created?

8   If you pursue this issue, it grows into a complex of closely related questions: what is created in art, what for, and how? The answers involve just about all the key concepts for a coherent philosophy of art: such concepts as *apparition,* or the image, *expressiveness, feeling, motif, transformation.* There are others, but they are all interrelated.

9   It is impossible to talk, in one lecture, about all the arts, and not end with a confusion of principles and illustrations. Since we are particularly concerned, just now, with the dance, let us narrow our discussion and center it about this art. Our first question, then, becomes: What do dancers create?

10   Obviously, a dance. As I pointed out before, they do not create the materials of the dance — neither their own bodies, nor the cloth that drapes them, nor the floor, nor any of the ambient space, light, musical tone, the forces of gravity, nor any other physical provisions; all these things they *use,* to create something over and above what is physically there: the dance.

11   What, then, is the dance?

12   The dance is an appearance; if you like, an apparition. It springs from what the dancers do, yet it is something else. In watching a dance, you do not see what is physically before you — people running around or twisting their bodies; what you see is a display of interacting forces, by which the dance seems to be lifted, driven, drawn, closed, or attenuated, whether it be solo or choric, whirling like the end of a dervish dance, or slow, cen-

tered, and single in its motion. One human body may put the whole play of mysterious powers before you. But these powers, these forces that seem to operate in the dance, are not the physical forces of the dancer's muscles, which actually cause the movements taking place. The forces we seem to perceive most directly and convincingly are created for our perception; and they exist only for it.

13   Anything that exists only for perception, and plays no ordinary, passive part in nature as common objects do, is a virtual entity. It is not unreal; where it confronts you, you really perceive it, you don't dream or imagine that you do. The image in a mirror is a virtual image. A rainbow is a virtual object. It seems to stand on the earth or in the clouds, but it really "stands" nowhere; it is only visible, not tangible. Yet it is a real rainbow, produced by moisture and light for any normal eye looking at it from the right place. We don't just dream that we see it. If, however, we believe it to have the ordinary properties of a physical thing, we are mistaken; it is an appearance, a virtual object, a sun-created image.

14   What dancers create is a dance; and a dance is an apparition of active powers, a *dynamic image*. Everything a dancer actually does serves to create what we really see; but what we really see is a virtual entity. The physical realities are given: place, gravity, body, muscular strength, muscular control, and secondary assets such as light, sound, or things (usable objects, so-called "properties"). All these are actual. But in the dance, they disappear; the more perfect the dance, the less we see its actualities. What we see, hear, and feel are the virtual realities, the moving forces of the dance, the apparent centers of power and their emanations, their conflicts and resolutions, lift and decline, their rhythmic life. These are the elements of the created apparition, and are themselves not physically given, but artistically created.

15   Here we have, then, the answer to our first question: what do dancers create? The dynamic image, which is the dance.

16   This answer leads naturally to the second question: for what is this image created?

17   Again, there is an obvious answer: for our enjoyment. But what makes us enjoy it as intensely as we do? We do not enjoy every virtual image, just because it is one. A mirage in the desert is intriguing chiefly because it is rare. A mirror image, being common, is not an object of wonder, and in itself, just as an image, does not thrill us. But the dynamic image created in dancing has a different character. It is more than a perceivable entity; this apparition, given to the eye, or to the ear and eye, and through them to our whole responsive sensibility, strikes us as something charged with feeling. Yet this feeling is not necessarily what any or all of the dancers feel. It belongs to the dance itself. A dance, like any other work of art, is a perceptible form that expresses the nature of human feeling — the rhythms and connections, crisis and breaks, the complexity and richness of what is sometimes called man's "inner life," the stream of direct experience, life as it feels to the living. Dancing is not a symptom of how the dancer happens to feel; for the dancer's

own feelings could not be prescribed or predicted and exhibited upon request. Our own feelings simply occur, and most people do not care to have us express them by sighs or squeals or gesticulation. If that were what dancers really did, there would not be many balletomaniacs to watch them.

18 What is expressed in a dance is an idea; an idea of the way feelings, emotions, and all other subjective experiences come and go — their rise and growth, their intricate synthesis that gives our inner life unity and personal identity. What we call a person's "inner life" is the inside story of his own history; the way living in the world feels to him. This kind of experience is usually but vaguely known, because most of its components are nameless, and no matter how keen our experience may be, it is hard to form an idea of anything that has no name. It has no handle for the mind. This has led many learned people to believe that feeling is a formless affair, that it has causes which may be determined, and effects that have to be dealt with, but that in itself it is irrational — a disturbance in the organism, with no structure of its own.

19 Yet subjective existence has a structure; it is not only met from moment to moment, but can be conceptually known, reflected on, imagined and symbolically expressed in detail and to a great depth. Only it is not our usual medium, discourse — communication by language — that serves to express what we know of the life of feeling. There are logical reasons why language fails to meet this purpose, reasons I will not try to explain now. The important fact is that what language does not readily do — present the nature and patterns of sensitive and emotional life — is done by works of art. Such works are expressive forms, and what they express is the nature of human feeling.

20 So we have played our second gambit, answering the second question: What is the work of art for — the dance, the virtual dynamic image? To express its creator's ideas of immediate, felt, emotive life. To set forth directly what feeling is like. A work of art is a composition of tensions and resolutions, balance and unbalance, rhythmic coherence, a precarious yet continuous unity. Life is a natural process of such tensions, balances, rhythms; it is these that we feel, in quietness or emotion, as the pulse of our own living. In the work of art they are expressed, symbolically shown, each aspect of feeling developed as one develops an idea, fitted together for clearest presentation. A dance is not a symptom of a dancer's feeling, but an expression of its composer's knowledge of many feelings.

21 The third problem on the docket — how is a dance created? — is so great that one has to break it down into several questions. Some of these are practical questions of technique — how to produce this or that effect. They concern many of you but not me, except in so far as solutions of artistic problems always intrigue me. The philosophical question that I would peel out of its many wrappings is: What does it mean to express one's idea of some inward or "subjective" process?

22 It means to make an outward image of this inward process, for oneself

and others to see; that is, to give the subjective events an objective symbol. Every work of art is such an image, whether it be a dance, a statue, a picture, a piece of music, or a work of poetry. It is an outward showing of inward nature, an objective presentation of subjective reality; and the reason that it can symbolize things of the inner life is that it has the same kinds of relations and elements. This is not true of the material structure; the physical materials of a dance do not have any direct similarity to the structure of emotive life; it is the created image that has elements and patterns like the life of feeling. But this image, though it is a created apparition, a pure appearance, is objective; it seems to be charged with feeling because its form expresses the very nature of feeling. Therefore, it is in *objectification* of subjective life, and so is every other work of art.

23   If works of art are all alike in this fundamental respect, why have we several great domains of art, such as painting and music, poetry and dance? Something makes them so distinct from each other that people with superb talent for one may have none for another. A sensible person would not go to Picasso to learn dancing or to Hindemith to be taught painting. How does dancing, for instance, differ from music or architecture or drama? It has relations with all of them. Yet it is none of them.

24   What makes the distinction among the several great orders of art is another of those problems that arise in their turn, uninvited, once you start from a central question; and the fact that the question of *what is created* leads from one issue to another in this natural and systematic way makes me think it really is central. The distinction between dancing and all of the other great arts — and of those from each other — lies in the stuff of which the virtual image, the expressive form, is made. We cannot go into any discussion of other kinds, but only reflect a little further on our original query: What do dancers create? What is a dance?

25   As I said before (so long before that you have probably forgotten), what we see when we watch a dance is a display of interacting forces; not physical forces, like the weight that tips a scale or the push that topples a column of books, but purely apparent forces that seem to move the dance itself. Two people in a *pas de deux* seem to magnetize each other; a group appears to be animated by one single spirit, one Power. The stuff of the dance, the apparition itself, consists of such nonphysical forces, drawing and driving, holding and shaping its life. The actual, physical forces that underlie it disappear. As soon as the beholder sees gymnastics and arrangements, the work of art breaks, the creation fails.

26   As painting is made purely of spatial volumes — not actual space-filling things but virtual volumes, created solely for the eye — and music is made of passage, movements of time, created by tone — so dance creates a world of powers, made visible by the unbroken fabric of gesture. That is what makes dance a different art from all the others. But as Space, Events, Time, and Powers are all interrelated in reality, so all the arts are linked by intricate relations, different among different ones. That is a big subject.

27   Another problem which naturally presents itself here is the meaning of *dance gesture;* but we shall have to skip it. We have had enough pursuit of meanings, and I know from experience that if you don't make an end of it, there is no end. But in dropping the curtain on this peep-show of philosophy, I would like to call your attention to one of those unexpected explanations of puzzling facts that sometimes arise from philosophical reflection.

28   Curt Sachs, who is an eminent historian of music and dance, remarks in his *World History of Dance* that, strange as it may seem, the evolution of the dance as a high art belongs to pre-history. At the dawn of civilization, dance had already reached a degree of perfection that no other art or science could match. Societies limited to savage living, primitive sculpture, primitive architecture, and as yet no poetry, quite commonly present the astonished ethnologist with a highly developed tradition of difficult, beautiful dancing. Their music apart from the dance is nothing at all; in the dance it is elaborate. Their worship is dance. They are tribes of dancers.

29   If you think of the dance as an apparition of interactive Powers, this strange fact loses its strangeness. Every art image is a purified and simplified aspect of the outer world, composed by the laws of the inner world to express its nature. As one objective aspect of the world after another comes to people's notice, the arts arise. Each makes its own image of outward reality to objectify inward reality, subjective life, feeling.

30   Primitive men live in a world of demonic Powers. Subhuman or superhuman, gods or spooks or impersonal magic forces, good or bad luck that dwells in things like an electric charge, are the most impressive realities of the savage's world. The drive to artistic creation, which seems to be deeply primitive in all human beings, first begets its forms in the image of these all-surrounding Powers. The magic circle around the altar or the totem pole, the holy space inside the Kiwa or the temple, is the natural dance floor. There is nothing unreasonable about that. In a world perceived as a realm of mystic Powers, the first created image is the dynamic image; the first objectification of human nature, the first true art, is Dance.

Commentary and questions

1. *Paragraphs 1-8:* This section is devoted to a definition of philosophy and art. Note the disparity in the lengths of the paragraphs. What purpose does this disparity serve? Paragraph 4 distinguishes types of statement. How is this distinction related to problems of aesthetic theory? See paragraph 5. What does Mrs. Langer mean by "coherent"?

2. *Paragraph 6:* How does Mrs. Langer seek to back up the central assertion of this paragraph? Does the discussion of "creation" in paragraph 7 satisfy her criteria for a "key question"?

3. *Paragraphs 9-14:* Here, where Mrs. Langer deals with the dance, does she successfully follow her own rule that philosophical questions must deal with word meanings?

4. *Paragraph 12:* Mrs. Langer opens with an assertion. How is it explained and developed? How does paragraph 10 prepare for this explanation? How does the definition of the dance as "appearance" or "apparition" differ from what the dancers actually do? What word does the author use to point up this difference?

5. *Paragraph 13:* Explain in your own words the fundamental distinction made in this paragraph.

6. *Paragraphs 16-20:* In what way do these paragraphs develop and extend the discussion of the dynamic image?

7. *Paragraph 17:* What assumption lies behind the question, "But what makes us enjoy it as intensely as we do?" Does Mrs. Langer explain this assumption? Select the key phrases in this paragraph that explain and isolate the dynamic image in *art*.

8. *Paragraph 20:* What distinction is made between art and life?

9. *Paragraph 22:* What idea previously established is developed here? Why do you think Mrs. Langer has returned to this idea?

10. *Paragraph 25:* This is a repetition of another question previously broached: what is a dance? Why is it repeated here? Has anything been added in the interim?

Topics for discussion and writing

I. Re-examine paragraphs 13 and 26. Then supply your own examples of a "virtual" image or "entity." A painting or piece of sculpture is an object and, in one sense, static. Can they be made to fit the author's concept of a "*dynamic image*"?

II. Which paragraphs state the problems Mrs. Langer deals with? Which ones support her assertions? Are the supporting paragraphs composed of factual statements or some other kind? What kind of illustrative material does she use? Does it differ from the kind used by Fry and Bell? Is it more or less generalized?

III. Examine paragraphs 25 and 28-30 and write a theme explaining the author's use of the term "Powers." What related terms does she use? Does the term have relationships to key terms used earlier in the essay? Does it have any relation to Bell's "significant form" and Fry's five elements which provoke emotion?

IV. Bell, Fry, and Mrs. Langer all propose some connection between the elements of art and human response to them. Write a theme listing these connections and comparing and contrasting them.

V. Write a theme analyzing and discussing the distinctions made by all three authors between art and life. How crucial are these distinctions? How do they differ from one another? How are they similar?

VI. Choose one of the three definitions of art and apply it to a painting, piece of sculpture, musical composition, building, or other artistic object with which you are familiar.

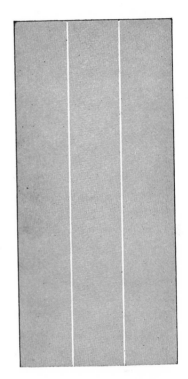

PART THREE

The whole composition

The whole composition is the writer's means of controlling and developing his material beyond the restrictions of statements or paragraphs. The accomplished writer will always pay close attention to his diction, to the form of his statements, and to the pattern of his paragraphs, but without a grasp of the entire range of the piece he is writing, the other efforts are of little use.

Moreover, words, phrases, sentences, and paragraphs are, by themselves, of only limited usefulness. A sentence, even a word, may in one sense be a "complete" thought, but, to speak illogically, there are degrees of completeness. The commands "Go" and "Come" are self-sufficient, but they yield only a minimum of information. At larger range, John Selden's remark, "A king is a thing men have made for their own sake for quietness' sake," is a much fuller statement, and by analysis of the diction we can tell a good deal about Selden's attitude toward kingship and the motives that cause political institutions. But without more information we cannot test the validity or plausibility of his opinion, for it covers too much ground with too few words and no evidence at all. (Review the section on statement in the introduction to Part II.) Similarly we may be told that Alexander the Great was the most successful military conqueror the world has ever known, but to be convinced we would need a full account of his life and some discussion of it in comparison to the careers of other conquerors.

Thus any extended piece of expository prose tends to corroborate and develop a general conclusion or thesis. Even in a long recital of particular details some principle will be present under which the details are organized, or else the writing will be incoherent. Quite frequently this organizing principle will be an idea the author wishes to demonstrate, in other words his *thesis*. Whether the thesis is stated openly and plainly or remains implicit and left to inference, it helps to govern the manner in which the author marshals his statements, his facts, opinions, assertions, his vocabulary. This is not to exclude other considerations that assist and modify the organization of the essay. A general thesis may be elaborated in different ways by different authors, as most of the selections will show. But if we regard *an* author's thesis as something more than a crude, rough generalization, that particular thesis will emerge for us as something quite central to that particular piece of writing. First of all, it will appear as the basic concept to which other concepts are secondary or subsidiary. It will be the main point the author

287

is trying to make. But that point may be complicated rather than simple, or the author may realize that he cannot discuss, for example, the soul of modern man without contrasting and comparative reference to the beliefs of the Middle Ages, or the attitudes of a free society without calling to mind the convictions of totalitarianism. A central thesis that can be expressed glibly and unequivocally may well be oversimplified. The reader should watch it closely.

On the other hand it may be difficult to grasp the presentation of an idea or series of ideas that are too fragmented, often a sign of incoherent thinking. There are at least two convenient ways of discovering and following an author's thesis: the first is to look for summary statements or ideas that are repeated through the essay (in other words, examine the topics to which an author returns); the second is to look for key words, those that not only appear frequently but also seem charged with more than casual significance. How and when an author repeats himself and how he develops such repetitions so that his concepts grow and become complete are sure indices of the directions in which he is moving and in which he hopes to carry the reader.

The organization of a central thesis, or, in other terms, the structure, is directly dependent upon the character of that thesis. In other words, structure is the particular manner by which a thesis is exposed. We have already anticipated the question of structure by mentioning above the matter of presentation. Structure is a fundamental element in presentation, and the type of structure an author employs depends upon several things — his purpose, his audience, and the demands of the subject.

Taking into consideration matters of subject, purpose, audience, and his own ability, the writer develops his subject either in the way it demands, or he selects what seems to him to be the best among several choices. Though each of these decisions is an individual one, any reader knows that certain patterns, apparently because they are especially useful, recur again and again. We can generalize about these recurring forms. Though the kinds of organization that follow are by no means exhaustive, they are central to a good deal of writing.

1. *Narrative or chronological.* Normally we expect to find narrative structure in fiction, but it is perfectly common in the essay or essay-length piece, as the selections on the French Revolution show. It is generally useful for biography and history, but it seldom stands alone, for the bare chronological recital of events can do little to render the significance of those events. Notice that J. B. Morton (pp. 328-329) modifies his narrative to discuss the personality of Desmoulins and evaluate his role in the French

Revolution. To do this, Morton has to depart from straight chronological narrative and organize his material according to another principle, if only temporarily.

2. *The description of an object or process.* Here again the type of organization is relatively simple in its basic form. One would ordinarily describe an industrial process from beginning to end. To do the reverse would be anticlimactic or perhaps insane. But the pieces on the Guggenheim Museum (pp. 213-219) remind us that one can begin anywhere in describing a building. Some definite principle is needed. The essays on evolution (pp. 367-392) also show considerable modifications of what might superficially appear to be an obvious plan of description.

3. *Inductive and deductive reasoning.* These are technical terms referring to two common methods of logical reasoning, but they can be, and very often are, basic principles in the structure of exposition. This is especially true of the inductive method. *Induction,* broadly speaking, describes the process of moving from separate facts to a conclusion that explains them all or shows their relationship to one another. Particulars are gathered together under a generalization, and because induction is so common a strategy in exposition, it is worthwhile to talk about it at some length. We might note first of all that this is the method by which Darwin (pp. 386-392) marshals his argument for a scientific law. Observed and classified facts are the very heart of his thinking. Without them, his concepts would remain untested hypotheses in an area of human inquiry where testing is possible. Had he not gathered and published his evidence, his work would have been labeled at most a good guess.

But an array of facts does not necessarily lead to a definite or irrefutable conclusion. Or, when they do, the immediate conclusion is not always the relevant issue. To take an example from one of the following groups of selections, the facts about fallout (measurable amount of radiation, where it occurs, how long it will last, and the like) when put together lead to certain obvious conclusions, one of them being that the testing of nuclear weapons increases the amount of radiation in the earth's atmosphere and in the natural environment. But what is important is the significance of this increase. In large part that significance is a matter of hypothesis or conjecture. Albert Schweitzer, using the inductive method, spends some time stating and reviewing a set of facts, but the inferences he draws from a consideration of these facts are matters for argument. Furthermore, Libby, who has read Schweitzer and is aware of the same facts, comes to quite different conclusions, and he presents his argument in quite a different way. Like Schweitzer he interprets fact according to a point of view he wishes to have confirmed, but unlike Schweitzer he makes his conclusion plain at the start and then presents fact to support it.

Thus, in the inductive process, facts and the *presentation* of conclusions do not follow each other in any order. Many writers will state their conclusions first as hypotheses or as a series of related questions which they will answer one by one on the basis of the evidence at hand. Other writers may delay their conclusions until all the facts have been presented. There is no set rule. The particular method used depends upon the demands of the particular subject and upon the audience. (For example, how much evidence can readers keep in mind before at least a tentative or partial generalization is made? Remember that the general concept usually governs the way in which evidence is presented.) Futhermore, the writer may have to explain away facts that seem to argue against his own concepts, and this necessity will usually make him modify his procedure (see 4. *Comparison and contrast,* below).

Deductive reasoning is less common in its pure form. Briefly, however, it is a method in which two propositions that are assumed to be "true" (that is, they are not argued or demonstrated) are combined so that they produce "logical" (inevitable) conclusions. Most readers have seen the standard example of deductive syllogism:

> PREMISE. All men are mortal.
> PREMISE. Socrates is a man.
> DEDUCTION. Socrates is mortal.

Note that no other deduction is possible on the basis of the two premises, but also note that we must accept the two premises as true before we can make the deduction. With false premises a perfectly correct deductive syllogism may lead to an utterly false conclusion.

> PREMISE. All apes are green.
> PREMISE. Socrates is an ape.
> DEDUCTION. Socrates is green.

The method is valid, but the deduction is not true, and this suggests the limitations of deduction as a method in serious expository discussion. Its value must always depend upon the inductive evidence that supports the premises. Deduction is seldom a feasible method by which to construct an entire essay.

Finally, induction and deduction remind us of the need for support of all general concepts. They further remind us that the sequence in which that support is arranged is equally crucial for both the clarity and the significance of whatever generalizations the writer tries to make.

4. *Comparison and contrast.* These two strategies are perhaps as common, and certainly as useful, as inductive reasoning. Indeed they are often the methods by which the inductive process is developed. Ideas, events, facts, characters, and objects may be likened to others or set in opposition to them. Comparison and contrast are notably useful for highlighting the significance a writer may wish to make clear. But, more important, they are a central method in argument, for writers of expository prose commonly attack their opponents at the same time they support their own arguments. The selections on education in Part I (pp. 54-91) argue opposing opinions, and necessarily they must in part contrast evidence and the conclusions drawn from it. Contrasting points of view also lie behind the pieces in "The work and the critic" (pp. 498-538). Comparison, and a special form of it, *analogy,* are frequently used in discussions of art and literature simply to place them in relation to other areas of human experience so that the ideas or interpretations the writer wishes to make can be established as clearly as possible, and the writers who discuss Billy Graham (pp. 339-363) use both comparison and contrast since it is necessary to regard him in the light of other members of his profession and according to the various standards the writers wish to invoke to evaluate him. (See also the discussion of metaphor in the introduction to Part I.)

But like induction and narrative and description, comparison and contrast are flexible tools of organization and are usually found mixed with one or more of the other methods. Classical rhetoric, which persisted through the Renaissance, decreed fairly inelastic rules for the construction of the oration or essay, but more recent centuries have seen exposition liberated. The careful reader will always examine the structure of an essay on its own terms and according to the author's purposes before he judges its success.

5. *The order of climax.* This is in reality a method that can be used concurrently with all the other general methods. If a number of facts or ideas differ in importance or persuasive appeal, the writer will often put the most important and most convincing items last, leading up to them so that his reader follows a trail of increasing interest. Only a writer who deliberately wants to avoid publication or understanding will carefully arrange his material in anticlimactic order. But it is entirely possible that the most important idea is the least glamorous, and when that happens the writer must exercise all his powers to make his thesis compatible without violating the truth as he sees it. One of the clues to the presence of a climactic order in an essay is to examine the pattern of emotionally charged language, for this is frequently the means by which the writer makes clear what he thinks is most important in his discussion. If metaphor and adjective and rhythm

become more intense as the discussion proceeds, we have a strong hint about the quality of the author's thinking and about what he wants us to accept. A careful study of Carlyle's account of the fall of the Bastille (pp. 318-323) will show a series of climaxes managed by figurative, emotionaly charged language.

These categories of organization are general and are offered here only as an introduction and guide to individual analysis of essay structure, which will be found in the questions and topics for discussion and writing appended to each selection. The rhetorical index lists particular examples of these general forms.

Finally there remain the matters of point of view and tone. Although they are clearest after the entire essay has been read, they must be watched constantly as the reader progresses.

Point of view is a term that contains several important notions. The simplest is probably narrative perspective. Here we demand appropriateness and consistency. If the author begins in the first person, we expect him to write from that point of view unless there is reason to change. Shifting from "I" to "one" can be confusing and annoying. We expect, too, that vocabulary and tone will fit with whatever person, whether first, second, or third, the author chooses. We expect him to deal with his audience consistently, too, not assuming them to be experts one moment and neophytes the next. Most writers are careful to maintain a consistent narrative perspective. The advantages are obvious.

Beyond narrative perspective there is a more complex area which we might call the author's viewpoint. The question we ask here, to extend our metaphor, is this: How does the author look at his material? The assumption implicit in the question, indeed in the term "viewpoint," is that every author distorts his material to some extent. The question the reader might ask, then, is what sorts and degrees of distortion the writer has introduced. There are two kinds: natural and intended distortion.

Natural distortion is the sort that a writer unconsciously introduces into his material. Our very necessity to express ideas in words is an example of natural distortion. For example, the question of whether light moves as waves or particles may grow out of language rather than natural phenomena. Historians of art forms borrow the language of biology and say that forms germinate, develop, flower, and wither. So fixed does the metaphor become that it is difficult for them to accept the idea that an art form may exist without going through some sort of period of puberty. Cultural conventions — our own attitudes toward women, old people, the insane, and criminals are examples — come to be regarded as norms of human conduct. Our cultural assumptions are such an easy burden that we hardly notice them at all. We regard the picture of the big-game hunter surrounded by his trophies as the natural order of things. But, as the lion remarked, nobody ever saw a picture painted by a lion.

There is another kind of natural distortion toward which we are less forgiving. This is the distortion introduced by self-interest. We rather expect philosophers to be partial to philosophy, but we nonetheless regard it as a failing. We must train ourselves to catch this sort of distortion, for it can be misleading. The writer unconsciously translates this distortion into suggestive language, catch-words, metaphors, and concepts he assumes without argument or definition. We must find and examine the unspoken or half-articulated assumptions which we are encouraged to accept without question. We may respond to Albert Schweitzer simply because he is on the side of virtue, but this itself is not enough.

There is also the matter of intended distortion. This is not a matter of immorality; it is the author's attempt to organize his material for maximum effectiveness. Four elements enter into an author's decision in how best to mold his material or distort it for his own reasons: (1) *Purpose.* Although it is hard actually to separate purpose from the other factors, yet it is the overriding consideration for any author. In one way or another every successful writer asks himself, "What do I want this piece of writing to do?" Most subsequent decisions are based on the answer to this question. (2) *Personality.* The author must decide whether he wants his own personality to enter into the writing or not. If he decides to use it, how will it be used? Since most authors use their own personalities in an emotive way, this characteristic becomes important in persuasive writing. Politicians obviously recognize the importance of the writer's personality. Tone, a part of personality, is important enough to require separate treatment later. (3) *Material.* This is patently a controlling factor. Some materials may demand one treatment and preclude another. It is difficult to be folksy about the nature of art, although this may be the natural tone for a pioneer reminiscing. The greatest fault in handling material is to oversimplify complex issues. (4) *Audience* is the final controlling factor. The taste, knowledge, background, and temperament of an audience are felt consciously or intuitively by most good writers.

These four elements affect one another and shape the whole composition. The writer considers these because the adjustments they dictate help make his work more effective. The good reader should take them into consideration, too. It is his purpose to identify the distortion these elements introduce and compensate for them. The author's constant effort is to place the object in the best light. The reader's constant effort should be to see the object clearly.

Purpose, personality, material, and audience help mold every aspect of the whole composition. Their effect can be seen notably in the decisions the author makes regarding tone, form, limitation of material, discrimination in presentation, and emphasis. *Tone* is taken up below, and *form* has already been discussed. *Limitation* of material comprehends the truncation or actual omission of material. This is a matter of considerable importance in argumentation and in popularization. An author who chooses to omit or depreciate material that bears on the other side is untrustworthy. So is an author who will oversimplify in order for his readers to "understand." He need not do this knowingly. Some of the most misleading writing that is done is published sincerely, honestly, and in good faith. Unfortunately sincerity is never enough. The *discrimination* an author shows is especially apparent in the way he categorizes and the form of support he uses. An author's intellectual weaknesses will usually show through his elegant verbiage if the reader will consider what points he chooses to support and the nature of the support itself. For example, an author whose highest appeal is to authority reveals a limitation in thought that may extend beyond the particular argument. *Emphasis* reveals what the author thinks is most important and sometimes what he thinks the reader regards as most important. Here again the reader must decide whether the material justifies the emphasis the writer gives.

Attention to these matters promotes active rather than passive reading. The close reader must consider what the author has done, but he must also consider what the author might have done. In a real sense he rewrites the essay as he reads. This is not to say that he regards the author's distortion as dishonest. A writer, like a painter, tries to make his audience see his subject as he himself sees it. He must impose organization. He should look from his own viewpoint. But the careful reader will not accept another's viewpoint without testing it first. The only way to do this is to read with a questioning mind.

An author's perspective or point of view is closely related to another element in exposition — *tone*. Tone is an indefinite term. Its meaning, the methods by which it is achieved, and the signals by which it can be recognized and described vary from writer to writer and from essay to essay. But style is not entirely anarchic, and most writers turn to the same basic resources, combining them differently, perhaps, to achieve particular effects. For the moment, "effect" is a convenient synonym for tone. It implies an impression made upon the reader, a reaction that he is stimulated to feel, and therefore it has to do with the less explicit elements in style. Some of these were discussed in the introduction to Part I (see especially pp. 3-8), but here we must discuss the suggestive elements in style as they work over an entire essay.

Tone is concerned first of all with the vocal, or spoken, qualities in writing. Conversational prose tends toward an informal familiar style, as if the author were speaking aloud. The absence of conversational elements may produce the opposite effect, but the vocal impression may remain as a quality much like oratory. Or formality may serve the author's desire to remain objective or give the impression of strict impartiality and logic. The length and complexity of sentences, matters affecting the rhythm of prose among other things, have a definite influence on the impression made by expository prose. In addition, the quality of the vocabulary can assist impressions. Slang will lead to informality; an academic or learned vocabulary will produce quite another effect.

The use of imagery and metaphor, or of highy colored and connotative language, in a consistent pattern or patterns throughout an essay is bound to produce specific tonal qualities, for, as we know, such language may have emotional effects quite apart from the designated meanings for words. Churchill's style is unmistakable because of its tone, because of its ability to suggest anger, approval, or contempt, to lead us to admire courage or despise nastiness. The energy and violence of Carlyle's prose attempt to involve us emotionally and immediately in the confused events of the fall of the Bastille. He wants us to feel what it was like to be there, to act, to shout, to be stirred and confused and angry and jubilant, and to this end he employs an astonishing variety of emotive techniques all at once: metaphor, epithet, Biblical language and allusion, violent adjectives, and energetic verbs. He calls names, he is gentle and brutal and exalted by turns.

However, the obvious presence of strong tonal qualities in the prose of Churchill and Carlyle should not mislead us into thinking that writers who are less connotative lack tone altogether. The writer who avoids conversation and language associated with it, who is sparing in his adjectives and metaphors and descriptive imagery, nevertheless is quite capable of managing tone. It may simply be quieter, less obtrusive, more in the background. If we look once more at Carlyle, who puts statements of fact in parentheses, and compare him with Darwin, who is eminently concerned with facts and the principles under which they are to be organized, it becomes clear that in the latter strong and abundant tones would be out of place. We must conclude, rather, that for Darwin the tone must be subdued, that the fact and its significance must occupy the foreground of discussion. His tone, therefore, can be called objective, relatively unemotional and detached. Darwin's personality is almost entirely out of the picture and the reader is not called upon for a primarily emotional response (although such may easily occur). Over its entire length the perspective and tone of the writing are meant to be detached and impersonal and the style at all levels reflects this purpose.

Perhaps the best way to begin to evaluate the tone of an entire essay is to examine pieces in which the tone is both obvious and consistent throughout. Carlyle has already been mentioned. The tone of Churchill's portrait of Trotsky (pp. 110-116) is largely ironic: Trotsky is supposed to be the dedicated revolutionary *par excellence;* Churchill paints him as an egotistical, self-seeking, squalidly greedy intriguer, and much of the style of the essay is pointed directly at this impression. George Jean Nathan's statements of his own belief seem intended to provoke shock and outrage. Perhaps they do. But, if tone is an effect consciously aimed at by the writer, it is also something he cannot always control, for the shades of connotation and emotional response change with the years and with the audience. What delights one group of readers will repel another. Furthermore, a writer may, through inadvertence or lack of skill, produce an effect quite contrary to the main burden of his thesis. Such inconsistencies, unless they are particularly glaring, require close reading and experience to discover them, but no reader should assume that the writing of the professional is always an unqualified success. An intelligent reader will always give as much attention to a writer's tone as to his organization and the validity of his ideas.

In summary we have remarked upon four main topics as crucial to the critical reading of the essay: (1) the essay as a developed thesis or central idea; (2) the problems of structure or organization (the means by which the elements in a thesis are arranged); (3) perspective or point of view, that is, the position from which a writer looks at his subject matter; and (4) tone, the effect or "feel" of prose beyond its intellectual or conceptual meaning. These categories are by no means absolute, nor do they exclude a host of other considerations involved in reading or writing. Rather they are offered as a convenience, as a means for approaching the essay analytically and critically, and for the practiced and attentive reader they are merely a point of departure.

LEATHERSTOCKING AND THE PROBLEM OF SOCIAL ORDER

Henry Nash Smith

Reprinted by permission of the publishers from Henry Nash Smith's Virgin Land: The American West as Symbol and Myth. *Cambridge, Mass.: Harvard University Press. Copyright, 1950, by the President and Fellows of Harvard College.*

ALTHOUGH Boone was not exactly the prototype of Cooper's Leatherstocking, there is a haunting similarity between the two figures. Cooper based a part of chapters X and XII of *The Last of the Mohicans* on a well-known exploit of Boone in conducting the rescue of Betsey and Fanny Callaway and Jemima Boone, his daughter, from the Cherokees.[1] Betsey Callaway, like Cora Munro in Cooper's novel, tried to aid her rescuers by breaking twigs to mark the trail, and was detected by her Indian guards.[2] The rescue also furnished Cooper with several other details for his story.[3]

2   Near the opening of *The Prairie* Cooper sets his stage by describing the migration of Americans from Ohio and Kentucky across the Mississippi immediately after the Louisiana Purchase. Although Boone actually settled in Missouri in 1799, Cooper names him among the emigrants of 1804:

> This adventurous and venerable patriarch was now seen making his last remove; placing the "endless river" between him and the multitude, his own success had drawn around him, and seeking for the renewal of enjoyments which were rendered worthless in his eyes, when trammelled by the forms of human institutions.[4]

In a footnote added to the revised edition, Cooper elaborates this passage with the remark that Boone emigrated beyond the Mississippi "because he found a population of ten to the square mile, inconvenient." [5] The aged Leatherstocking has likewise "been driven by the increasing and unparalleled advance of population, to seek a final refuge against society in the broad and tenantless plains of the west. . . ." [6]

3   The similarities between Boone and Leatherstocking were analyzed at length by a perceptive writer in *Niles' Register* in 1825, when Leatherstocking had appeared in only one novel, *The Pioneers*. The critic points out that both these heroes love the freedom of the forest, both take a passionate delight in hunting, and both dislike the ordinary pursuits of civilized men. As testimony to the fidelity of Cooper's characterization, the writer quotes a letter from a traveler through the Pennsylvania mountains who came upon herdsmen and hunters reminiscent both of Boone and of Leatherstocking. One of their number, celebrated throughout the West as having once been a companion of Boone, had set out for Arkansas when he was almost a hundred years old, and was reported to be still alive, a solitary hunter in the forest. A nephew of the emigrant who remained in Pennsylvania, himself athletic and vigorous at the age of seventy, shared Leatherstocking's love of hunting and his antipathy for "clearings" to such a marked degree that the traveler felt he must have sat as a model for Cooper.[7] A similar point was

---

1 Bakeless, *Daniel Boone*, p. 139. The reviewer of *The Pioneers* in the *Port Folio* (Fourth [Fifth] Series, XV, 232, March, 1823) remarked that Leatherstocking had been "modelled from the effigies of old Daniel Boone."
2 *The Last of the Mohicans: A Narrative of 1757*, 2 vols. (Philadelphia, 1826), I, 146.
3 Bakeless, *Daniel Boone*, pp. 133-139; *Mohicans*, I, 166-174.
4 *The Prairie: A Tale*, 2 vols. (Philadelphia, 1827), I, 14-15.
5 *The Prairie*, Red Rover ed. (New York, n. d.), p. 3n. Cooper has adopted Jefferson's estimate of the point at which density of population makes Americans "uneasy" (above, p. 10).
6 *The Prairie*, I, x.
7 *Niles' Register*, XXIX, 217 (December 3, 1825). The roving propensities of Leather-

made by the poet Albert Pike, who after graduating from Harvard went out the Santa Fé Trail and later settled in a very primtive Arkansas. "I cannot wonder that many men have chosen to pass their life in the woods," wrote Pike in 1834, "and I see nothing overdrawn or exaggerated in the character of Hawkeye and Bushfield." He listed as the prime attractions of the lonely hunter's life its independence, its freedom from law and restraint, its lack of ceremony.[8]

4   For at least one section of the reading public, then, Leatherstocking, like Boone, was a symbol of anarchic freedom, an enemy of law and order. Did this interpretation conform to Cooper's intention in drawing the character?

5   The original hunter of *The Pioneers* (1823) clearly expresses subversive impulses. The character was conceived in terms of the antithesis between nature and civilization, between freedom and law, that has governed most American interpretations of the westward movement. Cooper was able to speak for his people on this theme because the forces at work within him closely reproduced the patterns of thought and feeling that prevailed in the society at large. But he felt the problem more deeply than his contemporaries: he was at once more strongly devoted to the principle of social order and more vividly responsive to the ideas of nature and freedom in the Western forest than they were. His conflict of allegiances was truly ironic, and if he had been able — as he was not — to explore to the end the contradictions in his ideas and emotions, the Leatherstocking series might have become a major work of art. Despite Cooper's failures, the character of Leatherstocking is by far the most important symbol of the national experience of adventure across the continent.[9] The similarities that link Leather-

---

stocking had impressed an anonymous writer for *Niles' Register* within a few months after the publication of *The Pioneers:* "A settlement at the mouth of the *Columbia* has been seriously advocated in Congress, and will soon be made under the sanction of government; and, in a few years, we may expect that some persons *there*, feeling themselves too much crowded, like 'Leather Stocking' in the 'Pioneers,' will seek a country more *west* — Japan, perhaps, if good hunting could be expected therein!" (XXIV, 71, April 5, 1823).

[8] *Prose Sketches and Poems, Written in the Western Country* (Boston, 1834), p. 60. Bushfield was a Kentucky hunter in James K. Paulding's novel *Westward Ho!* (1832).

[9] Although critics often objected to the Indians of the Leatherstocking tales, they were enthusiastic about the old hunter from his first appearance. A reviewer in the generally unsympathetic *North American Review* called Leatherstocking "a bold and original conception . . . . upon the whole, the best piece of invention our author has ever produced; one, we may say, which deserves to be ranked in the first class of the creations of genius" (XXIII, 172, July, 1826). A later reviewer in this periodical, on the other hand, was cool toward the character (XXXII, 517, April, 1831). The *United States Review and Literary Gazette* said in 1827 that Cooper must mainly depend on Leatherstocking for his future fame (II, 307, July). Four years after Cooper had described the death of the hunter in *The Prairie*, the *American Monthly Magazine* of Boston declared, "in the whole range of fictitious writing, you will not find anything finer than Long Tom and Natty Bumpo [*sic*]" (II, 696, January, 1831). — The suggestion that the Leatherstocking series should be read in terms of "a tension between civilization and noncivilization" is interestingly set forth in Roy Harvey Pearce's article, "The Leatherstocking Tales Re-examined" (*South Atlantic Quarterly*, XLVI, 524-536, October, 1947). I have profited greatly in my discussion of Cooper from Mr. Pearce's observations.

stocking to both the actual Boone and the various Boones of popular legend are not merely fortuitous.

6   *The Pioneers* illustrates these aspects of Cooper's work with almost naïve directness. After a negligible first novel, *Precaution,* he had turned to the matter of the American Revolution in *The Spy,* which had a sensational success. The Preface to *The Pioneers,* his next book, has a jaunty air bespeaking the apprentice novelist's growing confidence. Cooper announces that he is now writing to please himself alone.[10] We may well believe him, for the scene is the Cooperstown of his childhood, and the character of Judge Marmaduke Temple, patron of the infant community, landed proprietor, justice of the peace, and virtual lord of the manor, has much in common with that of the novelist's father William Cooper. Not only did both William Cooper and Judge Temple buy land on the New York frontier and oversee the planting of a town on the shores of Lake Otsego; they resemble one another even in the minor detail of springing from Quaker forebears but having given up formal membership in the sect.[11] When an author turns to autobiographical material of this sort and introduces a central character resembling his father, one does not have to be very much of a Freudian to conclude that the imagination is working on a deeper level than usual. This is certainly the case in *The Pioneers.*

7   Still very much an amateur in the externals of his craft, Cooper contrived for his story of Cooperstown a flimsy plot that hinges upon a childish misunderstanding about Judge Temple's administration of the property of his old friend Major Effingham, but the plot is merely a framework to hold together a narrative focussed about an entirely different problem. The emotional and literary center of the story is a conflict between Judge Temple and the old hunter Leatherstocking which symbolizes the issues raised by the advance of agricultural settlement into the wilderness. In the management of this theme Cooper is at his best. From the opening scene, when Judge Temple claims as his own a deer that Leatherstocking's young companion has shot, until the moment when the Judge sentences the old hunter to a fine and imprisonment because of his resistance to the new game laws, the narrative turns constantly about the central issue of the old forest freedom versus the new needs of a community which must establish the sovereignty of law over the individual.[12] One aspect of the conflict is of course the question of a primitive free access to the bounty of nature — whether in the form of game or of land — versus individual appropriation and the whole notion of inviolable property rights. Not far in the background are the further issues of the rough equality of all men in a state of nature as against social stratification based on unequal distribution of property; and of formal institutional religion versus the natural, intuitive theology of Leatherstocking, who has little regard for theological niceties or the minutiae of ritual.

[10] *The Pioneers, or The Sources of the Susquehanna; A Descriptive Tale,* 2 vols. (New York, 1823), I, viii.
[11] *Ibid.,* I, 21, 27.
[12] *Ibid.,* I, 8-20; II, 206-215.

8   The profundity of the symbol of Leatherstocking springs from the fact that Cooper displays a genuine ambivalence toward all these issues, although in every case his strongest commitment is to the forces of order. The social compact, with all its consequences, is vividly and freshly realized, as it had to be realized with every new community planted in the wilderness. And all the aspects of authority — institutional stability, organized religion, class stratification, property — are exhibited as radiating from the symbol of the father. But if the father rules, and rules justly, it is still true that in this re-membered world of his childhood Cooper figures as the son. Thus he is able to impart real energy to the statement of the case for defiance and revolt.

9   But we are not concerned with Cooper's personal relation to his ma-terials so much as with his treatment of the themes arising from the advance of the agricultural frontier. The broader setting for the story is indicated in an exclamation of Elizabeth Temple: "The enterprise of Judge Temple is taming the very forests! How rapidly is civilization treading on the footsteps of nature!" [13] When Elizabeth, with a burst of womanly sympathy for the imprisoned Leatherstocking, declares he must be innocent because of his in-herent goodness, her father makes a crucial distinction: "Thou hast reason Bess, and much of it too, but thy heart lies too near thy head." The Judge himself means to pay Leatherstocking's fine, but he cannot brush aside the sentence of imprisonment which he imposed as the spokesman of necessary justice. He sends Elizabeth with a purse to visit the hunter and comfort him: ". . . say what thou wilt to the poor old man; give scope to the feelings of thy warm heart; but try to remember, Elizabeth, that the laws alone remove us from the condition of the savages; that he has been criminal, and that his judge was thy father." [14]

10   Another interesting scene occurs when the sonless Judge Temple invites Oliver Effingham to enter his household as a secretary. Oliver hesitates. Richard, the Judge's pompous factotum, says in an aside to Elizabeth, "This, you see, cousin Bess, is the natural reluctance of a half-breed to leave the savage state. Their attachment to a wandering life is, I verily believe, un-conquerable." The Judge remarks that the unsettled life of a hunter "is of vast disadvantage for temporal purposes, and it totally removes one from within the influences of more sacred things." But this rouses Leatherstocking, who bursts out:

> No, no, Judge . . . take him into your shanty in welcome, but tell him the real thing. I have lived in the woods for forty long years, and have spent five years at a time without seeing the light of a clearing, bigger than a wind-row in the trees, and I should like to know where you'll find a man, in his sixty-eighth year, who can get an easier living, for all your betterments, and your deer-laws: and, as for honesty, or doing what's right between man and man, I'll not turn my back to the longest winded deacon on your patent.

[13] *Ibid.*, I, 269.
[14] *Ibid.*, II, 228.

11   This states the issue as succinctly as possible. Cooper is unable to solve it, and resorts to a compromise statement that represents exactly his unwillingness or inabilty to accept the full implications of the conflict he has stated. The Judge answers, "nodding good-naturedly at the hunter": "Thou art an exception, Leatherstocking; for thou hast a temperance unusual in thy class, and a hardihood exceeding thy years. But this youth is made of materials too precious to be wasted in the forest." [15]

12   The Judge's reply expresses the unfailing regard for status which qualified Cooper's attitude toward the idea of nature as a norm. Leatherstocking, noble child of the forest, is nevertheless of inferior social status; whereas even in disguise, Oliver's gentle birth is palpable to the Judge's Falstaffian instinct. Leatherstocking began life as a servant of Major Effingham, and he is wholly illiterate. The fact that he speaks in dialect is a constant reminder of his lowly origin. It is true that the social status of the old hunter was not to prove significant during the long passages of adventure in *The Last of the Mohicans* and *The Prairie*, which deal with Indian warfare and the rescue of Cooper's distressed heroines from their captors. Here Leatherstocking's prowess with the rifle, his talents as a strategist, and his skill in following trails could be exploited with little regard for gradations in rank. But the problem of the hunter's status could not be permanently ignored. The response of readers to this symbol of forest freedom and virtue created a predicament for the novelist by revealing to him that his most vital character occupied a technically inferior position both in the social system and in the form of the sentimental novel as he was using it. The store of emotion associated with the vast wilderness in the minds of both Cooper and his audience was strikingly inharmonious with the literary framework he had adopted.

13   A more self-conscious or experimentally inclined writer might have found in this situation a challenge to devise a new form proceeding functionally from the materials. But Cooper was not the man to undertake a revolution, either in life or in literature. He chose a different course of action; he set about modifying the traditional form of the novel as far as he could without actually shattering it, and at the same time altering his materials as much as possible to make them fit.

14   Cooper's effort to solve his problem can be traced in the last two novels of the Leatherstocking series, *The Pathfinder* and *The Deerslayer*, which appeared in 1840 and 1841. In *The Prairie*, published thirteen years before, he had described the death of Leatherstocking, and had at that time meant to abandon the character forever. This decision seems to have been due in part to the technical difficulty mentioned above, for in later years Cooper told his daughter he wished he had left out of *The Prairie* the genteel hero and heroine, Inez de Certavallos and Captain Middleton, retaining only those characters who properly belonged to the locale.[16] But if the upper-class hero

---

[15] *Ibid.*, I, 254-255.
[16] Susan Fenimore Cooper, *Pages and Pictures, from the Writings of James Fenimore Cooper, with Notes* (New York, 1861), p. 157.

and heroine were to be omitted, and Leatherstocking was to be promoted to the post of official hero, how was the plot to be managed? It is at this point that Cooper's reluctance to break with the conventions of the sentimental novel becomes most glaringly apparent. A novel, according to canons which he considered binding, was a love story. The hero of the novel was the man who played the male lead in the courtship. If Leatherstocking was to be promoted to this rank, he must be made to fall in love with a heroine. In *The Pathfinder*, Cooper accordingly sets to work with great good will to exhibit Leatherstocking in love. The problem was to construct a female character, sufficiently refined and genteel to pass muster as a heroine, but sufficiently low in social status to receive the addresses of the hunter and scout without a shocking and indecent violation of the properties.

15   The object of Leatherstocking's affection, Mabel Dunham, is the daughter of a sergeant — not an officer — in the British army. When she is first introduced in the company of Cap, her seafaring uncle, who occupies "a station little, if any, above that of a common mariner," Cooper is careful to point out that Mabel is "a maiden of a class in no great degree superior to his own." [17] She is, therefore, technically accessible to the lower-class Leatherstocking. But before she can qualify as a heroine Mabel has to be given some of the attributes of gentility. Cooper explains elaborately that upon the death of her mother Mabel had been taken in charge by the widow of a field-officer of her father's regiment. Under the care of this lady Mabel had acquired "some tastes, and many ideas, which otherwise might always have remained strangers to her." The results of this association

> were quite apparent in her attire, her language, her sentiments, and even in her feelings, though neither, perhaps, rose to the level of those which would properly characterize a lady. She had lost the coarser and less refined habits and manners of one in her original position, without having quite reached a point that disqualified her for the situation in life that the accidents of birth and fortune would probably compel her to fill.[18]

In particular, Mabel had acquired a degree of sensibility that caused her to respond in approved fashion to the beauty of landscape — an index in Cooper almost as infallible as that of language for distinguishing the upper classes from the lower.

16   Ironically enough, the novelist's care in refining Mabel creates a fresh problem for him. The modifications of her character that qualify her for the role of heroine raise her somewhat above the actual range of Leatherstocking's manners and tastes. When Mabel's father proposes the marriage Leatherstocking is timid about it. He fears that a "poor ignorant woodsman" cannot hope to win the girl's affection. The sergeant compels the scout to admit that he is a man of experience in the wilderness, well able to provide

[17] *The Pathfinder; or, The Inland Sea*, 2 vols. (Philadelphia, 1840), I, 14.
[18] *Ibid.*, I, 114.

for a wife; a veteran of proved courage in the wars; a loyal subject of the King. But Leatherstocking still demurs: "I'm afeard I'm too rude, and too old, and too wild like, to suit the fancy of such a young and delicate girl, as Mabel, who has been unused to our wilderness ways, and may think the settlements better suited to her gifts and inclinations." Pressed still further, Leatherstocking makes an avowal that throws a flood of light on Cooper's conception of the social relationships prevailing within his standard tableau of a captured heroine in the process of being rescued by Leatherstocking and a genteel hero:

> I have travelled with some as fair, and have guided them through the forest, and seen them in their perils and in their gladness; but they were always too much above me, to make me think of them as more than so many feeble ones I was bound to protect and defend. The case is now different. Mabel and I are so nearly alike, that I feel weighed down with a load that is hard to bear, at finding us so unlike. I do wish, serjeant, that I was ten years younger [the scout was then presumably in his early thirties], more comely to look at, and better suited to please a handsome young woman's fancy!

In short, "I am but a poor hunter, and Mabel, I see, is fit to be an officer's lady." [19] She is indeed, as appears in the course of the story when the regimental quartermaster wants to marry her: or is she? Cooper subsequently causes this officer to prove a traitor, perhaps because of an unconscious impulse to punish him for his subversive disregard of class lines. In any event, when the actual moment of Leatherstocking's proposal arrives, Mabel's superior refinement is so unmistakable that it decides the issue. One of Cooper's very few valid comic inventions causes her, in her confusion, to use a more and more involved rhetoric that Leatherstocking cannot follow at all. He has to resort to his characteristic query, "Anan?" [20] The match is quite unsuitable and in the end Leatherstocking has the exquisite masochistic pleasure of giving his blessing to her union with Jasper Western, the young, handsome, and worthy Great Lakes sailor.[21]

[17] If Leatherstocking could hardly be imagined as married, however, a feeling for symmetry would suggest that he at least might be shown as himself hopelessly beloved. This is the formula of the last novel of the series, *The Deerslayer*, which removes the obstacle of the hero's age by going back to the period of his early youth and thus represents the utmost possible development of Leatherstocking into a hero of romance. In this story he is loved by Judith Hutter, beautiful daughter of a somewhat coarse backwoodsman. But Judith's reputation is stained by past coquetries: she is obviously not an appropriate mate for the chaste Leatherstocking, and eventually is consigned to an offstage marriage with a British officer.

[19] *Ibid.*, I, 135-136.
[20] *Ibid.*, II, 34-40.
[21] *Ibid.*, II, 214-225.

[18]   Despite these late experiments in depicting Leatherstocking in his youth, the persistent image of the hunter was that of his first appearance, as a man of venerable age. This trait of Leatherstocking was strengthened by whatever parallels were felt to exist between him and Daniel Boone. When John Filson's biography of Boone appeared in 1784, the Kentuckian, at fifty, already seemed a patriarchal figure, his active days of fighting in the past. The folk cult of Boone that developed after 1815 emphasized the picturesque conception of an octogenarian huntsman. Cooper himself gives testimony to the popular tendency to exaggerate Boone's age when he remarks in a note to the revised edition of *The Praire* that the famous hunter emigrated to Missouri "in his ninety-second year." [22] Boone was actually sixty-five when that event occurred. The many Western hunters created in the image of Leatherstocking who people Western fiction through most of the nineteenth century are characteristically of advanced age.

[19]   If Leatherstocking was, so to speak, intrinsically aged, this fact hindered his transformation into a hero of romance as seriously as did his low social status. Cooper was thus led to experiment with younger heroes who had Leatherstocking's vital relation to the forest, but were more easily converted into lovers. The character of Oliver Effingham in *The Pioneers* had early suggested the idea of a young hunter, wearing the garb and following the vocation of Leatherstocking. In *The Prairie* the impulse to double the role of the hunter in this fashion yields the character of Paul Hover, who, like Oliver, appears as an associate of Leatherstocking but is a real instead of merely a pretended child of the backwoods. Paul is a native of Kentucky and has a dialect that is the unmistakable badge of lowly status. It is true that he is merely a bee hunter rather than a hunter of deer and bear, but his sentiments concerning the rifle and his skill at marksmanship arouse Leatherstocking's enthusiastic approval. The most interesting thing about Paul is that, despite the presence in this novel of the official genteel hero and heroine, he is treated as an embryonic hero himself. He is young and handsome and virtuous, and in the end is allowed to marry Ellen Wade, who has carefully been given appearance, manners, speech, and sensibility superior to those of her crude companions — a distinct foreshadowing of Mabel Dunham's status and character in *The Pathfinder*. The Paul-Ellen love affair in *The Prairie*, in fact, seems to have furnished Cooper with the germ of his experiments in the two later novels.

[20]   Near the end of his life the novelist made a final effort to construct a story with a Western hero in *The Oak Openings* (1848). Like Paul Hover twenty years earlier, Ben Boden is a bee hunter of admirable character. In the absence of a genteel hero, however, he has to be refined somewhat beyond Paul Hover's level. This process is indicated in terms of the significant criterion of language. We are told twice in the first chapter that he used sur-

---

[22] *The Prairie,* Red Rover ed., p. 3n.

prisingly pure English for one in his social class, and he has the further genteel trait of highly moral views concerning whiskey.[23] Margaret Waring, the
heroine, like Ellen Wade, is related to a coarse frontiersman, but is made as
refined as possible within the iron limits of her status. Although *The Oak
Openings* is one of Cooper's weakest novels, the fault lies in his uncontrol-
lable tendency to preach on any current topic that happens to come into his
mind. The basic conception is very promising.

21   The novel begins as if Cooper were determined to see what might have
been made of *The Prairie* if he had carried out his project of omitting the
genteel hero and heroine. If this conjecture is valid, then Ben Boden represents Cooper's ultimate achievement in trying to use a man of the wilderness
as a technical hero. After the dangers of Indian warfare in early Michigan
have been endured by the young lovers, the novelist feels compelled to add
an epilogue that exhibits Ben Boden in his old age as a substantial farmer, a
man of influence in the community, and a state senator. This career "shows
the power of man when left free to make his own exertions." [24] But if Boden's
Jacksonian rise in the world gives retroactive sanction to Cooper's choice of
him as a hero, it dissolves whatever imaginative connection he may have had
with the mysterious and brooding wilderness.

22   Cooper's twenty-five years' struggle to devise a Wild Western hero capable of taking the leading role in a novel yielded the following results: (1)
Since the basic image of Leatherstocking was too old for the purposes of
romance, the novelist doubled the character to produce a young hunter
sharing the old man's habits, tastes, skills, and, to some extent, his virtues.
(2) The earliest of the young hunter companions of Leatherstocking, Oliver
Effingham, could be a hero because he was revealed as a gentleman temporarily disguised as a hunter. That is, the hero retained all his genteel prerogatives by hereditary right, and at the same time claimed the imaginative
values clustering about Leatherstocking by wearing a mask, a *persona* fashioned in the image of the old hunter. But this was so flagrant a begging of
the question that Cooper could not be satisfied with it. He therefore undertook further development of the young hunter produced by doubling the
character of Leatherstocking, and this process yielded (3) the Paul Hover-
Ben Boden type of hero, a young and handsome denizen of the wilderness,
following the gentler calling of a bee hunter and thus free from even the
justifiable taint of bloodshed involved in Leatherstocking's vocation. This
young Western hero is given a dialect less pronounced than that of Leatherstocking except in Leatherstocking's most exalted moments. His actual origin
is left vague. He is not a member of the upper class, but he is nowhere
specifically described as having once been a servant. Finally, the young hero
has none of the theoretical hostility to civilization that is so conspicuous in

---

23 *The Oak Openings; or, The Bee-Hunter*, 2 vols. (New York, 1848), I, 14, 18, 30-31.
24 *Ibid.*, II, 227.

Leatherstocking. These changes make it technically possible for a Wild Westerner to be a hero of romance, but they destroy the subversive overtones that had given Leatherstocking so much of his emotional depth.

Analysis

"Leatherstocking and the Problem of Social Order" illustrates the type of essay structure that announces itself openly, and it further reveals the complete use of documentation to support the author's assertions and conclusions.

In the broadest sense the structure of the essay is twofold: Paragraphs 1-8 explore the symbolic meaning of the pioneer or "Wild Western" hero and his interest for Cooper. Paragraphs 9-21 discuss Cooper's attempts to reconcile the pioneer hero with his "subversive," antisocial "overtones" to the conventions of the romantic novel. Paragraph 22 draws together and summarizes the two parts of the essay.

Within this framework, there are other elements of structure involving Smith's method of development. First of all, he moves from particular items to more general issues. Paragraphs 1 and 2 establish a similarity between Daniel Boone and Leatherstocking, at the same time mentioning the criteria behind that similarity. Paragraph 3 attempts to make the similarity more convincing by quotation of an independent critic. It further demonstrates that at least one contemporay saw Leatherstocking as a faithful copy of the real thing. Thus, the author is working through a comparative method as well as moving from the particular to the more general. Paragraph 4 is a transitional unit, summarizing briefly the previous paragraphs and preparing the way ahead by asking a question about Cooper's intention.

In paragraphs 5-8 Smith demonstrates Cooper's interest, and here the method is first to state the issue rather generally (paragraph 5). Paragraph 6 begins with the phrase, *"The Pioneers* illustrates . . ." and that illustration continues through paragraph 7. Paragraph 8 summarizes the author's conclusions about "The profundity of the symbol of Leatherstocking."

Paragraphs 5-8 are most concerned with establishing Cooper's own emotional interest in the Leatherstocking symbol, but Smith uses this as prelude to a more important question, the literary treatment of the symbol. This is the concern of paragraphs 9-22, and Smith once again works inductively, letting his examination of the details of Cooper's work lead into broader interpretive statements. Here also Smith begins to set up contrasts developed out of the symbolic conflict between natural and civilized values. These contrasts have already been mentioned but here Smith gives them more prominence, for now he is discussing the symbolic conflict as a problem of literary composition. The end of paragraph 12 and all of paragraph 13 witness the explicit emergence of this problem, showing also that Smith makes his transition to the later paragraphs of the essay a gradual one. Paragraph 13, like paragraph 4, is a signpost pointing both behind and before; it offers a brief reference to "this situation" and lays particular stress on Cooper's efforts to cope with it, thus establishing the basis for the remaining paragraphs.

Paragraphs 14-21 examine in detail Cooper's efforts to adjust the Wild Western hero to the requirements of the romantic or sentimental novel. Here Smith uses as evidence Cooper's later novels. We recall that his earlier discussion, showing *what* Cooper's problem was, is based on the earlier novels. To a certain extent, therefore, Smith's essay, or a large part of it, follows a chronological order established by the development of one of the major figures in Cooper's novels.

Here, then, are the main organizing devices in the essay:

(1) A broad division into two halves according to two halves of Smith's topic, and a further division into four parts (paragraphs 1-4, 5-8, 9-13, 14-22) which are punctuated by short transitional paragraphs.

(2) A fairly consistent movement from particular evidence to conclusions based on it. One of the four units of the essay, paragraphs 5-8, departs from this order, but the method is still basically inductive.

(3) He employs comparison and contrast, comparison to suggest the symbolic continuity between the historical figure of Boone and the literary figure of Leatherstocking, and contrast to stress the conflict of the symbolic meanings of the Wild Western hero with the demands of law and order in organized society. Note that, although Smith does not make it explicit, this conflict is paralleled on the literary level; the latter half of the essay is taken up with Cooper's efforts to fit the "subversive hero" into a fictional form (the romantic novel) dedicated to confirming the validity of the social order (see, for example, paragraphs 14-16, where Smith discusses Cooper's struggle to pair a socially acceptable heroine with Leatherstocking). Therefore, the nature of the problem Smith treats in his essay seems naturally to call for a pattern of contrast. This contrast is deepened in paragraph 8, where Smith interprets the interest in the Wild Western hero as a childhood impulse, opposed to the authoritarian, paternal figure of Cooper's father (and Colonel Effingham) who represents the order of society.

(4) A secondary principle of structure is chronological, following the use of Leatherstocking from the early through the late novels. This allows Smith to view Cooper's efforts as a changing and developing process and prevents oversimplification.

Our final consideration is the nature of Smith's supporting evidence. The footnotes clearly demonstrate that the author is willing to have his readers check up on him. He is confident of his facts, and since the purpose of his discussion is to demonstrate that the symbolism he ascribes to the figure of Leatherstocking is not a figment of his own imagination, the quotations from Cooper and others corroborate his interpretation. The nature of the evidence for Cooper's handling of Leatherstocking in the novels is somewhat different, and here Smith uses both paraphrase and quotation from some of the novels. These, too, can be checked for accuracy.

Smith's use of verifiable evidence also relates to his method of moving from the particular detail to general interpretive comment. Although it is true that an author who begins with particulars and stresses details is likely to give his readers a more vivid account of his subject, Smith has more than this to justify his method. The entire thesis of his essay is based on details: ultimately he wants to demonstrate that certain symbolic meanings existed both in Cooper's novels and in the public consciousness of the early nineteenth century and that they existed in a particular way. His demonstration would be less than convincing if he were inexact or resorted to uncorroborated general assertions. We thus have an essay whose structure and methods very closely mirror the author's purpose, and we have a motive for understanding the importance not only of *what* the author says, but also of *how* he says it.

July 14, 1789: THE CONTEMPORARY REPORTS, from *The Universal Magazine, The Gentleman's Magazine,* and *The French Revolution as Told by Contemporaries* · STORM AND VICTORY, Thomas Carlyle · BASTILLE, **J. M. Thompson** · THE BASTILLE FALLS, **J. B. Morton**

THE day of the fall of the Bastille is still celebrated in France as its most important national holiday. Through more than a century and a half the occasion has become a symbolic one, but when we look at accounts of what happened on that day it becomes clear that the specific meaning of that symbolism can vary drastically. Some of the early accounts were factually inaccurate in some details, but the major events are established now with some clarity. An agitated citizenry stole arms from the arsenal at the Invalides and marched on the fortress prison of the Bastille. It is clear that the prison had long been symbolic of tyranny, but, if we are to believe the statements that follow, its destruction did not necessarily mean the establishment of freedom. Therefore, we must examine what each writer says about the motives for the event, its causes, the motives of individuals centrally concerned, the character and quality of people's actions, singly and in groups.

Such an examination will move along the following lines: the type of statement used, the amount and kind of evidence supporting interpretation and conclusion, the kind of language used to persuade and influence readers, the selection and omission of detail and its motives.

Further notice should be given the historian's habit of dealing in terms of individuals or in terms of large groups of people or whole nations. Some of the selections also use atmosphere, general mood, vivid description and narrative to further their purposes. Each of these techniques may serve different ends.

Note: None of the selections is a complete essay, and some cover more ground than others. Nevertheless, enough material is here to test the ways in which a historical thesis or point of view can be developed, and the reader should give close attention to the ways in which historical narrative can be modified by or combined with other principles of organization.

THE CONTEMPORARY REPORTS   *The Universal Magazine*
The Gentleman's Magazine
The French Revolution as Told
by Contemporaries

From *The Universal Magazine* (London, July, 1789)

On Tuesday morning the hospital of invalids was summoned to surrender, and was taken possession of, after a slight resistance. All the cannon, small arms and ammunition were immediately seized upon, and every one who chose to arm himself was supplied with what was necessary. The cannon was distributed in different quarters of the town. In the evening a detachment with two pieces of cannon went to the Bastille, to demand the ammunition deposited there. A flag of truce had been sent before them, which was answered from within: but nevertheless the governor (the marquis de Launay) ordered the guard to fire, and several were killed. The populace, enraged at this proceeding, rushed forward to the assault, when the governor agreed to admit a certain number, on condition that they should not commit any violence. A detachment of about forty accordingly passed the drawbridge, which was instantly drawn up, and the whole party massacred. This breach of faith, aggravated by so glaring an instance of inhumanity, naturally excited a spirit of revenge and tumult not to be appeased. A breach was soon made in the gate, and the fortress surrendered. The governor, the principal gunner, the jailer, and two old invalids, who had been noticed as being more active than the rest, were seized and carried before the council assembled at the Hotel de Ville, by whom the marquis de Launay was sentenced to be beheaded, which was accordingly put in execution at the Place de Greve, and the other prisoners were also put to death. The Prevot des Marchands met with a similar fate, being suspected of betraying the citizens; and the heads of these persons were fixed on pikes, and carried round the city.

2   In the course of the same evening, the whole of the *Gardes Françaises* joined the Bourgeoisie, with all their cannon, arms, and ammunition.

3   Not more than four or five prisoners were found in the Bastille.

From *The Gentleman's Magazine* (London, July, 1789)

ON Tuesday [July 14] the scene opened in the same violent manner. Fresh troops kept constantly dropping in. Detachments, sent out of town on all sides, were continually returning with corn intended for the hostile troops, cannon, powder, &c. &c. Several wagons were intercepted destined for the King, and brought triumphantly into town, each of them drawn by six royal horses.

2 Before noon a body of 20,000 citizens, headed by the French guards, now joined by many of their officers who had previously taken an oath of fidelity, summoned the Hôtel des Invalides* in form with cannon (the Hôtel des Invalides is at 50 yards distance from the Military School, where there now were 4000 hostile troops with a park of artillery); the Governor surrendered, and immediate possession was taken of 52,000 stand of arms, cannon, ammunition, &c. and brought triumphantly into town.

3 On the other side of town the Bastille was summoned by 10 or 12,000 citizens, headed by the grenadiers of the French Guards; and on the Governor's holding out a white flag, and opening one of the gates, a party of young citizens, with some soldiers, incautiously entered. The Governor instantly drew up the drawbridge, and his troops, consisting of invalids and some auxiliary Swiss, fired through loop holes, and killed or wounded the whole party. About thirty were killed. Four times he attempted the same strategem, but not with the same success; at last the fortress was regularly attacked and cannonaded for three hours, and the ditches filled with straw, &c. &c. A breach was effected, and first mounted by a French grenadier; the Governor, the Marquis de Delaune, the Prince de Montbory, the Fort Major, &c. were made prisoners, and all the poor unhappy state prisoners, many of whom had languished for years in this execrable abode, released; among which number were Lord Mazarine, an Irish nobleman, who had been confined for debt near 30 years.

4 The great and important scene now followed — The Governor, the Prince, the Fort Major, and officers, were conveyed to the Hôtel de Ville, and, after a short trial, M. de Delaune and the Major were executed by first shooting them, and then cutting off their heads. Other officers next underwent the same fate.

5 In carrying the Bastille, about 300 were killed and wounded, besides those who perished through the artifice of the Governor.

---

* The Hôtel des Invalides was a hospital for invalided soldiers and in 1789 was being used to store arms and ammunition. The building still stands.

From *The French Revolution as Told by Contemporaries* (E. L. Higgins. Reprinted by permission of the publisher, Houghton, Mifflin Company.)

CAMILLE DESMOULINS AROUSES THE MOB (Desmoulins in *Le vieux cordelier*, No. 5)

1   It was half-past two; I came to sound out the people. My anger against the despots was turned into despair. I did not think the gatherings of people, although deeply moved or dismayed, sufficiently disposed to insurrection. Three young men appeared to me inspired with a more impetuous courage; they went hand in hand. I saw that they had come to the Palais-Royal with the same design as I; some passive citizens followed them. "Gentlemen," I said to them, "here is the beginning of a civic throng; one of us must do his duty, and mount a table to harangue the people." — "Get up here." — "I am willing." Immediately I was carried upon the table rather than allowed to mount it. Scarcely was I upon it than I saw myself surrounded by an immense crowd. Here is my short harangue, which I shall never forget.

2   "Citizens! there is not a moment to lose. I come from Versailles; M. Necker is dismissed: this dismissal is the tocsin of a Saint Bartholomew for patriots: this evening all the Swiss and German battalions will sally forth from the Champ-de-Mars to cut our throats. We have only one resource, to fly to arms, and wear cockades for the recognition of one another."

3   I had tears in my eyes, and spoke with a power that I have never been able to regain, or describe. My motion was received with unending applause. I continued, "What colors will you have?" Someone cried, "Choose!" "Will you have green, the color of hope, or the blue of Cincinnatus, color of American liberty and democracy?" Some voices were raised, "Green, the color of hope!" At that I cried, "Friends! the signal is given: there are spies and satellites of the police watching me. At least I will not fall into their hands alive." Then, drawing two pistols from my pocket, I said, "Let all citizens imitate me!" I descended stifled in embraces; some pressed me to their hearts; others bathed me with their tears: a citizen of Toulouse, fearing for my life, wished never to abandon me. Meanwhile they had brought me a green ribbon. I put it first in my hat, then distributed it among those who surrounded me.

PARIS ON JULY 14 (Extract from a letter of Jefferson to John Jay, Paris, July 19, 1789)

4   On the 14th, they [the committee of electors] sent one of their members (M. de Corny, whom we knew in America) to the Hôtel des Invalides, to ask arms for their bourgeois guard. He was followed by, or he found there, a great mob. The governor of the Invalides came out, and represented the impossibility of his delivering arms without the orders of those from whom he received them. De Corny advised the people then to retire, and retired himself; and the people took possession of the arms. It was remarkable that

not only the Invalides themselves made no opposition, but that a body of five thousand foreign troops, encamped within four hundred yards, never stirred.

(From Jean-François Marmontel, *Memoirs* [London, 1805], IV, 201)

5   The people then, in the presence of the troops of the Champ-de-Mars, ransacked with full license the Hôtel des Invalides. Twenty-eight thousand muskets were found there in the vaults of the dome; and with this booty, and the cannon of the esplanade drawn through Paris in triumph, the conquerors returned to the Hôtel de Ville. There they learned that the governor of the Bastille, the Marquis de Launay, summoned in his turn to furnish arms and ammunition, had answered that he had none. A general cry was instantly heard from every corner of the square, "Let's go and attack the Bastille!"

(From Jean-Joseph Dusaulx, *De l'insurrection Parisienne et de la prise de la Bastille* [Paris, 1822], pp. 332-333)

6   The first who advanced against the Bastille went there only to demand munitions and arms; they were threatened; they swore to triumph or die.

7   The crowd increased with every moment; it was augmented by citizens of every age and condition; officers, soldiers, firemen; women and priests; the greater part without arms and confusedly assembled.

8   One saw hastening thither even country people. One saw foreigners and warriors craving danger, warriors recently arrived from the various parts of the globe; some the evening before or even that very day, who had fought in two worlds, and had already contributed to several revolutions.

9   A young Greek, subject of the Grand Turk, there observed our enthusiasm and came back a Frenchman.

10   A number, as soon as they learned of the attack on the Bastille, went there for various motives; some, it is said, in the hope of pillage, but they were swept away. Others went there only to succor the wounded, or to save from the fury of the assailants relatives, friends, or those from whom they had, during their captivity, received consolations; so that humanity, gratitude, and filial piety were exercised at the risk of death.

THE ATTACK ON THE BASTILLE (Marmontel, IV, 202-206)

11   This resolution appeared to be sudden and unexpected among the people. But it was premeditated in the council of the chiefs of the Revolution. The Bastille, as a state prison, had always been odious on account of the iniquitous use to which the despotism of ministers had applied it under preceding reigns; and, as a fortress, it was formidable, particularly to those populous and mutinous faubourgs which its walls commanded, and which, in their riots, saw themselves under fire of the cannon of its towers. To agitate these multitudes at its will, and make them act boldly, the republican faction then ardently desired that they might be rid of this imposing object.

Honest men, even the most peaceful and most enlightened, wished too that
the Bastille might be destroyed, because they hated the despotism of which
it was the bulwark; and in this wish they consulted their personal security
more than their real safety; for the despotism of license is a thousand times
more dreadful than that of authority, and the unbridled populace is the most
cruel of tyrants. The Bastille, then, should not have been destroyed, but its
keys should have been deposited in the sanctuary of the laws.

12   The court thought it impregnable; it would have been so, or its attack
and siege would have cost rivers of blood had it been defended; but the man
to whom it was confided, the Marquis de Launay, would not, or dared not,
or could not use the means he had of rendering its resistance murderous;
and this populace, that so vilely assassinated him, owed him thanks and
praises.

13   De Launay had expected to intimidate the crowd; but it is evident that
he wished to spare it. He had fifteen pieces of cannon on the towers; and
whatever calumny may have said, to palliate the crime of his assassination,
not one single cannon shot was fired from these towers. There were besides,
in the interior of the castle, three cannon loaded with case shot, pointed in
front of the drawbridge. These would have made great slaughter at the
moment when the people came pouring in crowds into the first court; he
fired but one, and that but once. He was provided with firearms of every
kind, with six hundred musketoons, twelve rampart muskets carrying balls of
a pound and a half, and four hundred *biscaïens*. He had procured from the
arsenal abundance of ammunition, bullets, fifteen thousand cartridges, and
twenty thousand pounds of powder. In fine, he had collected on the two
towers of the drawbridge a mass of stones and broken iron, in order to crush
the besiegers if they should advance to the foot of the walls. But in all these
preparations to sustain a siege, he had forgotten provisions; and shut up in
his castle with eighty Invalides [pensioners], thirty-two Swiss soldiers, and
his staff, all the store he had on the day of the attack consisted of two sacks
of flour and a little rice; a proof that all the rest was only to inspire terror.

14   The small number of Swiss soldiers that had been sent to him were sure
men and well disposed to defend themselves; the Invalides were not so, and
he must have known that; but at least he ought not to have exposed them to
the fear of hunger. Too inferior to his situation, and in that stupor with
which the presence of danger strikes a weak mind, he looked on it with a
steadfast but troubled eye; and rather motionless with astonishment than
with resolution. Unhappily, not a man in the council supplied the foresight
that he wanted.

THE BASTILLE FALLS (Marmontel, IV, 206-210)

15   "The Bastille," said the brave Élie to me, "was not taken by main
strength. It surrendered even before it was attacked. It surrendered on the
promise I gave upon the honor of a French officer, and on the part of the
people, that not a man should be hurt if the fortress surrendered." This is

the simple fact, and such as Élie attests it to me. The following details of it are written as he dictates.

16   The forecourts of the Bastille had been abandoned. Some determined men having dared to break the chains of the drawbridge which barred the entrance into the first court, the people rushed in there in crowds; and deaf to the voice of the soldiers who, from the tops of the towers, forbore to fire on them, and cried out to them to retire, they persisted in advancing towards the walls of the castle. It was then that they were fired upon by the soldiers; and being put to flight, they saved themselves under the covert of the forecourts. One killed and a few wounded spread terror even to the Hôtel de Ville; multitudes came to demand urgently, in the name of the people, that deputations might be resorted to, in order to stop the carnage. Two of these deputations arrived, one by the arsenal, and the other by the side of the Fauborg Saint-Antoine. "Advance!" cried the Invalides to them from the tops of the towers. "We will not fire on you; advance with your flag. The governor is going down, the castle bridge will be let down in order to introduce you, and we will give hostages." The white flag was already hoisted on the towers, and the soldiers held their arms inverted in sign of peace. But neither of the deputations dared to advance so far as the last forecourt. At the same time, the crowd was pressing towards the drawbridge and firing from all sides. The besieged then had reason to think that these appearances of deputation were but a trick to surprise them; and after having cried in vain to the people not to advance, they found themselves obliged to fire in their turn.

17   The people, repulsed a second time, and furious at seeing some of their own body fall under the fire of the fortress, took that revenge in which it usually indulges. The barracks and shops of the forecourt were pillaged; the house of the governor was delivered to the flames. The firing of one cannon, loaded with case shot, and a discharge of musketry had driven back this crowd of robbers and incendiaries; when, at the head of a dozen brave citizens, Élie, advancing to the very edge of the ditch, cried out to the besieged to surrender, promising that not a man should be hurt. He then perceived a hand extended through an opening in a part of the drawbridge and presenting to him a note. This note was received by means of a plank that was held over the ditch; it was written in these words:

18   "We have twenty thousand pounds of powder. We will blow up the castle if you do not accept our capitulation.

DE LAUNAY"

19   Élie, after having read the note, cried out that he accepted it; and on the part of the fort, all hostilities ceased. However, De Launay, before he gave himself up to the people, wished that the capitulation should be ratified and signed at the Hôtel de Ville, and that, to secure his own safety and that of his soldiers, an imposing guard should receive and protect them. But the unfortunate Invalides, thinking to hasten their deliverance, did violence to the governor by crying out from the court, "The Bastille surrenders!"

20   It was then that De Launay, seizing the match of a cannon, threatened

to go and set fire to the powder magazine; and perhaps he was firmly resolved to do it. The sentinels who guarded the magazine presented to him
their bayonets; and in spite of himself, without further precaution or delay,
he saw himself forced to surrender.

THE SURRENDER (Memoir drawn up by the soldiers and non-commissioned
officers of the garrison)

21   It was then that M. de Launay asked the garrison what course should be
followed, that he saw no other than to blow himself up rather than to expose
himself to having his throat cut by the people, from the fury of which they
could not escape; that they must remount the towers, continue to fight, and
blow themselves up rather than surrender.

22   The soldiers replied that it was impossible to fight any longer, that they
would resign themselves to everything rather than destroy such a great
number of citizens, that it was best to put the drummer on the towers to beat
the recall, hoist a white flag, and capitulate. The governor, having no flag,
gave them a white handkerchief. Rouf and Roulard mounted the towers,
circuited the platform three times with the drummer beating the recall, all
of which lasted about a quarter of an hour; the people keeping up a continual
fire without paying any attention to the flag or the recall.

23   A quarter of an hour after the Invalides and the drummer had descended,
the besiegers, seeing that there was no longer any firing from any side of the
Bastille, advanced, while firing, to the interior bridge, crying out, "Lower the
bridge!" The Swiss officer spoke to them through a sort of loophole near
the drawbridge, and asked to march out with the honors of war; they replied,
"No." The said officer wrote out the capitulation and passed it through the
hole, saying that they desired to render themselves and lay down their arms,
on condition of a promise not to massacre the troop; there was a cry of,
"Lower your bridge; nothing will happen to you!"

(Marmontel, IV, 211-213)

24   The little drawbridge of the fort being first opened, Élie entered with
his companions, all brave and honorable men, and fully determined to keep
his word. On seeing him, the governor went up to him, embraced him, and
presented him with his sword, with the keys of the Bastille.

25   "I refused his sword," said Élie to me, "and took only the keys." His
companions received the staff and the officers of the garrison with the same
cordiality, swearing to serve them as a guard and defense; but they swore
in vain.

26   As soon as the great bridge was let down (and it is not known by what
hand that was done) the people rushed into the court of the castle and, full
of fury, seized on the troop of Invalides. The Swiss who were dressed only
in linen frocks escaped among the crowd, all the rest were arrested. Élie
and the honest men who had entered with him exerted all their efforts to

tear from the hands of the people the victims which they themselves had delivered to it. Ferocity held obstinately attached to its prey. Several of these soldiers, whose lives had been promised them, were assassinated; others were dragged like slaves through the streets of Paris. Twenty-two were brought to the Grève, and, after humiliations and inhuman treatment, they had the affliction of seeing two of their comrades hanged. When they were presented at the Hôtel de Ville, a furious madman said to them: "You deserve to be hanged; and you shall be so presently." Fortunately the French guards interceded for their pardon; the people suffered itself to be persuaded. But it was without pity for the officers of the garrison. De Launay, torn from the arms of those who wished to save him, had his head cut off under the walls of the Hôtel de Ville. In the midst of his assassins, he defended his life with the courage of despair; but he fell under their number. De Losme-Salbray, his major, was murdered in the same manner. The adjutant, Mirai, had been so, near the Bastille. Pernon, an old lieutenant of the Invalides, was assassinated on the wharf Saint-Paul, as he was going to the hall. Another lieutenant, Caron, was covered with wounds. The head of the Marquis de Launay was carried about Paris by this same populace that he would have crushed had he not been moved to pity.

27   Such were the exploits of those who have since been called the heroes and conquerors of the Bastille. On the 14th of July, 1789, about eleven o'clock in the morning, the people had assembled before it; at forty minutes after four it had surrendered. At half an hour after six the head of the governor was carried in triumph to the Palais-Royal. Among the number of the conquerors, which has been said to amount to eight hundred, many people have been mentioned who had not even approached the castle.

Commentary and questions

1. Compare the reporting of the facts. Which account is most complete? Which is most objective and unemotional?

2. Where do the sympathies of *The Universal Magazine* seem to lie? Note that its account of the death of de Launay and his officers agrees with that of *The Gentleman's Magazine,* but both disagree with later accounts.

3. What is the effect of the mention of "the poor, unhappy state prisoners"? Compare the statements of *The Universal Magazine* about these prisoners.

4. In *The French Revolution as Told by Contemporaries,* Desmoulins gives the impression that he was half-forced to address the throng. What details contribute to this impression? How far do the modern historians Thompson and Morton agree with his own version of the incident?

5. Are there any details that might lead you to believe that Desmoulins had colored his account to achieve specific effects? Compare his version with that of Carlyle (pp. 318-319).

6. Show the effect of Dusaulx' selection of detail. Why should he mention the young Greek?

7. Marmontel's account of the attack on the fortress contrasts the appearance of the action of the mob with the planning he says lay behind its actions. What do you infer about his attitude toward "the republican faction"? What is his estimate of de Launay's role in the attack? How much of his account is factual or narrative statement and how much is mainly analysis and interpretation? Does the evidence in the thirteenth paragraph confirm Marmontel's interpretation?

8. Paragraph 16 of Marmontel's account of the attack on the Bastille and its fall uses the reported statements of Élie. How much of Marmontel's point of view is left? Can he be said to have adopted Élie's attitude as his own?

9. The surrender is divided between reports by the soldiers of the garrison and Marmontel. The first report simply recounts what happened, but Marmontel's carefully distinguishes between Élie and his followers on the one hand and the mob on the other. What point of view toward the action of July 14 emerges from Marmontel's narrative? How would you estimate his political principles on the basis of this narrative?

Topics for discussion and writing

I. Examine the expository techniques of the selections in this group of contemporary accounts of the fall of the Bastille. Show how each important type of style furthers a political point of view or an attitude toward the events being described.

II. Make a list of the discrepancies between the various accounts. Do omissions and probable exaggerations seem convenient for emphasizing one interpretation or another of the event?

III. What evidence do you find in these writings that contemporaries were beginning to regard the fall of the Bastille as symbolically important? How would you describe that importance?

IV. The material in this group is necessarily brief. Which selections approach the status of complete essays? What methods of development do you find?

STORM AND VICTORY   Thomas Carlyle

From The French Revolution,
first published in 1837.

BUT SEE Camille Desmoulins, from the Café de Foy, rushing out, sibylline in face; his hair streaming, in each hand a pistol! He springs to a table: the Police satellites are eyeing him; alive they shall not take him, not they alive him alive. This time he speaks without stammering: — Friends! shall we die like hunted hares? Like sheep hounded into their pinfold; bleating for mercy, where is no mercy, but only a whetted knife? The hour is come; the supreme hour of Frenchman and Man; when Oppressors are to try conclusions with Oppressed; and the word is, swift Death, or Deliverance forever. Let such hour be *well*-come! Us, meseems, one cry only befits: To Arms! Let universal Paris, universal France, as with the throat of a whirlwind, sound only: To arms! — "To arms!" yell responsive the innumerable voices; like one great voice, as of a Demon yelling from the air: for all faces wax fire-eyed, all hearts burn up into madness. In such, or fitter words, does Camille evoke the Elemental Powers, in this great moment. — Friends, continues Camille, some rallying sign! Cockades; green ones; — the colour of Hope! — As with the flight of locusts, these green tree-leaves; green ribands from the neighbouring shops; all green things are snatched, and made cockades of. Camille descends from his table; "stifled with embraces, wetted with tears"; has a bit of green ribbon handed him; sticks it in his hat. And now to Curtius' Image-shop there; to the Boulevards; to the four winds, and rest not till France be on fire! . . .

2   — And now to the Bastille, ye intrepid Parisians! There grapeshot still threatens: thither all men's thoughts and steps are now tending.

3   Old De Launay, as we hinted, withdrew "into his interior" soon after midnight of Sunday. He remains there ever since, hampered, as all military gentlemen now are, in the saddest conflict of uncertainties. The Hôtel-de-Ville "invites" him to admit National Soldiers, which is a soft name for surrendering. On the other hand, His Majesty's orders were precise. His garrison is but eighty-two old Invalides, reinforced by thirty-two young Swiss; his walls indeed are nine feet thick, he has cannon and powder; but, alas, only one day's provision of victuals. The city, too, is French, the poor garrison mostly French. Rigorous old De Launay, think what thou wilt do!

4   All morning, since nine, there has been a cry every where: To the Bastille! Repeated "deputations of citizens" have been here, passionate for arms; whom De Launay has got dismissed by soft speeches through port-holes. Towards noon, Elector Thuriot de la Rosière gains admittance; finds De Launay indisposed for surrender; nay, disposed for blowing up the place rather. Thuriot mounts with him to the battlements: heaps of paving-stones, old iron and missiles lie piled; cannon all duly levelled; in every embrasure a cannon, — only drawn back a little! But outwards, behold, O Thuriot, how the multitude flows on, welling through every street: tocsin furiously pealing, of drums beating the *générale:* the Suburb Saint-Antoine rolling hitherward wholly, as one man! Such vision (spectral yet real) thou, O Thuriot, as from thy Mount of Vision, beholdest in this moment: prophetic of what other Phantasmagories, and loud-gibbering Spectral Realities, which thou yet beholdest not, but shalt! "*Que voulez-vous?*" said De Launay, turning pale at the sight, with an air of reproach, almost of menace. "Monsieur," said Thuriot, rising into the moral sublime, "what mean *you?* Consider if I could

not precipitate *both* of us from this height," — say only a hundred feet, exclusive of the walled ditch! Whereupon De Launay fell silent. Thuriot shows himself from some pinnacle, to comfort the multitude becoming suspicious, fremescent: then descends; departs with protest; with warning addressed also to the Invalides, — on whom, however, it produces but a mixed indistinct impression. The old heads are none of the clearest; besides, it is said, De Launay has been profuse of beverages (*prodigue des buissons*). They think they will not fire, — if not fired on, if they can help it; but must, on the whole, be ruled considerably by circumstances.

5   Wo to thee, De Launay, in such an hour, if thou canst not, taking some one firm decision, *rule* circumstances! Soft speeches will not serve; hard grapeshot is questionable; but hovering between the two is *un*questionable. Ever wilder swells the tide of men; their infinite hum waxing ever louder, into imprecations, perhaps into crackle of stray musketry, — which latter, on walls nine feet thick, cannot do execution. The Outer Drawbrige has been lowered for Thuriot; new *deputation of citizens* (it is the third, and noisiest of all) penetrates that way into the Outer Court: soft speeches producing no clearance of these, De Launay gives fire; pulls up his Drawbridge. A slight sputter; — which has *kindled* the too combustible chaos; made it a roaring fire-chaos! Bursts forth Insurrection, at sight of its own blood (for there were deaths by that sputter of fire), into endless rolling explosion of musketry, distraction, execration; — and over head, from the Fortress, let one great gun, with its grapeshot, go booming, to show what we *could* do. The Bastille is besieged!

6   On, then, all Frenchmen, that have hearts in your bodies! Roar with all your throats, of cartilage and metal, ye Sons of Liberty; stir spasmodically whatsoever of utmost faculty is in you, soul, body, or spirit; for it is the hour! Smite, thou Louis Tournay, cartwright of the Marais, old-soldier of the Regiment Dauphiné; smite at that Outer Drawbridge chain, though the fiery hail whistles round thee! Never, over nave or felloe, did thy axe strike such a stroke. Down with it, man; down with it to Orcus: let the whole accursed Edifice sink thither, and Tyranny be swallowed up forever! Mounted, some say, on the roof of the guard-room, some "on bayonets stuck into joints of the wall," Louis Tournay smites, brave Aubin Bonnemère (also an old soldier) seconding him: the chain yields, breaks; the huge Drawbridge slams down, thundering (*avec fracas*). Glorious: and yet, alas, it is still but the outworks. The Eight grim Towers, with their Invalide musketry, their paving stones and cannon-mouths, still soar aloft intact; — Ditch yawning impassable, stone-faced; the inner Drawbridge with its *back* towards us: the Bastille is still to take!

7   To describe this Siege of the Bastille (thought to be one of the most important in History) perhaps transcends the talent of mortals. Could one but, after infinite reading, get to understand so much as the plan of the

building! But there is open Esplanade, at the end of the Rue Saint-Antoine; there are such Forecourts, *Cour Avancée, Cour de l'Orme,* arched Gateway (where Louis Tournay now fights); then new drawbridges, dormant-bridges, rampart-bastions, and the grim Eight Towers; a labyrinthic Mass, high-frowning there, of all ages from twenty years to four hundred and twenty; — beleaguered, in this its last hour, as we said, by mere Chaos come again! Ordnance of all calibres; throats of all capacities; men of all plans, every man his own engineer: seldom since the war of Pygmies and Cranes was there seen so anomalous a thing. Half-pay Élie is home for a suit of regimentals; no one would heed him in coloured clothes: half-pay Hulin is haranguing Gardes Françaises in the Place de Grève. Frantic Patriots pick up the grapeshots; bear them, still hot (or seemingly so), to the Hôtel-de-Ville; — Paris, you perceive, is to be burnt! Flesselles is "pale to the very lips," for the roar of the multitude grows deep. Paris wholly has got to the acme of its frenzy; whirled, all ways, by panic madness. At every street-barricade, there whirls simmering a minor whirlpool, — strengthening the barricade, since God knows what is coming; and all minor whirlpools play distractedly into that grand Fire-Mahlstrom which is lashing round the Bastille.

8   And so it lashes and it roars. Cholat the wine-merchant has become an impromptu cannoneer. See Georget, of the Marine Service, fresh from Brest, ply the King of Siam's cannon. Singular (if we were not used to the like); Georget lay, last night, taking his ease at his inn; the King of Siam's cannon also lay, knowing nothing of *him,* for a hundred years. Yet now, at the right instant, they have got together, and discourse eloquent music. For, hearing what was toward, Georget sprang from the Brest Diligence, and ran. Gardes Françaises also will be here, with real artillery: were not the walls so thick! — Upwards from the Esplanade, horizontally from all neighbouring roofs and windows, flashes one irregular deluge of musketry, without effect. The Invalides lie flat, firing comparatively at their ease from behind stone; hardly through portholes, show the tip of a nose. We fall, shot; and make no impression!

9   Let conflagration rage; of whatsoever is combustible! Guard-rooms are burnt, Invalides mess-rooms. A distracted "Peruke-maker with two fiery torches" is for burning "the saltpetres of the Arsenal"; — had not a woman run screaming; had not a Patriot, with some tincture of Natural Philosophy, instantly struck the wind out of him (butt of musket on pit of stomach), overturned barrels, and stayed the devouring element. A young beautiful lady, seized escaping in these Outer Courts, and thought falsely to be De Launay's daughter, shall be burnt in De Launay's sight; she lies swooned on a paillasse: but again a Patriot, it is brave Aubin Bonnemère the old soldier, dashes in, and rescues her. Straw is burnt; three cartloads of it, hauled thither, go up in white smoke: almost to the choking of Patriotism itself; so that Élie had, with singed brows, to drag back one cart; and Réole the

"gigantic haberdasher" another. Smoke as of Tophet; confusion as of Babel; noise as of the Crack of Doom!

10   Blood flows; the aliment of new madness. The wounded are carried into houses of the Rue Cerisaie; the dying leave their last mandate not to yield till the accursed Stronghold fall. And yet, alas, how fall? The walls are so thick! Deputations, three in number, arrive from the Hôtel-de-Ville; Abbé Fauchet (who was of one) can say, with what almost superhuman courage of benevolence. These wave their Townflag in the arched Gateway; and stand, rolling their drum; but to no purpose. In such Crack of Doom, De Launay cannot hear them, dare not believe them: they return, with justified rage, the whew of lead still singing in their ears. What to do? The Firemen are here, squirting with their firepumps on the Invalides cannon, to wet the touchholes; they unfortunately cannot squirt so high; but produce only clouds of spray. Individuals of classical knowledge propose *catapults*. San-terre, the sonorous Brewer of the Suburb Saint-Antoine, advises rather that the place be fired, by a "mixture of phosphorus and oil-of-turpentine spouted up through forcing pumps": O Spinola-Santerre, hast thou the mixture *ready?* Every man his own engineer! And still the fire-deluge abates not: even women are firing, and Turks; at least one woman (with her sweetheart), and one Turk. Gardes Françaises have come: real cannon, real cannoneers. Usher Maillard is busy; half-pay Élie, half-pay Hulin rage in the midst of thousands.

11   How the great Bastille Clock ticks (inaudible) in its Inner Court there, at its ease, hour after hour; as if nothing special, for it or the world, were passing! It tolled One when the firing began; and is now pointing towards Five, and still the firing slakes not. — Far down, in their vaults, the seven Prisoners hear muffled din as of earthquakes; their Turnkeys answer vaguely.

12   Wo to thee, De Launay, with thy poor hundred Invalides! Broglie is distant, and his ears heavy: Besenval hears, but can send no help. One poor troop of Hussars has crept, reconnoitering, cautiously along the Quais, as far as the Pont Neuf. "We are come to join you," said the Captain; for the crowd seems shoreless. A large-headed dwarfish individual of smoke-bleared aspect, shambles forward, opening his blue lips, for there is sense in him; and croaks: "Alight then, and give up your arms!" The Hussar-Captain is too happy to be escorted to the Barriers, and dismissed on parole. Who the squat individual was? Men answer, It is M. Marat, author of the excellent pacific *Avis au Peuple!* Great truly, O thou remarkable Dogleech, is this thy day of emergence and new-birth: and yet this same day come four years ——! — But let the curtains of the Future hang.

13   What shall De Launay do? One thing only De Launay could have done: what he said he would do. Fancy him sitting, from the first, with lighted taper, within arm's length of the Powder-Magazine; motionless, like old Roman Senator, or Bronze Lamp-holder; coldly apprising Thuriot, and all men, by a slight motion of his eye, what his resolution was: — Harmless, he sat there, while unharmed; but the King's Fortress, meanwhile, could,

might, would, or should in nowise be surrendered, save to the King's Messenger: one old man's life is worthless, so it be lost with honour; but think, ye brawling *canaille*, how will it be when a whole Bastille springs skyward! — In such statuesque, taper-holding attitude, one fancies De Launay might have left Thuriot, the red Clerks of the Basoche, Curé of Saint-Stephen and all the tag-rag-and-bobtail of the world, to work their will.

14   And yet, withal, he could not do it. Hast thou considered how each man's heart is so tremulously responsive to the hearts of all men; hast thou noted how omnipotent is the very sound of many men? How their shriek of indignation palsies the strong soul; their howl of contumely withers with unfelt pangs? The Ritter Gluck confessed that the ground-tone of the noblest passage, in one of his noblest Operas, was the voice of the Populace he had heard at Vienna, crying to their Kaiser: Bread! Bread! Great is the combined voice of men; the utterance of their *instincts*, which are truer than their *thoughts:* it is the greatest a man encounters, among the sounds and shadows which make up this World of Time. He who can resist that, has his footing somewhere *beyond* Time. De Launay could not do it. Distracted, he hovers between two; hopes in the middle of despair; surrenders not his Fortress; declares that he will blow it up, seizes torches to blow it up, and does not blow it. Unhappy old De Launay, it is the death-agony of thy Bastille and thee! Jail, Jailoring, and Jailor, all three, such as they may have been, must finish.

15   For four hours now has the World-Bedlam roared: call it the World-Chimæra, blowing fire! The poor Invalides have sunk under their battlements, or rise only with reversed muskets: they have made a white flag of napkins; go beating the *chamade,* or seeming to beat, for one can hear nothing. The very Swiss at the Portcullis look weary of firing; disheartened in the fire-deluge: a porthole at the drawbridge is opened, as by one that would speak. See Huissier Maillard, the shifty man! On his plank, swinging over the abyss of that stone Ditch; plank resting on parapet, balanced by weight of Patriots, — he hovers perilous: such a Dove towards such an Ark! Deftly, thou shifty Usher: one man already fell; and lies mashed, far down there, against the masonry; Usher Maillard falls not: deftly, unerring he walks, with outspread palm. The Swiss holds a paper through his porthole; the shifty Usher snatches it, and returns. Terms of surrender: Pardon, immunity to all! Are they accepted? — "*Foi d'officier,* On the word of an officer," answers half-pay Hulin, — or half-pay Élie, for men do not agree on it, "they are!" Sinks the drawbridge, — Usher Maillard bolting it when down; rushes-in the living deluge: the Bastille is fallen! *Victoire! La Bastille est prise!*

Commentary and questions

1. *Paragraphs 1-6:* Although the style of these paragraphs is predominantly impressionistic, there are factual statements or references to specific actions or occurrences in the writing. Separate these and list them.

Compare them with such items of fact as you have gathered from the previous group of writings. Compare especially Carlyle's version of Desmoulins' speech with his own version. What differences do you find? Does Carlyle make him out a courageous figure?

What and whose points of view does Carlyle adopt in these paragraphs? What purpose does the illusion serve?

2. *Paragraphs 7-9:* Here a new point of view takes over. Is it Carlyle's own? Is it an attempt to objectify impressions previously established? Note the hyperbole and other means to strong, emotive language here. What attitude emerges from the use of this language?

3. *Paragraphs 10-15:* Describe the emotional or tonal structure of this passage. What types of language are used to move the feeling toward a climax? How does Carlyle vary or interrupt that movement? Why? Does the emotional structure match the pattern of the action that takes place?

Topics for discussion and writing

I. Discuss Carlyle's use of a shifting point of view. You might consider such purposes as verisimilitude, vividness, psychological insight, over-all impression.

II. List the major types of figurative, suggestive language Carlyle uses and give examples of each. You should consider metaphor, epithet, literary allusion, exclamation, vivid adjectives, and the like. Show how each serves a specific expository purpose.

III. Would it be accurate to call the structure of Carlyle's writing narrative? If not, what other structural patterns do you find?

IV. Write a theme describing Carlyle's attitude toward the events he treats and discuss his interpretation of them. Be specific in showing how you discover his attitude and interpretation.

V. Write a theme comparing Carlyle and Marmontel on the following points: (a) their interpretation of the fall of the Bastille; (b) their objectivity of interpretation; (c) their respective persuasiveness and the means each uses.

BASTILLE   J. M. Thompson

From The French Revolution *by J. M. Thompson. Copyright 1945 by Oxford University Press, Inc. (Originally published in 1943 by Basil Blackwell & Mott, Ltd., London.) Reprinted by permission. By permission of Basil Blackwell & Mott, Ltd., Oxford.*

THE NEWS spread dismay, too, amongst the crowds dancing at the *Fer à cheval,* or displaying their Sunday finery in the alleys of the Palais-Royal.

Here might be seen a lively irresponsible young man from Guise, Camille Desmoulins by name, a graduate of Louis-le-Grand, who had for the last eight years tried in vain to make a living as a barrister attached to the Paris *parlement*. About half-past three on this Sunday afternoon Desmoulins stood with a group of friends deploring the cowardice of the city in face of the king's attack, when three young men came along, holding hands, and crying *Aux armes!* He joined them, and was persuaded to mount a table and harangue the crowd. There were, he says, six thousand of them. His head was bursting with ideas, but he could not express them in an orderly way. He could only denounce the dismissal of Necker as an insult to the nation, and as the omen of another St. Bartholomew's Eve, a massacre of patriots. He ended by repeating the call to arms. "Let us take as our badge," he cried, "green cockades, the colour of hope!" He drew a pistol, and defied the police to arrest him. He would die a glorious death sooner than see France enslaved. . . .

2   Several times during the morning of Tuesday the 14th there were rumours that the royal troops were returning to the attack. The electors ordered barricades to be thrown up, and every step to be taken to block the entrances of the town. But soon it was found that the only soldiers to appear at the barriers were deserters from the king's troops; and the energies of the crowd turned to the search for arms and ammunition.

3   It had already been discovered that there were none at the Carthusian monastery to which Flesselles had directed attention, and none at the Arsenal, whose stores had been transferred two days before to the Town Hall and the Bastille. A deputation sent the previous evening to the Invalides, the Chelsea Hospital of Paris, reported that it contained enough muskets to arm thirty thousand citizens. A crowd gathered outside the building. The governor, the old Marquis de Sombreuil, tried to refuse admission, and was only prevented by lack of time and the insubordination of his men from carrying out the order given by the War Office a few days earlier to render the weapons unusable. Before he could do anything the crowd forced its way in, and seized all the arms it could find.

4   Next, powder. Part of the Arsenal supply had already been distributed at the Town Hall; most of it was known to be in the Bastille. The governor of this formidable old fortress, the Marquis de Launey, was making ineffectual preparations for defence. His ordinary garrison of a hundred Swiss Guards and pensioners (*Invalides*) had been reinforced a week before by thirty men of the Salis-Samade regiment; but he was seriously short of food. The sight of unaccustomed gun-muzzles thrust out between the antiquated battlements that overlooked their crowded streets set the inhabitants of Saint-Antoine in a ferment. Complaints were made; and at ten o'clock on the morning of the 14th deputies arrived from the municipality — the first of many such during the day — begging the governor not to fire on the people. De Launey received the delegates courteously, asked them to share

his *déjeuner,* and ordered the guns to be withdrawn. Meanwhile a crowd of sightseers had gathered in the unfortified outer court (*cour avancée*) of the fortress, and there was talk of an attack.

5   To prevent this, the municipality, about midday, sent a second deputation, under the elector Thuriot, to summon the governor, in the name of his country and nation, to surrender. De Launey took Thuriot up on to the battlements, to show him that the guns had been withdrawn. He guaranteed that, so long as the fortress was not attacked, its garrison would not fire. But he refused to surrender to a mob of civilians. Thuriot took this answer back to the Town Hall, and an order was given to proclaim it to the people: but as the herald raised the trumpet to his lips a sound of gunfire came from the direction of the Bastille.

6   No impartial account tells how hostilities began, or justifies the charge that de Launey fired treacherously on the crowd. But that he did so unnecessarily seems to be beyond doubt; and this provocation was the chief cause of what followed. About one o'clock a third deputation arrived from the Town Hall, with the proposal that a detachment of the *milice bourgeoise* should be admitted, to occupy the Bastille along with the royal troops. But these delegates were unable to reach the fortress; and when another party approached, in a vain hope of stopping hostilities, its drum and white flag were fired upon by the defenders.

7   The fighting now grew fierce and fatal. Between two and three in the afternoon the French Guard and the City Militia brought up guns, and an almost professional attack was made on the main defences of the fortress. Citizen volunteers led the way. It is related that Élie and Réole dragged away, at risk of their lives, some blazing hay-carts with which the garrison attempted to provide a smoke-screen; and that Hulin, with great daring, shot down the chains of the outer drawbridge. The attackers now occupied the inner approaches (*cour du gouverneur*), and the attack on the main drawbridge and gate could begin. In this close fighting the civilian assailants again showed a bravery which was acknowledged by their professional opponents, and lost heavily: eighty-three of them were killed outright, and eighty-eight wounded, fifteen fatally.

8   After two hours' cannonade, a white handkerchief fluttered from one of the towers, and a scrap of paper was pushed through a crack in the main gate. The assailants threw a plank over the moat. The first who tried to cross it fell and was killed. The second, a man whom history later knew as Stanislas Maillard, succeeded. The paper was found to contain a threat to blow up the fortress, if an honourable capitulation were not granted. The crowd were now determined to capture the place at all costs. Their guns opened again on the bridge and gateway. The governor was prevented from carrying out his threat by his own men, who insisted on surrender. At last the footbridge was lowered, and then the main drawbridge, and the crowd rushed in. The Bastille had fallen.

⁹ The people used its right of conquest to destroy the fortress, but not to plunder it. Doors, furniture, and wood-work of all kinds were demolished. Papers were tossed out of the windows. The dungeons were opened, and the prisoners found in them — only seven remained since Malesherbes' merciful visitation of 1775 — were released. Two of them, said to be the Comte d'Auche and Major White (Whyte de Malleville), an Englishman, were taken to the house of Santerre, the popular brewer of Saint-Antoine, and spent the night there. One had to be removed to an asylum; the other appeared at a window on the 17th, and waved his hat when the king passed by. De Launey, saved from immediate vengeance by Maillard, Élie, and Hulin, was pursued through the streets, and murdered by an angry crowd, before his protectors could convey him to the Town Hall. His fate was shared by three of his officers and three of his men. Flesselles was shot down as he left the Town Hall to answer the charges of treachery brought against him.

¹⁰ Amid the almost incessant ringing of bells and firing of muskets, the shouting of excited crowds and the marching to and fro of the City Militia to which Paris had by this time grown accustomed, the siege of the Bastille passed almost unnoticed outside the remote district in which it took place. Dr. Rigby of Norwich, who was staying in Paris at the time, was first made aware of what had happened when he met an immense crowd marching, or rather running — such is the impression produced by the rapid step of a French mob, or of a French regiment — along the rue Saint-Honoré towards the Palais-Royal. As it came nearer, he saw "a flag, some large keys, and a paper elevated on a pole above the crowd, in which was inscribed *La Bastille est prise et les portes sont ouvertes!*" This sight was greeted with "shouts and shrieks, leaping and embracing, laughter and tears," and every sign of frantic joy. But in a few moments another crowd followed. It was welcomed with equal signs of joy, but produced a very different impression upon the English visitor; for instead of trophies of victory it carried trophies of revenge — the bleeding heads of de Launey and Flesselles raised aloft on pikes.

¹¹ The capture of the Bastille seemed miraculous to an age accustomed to scoff at miracles. That a massive medieval castle like Conway or Corfe, strengthened with guns and a garrison, should have surrendered after a few hours' fighting to a civilian crowd stiffened by a few soldiers, might well puzzle a professional mind. There was little food in the fortress; but the garrison was not starved out. Both besiegers and besieged realized that, if the affair dragged on, de Broglie's troops would be bound to intervene. The civilians had a few guns: but what could they have done against so rock-like a building? The governor soon lost what little discretion he possessed: but he need never have surrendered. The day was, in fact, won, not by guns or gunpowder, but by the moral force of the people. It was the enthusiasm of the people which inspired Hulin and his fellows with legendary courage. It was disdain of the people which inspired de Launey's threat to blow up

the fortress. It was sympathy with the people which forced the garrison to surrender. The apparent miracle was the result of unwonted but not unnatural causes. . . .

Commentary and questions

1. *Paragraphs 1-5:* The tone here is largely quiet and neutral. Compare it to that of Carlyle. Which is a more effective beginning? Which gives the better account of Desmoulin's speech?

2. *Paragraph 6:* Thompson blames de Launey for the bloodshed and violence. What evidence does he present? Find the specific places where he differs from Marmontel and Carlyle. Where do they all agree?

3. *Paragraph 8:* Compare this paragraph with Marmontel's version of the same incident. What does Thompson omit? Is there any motive for this omission that you can discover in the purpose of Thompson's account?

4. *Paragraph 9:* This clearly establishes Thompson's sympathies. Why is his version of the treatment of the officers of the garrison merely factual? Does he omit anything noticed by the other writers? Does he include anything they omit?

5. *Paragraph 11:* What evidence do you find for Thompson's assertion that "the day was, in fact, won, not by guns or gunpowder, but by the moral force of the people." Do Marmontel and Carlyle directly or indirectly charge de Launey with "disdain of the people."

Topics for discussion and writing

I. Analyze the structure of Thompson's account of the fall of the Bastille. By necessity there must be a primary narrative order to the discussion. What other organizing principles do you find?

II. By comparison to Marmontel and Carlyle, Thompson's use of figurative or colored language is mild. What techniques does Thompson use to develop his interpretation of events?

III. Is Thompson's preference for the "people" a fundamental unproved assumption or a position he argues and demonstrates? Give evidence for your answer.

THE BASTILLE FALLS   J. B. Morton

From J. B. Morton, The Bastille Falls and Other Studies of the French Revolution, *1936. Reprinted by permission of Longmans, Green and Co.*

IT WAS the day of Camille Desmoulins. History has set his name at the beginning of the insurrection, and though his part as a leader has been over-dramatised, though he was but one voice among many, he remains for us the will of the people upon that day. He gathered up all the vague fear and protest and anger of those hours, and clothed them in a few simple phrases, telling the people plainly what they knew by instinct — that this matter would only be settled by fighting, that the enemy was armed and ready, and that they, too, must find arms. If we must reject the picturesque story of the leaves torn from the trees, we can remember that on this day he was not a poet (which might, perhaps, have been his destiny) but, what was needed more, a man of action. If he himself, in the accounts he wrote of the day, exaggerated the importance of his rôle, we must not forget that he was inordinately vain, that he knew himself for a follower and not a leader, and was probably amazed at his own daring and at its result, and that many historians have given him a more romantic legend than he hoped to give himself. What is clear is that he had a share in rousing the people to the required pitch of rage. To make him responsible for the anarchy of two days and nights and for the attack on the Bastille is to exaggerate his influence.

2   He left many allusions to his actions on July 12, both in his speeches and his writings, but only three accounts of any length or detail. In the third and last of the three he allowed it to be understood that it was he who brought the news from Versailles of the dismissal of Necker. By that time he had forgotten the letter which he wrote to his father on July 16, four days after the insurrection. In this letter he describes Paris in consternation at the news by the time — three o'clock — he reached the Palais Royal. And many who have written of this day have tended to ignore important parts of the letter, for obvious reasons. In it he describes his arrival at the Palais Royal in the afternoon, and his disappointment because, in spite of the news, no active steps were being taken. The crowd was noisy and angry, but there seemed to be nobody to lead them. He himself stood in the midst of a group, deploring the cowardice and lack of initiative, and haranguing all who cared to listen, when there came by three young men crying "To arms!" Camille joined them, and, seeing his enthusiasm, they encouraged him to mount a table and to address the crowd. Carried away by excitement he leapt on to the table and delivered the speech which has remained as famous as the three young men have remained obscure. He told his audience that the dismissal of Necker was an earnest of what was to come. For this very night, said he, for all they knew, the Court might be preparing a second St. Bartholomew. He cried "To arms!" and bade them choose for their badge a cockade of green, the colour of spring and hope. To his own hat he fastened a green ribbon, and then, catching sight of police spies, he brandished a pistol, and cried that they should not take him alive; that he knew how to die a glorious death; that the only misfortune which could befall him was to see his country enslaved.

3   His speech and the fire with which it was delivered had an instantaneous effect. The crowd pressed round him cheering and applauding. They

said they would give him a bodyguard, that they would not leave him, that they would follow whither he had a mind to lead them. And he replied that he had no desire to lead them, that it was enough for him to be in the ranks. . . .

4   Early on this morning Desmoulins was among those who raided the Invalides, and seized a store of muskets (not 100,000 as he reported, but nearer 30,000). It was said that there were more in the Bastille. The word passed from lip to lip, and soon the mixed crowd was on its way: shop-keepers anxious to restore order, released criminals, vagabonds from the provinces, sightseers, men who had been genuinely moved by the speeches of the agitators. This wild army, with four or five different purposes, ad-vanced against the old dungeon of the St. Antoine quarter, crying "Vive le Roi!" On this note of comedy the Revolution began.

5   To those who had listened to the agitators the old dark prison-fortress of Charles VI was something more than an arsenal which might give them a further supply of arms. It was the solid presence of the old régime, and its grey stones were a monument to the tyranny of monarchy. The word sug-gested the *lettre de cachet*, that swift weapon of arbitrary power, and called up visions of men left to rot through the years in dark dungeons. Several of the *cahiers* from the electoral districts had demanded its destruction. Its presence, and all it represented, was one of the grievances of the electoral bodies. The people of the faubourg St. Antoine, on the move like all Paris on this Tuesday morning, could see the cannon in their high embrasures. The muzzles pointed at the quarter. If those guns spoke and the troops which encircled Paris began to close in, what would become of them all? They imagined the strong garrison standing to arms in the forecourts, and they sent a deputation to the Town Hall to demand the withdrawal of the cannon which threatened them. The deputation was brought before the Committee, in permanent session, and steps were taken to attend to the grievance of the people. Three officials were despatched to the Bastille, and admitted to the presence of old de Launey, the governor. They repeated the complaint, which must have seemed like a rather foolish joke to de Launey, who was under no illusions as to the military quality of his artillery. He pointed out that his fifteen pieces were as old as the hills, and were used occasionally to fire a salvo on some festive occasion. As for his garrison, he had some 120 men, the majority of them old Invalides, and the rest of them Swiss. In the current year he had received one prisoner — a voluntary one — Réveillon the paper-maker of their own faubourg St. Antoine, who could think of no safer asylum. The victims of the King's tyranny at present imprisoned in the cells numbered seven. They were two lunatics, four forgers, and a young nobleman convicted of incest.

6   However, de Launey promised to withdraw his cannon, and was given, in return, an assurance that no attack would be made on the Bastille. Nevertheless, when he had ordered meat and drink to be set before the

deputies, he realised that the situation was difficult. He had heard all the rumours of attack, but he had failed to provision his garrison. There was, of course, no question of a mere mob being able to capture a fortress, but what means would he have of dispersing them? He saw, when the deputation left, that a crowd of people had penetrated, with the spokesmen of the Town Hall, past the outer court, and near enough to the Governor's house to be heard. They were separated from the fortress itself only by a ditch of some thirty yards in width. When these people saw the cannon withdrawn from their positions, they thought that the gunners were about to load. The leaders among them, or those with the loudest voices, counselled an attack on the fortress. The news of what was toward passed back through the crowded streets in every direction, and so came to the ears of the lawyer Thuriot de la Rozière, who, with two others, immediately demanded an audience of the Governor. He was courteously received, alone, and advised de Launey to surrender in the name of the Nation. Then, in the main court, he addressed the garrison. After this he climbed to the towers, and the two men looked out across the St. Antoine quarter and saw that the dense masses were moving towards them. Beneath them the outer courts were seething; and when they turned about they saw that the narrow streets were filled with slow-moving crowds. From below a continuous murmur came up, which now and then, in one spot or another, became fiercer and shriller. De Launey knew that he was beleaguered, and Thuriot noted that not only had the cannon been withdrawn, but the embrasures had been blocked with billets of wood, so that the crowds should not see the muzzles of the withdrawn guns. Once more, after descending to the main court, Thuriot harangued the troops, and advised them to surrender. But whatever their feelings, de Launey was still in command. He promised not to fire upon the mob save in self-defence. It was about half-past twelve when Thuriot left the Governor.

7 In the streets a soldier named Elie had been singled out by one section of the crowd. They told him that if the authorities would not hand over arms and ammunition they were determined to storm the fortress, and they asked him how he would set about it. He told them that they must get guns from the French Guards, and that they must spread the news everywhere that the Bastille was to be stormed.

8 All this while the mob was pressing in by the triple gate of St. Anthony, and along the covered way, past the first guard-room, to that open space which was called the Passage. This was a kind of miniature village outside the actual fortress. On one side were the barracks of the Invalides, and on the other a line of taverns, barbers' shops, grocers' shops, and so on. It was a public place, with a narrow opening on the right, leading to an inner court and to the streets. On the left was an alley leading to a drawbridge over the outer ditch. Beyond this drawbridge there were two gates, one for pedestrians, another for carriages, leading into another court, where the

Governor had his house, and where was the armoury. From here a long avenue ran to the main moat, guarded by the great drawbridge which covered the gate of the dark interior court of the Bastille itself. On the right of this avenue were the kitchens, and a bathroom for the Governor's wife. At the end of it rose the two southern towers, Comté and Basinière, bastions of the main court.

9   De Launey had withdrawn his small garrison into an inner court, and had raised the drawbridge that communicated with the court in front of his house. But the crowd was by now desperate. Two soldiers, Bonnemère and Tournay, clambered on to the roof of a shop and hacked at the chains of the drawbridge with hatchets. No shot was fired at them. They were ordered to withdraw, but they went on with their work, encouraged by the howls of those who were near enough to see what was going on. At length the chains were severed, the drawbridge fell with a crash, and the mob swarmed across, firing wildly as they came. At that critical moment de Launey gave the order to fire, and the rabble wavered, broke and came pouring back, throwing the dense mass behind them into a panic.

10   While the mob had been waiting to rush the drawbridge, Thuriot was at the Town Hall, reporting the state of affairs. It was decided that a proclamation should be made in the Place de Grève, informing the people of de Launey's promise not to open fire except in self-defence. It was about one o'clock when the trumpeter came out on to the steps of the Town Hall, but as he raised the trumpet to his lips, all heads turned from him. There was a sound of firing, and it came from the direction of the Bastille. Soon afterwards the wounded began to arrive, and with them the false tales of de Launey's treachery. By evening the lie was all over Paris. De Launey had ordered the drawbridge to be lowered, had made friendly overtures to the people, and had then fired on them. No serious historian accepts this nonsense to-day.

11   It was decided that another deputation should be sent to the Bastille, to ask de Launey to accept the protection of a force of militia. The party was unable to carry out its mission, as it arrived when the mob, momentarily routed, had returned to the attack. White handkerchiefs were waved, but nobody took any notice. For the business was settling down into a siege. The French Guards arrived, bringing guns. The fire of the garrison, now lining the towers, was returned by men who crowded in the doorways of shops, or behind chimney-pots, or at the dark edge of the little tunnel that led from the rue St. Antoine to the Arsenal. By three o'clock five guns had arrived. Five more were on the way, with the mixed band of civilians and soldiers commanded by Hulin. By the Arsenal garden another crowd advanced, the men of the faubourg St. Marceau, armed with scythes and forks and spades, and their leader, Acloque the brewer, had the greatest difficulty in persuading them to take cover behind a line of trees. Another brewer, Santerre, led the St. Antoine contingent. He had commandeered a number

of dung-carts. He lit the contents, and the heavy smoke provided a screen for his movements.

12 What had begun as an assembly of angry crowds, without leaders and without a plan, had by four o'clock changed to an organised siege. Hulin and Elie, soldiers, had taken matters in hand, and others, in various parts of the huge, heaving host, had discovered in themselves a quality of leadership — among whom two of the strangest characters of the Revolution. The first was a peasant girl named Anne-Joseph Terwagne, from Marcourt, in Luxembourg, twenty-six years of age. After playing a spectacular part on this day, on October 5 and on August 10, she lost her wits, and died insane in 1817. The second was the tall usher Maillard, also aged twenty-six, and destined to leave his name for ever connected with October 5 and the September massacres. He died of tuberculosis in the spring of 1794. Maillard was with Hulin and Elie and the men who planned and carried out the first determined assault on the Bastille itself. They pushed in from the south, dragging forward their pieces of artillery across the Cour du Gouvernement, which led to the last drawbridge covering the gates into the main courtyard. Here, however, they found Santerre's wagons in the way. A party led by Elie himself, in his old uniform of the Queen's Regiment, dragged them back under fire, losing two of their number. The guns were rapidly hauled forward, and behind them came rank upon rank of soldiers and civilians. A hundred feet above them rose the two southern round towers, Comté and Basinière, from which the defenders threw down paving-stones and lumps of iron. De Launey himself took part in this attempt to beat back the invaders. But there was a spirit in them now, and eye-witnesses on either side testify to the astounding courage, not merely of the soldiers, but of workmen and shopkeepers, often unarmed, and entirely unused to fighting. Their losses alone might have terrified them, but they pressed on until they were within a few yards of the last drawbridge and the gate into the inner court. De Launey took counsel with his officers. He was for blowing up the Tour de la Liberté, in which the ammunition was kept, and himself with it, but two of his officers prevented him. Capitulation was decided on, in face of the threat of Hulin's cannon, now firing point-blank on the entrance gates.

13 It is true that the Bastille was not captured by force, but surrendered; but the attackers lost more than eighty dead, and more than seventy wounded.

14 It was about five o'clock when the white flag appeared on the Basinière tower, but the assailants went on firing. Presently, at a loophole beside the last of the drawbridges appeared the face of a Swiss. An arm, holding a paper, was stretched through the hole. But there was nobody near enough to read what the writing said. Somebody fetched a plank, and while it was held down, in the manner of a seesaw, at one end, and rested, at the other, on a narrow parapet, a man crawled along it to get the paper. He lost his footing and fell into the stone ditch. Young Maillard took his place, and

returned with the terms. In a few blunt words de Launey informed the attackers that if they refused to accept his surrender he would blow up the
powder-magazine, the garrison and the enemy. Of the conflicting accounts
of what followed, that of Louis de Flue, the officer of the Swiss who actually
handed the paper through the hole, is the most likely to be true. De Flue
had stood in the Salle du Conseil with de Launey, trying to persuade him to
fight on, since the fortress had suffered no damage, but de Launey would
not listen. The paper was delivered to Elie, but while those nearest gathered
round him to read the terms, the mob behind continued to shout "No capitulation." De Flue withdrew, and posted himself on the left of the main entrance, outside the guard-room, having reported to de Launey the way in
which the crowd had received the offer of surrender. Apparently the crowd
did not know that Elie had accepted the surrender and had given his word of
an officer that no harm should come to the garrison. Obviously only those
of the attackers nearest to him could have heard him shout the acceptance
of the terms. Anyhow the last drawbridge was lowered, and the mob, infuriated by the resistance of the defenders, came tumbling across into the
main court — Maillard among the first. He and Arné, a grenadier, seized the
Governor and snatched from him the swordstick with which he would have
ended his life. The people howled for his instant execution, while Hulin
and Elie tried to protect him. He and his staff were dragged to the Town
Hall, and the dregs of the mob smashed up furniture, massacred any of the
garrison they could find and destroyed or burned the archives. The seven
prisoners were freed, and carried through the streets in triumph. The
moment of discipline and order which had preceded the capitulation, when
Hulin and Elie had matters in hand, had given place to the wildest confusion again. People were firing on each other in the courts of the fortress,
nobody knowing friend from enemy. Those who were taken to the Town
Hall were stoned and kicked and beaten all along the way. De Launey,
already badly wounded, was murdered in the Place de Grève. He fell fighting like a lion, and a cook's apprentice named Desnot severed the head from
the body with a penknife and carried it about the streets on a three-pronged
fork, having nerved himself with a drink of brandy and gunpowder. His
defence was that he had hoped to obtain a medal for his patriotic action.
De Flesselles was shot dead on the steps of the Town Hall. He was at work
in the building when the mob burst into the Council Chamber, crying that
the Bastille had fallen. Elie was with them, covered with blood, his sword
bent and buckled. He was the hero of the moment. They offered him the
silver plate of the Governor, which they had brought hither, as well as
scraps of old armour, and the flag of the Bastille. De Flesselles watched in
silence, and he was pale as death. Elie, erect on a table, tried to make his
voice heard. In a passion of despair he took his sword in both hands and
broke it across his chest, while, all around him, the surging throng greeted

with yells the arrival of Invalides or Swiss, who were taken outside to be hanged or shot. The cry of "A la lanterne!" stupefied those who did not know what scourge had been loosed on Paris. The French Guards were too few to restrain the mob. Elie succeeded in saving the lives of a few, when he could shout loudly enough to be heard. But it was not long before de Flesselles himself became the centre of attention. Some were for shutting him up in the Châtelet, others were for taking him to the Palais Royal, and hearing what he had to say in his own defence against the charge of treason. He was dragged from the Council Chamber, and on the steps of the Town Hall a young man shot him dead. His head, with that of de Launey, was carried to the garden of the Palais Royal, and paraded with the keys of the Bastille.
15 That evening Louis XVI wrote in his private diary the one word "Rien."

16 In the capture of the Bastille there was tremendous courage, but little of the glory which the Constituent Assembly claimed for the day of July 14. The majority of the mob probably thought that de Launey was a traitor who deserved death. In any case, they could claim that Hulin and Elie had no mandate from them to accept a surrender couched in such proud terms. They would have insisted on, and would have obtained, unconditional surrender. But the day began, as it ended, with anarchy. Hulin's attack had been a brief interlude. The rest was, first, the turbulence of criminals and vagabonds, and afterwards the savagery of men maddened by the sight of blood. The peaceful citizens who had marched on the Bastille to demand arms soon found themselves an uncomfortable minority in a crazy army. And some of them lived to boast that they too had had a share in that glorious day's work. Within forty-eight hours the Constituent Assembly passed from terror of the Court to terror of the people, and from terror of the people to a feeling of relief. In another forty-eight hours those who had barred their doors and shuttered their windows against thieves and rioters were astonished to hear that Paris had been full, not of bandits, but of heroes. And the agitators who had talked of plunder and riches talked now of glory and liberty. As for Desmoulins, who had picked out for himself at the Invalides a musket with a bayonet, and two pistols, and had "Rushed up at the first cannon-shot, but the Bastille was already taken" — Desmoulins was spoken of as one of the principal authors of the whole affair. "Perhaps," he says to his father in a letter of September 20, "Perhaps I saved Paris from complete ruin and the nation from the most horrible servitude." Anyhow, his name stands at the commencement of what was done on that day, and he will be spoken of through the years whenever men speak of July 14.

Commentary and questions

1. *Paragraphs 1-3:* Morton's account of Desmoulin's speech is somewhat lengthier than those of other writers in this selection. Compare their in-

terpretations of the significance of that speech. Which interpretation seems to be the most balanced? For what differing purposes do the several authors use the speech?

2. *Paragraph 4:* What does this description of the crowd marching on the Bastille convey? What do you think Morton's attitude is? Does he see the crowd as directed and purposeful, uncertain and propelled by emotion, or suffering from mixed and contradictory impulses. What makes him call the incident a "note of comedy"?

3. *Paragraph 5:* What purpose does the description serve here? What apparent facts are mentioned that none of the other writers use?

4. *Paragraph 6:* Does Morton's account of de Launey's actions contradict any of the others you have read? In what particulars does he differ?

5. *Paragraphs 10-13:* Isolate statements of fact, interpretation or analysis, suppositions, and conclusions in this passage. What is the effect of paragraph 13?

6. *Paragraph 14:* Compare Morton's account of the attempted surrender and the mob with those of Carlyle, Marmontel, and Thompson. How does the emphasis of each accord with or differ from the others?

7. *Paragraph 15:* Discuss the placement and effect of this sentence.

8. *Paragraph 16:* What interpretations of the fall of the Bastille and the events of July 14 does Morton mention or allude to? What is his own point of view?

Topics for discussion and writing

I. Note the places where Morton interrupts his narrative. What does he substitute? Why?

II. List the events and incidents recounted by Morton for July 14, 1789. What does he mention that is not included by the other authors? Does this added material in any way support conclusions that differ from those of the other writers?

III. Compare Carlyle, Thompson, and Morton in their estimates of the character and role of Desmoulins. You should, of course, make reference to Desmoulin's own account of his speech.

IV. Write a theme comparing the accounts of the role of de Launey, the commander of the Bastille garrison. Which do you think is the most disinterested and balanced account? Do the authors use de Launey for differing purposes?

V. Write a theme discussing the attitudes of Marmontel, Carlyle, Thompson, and Morton toward the crowd that attacked the Bastille. Pay close attention to the language used to describe that crowd and its actions.

VI. Choose three of the accounts and compare their use of figurative language.

VII. Make two lists: (a) of the facts on which all the accounts agree; (b) of those upon which there is apparent disagreement (you should include omissions). Then write a theme discussing the use of facts in the writing of history. What considerations govern the use of facts? To what extent may facts be variously interpreted? For this last question you might take an incident upon which several or all of the writers agree as regards its status as a fact but upon which they differ in interpretation.

VIII. Write a theme discussing three or more of the authors' use of individual characters.

Billy Graham—pro and con: WHEN BILLY GRAHAM
SAVED SCOTLAND, R. B. Robertson · THE REAL BILLY GRAHAM, David H. C.
Read · DIFFERING POINTS OF VIEW ON BILLY GRAHAM, Reinhold Niebuhr and
John Sutherland Bonnell

CONTROVERSY over the accomplishments and value of such
a public figure as Billy Graham is bound to involve strong opinion and conviction. The following selections are divided equally among writers for and
against Billy Graham. Neither group offers any substantial body of objective
facts upon which to base logical judgment, because few such facts exist.
In reality, these authors are not interested in what the introduction to Part
II calls "statements of fact." The important matters in discussing Billy
Graham are not matters that can be observed or measured.

There is another kind of statement, that in which the writers who have
observed Graham at first hand report his effect on his audiences, but these
are impressions and conclusions, not observed facts. Robertson and Read
both rely upon their impressions to convince their readers that what they
say is valid, but these impressions can never be tested impartially or con-
clusively. Niebuhr and Bonnell argue the issue against a much broader
background, the religious value of the evangelism Graham practices. Although Bonnell rests part of his case on his assessment of the genuineness of
Graham as a human being (a point Niebuhr does not debate), their differences center in their attitudes toward evangelism in general.

But they, too, offer little concrete evidence in support of their views.
This means that all four selections rely on techniques of argument aimed
at influencing the reader's opinion solely on a persuasive basis: irony, humor,
narrative description, broadly connotative terms, character analysis, and
inference are the raw materials of these authors' appeals (though this list
by no means exhausts the persuasive techniques used here). Of course, all
four writers expect their readers to be moderately informed about Graham
and evangelism.

The fact that this section includes essays for and against would seem to imply that there are only two sides to this question. For the reader who wishes to take a stand there are, of course, alternatives to the simple for and against, though these positions are not represented by essays here.

WHEN BILLY GRAHAM
SAVED SCOTLAND

R. B. Robertson

First published in The Atlantic Monthly. *Reprinted with some changes from* Of Sheep and Men, *by permission of Alfred A. Knopf, Inc. Copyright 1957 by R. B. Robertson.*

DURING the closed season for sin, which synchronizes pretty exactly with the lengthening evenings and the end of the winter run of salmon, religion becomes the principal pastime of our parish, as it has always been the principal national pastime of the Scots. So, when Evangelist Billy Graham picked on our little country of Scotland for one of his biggest jamborees to date, he was not bringing an unknown commodity to our people.

2   It might have seemed that way on superficial examination. For example, only eight persons attended the morning service in our village kirk the Sunday before the Billy Graham All-Scotland Crusade began. This had always been about the average attendance, and it was a fair index of the strength and popularity of organized religion as presented by the Church of Scotland in our area today, but not of the religious interest of the people. The question "Are ye gaun tae Billy Graham?" showed that. My wife and I were asked that question one hundred and eighty-six times inside the week.

3   We already knew the official attitude toward the Graham Crusade of the Kirk of Scotland. There was a day when the "Sword of Gideon," as it calls itself, would have smitten, as only the Scottish Kirk could smite, anyone holding to doctrines differing from its own who tried to interfere on a national scale with the spiritual and religious life of Scotland. Yet here it was today saying: "Please, Billy, come and save Scotland!" Here was our world-famous band of clergy voluntarily and gladly taking back seats to a foreign preacher who was by no means an intellectual theologian, assisted by a trombonist, a crooner, and a stunt organizer. Truly the Sword of Gideon had crumbled into rust!

4   But what was "oor Meenister" going to do? We soon found out.

5   "Oor Meenister" is not of the Kirk of Scotland, but of that dissident and fiercer body, the *Free* Church of Scotland, which is so strictly Calvinistic that it believes the national church is "halfway to Rome."

6   But, like his "high church" colleagues, he was going to admit that his eight years' training for, and fifteen years in, the ministry had been in vain.

He was going to admit his incompetence and his inability to attend to the spiritual welfare and salvation of the small group of souls in the parish committed to his care. He was going to Billy Graham, and he was taking along with him as many of us, church members and sinners alike, as he could persuade to accompany him on his bus to Glasgow, there to have done on us in an hour and a half the job we had been paying him to do for fifteen years. A special bus would leave at two thirty on Tuesday. We were to bring sandwiches and a flask of tea, or such refreshment as we required on the three-hour journey. A collection would be taken on the bus, which would be our parish contribution to the All-Scotland Crusade.

7   My wife and I were first on the bus. We sat, as sinners do on such occasions, in the back seat and watched the salvation-seekers from our village arrive.

8   There came first Hamish Dundas. Hamish is perhaps our most solid parishioner. He keeps the local smithy six days a week and haggles over the price of a shoe nail as though it were made of uranium. But on Sunday a metamorphosis takes place and Hamish changes from his old overalls into dark suit, high stiff collar, and black tie, his uniform as leading member of the kirk session. He keeps the seventh day holy as only an elder of the Free Scottish Church can keep it, carrying out his elderly offices for the adults, teaching Sunday school to our fourteen village children and Bible class for our five adolescents. Between times on the Sabbath he conducts family worship for his wife and mother and sister, provided, that is, that no godless Englishman, breaking the Sabbath by jaunting over the Border, needs his horse shod — and provided the salmon are "no' runnin'."

9   A Scottish elder's womenfolk follow him around with a dumb apathy and self-effacement similar to that of Oriental women cowed through the ages by their lords. So when the black-hatted, black-coated Hamish entered the bus and took, as befitted his station, the front seat, two silent purdahed figures, his wife and daughter, slipped unobtrusively in behind him.

10   Next came Auld Kenneth's two sisters, staunch kirkwomen both, the elder the leader of the parish temperance movement and the younger the secretary of the parochial branch of every society for the abolition of everything else. They negotiated their skirts up the three steps into the bus with the practiced dexterity of legless nuns and succeeded in making the two well-upholstered and luxurious seats directly behind the Dundas family look like uncomfortable pews.

11   Auld Kenneth himself arrived a minute later, easing his weather-beaten neck in its unaccustomed collar, but carrying as always his battered old-lambin' stick, and accompanied by his two scrawny collie bitches. These, at the words "Come by, Meg! Come by, Tim!" leaped onto the bus and stood motionless in the aisle, awaiting their master's instructions on how to deal with the few sheep already collected in this peculiar pen.

12   "Ye canna bring your dogs, Kenneth," came Hamish's elderly edict from the front seat.

13   "An' why for no'?" expostulated Auld Kenneth in bewilderment. "They aye come tae kirk wi' me. Can they no come tae Billy Graham?"

14   "Ye canna bring your dogs, Kenneth," the kirk session repeated its decree. Kenneth glanced from his collies to Hamish, then back again, as if of two minds whether to order them to "haud that ane oot o' here!" (which they would have done at a flick of Kenneth's calloused hand). But instead he submitted to ecclesiastical authority, and at a toss of his head and the traditional "That'll do," his dogs bounded out of the bus and away back up the glen to his cottage five miles away.

15   Then the village adolescents burst into the bus — all five of them. Headed by Flossie, Tam's sixteen-year-old, and her pal, the diker's daughter, they giggled their way aboard, throwing loud "hellos" in all directions, and scrambled toward the rear seats, as far from respectability as they could get. There was some jostling among the three lads following the girls, for each of them had the idea of spending the next three hours in the seat next to Flossie. But she outmaneuvered them all and settled in the back corner opposite us, with the diker's daughter as a barrier between herself and the thrustful young males. Two of these dived into the seat in front of the girls and immediately turned around to kneel on the seat.

16   The third lad, the little red-headed gowk, Wee Ecky, was forgotten by the others and sat farther forward alone, feeling as far out of things as only a fifteen-year-old tagging along with sixteen-year-olds can feel.

17   Mrs. Chisholm came next. Nobody in the village really knows Mrs. Chisholm. She speaks only to the Minister and to the village children, always calling the latter "my poor wee things" and weeping over them even when she encounters them in the midst of their boisterous enjoyment. The children, in defense, call her "Greetin' Gertie," because of her proclivity for weeping, and clam up at her approach. The more charitable adult villagers have tried to be kind to her and to find out how they can help her to bear the ghastly and apparently uncommunicable sorrow that is bespoken by her every gesture. They have been obliged to desist and to admit that she is "a wee bit nervous," but they excuse this euphemistically described Border condition by pointing out that "of course she's at a difficult time o' life."

18   Mrs. Chisholm hurried into the bus with a pseudo-tense jerkiness and slumped silently into the loneliest seat she could find, more oblivious to than oblivious of the thirteen pairs of eyes watching her. All of us fell silent too, even Flossie and her noisy friends, for they, of course, had been "poor wee things" only two or three lambing seasons before.

19   Hamish Dundas' clearing his throat in his dignified elderly way was insufficient to bring life back to the bus after Greetin' Gertie's arrival, and we all hoped that the next to come would be somebody less deflating.

20   It was. But unfortunately it was so explosive that we became if possible even more silent. For it was none other than Old Jerry Nolan.

2

1   Now this was a Scottish bus, organized by the Free Church of Scotland, under the personal supervision of the Minister (it was high time he appeared, with people such as Jerry stepping aboard!) and it was proceeding to the All-Scotland Crusade meeting, the main purpose of which was to save Scotland from Sin and bring it back into the arms of the True Kirk. And here was this Nolan, getting on the bus with a friendly smile and a greeting from everybody, from the elder in the front seat to the sinners in the back, and sitting down near Auld Kenneth Lindsay without any apology or explanation at all. It was outrageous!

2   For Jerry, I should explain, is an Irishman. Nobody can blame him for that, of course, and no doubt there are some good Irishmen, the same as there are good Russians and even, they say, good Englishmen. But he's not only an Irishman, he's the *barman* at the House of Sin. The chief wrecker of homes in the parish. The man who provides the Minister with excoriative material, spoken under ecclesiastical privilege, for at least fifty sermons every year. Where does this man Nolan think our bus is going? To Phil the Fluter's Ball, or Finnegan's Wake, or somewhere? Because, far worse than being a barman, the man's a Catholic! Indeed, this was Saladin walking into the tent of the King Richard of the All-Scotland Crusade. *Where* was the Minister?

3   The next comer, fortunately for the peace of Christendom and the safety of her Majesty's lieges in Scotland, was not the Minister but (we all breathed again) Barry Caven.

4   I don't think Barry had any advance intention of "gaun tae Billy Graham," for Barry's religion, as far as anybody knows, is something akin to early Druidism. But as he passed down the lane where the bus was filling up, some Pictish instinct told him that here was just the kind of human tangle which, by adding his mysterious presence, he liked to complicate still further. So he took a seat.

5   Like us and the adolescents, but for a different reason, he sat far back.

6   One of Barry Caven's most disconcerting traits is making people talk about the subject that is uppermost in their minds but which they think it would be tactless and in bad taste to discuss. If Barry goes to a funeral, he talks about death all the time. In the presence of millionaires, he always talks about money, and if he entered a convent he would immediately open a discussion on sex.

7   This being a religious excursion on which we were embarking, it seemed to Barry that we should discuss modern ritual, and with a dead-pan face he inquired of Hamish Dundas his opinion concerning total immersion of the adult as opposed to baptism of the infant as a necessary prelude to salvation. Hamish, whose ancestors had fought and died on the Border hills in attack on and defense of minor liturgical issues, reddened slightly, but gave the Free Kirk's present party-line reply concerning its doctrinal differences with Billy Graham: that the Kirk did not want to stress the incongruities of its association with the Baptists, for Billy was an honorable man, and his team of evangelists . . . "So are they all, all honorable men!" concluded Barry Caven for him; then turning to Jerry Nolan, to whom nobody had yet spoken, he inquired whether Old Jerry thought that there was at least a psychological if not a doctrinal resemblance between the Roman confessional and Graham's technique of collecting penitents before him and remitting their sins.

8   Jerry's reply, which might have caused an uproar in our predominantly Presbyterian bus, was fortunately lost in the bustle attending the arrival, only half an hour late, of the Minister.

9   "Good day, everybody! Good day!" The Minister beamed. "What a fine turnout! Billy will be proud of the response of our parish to his Crusade. Now let me see how many we are. . . . Counting myself, I make it seventeen souls and the driver."

10   "That makes eighteen," said Barry in a loud, clear voice.

11   "Nearly a tithe of the parish! Now let me see who we are. Mr. Dundas, and of course Mrs. Dundas, and Miss Dundas, and the Miss Lindsays — all my old faithfuls — and you too, Kenneth, though I haven't seen you in kirk for a week or two." (The old herd fidgeted uncomfortably and gazed glumly at his feet like a reproved ten-year-old.) "Now who have we here? . . . Oh! . . ." His shortsighted eyes had focused on Jerry. They blinked slowly three times, then passed quickly on to Mrs. Chisholm. "Ah! Dear lady. I thought you would answer the call. And there's Flossie, and the other young people. I hope you've all brought your Bibles with you. Billy Graham teaches that we should base even our everyday lives on the Bible."

12   "Jack Calvin and good old Johnnie Knox had the same idea a while ago," remarked Barry Caven, thereby bringing the ministerial gaze to bear on him at last.

13   "Now who have we here? Why! By . . . by . . . hookey! It's Mr. Caven!" The shock of finding Jerry Nolan on the bus had not yet worn off, and this time the poor Minister could not conceal his amazement. "I didn't know, Mr. Caven, that you . . . ah . . . that you . . . well, anyway, welcome to our company! Billy has asked us to bring anybody and everybody. And many outside the Church may have their lives changed this evening. I hear that even an actress heard Billy's call last night, forsook her disgraceful way of life, so there's no reason why a . . . ah . . ."

14   "Tramp?" suggested Barry helpfully.

15   ". . . why other unconventional souls shouldn't hear the call," the Minister finished hurriedly.

16   "If the Billy Graham Evangelical Association, Inc., is calling on us to forsake this world's goods, tell 'em I heard the call at Capernaum two thou-

sand years ago," said Barry, but the Minister evaded this dangerous topic by turning to may wife and myself with a brief nod of recognition, then ordered the driver to start his bus. But there were two further incidents before we got out of the village.

3

1 Down the lane a ragged, trousered, but obviously female figure, well known to us all, stepped out and held the bus for a few moments. This was Mrs. Tam. She spoke to Flossie through the window, ignoring the Minister's obvious irritation.

2 "After the meetin' gang oot tae the shops, Flossie, an' get me a jar o' potted shrimps."

3 "Okay, Mither," replied Flossie; then added, to the amusement of all those in the rear seats, "But what if I get convairted tae Christ, Mither? Then I'll hae to stay behind and get coonseled, an' the shops'll a' be shut."

4 "Ye can get convairted tae ony bluidy thing ye like, but dinna come hame withoot they potted shrimps," admonished our village doyenne.

5 "Wouldn't you care to join us, Mrs. Elliot?" It was not the Minister, but Barry Caven, who issued the invitation. "We may all have our lives changed tonight."

6 "Ye're a' bluidy daft, that's what ye are," replied the doyenne, and waved the bus on.

7 The second interruption occurred at the House of Sin. Passing that establishment, the Minister, the elder, and the church members, as is their custom, all averted their eyes and found something very interesting to engage their attention in the blank empty field on the other side of the road, so they did not see the aging red-faced citizen in a greasy old tweed cap and plus fours who dashed out of the bar door waving a battered blue paper-backed book with as much vehemence as an evangelist waves a Bible. The driver saw him, however, and braked hard to allow him to jump aboard and slump down, breathing heavily, in the seat beside Auld Kenneth. We were finally off.

8 None of us knew Old Greasy Cap, which was rather astonishing, for we know everybody within ten miles of our village. The respectable folk in the front seats turned to take one look at him, noted with obvious horror his choice of attire for church-going, and turned back quickly. The rear seats began a whispered colloquy in an effort to diagnose him. Even Barry Caven was stumped. It was agreed that if we could see the name of the unusual-looking scripture he was clutching, that would furnish the main clue, so my wife was detailed to find out the nature of this well-thumbed tract before we reached Billy Graham.

9 Interest in our latest-joined pilgrim was temporarily banished when the Minister announced that, as there would be no time for attending to the

inner man when we arrived in Glasgow, we had better all partake of the sustenance he hoped we had brought with us. Owing to the unusual circumstances, he would dispense with the saying of grace and the blessing of food, but before we opened our flasks of tea, Mr. Dundas would take up a collection, which would be our parish contribution to the All-Scotland Crusade.

10 Hamish removed his black hat with alacrity and moved around the bus. When he came to Barry Caven, with mute but irresistible demand, I tried to slip Barry a shilling under the seat. But Barry pushed it away and announced with quiet dignity and without excuse, "I have no money."

11 It then transpired that the Minister, owing to the pressure of work connected with the evangelical revival in our parish, had omitted to bring his own sustenance.

12 "But," he said, fixing my wife with a look of Pickwickian benevolence, "I have no doubt that one of the ladies will allow me a sip of tea from her flask."

13 I was the only person on the bus who knew how awkward was this particular situation, for the flask was filled, not with tea, but with a pint of exquisitely cold and very dry martinis. Barry saved the day by telling the Minister that my wife had already promised *him* a cup from her flask; and as soon as the reverend gentleman had gone scrounging elsewhere, Barry reached over the back of the seat for his cup of tea, which he had great difficulty in holding steadily for the next two minutes.

14 When we had munched our sandwiches and emptied our flasks, a somnolent silence settled over the bus awhile. It was broken by the unknown pilgrim, who leaned his greasy cap close to Auld Kenneth's well-brushed Sunday bowler and shouted in his ear:

15 "It should be a guid meetin'."

16 "Aye!" Kenneth allowed that it would. "I hear they're expectin' fifteen thoosand."

17 "Are they noo! I didna ken it held that many."

18 "Oh, aye!" maintained Kenneth. "An' it's tae be on the televeesion as weel."

19 "Is it indeed! If I'd kent that, I'd hae bided at hame. It micht hae been cheaper."

20 Bowler Hat looked at Greasy Cap reprovingly, and Hamish the elder turned half around in his seat.

21 "I dinna think it's oor money they're after," they both said together, and Hamish added: "I think the success o' the meetin' is tae be judged by the number that gaes up."

22 "Oh, aye! That's so," conceded Greasy Cap. "And there should be a lot of stairters the day. There's twa-three young 'uns I'm interested in, an' if they dinna gae up the day, it'll brak my heart."

23 The trend of this conversation had me puzzled, so I turned to my wife,

only to find her equally perplexed. But I noted a look of delighted comprehension coming over the face of Barry Caven, so I raised my eyebrows in inquiry.

24   "The book," whispered Barry with huge glee. "That blue Bible! I can guess now what it is!"

25   Barry refused to explain further, and the remainder of the journey to Glasgow passed somewhat tediously.

4

1   At Kelvin Hall, which is Scotland's largest place of assembly, we found hundreds of buses exactly like our own, but bearing the names of widely dispersed villages all over the country. As each bus arrived, the bodies, if not yet the souls, of its occupants were immediately grabbed by the Billy Graham Evangelical Association, Inc., and we found ourselves under a discipline as strict as that of the barrack square or the stockyard. Our group was placed under the command of a ferociously cordial young Christian who handed each of us a yellow ticket before marching us into the hall to our appointed seats near the front. "Watch Greasy Cap," Barry whispered to me.

2   Our unknown pilgrim had grabbed his yellow ticket from the young man, glanced down at it covertly behind his hand, then looked wonderingly back into the innocent face of the steward.

3   "He's looking at it as though it were a half-crown tip he'd got at the entrance to the race-course," I commented, and Barry burst into a long-pent-up laugh.

4   "And that's exactly what he thinks it is! He thought he was getting on the bus for the Lanark Races, and he's never heard of the All-Scotland Handicap. I wouldn't be surprised if that book under his arm is —"

5   "It's *Ruff's Guide to the Turf*," announced my wife, who had sidled up as instructed to read the title.

6   Inside the hall we were surrounded by ferociously cordial stewards, or "Collie Dogs" as they had already been named by Barry Caven.

7   "We're outnumbered about three to one," he said anxiously, "and I don't want to sit right up in the middle of the pen with the others. But there's always one or two sheep get through the line of dogs, so come on!" and, grabbing my wife and myself by the arms, he doubled on his tracks and we managed to retreat about ten rows before we were borne down by reinforcements of Collies.

8   From our new position we had a better view of the thousands of Scottish villagers being herded in toward the pound, and we could see better the props and effects which were to assist in their redemption. Some fifteen thousand people were soon collected under the roof, but a thousand or two who had failed to pass the screening to which we were all subjected on entering had been penned in annexes to watch the proceedings on television,

perhaps because they were bad security risks who might try to contradict Billy, or perhaps because their souls were such that even Billy in the flesh could not save them. Curiously enough, the only member of our party wheeled into the annex was Jerry Nolan, the Catholice barman, whom one of the Collie Dogs had spotted with unerring instinct. Greasy Cap had got through the screen, probably because he would be a magnificent showpiece on the sinners' parade at the finale; but two of the Collies had been specially detailed to keep an eye on him.

9   In the center of the fifteen thousand gaping Scots was a large, solid-looking, black-draped rostrum. "Just like the Kaaba!" commented Barry Caven, who had no doubt seen that famous shrine in his wanderings.

10   Behind this was a choir of two thousand, the males on the left all dressed like Hamish Dundas and the females on the right dressed in white like Aimee McPherson's Angels. Some attempt had been made to ease the eye a bit by putting the younger choristers at the front and sides, like icing around a cake, but the choral core was a few hundred middle-aged songsters, collected from the Glasgow churches, over whom the lights had been arranged in such a way as to dim their appearance though not their voices.

11   The choir was already in action when we arrived. They were being led, or energetically followed, by an athletic young man who seemed to be throwing an imaginary medicine ball to basses, tenors, then altos, but most often to the sopranos.

12   The other scenery of interest included sundry cranes, trolleys, scaffoldings, traffic lights, and all the impedimenta one would normally expect to find on a Clydeside wharf rather than in the House of God. This, we were told by another sinner whom Barry had instinctively selected as a conversational companion, was the TV, moving-picture, and land-line apparatus, which was going to carry "The Message" to about fifteen per cent of the population of Scotland, assembled in town halls, village churches, and schoolhouses in highlands and lowlands and islands.

13   But our fifteen thousand fellow Scots interested us even more than the evangelistic paraphernalia. The uniformity of the types represented was frightening. "I can see at least five hundred Flossies between me and the Kaaba," my wife whispered. "Each one accompanied by one or more gawky boy friends. And there's at least fifty Greetin' Gerties sprinkled among them."

14   The beginning of the service then interrupted our audience analysis.

5

1   A Billy Graham gospel gathering need be described only to the incurious and sensible few who have never left the Plain of Philistia, for the procedure, the music, and often enough the sermon, are identical, whether the performance takes place in Glasgow, or Paris, or London, or Delhi, or Madison Square Garden. At the sound of the last tone of some unseen time ma-

chine, the Medicine Ball Man faces about smartly and orders us all to Rise and Pray.

2   "Every head bowed! Every eye closed!"

3   "And keep the barrel of the rifle on the toe of the right boot, not in the bluidy mud!" muttered Barry Caven as he rose, causing some unseemly mirth among a few ex-service sinners around us who had paraded under Sergeants in Charge of Funeral Parties in the past.

4   We were kept standing during a long prayer, a Bible reading, a bit of community singing, and an admonition to be good and not whisper or cough — about twenty-five minutes in all — and then, having been advised to reach into our hip pockets for our wallets before sitting down, we were allowed to slump gratefully into our seats.

5   "Here comes the Sunday-school superintendent," whispered Barry as the leading man made his blatantly unobtrusive entry on stage and sat down modestly in a corner of the Kaaba.

6   The collection was then taken up by the Collie Dogs so smoothly and efficiently that there were men staggering out the doors of the hall laden with sackfuls of money almost before the organist had reached the second bar of his palliative music; then the chief crooner of the Crusade gave us a number; and then, at last, the main act was on.

7   The sermon is a sort of national institution in Scotland, and it is expected to fit a pattern which has been precisely defined since John Knox preached the first. It must consist of six parts: the Text, followed by a Firstly (explanation), a Secondly (theology), a Thirdly (illustration), and two Finally Brethrens, the first of which should give us a brief tantalizing glimpse of the Heaven we have undoubtedly forfeited because of our sins or because we are not of the Elect, and the second a much longer description of the Hell we are undoubtedly doomed to for all eternity.

8   Graham, perhaps because he is at least partly of our race, followed the pattern pretty closely. For good measure he gave us three Texts, a sort of triple dip, then fifteen minutes of explanation which would have satisfied those with an IQ even as high as 80. His Secondly, or theological argument, was that the Bible said so, and if we did not accept that as a good enough authority, Billy Graham said so too, and we could come to him and say, "But look, Billy —" if we wanted to. (Already I could see several little Flossies around us deciding to take him up on this offer.) His Thirdly was a masterly bit of soap opera, well relayed through the electronic pulpit, during which we met the Graham family in cozy intimacy. At the end we loved the beautiful wife even more than we love Lucy, and we felt we had known the wonderful children, especially "little Ruth, whom we always call Bonny," all their lives.

9   The first, or glimpse-of-Heaven, peroration was rather vague, leaving us with the impression that Heaven, if not actually in the Blue Ridge mountains of North Carolina, bears a distinct resemblance to that balmy district.

But the second peroration was the masterpiece. Hell, we gathered, was an even worse place than Glasgow on a wet March night, and we were given such a vivid impression of it that some of us could not help thinking if ever BGEA, Inc., goes bust, one at least of its sermon writers has a job ready waiting for him as a contributor to horror stories.

10   But, unlike the Scots ministers, Billy gave us a letout. If, he invited us, we would get up now out of our seats and come forward, while the choir sang softly, and stand reverently before him, it was North Carolina for us, and hundred-year-long chats with big blond Billy Graham. If we didn't — and here he looked directly at Barry Caven and raised the big Bible which was his principal prop as though to bang all the sinners in the hall over the head — if we didn't, it would be Glasgow, and all the additional horrors he had mentioned, for all eternity. And we would never have the chance to choose again.

11   "Come . . ." he went on, in a voice Coué would have envied. "Come . . . *God* is speaking to you now, right at this very moment. Come . . . *you* come and talk to God, just as you would talk to *me*. Come, all of you. *Jesus* is here, right *here* . . ."

12   A hush, a low humming noise from the choir, the Bible is slowly lowered to the lectern, and the splendid golden head is lowered in prayer. There is a smothered snuffling from a thousand young female nasopharynges within earshot of us, the owners of which are probably dreaming of an eternity in Heaven, N.C., with this godlike male — and then!

13   "*Jesus Christ!*"

14   Every Collie within a hundred yards of us looked sharply up in our direction, and to my horror I realized the ejaculation had come from my wife.

15   "Jesus Christ!" she repeated, less audibly this time. "There goes Flossie!"

16   And sure enough, there went Flossie, weeping and stumbling down the aisle to get to the Throne of Grace before her contemporaries stole all the best places.

17   They were not long in following her lead. From all parts of the hall a hundred Flossies surged forward, not screaming and kicking and shouting "Love me, Billy!" as they had no doubt all done on other occasions, but this time trying to outdo each other in reverence, though elbowing each other as reverently as they could to get into the front row.

18   We felt almost proud of the initiative shown by our parish, especially when we saw Greetin' Gertie make the next move. With both hands clutched to her breasts, she leaped from her seat, pushed away a Collie Dog who tried to head her off, and *ran* down the aisle. As soon as she was under the arc light in front of the Kaaba and within speaking distance of the Muezzin calling to her, she tried, unconsciously no *doubt*, to outsmart the Flossies. A stumble, a shudder of obvious agony, an earsplitting noise which yet succeeded in remaining a moan rather than a shriek, and she assumed a moder-

ately comfortable horizontal position behind the assembled adolescents.
19 At this moment I admired Graham's pulpit technique, or audience know-how, or whatever it is. He did not move a muscle. The piercing blue eyes were closed; the well-coiffured head was bowed.

20 And just as well!

21 For there were already fifty more Greetin' Gerties staggering down the aisles, like boxers unconscious on their feet. And, had Graham shown a flicker of Christlike compassion for our poor Mrs. Chisholm, there would have been so many women of menopausal age littering the deck that the hundreds of ambulance men present would not have been able to carry out the wounded quick enough. But Graham, by his immobility, let them know that reverence would gain his attention quicker than released repressions, so the Greetin' Gerties braked hard.

22 And then, perhaps because he peeked, or perhaps because he knew from previous experience, he seemed to realize that there was, as Barry put it, "a much higher proportion of yowe-lambs than tup-hoggs in the pen so far," for the next appeal went out to the males. The therapeutic monotone rose again above the music.

23 "Come . . . there are many in this hall carrying a burden of secret sin . . . come and cast it down here . . . here, before me . . . old and young, men and boys . . ."

24 No elderly gentlemen answered this call, but again our village was in the van. This time it was fifteen-year-old Wee Ecky, Flossie's youngest and gawkiest suitor. With a face as red as it was determined, and trying to make himself even less conspicuous than he was, Ecky slipped into the ring, and several score other young lads made their embarrassed way forward to lay their secret sin at the feet of this Hero of the Christian Union.

25 "That's a damned shame," was Barry's rather angry comment this time. "Five minutes' chat with an intelligent schoolmaster or the village doctor would have solved the problems of any of these laddies."

26 Next came the call for those who had already made the "Decision" but wanted to take the opportunity to rededicate their lives. This was Hamish Dundas' signal. At an approving nod from the Minister, he arose and strode down the aisle "in solemn sanctimonious state," his dutiful women behind him. And, lest there be any of the fifteen thousand observers so undiscerning as to mistake this for a repentant sinner instead of a rededicating kirk elder, he withdrew his large Bible from under his armpit and clutched it to his tummy, rather as Moses must have clutched the second edition of the Tablets as he came down the mountain.

27 Other Moses-like figures, followed by their grim odalisques, were converging from all directions. The crowd around the Kaaba now began to look as though the queues for a Roy Rogers film, the outpatient department of a psychiatric clinic, and the General Assembly of the Kirk of Scotland had become unaccountably commingled.

28 But Billy hadn't scraped the bottom of Scotland's hallelujah barrel yet. He knew that there were several hundred Auld Kenneth Lindsays in his audience, and again I admired his craft as he urged their women to bring them forward. Auld Kenneth, I am sure, had no more intention of declaring for Christ than for Confucius, but his women hauled him up. Halfway down the aisle, he "minded that he'd left his hat and stick on the seat" and had to go back for them — more, I feel, to gain time to cover his embarrassment than because he wanted to appear before his Saviour properly dressed.

29 That left only four in the parish pew ahead of us. The Minister at one end, Greasy Cap at the other, and the two sixteen-year-old boys in the middle. Billy had slipped up badly in his attempt to lure those boys into the fold. He had told them that if they came forward, they would be "Babes in Christ," and no sixteen-year-old was going to stand for that, however much he loved Flossie and wanted to accompany her into the mysterious inner room of the temple, where she was going to be "coonseled."

30 The night's quota had now been reached, so the handsome gospeler swung himself off the rostrum and disappeared. The Babes in Christ, now guarded by a veritable regiment of Collie Dogs, were paraded ostentatiously before the thousands of us who had missed forever our chance of salvation, and then led on into eternal life, which lay somewhere through a rather dingy door at the back of Kelvin Hall. Then, as a sort of sublime *non sequitur*, a minister of the Kirk blessed all of us who were left, "now, henceforth, and forever more," and the show was over.

31 The pubs in the vicinity of Kelvin Hall were crowded that night as they had not been seen since the Cup Final.

32 Billy Graham has gone from Scotland now.

33 The Kirk's assessment of the results of the All-Scotland Crusade have not yet been published, but the report and statistics of the effect on our Free Kirk parish are available. Here they are:

TOTAL NUMBER OF CRUSADERS	15
DECISIONS	4
REDEDICATIONS	5
UNCONVERTED	6

34 The Minister preached to a congregation of eight souls the Sunday after the Crusade, and none of the "convairted" showed up, even though, I am told, he preached in an attempted American accent with a hint of a Southern drawl, and banged his Bible on the pulpit four times.

35 The All-Scotland Crusade had made its assault on our parish, as it had on the rest of the country, and had passed on elsewhere.

36 "I tellt ye ye were a' bluidy daft," commented Mrs. Tam.

Commentary and questions

Section 1

1. *Paragraph 1:* What is the effect of the phrases "closed season for sin" and "religion becomes the principal pastime"? What kind of statement is involved here?

2. *Paragraphs 2-4:* These are a description of the attitudes of church and public before Billy Graham's visit. What is the author's point of view, and how does he make it apparent?

3. *Paragraph 7-Section 3, Paragraph 8:* The author describes very fully a series of individuals as they board the bus. What is the purpose of this technique? Is there any significance in the order in which these individuals appear? Is there any incongruity between the occasion and the characters of these people as Robertson presents them?

Section 3

4. *Paragraphs 12-13:* Do the minister's attempt to share Mrs. Robertson's tea and the fact that her flask contains something else have anything to do with the author's central purpose or is it a useless digression?

Section 4

5. A greasy, mysterious stranger was introduced in the previous section; here he turns out to be a follower of the races. What is the purpose of this bit of surprise?

6. Note that throughout this section Robertson refers to the audience as "sheep," a metaphor traditional in religious terminology (the term "pastor" means "shepherd," and a congregation is often referred to as a "flock"). What is the effect of this metaphor? Does it contribute to the general tone of Robertson's description of the meeting? How? Does the phrase "Collie Dogs" in any way assist Robertson's particular use of the sheep metaphor?

Section 5

7. *Paragraph 1:* Note the phrase "incurious and sensible few who have never left the Plain of Philistia." How does the allusion substantiate what we know of the author's attitude toward Graham and his crusade?

8. Barry Caven is one of the recurrent characters in this piece. Are his comments and observations in this section and elsewhere close to the author's own opinions? If so, why does he state them through the voice of another?

9. *Paragraphs 7-10:* Robertson's analysis of Graham's sermon stresses its conventionality, but its main purpose seems to be an evaluation of Graham and his religious convictions. How is this achieved? How would you describe Graham's beliefs as they are presented here?

10. *Paragraph 13:* Mrs. Robertson's exclamation is clearly intended to shock the reader. How does it prepare for the reappearance of Flossie?

11. *Paragraph 17 and following:* Robertson generalizes by terming the younger females in the audience "Flossies." How does this generalization contribute to the expression of the author's point of view? Is he building on the experience of his readers? How?

12. *Paragraph 22:* Analyze the phrase "therapeutic monotone." How is Robertson using language here?

13. *Paragraph 27:* The wives of the righteous are called "odalisques"? Why does Robertson use this word? What are its connotations in this context?

14. After this piece came out readers objected that it was unfair to Billy Graham. Such an objection assumes Robertson intended to be fair. What, from the evidence of the essay, was his intention?

Topics for discussion and writing

I. The basic organization of this selection is narrative, but behind the narrative are attitudes and concepts. Are they developed in any other order? Describe this development if you think it significant.

II. Evaluate Robertson's use of personal observation of the events he takes up. How convincing is his eye-witness account? Do you think he exaggerates in any place? If so, how, precisely, and how do you know that he is exaggerating?

III. Much of Robertson's technique is "indirect" or "suggestive" as these terms are used in Part I of this anthology (see pp. 5, 7-8, 35-38). Write a theme describing and evaluating Robertson's use of humor, irony, narrative suspense, the incongruous placing of details, character portrayal. Relate these methods to Robertson's main thesis.

IV. Write a theme explaining some of the advantages Robertson gains from using an ironic approach.

THE REAL BILLY GRAHAM David H. C. Read

From The Atlantic Monthly, *Vol.* 200 (*September,* 1957). *Copyright* 1957. *Reprinted by permission of the author.*

"Would you like a ticket for the new show at the Harringay Rink?" said a friend of mine one day in 1954 when I was in London on a visit from Scotland. "It's called *God on Ice.*" That is how I came to receive my first impression of Billy Graham. It was at the beginning of his London campaign, and in Scotland not much more than his name and a vaguely prejudicial aroma of American evangelism had reached us. London church circles were cynical, but I noted a different attitude in one or two people who had been to Harringay. "This isn't the kind of pseudo-religious jamboree we expected," they said. "Go and see."

2   So I went. The meeting was orderly, the stewards quietly efficient, the singing excellent of its kind. The arena was well spiked with Bible-carrying Christians, but the general impression was of a real cross section of the population. The proportion of men was greater than in most English churches.

3   When the tall young man from North Carolina strode forward to the rostrum, I had not the slightest idea what to expect. His first remarks revealed an attractive voice, a pleasant personality, and a sense of humor. Then he announced his theme — "Justification by Faith" — and launched into a forty-five-minute rapid-delivery exposition. I sat entranced — not because of any unusual brilliance of thought or language; on the contrary. I had just written a book, *The Communication of the Gospel*, in which I had suggested that the time had come for a radically new vocabulary and method of preaching for this age, but here was a man using all the battered phrases of evangelism, basing his address on a theological dogma supposed to be meaningless to the average man — and communicating as no one I had ever heard. How was it done? There was a directness and a sympathy that struck through the conventional phrases; there was undoubted charm; the voice was pleasant. But one thing stood out: the man was genuine. He believed what he said. He was concerned about God and the people in front of him, and not chiefly with Billy Graham.

4   Then came the part I expected to find embarrassing. He made the appeal to come forward. I have seen this done in the manner of a spiritual auctioneer with waving hands and throbbing voice, bidding for souls on the crest of an emotional upheaval. Here there was so little tension and excitement at the end of the address that I found it hard to believe that anyone would move from his seat. Then, in hundreds, they began to move — silently, reverently, seriously. No one fainted. No one shouted. No one, as far as I could see, was weeping. It made me think of an Episcopal congregation going forward to receive the bread and wine. They stood there for a moment or two and then passed out to the back of the hall. The meeting was over.

5   A year later I was in the Kelvin Hall, Glasgow. My impressions were exactly the same. The Scottish crowd was as quiet as a meeting of the General Assembly on a dull morning. There had been some teen-age adulation when Billy arrived in Glasgow, but within the hall you could have heard an amen drop. But there wasn't one — not even an audible ejaculation from a skeptic's wife. And there wasn't a "Greetin' Gertie" within sight. Recent visits to Madison Square Garden give me the same picture. The majority of those going forward seem to be sober citizens, with a remarkable percentage in the upper-middle years.

6   It is possible to go to a Graham meeting and come away with a different impression. Some people are unmoved; some are repelled by the traditional piety of platform and choir; some are concerned at an oversimplification of

the Christian challenge. But the majority of my friends, believers and un-believers, have had an impression similar to mine.

7   It seems at first sight quite incomprehensible that anyone should have seen at the Kelvin Hall anything resembling what Dr. Robertson described in his brilliant fantasy "When Billy Graham Saved Scotland." Then one realizes just how the raw material of a Crusade meeting has been doctored for the delectation of those who have never been there. The trick is simple enough and when used with skill produces an extremely funny story — funny, unless one happens to believe that Billy Graham is not a religious racketeer but the vehicle and symbol of a significant religious movement in our age. It could be done with any church service, political meeting, or rally of the Rationalists' Association. Call the ushers "Collie Dogs" and their courtesy "ferociously cordial," make their every motion sinister, set free a rich Freudian imagination as you survey the audience, call the singer a "crooner," the conductor a "Medicine Ball Man"; when the speaker is lively call it "a masterly bit of soap opera," when he is quiet make him "ostentatiously unobtrusive" — and, of course, never let the reader forget that the audience, as distinguished from the writer and reader, are a flock of silly sheep.

8   The trouble with this method applied to a major religious phenomenon of our times is that it diverts attention from really serious criticism. A satirical flight that bears little relation either to Billy Graham or to the Church of Scotland will amuse those who have as meager a knowledge of either as Dr. Robertson and as violent an aversion to any form of "popular religion." It will infuriate all, from eggheads to dimwits, who have found in the Crusades a genuine religious experience. What is needed is sober and fair criticism. For there is a real danger already apparent (not in Billy Graham, but in some of his followers) in the fanaticism which says, "If you're not 100 per cent for Billy Graham you're an atheist — and probably subversive too." This is as unfortunate as the opposite tendency to dismiss the Crusades with an empty laugh. On a subject of world-wide implications the public ought not to be asked to choose between a Robertsonian ridicule and a fanatical Graham-cult. This is why the story needs to be told of the hesitations of the Churches and why leaders in the Church of England, the Church of Scotland, and the major denominations of the U.S.A. have mostly come to a position of support for the Crusades.

9   According to Dr. Robertson the Kirk in Scotland, on its beam ends, threw theological principle to the winds and cried for help across the Atlantic. It is impossible to take seriously at any point the caricature of the Kirk he presents. I have been a parish minister in the Scottish Borders and can assure American readers that neither ministers' sermons, elders' wives, nor the attitudes toward the theater and the pub bear the slightest resemblance to this hallucination. Those who have enjoyed reading about the impact made by a mythical American evangelist on a Kirk that exists only in

the more lurid pages of some dated Scottish novelists may be interested to know of the reaction of the real Church of Scotland to the real Billy Graham.

2

1   Since World War II the Church of Scotland has shown a small but steady increase in membership and church attendance, and a marked revival of missionary zeal. The latter has found domestic expression in a movement known as "Tell Scotland." This is an effort, in coöperation with other denominations, to encourage local congregations to "do the work of an evangelist" — that is, to attempt by visitation, cell groups, parish missions, and other experiments, to alert the whole population to the relevance of the Christian Faith. I was serving on the steering panel of this movement when the suggestion was made of a Graham campaign in Scotland. Our immediate reaction was that a big evangelistic effort centered on one place and featuring an imported speaker would counteract the emphasis we had been seeking to lay on local responsibility and initiative. We also had considerable hesitation about the methods that might be used.

2   By this time the Harringay Crusade in London was under way. Observers reported back to Scotland. Many had an opportunity to meet Graham and his team. Finally the decision was made to move, in the General Assembly, that the invitation to the Glasgow Crusade be extended by the "Tell Scotland" movement and given the blessing of the Kirk. In the ensuing debate Dr. George MacLeod (the present Moderator) made an incisive plea against the proposal, but after full debate the motion was carried by a large majority. So, in a mood of sober reflection, Billy Graham was invited to Scotland.

3   What led some of us to change our minds about the wisdom of issuing the invitation? There were two main factors.

4   The first was the growing conviction that perhaps, after all, "mass-evangelism" was not a dirty word. We were trying new ways. Was it not possible that an old way, even with some modern techniques that would shock the conservative Scot, would break through to some whom we were obviously failing to reach? It had happened before. There is, after all, some mass-evangelism in the New Testament. And there were Saint Francis, Savonarola, Thomas Chalmers, John Wesley, and a dozen others.

5   The idea of raising an ecclesiastical tariff barrier on an American evangelist on the grounds that to receive him was a confession of pastoral bankruptcy never entered a ministerial head. A great Scottish churchman and scholar of a previous generation — Henry Drummond — had been one of the first to welcome Dwight L. Moody, and had given enthusiastic support to a type of evangelism that was entirely foreign to his nature. And the results of the Moody Crusade were still with us. The theological stretch from Drummond to Moody was no greater than between us and Graham, and in

each case we were at one on the central affirmations to which the Church is committed in its creeds.

6   The decisive point was our estimation of Graham himself and the way he had conducted his Crusades. Long before he came to Scotland the British public had been making up its mind about this young evangelist. The cards were stacked against him when he came. One touch of "I've come to save Britain," one word of criticism of cherished institutions, secular or ecclesiastic, one gesture of insincerity and religious racketeering, and he would have gone to that limbo of hollow laughter the British reserve for such intruders. It took only a few weeks for Billy to disabuse the critics and win for himself a place in the affection of the public that has been given to few foreign guests and to no other visiting evangelist in living memory.

7   My brother-in-law, who is on the London stage ("a disgraceful way of life" in the eyes of Dr. Robertson's Kirk), has told me that a little satirical piece prepared for Billy's arrival went down well in an intimate revue for the first few days. Then the audience stopped laughing, the performers felt embarrassed, and eventually the number was eliminated. The London public had sensed that what was going on at Harringay was too real for mockery, too genuine for slick wisecracks.

8   Months later I was passing by High Street in Edinburgh where a large crowd was watching the various notables of Kirk and State emerging from St. Giles to proceed to the opening of the General Assembly. In the middle of the robed and bemedaled representatives of the Church, the Government, the Law, and the Armed Forces was a tall figure looking somewhat nervous in a black frock coat. The word flashed around the crowd, "Billy Graham!" and a buxom woman — one of the incarnations of Scottish caution and common sense locally described as a "Canongate wifie" — turned to me and said, "Yon's the man for me." I had no inclination to reply, "Away! Ye're a' bluidy daft."

9   I watched Billy in action in Scotland. I saw how he listened to local advice, was sensitive to the traditions of the Kirk, talked freely and naturally to all ranks of our grimly democratic society, and never for one minute suggested that what he was doing was more important than the year-round labor of the remotest parish kirk. The ministers who met him were charmed by his modesty and invigorated by his enthusiasm. His address by special invitation one morning to the General Assembly was a triumph of tact. He spoke for precisely one minute. The highest court of the Church of Scotland, never an easy or patient body to address, expressed the same gratitude and commendation as the Archbishop of Canterbury had already done on behalf of the Southern Establishment.

10   Dr. Johnson found "the merriment of persons highly offensive." Dr. Robertson seems to find equally offensive the human touch by which Billy Graham communicates with the ordinary man. But the spontaneous friendliness of the man overflowed into many homes in Scotland where it was not

resented. The televised meeting had a profound effect on the entire nation
from palace to cottage on Good Friday, 1955.

11   It was this growing respect for a dedicated man with an astonishing gift
for making people listen that led me, as Chaplain to Edinburgh University
at that time, to invite him to address a lunch-hour meeting of students and
faculty. If Graham had made an impression of bogus, big-business religion;
if he had displayed a fundamentalism of the "if you don't pronounce *shib-
boleth* like me you're damned" type, no popular notoriety would have persuaded me to present him to the students.

12   He came right in the middle of the tumultuous period that precedes a
Scottish Rectorial Address and spoke in a hall where some distinguished men
have received a more than rowdy welcome on these occasions. The Principal
took the chair. The hall was packed. No one knew what might happen, but
the evangelist was received with polite respect and was applauded when he
rose to speak. The address lasted the exact eighteen minutes we had asked
for, and when he sat down there was a profound and remarkable silence.
There was no appeal, no dramatics, no sob stuff. But I count the meeting as
one of the most effective I have known. Still puzzled by the response to a
message that has little novelty or intellectual weight, I asked one science
student who, as a result of the meeting, joined my confirmation class what
in fact Billy Graham had done. "He jolted me out of my indifference," he
said. For that, on a wide scale, if for nothing else, Scotland was grateful.

13   The Church of Scotland respected Billy Graham for reasons very different from the suggestions of Dr. Robertson. The theory that every Scot expects a sermon to have six parts of which the last is devoted to the horror
of hell belongs to a world of entirely bogus imagination, as does the picture
of a Graham who follows this pattern. I have listened to sermons in Scotland
for forty years without hearing one single description of hell anywhere at
any time. Our respect for Graham was based on his complete loyalty in coöperation with the Churches. This is a man who could have had a fatally
divisive effect, creating a Graham-sect and damning the established
Churches. He *could* have — but this is not the real Billy Graham.

14   The results? Those who responded to the appeals (Graham does not
call them "converts"; still less does he profess to "remit their sins") were
related wherever possible to the local parishes. As might be expected,
ministers found that many were already loyal members, a few were victims
of a passing emotion, others (not vast numbers) had genuinely come to a
living faith for the first time. Percentages of lapse were not strikingly different from what all ministers experience in confirmation classes. But the "Tell
Scotland" movement found that its original decision justified the Crusade
and had not thrown it out of its stride, but had given it new momentum.

15   Like many others, I have now sufficient evidence from London, Glasgow,
and New York to show that men and women of remarkably divergent background and education have found in Billy Graham's Crusades a genuine

Christian experience, and thousands have sensed in them a real Presence
they could acknowledge but not understand.

16 We might end with some *real* statistics.

17 According to an impartial survey conducted in Glasgow, the average
adult attendance in Protestant churches on the same three consecutive Sun-
days in successive years was:

> in 1954 (before the Crusade) 56,503
> in 1955 (during the Crusade) 67,078
> in 1956 (a year after)   62,224

In other words, church attendance jumped by over 10,000 during the Crusade, slumped somewhat thereafter, but was still 5721 ahead of 1954. Not
so "bluidy daft" after all.

Commentary and questions

Section 1

1. Read is undertaking one of the most difficult kinds of argument —
refutation of ironic statement, of statement by description, of apparently
tolerant sympathy, and of words loaded with connotative meanings. He
has the additional burden of being serious about a humorous article. His
strategy is to attack selected targets. If he can convince his reader that
Robertson is ignorant of certain obvious facts about Scottish religion, unfair in his presentation of certain scenes, and inaccurate in his estimate
of Graham's effect, he can relegate Robertson's article to the realm of
"fantasy." What alternative strategies might he have followed?

2. *Paragraph 2:* Read describes the "stewards" as "quietly efficient."
Compare this to Robertson's phrase "Collie Dogs." Each phrase depends
upon connotation for its impact. Analyze these connotations.

Read remarks that Graham's audience was a "real cross section of
the population." Does this differ from Robertson's account of the same
audience? How?

3. *Paragraph 3:* What kind of statement is "The man was genuine" (see
Part II, pp. 161-163)?

How do Robertson's remarks influence Read's statements in this
paragraph? How many of them does Read challenge? Does he take issue
with the most damaging of Robertson's criticisms?

4. *Paragraph 5:* "Not even an audible ejaculation from a skeptic's wife."
What is Read trying to suggest by this sentence about the value of
Robertson's testimony?

"The majority of those going forward seemed to be sober citizens,
with a remarkable percentage in the upper-middle years." What element
in Robertson's account prompts this statement? Why does Read use the
cautious word "seemed"? How precise is his numerical description of
the crowd?

5. *Paragraph 7:* Read calls Robertson's article "brilliant fantasy." In what way does he use the word "brilliant"? How just and accurate is his account of Robertson's stylistic techniques?

6. *Paragraphs 8-9:* Read suggests that Robertson is inaccurate. What evidence does he give for this judgment? Is his desire for a moderate appraisal of Billy Graham consistent with his own attitude toward the evangelist and his work?

Section 2

7. Is the "evidence" any more objective or authoritative than Robertson's? How does the author's attempt to create an image of his own personality work as part of the argument here?

8. *Paragraph 1:* Read gives an account of the recent history of the Church of Scotland. This is apparently one of the few objectively factual sections in the two articles. How damaging is it to Robertson's case if Read can show him to be ignorant of facts of Scottish culture?

9. *Paragraph 10:* The assertion "The televised meeting had a profound effect" is unsupported. Does this injure its value as convincing statement?

10. Read concludes his article with statistics, noting that Church attendance "slumped somewhat" the year following Billy Graham's crusade. Is this phrase consistent with the percentage of decline in attendance indicated by the figures?

Topics for discussion and writing

I. Write a comparative analysis of Robertson's and Read's positions on Billy Graham assessing the relative values of their arguments and points of view. What biases or prejudices or basic assumptions can you discover in each that might influence their conclusions?

II. What is the relative weight of Read's use of factual evidence, unsupported opinion, personal reporting and anecdote, generalization, irony?

III. Without regard to your own opinion of Billy Graham, which of the authors is most effective in his technique of argument? What are the weaknesses in technique of the author you prefer?

DIFFERING POINTS OF VIEW ON BILLY GRAHAM

Reinhold Niebuhr and John Sutherland Bonnell

Reprinted from Life. *Copyright, 1957, Time, Inc. Reprinted by permission of the authors.*

REINHOLD NIEBUHR

1   The growing success of the evangelist, Billy Graham, and the crowds he draws to Madison Square Garden may be explained in terms of his un-

doubted gifts. This handsome, youthful, modest and obviously sincere evangelist is better than any evangelist of his kind in American history.

2 But there are Christians who, while respecting Graham's personal honesty, have their reservations about mass evangelism. Its success depends upon oversimplifying every issue of life. This in turn means appeal to the Scripture in terms which negate all the achievements of Christion historical scholarship. Graham admits that success eluded him until he could say merely, "The Bible says . . ." Such a formula of salvation must also be simple and not include any of life's many ambiguities.

3 Thus Graham declares: "Every human problem can be solved and every hunger satisfied and every potential can be fulfilled when a man encounters Jesus Christ and comes in vital relation to God in him."

4 Perhaps because these solutions are rather too simple in any age, but particularly so in a nuclear one with its great moral perplexities, such a message is not very convincing to anyone — Christian or not — who is aware of the continual possibilities of good and evil in every advance of civilization, every discipline of culture, and every religious convention. Graham offers Christian evangelism even less complicated answers than it has ever before provided.

5 Graham exemplifies a typically frontier American evangelism which has long flourished here. It sprang from the Protestant sects which at the time of the Reformation insisted that a man's "old self" must be shattered in an encounter with Christ as a personal experience. These sects admitted to membership only those who had made an explicit "decision for Christ." They criticized the liturgy, leadership and theology of more formal church bodies, both Protestant and Roman Catholic. Indeed, they criticized all cultural disciplines — including theology — which did not make the Gospel seem simple, straightforward and almost entirely dependent on the individual Christian's evangelistic zeal.

6 In America these sects became the most powerful churches, chiefly by conquering the frontier, where their uncomplex message was particularly relevant to frontier conditions. Such evangelism, with its continual emphasis on the individual saving his own soul, neglected to explore the social dimensions of the Gospel. Graham typifies the great majority of American evangelists; though he has sound personal views on racial segregation and other social issues of our time, he almost ignores all of them in his actual preaching. As a result, although Graham claims that his present crusade is aimed at New York City, relatively few New Yorkers attend the Garden meetings. The bulk of his nightly audience comes from out of town.

7 At the turn of the century, Dwight Moody conducted revivals both here and in England and proved for the first time that American evangelism could be an export article. Since Moody's time, the chasm between Christian pietism and modern scientific culture has greatly widened. A generation ago Billy Sunday, the ex-ballplayer, combined an evangelical message with

fierce opposition to the saloon in a fashion which made the prohibition movement appear the chief moral outlet for man's religious impulse. Compared
to Sunday, Graham's campaign seems a pure gain, even among those who
find Graham's approach to life's problems far too simple and narrow. To his
credit, Graham is also free of every vulgarity and of the commercialism
which marred Sunday's plea for "offerings."

8   Graham is honest and describes the signers of his decision cards as
"inquirers" rather than "converts." It would be interesting to know how
many of those attracted by his evangelistic Christianity are attracted by the
obvious fact that this new evangelism is much blander than the old. For it
promises a new life, not through painful religious experience but merely by
signing a decision card. Thus, a miracle of regeneration is promised at a
painless price by an obviously sincere evangelist. It is a bargain.

JOHN SUTHERLAND BONNELL

1   On the strength of many intimate talks with Billy Graham, I can say
that among religious leaders I have never met a more dedicated and truly
humble man — and he has succeeded in maintaining this humility despite
all the publicity and adulation he receives.

2   "My unceasing prayer," he has said to me, "is that God will keep me
humble. If the day ever comes when I shall be more interested in promoting
Billy Graham than in proclaiming Christ, that day will mark the end of any
power of effectiveness I possess. God will abandon me, for He has said, 'My
glory will I not give to another.' "

3   Two years ago, during his all-Scotland crusade, I asked him "Billy, when
will you begin a crusade in New York?"

4   He said, "I am not yet ready for that. I want more time for study and
prayer before tackling that project."

5   For several weeks now the long-awaited crusade has been under way
in New York. Judging by the number of "decisions for Christ" recorded up
to the present we can assume that by the close of the crusade on July 21,
there will be about 35,000 such decisions.

6   How shall we evaluate these developments? What may we expect to
achieve in New York as a result of this tremendous effort? It is too early yet
to make a final appraisal of this particular crusade, but certain trends are already discernible.

7   *One.* The greatest impact will be felt in the churches of New York. It
may well be that most of the people going forward will be active members
of New York churches rather than the unchurched. Now this is not something to be deplored. The spiritual life of many a New York church will be
strengthened by the presence of these dedicated members. For years to come
these churches will be vitalized by the influence of the crusade, as the

churches of Britain for decades felt the impact of the revival they made under Dwight. L. Moody's leadership.

8   *Two.* The most readily discernible contribution is the creation of a spiritual climate favorable to religious decision. Several ministers have told me that prospective members within their own congregations on whom they have spent much time and effort without result came to an immediate and affirmative decision after attending one or more of the Graham meetings. They are now active church members. Some New Yorkers previously reticent on spiritual matters are now freely discussing religion. This will simplify the task of the large force of lay men and women who will participate in a citywide program of visitation evangelism to be launched in October.

9   *Three.* Many persons who have attended the meetings at Madison Square Garden have been deeply impressed and not a few of them have, in their own hearts, rededicated themselves to Christ without going forward to the platform. I have talked with scores of such persons whose religious training and outlook kept them from this public demonstration of their inner resolve. There is good reason to believe that for every one who goes to the counseling room there are two others in the vast arena who have made a new covenant with Christ. If this be true it widens very considerably the area of positive results.

10   *Four.* Christian laymen and ministers are concerned that the crusade, up to this point, has not reached more of the unchurched. The emphasis of Billy and his team has been too uniformly on an individualistic gospel with no sufficient recognition of un-Christian social conditions and practices in our city and nation. Little public attention has been given to Negro, Puerto Rican and other socioreligious challenges which deeply concern so many. New Yorkers both within and without the churches are especially sensitive to these issues and respond more readily to an inclusive gospel.

11   Whatever limitations may be found in the Billy Graham crusade in New York are nevertheless far outweighed by the results he has achieved in the area. As a pastor for 22 years of a historic church in the center of Manhattan I am profoundly grateful to God for Billy Graham and his crusade.

Commentary and questions

Reinhold Niebuhr

1. *Paragraph 1:* Niebuhr seems to praise Billy Graham, but Niebuhr's article is critical as a whole. Why then does he make this concession? Examine and comment on the italicized words: "better than any *evangelist of his kind* in American history."

2. *Paragraph 2:* Niebuhr has "reservations about mass evangelism," and accuses Billy Graham of "oversimplifying every issue of life." For the purposes of this article which seems to be the more important point? Which does Niebuhr develop most persistently? What is the force and tone of "reservations"?

3. *Paragraph 3:* Niebuhr quotes Graham to support the charge of over-simplification. Does the quotation accomplish that purpose?

4. *Paragraph 4:* In pursuing the charge of oversimplification Niebuhr implies that ours is a complex age. Is this adequate to convince us? What do you think he means?

Does Niebuhr use the term "evangelism" in the same context as in previous paragraphs? Has the term acquired any added meaning or connotation here?

5. *Paragraph 5:* In referring to a "typically frontier American evangelism" Niebuhr seems to be evaluating Graham against a historical background. What is the effect of this technique? How much information does Niebuhr assume that his readers have? Does the historical approach have anything to do with his "reservations about mass evangelism" in paragraph 2?

6. *Paragraph 7:* Graham is compared favorably to Billy Sunday. Does this concession weaken Niebuhr's argument?

7. *Paragraph 8:* What is meant by the phrase "this new evangelism is much blander than the old"? What does the statement "It is a bargain" suggest about Graham's supporters?

John Sutherland Bonnell

8. Like Robertson and Read, Bonnell opens with personal anecdote. What is his purpose?

9. Like Niebuhr, Bonnell quotes Graham. How does his use in paragraph 2 of Graham's own words differ? Is it effective?

10. *Paragraph 5:* Bonnell uses figures in referring to Graham's New York crusade. How effective are these as factual, statistical evidence?

11. *Paragraphs 7-10:* The section lists four points in evaluating Graham's New York crusade, three of them favorable. How precise is each point? To what extent is each supported by argument or evidence? To what extent does each contribute to Bonnell's main thesis?

Topics for discussion and writing

Reinhold Niebuhr

I. State the premises for Niebuhr's criticism of Graham and outline the structure of his argument.

II. Give a brief account of Niebuhr's use of the word "evangelism." Does he make his meanings plain? What concept of religion can you infer that Niebuhr himself holds?

III. How does Niebuhr's technique of argument differ from the other three writers in this group of selections?

John Sutherland Bonnell

IV. What does Bonnell mean by the phrase "spiritual life?" How precisely is this term defined?

V. What is meant by the phrase "area of positive results" in paragraph 9? The phrase seems to be used with the assumption that readers will react automatically to it. Examine Bonnell's article for other phrases or words used in this way. How heavily does Bonnell rely upon the connotative effects of his statements?

VI. Read, Niebuhr, and Bonnell all agree that Graham is sincere and honest. Write a theme summarizing their specific points of disagreement. Do they disagree about the same issues or does each select a different aspect of Graham and his work to deal with?

VII. Any discussion of religion is bound to involve the emotions of readers and writers. To what extent do the four authors in this group of writings deliberately play upon and cultivate the reader's emotions? To what extent do they attempt to allay them? Is there any appeal to prejudice? Write a theme analyzing these issues.

VIII. Write a theme describing the techniques of an evangelist. Compare them and the audience's reaction to nonevangelistic techniques. What basic approaches to religion do you find in each?

Evolution: THE SNOUT, Loren Eiseley · THE PATH OF BIOLOGICAL PROGRESS, Julian S. Huxley · THE STRUGGLE FOR EXISTENCE, Charles Darwin

A TOPIC so broad and intricate as evolution can never be fairly represented in a few short selections. What is important for the purposes of this book is the chance to observe and analyze the ways in which three scientists treat aspects of evolution. The selections from Darwin, Eiseley, and Julian Huxley (the grandson of Thomas Huxley, the great nineteenth-century apologist for Darwin's theories) give expression to important generalized principles of biological change. Their writings do not coincide on all specific points, nor do they argue with one another. And there are other differences between them. Darwin is separated from Eiseley and Huxley by nearly one hundred years; in the interval a number of discoveries have been made — notably those concerning the laws of mutation. Furthermore, Darwin has for all practical purposes nothing to say about man, while Eiseley and Huxley are intimately concerned with man's place in the evolutionary process.

But these discrepancies should not be permitted to cloud the fundamental unity of focus in all three writers: They are commonly interested in describing and explaining the objective forces at work in existence. They are all concerned with adjusting general principles or laws to specific facts. All three resort to familiar expository strategies to make their topics coherent and even interesting — Eiseley and Huxley are especially aware of an audience of educated readers without technical knowledge but sufficiently curious and intelligent to respond to an adult type of explanation.

Perhaps of greatest value to the student is to observe the means each writer uses to compress general concepts into a restricted space. Here we must note what the writers assume their audience knows, what they most emphasize and repeat, and what they subordinate. The selection from *Origin of Species* is probably the most general because Darwin takes an entire book to detail what he states in broad terms here. Nevertheless, the excerpt does contain illustrative examples. Eiseley can assume our knowledge that struggle exists and concentrate on one important phase of that struggle in one period of geologic time. Huxley, on the other hand, brings us back to a wider perspective in time, examining biological change as progress.

Finally, all three writers in one fashion or another are concerned with definition, the definition of their terms and through them the definition of the scientific principles they wish to make clear. But here again we find different definitive procedures. Darwin wishes to distinguish "Natural Selection" from types of change produced by human planning, and he even has the unscientific courage to exalt nature over man. Eiseley is the most indirect of the three: We must discover his particular meanings by implication and through the context. Open and exact definition is not part of his scheme. Huxley is the most persistent in making his key terms clear. Not content with the notion that nature operates by the improvement of species of animal life, he tries to isolate progress as a special and important kind of improvement. The reader should pay careful attention to his reasons.

The previous paragraph should suggest that the brief and summary expression of a general scientific principle does not consist solely in persuasive or clear broad statement. It is also a process of making distinctions, and such distinctions are made for specific purposes. These purposes may involve the special point of view the writer wishes to put across, the attitude toward the subject he wishes his audience to adopt, or they may be the first step toward a detailed explanation of the topic, breaking it down into more and more particular segments. The development of a valid generality — whether the principle of organization is narrative, inductive, deductive, comparative, contrastive, or a combination of any number of them — must involve some degree and kind of detail.

(*Note:* The reader should make frequent use of the dictionary for this group of readings.)

THE SNOUT   Loren Eiseley

I HAVE long been an admirer of the octopus. The cephalopods are very old, and they have slipped, protean, through many shapes. They are the wisest of the mollusks, and I have always felt it to be just as well for us that they never came ashore, but — there are other things that have.

2   There is no need to be frightened. It is true some of the creatures are odd, but I find the situation rather heartening than otherwise. It gives one a feeling of confidence to see nature still busy with experiments, still dynamic, and not through nor satisfied because a Devonian fish managed to end as a two-legged character with a straw hat. There are other things brewing and growing in the oceanic vat. It pays to know this. It pays to know there is just as much future as there is past. The only thing that doesn't pay is to be sure of man's own part in it.

3   There are things down there still coming ashore. Never make the mistake of thinking life is now adjusted for eternity. It gets into your head — the certainty, I mean — the human certainty, and then you miss it all: the things on the tide flats and what they mean, and why, as my wife says, "they ought to be watched."

4   The trouble is we don't know what to watch for. I have a friend, one of these Explorers Club people, who drops in now and then between trips to tell me about the size of crocodile jaws in Uganda, or what happened on some back beach in Arnhem Land.

5   "They fell out of the trees," he said. "Like rain. And into the boat."

6   "Uh?" I said, noncommittally.

7   "They did *so*," he protested, "and they were hard to catch."

8   "Really —" I said.

9   "We were pushing a dugout up one of the tidal creeks in northern Australia and going fast when *smacko* we jam this mangrove bush and the things come tumbling down.

10   "What were they doing sitting up there in bunches? I ask you. It's no place for a fish. Besides that they had a way of sidling off with those pop-eyes trained on you. I never liked it. Somebody ought to keep an eye on them."

11   "Why?" I asked.

12   "I don't know why," he said impatiently, running a rough, square hand through his hair and wrinkling his forehead. "I just mean they make you feel that way, is all. A fish belongs in the water. It ought to stay there — just as we live on land in houses. Things ought to know their place and stay in it, but those fish have got a way of sidling off. As though they had mental reservations and weren't keeping any contracts. See what I mean?"

13   "I see what you mean," I said gravely. "They ought to be watched. My wife thinks so too. About a lot of things."

14   "She does?" He brightened. "Then that's two of us. I don't know why, but they give you that feeling."

15   He didn't know why, but I thought that I did.

II

16   It began as such things always begin — in the ooze of unnoticed swamps, in the darkness of eclipsed moons. It began with a strangled gasping for air.

17 The pond was a place of reek and corruption, of fetid smells and of oxygen-starved fish breathing through laboring gills. At times the slowly contracting circle of the water left little windrows of minnows who skittered desperately to escape the sun, but who died, nevertheless, in the fat, warm mud. It was a place of low life. In it the human brain began.

18 There were strange snouts in those waters, strange barbels nuzzling the bottom ooze, and there was time — three hundred million years of it — but mostly, I think, it was the ooze. By day the temperature in the world outside the pond rose to a frightful intensity; at night the sun went down in smoking red. Dust storms marched in incessant progression across a wilderness whose plants were the plants of long ago. Leafless and weird and stiff they lingered by the water, while over vast areas of grassless uplands the winds blew until red stones took on the polish of reflecting mirrors. There was nothing to hold the land in place. Winds howled, dust clouds rolled, and brief erratic torrents choked with silt ran down to the sea. It was a time of dizzying contrasts, a time of change.

19 On the oily surface of the pond, from time to time a snout thrust upward, took in air with a queer grunting inspiration, and swirled back to the bottom. The pond was doomed, the water was foul, and the oxygen almost gone, but the creature would not die. It could breathe air direct through a little accessory lung, and it could walk. In all that weird and lifeless landscape, it was the only thing that could. It walked rarely and under protest, but that was not surprising. The creature was a fish.

20 In the passage of days the pond became a puddle, but the snout survived. There was dew one dark night and a coolness in the empty stream bed. When the sun rose next morning the pond was an empty place of cracked mud, but the Snout did not lie there. He had gone. Down stream there were other ponds. He breathed air for a few hours and hobbled slowly along on the stumps of heavy fins.

21 It was an uncanny business if there had been anyone there to see. It was a journey best not observed in daylight, it was something that needed swamps and shadows and the touch of the night dew. It was a monstrous penetration of a forbidden element, and the Snout kept his face from the light. It was just as well, though the face should not be mocked. In three hundred million years it would be our own.

22 There was something fermenting in the brain of the Snout. He was no longer entirely a fish. The ooze had marked him. It takes a swamp-and-tide-flat zoologist to tell you about life; it is in this domain that the living suffer great extremes, it is here that the water-failures, driven to desperation, make starts in a new element. It is here that strange compromises are made and new senses are born. The Snout was no exception. Though he breathed and walked primarily in order to stay in the water, he was coming ashore.

23 He was not really a successful fish except that he was managing to stay alive in a noisome, uncomfortable, oxygen-starved environment. In fact the time was coming when the last of his kind, harried by more ferocious and

speedier fishes, would slip off the edge of the continental shelf, to seek safety in the sunless abysses of the deep sea. But the Snout was a fresh-water Crossopterygian, to give him his true name, and cumbersome and plodding though he was, something had happened back of his eyes. The ooze had gotten in its work.

III

24   It is interesting to consider what sort of creatures we, the remote descendants of the Snout, might be, except for that green quagmire out of which he came. Mammalian insects perhaps we should have been — solid-brained, our neurones wired for mechanical responses, our lives running out with the perfection of beautiful, intricate, and mindless clocks. More likely we should never have existed at all. It was the Snout and the ooze that did it. Perhaps there also, among rotting fish heads and blue, night-burning bog lights, moved the eternal mystery, the careful finger of God. The increase was not much. It was two bubbles, two thin-walled little balloons at the end of the Snout's small brain. The cerebral hemispheres had appeared.

25   Among all the experiments in that dripping, ooze-filled world, one was vital: the brain had to be fed. The nerve tissues are insatiable devourers of oxygen. If they do not get it, life is gone. In stagnant swamp waters, only the development of a highly efficient blood supply to the brain can prevent disaster. And among those gasping, dying creatures, whose small brains winked out forever in the long Silurian drought, the Snout and his brethren survived.

26   Over the exterior surface of the Snout's tiny brain ran the myriad blood vessels that served it; through the greatly enlarged choroid plexuses, other vessels pumped oxygen into the spinal fluid. The brain was a thin-walled tube fed from both surfaces. It could only exist as a thing of thin walls permeated with oxygen. To thicken, to lay down solid masses of nervous tissue such as exist among the fishes in oxygenated waters was to invite disaster. The Snout lived on a bubble, two bubbles in his brain.

27   It was not that his thinking was deep; it was only that it had to be thin. The little bubbles of the hemispheres helped to spread the area upon which higher correlation centers could be built, and yet preserve those areas from the disastrous thickenings which meant oxygen death to the swamp dweller. There is a mystery about those thickenings which culminate in the so-called solid brain. It is the brain of insects, of the modern fishes, of some reptiles and all birds. Always it marks the appearance of elaborate patterns of instinct and the end of thought. A road has been taken which, anatomically, is well-nigh irretraceable; it does not lead in the direction of a high order of consciousness.

28   Wherever, instead, the thin sheets of gray matter expand upward into the enormous hemispheres of the human brain, laughter, or it may be sorrow, enters in. Out of the choked Devonian waters emerged sight and sound

and the music that rolls invisible through the composer's brain. They are there still in the ooze along the tideline, though no one notices. The world is fixed, we say: fish in the sea, birds in the air. But in the mangrove swamps by the Niger, fish climb trees and ogle uneasy naturalists who try unsuccessfully to chase them back to the water. There are things still coming ashore.

IV

29   The door to the past is a strange door. It swings open and things pass through it, but they pass in one direction only. No man can return across that threshold, though he can look down still and see the green light waver in the water weeds.

30   There are two ways to seek the doorway: in the swamps of the inland waterways and along the tide flats of the estuaries where rivers come to the sea. By those two pathways life came ashore. It was not the magnificent march through the breakers and up the cliffs that we fondly imagine. It was a stealthy advance made in suffocation and terror, amidst the leaching bite of chemical discomfort. It was made by the failures of the sea.

31   Some creatures have slipped through the invisible chemical barrier between salt and fresh water into the tidal rivers, and later come ashore; some have crept upward from the salt. In all cases, however, the first adventure into the dreaded atmosphere seems to have been largely determined by the inexorable crowding of enemies and by the retreat further and further into marginal situations where the oxygen supply was depleted. Finally, in the ruthless selection of the swamp margins, or in the scramble for food on the tide flats, the land becomes home.

32   Not the least interesting feature of some of the tide-flat emergents is their definite antipathy for the full tide. It obstructs their food-collecting on the mud banks and brings their enemies. Only extremes of fright will drive them into the water for any period.

33   I think it was the great nineteenth-century paleontologist Cope who first clearly enunciated what he called the "law of the unspecialized," the contention that it was not from the most highly organized and dominant forms of a given geological era that the master type of a succeeding period evolved, but that instead the dominant forms tended to arise from more lowly and generalized animals which were capable of making new adaptations, and which were not narrowly restricted to a given environment.

34   There is considerable truth to this observation, but, for all that, the idea is not simple. Who is to say without foreknowledge of the future which animal is specialized and which is not? We have only to consider our remote ancestor, the Snout, to see the intricacies into which the law of the unspecialized may lead us.

35   If we had been making zoological observations in the Paleozoic Age, with no knowledge of the strange realms life was to penetrate in the future, we would probably have regarded the Snout as specialized. We would have

seen his air-bladder lung, his stubby, sluggish fins, and his odd ability to wriggle overland as specialized adaptations to a peculiarly restricted environmental niche in stagnant continental waters. We would have thought in water terms and we would have dismissed the Snout as an interesting failure off the main line of progressive evolution, escaping from his enemies and surviving successfully only in the dreary and marginal surroundings scorned by the swift-finned teleost fishes who were destined to dominate the seas and all quick waters.

36 Yet it was this poor specialization — this bog-trapped failure — whose descendants, in three great movements, were to dominate the earth. It is only now, looking backward, that we dare to regard him as "generalized." The Snout was the first vertebrate to pop completely through the water membrane into a new dimension. His very specializations and failures, in a water sense, had preadapted him for a world he scarcely knew existed.

v

37 The day of the Snout was over three hundred million years ago. Not long since I read a book in which a prominent scientist spoke cheerfully of some ten billion years of future time remaining to us. He pointed out happily the things that man might do throughout that period. Fish in the sea, I thought again, birds in the air. The climb all far behind us, the species fixed and sure. No wonder my explorer friend had had a momentary qualm when he met the mudskippers with their mental reservations and lack of promises. There is something wrong with our world view. It is still Ptolemaic, though the sun is no longer believed to revolve around the earth.

38 We teach the past, we see farther backward into time than any race before us, but we stop at the present, or, at best, we project far into the future idealized versions of ourselves. All that long way behind us we see, perhaps inevitably, through human eyes alone. We see ourselves as the culmination and the end, and if we do indeed consider our passing, we think that sunlight will go with us and the earth be dark. We are the end. For us continents rose and fell, for us the waters and the air were mastered, for us the great living web has pulsated and grown more intricate.

39 To deny this, a man once told me, is to deny God. This puzzled me. I went back along the pathway to the marsh. I went, not in the past, not by the bones of dead things, not down the lost roadway of the Snout. I went instead in daylight, in the Now, to see if the door was still there, and to see what things passed through.

40 I found that the same experiments were brewing, that up out of that ancient well, fins were still scrambling toward the sunlight. They were small things, and which of them presaged the future I could not say. I saw only that they were many and that they had solved the oxygen death in many marvelous ways, not always ours.

41 I found that there were modern fishes who breathed air, not through

a lung but through their stomachs or through strange chambers where their gills should be, or breathing as the Snout once breathed. I found that some crawled in the fields at nightfall pursuing insects, or slept on the grass by pond sides and who drowned, if kept under water, as men themselves might drown.

⁴² Of all these fishes the mudskipper *Periophthalmus* is perhaps the strangest. He climbs trees with his fins and pursues insects; he snaps worms like a robin on the tide flats; he sees as land things see, and above all he dodges and evades with a curious popeyed insolence more suggestive of the land than of the sea. Of a different tribe and a different time he is, nevertheless, oddly reminiscent of the Snout.

⁴³ But not the same. There lies the hope of life. The old ways are exploited and remain, but new things come, new senses try the unfamiliar air. There are small scuttlings and splashings in the dark, and out of it come the first croaking, illiterate voices of the things to be, just as man once croaked and dreamed darkly in that tiny vesicular forebrain.

⁴⁴ Perpetually, now, we search and bicker and disagree. The eternal form eludes us — the shape we conceive as ours. Perhaps the old road through the marsh should tell us. We are one of many appearances of the thing called Life; we are not its perfect image, for it has no image except Life, and life is multitudinous and emergent in the stream of time.

Commentary and questions

1. *Paragraph 1:* Eiseley's opening is deliberately personal and conversational. His statements seem oddly out of place in scientific writing, and he has a vague and oblique means of introducing his topic. For example, notice the phrase "things" that "came ashore." What is his purpose in using this style?

2. *Paragraph 2:* The manner of the previous paragraph is continued, but is his development of the topic really unorthodox? Notice that the "things" are now identified as Devonian fish and are connected rather humorously to man. The precise connection is not yet made clear, but a certain type of information is conveyed. Describe it.

  Note the use of the metaphor "oceanic vat." Try to explain its connotations. What other words in the paragraph suggest a type of activity?

3. *Paragraph 3:* Eiseley argues against "human certainty." Restate Eiseley's point of view in other words.

4. *Paragraphs 4-15:* These are devoted to conversation and personal anecdote. Why does Eiseley adopt the techniques of the fiction writer? What does he convey that he might not by a more straightforward expository style?

  The phrase "they ought to be watched" is unexplained. How does Eiseley intend it? Does his point of view differ from that of his wife? How?

  Note that the first fifteen paragraphs are introductory, but that they give little specific information about Devonian fish or the process of coming ashore. Quite clearly Eiseley's purpose here is not informative. How can his purpose be described? Compare this introduction to Huxley's attempt to establish a point of view toward biological change (pp. 375-877).

5. *Paragraph 16:* This second section of "The Snout" is openly narrative and evokes the atmosphere of the swamp. Since Eiseley has already made a tentative connection between primitive animal life and man, one might conclude that these paragraphs are a deliberate effort to provoke our disgust about our own remote origins. Is this an accurate reading of Eiseley's purpose? Cite the words and statements that lead you to this opinion.

6. *Paragraph 17:* Beginning here there are a number of clues that Eiseley wishes to do more than tell a story. Indirectly he begins to explain things, though he offers no evidence for the assertion "In it the human brain began." Also, his purpose may go beyond vivid, colorful explanation. He may be arguing for a certain perspective on evolution, or that part of it dealing with human origins. Examine the means he uses and paraphrase his concepts.

7. *Paragraphs 18-20:* Examine the vocabulary, especially the repeated words. What impression do they create? Do they add explanatory information or express Eiseley's point of view in more detail?

8. *Paragraphs 21-22:* Is the emergence of a fish onto land "a monstrous penetration of a forbidden element"? What does the phrase suggest about Eiseley's attitude toward significant evolutionary change? Do the phrases "water failures," "great extremes," and "driven to desperation" convey any specific concept of the evolutionary process?

Note the paradox in the last sentence of paragraph 22. Explain it in your own words.

9. *Paragraph 23:* This completes the author's narrative. Recapitulate his plan of development so far. What main concepts has he established? What connotative values has he tried to convey?

10. *Paragraph 24:* What words and phrases establish a connection with the previous section? How has the nature of the style changed?

11. *Paragraphs 25-28:* Why does Eiseley concentrate on a description of the Snout's brain?

12. *Paragraph 28:* What is the purpose and effect of the phrase "laughter, or it may be sorrow, enters in"?

"There are things still coming ashore." Does this familiar phrase have more meaning behind it now than when it was first used? Explain.

13. *Paragraph 29:* This begins a third stage in the development of Eiseley's thesis. The first two have involved the establishment of a point of view toward evolutionary change and a description of the conditions under which a particular type of significant change took place. Now Eiseley is still careful to keep these two aspects of his subject in view,

but he adds a new element to the discussion: the notion that change cannot be reversed. Does any new stylistic technique appear? Is there any change in tone?

14. *Paragraphs 30-31:* Eiseley repeats material already covered. Does he add anything new? Why does he indulge in summary here?

15. *Paragraphs 34-36:* Eiseley dwells on the unlikeliness of the Snout as an ancestor of man. Has he prepared the reader in any way for this notion?

16. *Paragraph 37:* This begins a fifth section in the essay. Eiseley uses a friend to represent a point of view which he argues against. Paraphrase both attitudes. How has Eiseley established his own position in previous paragraphs? Is there any factual basis for his argument?

17. *Paragraph 38:* Describe Eiseley's contrast between the past and the future. Is he trying to put limitations on human knowledge and human insight? Is he suggesting that the processes of nature are essentially mysterious? Compare his attitude to Darwin's assertion of the superiority of nature over man (pp. 386-387).

18. *Paragraphs 39-44:* Eiseley evokes the present. Relate the concept he expresses here to his description of the Snout emerging from the water.

Topics for discussion and writing

I. Write an essay discussing the relative importance of elements of style in Eiseley's essay: narrative, connotation, the repetition of key phrases, the use of shock or surprise, humor.

II. Write a theme paraphrasing Eiseley's point of view toward the significance of evolutionary change.

III. Does Eiseley's insistence on the desperate struggle of the Snout to escape from the water correspond to Darwin's account of "the struggle for existence"?

IV. How would you describe Eiseley's main purpose? Is it explanatory, informative, persuasive, or is it simply to evoke emotion?

THE PATH OF BIOLOGICAL PROGRESS

Julian S. Huxley

Reprinted from Evolution in Action *by Julian S. Huxley, by permission of Harper & Brothers. Copyright 1953 by Julian S. Huxley. Canadian rights granted by A. D. Peters, 10 Buckingham Street, Adelphi, W.C.2, England.*

IT IS easy to confuse the two ideas of progress and improvement; so, at the risk of repeating myself tediously, I want to remind you of a few salient points. There are all kinds of biological improvement. There are adaptations which benefit certain individuals at the expense of the species; minor adjustments of the species; specializations of a type for a particular way of life; and advances in the general efficiency of biological machinery. But improvements are not something ready-made, they are trends in time. And most of them turn out to be finite; sooner or later, they come to a stop. Occasionally, one line of advance continues after related lines have come to a stop; and then you get what I called successional replacement, where a later deployment replaces an earlier one as a dominant type. The fact of replacement is itself a demonstration that there has been general improvement or advance. Putting the matter in another way, there is continuity of improvement between one group and its successor, as for instance between reptiles and mammals. We need a term for the sum of these continuities through the whole of evolutionary time, and I prefer to take over a familiar word like *progress* instead of coining a special piece of esoteric jargon.

2 In the light of these considerations, the human species, as the latest successional deployment, represents the furthest step yet taken in evolutionary progress. This is not just anthropomorphic wish-fulfillment, but a direct and necessary deduction from biological fact. Man may not be the measure of all things, but the difference between man and the simplest organisms is certainly the measure of biological progress. However, though biological progress has culminated in man, progress had been going on during the hundreds of millions of years before man came into existence. It was there, merely waiting to be detected.

3 It was with these distinctions in mind that in my third chapter I threw out a brief definition of biological progress, as "improvement which permits or facilitates further improvement, or, if you prefer, as a series of advances which do not stand in the way of further advances." Progress could also well be defined as the way which leads to ever-fresh realizations of new possibilities for living substance. But we have to consider its results as well. During the course of biological progress there is a trend toward increased efficiency in dealing with the challenge of the environment, and an increased independence of the changes going on in it. Both of these involve increased complexity of organization and efficiency of working. In particular there is a trend towards more harmonious integration of the individual organism as a whole. Progress, from this aspect, is characterized by an increase of variety-in-unity. Finally, and in a way most important, biological progress is marked by the intensification and improvement of mental capacity and its results, in particular knowledge and the organization of knowledge.*

* Simpson, in *The Meaning of Evolution*, gives a number of definitions and criteria of biological progress. Some of them, as he himself says, seem to be too general: thus the sheer increase in the total amount of living matter cannot be much of a criterion in considering the status of any particular group. On the other hand, to call specialization a form of progress would appear to me to confuse progress, which is rare, with improvement, which is common. He criticizes the idea of defining progress in relation to

4   Another way of putting the matter is to say that progress is constantly leading life into regions of new evolutionary opportunity. Like other kinds of biological improvement, it goes in a series of well-marked steps. Its path follows a general direction, but sometimes makes surprising twists and turns. Each new deployment, after steadily advancing over its new terrain, comes to an impasse. There is sometimes a path out of the impasse, but it is generally a devious one; it is through its twists and turns that life finds its way into a new field of maneuver; and this marks the beginning of another distinct step of progress. It is not too hard to chart the general direction of progress, but it is extremely difficult to prophesy the detailed course it will have to take to get from one step to the next. On the other hand, once we can look back on the facts we realize that it could have happened in no other way. Progress is inevitable as a general fact; but it is unpredictable in its particulars.

5   The nature of the process can only be understood in detail by describing how it actually happens, and studying the way in which it is related to all the rest of the evolutionary process. The best way to visualize these relations is to think of evolution as a tree, but a tree with a rather peculiar manner of growth. It grows on the whole upward, but with a succession of branchings representing the different major deployments of life. Some of these branches run more or less straight upward, some diagonally, and some more or less straight outward; but in each of them the final twigs do not reach above a certain level, and fewer and fewer branches attain the upper levels.

6   Just as there is no such thing as absolute motion — merely motion relative to some other motion — so there is no such thing as progress in the abstract. It can only be defined, or indeed described, in relation to other kinds of evolutionary change, and we must take into account the restrictions and the dead ends of improvement as well as the onward continuity of its advance. Look at the history of living substance from this angle: what is the general direction of overall improvement; how did life reach this or that necessary new step or level of progress; and how on each new level did it come up against limitations or into dead ends? We want to know the prerequisites, the accompaniments, and the consequences of progress.

7   I once tried to list the series of all the major steps in biological progress, but gave it up when I got to the fortieth. Here all I can do is to pick out a few illuminating instances. Before beginning on this I must make one point. The story of life's advance is not made up out of the imagination;

---

the possibility of further progress, on the grounds that this "cannot . . . be used to define progress going on or accomplished in the past." But this objection falls to the ground when we think of progress as a process and not merely as a series of static stages.

In general, it is refreshing to find that, while rightly rejecting any mystic "perfecting principle" inherent in life, this eminent paleontologist agrees that progress has occurred during evolution, though it is not universal; and that it is not unscientific anthropomorphism to regard man as standing high on any scale of evolutionary progress.

even though the evidence is often indirect or circumstantial, it is none the less evidence. The biologist knows that evolution has happened. He looks at the results of it, as many of them as possible, and then reconstructs the picture of its course which will best fit the facts. When the facts are available in the shape of actual fossils, his picture will be more detailed and more accurate. But the facts of comparative anatomy and embryology and biochemistry and genetics are equally relevant, and any picture which fits them will not be a false picture; it will give a reasonable approximation to the truth.

8   One of the earliest necessary steps in progress was the reduction of the rate at which mutation occurs. I remember the surprise with which I first realized this fact. We know that mutation rate can be controlled genetically: genes have been discovered which alter the rates of mutation of other genes, though we do not yet know just how this is effected. We also know that any molecule so immensely large and complicated as a gene would be expected to undergo changes in its chemical structure — in other words to mutate — at a rate too high for reasonable genetic stability, and certainly much higher than all normal mutation rates actually found. Selection must have mutations to build with; but if the mutation rate is too high, the building will keep falling apart. The necessary reduction of mutation rate to a manageable level seems to have been one of the very first steps in progress. With the possible exception of some of the viruses (perhaps not fully fledged organisms at all), this step was taken by all forms of life.

9   The first forms of life can have been little more than naked genes; an early step in progress was from this simplicity to the cellular level of organization. A cell, for our purpose, is a microscopic but highly complicated unit of living substance, enclosing a nucleus with an accurately self-producing genetic outfit in it — in other words, chromosomes with an array of different genes along their length, and a mechanism for distributing them accurately each time the cell divides. This seems to have been combined, probably from the outset, with another vital step, the development of sex — in other words, a mechanism for recombining mutant genes from different lines. It used to be supposed, until very recently, that the whole enormous group of bacteria were so primitive that they possessed neither chromosomes nor sex. One of the most spectacular discoveries of the past few years is the fact that, in their chromosomes and their mechanisms of sexual recombination, they possess essentially the same genetic equipment as you or I or any other organism.

10   Next, I want to say a word about the step to the many-celled condition in animals. This was indispensable for the attainment of more than microscopic size and more than an elementary degree of division of labor among the tissues and organs of the body. But it was not universally taken. The protozoa are organized on the basis of a single cell unit; but they are among the most successful of animals, swarming in the sea, in the soil, in fresh

water, in the interiors of other animals. This fact well illustrates the difference between success and advance. There is room in the world for microscopic animals as well as large ones. The protozoa fill a large part of the microscopic niche very successfully, and in a way that would be impossible for animals of larger bulk. Theoretically, the step to the many-celled condition could have been taken in two rather different ways — either by way of a colony of separate cells, or by the cutting up of a single highly differentiated cell with several nuclei in it, into a number of cellular units. It looks as if the first was the method adopted by the sponges. In any case, the sponges have remained throughout their evolution as rather loosely knit aggregates of cells; and they have never evolved such elementary prerequisites of further progress as a mouth or a nervous system. They represent a branch that came inevitably to a dead end.

11   Professor Hadzi of Yugoslavia has recently made the interesting suggestion that the rest of the many-celled animals, the so-called Metazoa, owe their origin to the second method. He suggests that they originated from some complicated protozoan belonging to the group of ciliates, of which the *Paramecium* I mentioned in my last chapter is an example. It would then have had to cut itself up into a number of cellular units, each with a nucleus, the process culminating in the emergence of an extremely small and simple kind of worm. We find such creatures today among the Flatworms. They consist of little more than a layer of cells on the outside, equipped with cilia or microscopic whiplashes for movement, and a mouth leading in, not to a digestive cavity, but to a densely packed mass of cell units which pick up the food mechanically like so many amoebae. This suggestion is far from being generally accepted, but it is useful to help one to picture the way in which this step of progress might actually have been achieved.

12   The next indispensable step involves three apparently different but actually interconnected developments. These are bilateral symmetry; the exploration of the environment for food by forward movement; and finally the formation of a head — the gradual concentration, in the front part of the body, of the mouth, the primitive brain, and the main sense organs. We are apt to take these improvements for granted; but, though they were indispensable for progress, they were not present in the great majority of earlier forms of life, and one or other of them has often been abandoned during the further evolution of animals. This happened with all the creatures that took to a fixed existence, or went over from active searching for food to filter feeding or tentacle feeding, to random crawling or floating — sea anemones and jellyfish, sea lilies and clams, sea urchins and barnacles. And it is quite clear that any animals that lost any one of this set of improvements were thereby put out of the path of further progress. Headless animals are often successful; but they are in a blind alley.

13   One way of escaping from blind alleys may be that which has been given the rather formidable name of *Paedomorphosis* — prolonging an early

developmental stage into adult life and going on from there. I have already mentioned the likelihood that insects may be thus derived from the newly hatched stage of myriapods, with its three pairs of legs. Garstang has made the more drastic suggestion that the free-swimming larva of some bottom-living form related to the echinoderms may have, by paedomorphosis, provided the starting point for the evolution of the great group of vertebrates. This is highly speculative, and may never be confirmed by other evidence; but it is worth bearing in mind as a possibility. Certainly the vertebrate plan of construction has more affinities in this quarter than with the plan of any adult invertebrate type.

14   Now I must make a big jump. In the next stage of animal progress, over hundreds of millions of years, there must have been parallel advances in many different lines — advances in efficiency and in integrated complexity. Thus, the three main groups which have evolved out of the early many-celled Metazoa — the molluscs, the arthropods and the vertebrates — all developed highly organized digestive and circulatory systems, highly efficient tissues like muscles and nerves, and highly elaborate sense organs, like pattern-forming eyes, while they were still aquatic. It comes as something of a shock to realize that this could not have been achieved without death, in the sense of the obligatory death of all the body except its germ cells. The distinction between non-reproducing individual body or *soma* and immortal reproductive tissue or *germ plasm*, first made by Weismann, is an important one, even though it is not always quite so clear-cut as he supposed. In protozoa, death in this sense does not exist: the individual simply divides into two. In Metazoa the separation begins; and it grows sharper during their evolution. It grows sharper in two rather different ways. The continuing sexual germ plasm becomes more rigidly separated at an early stage in development. And the somatic tissues lose their capacity for non-sexual reproduction. Many polyps and worms, for instance, can still reproduce by fission or make new individuals by budding. But even this seems to be impossible after a certain level of organization has been reached. At any rate it never occurs in animals with a highly organized body consisting of specialized tissues. For the Metazoa, death was thus a prerequisite for further progress; it is the price life had to pay for individuality and the efficiency of its biological machinery: and we continue to pay that price.

15   Among the molluscs and the arthropods are to be found some very successful groups, like the snails or the crabs or the insects: the insects indeed are in one way the most successful of all types, in that they have given rise to more different species than any other. But of all these none was capable of indefinite progress. This was reserved for the vertebrates. The earliest vertebrates had many prerequisites for further progress. They were active searchers for food; their method of swimming with the aid of a tail gave them greater speed and power than any of their competitors; and they were capable of growing to a larger size. Perhaps I should say that the scale of

their construction is larger than that of any other kind of animal. The smallest vertebrate is hundreds or thousands of times larger than the smallest mollusc or arthropod, and no mollusc attains even one-tenth, no arthropod even one-hundredth, of the bulk of the biggest fish, still less of the biggest mammals.

16 Further, a point which is often forgotten, their organization is more flexible. Their skeleton is made of living and adjustable material, like bone and cartilage, instead of dead secretions; and their tendons can adapt themselves to the tensions to which they are subjected during growth. Thus their whole structural framework can grow and adjust itself continuously, instead of molting from one predetermined piece of body armor into another, as in arthropods. In addition, they are capable of attaining a much greater flexibility of behavior. They have evolved an internal environment which is both more flexible and more independent of outer changes than that of any other group. The blood stream of higher vertebrates regulates its chemical composition with extraordinary accuracy, and in this way, as well as by its self-regulatory mechanism of temperature control, lays the foundation for a high degree of continuity and accuracy of mental activities. Meanwhile the development of the system of endocrine glands, secreting hormones into the blood, makes possible a new and more flexible integration.

17 Before the appearance of the early vertebrates we have reached the stage at which evolution is documented by well-preserved fossils — the stage comparable to that of recorded history in the affairs of man. Accordingly, we can now often detect the actual twists and turns of progress. Take the successful occupation of the land by animals — a step which only occurred well in the last quarter of evolutionary time. On land, the animal is confronted with a greater range and rapidity of change in environmental conditions than in water. This means a need for greater acuteness and range of sense organs, and puts a premium on learning rapidly by experience. On land, again, not only was there an obvious advantage in attaining a high constant body temperature, but it was easier, for various physiological reasons, to attain it. The stimuli of land life thus provided various opportunities for progress; and only the vertebrates were capable of taking full advantage of those opportunities. Even the insects could not climb these further steps — they are too small to have a constant temperature or to be very intelligent, and too rigidly made for flexibility of structure or behavior. In passing, their inflexibility and their small size are the reasons for the enormous number of their species — each species tends to have a smaller coverage, so to speak, of the environment.

18 However, for the vertebrates to achieve land life they had to pass through a narrow and devious channel, some three hundred million years ago, during the Devonian period. There were various prerequisites for this step in progress. In the first place, there had to be a change in climate — a desiccation which led to a drying out of the fresh waters of the world. Then,

the invaders of the land, the future ancestors of ourselves, had to be fresh-water fish; marine fish were out of the running. They had still to retain lobe-shaped fins, widely spaced out along the body, on which they rested while on the bottom of the water; so all fish which had specialized for streamlined speed in open waters were out of the running also. Finally, they had to have a swim bladder which was open to the gullet, and was therefore capable of acting as an accessory organ of respiration by gulping in air.

[19]   In the Devonian period there was a whole group of fish of this type, adapted to bottom living in stagnant fresh waters — the lungfish, in the broad sense of the word. When they were caught in increasingly stagnant water by the change of climate, they could survive by getting from one pool to another in case of need. In those which adopted this method, the air blad-der became a little more of a lung; their fins became better able to support their weight when out of water. So the first step in the conquest of the land was, strictly speaking, not an adaptation to land life at all, but merely an adaptation for continuing aquatic life by getting from one pool of water to another as quickly as possible. However, once this step had been taken, a new evolutionary opportunity was open. By means of minor further im-provements their fins could become walking legs, and their air bladders could become nothing but lungs. With these improvements the animals were able to spend the whole of their adult life out of water, so long as they spent it in moist conditions.

[20]   Another striking twist in the path of progress occurred during the origin of the mammals. They had, it seems, to pass through a phase of their exist-ence as small and insignificant nocturnal creatures, in the course of which they lost the capacity for color vision. Their very insignificance enabled them to survive during the long period when the land was dominated by powerful and specialized types of reptile. Their opportunity came when a great moun-tain-building revolution occurred, at the close of the Mesozoic epoch. The accompanying changes in climate, and in the distribution of land and sea, eventually resulted in the extinction of many of their reptilian competitors and put the rest at a disadvantage. The mammals were then able to profit by their new combination of capacities — temperature regulation, and car-ing for their young; and so were able to emerge into the light of day, and to spread and multiply exceedingly, though they seem not to have reac-quired color vision until the emergence of monkeys and apes.

[21]   Meanwhile, the birds had replaced the pterodactyls as conquerors of the air, and during the subsequent period they arrived at a delicacy of temperature regulation equal to that of the mammals. They also became capable of speeds greater than that of any other organism — speeds which were only excelled by airplanes a bare twenty years ago. They were very successful, and they achieved a number of important advances, but they cut themselves off from progress by their specialization. Their fore limbs are so thoroughly specialized as flying organs that they have become un-

usable for any other function; they are incapable of use as hands, and hands were a prerequisite for further progress.

22 Long before the end of the Cenozoic epoch, most of the possibilities available to living substance had been exhausted, in one animal group or another. Speed I have just mentioned. Size had reached a point where it became self-defeating; the chemical composition of the blood had become fully constant; the efficiency of nervous conduction, of sense organs, of digestive systems, and of mechanical construction had all reached limits of one sort or another. Only one feature remained capable of improvement — brain organization and behavior. Only a greater flexibility of behavior, and a higher organization of awareness, enabled living substance to become capable of conceptual thought and symbolic language; and these, as we saw, are the two distinguishing marks of man, and the basis of the latest deployment of life.

23 Here again the new step could not be reached except through a tortuous channel. The precursor of man had to pass through the stage of being a monkey. It had to give up the usual practice of mammals, of producing many young at a birth. As J. B. S. Haldane has pointed out, the presence of many young in the uterus gives rise to an acute struggle for existence between them before birth; and in this competition, general rapidity of growth and development is at a premium. Only in creatures which normally produce one young at a birth was it possible for the general rate of development to be slowed down, so as to provide a long learning period. Monkeys live in trees, and they use their hands as well as feet for climbing. They also use their hands for manipulating their food, and have developed binocular vision for its better detection. This combination of handling and seeing was necessary for the better organization of experience. Tree life thus laid the foundation both for our clearer definition of objects by conceptual thought, and for our fuller control of them by tools and machines tens of millions of years later. However, two further turnings had to be taken before this could come about. First, monkeys had to become apes. Apes get around mainly by swinging with their arms, not by climbing with all four limbs. This made it possible for their hind limbs to become differentiated as supporting feet. Finally, it was necessary for the apes to descend from the trees. This paved the way for the fully erect posture of our own species; and made possible the freeing of the hands for the sole job of manipulation. And this, in turn, was the prerequisite for the last step in biological progress — the attainment of true speech and conceptual thinking.

24 Looking back into the past we see clearly enough that conceptual thought could only have arisen in an animal as against a plant; in a multicellular animal; in an actively feeding animal, with bilateral symmetry and a head; in one with a highly differentiated bodily organization, which was therefore doomed to die; in a vertebrate as against a mollusc or an arthropod; in a land vertebrate as against a fish; and among land vertebrates, only in a

placental mammal with a constant temperature. And finally, it could have arisen only in a mammal which had become gregarious, which had a long period of learning and experience, which produced only one young at a birth, and which had recently become terrestrial after a long spell of life in the trees. Clearly, the path of progress is both devious and unique!

Commentary and questions

1. *Paragraph 1:* Huxley begins at once with a definition of the key term in the title of his essay. "Progress" is often used as what we call a "value" word; we tend to think of progress as something desirable. Does Huxley's definition include or omit this sense? Why does he dissociate "progress" from "improvement"? Explain the distinction in your own words.

2. *Paragraph 2:* In placing man in the line of biological progress, what does Huxley mean by saying "This is not just anthropomorphic wish-fulfillment"? Is he in conflict with Eiseley's effort to picture man as simply one stage in a broad pattern of biological change?

3. *Paragraph 3:* This continues the definition of progress by breaking it down into four elements. How do these fit Huxley's more general definition in paragraph 1? Are they all directly related to the concept of "indefinite improvement"?

4. *Paragraph 4:* The restatement of previous material lifts the discussion to a more general level and broadens the area in which the notion of progress is to be applied. How, precisely, is this broadening applied? In what areas? What new concept is added to Huxley's thesis?

5. *Paragraph 5:* What motive does Huxley have for introducing the analogy to a tree and its branches? How much of the concept behind the analogy has been stated before?

6. *Paragraph 6:* Huxley mentions that progress is relative to "other kinds of evolutionary change." Has he listed any other kinds? What are they?

Note also that the burden of this paragraph is an argument for the scientific truth of the theory of progressive change. How does Huxley understand scientific truth? How fully does he explain it? What words are most important in his argument?

7. *Paragraph 8:* Huxley introduces the first of four important stages which he goes on to list. How fully is the "reduction of the rate at which mutation occurs" described? Why are no figures given? Why is this stage placed first — is it first in time or is it a more fundamental or more general step than the others?

8. *Paragraph 10:* Is the "step to the many-celled condition in animals" a necessity for success? For progress? Explain.

9. *Paragraph 12:* The three developments listed also involve mutation, but describe its physical manifestations, the results of cellular special-ization. How are these important for "progress"? How does Huxley make use of contrast in this paragraph?

10. *Paragraph 14:* The fourth "stage of animal progress" is death. How does this stage differ from the others? Is it a cellular function? What is the vital distinction between types of reproduction? How is this distinction related to the concept of specialization noted in paragraphs 9 and 10?

11. *Paragraph 15:* Huxley makes it clear that the four major steps he has outlined are also organized to permit him to distinguish more and more sharply between forms of life capable of "indefinite progress" from those which may be "successful" but are capable of only "finite" improvement (see paragraph 1). Are these stages also arranged according to geological chronology? In other words, does Huxley indicate that any of the steps come later in geological time than others?

12. *Paragraph 16:* This is a list of vertebrate characteristics useful for progress. Why must these details be mentioned after Huxley has outlined his four steps in biological progress? What is the key word in this paragraph? How is it important to the unity of the paragraph?

13. *Paragraph 17:* Why has Huxley waited until now to mention the evidence for the principles he has discussed? How precise and detailed is this evidence?

14. *Paragraphs 18-23:* Huxley explains the prerequisites and conditions necessary for the successful transition of animal life from sea to land. Compare Huxley's account to Eiseley's, noting the differences in style, approach, amount of detail, and any similarities and differences in their basic concepts of the principles according to which this evolutionary change took place. As a sample inquiry, the reader might ask whether Eiseley presents the emergence of fish onto land as a form of "progress."

What overtones and connotative values does Huxley ascribe to the change? Do these have any relation to Darwin's understanding of the process of natural selection? (See pp. 386-392.)

15. *Paragraph 23:* Huxley summarizes aspects of the progress of mammals. Which and how many of the four major stages listed in paragraphs 8-12 come into play here?

16. *Paragraph 24:* Huxley's conclusion looks back over the entire selection. What elements in his discussion does he particularly emphasize here? Are they entirely factual?

Topics for discussion and writing

I. It is fair to say that Huxley's essay is a generalized explanation of a very broad topic. To what sort of audience is that explanation addressed? What elements in his style and organization are clues to the nature of his audience?

II. Definition is clearly an important part of Huxley's plan. Would you characterize the entire essay as a definition of "progress"? What other purposes besides the definitive do you notice?

III. Make a topic outline of Huxley's essay, indicating important generalization and subordination.

IV. Write a theme discussing the specific areas in which Huxley and Eiseley discuss similar or closely related topics. Discuss the important stylistic differences between them and the apparent purposes behind those differences.

V. Write a theme in which you define evolutionary change as both authors present it. What purposes seem to influence their understanding of evolutionary change and the contexts within which they discuss it?

THE STRUGGLE FOR EXISTENCE   Charles Darwin

From Origin of Species, *first published in 1859.*

BEFORE entering on the subject of this chapter, I must make a few preliminary remarks, to show how the struggle for existence bears on Natural Selection. It has been seen in the last chapter that amongst organic beings in a state of nature there is some individual variability: indeed I am not aware that this has ever been disputed. It is immaterial for us whether a multitude of doubtful forms be called species or sub-species or varieties, what rank, for instance, the two or three hundred doubtful forms of British plants are entitled to hold, if the existence of any well-marked varieties be admitted. But the mere existence of individual variability and of some few well-marked varieties, though necessary as the foundation for the work, helps us but little in understanding how species arise in nature. How have all those exquisite adaptations of one part of the organisation to another part, and to the conditions of life, and of one organic being to another being, been perfected? We see these beautiful co-adaptations most plainly in the woodpecker and the mistletoe; and only a little less plainly in the humblest parasite which clings to the hairs of a quadruped or feathers of a bird; in the structure of the beetle which dives through the water: in the plumed seed which is wafted by the gentlest breeze; in short, we see beautiful adaptations everywhere and in every part of the organic world.

2   Again, it may be asked, how is it that varieties, which I have called incipient species, become ultimately converted into good and distinct species, which in most cases obviously differ from each other far more than do the varieties of the same species? How do those groups of species, which constitute what are called distinct genera, and which differ from each other more than do the species of the same genus, arise? All these results, as we shall more fully see in the next chapter, follow from the struggle for life. Owing to this struggle, variations, however slight and from whatever cause proceeding, if they be in any degree profitable to the individuals of a spe-

cies, in their infinitely complex relations to other organic beings and to their physical conditions of life, will tend to the preservation of such individuals, and will generally be inherited by the offspring. The offspring, also, will thus have a better chance of surviving, for, of the many individuals of any species which are periodically born, but a small number can survive. I have called this principle, by which each slight variation, if useful, is preserved, by the term Natural Selection, in order to mark its relation to man's power of selection. But the expression often used by Mr. Herbert Spencer of the Survival of the Fittest is more accurate, and is sometimes equally convenient. We have seen that man by selection can certainly produce great results, and can adapt organic beings to his own uses, through the accumulation of slight but useful variations, given to him by the hand of Nature. But Natural Selection, as we shall hereafter see, is a power incessantly ready for action, and is as immeasurably superior to man's feeble efforts, as the works of Nature are to those of Art.

3 We will now discuss in a little more detail the struggle for existence. In my future work this subject will be treated, as it well deserves, at greater length. The elder De Candolle and Lyell have largely and philosophically shown that all organic beings are exposed to severe competition. In regard to plants, no one has treated this subject with more spirit and ability than W. Herbert, Dean of Manchester, evidently the result of his great horticultural knowledge. Nothing is easier than to admit in words the truth of the universal struggle for life, or more difficult — at least I have found it so — than constantly to bear this conclusion in mind. Yet unless it be thoroughly engrained in the mind, the whole economy of nature, with every fact on distribution, rarity, abundance, extinction, and variation, will be dimly seen or quite misunderstood. We behold the face of nature bright with gladness, we often see superabundance of food; we do not see or we forget, that the birds which are idly singing round us mostly live on insects or seeds, and are thus constantly destroying life; or we forget how largely these songsters, or their eggs, or their nestlings, are destroyed by birds and beasts of prey; we do not always bear in mind, that, though food may be now superabundant, it is not so at all seasons of each recurring year.

The Term, Struggle for Existence, Used in a Large Sense

4 I should premise that I use this term in a large and metaphorical sense including dependence of one being on another, and including (which is more important) not only the life of the individual, but success in leaving progeny. Two canine animals, in a time of dearth, may be truly said to struggle with each other which shall get food and live. But a plant on the edge of a desert is said to struggle for life against the drought, though more properly it should be said to be dependent on the moisture. A plant which annually produces a thousand seeds, of which only one of an average comes to maturity, may be more truly said to struggle with the plants of the same

and other kinds which already clothe the ground. The mistletoe is dependent on the apple and a few other trees, but can only in a far-fetched sense be said to struggle with these trees, for, if too many of these parasites grow on the same tree, it languishes and dies. But several seedling mistletoes, growing close together on the same branch, may more truly be said to struggle with each other. As the mistletoe is disseminated by birds, its existence depends on them, and it may metaphorically be said to struggle with other fruit-bearing plants, in tempting the birds to devour and thus disseminate its seeds. In these several senses, which pass into each other, I use for convenience' sake the general term of Struggle for Existence.

Geometrical Ratio of Increase

5   A struggle for existence inevitably follows from the high rate at which all organic beings tend to increase. Every being, which during its natural lifetime produces several eggs or seeds, must suffer destruction during some period of its life, and during some season or occasional year, otherwise, on the principle of geometrical increase, its numbers would quickly become so inordinately great that no country could support the product. Hence, as more individuals are produced than can possibly survive, there must in every case be a struggle for existence, either one individual with another of the same species, or with the individuals of distinct species, or with the physical conditions of life. It is the doctrine of Malthus applied with manifold force to the whole animal and vegetable kingdoms; for in this case there can be no artificial increase of food, and no prudential restraint from marriage. Although some species may be now increasing, more or less rapidly, in numbers, all cannot do so, for the world would not hold them.

6   There is no exception to the rule that every organic being naturally increases at so high a rate, that, if not destroyed, the earth would soon be covered by the progeny of a single pair. Even slow-breeding man has doubled in twenty-five years, and at this rate, in less than a thousand years, there would literally not be standing-room for his progeny. Linnæus has calculated that if an annual plant produced only two seeds — and there is no plant so unproductive as this — and their seedlings next year produced two, and so on, then in twenty years there would be a million plants. The elephant is reckoned the slowest breeder of all known animals, and I have taken some pains to estimate its probable minimum rate of natural increase; it will be safest to assume that it begins breeding when thirty years old, and goes on breeding till ninety years old, bringing forth six young in the interval, and surviving till one hundred years old; if this be so, after a period of from 740 to 750 years there would be nearly nineteen million elephants alive, descended from the first pair.

7   But we have better evidence on this subject than mere theoretical calculations, namely, the numerous recorded cases of the astonishingly rapid increase of various animals in a state of nature, when circumstances have been

favourable to them during two or three following seasons. Still more striking is the evidence from our domestic animals of many kinds which have run wild in several parts of the world; if the statements of the rate of increase of slow-breeding cattle and horses in South America, and latterly in Australia, had not been well authenticated, they would have been incredible. So it is with plants; cases could be given of introduced plants which have become common throughout whole islands in a period of less than ten years. Several of the plants, such as the cardoon and a tall thistle, which are now the commonest over the wide plains of La Plata, clothing square leagues of surface almost to the exclusion of every other plant, have been introduced from Europe; and there are plants which now range in India, as I hear from Dr. Falconer, from Cape Comorin to the Himalayas, which have been imported from America since its discovery. In such cases, and endless others could be given, no one supposes, that the fertility of the animals or plants has been suddenly and temporarily increased in any sensible degree. The obvious explanation is that the conditions of life have been highly favorable, and that there has consequently been less destruction of the old and young, and that nearly all the young have been enabled to breed. Their geometrical ratio of increase, the result of which never fails to be surprising, simply explains their extraordinarily rapid increase and wide diffusion in their new homes.

8   In a state of nature almost every full-grown plant annually produces seed, and amongst animals there are very few which do not annually pair. Hence we may confidently assert, that all plants and animals are tending to increase at a geometrical ratio, — that all would rapidly stock every station in which they could anyhow exist, — and that this geometrical tendency to increase must be checked by destruction at some period of life. Our familiarity with the larger domestic animals tends, I think, to mislead us: we see no great destruction falling on them, but we do not keep in mind that thousands are annually slaughtered for food, and that in a state of nature an equal number would have somehow to be disposed of.

9   The only difference between organisms which annually produce eggs or seeds by the thousand, and those which produce extremely few, is, that the slow-breeders would require a few more years to people, under favourable conditions, a whole district, let it be ever so large. The condor lays a couple of eggs and the ostrich a score, and yet in the same country the condor may be the more numerous of the two; the Fulmar petrel lays but one egg, yet it is believed to be the most numerous bird in the world. One fly deposits hundreds of eggs, and another, like the hippobosca, a single one; but this difference does not determine how many individuals of the two species can be supported in a district. A large number of eggs is of some importance to those species which depend on a fluctuating amount of food, for it allows them rapidly to increase in number. But the real importance of a large number of eggs or seeds is to make up for much destruction

at some period of life; and this period in the great majority of cases is an early one. If an animal can in any way protect its own eggs or young, a small number may be produced, and yet the average stock be fully kept up; but if many eggs or young are destroyed, many must be produced, or the species will become extinct. It would suffice to keep up the full number of a tree, which lived on an average for a thousand years, if a single seed were produced once in a thousand years, supposing that this seed were never destroyed, and could be ensured to germinate in a fitting place. So that, in all cases, the average number of any animal or plant depends only indirectly on the number of its eggs or seeds.

10   In looking at Nature, it is most necessary to keep the foregoing considerations always in mind — never to forget that every single organic being may be said to be striving to the utmost to increase in numbers; that each lives by a struggle at some period of its life; that heavy destruction inevitably falls either on the young or old, during each generation or at recurrent intervals. Lighten any check, mitigate the destruction ever so little, and the number of the species will almost instantaneously increase to any amount.

Nature of the Checks to Increase

11   The causes which check the natural tendency of each species to increase are most obscure. Look at the most vigorous species; by as much as it swarms in numbers, by so much will it tend to increase still further. We know not exactly what the checks are even in a single instance. Nor will this surprise any one who reflects how ignorant we are on this head, even in regard to mankind, although so incomparably better known than any other animal. This subject of the checks to increase has been ably treated by several authors, and I hope in a future work to discuss it at considerable length, more especially in regard to the feral animals of South America. Here I will make only a few remarks, just to recall to the reader's mind some of the chief points. Eggs of very young animals seem generally to suffer most, but this is not invariably the case. With plants there is a vast destruction of seeds, but, from some observations which I have made, it appears that the seedlings suffer most from germinating in ground already thickly stocked with other plants. Seedlings, also, are destroyed in vast numbers by various enemies; for instance, on a piece of ground three feet long and two wide, dug and cleared, and where there could be no choking from other plants, I marked all the seedlings of our native weeds as they came up, and out of 357 no less than 295 were destroyed, chiefly by slugs and insects. If turf which has long been mown, and the case would be the same with turf closely browsed by quadrupeds, be let to grow, the more vigorous plants gradually kill the less vigorous, though fully grown plants; thus out of twenty species growing on a little plot of mown turf (three feet by four) nine species perished, from the other species being allowed to grow up freely.

12   The amount of food for each species of course gives the extreme limit to which each can increase; but very frequently it is not the obtaining food, but the serving as prey to other animals, which determines the average numbers of a species. Thus, there seems to be little doubt that the stock of partridges, grouse, and hares on any large estate depends chiefly on the destruction of vermin. If not one head of game were shot during the next twenty years in England, and, at the same time, if no vermin were destroyed, there would, in all probability, be less game than at present, although hundreds of thousands of game animals are now annually shot. On the other hand, in some cases, as with the elephant, none are destroyed by beasts of prey; for even the tiger in India most rarely dares to attack a young elephant protected by its dam.

13   Climate plays an important part in determining the average numbers of a species, and periodical seasons of extreme cold or drought seem to be the most effective of all checks. I estimated (chiefly from the greatly reduced numbers of nests in the spring) that the winter of 1854-5 destroyed four-fifths of the birds in my own grounds; and this is a tremendous destruction, when we remember that ten per cent. is an extraordinarily severe mortality from epidemics with man. The action of climate seems at first sight to be quite independent of the struggle for existence; but in so far as climate chiefly acts in reducing food, it brings on the most severe struggle between the individuals, whether of the same or of distinct species, which subsist on the same kind of food. Even when climate, for instance extreme cold, acts directly, it will be the least vigorous individuals, or those which have got least food through the advancing winter, which will suffer most. When we travel from south to north, or from a damp region to a dry, we invariably see some species gradually getting rarer and rarer, and finally disappearing; and the change of climate being conspicuous, we are tempted to attribute the whole effect to its direct action. But this is a false view; we forget that each species, even where it most abounds, is constantly suffering enormous destruction at some period of its life, from enemies or from competitors for the same place and food; and if these enemies or competitors be in the least degree favoured by any slight change of climate, they will increase in numbers; and as each area is already fully stocked with inhabitants, the other species must decrease. When we travel southward and see a species decreasing in numbers, we may feel sure that the cause lies quite as much in other species being favored, as in this one being hurt. So it is when we travel northward, but in a somewhat lesser degree, for the number of species of all kinds, and therefore of competitors, decreases northwards; hence in going northwards, or in ascending a mountain, we far oftener meet with stunted forms, due to the *directly* injurious action of climate, than we do in proceeding southwards or in descending a mountain. When we reach the Arctic regions, or snow-capped summits, or absolute deserts, the struggle for life is almost exclusively with the elements.

¹⁴   That climate acts in main part indirectly by favoring other species, we clearly see in the prodigious number of plants which in our gardens can perfectly well endure our climate, but which never become naturalized, for they cannot compete with our native plants nor resist destruction by our native animals.

¹⁵   When a species, owing to highly favorable circumstances, increases inordinately in numbers in a small tract, epidemics — at least, this seems generally to occur with our game animals — often ensue; and here we have a limiting check independent of the struggle for life. But even some of these so-called epidemics appear to be due to parasitic worms, which have from some cause, possibly in part through facility of diffusion amongst the crowded animals, been disproportionally favored: and here comes in a sort of struggle between the parasite and its prey.

¹⁶   On the other hand, in many cases, a large stock of individuals of the same species, relatively to the numbers of its enemies, is absolutely necessary for its preservation. Thus we can easily raise plenty of corn and rape-seed, &c., in our fields, because the seeds are in great excess compared with the number of birds which feed on them; nor can the birds, though having a superabundance of food at this one season, increase in number proportionally to the supply of seed, as their numbers are checked during winter; but any one who has tried, knows how troublesome it is to get seed from a few wheat or other such plants in a garden: I have in this case lost every single seed. This view of the necessity of a large stock of the same species for its preservation, explains, I believe, some singular facts in nature such as that of very rare plants being sometimes extremely abundant, in the few spots where they do exist; and that of some social plants being social, that is abounding in individuals, even on the extreme verge of their range. For in such cases, we may believe, that a plant could exist only where the conditions of its life were so favourable that many could exist together, and thus save the species from utter destruction. I should add that the good effects of intercrossing, and the ill effects of close interbreeding, no doubt come into play in many of these cases; but I will not here enlarge on this subject.

Commentary and questions

1. *Paragraph 1:* What crucial question does Darwin raise? Why does he say it is immaterial whether doubtful forms be called species or subspecies or varieties? What links the woodpecker and the plumed seed?

As a secondary matter the reader should notice that some of Darwin's terms go beyond the task of explanation and suggest his own personal attitude toward the laws of nature.

2. *Paragraph 2:* This is a continuation of the posing of problems begun in the first. Notice the phrase "All these results." List the items Darwin classifies under "results." What, then, does Darwin include under cause?

The latter part of the paragraph is a definition of Natural Selection. How complete is this definition?

3. *Paragraph 3:* What terms are used to paraphrase "the struggle for existence"? What, according to Darwin, is the importance of the general concept to which this phrase refers? How does Darwin use contrast at the end of the paragraph?

4. *Paragraph 4:* In explaining why and how he uses the term "the struggle for existence," Darwin says that it is metaphorical. Precisely how is this true? What unexpected meanings do you find in his explanation of the term? Does this concept of struggle include anything not specifically mentioned by Huxley and Eiseley in their use of the term? Examine the structure and completeness of Darwin's definition of "the struggle for existence." How fully does it coincide with the principles of definition discussed in the introduction to Part I (pp. 16-35)?

5. *Paragraphs 5-6:* Darwin's connection between the ratio of increase in organic beings to the struggle for existence is an example of deductive reasoning. Examine the next to last sentence in the paragraph to observe a key premise. State Darwin's premises and conclusion in your own words. To do so, you must note the places where one or more are repeated.

One of Darwin's premises — "the rule that every organic being naturally increases at so high a rate . . . , that . . . the earth would soon be covered by the progeny of a single pair" — is supported inductively. Paragraphs 4, 5, and 8 are an excellent example of the interdependence of the deductive and inductive processes, the latter group being taken up with evidence for the premise of geometrical increase. But the evidence involves more than a simple accumulation of similar details. What subordinate considerations does Darwin mention to bolster his assertion? What is the significance of the rate of time it takes organic beings to reproduce?

6. *Paragraph 8:* Darwin introduces a principle working against uninhibited increase, that of destruction. How precisely does destruction work in nature, according to this paragraph?

7. *Paragraphs 9-14:* This section specifies the workings of destruction as a general principle in organic life. How many types of destruction does Darwin list? Does he assign special importance to any one type? Paraphrase the main points of these paragraphs.

Topics for discussion and writing

I. The organization of this selection is straightforward. How would you categorize it?

II. Summarize the general points Darwin makes. What kinds of detail does he use to clarify these generalities? The reader should consider example, comparison, contrast, and repetition, among others.

III. Write a theme explaining the attitudes of Darwin, Huxley, and Eiseley toward the concept of struggle. Is the concept expressed metaphorically by all three writers? Does struggle involve competition and hostility (either to environment or other living things) alone? What connotative overtones or inferences does each writer make use of?

IV. Write a theme discussing the differences in the three writers' understanding of the significance of man in the processes of evolutionary change. What do Huxley and Eiseley emphasize that Darwin does not? What assumptions lie behind the point of view of each writer? What inferences may be drawn from their views?

V. Discuss the amount of subjectivity or bias in the essays of the three writers. What specific elements of style indicate these biases?

VI. Write an essay analyzing the various types of statements used for support by one or more of these writers. Show what types predominate and how far these types seem to determine characteristics of the essay.

Science, conscience, and nuclear tests: A DEC-
LARATION OF CONSCIENCE, Albert Schweitzer · AN OPEN LETTER TO DR.
SCHWEITZER, Willard F. Libby · WHAT IS A "SMALL" RISK?, Harrison Brown

THE ENERGY with which any issue is debated depends a good deal upon its timeliness and the degree of seriousness with which the public mind regards it. Few national or international problems are more urgent than that of the effects of atomic fallout, and that urgency is mirrored in various ways by the writers in this group of essays: The tone of their language shows an obvious and strenuous effort at sobriety, but one may detect a note of urgency beneath the surface, and sometimes on the surface.

Perhaps even more important is the influence public attitudes toward fallout have over the styles of these writers. They are not simply arguing against each other; and mixed with their efforts to draw valid conclusions from the scientific evidence they use are clear and strong appeals to public opinion. Thus, it is nearly impossible to divorce the merits of the problem of fallout from the public understanding of it.

Nevertheless, the reader who wants to assess the value of the arguments used must first concern himself with the matter of inductive logic, for all three authors are more or less concerned with a body of scientific data and hypotheses, and a useful way to test the comparative validity of the three essays is to examine their use of this material. How specifically do they present the evidence? How thoroughly do they cover the possible inferences and conclusions that may be drawn from it? And, finally, how much does each sacrifice logical exactness to appeal to the public?

Like most serious discussion, the writings in this group depend upon the senses in which various key words are used. Here the reader's experience with and sensitivity to the problem of definitions — implicit and explicit — will help in evaluating the premises upon which arguments are based and the unarticulated concepts that lurk between the lines. Paramount in all the essays are the meanings given to "danger." What does it mean in concrete terms? How can it be made precise? How can degrees of "danger" be estimated? These matters suggest the direction in which the three authors move.

Behind each of these accounts lies the recognition that there are really three different problems: (1) Does continued atomic testing create a hazard to human beings? This is a scientific question, and it is a complex question because it is not enough to say yes or no. The answer must also say how much and then define what is hazardous to human beings. (2) The second question is this: Is the continuation of tests a military necessity? Here again the answer is complex. Yes and no are not enough. The matter of degree enters and in addition the all-important hypothetical situation — if all other countries stopped testing. . . . (3) Now a third point arises. At what point does the harm done to human beings outweigh military necessity? At what point does military necessity outweigh the harm done to human beings? The answers to these questions are based partly on the first two, but just as essentially on the moral assumptions of the person who answers.

One of the interesting facts in arguments of this sort is that the moral assumptions of the debaters are often so taken for granted by themselves that they argue ostensibly on scientific grounds. But the whole argument is provoked by the fact that military compulsion creates moral problems. Where the debater does not examine his own assumptions, the reader must.

(*Note:* Since these articles were published in 1957, they should not be regarded as the latest word on fallout.)

A DECLARATION OF CONSCIENCE   Albert Schweitzer

Albert Schweitzer, "A Declaration of Conscience," Saturday Review, *Vol. 40* (*May 18, 1957*). *By permission of the publishers.*

SINCE March 1, 1954 hydrogen bombs have been tested by the United States at the Pacific Island of Bikini in the Marshall group and by Soviet Russia in Siberia. We know that testing of atomic weapons is something quite different from testing of non-atomic ones. Earlier, when a new type of giant gun had been tested, the matter ended with the detonation. After the explosion of a hydrogen bomb that is not the case. Something remains in the air, namely, an incalculable number of radioactive particles emitting radioactive rays. This was also the case with the uranium bombs dropped on

Nagasaki and Hiroshima and those which were subsequently tested. However, because these bombs were of smaller size and less effectiveness compared with the hydrogen bombs, not much attention was given to this fact.

2   Since radioactive rays of sufficient amount and strength have harmful effects on the human body, it must be considered whether the radiation resulting from the hydrogen explosions that have already taken place represents a danger which would increase with new explosions.

3   In the course of the three-and-a-half years that have passed since then [the test explosions of the early hydrogen bombs] representatives of the physical and medical sciences have been studying the problem. Observations on the distribution, origin, and nature of radiation have been made. The processes through which the human body is harmfully affected have been analyzed. The material collected, although far from complete, allows us to draw the conclusion that radiation resulting from the explosions which have already taken place represents a danger to the human race — a danger not to be underrated — and that further explosions of atomic bombs will increase this danger to an alarming extent.

4   This conclusion has repeatedly been expressed, especially during the last few months. However, it has not, strange to say, influenced public opinion to the extent that one might have expected. Individuals and peoples have not been aroused to give to this danger the attention which it unfortunately deserves. It must be demonstrated and made clear to them.

5   I raise my voice, together with those of others who have lately felt it their duty to act, through speaking and writing, in warning of the danger. My age and the generous understanding so many people have shown of my work permit me to hope that my appeal may contribute to the preparing of the way for the insights so urgently needed.

6   My thanks go to the radio station in Oslo, the city of the Nobel Peace Prize, for making it possible for that which I feel I have to say to reach far-off places.

7   What is radioactivity?

8   Radioactivity consists of rays differing from those of light in being invisible and in being able to pass not only through glass but also through thin metal discs and through layers of cell tissue in the human and animal bodies. Rays of this kind were first discovered in 1895 by the physicist Wilhelm Röentgen of Munich, and were named after him.

9   In 1896 the French physicist Henry Becquerel demonstrated that rays of this kind occur in nature. They are emited from uranium, an element known since 1786.

10   In 1898 Pierre Curie and his wife discovered in the mineral pitchblende, a uranium ore, the strongly radioactive element radium.

11   The joy caused by the fact that such rays were at the disposal of humanity was at first unmixed. It appeared that they influence the relatively

rapidly growing and relatively rapidly decaying cells of malignant tumors and sarcomas. If exposed to these rays repeatedly for a longer period, some of the terrible neoplasms can be destroyed.

12   After a time it was found, however, that the destruction of cancer cells does not always mean the cure of cancer and also, that the normal cells of the body may be seriously damaged if long exposed to radioactivity.

13   When Mme. Curie, after having handled uranium ore for four years, finally held the first gram of radium in her hand there appeared abrasions in the skin which no treatment could cure. With the years she grew steadily sicker from a disease caused by radioactive rays which damaged her bone marrow and through this her blood. In 1934 death put an end to her suffering.

14   Even so, for many years we were not aware of the grave risks involved in X-rays to those constantly exposed to them. Through operating X-ray apparatus thousands of doctors and nurses have incurred incurable diseases.

15   Radioactive rays are material things. Through them the radioactive element constantly and forcefully emits tiny particles of itself. There are three kinds. They are named after the three first letters of the Greek alphabet, *alpha, beta, gamma*. The gamma rays are the hardest ones and have the strongest effect.

16   The reason why elements emit radioactive rays is that they are in a continuous state of decaying. The radioactivity is the energy liberated little by little. There are other elements besides uranium and radium which are radioactive. To the radiation from the elements in the earth is added some radiation from space. Fortunately, the air mass 400 kilometers high that surrounds our earth protects us against this radiation. Only a very small fraction of it reaches us.

17   We are, then, constantly being exposed to radioactive radiation coming from the earth and from space. It is so weak, however, that it does not hurt us. Stronger sources of radiation, as for instance X-ray machines and exposed radium, have, as we know, harmful effects if one is exposed to them for some time.

18   The radioactive rays are, as I said, invisible. How can we tell that they are there and how strong they are?

19   Thanks to the German physicist Hans Geiger, who died in 1945 as a victim to X-rays, we have an instrument which makes that possible. This instrument is called the Geiger counter; it consists of a metal tube containing rarefied air. In it are two metal electrodes between which there is a high potential. Radioactive rays from the outside affect the tube and release a discharge between the two electrodes. The stronger the radiation the quicker the discharges follow one another. A small device connected to the tube makes the discharge audible. The Geiger counter performs a veritable drumroll when the discharges are strong.

20   There are two kinds of atom bomb — uranium bombs and hydrogen bombs. The effect of an uranium bomb is due to a process which liberates

energy through the fission of uranium. In the hydrogen bomb the liberation of energy is the result of the transformation of hydrogen into helium.

21   It is interesting to note that this latter process is similar to that which takes place in the center of the sun, supplying it with the self-renewing energy which it emits in the form of light and heat.

22   In principle, the effect of both bombs is the same. But according to various estimates the effect of one of the latest hydrogen bombs is 2,000 times stronger than the one which was dropped on Hiroshima.

23   To these two bombs has recently been added the cobalt bomb, a kind of super atom-bomb. It is a hydrogen bomb surrounded by a layer of cobalt. The effect of this bomb is estimated to be many times stronger than that of hydrogen bombs that have been made so far.

24   The explosion of an atom bomb creates an unconceivably large number of exceedingly small particles of radioactive elements which decay like uranium or radium. Some of these particles decay very quickly, others more slowly, and some of them extraordinarily slowly. The strongest of these elements cease to exist only ten seconds after the detonation of the bomb. But in this short time they may have killed a great number of people in a circumference of several miles.

25   What remains are the less powerful elements. In our time it is with these we have to contend. It is of the danger arising from the radioactive rays emitted by these elements that we must be aware.

26   Of these elements some exist for hours, some for weeks, or months, or years, or millions of years, undergoing continuous decay. They float in the higher strata of air as clouds of radioactive dust. The heavy particles fall down first. The lighter ones will stay in the air for a longer time or come down with rain or snow. How long it will take before everything carried up in the air by the explosions which have taken place till now has disappeared no one can say with any certainty. According to some estimates, this will be the case not earlier than thirty or forty years from now.

27   When I was a boy I witnessed how dust hurled into the air from the explosion in 1883 of the island Krakatoa in the Sunda group was noticeable for two years afterwards to such an extent that the sunsets were given extraordinary splendor by it.

28   What we can state with certainty, however, is that the radioactive clouds will constantly be carried by the winds around the globe and that some of the dust, by its own weight, or by being brought down by rain, snow, mist, and dew, little by little, will fall down on the hard surface of the earth, into the rivers, and into the oceans.

29   Of what nature are these radioactive elements particles of which were carried up in the air by the explosion of atom bombs and which are now falling down again?

30   They are strange variants of the usual non-radioactive elements. They have the same chemical properties, but a different atomic weight. Their

names are always accompanied by their atomic weights. The same element can occur in several radioactive variants. Besides Iodine 131, which lives for sixteen days only, we have Iodine 129, which lives for 200,000,000 years.

31 Dangerous elements of this kind are: Phosphorus 32, Calcium 45, Iodine 131, Iron 55, Bismuth 210, Plutonium 239, Cerium 144, Strontium 89, Caesium 137. If the hydrogen bomb is covered by cobalt, Cobalt 60 must be added to the list.

32 Particularly dangerous are the elements combining long life with a relatively strong efficient radiation. Among them Strontium 90 takes the first place. It is present in very large amounts in the radioactive dust. Cobalt 60 must also be mentioned as particularly dangerous.

33 The radioactivity in the air, increased through these elements, will not harm us from the outside, not being strong enough to penetrate the skin. It is another matter with respiration, through which radioactive elements can enter our bodies. But the danger which has to be stressed above all the others is the one which arises from our drinking radioactive water and our eating radioactive food as a consequence of the increased radioactivity in the air.

34 Following the explosions of Bikini and Siberia rain falling over Japan has, from time to time, been so radioactive that the water from it cannot be drunk. Not only that: Reports of radioactive rainfall are coming from all parts of the world where analyses have recently been made. In several places the water has proved to be so radioactive that it was unfit for drinking.

35 Well-water becomes radioactive to any considerable extent only after longer periods of heavy rainfall.

36 Wherever radioactive rainwater is found the soil is also radioactive — and in a higher degree. The soil is made radioactive not only by the downpour, but also from radioactive dust falling on it. And with the soil the vegetation will also have become radioactive. The radioactive elements deposited in the soil pass into the plants, where they are stored. This is of importance, for as a result of this process it may be the case that we are threatened by a considerable amount of radioactive elements.

37 The radioactive elements in grass, when eaten by animals whose meat is used for food, will be absorbed and stored in our bodies.

38 In the case of cows grazing on contaminated soil, the absorption is effected when we drink their milk. In that way small children run an especially dangerous risk of absorbing radioactive elements.

39 When we eat contaminated cheese and fruits the radioactive elements stored in them are transferred to us.

40 What this storing of radioactive material implies is clearly demonstrated by the observations made when, on one occasion, the radioactivity of the Columbia River in North America was analyzed. The radioactivity was caused by the atomic plants at Hanford, which produce plutonium for atomic bombs and which empty their waste water into the river. The radio-

activity of the river water was insignificant. But the radioactivity of the river plankton was 2,000 times higher, that of the ducks eating plankton 40,000 times higher, that of the fish 15,000 times higher. In young swallows fed on insects caught by their parents in the river the radioactivity was 500,000 times higher, and in the egg yolks of water birds more than 1,000,-000 times higher.

41   From official and unofficial sources we have been assured, time and time again, that the increase in radioactivity of the air does not exceed the amount which the human body can tolerate without any harmful effects. This is just evading the issue. Even if we are not directly affected by the radioactive material in the air, we are indirectly affected through that which has fallen down, is falling down, and will fall down. We are absorbing this through radioactive drinking water and through animal and vegetable food-stuffs, to the same extent as radioactive elements are stored in the vegetation of the region in which we live. Unfortunately for us, nature hoards what is falling down from the air.

42   None of the radioactivity of the air, created by the explosion of atom bombs, is so unimportant that it may not, in the long run, become a danger to us through increasing the amount of radioactivity stored in our bodies.

43   What we absorb of radioactivity is not spread evenly in all cellular tissue. It is deposited in certain parts of our body, particularly in the bone tissue and also in the spleen and in the liver. From those sources the organs which are especially sensitive to it are exposed to radiation. What the radia-tion lacks in strength is compensated for by time. It works day and night without interruption.

44   How does radiation affect the cells of an organ?

45   Through being ionized, that is to say, electrically charged. This change means that the chemical processes which make it possible for the cells to do their job in our body no longer function as they should. They are no longer able to perform the tasks which are of vital importance to us. We must also bear in mind that a great number of the cells of an organ may degenerate or die as a result of radiation.

46   What are the diseases caused by internal radiation? The same diseases that are known to be caused by external radiation.

47   They are mainly serious blood diseases. The cells of the red bone mar-row, where the red and the white blood corpuscles are formed, are very sensitive to radioactive rays. It is these corpuscles, found in great numbers in the blood, which make it possible for it to play such an important part. If the cells in the bone marrow are damaged by radiation they will produce too few or abnormal, degenerating blood corpuscles. Both cases lead to blood diseases and, frequently, to death. These were the diseases that killed the victims of X-rays and radium rays.

48   It was one of these diseases that attacked the Japanese fishermen who were surprised in their vessel by radioactive ashes falling down 240 miles from Bikini after the explosion of an hydrogen bomb. With one exception,

they were all saved, being strong and relatively mildly affected, through continuous blood transfusions.

49   In the cases cited the radiation came from the outside. It is unfortunately very probable that internal radiation affecting the bone marrow and lasting for years will have the same effect, particularly since the radiation goes from the bone tissue to the bone marrow. As I have said, the radioactive elements are by preference stored in the bone tissue.

50   Not our own health only is threatened by internal radiation, but also that of our descendants. The fact is that the cells of the reproductive organs are particularly vulnerable to radiation which in this case attacks the nucleus to such an extent that it can be seen in the microscope.

51   To the profound damage of these cells corresponds a profound damage to our descendants.

52   It consists in stillbirths and in the births of babies with mental or physical defects.

53   In this context also, we can point to the effects of radiation coming from the outside.

54   It is a fact — even if the statistical material being published in the press needs checking — that in Nagasaki, during the years following the dropping of the atom bomb, an exceptionally high occurrence of stillbirths and of deformed children was observed.

55   In order to establish the effect of radioactive radiation on posterity, comparative studies have been made between the descendants of doctors who have been using X-ray apparatus over a period of years and descendants of doctors who have not. The material of this study comprises about 3,000 doctors in each group. A noticeable difference was found. Among the descendants of radiologists a percentage of stillbirths of 1.403 was found, while the percentage among the non-radiologists were 1.222.

56   In the first group 6.01 per cent of the children had congenital defects, while only 4.82 per cent in the second.

57   The number of healthy children in the first group was 80.42 per cent; the number in the other was significantly higher, viz. 83.23 per cent.

58   It must be remembered that even the weakest of internal radiation can have harmful effects on our descendants.

59   The total effect of the damage done to descendants of ancestors who have been exposed to radioactive rays will not, in accordance with the laws of genetics, be apparent in the generations coming immediately after us. The full effects will appear only 100 or 200 years later.

60   As the matter stands we cannot at present cite cases of serious damage done by internal radiation. To the extent that such radiation exists it is not sufficiently strong and has not lasted long enough to have caused the damage in question. We can only conclude from the harmful effects known to be caused by external radiation to those we must expect in the future from internal radiation.

61   If the effect of the latter is not as strong as that of the former, it may

become so, through working little by little and without interruption. The final result will be the same in both cases.

62 Their effects add up.

63 We must also remember that internal radiation does not have to, in contrast to that coming from the outside, penetrate layers of skin, tissues, and muscles to hit the organs. It works at close range and without any weakening of its force.

64 When we realize under what conditions the internal radiation is working, we cease to underrate it. Even if it is true that, when speaking of the dangers of internal radiation, we can point to no actual case, only express our fear, that fear is so solidly founded on facts that it attains the weight of reality in determining our attitude. We are forced to regard every increase in the existing danger through further creation of radioactive elements by atom bomb explosions as a catastrophe for the human race, a catastrophe that must be prevented.

65 There can be no question of doing anything else, if only for the reason that we cannot take the responsibility for the consequences it might have for our descendants.

66 They are threatened by the greatest and most terrible danger.

67 That radioactive elements created by us are found in nature is an astounding event in the history of the earth and of the human race. To fail to consider its importance and its consequences would be a folly for which humanity would have to pay a terrible price. We are committing a folly in thoughtlessness. It must not happen that we do not pull ourselves together before it is too late. We must muster the insight, the seriousness, and the courage to leave folly and to face reality.

68 This is at bottom what the statesmen of the nations producing atomic bombs are thinking, too. Through the reports they are receiving they are sufficiently informed to form their own judgments, and we must also assume that they are alive to their responsibility.

69 At any rate, America and Soviet Russia and Britain are telling one another again and again that they want nothing more than to reach an agreement to end the testing of atomic weapons. At the same time, however, they declare that they cannot stop the tests as long as there is no such agreement.

70 Why do they not come to an agreement? The real reason is that in their own countries there is no public opinion asking for it. Nor is there any such public opinion in other countries, with the exception of Japan. This opinion has been forced upon the Japanese people because, little by little, they will be hit in a most terrible way by the evil consequences of all the tests.

71 An agreement of this kind presupposes reliability and trust. There must be guarantees preventing the agreement from being signed by anyone intending to win important tactical advantages foreseen only by him.

72 Public opinion in all nations concerned must inspire and accept the agreement.

73 When public opinion has been created in the countries concerned and

among all nations, an opinion informed of the dangers involved in going on with the tests and led by the reason which this information imposes, then the statesmen may reach an agreement to stop the experiments.

74 A public opinion of this kind stands in no need of plebiscites or of forming of committees to express itself. It works through just being there.

75 The end of further experiments with atom bombs would be like the early sunrays of hope which suffering humanity is longing for.

Commentary and questions

1. *Paragraphs 1-6:* These are general and introductory. Schweitzer's statements are comparatively objective and unemotional, but they bring in the main issues to be covered in the body of the essay: the "harmful" effects of radiation. Does Schweitzer in any way anticipate his conclusions here? Does he appeal emotionally to his audience in any way?

2. *Paragraphs 7-16:* This section is in reality a definition, beginning as it does with the question, "What is radioactivity?" But the definition involves a broad coverage of scientific fact. Why does Schweitzer take so many pains with background information at this time? How much of what he says can be assumed to be familiar to an educated audience?

Schweitzer lists both the advantages and disadvantages of radiation. Does he place any special emphasis on one or the other? What words or statements in this section help him to continue the thread of his argument as it is outlined in the first six paragraphs?

3. *Paragraphs 17-43:* These go on to deal with the harmful effects of radiation in considerable detail and ought to be compared with the other authors' handling of the same topic, after all the essays have been read. In the meantime, it will be useful to make a concise statement of what Schweitzer means by the phrases "dangerous" and "harmful." He lists effects that may occur. Does he adequately cover the area of definition necessary for these terms in this context? Examine the following statements: "Strontium-90 takes the first place"; "Cobalt 60 must also be mentioned as particularly dangerous" (paragraph 32); "small children run an especially dangerous risk of absorbing radioactive elements" (paragraph 38). In their context are these statements given explicit meaning? Are they merely sober, objective statements of fact or does Schweitzer use them for emotional appeal as well?

4. *Paragraph 41:* Study the phrase "has fallen down, is falling down, and will fall down." Does this represent any change in the tone of Schweitzer's style?

5. *Paragraphs 42-62:* These carry still further the detailed study of the harmful effects of fallout. It is clear by this time that one of Schweitzer's strategies is to move steadily from general to increasingly particular statements. Does he "let the facts speak for themselves" or does he use additional means to direct the reader's response to the "facts"?

6. *Paragraph 61:* What is the purpose of repeating previous statements here?

7. *Paragraph 66:* Is there any purpose behind the brevity here? Does it represent any change in tone or style?

8. *Paragraphs 68-75:* Here Schweitzer deals with the wider political and social implications of the problem of fallout and forsees a solution in the exercise of public opinion. How convincing is this conclusion? Has it been prepared for? How may the style of Schweitzer's conclusion be described?

Topics for discussion and writing

I. Outline Schweitzer's essay in the following ways: (a) Reduce each paragraph to one sentence (in some cases one sentence may serve for more than one paragraph); (b) summarize in one paragraph Schweitzer's main thesis; (c) separate the elements of the essay into the following categories — hypotheses, types of evidence, inferences and conclusions based on the evidence, unsupported assertions. Rank each item in these categories according to its relative importance.

II. Write a short theme outlining and discussing Schweitzer's use of the word "dangerous" (or "harmful").

III. Discuss Schweitzer's persuasive techniques: use of metaphor, connotative or suggestive language, changes in tone, the climactic presentation of evidence.

IV. Why does Schweitzer call the piece "A Declaration of Conscience"? The reaction to this declaration indicated many people felt Schweitzer had brought moral forces to bear on the problem. Write an essay explaining what Schweitzer's underlying moral assumptions are and how they are conveyed to the reader.

AN OPEN LETTER TO DR. SCHWEITZER

Willard F. Libby

From Saturday Review, *Vol. 40* (*May 25, 1957*). *Reprinted by permission of* Saturday Review *and the author.*

To Dr. Albert Schweitzer,
Lambarene Hospital,
Lambarene, Gabon,
French Equatorial Africa

Washington, D.C.
April 25, 1957

Dear Dr. Schweitzer:

1   I am writing you as a scientist, to present data bearing on a scientific fact: The degree of hazard to humanity from radioactive fallout from nuclear weapons tests.

2   In the press on April 24, I read your statement from Oslo on the hazards of nuclear weapons testing, and in this way learned of your fears that the present testing program may be dangerous. Since I have spent much time during the past several years in the study of this question, I am taking the liberty of writing you. Also, since your statement was issued to news media and received wide public attention, I am making this letter public in the belief that every possible action should be taken to increase public understanding on the important question of weapons testing.

3   Your belief in the sanctity of life, and the dedication with which you have devoted your own life and talents to unselfish causes, have made a deep impression on the minds of persons throughout the world. Your concern over the possible effects of nuclear tests is characteristic of the humane and sensitive qualities which you always have displayed, and for which you are justly honored. Along with these qualities, I know you have the intellectual strength and integrity to seek the truth wherever it lies. It is in this spirit that I write you, believing that you will welcome whatever facts I may be able to provide regarding radioactive fallout from weapons testing.

4   I do not know what data you have utilized in studying this question, but I seriously doubt, from the evidence of your statement, that you have had access to the most recent information. Immediately after reading your statement I sent you a copy of a speech which I gave recently regarding what we know from scientific studies on fallout radiation and its effects. I am enclosing with this letter a copy of a paper which I am presenting on April 26 before the American Physical Society. I hope these documents will be of use to you. They demonstrate that an intensive effort has been made to calculate on theoretical grounds, and to determine from sample collections, the actual levels of radioactivity in the soil, in water, in food products, and in human bodies as a result of weapons tests.

5   If you have gained the impression that United States official statements do not take into account the possible hazard from internal radiation — and I fear from your statement that you have — I hasten to assure you that this is not the case. Government statements have dealt extensively with this matter. It has likewise been considered at length in a report prepared by scores of eminent scientists for the National Academy of Sciences, and in England by the British Medical Research Council, both reports appearing in June of last year.

6   Particularly since the summer of 1953 the Atomic Energy Commission has conducted an intensive study of world-wide fallout which has revealed most of the information now available on this subject. These studies have included analysis of soil, plants, foods, and other materials from many parts of the world. The United States Government has furnished this information without reserve to the United Nations Scientific Committee on Atomic Radiation, which was established at the recommendation of the United States and which has studied data provided by other countries.

7 Although there are some differences in findings of scientists in this country and abroad, there is general agreement upon the approximate magnitude of the fallout and the rate at which it is descending from the stratosphere. Perhaps there is less agreement about the magnitude of the physiological effects which can be expected to result from fallout radiation. Nevertheless, it is very generally agreed, among those who have studied the question, that the radiation exposures from fallout are very much smaller than those which would be required to produce observable effects in the population. The U.S. Government agencies have been continuously concerned with maintaining this condition of very small test radiation and have never neglected study and action to reduce it.

8 I do not mean to say that there is no risk at all. What I should like to demonstrate to you is that the risk is extremely small compared with other risks which persons everywhere take as a normal part of their lives. At the same time, I ask you to weigh this risk against what I believe would be the far greater risk — to freedom-loving people everywhere in the world — of not maintaining our defenses against the totalitarian forces at large in the world until such time as safeguarded disarmament may be achieved. Of course, a workable, safeguarded system of international disarmament is a paramount objective of the United States Government, and one which we must work for and hope and pray will be achieved.

9 To go into more detail on the question of risk from world-wide radioactive fallout, there are two possible hazards. The first is the genetic hazard due to radiation of the reproductive organs by penetrating gamma radiation, and the second is the hazard due to the irradiation of the bones by assimilated strontium-90, taken up largely through food. These two possible hazards should not be confused; there is no reason to fear genetic hazard from strontium-90, since it accumulates in the bones and does not appreciably irradiate the reproductive organs.

10 In order to understand the degree of these hazards, it is necessary to compare the amount of radiation dosage received from fallout with the amount of radiation dosage normally received by all living things because of the natural radioactivity in the environment. In this way, it is possible to put the hazards from weapons testing into the context of normal human experience.

11 When this kind of comparison is made, it becomes apparent that we all carry in our bodies, and have in our surroundings, amounts of radioactivity very much larger than those derived from radioactive fallout.

12 Cosmic rays, which come from outer space, have their radiation effect progressively diluted as they pass through the atmosphere. Thus, a person living at an altitude of about one mile above sea level receives a dosage of cosmic rays approaching double that of a person who lives at sea level. There are other variations in the natural "background" dosages. For example, people living in certain localities of uranium or thorium mineralization will receive much more radiation than the average, and their ancestors have received these much higher doses over centuries in many parts of the world. Living in a brick house, rather than in a wooden house, will, with certain kinds of bricks in certain parts of the world, increase radiation exposure many times over that from test fallout.

13 The additional radiation dosages which persons receive from fallout are small compared to these natural dosages and even the variations in the natural dosages. To be specific, the dosage to new bone as in children which results from strontium-90 at present is about the same as the additional dosage which a resident at sea level would receive from cosmic rays if he moved from a beach to the top of a hill a few hundred feet high.

14 There is no question that excessive dosages of radioactive strontium can cause bone cancer and leukemia in animals, so we should not casually dismiss the possibility of harmful results from test fallout. However, keeping in mind that populations are exposed to natural radiations considerably greater than the fallout dosages, we can attempt to determine whether these have caused any detectable effects. We can examine, for example, whether there is any obvious increase in the rate of occurrence of bone cancer and leukemia in populations living at higher altitudes or in regions of uranium mineralization, etc.

15 Examination of available records does not disclose any such effects. However, vital statistics have not always been carefully kept, and further studies are being carried on under the egis of the United Nations Committee to determine whether any such effects can be detected. One fact is apparent, however — it certainly is not our normal experience that people can appreciably increase the occurrence of these dread diseases by moving to a higher altitude or by moving from a sedimentary soil, where the uranium content is low, to an igneous or granitic surface, where the uranium content is very much higher, or by moving from a wooden to a brick or concrete house.

16 Another way of evaluating the possible risk from strontium-90 in fallout is through comparison with the permissible concentration of strontium-90 recommended by authoritative groups. The permissive amount of strontium-90 for atomic energy workers in the United States is about 2,000 times the present strontium-90 content of new bone in the United States resulting from fallout. (Strontium-90 concentrations in the rest of the world are generally lower than those in the United States.) Authoritative groups have recommended that, on grounds of general prudence, the permissible limit for whole populations be one-tenth of that for atomic energy workers.

17 On this basis, the present level for new bone, that is, in children, in the United States is somewhat less than 1 per cent of the maximum permissible concentration for the population.

18 Perhaps a word of explanation should be given regarding these maximum permissible concentrations. As you know, scientists do not speak of "risks" or "hazards" in the sense that the words ordinarily are used. They try

to measure possibilities almost to the limits of the finite; therefore, "risk" includes the possibility of effects far beyond the range of the probable or detectable. The maximum permissible concentrations are not safety limits; rather, they indicate that at considerably large concentrations, perhaps tenfold greater, there would be definitely detectable effects.

19   So far, I have been discussing principally the possible risks from radioactive strontium. Radioactive fallout includes other materials which do not accumulate inside the body, but do emit penetrating radiation which can irradiate the sex organs and other parts of the whole body from the outside. Such radiations can produce genetic mutations.

20   Again, in evaluating the possibility of genetic effects from fallout, we should try to compare it with normal experience. The external dosages from fallout, that is, those which might cause genetic effects, have averaged between one- and five-thousandths of one roentgen per year in the United States during the last three or four years. This figure should be compared with a normal dosage of 150 thousandths of one roentgen per year from cosmic rays and natural radioactive materials in the environment. In other words, the external fallout radiation has been from 0.7 per cent to about 3 per cent of the natural radiation exposure.

21   As another example, in certain countries of the world a brick house might easily have enough natural radioactive material in the walls to give up to 40 thousandths of a roentgen more exposure per year than a wooden house and a concrete block house gives about 100 thousandths of a roentgen more annually. These dosages range between eight and 100 times the dosage due to test fallout.

22   Obviously, the genetic effect of fallout radiation must be very small compared with the genetic effect of natural radiation.

23   As you pointed out in your statement, radioactivity from tests which already have been held is present in the stratosphere, from which it will descend for years to come. The radioactivity of this material constantly is decreasing through normal radioactive decay. The tiny radioactive particles fall so slowly from the stratosphere that the continuing fallout in the United States just about compensates for the radioactive decay of the radiostrontium already deposited. Therefore, the present level of radiostrontium in the soil is about as much as we shall ever have from tests already fired.

24   Continued testing would not increase radioactivity on a straight additive basis, since an equilibrium would be established between the added radioactivity and radioactive decay. If tests were to continue until 1983 at the rate of the past five years, levels in the United States would be expected to reach about four times their present values. Levels about six times the present ones would be reached by the year 2011 if testing were to continue for that long a time.

25   I hope that I have provided enough information to demonstrate that the risk from nuclear testing at the present rate is small. Of course, a great

amount of more detailed information is available, and I shall be glad to
supply it to you if you wish. No scientist contends that there is no risk. We
accept risk as payment for our pleasures, our comforts, and our material
progress. Here the choice seems much clearer — the terrible risk of abandoning the defense effort which is so essential under present conditions to
the survival of the free world against the small controlled risk from weapons
testing.

Sincerely yours,

W. F. Libby

WHAT IS A "SMALL" RISK?   Harrison Brown

From Saturday Review, *Vol. 40*
(*May 25, 1957*). *Reprinted by
permission of* Saturday Review
and the author.

THE Atomic Energy Commission is convinced that continued testing of H-
bombs is necessary for the defense of the United States. Upon Dr. Willard
Libby's shoulders has fallen the task of assuring the world that continued
testing is safe. It has been next to impossible for anyone of any consequence
to voice doubts or fears concerning radiation hazards and H-bomb testing
without a new letter or article from Dr. Libby quickly appearing, assuring
the reader in carefully worded sentences that everything will be all right.
Dr. Schweitzer is the latest addition to a long list of distinguished individuals who have received such reassurance.

2   Dr. Libby's reassurances seem to make sense. He appears to approach
the problem objectively. He outlines in simple terms the basic aspects of the
problem and the numbers which emerge all seem to be small. His writing
expresses both surprise and the deepest of sorrow when individuals refer to
the dangers involved in H-bomb testing. He is a reputable and competent
scientist who holds a position of respect and authority and who is listened
to.

³   For a long time Dr. Libby contended that there were no dangers of any
consequence involved in H-bomb fallout, if we continued testing at the
present rate. Recently, however, there has been a change of tone. In his
letter to Dr. Schweitzer he admits that there is some risk, although he hastily
adds that the risk is "extremely small compared with other risks which persons everywhere take as a normal part of their lives." He then asks Dr.
Schweitzer to "weigh this risk against what I believe would be the far greater
risk — to freedom-loving people everywhere in the world — of not maintaining our defenses against the totalitarian forces at large in the world. . . ."

4   Dr. Libby's letter to Dr. Schweitzer begs at least two major questions.

Do we really know what the risks are in sufficient detail so that we can be as confident as Dr. Libby appears to be? And what does he mean when he says that the risk is "extremely small?"

5   It seems to me that from the beginning Dr. Libby has been so convinced that H-bomb tests must be continued *a priori* he has taken the attitude that the risks are small, even though he has rather clearly not known in detail what those risks are. This attitude, of assuming that the risks are small and then setting out to prove it, seems to me to be the foundation for the approach of the AEC to the entire fallout problem. It is illustrated by an incident which took place when Dr. Libby, upon hearing of my own concern about the fallout problem, asked me to come to Washington to discuss the matter with him. Upon my arrival in his office he leaned back in his chair and said (as nearly as I can remember): "All right, convince me that it's dangerous." I replied that in view of the nature of the problem it would be far more appropriate if he were to convince me that fallout is safe.

6   So marked has this conditioning been that a really serious danger involving fallout was overlooked by Dr. Libby, who has scores of scientists working on the problems of fallout. This danger was uncovered by a lone geneticist, Professor E. B. Lewis of the California Institute of Technology, who found that the incidence of leukemia is increased with exposure to low-dosage radiation. If Lewis's results are correct then it appears that the incidence of leukemia will almost certainly be increased appreciably as a result of H-bomb tests.

7   Briefly, Dr. Lewis, whose study appears this week in *Science,* has found that a substantial fraction of the leukemia which we see about us is induced by the natural radiation which our bodies constantly receive from a diversity of sources and from which we cannot hide — cosmic rays, radioactive elements in rocks, bricks and concrete, radioactive gas in the atmosphere, radioactivity in our bones. He estimates that perhaps 20 per cent of all leukemia cases are produced in this way and that there is no "threshold" of radiation dosage below which leukemia does not appear. Each small bit of radiation which an individual receives increases by a calculable amount the likelihood of his dying of this dread and incurable disease.

8   Let us now estimate, on the basis of this finding, the possible effect of fallout upon the world-wide incidence of leukemia. Dr. Libby has stated that the present concentration of strontium-90 in children in the United States is "somewhat less than 1 per cent of the maximum permissible concentration for the population." The latter in turn is one-tenth the permissible amount of strontium-90 for atomic energy workers in the United States. If we assume that 20 per cent of all existing leukemia has been induced by radiation, then it can be shown that in the absence of further explosions, the leukemia rate will go up about 0.1 per cent. If testing continues at the present rate for the next few decades, the leukemia rate may increase by about 0.5 per cent. If we were to permit tests at a rate such that doses of strontium-90 were re-

ceived equal to that which have been declared "safe" for the population as a whole by a committee of the National Academy of Sciences, leukemia incidence might increase 10 per cent.

9   A person who subscribes to the AEC philosophy might phrase the effects of continued testing upon the incidence of leukemia as follows: "This effect is so small that it cannot be detected with certainty in death statistics. Clearly the risk is far less than most other risks which we face as payment for our pleasures, our comfort, or our material progress." Many of us, however, might prefer to phrase the consequences in other terms: "Continued testing at the present rate may well result in the death each year from leukemia of nearly 10,000 persons who would not otherwise have died."

10   Here we come to the root of the argument concerning H-bomb fallout. What constitutes a large risk? When we say that the leukemia rate is increased by only 0.5 per cent, the number appears small. But when we say that 10,000 *individuals* are killed each year — individuals of all nationalities who work, love, and laugh and who want to live as much as do you and I — the number suddenly seems very large. But we can seldom point to a particular death and say "that death was caused by fallout." In the very nature of fallout, living people are transformed into statistics. Seldom can we say that so-and-so was killed by radiation. Instead we must say that there is a 10 per cent probability that he was killed in this way.

11   We would not dream of lining thousands of people against a wall and shooting them down in order to test a new machine gun. But this, in effect, is what the U.S., the U.S.S.R., and the U.K. do when they test these fantastic new weapons. We do not know *who* the people are who are afflicted, but we know that with little question many people are killed as a result of these actions.

12   I would like to stress that leukemia is but a single manifestation of danger caused by low-dosage radiation. Are there others? We don't know, but it would be surprising if there were not. And if there are it seems unlikely that the AEC will discover them if they continue to operate within the framework of their present philosophy.

13   I believe that in this area we must be guided as much by our ignorance as by our knowledge. There is much yet to be learned concerning both the immediate and long-range effects of radiation fallout. And I cannot help feeling that as the testing nations follow their present path, as their actions result indiscriminately in the deaths of persons all over the world, and as they continue to pursue an elusive security, they lose what is perhaps the most important element of true security — their human dignity.

Commentary and questions

An Open Letter to Dr. Schweitzer

1. Why is the letter "open"? Does this suggest anything about Libby's purpose in writing?

2. *Paragraph 1:* What is the effect of the statement "I am writing you as a scientist"?

3. *Paragraph 3:* Why does Libby take pains to pay tribute to Schweitzer? What is implied in the statement "you will welcome whatever facts I may be able to provide"?

4. *Paragraph 4:* What are the implications here? What weakness in Schweitzer's essay does "actual levels of radioactivity" imply?

5. *Paragraph 7:* Examine the statement "It is very generally agreed . . . that the radiation exposures from fallout are very much smaller than those which would be required to produce observable effects in the population." Notice the qualifications in the statement. How may they be interpreted? What inferences does Libby want the reader to draw from his statement? Can any other inferences be drawn?

6. *Paragraph 8:* Libby suggests that the risk from fallout is "small" compared to those we take every day. See Harrison Brown's restatement of Libby's last paragraph (paragraph 9 above). Is Brown's rephrasing fair to the original statement?

7. *Paragraph 9:* Does Libby produce any evidence for the statement that there is "no reason to fear genetic hazard from strontium-90"?

8. *Paragraph 10:* What are the connotations of the phrase "natural" radioactivity? How close to Libby's main argumentative strategy is the topic of "natural" radiation?

9. *Paragraphs 13-15:* How much of the argument is negative?

10. *Paragraph 16:* What is the effect of the phrase "authoritative groups"?

What is a "Small" Risk?

11. *Paragraphs 1-2:* Why does Brown begin by attacking Libby rather than his arguments? Why does he neglect to add supporting detail to his attack?

12. *Paragraph 4:* Brown states that Libby "begs at least two major questions." Does Brown's judgment of what constitutes the major issues in the dispute over fallout expose the heart of the issue? Does Libby beg the questions?

13. *Paragraph 5:* Brown extends his attack on Libby, questioning his logic and trying to shift the burden of proof. How does this strategy depend upon definition? Is there a third alternative to the question of which writer ought to offer the proof?

14. *Paragraph 6:* How does Brown make Libby responsible for failing to disclose the discoveries of E. B. Lewis? Is there an adequate way of explaining this situation without blaming Libby?

15. *Paragraphs 7-9:* Do Brown's facts about leukemia make the discussion of what constitutes risk or danger more precise?

16. *Paragraph 10:* Brown tries to illuminate the question of "what constitutes a large risk." What factors does he suggest govern our estimate of the degree of risk? Are statistics alone any help in this estimate? Which kind of figure does Brown prefer to use? Notice Brown's language in this paragraph. Does it suggest a subjective or objective approach to the problem of risk?

17. *Paragraph 11:* Is the machine gun analogy valid?

18. *Paragraph 12:* Brown uses leukemia as an example of the kind of danger we might expect from fallout. Is this one example enough to make a convincing point? Why has Brown chosen leukemia in preference to some other disease?

Topics for discussion and writing

An Open Letter to Dr. Schweitzer

I. Write a theme comparing Libby's understanding of "risk" with Schweitzer's use of "dangerous." Why does Libby use "risk" predominantly? Is there any essential difference in the two terms?

II. Make an outline of Libby's essay. How would you describe his strategy?

III. Discuss the tone of Libby's argument. Is tonal suggestion more important than inductive reasoning in the essay? How precise is Libby's factual information compared to the other three writers?

IV. Write a theme comparing the essays by Schweitzer and Libby in their use of uncolored words and emotive words.

V. Write a theme showing exactly how Schweitzer erred according to Libby.

What is a "Small" Risk?

VI. Brown's criticism of Libby's letter uses the issue of definition as its central strategy. Does Brown adequately define "risk" or is he as imprecise as he accuses Libby of being? What is the basis for Brown's understanding of the meaningful value of "risk"?

VII. Trace the connotations Brown attaches to the key words in his essay. Do they constitute a pattern?

VIII. Write a theme comparing Libby and Brown for the comprehensiveness with which each handles the problem of fallout. How much do they focus on single, concentrated points? How do they compare with Schweitzer in the breadth and thoroughness of their treatments?

IX. What points that Libby makes does Brown ignore?

X. Take one point that Schweitzer, Libby, and Brown all cover ("risk," for example) and write a theme listing their differences in definition, treatment, and opinion.

The concurrent majority: THE CONCURRENT MAJORITY,
John C. Calhoun · JOHN C. CALHOUN — REALIST, Vernon L. Parrington ·
UNWRITTEN RULES OF AMERICAN POLITICS, John Fischer

Two crucial problems that must be faced in school and out
of school are understanding another man's ideas and applying them to a
new situation. Here the man with the ideas is John C. Calhoun, and the
first purpose is to grasp what he means by the concurrent majority. The
second essay tries to do more. Vernon L. Parrington is a historian of ideas,
and he moves from what Calhoun says to an interpretation of his motives.
He also passes judgment on Calhoun's thinking, and here it might be well
to say that Parrington is a follower of Jefferson, not Calhoun. The third
writer, John Fischer, is just as concerned to understand Calhoun, but he
regards this as simply a preliminary. His main purpose is to apply the principle of the concurrent majority to an explanation of the workings of modern
American politics. Both Parrington and Fischer make use of other Calhoun
material as well as his *A Disquisition on Government,* from which the following selection was taken.

The styles of these three men contrast notably. Calhoun's reasoned
prose offers abstract statements without specific examples. It is his province
to inform, not amuse. Fischer, in a style and manner popular in our own
time, is almost at the other extreme. He convinces in terms of specific examples. Diction, comment, and selected details add an urbane lightness to
an article which has a serious purpose. Parrington, writing a history of
American thought, must write compactly. He depends, then, as much upon
assertion and impression as upon marshaled facts and examples. The demand
to say much in a short space invites, if it does not require, persuasive as well
as informative language.

415

THE CONCURRENT MAJORITY   John C. Calhoun

From A Disquisition on Government, *first published in 1854.*

How government, then, must be constructed, in order to counteract, through its organism, this tendency on the part of those who make and execute the laws to oppress those subject to their operation, is the next question which claims attention.

2   There is but one way in which this can possibly be done; and that is, by such an organism as will furnish the ruled with the means of resisting successfully this tendency on the part of the rulers to oppression and abuse. Power can only be resisted by power, — and tendency by tendency. Those who exercise power and those subject to its exercise, — the rulers and the ruled, — stand in antagonistic relations to each other. The same constitution of our nature which leads rulers to oppress the ruled, — regardless of the object for which government is ordained, — will, with equal strength, lead the ruled to resist, when possessed of the means of making peaceable and effective resistance. Such an organism, then, as will furnish the means by which resistance may be systematically and peaceably made on the part of the ruled, to oppression and abuse of power on the part of the rulers, is the first and indispensable step toward *forming* a constitutional government. And as this can only be effected by or through the right of suffrage, — (the right on the part of the ruled to choose their rulers at proper intervals, and to hold them thereby responsible for their conduct), — the responsibility of the rulers to the ruled, through the right of suffrage, is the indispensable and primary principle in the *foundation* of a constitutional government. When this right is properly guarded, and the people sufficiently enlightened to understand their own rights and the interests of the community, and duly to appreciate the motives and conduct of those appointed to make and execute the laws, it is all-sufficient to give to those who elect, effective control over those they have elected.

3   I call the right of suffrage the indispensable and primary principle; for it would be a great and dangerous mistake to suppose, as many do, that it is, of itself, sufficient to form constitutional governments. To this erroneous opinion may be traced one of the causes why so few attempts to form constitutional governments have succeeded; and why, of the few which have, so small a number have had durable existence. It has led, not only to mistakes in the attempts to form such governments, but to their overthrow, when they have, by some good fortune, been correctly formed. So far from being, of itself, sufficient, — however well guarded it might be, and however enlightened the people, — it would, unaided by other provisions, leave the government as absolute, as it would be in the hands of irresponsible rulers; and with a tendency, at least as strong, toward oppression and abuse of its power; as I shall next proceed to explain.

4   The right of suffrage, of itself, can do no more than give complete con-

trol to those who elect over the conduct of those they have elected. In doing this, it accomplishes all it possibly can accomplish. This is its aim, — and when this is attained, its end is fulfilled. It can do no more, however enlightened the people, or however extended or well guarded the right may be. The sum total, then, of its effects, when most successful, is to make those elected, the true and faithful representatives of those who elected them, — instead of irresponsible rulers, as they would be without it; and thus, by converting it into an agency, and the rulers into agents, to divest government of all claims to sovereignty, and to retain it unimpaired to the community. But it is manifest that the right of suffrage, in making these changes, transfers, in reality, the actual control over the government from those who make and execute the laws, to the body of the community; and, thereby, places the powers of the government as fully in the mass of the community as they would be if they, in fact, had assembled, made, and executed the laws themselves, without the intervention of representatives or agents. . . .

5   If the whole community had the same interests, so that the interests of each and every portion would be so affected by the action of the government, that the laws which oppressed or impoverished one portion, would necessarily oppress and impoverish all others, — or the reverse, — then the right of suffrage, of itself, would be all-sufficient to counteract the tendency of the government to oppression and abuse of its powers; and, of course, would form, of itself, a perfect constitutional government. . . .

6   But such is not the case. On the contrary, nothing is more difficult than to equalize the action of the government, in reference to the various and diversified interests of the community; and nothing more easy than to pervert its powers into instruments to aggrandize and enrich one or more interests by oppressing and impoverishing the others; and this too, under the operation of laws couched in general terms; — and which, on their face, appear fair and equal. Nor is this the case in some particular communities only. It is so in all; the small and the great, — the poor and the rich, — irrespective of pursuits, productions, or degrees of civilization; — with, however, this difference, that the more extensive and populous the country, the more diversified the condition and pursuits of its population, and the richer, more luxurious, and dissimilar the people, the more difficult is it to equalize the action of the government, — and the more easy for one portion of the community to pervert its powers to oppress and plunder the other.

7   Such being the case, it necessarily results, that the right of suffrage, by placing the control of the government in the community must, from the same constitution of our nature which makes government necessary to preserve society, lead to conflict among its different interests, — each striving to obtain possession of its powers, as the means of protecting itself against the others; — or of advancing its respective interests, regardless of the interests of others. For this purpose, a struggle will take place between the various interests to obtain a majority, in order to control the government. If no one

interest be strong enough, of itself, to obtain it, a combination will be formed between those whose interests are most alike; — each conceding something to the others, until a sufficient number is obtained to make a majority. The process may be slow, and much time may be required before a compact, organized majority can be thus formed; but formed it will be in time, even without preconcert or design, by the sure workings of that principle or constitution of our nature in which government itself originates. When once formed, the community will be divided into two great parties, — a major and minor, — between which there will be incessant struggles on the one side to retain, and on the other to obtain the majority and, thereby, the control of the government and the advantages it confers. . . .

8   As, then, the right of suffrage, without some other provision, cannot counteract this tendency of government, the next question for consideration is — What is that other provision? This demands the most serious consideration; for of all the questions embraced in the science of government, it involves a principle, the most important and the least understood; and when understood, the most difficult of application in practice. It is, indeed, emphatically, that principle which *makes* the constitution, in its strict and limited sense.

9   From what has been said, it is manifest, that this provision must be of a character calculated to prevent any one interest, or combination of interests, from using the powers of government to aggrandize itself at the expense of the others. Here lies the evil: and just in proportion as it shall prevent, or fail to prevent it, in the same degree it will effect, or fail to effect the end intended to be accomplished. There is but one certain mode in which this result can be secured; and that is, by the adoption of some restriction or limitation, which shall so effectually prevent any one interest, or combination of interests, from obtaining the exclusive control of the government, as to render hopeless all attempts directed to that end. There is, again, but one mode in which this can be effected; and that is, by taking the sense of each interest or portion of the community, which may be unequally and injuriously affected by the action of the government, separately, through its own majority, or in some other way by which its voice may be fairly expressed; and to require the consent of each interest, either to put or to keep the government in action. This, too, can be accomplished only in one way, — and that is, by such an organism of the government, — and, if necessary for the purpose, of the community also, — as will, by dividing and distributing the powers of government, give to each division or interest, through its appropriate organ, either a concurrent voice in making and executing the laws, or a veto on their execution. It is only by such an organism, that the assent of each can be made necessary to put the government in motion; or the power made effectual to arrest its action, when put in motion; — and it is only by the one or the other that the different interests, orders, classes, or portions, into which the community may be divided, can be protected, and all conflict

and struggle between them prevented, — by rendering it impossible to put or to keep it in action, without the concurrent consent of all. . . .

10   It results, from what has been said, that there are two different modes in which the sense of the community may be taken; one, simply by the right of suffrage, unaided; the other, by the right through a proper organism. Each collects the sense of the majority. But one regards numbers only, and considers the whole community as a unit, having but one common interest throughout; and collects the sense of the greater number of the whole, as that of the community. The other, on the contrary, regards interests as well as numbers; — considering the community as made up of different and conflicting interests, as far as the action of the government is concerned; and takes the sense of each, through its majority or appropriate organ, and the united sense of all, as the sense of the entire community. The former of these I shall call the numerical, or absolute majority; and the latter, the concurrent, or constitutional majority. I call it the constitutional majority, because it is an essential element in every constitutional government, — be its form what it may. So great is the difference, politically speaking, between the two majorities, that they cannot be confounded, without leading to great and fatal errors; and yet the distinction between them has been so entirely overlooked, that when the term *majority* is used in political discussions, it is applied exclusively to designate the numerical, — as if there were no other. . . .

11   The first and leading error which naturally arises from overlooking the distinction referred to, is, to confound the numerical majority with the people; and this so completely as to regard them as identical. This is a consequence that necessarily results from considering the numerical as the only majority. All admit, that a popular government, or democracy, is the government of the people; for the terms imply this. A perfect government of the kind would be one which would embrace the consent of every citizen or member of the community; but as this is impracticable, in the opinion of those who regard the numerical as the only majority, and who can perceive no other way by which the sense of the people can be taken, — they are compelled to adopt this as the only true basis of popular government, in contradistinction to governments of the aristocratical or monarchical form. Being thus constrained, they are, in the next place, forced to regard the numerical majority, as, in effect, the entire people; that is, the greater part as the whole; and the government of the greater part as the government of the whole. It is thus the two come to be confounded, and a part made identical with the whole. And it is thus, also, that all the rights, powers, and immunities of the whole people come to be attributed to the numerical majority; and, among others, the supreme, sovereign authority of establishing and abolishing governments at pleasure.

12   This radical error, the consequence of confounding the two, and of regarding the numerical as the only majority, has contributed more than any other cause, to prevent the formation of popular constitutional governments,

— and to destroy them even when they have been formed. It leads to the conclusion that, in their formation and establishment, nothing more is necessary than the right of suffrage, — and the allotment to each division of the community a representation in the government, in proportion to numbers. If the numerical majority were really the people; and if, to take its sense truly, were to take the sense of the people truly, a government so constituted would be a true and perfect model of a popular constitutional government; and every departure from it would detract from its excellence. But as such is not the case, — as the numerical majority, instead of being the people, is only a portion of them, — such a government, instead of being a true and perfect model of the people's government, that is, a people self-governed, is but the government of a part, over a part, — the major over the minor portion. . . .

13   I shall next proceed to explain, more fully, why the concurrent majority is an indispensable element in forming constitutional governments; and why the numerical majority, of itself, must, in all cases, make governments absolute.

14   The necessary consequence of taking the sense of the community by the concurrent majority is, as has been explained, to give to each interest or portion of the community a negative on the others. It is this mutual negative among its various conflicting interests, which invests each with the power of protecting itself; — and places the rights and safety of each, where only they can be securely placed, under its own guardianship. Without this there can be no systematic, peaceful, or effective resistance to the natural tendency of each to come into conflict with the others: and without this there can be no constitution. It is this negative power, — the power of preventing or arresting the action of the government, — be it called by what term it may, — veto, interposition, nullification, check, or balance of power, — which, in fact, forms the constitution. They are all but different names for the negative power. In all its forms, and under all its names, it results from the concurrent majority. Without this there can be no negative; and, without a negative, no constitution. The assertion is true in reference to all constitutional governments, be their forms what they may. It is, indeed, the negative power which makes the constitution, and the positive which makes the government. The one is the power of acting; — and the other the power of preventing or arresting action. The two, combined, make constitutional governments.

15   But, as there can be no constitution without the negative power, and no negative power without the concurrent majority; — it follows, necessarily, that where the numerical majority has the sole control of the government, there can be no constitution; as constitution implies limitation or restriction, — and, of course, is inconsistent with the idea of sole or exclusive power. And hence, the numerical, unmixed with the concurrent majority, necessarily forms, in all cases, absolute government.

16   It is, indeed, the single, or *one power*, which excludes the negative, and constitutes absolute government; and not the *number* in whom the power is vested. The numerical majority is as truly a *single power*, and excludes the negative as completely as the absolute government of one, or of the few. The former is as much the absolute government of the democratic, or popular form, as the latter of the monarchical or aristocratical. It has, accordingly, in common with them, the same tendency to oppression and abuse of power.

17   Constitutional governments, of whatever form, are, indeed, much more similar to each other, in their structure and character, than they are, respectively, to the absolute governments, even of their own class. All constitutional governments, of whatever class they may be, take the sense of the community by its parts, — each through its appropriate organ; and regard the sense of all its parts, as the sense of the whole. They all rest on the right of suffrage, and the responsibility of rulers, directly or indirectly. On the contrary, all absolute governments, of whatever form, concentrate power in one uncontrolled and irresponsible individual or body, whose will is regarded as the sense of the community. And, hence, the great and broad distinction between governments is, — not that of the one, the few, or the many, — but of the constitutional and the absolute.

18   From this there results another distinction, which, although secondary in its character, very strongly marks the difference between these forms of government. I refer to their respective conservative principle; — that is, the principle by which they are upheld and preserved. This principle, in constitutional governments, is *compromise;* — and in absolute governments, is *force;* — as will be next explained.

19   It has been already shown, that the same constitution of man which leads those who govern to oppress the governed, — if not prevented, — will, with equal force and certainty, lead the latter to resist oppression, when possessed of the means of doing so peaceably and successfully. But absolute governments, of all forms, exclude all other means of resistance to their authority, than that of force; and, of course, leave no other alternative to the governed, but to acquiesce in oppression, however great it may be, or to resort to force to put down the government. But the dread of such a resort must necessarily lead the government to prepare to meet force in order to protect itself; and hence, of necessity, force becomes the conservative principle of all such governments.

20   On the contrary, the government of the concurrent majority, where the organism is perfect, excludes the possibility of oppression, by giving to each interest, or portion, or order, — where there are established classes, — the means of protecting itself, by its negative, against all measures calculated to advance the peculiar interests of others at its expense. Its effect, then, is, to cause the different interests, portions, or orders, — as the case may be, — to desist from attempting to adopt any measure calculated to promote the prosperity of one, or more, by sacrificing that of others; and thus to force them

to unite in such measures only as would promote the prosperity of all, as the only means to prevent the suspension of the action of the government; — and, thereby, to avoid anarchy, the greatest of all evils. It is by means of such authorized and effectual resistance, that oppression is prevented, and the necessity of resorting to force superseded, in governments of the concurrent majority; — and, hence, compromise, instead of force, becomes their conservative principle.

21   It would, perhaps, be more strictly correct to trace the conservative principle of constitutional governments to the necessity which compels the different interests, or portions, or orders, to compromise, — as the only way to promote their respective prosperity, and to avoid anarchy, — rather than to the compromise itself. No necessity can be more urgent and imperious, than that of avoiding anarchy. It is the same as that which makes government indispensable to preserve society; and is not less imperative than that which compels obedience to superior force. Traced to this source, the voice of a people, — uttered under the necessity of avoiding the greatest of calamities, through the organs of a government so constructed as to suppress the expression of all partial and selfish interests, and to give a full and faithful utterance to the sense of the whole community, in reference to its common welfare, — may, without impiety, be called *the voice of God*. To call any other so, would be impious. . . .

Commentary and questions

1. *Paragraph 1:* Calhoun states the problem before the solution. What is his assumption about all governments? Is this assumption fact or opinion?

2. *Paragraphs 2-4:* What assumption in the minds of his readers persuades Calhoun to deal at the outset with suffrage?

3. *Paragraphs 6-7:* Paragraph 7 develops logically out of paragraph 6. Is there any proof for the assertions of paragraph 6? Do these assertions require proof? Are they susceptible of proof? How could they be supported?

4. *Paragraph 9:* Follow its development by noting the successive deductions. The inevitability of the conclusion of this paragraph is dependent on there being "but one certain mode" for accomplishing each desired end. Can you break the logical structure of the thought?

5. *Paragraph 15:* Examine the syllogism. Are its terms properly supported in the earlier paragraph?

6. *Paragraph 18:* What does "conservative" mean?

7. *Paragraphs 18-21:* Is the opposition between "force" and "compromise" adequately explained and supported?

Topics for discussion and writing

I. Write a paper in which you state and defend from evidence in the essay the underlying assumptions that Calhoun holds about government.

II. Most modern writers avoid categorical assertions and broad statements. Discuss Calhoun's use of them in this essay and the effect Calhoun apparently expects them to produce.

III. Write a paper in which you analyze the chief kinds of paragraph structure used by Calhoun and show how it relates to his purpose and the argumentative structure of his essay.

IV. Write a paper explaining Calhoun's concept of constitutional government.

JOHN C. CALHOUN — REALIST   Vernon L. Parrington

From Main Currents in American Thought, *Volume 2, by Vernon L. Parrington, copyright, 1927, by Harcourt, Brace and Company, Inc.; renewed by Vernon L. Parrington, Jr., Louise P. Tucker, Elizabeth P. Thomas. Reprinted by permission of the publishers.*

JOHN C. CALHOUN was a man who set his face like flint againt every northern middle-class ambition, and with his dream of a Greek democracy steered his beloved South upon the rocks. A truly notable figure was this ascetic Carolinian. In the passionate debates over slavery he daily matched powers with Webster and Clay and proved himself intellectually the greatest of the three. He is the one outstanding political thinker in a period singularly barren and uncreative. . . . Whatever road one travels one comes at last upon the austere figure of Calhoun, commanding every highway of the southern mind. He subjected the philosophy of the fathers to critical analysis; pointed out wherein he conceived it to be faulty; cast aside some of its most sacred doctrines; provided another foundation for the democratic faith which he professed. And when he had finished the great work of reconstruction, the old Jeffersonianism that had satisfied the mind of Virginia was reduced to a thing of shreds and patches, acknowledged by his followers to have been a mistaken philosophy, blinded by romantic idealism and led astray by French humanitarianism. To substitute realism for idealism, to set class economics above abstract humanitarianism, was the mission to which Calhoun devoted himself. He undid for the plantation South the work of his old master. Speaking in the name of democracy, he attacked the foundations on which the democratic movement in America had rested, substituting for its libertarian and equalitarian doctrines conceptions wholly alien and antagonistic to western democracy, wholly Greek in their underlying spirit. . . .

2   Calhoun's contribution to political theory — a contribution that elevates him to a distinguished place among American political thinkers — was the child of necessity, and received its particularist bias from the exigencies of sectional partisanship. With the rapid expansion of the nation westward, and the consequent augmenting of a potentially hostile free-soil power, the South was doomed to become increasingly a minority voice in the councils of government; and if it were to preserve its peculiar institution it must find more adequate means of self-protection than it had enjoyed hitherto. The tendencies most to be feared, in his judgment, were the spontaneous drift towards consolidation, and an uncritical faith in numerical majorities. He was convinced that America had too thoughtlessly accepted the principle of political democracy as a sufficient safeguard against the danger of arbitrary government. Soon or late it must discover, what the South already was discovering, that numerical democracy, unrestrained by constitutional limitations on its will, is no friend to political justice. The critical test of every government is the measure of protection afforded its weakest citizen; and judged by this test a democratic state, when power has come to be centralized in few hands, may prove to be no other than a tyrant. Irresponsible in its unrestraint, the majority vote may easily outdo an Oriental despot in arbitrary rule, and the more power it wields the more ruthless will be its disregard of minority opinion. The political philosopher who proposes to formulate an ideal democratic system of government, therefore, must deal critically with this fundamental problem of political justice, for upon the solution will turn the excellence and permanence of every democracy. It was to this baffling problem that Calhoun addressed himself. . . .

3   The perennial problem of constitutional government, then, in Calhoun's philosophy, remains what it was seen to be by the Federalist followers of Montesquieu — the problem of restraining government by constitutional checks to the end that it be kept just. Existing machinery having demonstrated its inadequacy, it remained to provide more effective. Freedom Calhoun regarded as the crown jewel of civilization, hardly won, easily lost. But freedom was not to be measured by *habeas corpus* acts and similar legal restraints on tyranny; it was freedom from legal exploitation and statutory dictatorship. "The abuse of delegated power, and the tyranny of the stronger over the weaker interests, are the two dangers, and the only two to be guarded against; and if this be done effectually, liberty must be eternal. Of the two, the latter is the greater and most difficult to resist" (*Works,* Vol. VI, p. 32). In more definite terms the problem is thus stated:

4   Two powers are necessary to the existence and preservation of free
     States: a power on the part of the ruled to prevent rulers from abusing

their authority, by compelling them to be faithful to their constituents, and which is effected through the right of suffrage; and a power to compel the parts of society to be just to one another, by compelling them to consult the interest of each other — which can only be effected . . . by requiring the concurring assent of all the great and distinct interests of the community to the measures of the Government. This result is the sum-total of all the contrivances adopted by free States to preserve their liberty, by preventing the conflicts between the several classes or parts of the community. (*Ibid.*, Vol. VI, pp. 189-190.)

5   In elaboration of the second phase of the problem Calhoun contributed the principle on which his reputation as a political thinker must rest — the doctrine of a concurrent majority. He found his solution in an expansion of the principle of democracy — recovering the true principle, he was fond of insisting — by superimposing upon the consolidated, indiscriminate numerical majority the will of a geographical majority; or in other words, by a special form of sectional referendum.

6   It results, from what has been said, that there are two different modes in which the sense of the community may be taken: one, simply, by the right of suffrage, unaided; the other, by the right through a proper organism. Each collects the sense of the majority. But one regards numbers only, and considers the whole community one unit, having but one common interest throughout; and collects the sense of the greater number of the whole, as that of the community. The other, on the contrary, regards interests as well as numbers; — considering the community as made up of different and conflicting interests as far as the action of the government is concerned; and takes the sense of each, through its majority or appropriate organ, and the united sense of all, as the sense of the entire community. The former of these I call the numerical, or absolute majority; and the latter, the concurrent, or constitutional majority. ("A Disquisition on Government," in *Works*, Vol. I, p. 28.)

7   In such speculation on the possibility of achieving political justice by the machinery of representation, Calhoun was face to face with a revolutionary conception — the conception of proportional economic representation. The idea was implicit in his assumption of an existing economic sectionalism that must find adequate expression through political agencies. He had come to understand the futility of a miscellaneous numerical majority; he had only to go back to eighteenth-century philosophy and substitute economic classes for economic sectionalism, finding his social cleavages in economic groups instead of geographical divisions, to have recast the whole theory of representation. Clearly, he had made enormous strides in his thinking. He had long since put behind him the philosophy of Jefferson. He had subjected the principle of democracy to critical scrutiny. But instead of rejecting it as an unworkable hypothesis, as the Hamiltonian Federalists had done, he proposed to establish it on a sound and permanent basis. The ideal of democracy he conceived to be the noblest in the whole field of political

thought, but misunderstood and misapplied as it had been in America, it had
become the mother of every mischief. This betrayal of democracy he laid at
the door of the Jeffersonians. They had accepted too carelessly the romantic
dogmas of the French school, and had come to believe that democracy was
synonymous with political equalitarianism.

8   It was this false notion that had debased the noble ideal, and delivered
it over to the hands of the mob. To assert that men are created free and
equal is to fly in the face of every biological and social fact. The first business
of the true democrat, therefore, was to reëxamine the nature of democracy
and strip away the false assumptions and vicious conclusions that had done
it incalculable injury. The Greeks, he pointed out, understood its essential
nature better than the moderns. Democracy assumes a co-partnership among
equals. Its only rational foundation is good will, and it can function only
through compromise. From this it follows that in a society composed of high
and low, capable and weak, worthy and unworthy — as every historical society has been composed — a universal democracy is impractical. The numerous body of social incompetents will suffer one of two fates: they will
be exploited by the capable minority under the guise of free labor, or they
will be accepted as the wards of society and protected by the free citizens —
they must inevitably become either wage slaves or bond slaves, in either
case incapable of maintaining the rights of free members of the commonwealth. Democracy is possible only in a society that recognizes inequality as
a law of nature, but in which the virtuous and capable enter into a voluntary
co-partnership for the common good, accepting wardship of the incompetent
in the interests of society. This was the Greek ideal and this ideal had
created Greek civilization.

9   Calhoun was thus brought face to face with the natural-rights theory,
which the glowing rhetoric of the Declaration of Independence had disseminated throughout America, and which lay as a virus at the heart of Jackso-
nianism. To destroy that theory, he believed, was a necessary preliminary to
any rational theory of democracy, and he turned to the business with characteristic frankness. Upon the venerable dogmas he threw the light of his
realism, subjecting them to critical analysis. The origin of government in
compact was only a myth. The amiable being known as man in a state of
nature, whose portrait had been drawn by the French romantics, he discovered in neither social nor biological history. The true origin of government,
he asserted in common with John Adams, is to be found in practical necessity; government arises, as Hobbes had pointed out, from the universal fact
of human selfishness. It has always been found necessary to lodge coercive
powers in certain hands as a social protection against individual aggression;
and since all men are impelled by self-interest, political systems are determined in form and scope by this universal instinct. Without government
there is anarchy; with government there is potential tyranny. The crucial
problem to be solved by the political philosopher, hence, is to determine the
just delimitation between sovereign power and individual liberty; the one

protecting the rights of the whole, the other keeping open fresh opportunity to advance.

Commentary and questions

1. *Paragraph 1:* Does the opening convey a favorable, unfavorable, or neutral impression of Calhoun? Explain the basis for your opinion.

2. *Paragraph 2:* Parrington speaks of a "particularist bias." Can this be supported from the selection? Can the assertion that Calhoun's work was a "child of necessity" be supported? Can you support the assertion that Calhoun feared "the spontaneous drift towards consolidation, and an uncritical faith in numerical majorities." Go through this paragraph and separate Calhoun's explicit statements, the assumptions behind Calhoun's statements, statements that seem to be logical applications of Calhoun's ideas to particular situations, and the motives that Parrington attributes to Calhoun.

3. *Paragraph 5:* Is the idea of a "geographical" majority explicit in Calhoun's *Disquisition?* Does Calhoun specifically name any of the diverse interests whose powers he discusses?

4. *Paragraphs 7-8:* Examine the language here and compare it to Calhoun's language.

Topics for discussion and writing

I. Write a summary statement for each of Parrington's paragraphs. What in Parrington's writing makes this a difficult task in several instances?

II. Write a paper in which you analyze the attitude of Parrington toward Calhoun and his work.

III. Parrington places Calhoun's *Disquisition* against a contemporary background. Write an essay in which you explain Parrington's chief contributions to your understanding of Calhoun's *Disquisition.*

IV. Write an essay in which you explain whether or not you think Parrington's explanation is a fair and accurate presentation of Calhoun's ideas.

UNWRITTEN RULES OF AMERICAN POLITICS

John Fischer

From Harper's Magazine, *Vol. 197 (Nov., 1948). Copyright 1948, by Harper & Brothers. Reprinted by permission of the author.*

THE safest bet anybody could make on this month's election is that the Progressive party will begin to come unraveled before the last votes are counted. The Communists, of course, have practically guaranteed that. The slick assurance with which they took over the management of the new party already has scared away a good many of the innocent idealists who ran a-whooping to join Gideon's Army at the beginning of the campaign. By Christmas nearly all the rest (perhaps including Henry Wallace himself) can be expected to drop out of the ranks, nursing purple bruises of disillusionment. The remaining core of incurable fellow travelers most likely will dwindle, eventually, into a kind of Soviet counterpart of the late German-American Bund.

2   Even if Mr. Wallace weren't toting the red albatross around his neck, however, his enterprise almost certainly would fail to develop into a major party. For it violates the unwritten but enduring rules of American politics — and no group which ignored these rules has ever been able to grow out of the nursery stage.

3   Earlier efforts to form a third party — about one a generation — have fallen into much the same pattern. In particular, the basic argument for a third party always remains the same. It is a persuasive argument, especially for well-meaning people who have not had much first-hand experience in politics. It runs something like this:

4   "Both of the traditional American parties are outrageous frauds. Neither the Republicans nor the Democrats have any fundamental principles or ideology. They do not even have a program. In every campaign the platforms of both parties are simply collections of noble generalities, muffled in the vaguest possible language; and in each case the two platforms are very nearly identical.

5   "Obviously, then, both parties are merely machines for grabbing power and distributing favors. In their lust for office they are quite willing to make a deal with anybody who can deliver a sizable block of votes. As a result, each party has become an outlandish cluster of local machines and special interest groups which have nothing in common except a lecherous craving for the public trough.

6   "This kind of political system" — so the argument runs — "is clearly meaningless. A man of high principles can never hope to accomplish anything through the old parties, because they are not interested in principle. Moreover, the whole arrangement is so illogical that it affronts every intelligent citizen. Consequently, it is the duty of every liberal to work for a tidier and more sensible political system.

7   "We ought to separate the sheep from the goats — to herd all the progressives on one side of the fence and all the conservatives on the other. Then politics really will have some meaning; we will know who the enemy is and where he stands; every campaign can be fought over clearly-defined issues. The Europeans, who are more sophisticated politically than we simple Americans, discovered this long ago, and in each of their countries they have arranged a neat political spectrum running from Left to Right.

8   "As a first step toward such a logical scheme of politics, we need to

organize a progressive party with a precise ideology and a clearly formulated program." (Nowadays the implication usually is that such a program must be more or less Marxist, whether in the Communist or Social Democratic tradition.) "Such a party will rally together the labor movement, the farmers, and the white-collar liberals — and then it should have little trouble in defeating the reactionary business men who have long held such strategic positions in our old-fashioned political system."

9   That, I believe, is a reasonably fair statement of the position taken by most of the supporters of Mr. Wallace. It is much the same as that once taken by the followers of Theodore Roosevelt and old Bob LaFollette, and a similar case has been argued in season and out by most of the splinter groups of the American left.

10   It sounds so plausible — at least on the surface — that it is hard to see why the idea has never made much headway. Indeed, many veteran third party enthusiasts have been able to account for their failure only by assuming a perverse and rock-headed stupidity among the American electorate. This, in turn, sometimes leads to a secret conviction that the dopes don't know what is good for them — and that what this country needs is a Strong Leader or a small, tough party of the enlightened, which can herd the ignorant masses up the road to Utopia whether they like it or not.

11   There is, however, one other possible explanation for the chronic failure of the third-party argument: maybe there is something wrong with the idea itself. Maybe it never gets to first base, not because the American voter is a hopeless dullard, but simply because he rejects instinctively a notion which doesn't make sense in terms of his own experience.

12   It can be argued, indeed, that a third party movement usually is an attempt to transplant a European concept of politics into an American setting — and that it fails because our own political tradition is more vigorous, more deeply rooted, and far better suited to our own peculiar needs. Such attempts often serve a useful purpose, as we shall see; but it is not the purpose which the evangels of the new party have in mind. Their whole endeavor, in fact, springs out of a profound misunderstanding of the way in which the American political system works.

13   Moreover, it seems to me that a careful look will show that our native scheme of politics is a more complex and subtle conception than the crude blacks and whites of the European ideological parties. And finally there is considerable evidence that our own system — in spite of certain dangerous weaknesses — has on the whole worked out more successfully than the European.

II

1   Perhaps it is the very subtlety of the American political tradition which is responsible for the almost universal misunderstanding of it abroad. Every practicing American politician grasps its principles by instinct; if he does

not, he soon retires into some less demanding profession. Moreover, the overwhelming majority of citizens have a sound working knowledge of the system, which they apply every day of their lives — though many of them might have a hard time putting that knowledge into words. There are almost no foreigners, however (except perhaps D. W. Brogan), who really understand the underlying theory. Even the editors of the London *Economist* — probably the most brilliant and well-informed group of journalists practicing anywhere today — display their bewilderment week after week. To them, and to virtually all other European observers, our whole political scene looks arbitrary, irrational, and dangerous.

2   Another reason for this misunderstanding lies in the fact that surprisingly little has been written about the rules of American politics during our generation. The newspapers, textbooks, and learned journals are running over with discussions of tactics and mechanics — but no one, so far as I know, has bothered to trace out the basic tradition for a good many years.

3   In fact, the most useful discussion of this tradition which I have come across is the work of John C. Calhoun, published nearly a century ago. Today of course he is an almost forgotten figure, and many people take it for granted that his views were discredited for good by the Civil War. I know of only one writer — Peter F. Drucker of Bennington College — who has paid much attention to him in recent years. It was he who described Calhoun's ideas as "a major if not the only key to the understanding of what is specifically and uniquely American in our political system"; and I am indebted to Dr. Drucker for much of the case set forth here.

4   Calhoun summed up his political thought in what he called the Doctrine of the Concurrent Majority. He saw the United States as a nation of tremendous and frightening diversity — a collection of many different climates, races, cultures, religions, and economic patterns. He saw the constant tension among all these special interests, and he realized that the central problem of American politics was to find some way of holding these conflicting groups together.

5   It could not be done by force; no one group was strong enough to impose its will on all the others. The goal could be achieved only by compromise — and no real compromise could be possible if any threat of coercion lurked behind the door. Therefore, Calhoun reasoned, every vital decision in American life would have to be adopted by a "concurrent majority" — by which he meant, in effect, a unanimous agreement of all interested parties. No decision which affected the interests of the slaveholders, he argued, should be taken without their consent; and by implication he would have given a similar veto to every other special interest, whether it be labor, management, the Catholic church, old-age pensioners, the silver miners, or the corn-growers of the Middle West.

6   Under the goad of the slavery issue, Calhoun was driven to state his doctrine in an extreme and unworkable form. If every sectional interest had

been given the explicit legal veto power which he called for, the govern‑ ment obviously would have been paralyzed. (That, in fact, is precisely what seems to be happening today in the United Nations.) It is the very essence of the idea of "concurrent majority" that it cannot be made legal and official. It can operate effectively only as an informal, highly elastic, and generally accepted understanding. Perhaps the best example is the Quaker church meeting, where decisions are not reached by formal vote at all, but rather by a give-and-take discussion which continues until "the sense of the meet- ing" jells and is accepted by everybody present.

7   Moreover, government by concurrent majority can exist only when no one power is strong enough to dominate completely, *and then only when all of the contending interest groups recognize and abide by certain rules of the game.*

8   These rules are the fundamental bond of unity in American political life. They can be summed up as a habit of extraordinary toleration, plus "equality" in the peculiar American meaning of that term which cannot be translated into any other language, even into the English of Great Britain. Under these rules every group tacitly binds itself to tolerate the interests and opinions of every other group. It must not try to impose its views on others, nor can it press its own special interests to the point where they seriously endanger the interests of other groups or of the nation as a whole.

9   Furthermore, each group must exercise its implied veto with respon- sibility and discretion; and in times of great emergency it must forsake its veto right altogether. It dare not be intransigent or doctrinaire. It must make every conceivable effort to compromise, relying on its veto only as a last resort. For if any player wields this weapon recklessly, the game will break up — or all other players will turn on him in anger, suspend the rules for the time being, and maul those very interests he is trying so desperately hard to protect. That was what happened in 1860, when the followers of Calhoun carried his doctrine to an unbearable extreme. Much the same thing, on a less violent scale, happened to American business in- terests in 1933 and to the labor unions in 1947.

10   This is the somewhat elusive sense, it seems to me, in which Calhoun's theory has been adopted by the American people. But elusive and subtle as it may be, it remains the basic rule of the game of politics in this country — and in this country alone. Nothing comparable exists in any other nation, although the British, in a different way, have applied their own rules of responsibility and self-restraint.

11   It is a rule which operates unofficially and entirely outside the Con- stitution — but it has given us a method by which all the official and Con- stitutional organs of government can be made to work. It also provides a means of selecting leaders on all levels of our political life, for hammering out policies, and for organizing and managing the conquest of political power.

1   The way in which this tradition works in practice can be observed most easily in Congress. Anyone who has ever tried to push through a piece of legislation quickly discovers that the basic units of organization on Capitol Hill are not the parties, but the so-called blocs, which are familiar to everyone who reads a newspaper. There are dozens of them — the farm bloc, the silver bloc, the friends of labor, the business group, the Midwestern isolationists, the public power bloc — and they all cut across party lines.

2   They are loosely organized and pretty blurred at the edges, so that every Congressman belongs at different times to several different blocs. Each of them represents a special interest group. Each of them ordinarily works hand-in-hand with that group's Washington lobby. In passing, it might be noted that these lobbies are by no means the cancerous growth which is sometimes pictured in civics textbooks. They have become an indispensable part of the political machine — the accepted channel through which American citizens make their wishes known and play their day-to-day role in the process of government. Nor is their influence measured solely by the size of the bankrolls and propaganda apparatus which they have at their disposal. Some of the smallest and poorest lobbies are often more effective than their well-heeled rivals. For example, Russell Smith, the one-man lobby of the Farmers Union, was largely responsible for conceiving and nursing through Congress the Employment Act of 1946, one of the most far-reaching measures adopted since the war.

3   Now it is an unwritten but firm rule of Congress that no important bloc shall ever be voted down — under normal circumstances — on any matter which touches its own vital interests. Each of them, in other words, has a tacit right of veto on legislation in which it is primarily concerned. The ultimate expression of this right is the institution — uniquely American — of the filibuster in the Senate. Recently it has acquired a bad name among liberals because the Southern conservatives have used it ruthlessly to fight off civil rights legislation and protect white supremacy. Not so long ago, however, the filibuster was the stoutest weapon of such men as Norris and the LaFollettes in defending many a progressive cause — and under the Dewey regime, the surviving handful of liberal Senators may well have occasion to use it again.

4   Naturally no bloc wants to exercise its veto power except when it is absolutely forced to — for this is a negative power, and one which is always subject to retaliation. Positive power to influence legislation, on the other hand, can be gained only by conciliation, compromise, and endless horse-trading.

5   The farm bloc, for instance, normally needs no outside aid to halt the passage of a hostile bill. As a last resort, three or four strong-lunged statesmen from the corn belt can always filibuster it to death in the Senate. If the bloc wants to put through a measure to support agricultural prices, however, it can succeed only by enlisting the help of other powerful special interest groups. Consequently, it must always be careful not to antagonize any potential ally by a reckless use of the veto; and it must be willing to pay for such help by throwing its support from time to time behind legislation sought by the labor bloc, the National Association of Manufacturers, or the school-teachers' lobby.

6   The classic alliance of this sort was formed in the early days of the New Deal, when most of the Roosevelt legislation was shoved onto the statute books by a temporary coalition of the farm bloc and urban labor, occasionally reinforced by such minor allies as the public power group and spokesmen for the northern Negroes. Mr. Roosevelt's political genius rested largely on his ability to put together a program which would offer something to each of these groups without fatally antagonizing any of them, and then to time the presentation of each bill so that he would always retain enough bargaining power to line up a Congressional majority. It also was necessary for him to avoid the veto of the business group, which viewed much of this legislation as a barbarous assault upon its privileges; and for this purpose he employed another traditional technique, which we shall examine a little later.

7   This process of trading blocs of votes is generally known as log-rolling, and frequently it is deplored by the more innocent type of reformer. Such pious disapproval has no effect whatever on any practicing politician. He knows that log-rolling is a sensible and reasonably fair device, and that without it Congress could scarcely operate at all.

8   In fact, Congress gradually has developed a formal apparatus — the committee system — which is designed to make the log-rolling process as smooth and efficient as possible. There is no parallel system anywhere; the committees of Parliament and of the Continental legislative bodies work in an entirely different way.

9   Obviously the main business of Congress — the hammering out of a series of compromises between many special interest groups — cannot be conducted satisfactorily on the floor of the House or Senate. The meetings there are too large and far too public for such delicate negotiations. Moreover, every speech delivered on the floor must be aimed primarily at the voters back home, and not at the other members in the chamber. Therefore, Congress — especially the House — does nearly all its work in the closed sessions of its various committees, simply because the committee room is the only place where it is possible to arrange a compromise acceptable to all major interests affected.

10   For this reason, it is a matter of considerable importance to get a bill before the proper committee. Each committee serves as a forum for a particular cluster of special interests, and the assignment of a bill to a specific committee often decides which interest groups shall be recognized

officially as affected by the measure and therefore entitled to a hand in its drafting. "Who is to have standing before the committee" is the technical term, and it is this decision that frequently decides the fate of the legislation.

I V

1   Calhoun's principles of the concurrent majority and of sectional compromise operate just as powerfully, though sometimes less obviously, in every other American political institution. Our cabinet, for example, is the only one in the world where members are charged by law with the representation of special interests — labor, agriculture, commerce, and so on. In other countries, each agency of government is at least presumed to act for the nation as a whole; here most agencies are expected to behave as servants for one interest or another. The Veterans' Administration, to cite the most familiar case, is frankly intended to look out for Our Boys; the Maritime Commission is the spokesman for the shipping industry; the National Labor Relations Board, as originally established under the Wagner Act, was explicitly intended to build up the bargaining power of the unions.

2   Even within a single department, separate agencies are sometimes set up to represent conflicting interests. Thus in the Department of Agriculture under the New Deal the old Triple-A became primarily an instrument of the large-scale commercial farmers, as represented by their lobby, the Farm Bureau Federation; while the Farm Security Administration went to bat for the tenants, the farm laborers, and the little subsistence farmers, as represented by the Farmers Union.

3   This is one reason why federal agencies often struggle so bitterly against each other, and why the position of the administration as a whole on any question can be determined only after a long period of inter-bureau squabbling and compromise. Anyone who was in Washington during the war will remember how these goings-on always confused and alarmed our British allies.

4   Calhoun's laws also govern the selection of virtually every candidate for public office. The mystery of "eligibility" which has eluded most foreign observers simply means that a candidate must not be unacceptable to any important special interest group — a negative rather than a positive qualification. A notorious case of this process at work was the selection of Mr. Truman as the Democrat's Vice Presidential candidate in 1944. As Edward J. Flynn, the Boss of the Bronx, has pointed out in his memoirs, Truman was the one man "who would hurt . . . least" as Roosevelt's running mate. Many stronger men were disqualified, Flynn explained, by the tacit veto of one sectional interest or another. Wallace was unacceptable to the business men and to many local party machines. Byrnes was distasteful to the Catholics, the Negroes, and organized labor. Rayburn came from the wrong part of the country. Truman, however, came from a border state, his

labor record was good, he had not antagonized the conservatives, and — as Flynn put it — "he had never made any 'racial' remarks. He just dropped into the slot."

5 The same kind of considerations govern the selection of candidates right down to the county, city, and precinct levels. Flynn, one of the most successful political operators of our time, explained in some detail the complicated job of making up a ticket in his own domain. Each of the main population groups in the Bronx — Italians, Jews, and Irish Catholics — must be properly represented on the list of nominees, and so must each of the main geographical divisions. The result is a ticket which sounds like the roster of the Brooklyn Dodgers: Loreto, Delagi, Lyman, Joseph, Lyons, and Foley.

6 Comparable traditions govern the internal political life of the American Legion, the Federation of Women's Clubs, university student bodies, labor unions, Rotary Clubs, and the thousands of other quasi-political institutions which are so characteristic of our society and which give us such a rich fabric of spontaneous local government.

7 The stronghold of Calhoun's doctrine, however, is the American party — the wonder and despair of foreigners who cannot fit it into any of their concepts of political life.

8 The purpose of European parties is, of course, to divide men of different ideologies into coherent and disciplined organizations. The historic role of the American party, on the other hand, is not to divide but to unite. That task was imposed by simple necessity. If a division into ideological parties had been attempted, in addition to all the other centrifugal forces in this country, it very probably would have proved impossible to hold the nation together. The Founding Fathers understood this thoroughly; hence Washington's warning against "factions."

9 Indeed, on the one occasion when we did develop two ideological parties, squarely opposing each other on an issue of principle, the result was civil war. Fortunately, that was our last large-scale experiment with a third party formed on an ideological basis — for in its early days that is just what the Republican party was.

10 Its radical wing, led by such men as Thaddeus Stevens, Seward, and Chase, made a determined and skillful effort to substitute principles for interests as the foundations of American political life. Even within their own party, however, they were opposed by such practical politicians as Lincoln and Johnson — men who distrusted fanaticism in any form — and by the end of the Reconstruction period the experiment had been abandoned. American politics then swung back into its normal path and has never vered far away from it since. Although Calhoun's cause was defeated, his political theory came through the Civil War stronger than ever.

11 The result is that the American party has no permanent program and no fixed aim, except to win elections. Its one purpose is to unite the largest

possible number of divergent interest groups in the pursuit of power. Its unity is one of compromise, not of dogma. It must — if it hopes to succeed — appeal to considerable numbers on both the left and the right, to rich and poor, Protestant and Catholic, farmer and industrial worker, native and foreign born.

12   It must be ready to bid for the support of any group that can deliver a sizable chunk of votes, accepting that group's program with whatever modifications may be necessary to reconcile the other members of the party. If sun worship, or Existentialism, or the nationalization of industry should ever attract any significant following in this country, you can be sure that both parties would soon whip up a plank designed to win it over.

13   This ability to absorb new ideas (along with the enthusiasts behind them) and to mold them into a shape acceptable to the party's stand-patters is, perhaps, the chief measure of vitality in the party's leadership. Such ideas almost never germinate within the party itself. They are stolen — very often from third parties.

14   Indeed, the historic function of third parties has been to sprout new issues, nurse them along until they have gathered a body of supporters worth stealing, and then to turn them over (often reluctantly) to the major parties. A glance at the old platforms of the Populists, the Bull Moosers, and the Socialists will show what an astonishingly high percentage of their once-radical notions have been purloined by both Republicans and Democrats — and enacted into law. Thus the income tax, child-labor laws, minimum wages, regulation of railroads and utilities, and old-age pensions have all become a part of the American Way of Life. In similar fashion, Mr. Wallace has forced both the old parties to pay a good deal more attention to such matters as civil rights than they ever would have done on their own initiative. He has compelled them to bid — and to bid high — for a handsome block of Negro votes.

15   While each major party must always stand alert to grab a promising new issue, it also must be careful never to scare off any of the big, established interest groups. For as soon as it alienates any one of them, it finds itself in a state of crisis.

16   For sixteen years the Republicans lost much of their standing as a truly national party because they had made themselves unacceptable to labor. Similarly, the Democrats during the middle stage of the New Deal incurred the wrath of the business interests. Ever since Mr. Truman was plumped into the White House, the Democratic leadership has struggled desperately — though rather ineptly — to regain the confidence of business men without at the same time driving organized labor out of the ranks. It probably would be safe to predict that if the Republican party is to regain a long period of health, it must within the next four years make an equally vigorous effort to win back the confidence of labor. For the permanent veto of any major element in American society means political death — as the ghosts of the Federalists and Whigs can testify.

V

1   The weaknesses of the American political system are obvious — much more obvious, in fact, than its virtues. These weaknesses have been so sharply criticized for the past hundred years, by a procession of able analysts ranging from Walter Bagehot to Thomas K. Finletter, that it is hardly necessary to mention them here. It is enough to note that most of the criticism has been aimed at two major flaws.

2   First, it is apparent that the doctrine of the concurrent majority is a negative one — a principle of inaction. A strong government, capable of rapid and decisive action, is difficult to achieve under a system which forbids it to do anything until virtually everybody asquiesces. In times of crisis, a dangerously long period of debate and compromise usually is necessary before any adminstration can carry out the drastic measures needed. The depression of the early thirties, the crisis in foreign policy which ended only with Pearl Harbor, the equally great crisis of the Marshall program a few months ago all illustrate this recurring problem.

3   This same characteristic of our system gives undue weight to the small but well-organized pressure group — especially when it is fighting *against* something. Hence a few power companies were able to block for twenty years the sensible use of the Muscle Shoals dam which eventually became the nucleus of TVA, and — in alliance with the railroads, rail unions, and Eastern port interests — they are still holding up the development of the St. Lawrence Waterway. Even more flagrant examples are the silver and wool blocs, each representing only a tiny fraction of the American people. The first has been looting the Treasury for a generation by a series of outrageous silver subsidy and purchase laws. The second, in league with a handful of stockmen, may yet get away with the wholesale land grab which Mr. Bernard DeVoto has repeatedly discussed in these columns.

4   The negative character of our political rules also makes it uncommonly difficult for us to choose a President. Many of our outstanding political operatives — notably those who serve in the Senate — are virtually barred from a Presidential nomination because they are forced to get on record on too many issues. Inevitably they offend some important interest group, and therefore become "unavailable." Governors, who can keep their mouths shut on most national issues, have a much better chance to reach the White House. Moreover, the very qualities of caution and inoffensiveness which make a good candidate — Harding and Coolidge come most readily to mind — are likely to make a bad President.

5   An even more serious flaw in our scheme of politics is the difficulty in finding anybody to speak for the country as a whole. Calhoun would have argued that the national interest is merely the sum of all the various special interests, and therefore needs no spokesmen of its own — but in this case he clearly was wrong.

6   In practice, we tend to settle sectional and class conflicts at the expense

of the nation as a whole — with results painful to all of us. The labor troubles in the spring of 1946, for instance, could be settled only on a basis acceptable to *both* labor and management: this is, on the basis of higher wages *plus* higher prices. The upshot was an inflationary spiral which is damaging everybody — and at this writing there is a good deal of mournful evidence that the process is about to be repeated. Countless other instances, from soil erosion to the rash of billboards along our highways, bear witness to the American tendency to neglect matters which are "only" of national interest, and therefore are left without a recognized sponsor.

7   Over the generations we have developed a series of practices and institutions which partly remedy these weaknesses, although we are still far from a complete cure. One such development has been the gradual strengthening of the Presidency as against Congress. As the only man elected by all the people, the President inevitably has had to take over many of the policy-making and leadership functions which the Founding Fathers originally assigned to the legislators. This meant, of course, that he could no longer behave merely as an obedient executor of the will of Congress, but was forced into increasingly frequent conflicts with Capitol Hill.

8   Today we have come to recognize that this conflict is one of the most important obligations of the Presidency. No really strong executive tries to avoid it — he accepts it as an essential part of his job. If he simply tries to placate the pressure groups which speak through Congress, history writes him down as a failure. For it is his duty to enlist the support of many minorities for measures rooted in the national interest, reaching beyond their own immediate concern — and, if necessary, to stand up against the ravening minorities for the interest of the whole.

9   In recent times this particular part of the President's job has been made easier by the growth of the Theory of Temporary Emergencies. All of us — or nearly all — have come around to admitting that in time of emergency special interest groups must forego their right of veto. As a result, the President often is tempted to scare up an emergency to secure legislation which could not be passed under any other pretext. Thus, most of the New Deal bills were introduced as "temporary emergency measures," although they were clearly intended to be permanent from the very first; for in no other way could Mr. Roosevelt avoid the veto of the business interests.

10   Again, in 1939 the threat of war enabled the President to push through much legislation which would have been impossible under normal circumstances. And Mr. Truman recently found it necessary to present the Greco-Turkish situation under the guise of a world crisis, in order to get authority and funds to carry out a rather small, routine police operation.

VI

1   Because we have been so preoccupied with trying to patch up the flaws in our system, we have often overlooked its unique elements of

strength. The chief of these is its ability to minimize conflict — not by suppressing the conflicting forces, but by absorbing and utilizing them. The result is a society which is both free and reasonably stable — a government which is as strong and effective as most dictatorships, but which can still adapt itself to social change.

2 The way in which the American political organism tames down the extremists of both the left and right is always fascinating to watch. Either party normally is willing to embrace any group or movement which can deliver votes — but in return it requires these groups to adjust their programs to fit the traditions, beliefs, and prejudices of the majority of the people. The fanatics, the implacable radicals cannot hope to get to first base in American politics until they abandon their fanaticism and learn the habits of conciliation. As a consequence, it is almost impossible for political movements here to become entirely irresponsible and to draw strength from the kind of demagogic obstruction which has nurtured both Communist and Fascist movements abroad.

3 The same process which gentles down the extremists also prods along the political laggards. As long as it is in a state of health, each American party has a conservative and a liberal wing. Sometimes one is dominant, sometimes the other — but even when the conservative element is most powerful, it must reckon with the left-wingers in its own family. At the moment the Republican party certainly is in one of its more conservative phases; yet it contains such men as Senators Morse, Aiken, Flanders, Tobey, and Baldwin, who are at least as progressive as most of the old New Dealers. They, and their counterparts in the Democratic party, exert a steady tug to the left which prevents either party from lapsing into complete reaction.

4 The strength of this tug is indicated by the fact that the major New Deal reforms have now been almost universally accepted. A mere ten years ago, the leading Republicans, plus many conservative Democrats, were hell-bent on wiping out social security, TVA, SEC, minimum-wage laws, rural electrification, and all the other dread innovations of the New Deal. Today no Presidential aspirant would dare suggest the repeal of a single one of them. In this country there simply is no place for a hard core of irreconcilable reactionaries, comparable to those political groups in France which have never yet accepted the reforms of the French Revolution.

5 This American tendency to push extremists of both the left and right toward a middle position has enabled us, so far, to escape class warfare. This is no small achievement for any political system; for class warfare cannot be tolerated by a modern industrial society. If it seriously threatens, it is bound to be suppressed by some form of totalitarianism, as it has been in Germany, Spain, Italy, Russia, and most of Eastern Europe.

6 In fact, suppression might be termed the normal method of settling conflicts in continental Europe, where parties traditionally have been drawn

up along ideological battle lines. Every political campaign becomes a religious crusade; each party is fanatically convinced that it and it alone has truth by the tail; each party is certain that its opponents not only are wrong, but wicked. If the sacred ideology is to be established beyond challenge, no heresy can be tolerated. Therefore it becomes a duty not only to defeat the enemy at the polls, but to wipe him out. Any suggestion of compromise must be rejected as treason and betrayal of the true faith. The party must be disciplined like an army, and if it cannot win by other means it must be ready to take up arms in deadly fact.

7   Politics thus becomes merely a prelude to civil war — and all too often the prelude is short. In Italy the Partisan brigades are drilling today on the same parade grounds where Mussolini's Blackshirts once trained for their march on Rome. And in France both Communists and DeGaullists are reported to be squirreling away Bren guns against the day when each expects to "save the Republic" from the other.

8   Under this kind of political system the best that can be hoped for is a prolonged deadlock between parties which are too numerous and weak to exterminate one another. The classic example is prewar France, where six revolutions or near-revolutions broke out within a century, where cabinets fell every weekend, and no government could ever become strong enough to govern effectively. The more usual outcome is a complete victory for one ideology or another, after a brief period of electioneering, turmoil, and fighting in the streets; then comes the liquidation of the defeated.

9   Because this sort of ideological politics is so foreign to our native tradition, neither Socialists, Communists, nor Fascists have ever been accepted as normal parties. So long as that tradition retains its very considerable vitality, it seems to me unlikely that any third party founded on an ideological basis can take root. The notion of a ruthless and unlimited class struggle, the concept of a master race, a Fascist élite, or a proletariat which is entitled to impose its will on all others — these are ideas which are incompatible with the main current of American political life. The uncompromising ideologist, of whatever faith, appears in our eyes peculiarly "un-American," simply because he cannot recognize the rule of the concurrent majority, nor can he accept the rules of mutual toleration which are necessary to make it work. Unless he forsakes his ideology, he cannot even understand that basic principle of American politics which was perhaps best expressed by Judge Learned Hand: "The spirit of liberty is the spirit which is not too sure that it is right."

Commentary and questions

Section I

1. Fischer's article was published in 1948. His readers at that time would have understood Section I as especially germane to the Progressive Party. Is Section I introductory only in the sense that it brings the subject up, piquing the reader's interest and preparing him for what follows, or is it an essential part of the presentation?

2. Does the last paragraph of Section I contain the thesis of the essay? State the thesis in your own words.

Section II

3. *Paragraph 4:* Would you agree that Calhoun "realized that the central problem of American politics was to find some way of holding these conflicting groups together"? State in your own words what you believe Calhoun considered the central problem of government to be.

4. *Paragraph 5:* Do you agree with Fischer's "by implication"?

5. *Paragraph 6:* Fischer refers to writings other than the *Disquisition*. Why does he say "It is the very essence of the idea of 'concurrent majority' that it cannot be made legal and official"?

6. *Paragraph 7:* What is the assumption behind the statement that the "concurrent majority can exist only when no one power is strong enough to dominate completely"?

7. What is the purpose of the second section?

Other Sections

8. What is the purpose of the third section? Is the thesis for the section stated explicitly?

9. State the thesis and outline Section IV.

10. What is the relation of Section V to Section VI? Why are they arranged in this order?

Topics for discussion and writing

I. Calhoun's method of presentation and Fischer's are both effective and different. Write an essay in which you contrast the way they have presented their ideas.

II. Write an essay comparing Calhoun's explanation of the concurrent majority to Fischer's explanation.

III. Write an essay analyzing the language and tone of Fischer's essay.

IV. Compare the paragraph structure in Fischer with that in Calhoun and Parrington. Explain the differences and explain whether each is appropriate in its essay.

V. Write a theme explaining the meaning of "compromise" as each of the three authors understands it. Which gives it the most complete meaning? What, if any, limitations on compromise as a political principle do they mention? Do all of them see compromise as opposed to the exercise of central political authority?

VI. Note the places where Fischer reveals his own political sympathies. Do they in any way affect the validity of his main thesis?

The modern temper: THE GENESIS OF A MOOD, Joseph Wood Krutch · THE SOUL OF MAN UNDER MODERNISM, Irwin Edman · FREEDOM: A FIGHTING FAITH, Arthur M. Schlesinger, Jr. · OUR PRESENT DISCONTENTS, Crane Brinton · ONE MAN'S BELIEF, George Jean Nathan

SPECULATIVE generalization of the sort represented in this group of essays is difficult to write well and difficult to estimate. The speculative writer must assume that there is such an entity as "modern man," and he must also assume that his readers will understand that the term does not designate all modern men or nations or societies or even all men in a given society. There are, of course, Americans, Englishmen, Frenchmen, and Austrians who simply would not fit the statements made by these authors about the modern mind, the modern soul, or the modern temper. Any intelligent reader can think of particulars that would seem to contradict the basic generalizations in these essays.

Nevertheless, such exceptions may be beside the point. Quite clearly the authors are speaking of dominant or characteristic trends, states of mind, belief, and attitude about what Brinton calls the "Big Questions." Each writer must isolate the qualities that, in his judgment, are dominant and characteristic. Such discrimination is a basic part of the speculative process. We may quarrel with the writer's judgment and what it chooses to discuss, but we must have reasonable and authoritative grounds for doing so.

The validity of speculative thinking can never be tested as the validity of a fact can be tested. But this does not mean that one opinion is as good as another. It does mean that the reader must use his judgment in a different way. Ideally the critical reader should have enough information to judge how well the writer has selected his examples and supporting instances. For the diligent student this is not so difficult as it may seem; Krutch, Edman, Schlesinger, and Brinton all refer frequently to other writers whose work is the common property of educated men, and some of this reference is simply for vivid and persuasive statement. Then, the thesis of the speculative writer can itself be judged. Is it consistent? Does it deal adequately with possible objections? Does it handle the conditions it discusses in the simplest and most comprehensive way?

In each essay the organization is reasonably complex. No single type of expository technique excludes others, although distinction and contrast are fairly common in all the pieces. But there are also analogy, example, definition of terms, restatement, and the development of suggestion. Furthermore, the reader will do well to examine key words and phrases, both those peculiar to the individual authors and those common to two or more. The development of such terms, the associations and concepts they accumulate as they move along, is a crucial area of expository technique, for it exposes the author's use of his main ideas, his consistency or lack of it, and his ability to maintain a difficult concept intact through an essay of some range and length.

On the surface Nathan's essay is quite different from the others, in style, content, and purpose. It is a witty, belligerent, apparently honest record of the beliefs of one man. Nathan may or may not be typical of the twentieth-century literate American, but some of his attitudes reflect the states of mind the other authors discuss. And at least his voice is loud and insistent.

THE GENESIS OF A MOOD   Joseph Wood Krutch

From The Modern Temper, copyright, 1929, by Harcourt, Brace and Company, Inc.; renewed by Joseph Wood Krutch. Reprinted by permission of the publishers.

IT IS ONE OF Freud's quaint conceits that the child in its mother's womb is the happiest of living creatures. Into his consciousness no conflict has yet entered, for he knows no limitations to his desires and the universe is exactly as he wishes it to be. All his needs are satisfied before even he becomes aware of them, and if his awareness is dim that is but the natural result of a complete harmony between the self and the environment, since, as Spencer pointed out in a remote age, to be omniscient and omnipotent would be to be without any consciousness whatsoever. The discomfort of being born is the first warning which he receives that any event can be thrust upon him; it is the first limitation of his omnipotence which he perceives, and he is cast upon the shores of the world wailing his protest against the indignity to which he has been subjected. Years pass before he learns to control the expression of enraged surprise which arises within him at every unpleasant fact with which he is confronted, and his parents conspire so to protect him that he will learn only by very slow stages how far is the world from his heart's desire.

2   The cradle is made to imitate as closely as may be the conditions, both physical and spiritual, of the womb. Of its occupant no effort is demanded, and every precaution is taken to anticipate each need before it can arise. If, as the result of any unforeseen circumstance, any unsatisfied desire is born, he need only raise his voice in protest to cause the entire world in so far as he knows it — his nurse or his parents — to rush to his aid. The whole of his physical universe is obedient to his will and he is justified by his experience in believing that his mere volition controls his destiny. Only as he grows older does he become aware that there are wills other than his own or that there are physical circumstances rebellious to any human will. And only after the passage of many years does he become aware of the full extent of his predicament in the midst of a world which is in very few respects what he would wish it to be.

3   As a child he is treated as a child, and such treatment implies much more than the physical coddling of which Freud speaks. Not only do those who surround him co-operate more completely than they ever will again to satisfy his wishes in material things, but they encourage him to live in a spiritual world far more satisfactory than their own. He is carefully protected from any knowledge of the cruelties and complexities of life; he is led to suppose that the moral order is simple and clear, that virtue triumphs, and that the world is, as the desires of whole generations of mankind have led them to try to pretend that it is, arranged according to a pattern which would seem reasonable and satisfactory to human sensibilities. He is prevented from realizing how inextricably what men call good and evil are intertwined, how careless is Nature of those values called mercy and justice and righteousness which men have come, in her despite, to value; and he is, besides, encouraged to believe in a vast mythology peopled with figments which range all the way from the Saints to Santa Claus and which represent projections of human wishes which the adult has come to recognize as no more than projections but which he is willing that the child, for the sake of his own happiness, should believe real. Aware how different is the world which experience reveals from the world which the spirit desires, the mature, as though afraid that reality could not be endured unless the mind had been gradually inured to it, allow the child to become aware of it only by slow stages, and little by little he learns, not only the limitations of his will, but the moral discord of the world. Thus it is, in a very important sense, true that the infant does come trailing clouds of glory from that heaven which his imagination creates, and that as his experience accumulates he sees it fade away into the light of common day.

4   Now races as well as individuals have their infancy, their adolescence, and their maturity. Experience accumulates not only from year to year but

from generation to generation, and in the life of each person it plays a little larger part than it did in the life of his father. As civilization grows older it too has more and more facts thrust upon its consciousness and is compelled to abandon one after another, quite as the child does, certain illusions which have been dear to it. Like the child, it has instinctively assumed that what it would like to be true is true, and it never gives up any such belief until experience in some form compels it to do so. Being, for example, extremely important to itself, it assumes that it is extremely important to the universe also. The earth is the center of all existing things, man is the child and the protégé of those gods who transcend and who will ultimately enable him to transcend all the evils which he has been compelled to recognize. The world and all that it contains were designed for him, and even those things which seem noxious have their usefulness only temporarily hid. Since he knows but little he is free to imagine, and imagination is always the creature of desire.

II

5   The world which any consciousness inhabits is a world made up in part of experience and in part of fancy. No experience, and hence no knowledge, is complete, but the gaps which lie between the solid fragments are filled in with shadows. Connections, explanations, and reasons are supplied by the imagination, and thus the world gets its patterned completeness from material which is spun out of the desires. But as time goes on and experience accumulates there remains less and less scope for the fancy. The universe becomes more and more what experience has revealed, less and less what imagination has created, and hence, since it was not designed to suit man's needs, less and less what he would have it be. With increasing knowledge his power to manipulate his physical environment increases, but in gaining the knowledge which enables him to do so he surrenders insensibly the power which in his ignorance he had to mold the universe. The forces of nature obey him, but in learning to master them he has in another sense allowed them to master him. He has exchanged the universe which his desires created, the universe made for man, for the universe of nature of which he is only a part. Like the child growing into manhood, he passes from a world which is fitted to him into a world for which he must fit himself.

6   If, then, the world of poetry, mythology, and religion represents the world as a man would like to have it, while science represents the world as he gradually comes to discover it, we need only compare the two to realize how irreconcilable they appear. For the cozy bowl of the sky arched in a protecting curve above him he must exchange the cold immensities of space and, for the spiritual order which he has designed, the chaos of nature. God he had loved *because* God was anthropomorphic, because He was made in man's own image, with purposes and desires which were human and hence

understandable. But Nature's purpose, if purpose she can be said to have, is no purpose of his and is not understandable in his terms. Her desire merely to live and to propagate in innumerable forms, her ruthless indifference to his values, and the blindness of her irresistible will strike terror to his soul, and he comes in the fullness of his experience to realize that the ends which he proposes to himself — happiness and order and reason — are ends which he must achieve, if he achieve them at all, in her despite. Formerly he had believed in even his darkest moments that the universe was rational if he could only grasp its rationality, but gradually he comes to suspect that rationality is an attribute of himself alone and that there is no reason to suppose that his own life has any more meaning than the life of the humblest insect that crawls from one annihilation to another. Nature, in her blind thirst for life, has filled every possible cranny of the rotting earth with some sort of fantastic creature, and among them man is but one — perhaps the most miserable of all, because he is the only one in whom the instinct of life falters long enough to enable it to ask the question "Why?" As long as life is regarded as having been created, creating may be held to imply a purpose, but merely to have come into being is, in all likelihood, merely to go out of it also.

7   Fortunately, perhaps, man, like the individual child, was spared in his cradle the knowledge which he could not bear. Illusions have been lost one by one. God, instead of disappearing in an instant, has retreated step by step and surrendered gradually his control of the universe. Once he decreed the fall of every sparrow and counted the hairs upon every head; a little later he became merely the original source of the laws of nature, and even today there are thousands who, unable to bear the thought of losing him completely, still fancy that they can distinguish the uncertain outlines of a misty figure. But the rôle which he plays grows less and less, and man is left more and more alone in a universe to which he is completely alien. His world was once, like the child's world, three-quarters myth and poetry. His teleological concepts molded it into a form which he could appreciate and he gave to it moral laws which would make it meaningful, but step by step the outlines of nature have thrust themselves upon him, and for the dream which he made is substituted a reality devoid of any pattern which he can understand.

8   In the course of this process innumerable readjustments have been made, and always with the effort to disturb as little as possible the myth which is so much more full of human values than the fact which comes in some measure to replace it. Thus, for example, the Copernican theory of astronomy, removing the earth from the center of the universe and assigning it a very insignificant place among an infinitude of whirling motes, was not merely resisted as a fact but was, when finally accepted, accepted as far as possible without its implications. Even if taken entirely by itself and without the whole system of facts of which it is a part, it renders extremely improbable the assumption, fundamental in most human thought, that the universe has man as its center and is hence understandable in his terms, but this

implication was disregarded just as, a little later, the implications of the theory of evolution were similarly disregarded. It is not likely that if man had been aware from the very beginning that his world was a mere detail in the universe, and himself merely one of the innumerable species of living things, he would ever have come to think of himself, as he even now tends to do, as a being whose desires must be somehow satisfiable and whose reason must be matched by some similar reason in nature. But the myth, having been once established, persists long after the assumptions upon which it was made have been destroyed, because, being born of desire, it is far more satisfactory than any fact.

9   Unfortunately, perhaps, experience does not grow at a constant, but at an accelerated, rate. The Greeks who sought knowledge, not through the study of nature but through the examination of their own minds, developed a philosophy which was really analogous to myth, because the laws which determined its growth were dictated by human desires and they discovered few facts capable of disturbing the pattern which they devised. The Middle Ages retreated still further into themselves, but with the Renaissance man began to surrender himself to nature, and the sciences, each nourishing the other, began their iconoclastic march. Three centuries lay between the promulgation of the Copernican theory and the publication of the *Origin of Species,* but in sixty-odd years which have elapsed since that latter event the blows have fallen with a rapidity which left no interval for recovery. The structures which are variously known as mythology, religion, and philosophy, and which are alike in that each has as its function the interpretation of experience in terms which have human values, have collapsed under the force of successive attacks and shown themselves utterly incapable of assimilating the new stores of experience which have been dumped upon the world. With increasing completeness science maps out the pattern of nature, but the latter has no relation to the pattern of human needs and feelings.

10   Consider, for example, the plight of ethics. Historical criticism having destroyed what used to be called by people of learning and intelligence "Christian Evidences," and biology having shown how unlikely it is that man is the recipient of any transcendental knowledge, there remains no foundation in authority for ideas of right and wrong; and if, on the other hand, we turn to the traditions of the human race anthropology is ready to prove that no consistent human tradition has ever existed. Custom has furnished the only basis which ethics have ever had, and there is no conceivable human action which custom has not at one time justified and at another condemned. Standards are imaginary things, and yet it is extremely doubtful if man can live well, either spiritually or physically, without the belief that they are somehow real. Without them society lapses into anarchy and the individual becomes aware of an intolerable disharmony between himself and the universe. Instinctively and emotionally he is an ethical ani-

mal. No known race is so low in the scale of civilization that it has not attributed a moral order to the world, because no known race is so little human
as not to suppose a moral order so innately desirable as to have an inevitable
existence. It is man's most fundamental myth, and life seems meaningless to
him without it. Yet, as that systematized and cumulative experience which
is called science displaces one after another the myths which have been generated by need, it grows more and more likely that he must remain an ethical
animal in a universe which contains no ethical element.

III

¹¹   Mystical philosophers have sometimes said that they "accepted the
universe." They have, that is to say, formed of it some conception which answered the emotional needs of their spirit and which brought them a sense
of being in harmony with its aims and processes. They have been aware of
no needs which Nature did not seem to supply and of no ideals which she
too did not seem to recognize. They have felt themselves one with her because they have had the strength of imagination to make her over in their
own image, and it is doubtful if any man can live at peace who does not thus
feel himself at home. But as the world assumes the shape which science gives
it, it becomes more and more difficult to find such emotional correspond-
ences. Whole realms of human feeling, like the realm of ethics, find no place
for themselves in the pattern of nature and generate needs for which no satisfaction is supplied. What man knows is everywhere at war with what he
wants.

¹²   In the course of a few centuries his knowledge, and hence the universe
of which he finds himself an inhabitant, has been completely revolutionized,
but his instincts and his emotions have remained, relatively at least, un-
changed. He is still, as he always was, adjusted to the orderly, purposeful,
humanized world which all peoples unburdened by experience have figured
to themselves, but that world no longer exists. He has the same sense of dignity to which the myth of his descent from the gods was designed to minister,
and the same innate purposefulness which led him to attribute a purpose
to nature; but he can no longer think in terms appropriate to either. The
world which his reason and his investigation reveal is a world which his
emotions cannot comprehend.

¹³   Casually he accepts the spiritual iconoclasm of science, and in the detachment of everyday life he learns to play with the cynical wisdom of biology
and psychology, which explain away the awe of emotional experience just as
earlier science explained away the awe of conventional piety. Yet, under the
stress of emotional crises, knowledge is quite incapable of controlling his
emotions or of justifying them to himself. In love, he calls upon the illusions
of man's grandeur and dignity to help him accept his emotions, and faced
with tragedy he calls upon illusion to dignify his suffering; but lyric flight is
checked by the rationality which he has cultivated, and in the world of

metabolism and hormones, repressions and complexes, he finds no answer for his needs. He is feeling about love, for example, much as the troubadour felt, but he thinks about it in a very different way. Try as he may, the two halves of his soul can hardly be made to coalesce, and he cannot either feel as his intelligence tells him that he should feel or think as his emotions would have him think, and thus he is reduced to mocking his torn and divided soul. In the grip of passion he cannot, as some romanticist might have done, accept it with a religious trust in the mystery of love, nor yet can he regard it as a psychiatrist, himself quite free from emotion, might suggest — merely as an interesting specimen of psychical botany. Man *qua* thinker may delight in the intricacies of psychology, but man *qua* lover has not learned to feel in its terms; so that, though complexes and ductless glands may serve to explain the feelings of another, one's own still demand all those symbols of the ineffable in which one has long ceased to believe.

14   Time was when the scientist, the poet, and the philosopher walked hand in hand. In the universe which the one perceived the other found himself comfortably at home. But the world of modern science is one in which the intellect alone can rejoice. The mind leaps, and leaps perhaps with a sort of elation, through the immensities of space, but the spirit, frightened and cold, longs to have once more above its head the inverted bowl beyond which may lie whatever paradise its desires may create. The lover who surrendered himself to the Implacable Aphrodite or who fancied his foot upon the lowest rung of the Platonic ladder of love might retain his self-respect, but one can neither resist nor yield gracefully to a carefully catalogued psychosis. A happy life is a sort of poem, with a poem's elevation and dignity, but emotions cannot be dignified unless they are first respected. They must seem to correspond with, to be justified by, something in the structure of the universe itself; but though it was the function of religion and philosophy to hypostatize some such correspondence, to project a humanity upon nature, or at least to conceive of a humane force above and beyond her, science finds no justification for such a process and is content instead to show how illusions were born.

15   The most ardent love of truth, the most resolute determination to follow nature no matter to what black abyss she may lead, need not blind one to the fact that many of the lost illusions had, to speak the language of science, a survival value. Either individuals or societies whose life is imbued with a cheerful certitude, whose aims are clear, and whose sense of the essential rightness of life is strong, live and struggle with an energy unknown to the skeptical and the pessimistic. Whatever the limitations of their intellects as instruments of criticism, they possess the physical and emotional vigor which is, unlike critical intelligence, analogous to the processes of nature. They found empires and conquer wildernesses, and they pour the excess of their energy into works of art which the intelligence of more sophisticated peoples continue to admire even though it has lost the faith in life which is requisite

for the building of a Chartres or the carving of a Venus de Milo. The one was not erected to a law of nature or the other designed to celebrate the libido, for each presupposed a sense of human dignity which science nowhere supports.

16   Thus man seems caught in a dilemma which his intellect has devised. Any deliberately managed return to a state of relative ignorance, however desirable it might be argued to be, is obviously out of the question. We cannot, as the naïve proponents of the various religions, new and old, seem to assume, believe one thing and forget another merely because we happen to be convinced that it would be desirable to do so; and it is worth observing that the new psychology, with its penetrating analysis of the influence of desire upon belief, has so adequately warned the reason of the tricks which the will can play upon it that it has greatly decreased the possibility of beneficent delusion and serves to hold the mind in a steady contemplation of that from which it would fain escape. Weak and uninstructed intelligences take refuge in the monotonous repetition of once living creeds, or are even reduced to the desperate expedient of going to sleep amid the formulae of the flabby pseudo-religions in which the modern world is so prolific. But neither of these classes affords any aid to the robust but serious mind which is searching for some terms upon which it may live.

17   And if we are, as by this time we should be, free from any teleological delusion, if we no longer make the unwarranted assumption that every human problem is somehow of necessity solvable, we must confess it may be that for the sort of being whom we have described no survival is possible in any form like that which his soul has now taken. He is a fantastic thing that has developed sensibilities and established values beyond the nature which gave him birth. He is of all living cratures the one to whom the earth is the least satisfactory. He has arrived at a point where he can no longer delude himself as to the extent of his predicament, and should he either become modified or disappear the earth would continue to spin and the grass to grow as it has always done. Of the thousands of living species the vast majority would be as unaware of his passing as they are unaware now of his presence, and he would go as a shadow goes. His arts, his religions, and his civilizations — these are fair and wonderful things, but they are fair and wonderful to him alone. With the extinction of his poetry would come also the extinction of the only sensibility for which it has any meaning, and there would remain nothing capable of feeling a loss. Nothing would be left to label the memory of his discontent "divine," and those creatures who find in nature no lack would resume their undisputed possession of the earth.

18   Anthropoid in form some of them might continue to be, and possessed as well of all of the human brain that makes possible a cunning adaptation to the conditions of physical life. To them nature might yield up subtler secrets than any yet penetrated; their machines might be more wonderful and their bodies more healthy than any yet known — even though there had

passed away, not merely all myth and poetry, but the need for them as well. Cured of his transcendental cravings, content with things as they are, accepting the universe as experience had shown it to be, man would be freed of his soul and, like the other animals, either content or at least desirous of nothing which he might not hope ultimately to obtain.

19   Nor can it be denied that certain adumbrations of this type have before now come into being. Among those of keener intellect there are scientists to whom the test tube and its contents are all-sufficient, and among those of coarser grain, captains of finance and builders of mills, there are those to whom the acquirement of wealth and power seems to constitute a life in which no lack can be perceived. Doubtless they are not new types; doubtless they have always existed; but may they not be the strain from which Nature will select the coming race? Is not their creed the creed of Nature, and are they not bound to triumph over those whose illusions are no longer potent because they are no longer really believed? Certain philosophers, clinging desperately to the ideal of a humanized world, have proposed a retreat into the imagination. Bertrand Russell in his popular essay, *A Free Man's Worship,* Unamuno and Santayana *passim* throughout their works, have argued that the way of salvation lay in a sort of ironic belief, in a determination to act as though one still believed the things which once were really held true. But is not this a desperate expedient, a last refuge likely to appeal only to the leaders of a lost cause? Does it not represent the last, least substantial, phase of fading faith, something which borrows what little substance it seems to have from a reality of the past? If it seems half real to the sons of those who lived in the spiritual world of which it is a shadow, will it not seem, a little further removed, only a faint futility? Surely it has but little to oppose to those who come armed with the certitudes of science and united with, not fleeing from, the nature amid which they live.

20   And if the dilemma here described is itself a delusion, it is at least as vividly present and as terribly potent as those other delusions which have shaped or deformed the human spirit. There is no significant contemporary writer upon philosophy, ethics, or aesthetics whose speculations do not lead him to it in one form or another, and even the less reflective are aware of it in their own way. Both our practical morality and our emotional lives are adjusted to a world which no longer exists. In so far as we adhere to a code of conduct, we do so largely because certain habits still persist, not because we can give any logical reason for preferring them, and in so far as we indulge ourselves in the primitive emotional satisfactions — romantic love, patriotism, zeal for justice, and so forth — our satisfaction is the result merely of the temporary suspension of our disbelief in the mythology upon which they are founded. Traditionalists in religion are fond of asserting that our moral codes are flimsy because they are rootless; but, true as this is, it is perhaps not so important as the fact that our emotional lives are rootless too.

21   If the gloomy vision of a dehumanized world which had just been evoked is not to become a reality, some complete readjustment must be made, and at least two generations have found themselves unequal to the task. The generation of Thomas Henry Huxley, so busy with destruction as never adequately to realize how much it was destroying, fought with such zeal against frightened conservatives that it never took time to do more than assert with some vehemence that all would be well, and the generation that followed either danced amid the ruins or sought by various compromises to save the remains of a few tottering structures. But neither patches nor evasions will serve. It is not a changed world but a new one in which man must henceforth live if he lives at all, for all his premises have been destroyed and he must proceed to new conclusions. The values which he thought established have been swept away along with the rules by which he thought they might be attained.

22   To this fact many are not yet awake, but our novels, our poems, and our pictures are enough to reveal that a generation aware of its predicament is at hand. It has awakened to the fact that both the ends which its fathers proposed to themselves and the emotions from which they drew their strength seem irrelevant and remote. With a smile, sad or mocking, according to individual temperament, it regards those works of the past in which were summed up the values of life. The romantic ideal of a world well lost for love and the classic ideal of austere dignity seem equally ridiculous, equally meaningless when referred, not to the temper of the past, but to the temper of the present. The passions which swept through the once major poets no longer awaken any profound response, and only in the bleak, tortuous complexities of a T. S. Eliot does it find its moods given adequate expression. Here disgust speaks with a robust voice and denunciation is confident, but ecstasy, flickering and uncertain, leaps fitfully up only to sink back among the cinders. And if the poet, with his gift of keen perceptions and his power of organization, can achieve only the most momentary and unstable adjustments, what hope can there be for those whose spirit is a less powerful instrument?

23   And yet it is with such as he, baffled, but content with nothing which plays only upon the surface, that the hope for a still humanized future must rest. No one can tell how many of the old values must go or how new the new will be. Thus, while under the influence of the old mythology the sexual instinct was transformed into romantic love and tribal solidarity into the religion of patriotism, there is nothing in the modern consciousness capable of effecting these transmutations. Neither the one nor the other is capable of being, as it once was, the *raison d'être* of a life or the motif of a poem which is not, strictly speaking, derivative and anachronistic. Each is fading, each becoming as much a shadow as devotion to the cult of purification through self-torture. Either the instincts upon which they are founded will achieve new transformations or they will remain merely instincts, regarded as having no particular emotional significance in a spiritual world which, if

it exists at all, will be as different from the spiritual world of, let us say, Robert Browning as that world is different from the world of Cato the Censor.

24 As for this present unhappy time, haunted by ghosts from a dead world and not yet at home in its own, its predicament is not, to return to the comparison with which we began, unlike the predicament of the adolescent who has not yet learned to orient himself without reference to the mythology amid which his childhood was passed. He still seeks in the world of his experience for the values which he had found there, and he is aware only of a vast disharmony. But boys — most of them, at least — grow up, and the world of adult consciousness has always held a relation to myth intimate enough to make readjustment possible. The finest spirits have bridged the gulf, have carried over with them something of a child's faith, and only the coarsest have grown into something which was no more than finished animality. Today the gulf is broader, the adjustment more difficult, than ever it was before, and even the possibility of an actual human maturity is problematic. There impends for the human spirit either extinction or a readjustment more stupendous than any made before.

Commentary and questions

1. *Paragraphs 1-4:* Krutch re-creates, rather poetically, what it is like to be born, to pass from comfortable security to anxiety and uncertainty, and uses this re-creation as an analogy to the life of races. What is the purpose of the analogy? Is it a means of proof, or an attempt to represent certain concepts vividly? What particular contrasts does Krutch outline here? What values does he give these contrasts? Why does he emphasize the emotional, connotative side of them? Explain the phrase in paragraph 4: "Imagination is always the creature of desire." How would you describe Krutch's own point of view toward general human nature?

2. *Paragraph 5:* What does "fancy" mean? Why does Krutch oppose it to experience?

Do you notice anything odd about the statement that "Connections, explanations, and reasons are supplied by the imagination"? What does it suggest about Krutch's understanding of the contrast of ideality and reality? How does Krutch link this contrast to the theme of maturity or growth? Paraphrase the central idea or ideas of this paragraph.

3. *Paragraph 6:* This develops a further set of related contrasts, and adds meanings to the term "fancy." Explain how Krutch develops the concepts outlined in the first five paragraphs. What is the relationship suggested here and in paragraph 7 between the history of man's belief in God and his position in the modern world?

4. *Paragraphs 8-9:* Krutch intensifies the development of his thesis of man's aloneness and dissatisfaction by compressed historical survey and by contrast. What is the central contrast of these paragraphs?

5. *Paragraphs 10-14:* How is the central contrast of paragraphs 8-9 developed in this section? What concepts are added to it? How does Krutch relate this development to the first five paragraphs?

6. *Paragraph 15:* Up to this point Krutch has been writing as if traditional beliefs were no longer useful, but now he talks about their "survival value." Why does he suggest that they have this value?

7. *Paragraphs 16-20:* In your own words, what is the "dilemma" Krutch refers to? What is Krutch's own attitude toward current religious belief? Does he equate it with the beliefs of the past? Analyze the tone of the language in this section. Has it any relation to the tone of the beginning of the essay?

8. *Paragraphs 21-24:* Krutch argues here for a "humanized" future. On what basis does he suggest that it is possible? What does he mean by "humanized"? Does he define the term explicitly or implicitly?

Topics for discussion and writing

I. Krutch makes ample use of a contrast between the present and the past. Precisely how does he differentiate them? How central are his distinctions to his argument?

II. How much of Krutch's persuasiveness is due to his use of tonal values? How much can you derive of Krutch's own attitude from the tone of his essay? How would you describe that attitude: disillusioned, ironic, detached, concerned, anxious? Do you think that Krutch sees himself as sharing the modern mood he describes?

III. Write a theme describing Krutch's view of the modern "mood." Indicate what you think are the most important elements in that mood.

IV. Write a paper explaining what the subjects of each of the three sections are, their relation to one another, and their relation to the main theme of the essay.

THE SOUL OF MAN UNDER MODERNISM

Irwin Edman

From The Contemporary and His Soul, *by Irwin Edman. Copyright 1931 by Irwin Edman and 1959 by Meta Markel. Reprinted by permission of The Viking Press, Inc.*

THERE is probably no epithet that is more unfashionable in contemporary discourse than the word soul, no theme less congenial to the current imagination than salvation. The newer psychologies have substituted complex inquiries into the mechanisms of behaviour for the traditional notion of a presiding essence or psyche that governs a man's actions or that truly constitutes his essential being. The new moralities, in their concern with how a man may best live in this world, seem remote enough from the mediaeval problem of how he was to save his soul in the next.

2   Yet there would seem to be little question that, for all the difference in language, the concerns of the contemporary are precisely what those of his ancestor were, his soul and its salvation. Precisely because, as Walter Lippmann observes, "whirl is king," there has been endless brooding speculation, often masquerading as science, on the soul of man and its destiny. Precisely because all those interests, values and aspirations which commonly go by the name of soul, seem threatened by the passing of ancient traditions and the rise of unprecedented new circumstances, there has been a perplexed concern over the destiny of that spirit, its hopes, its future or its possible extinction. The whole of the modern temper has been a fretful canvassing of the conditions of the soul of man under mechanism, industry and latter-day worldliness. The question remains now what it always has been, What must we do to be saved? The psychologists have redefined soul and the moralists have recharted salvation, but Watson and Freud have been trying to describe what Thomas Aquinas so differently and less ambiguously defined; Joseph Wood Krutch and Lewis Mumford and Lippmann and Bertrand Russell have been trying in terms of a new world to find a new itinerary by which the confused or tormented contemporary may find his way, if not to bliss, at least to peace.

3   Now the mediaeval moralist when he spoke of the soul knew definitely, though abstractly, what he meant by it; the mediaeval theologian knew well enough what he meant by salvation. The disembodied principle of intelligence, pure and angelic, was to find peace in the eternal beatitude of beholding that pure and absolute Being which is God. The modern is blinded to the fact that he is concerned for his soul and for its salvation by the fact that he scarcely believes in the first, and because there is such a confusion of tongues and doctrines with regard to the second.

4   There is, indeed, in the first place, a very considerable current of belief that no soul of man — about whose salvation, none the less, the modern man worries so interminably — exists at all. The gradual extension of the mechanistic hypothesis came in time to pass from the stars and atoms to the natural life of man.

5   Of that tendency the latest, most extreme and — in its extreme instances — absurd form is Behaviourism. The mechanistic hypothesis is simply the hypothesis that all that used, properly speaking, to be characteristic of the soul can be explained — and explained away — by the externals of behaviour. Love and rapture, aspiration and defeat of aspiration, brooding happiness, joy and sorrow, all the awareness induced by the friction of the self and the world, of the life of man with the conditions in which that life is furthered or frustrated — all these, we have been now asked to believe, are to be understood in terms of glands and reflexes, of complexes and inhibitions. It is no longer for most people a question whether the soul is immortal or

not: they question its very existence. There is a personality about which a man is at once proud and ashamed, that self which seems to survive somehow — self recognized amid so many vicissitudes and transformations. But that self has suffered at the hands of psychologists and sociologists a thousand dissolutions. It is disintegrated into the statistics of the laboratory, into the formulas of the psycho-analysts and the sociologists. In very truth it is difficult these days for a man to call his soul his own.

6   Yet parallel to this disintegration of the psyche, there has come in contemporary thought an unprecedented meditation upon the self. No Pauline apostle, awake to the conviction of sin, could be more completely agonized about the self than is the contemporary harassed by his doubts and exasperations. What is the inferiority complex but the traditional sense of sin, what mediaeval ever sensed himself more lost than does the modern awakened to the transcience or emptiness of love or life or nature, the shipwreck of a world where there is nothing left to worship or adore? No Augustine, canvassing for three long books of his Confessions the quarrel in him between will and desire, could feel more deeply than do many contemporaries the quarrel in them between love and lust, between the flesh and the spirit. No Christian mystic could be more harassed than Proust over the evanescence of sensations and of memories and the struggle to keep hold of some portion of the self that will survive the flux of time.

7   But even more exact is the parallel between the modern and the mediaeval in the exacerbated reflection upon the self defeated by wordliness and by the world. St. Paul long ago scolded and implored the Christians at Corinth and at Rome to keep the spirit undefiled by the flesh. The contemporary sees on all sides everything that he has in the past subsumed under the category of the spirit of man being assailed, soiled and frustrated by things, by nature and by society. There is no quiet realm of eternity in which the balance may be rectified. Love defeated in this world is defeated for ever, and it is in *this* world that love and every other idealism is defeated. They are defeated, indeed, not simply by the fact that they are crushed, but by the fact that the conditions of modern industrial and social life generate a mood in which those very higher values come to seem negligible or futile or ridiculous. One begins by doubting the existence of the soul; one ends by doubting whether its interests can be fulfilled, or whether in the long run they matter. The soul becomes lost in the world, and ends by itself becoming worldly.

8   It is from such worldliness that, as in the past, salvation is being sought. The whole attempt of contemporary reflection may be said to be that of finding some way of life whereby the modern may find integrity or peace. Now peace is precisely what the mediaeval theologian promised the believer. If one's character, one's moral habits should become purified and one's mind should attain clarity, one would have gained integrity in this world and peace in the next. The current moralities are less concerned with

integrity than with integration, less with peace than with adult adjustment. But integrity is what they are after and peace is what they want. If, we are promised, one could come to know reality, including the realities of one's own nature, one could face both one's self and the conditions of all mortal existence with equanimity, perhaps with happiness. St. Bonaventura could indicate the itinerary of the mind to God. A hundred current writers, in novels, plays and moral essays, are trying to find the road also to a kind of peace. Or they are, perhaps, obsessed, as is Aldous Huxley, with the novel psychical and material obstacles to salvation.

9   It were best, perhaps, to canvass briefly those enemies of the soul of man — meaning by that expression the enemies of his moral and aesthetic interests — about which the contemporary is peculiarly distressed. Most serious, beyond question, is the fact that the new psychologies, especially as practiced or implied by men of letters, have made man not so much disbelieve in his own spirit as lose his respect for it. The net effect of recent inquiry, and especially of recent literary discussion, has been to make the modern incredibly scornful of his own idealisms. Love is seen to be simply lust on parade. Generosity becomes the assertion, roundabout and polite, of the desire for attention or for praise; and reason itself is found to be mostly arguments superficially good for motives irrefutably bad. It is with such mordant analysis, or illustrations of it, that a hundred recent novels are filled. We are taught to behold and to consider not those elements of human nature which might give us an inkling of potential glory, but rather those aspects or evidences of it that teach us to range ourselves with apes and peacocks rather than with heroes or angels. It is not so much life that is beastly as we that are.

10   It is a question too complex for consideration here how much we live and are sustained by romantic projections of ourselves, how much what we are or what we hope to be is dependent on the view that we imagine other people to have of us. Certain psychologists, notably Freud in his recent utterances, would have us account for much unhappiness by a sense of guilt that grows instead of decreases with the civilization of mankind. It remains certainly true, when we can only figure ourselves to ourselves as shoddy little poseurs, cringing, lustful, avaricious and vain, that there comes upon us, as there came upon the early Christians, a sense of unpardonable sin. The salt, our own salt, has lost its savour. We are vessels of corruption; we are bodies of this death; there is nothing in ourselves to save; worse still, there is nothing worth rescue.

11   Little, one is tempted to say, has more crucified the contemporary meditating upon himself, than this sense of irremediable evil, of something beyond salvage and not deserving it. It is not for nothing that three centuries of modern philosophy have coloured and poisoned with subjectivity our estimates of the nature of things and the goods in nature. How can anything be estimable when we who do the estimating are seen to be suspect and

compact of self-deceit and self-fraud, self-loathing and self-destruction? At least, our believing predecessors, if they saw no worth in themselves, knew where else to look for it. If they were obsessed with the yoke of sin, they knew where grace was abounding. We know, too, or make confused gestures toward knowing. Some simple faith tells us that some simple formula will cure us of an inferiority complex. Some innocence makes us believe that a formula of "disinterestedness" or "adult adjustment," of "objectivity" or "socialization," will cure us of the agony of aimlessness or of despair. There will be occasion later to inquire into some of these new faiths, these reliances at once touching and fantastic. It is sufficient for the present that the fact be noted that the new age still cherishes the ancient tribulation.
12   It has simply found new reasons for disbelieving in its own essential goodness or in its own power to rescue itself from confounding and distress.
13   But if the current imagination is troubled by disbelief in its own worth or its own values, it has still other enemies of the soul to reckon with. Traditional Christianity, with a shrewd instinct, saw itself, as all forthright religions have seen themselves, as standing foursquare against worldliness and the world. The current plaint — it is not a new one — is that the world is too much with us. But it is a new realm that impinges upon and oppresses us, an order in which speed, luxury and mechanization play an unprecedented part. Luxury is clearly not a novelty; the satirists of ancient Rome had it as their subject matter. But material comfort and physical indulgence have probably never before been available to so many nor have they been before to so many a predominant obsession. Even in a palace, said Marcus Aurelius, it is possible to live well. But, as the ancient sage pointed out, it required a special effort under the circumstances. And there have been few epochs and few parts of the world where the opportunity to battle against the enticements of material well-being were as open to as many as they are, or until recently have been, in America. The spiritual life need not be lived in sackcloth, but it can scarcely be led among the engulfing trivialities and distractions of middle-class contemporary society. Much of the criticism of Main Street and the country club is nothing but a reassertion of the traditional criticism of the flesh and the fleshpots by those who stand for something nobler, subtler and serener than the prevailing mores of the society in which they live. A hundred little Savonarolas are asking us to burn a thousand evidences of our corruption. And on a thousand Main Streets and on the verandahs of a thousand country clubs, a sudden pang of emptiness and vanity has assailed the occasional sensitive inhabitants and convicted them of a life void of meaning.
14   In the eighteenth century Rousseau won a prize by proving that all the arts and sciences had done for civilization was to degrade the spirit and corrupt the hearts and manners of mankind. Some new Rousseau might arise — he is, indeed, in a thousand forms arising — to tell us how much comfort, convenience and material excitement have corrupted the life of the spirit,

how they have made at once difficult and suspect the living, if not constantly at least consistently, in the society of beautiful and eternal things.
15   The obvious defeat that the soul suffers in an age when speed is every man's commonplace, has received enough detailed attention not to need repetition. But the restlessness of the modern temper and its mobility are not disconnected. Where there is nothing to cling to, or lovingly to brood upon, a restlessness of spirit is induced and a restlessness of body follows. It is not the mere physical exhilaration of speed that has made the automobile and the aeroplane popular. There is an intellectual excitement about motion, at once a stimulant and a narcotic. One derives from it a hurried sense of accomplishment; the sense of being en route, of seeing and doing many things quickly, conceals the emptiness of one's being and the scenes among which one superficially moves.
16   But most serious of the enemies of the soul of man, in the eyes of reflective observers, is standardization. It is futile to inquire how much the machine age and machine methods have rendered impossible that individuality in which alone any life acquires dignity, interest and character. There is no reason to suppose that the refrigerator and the automobile impede the good life. But there is very good reason for suspecting the subtler forms of mechanization, the regimentation brought about by mass schooling, the standard provision by routine thousands of amusements designed for mediocre millions, the chain stores of culture designed to make available to an innumerable democracy what is in essence possible only to an intellectually aristocratic few. It is not simply that the glitter of false goods is distracting the contemporary from his characteristic intellectual and aesthetic interests, but that the currency of these themselves is being debased. The very essence of intelligence is discrimination, the character of taste is to *have* character and definition, and these are being imperilled by the spread of an education whose standards are mediocrity, and whose appeal is merely promiscuous.
17   In his discovery of a fundamental lack of confidence in his own values, in the threatened extinction of even these by the special, novel conditions of current life, the contemporary has cause enough for confusion and despair. But he is even less comforted when he looks abroad, as it were, to nature itself, or at least to those contemporary versions of it to which his reading and his conversation expose him. The nineteenth century has bequeathed to us a cult of disillusion, a nightmare of an alien world, from which (*vide* as recent a work as Joseph Wood Krutch's *The Modern Temper*) we find it extraordinarily difficult to recover. There are, however, special recent variations of the modern malaise that need examination. It did not require the twentieth century to discover the sorrowful character of time. Poets, beginning with Eccleciastes, have bewailed the devouring mouth of time which consumes all things, including — and this is the tragedy — all that is most precious and beautiful. Time is merely another name for change, and change, in the imagination of a creature looking for stability and peace, is

freighted with the peril of destruction. The Greeks gave expression again and again, but especially in their philosophy, to the terror and the pre-cariousness of a temporal world. What else is Plato's passion for the per-manence of the Heaven of Eternal Ideas but the protest of the poet-philos-opher erecting a realm that abides for ever to free the mind from the sadness and defeat of one that is constantly passing away. The Christian theme — Augustine's *Confessions* are full of it — was again and again the peace of God's eternity contrasted with the vanishing illusions of time.

18   But it remained for the modern to explore more exactly into the nature of time itself, and to derive a private sting of melancholy from the explora-tions. For time cannot any longer be considered simply as the illusory char-acter of a merely shadow world. It seems to be woven into the very character of ultimate existence. Nature is ultimately nothing but the flow of all ex-perience, and all experience is set, as it were, in the moving matrix of time. The permanent is seen to be simply a pause in reflection, a stability which action momentarily achieves. Even space and the physical world have, in the hands of the contemporary physicist, become a pictorial expression, a visual function of time.

19   There are thinkers (John Dewey is one of them) who find an exhilara-tion in the discovery of the essentially temporal character of the universe. Only in an unfinished world, they are constantly reminding us, is improve-ment possible; only where all is genuinely unfinished can something yet be done. In so insisting, they are giving expression to a pioneer and exploratory mood which three centuries of invention and discovery have not sufficed to exhaust. For many, time still remains time to do, to accomplish, to make a difference and to make over a civilization. For many, change means the excitement of novelty, the suspense of a possible unprecedented goodness or beauty, the revelation of some as yet undreamed-of good. "There will," Wil-liam James remarked, "be news in Heaven." For the perpetually young — or the perpetually adolescent — the omnipresence of the fact of time in contem-porary thinking holds not terror but encouragement, not a dusk but a dawn.

20   There is no doubt but the discovery of, the emphasis upon, change has about it a certain glory, at once stalwart and romantic. But the more intro-spective have found in this consideration that time has forced upon them less occasion for congratulation. For change remains change, and change as often means loss as gain, and once in every life it means extinction. More-over, if time alone be real, as in certain quarters we are led to believe that it is, then nothing else is really so. This discovery may be the fruit of a subtle metaphysics, as it is in Bergson, but it is an insight that any sensitive person can make for himself, and one to which his life and memory rather than any speculation have led him. For the philosophers have simply confirmed what the sensitive have long known. Mutation is discovered first not among things but in one's self, one's loves, one's friends and one's memories. The appeal, half delicious, half depressing, that the writings of Marcel Proust have for

many readers lies in the skillful way he has of evoking past time and its realities, perishing and precarious, of our memories. The instant, so lovely and so living, is qualified by memories of the past that is irrevocably gone. We scarcely live at all, save in the illusions, the distorted perspectives of memory, and the imaginations of which the materials of memory form a large and illusive part. Our life is a succession of, or rather a river of, indistinguishable instants, each scarcely isolable from its predecessors and each in turn unreal. Time, by whose indeterminate future we were to save ourselves, turns out to be the river in which those constantly vanishing moments we call ourselves must drown.

21   From these and similar awarenesses the contemporary, though he would shun the expression, is looking about to be saved. Christianity, when it spread with such surprising rapidity over the Graeco-Roman world, was not the only cult that promised the believer repose if not bliss. All these mystery religions had a widespread and intelligible appeal, Christianity itself in its Pauline form being likewise a mystery.

22   It was a time of general despair, what Gilbert Murray has aptly termed "the failure of nerve." There was no hope in civic righteousness or personal virtue. He who would believe in the Lord and follow His Way — and this was all that was essentially necessary — would be saved. The old life, compact and secure, of the Greek city state had broken up, and personal success was largely on the knees of whatever gods or atoms there were; it was no longer a matter of ordered virtue but of capricious fate.

23   A not dissimilar situation confronts us at the present time. Just before the war a faith in a Wellsian code of co-operative science captured the imagination of ardent young liberals. The war destroyed that hope along with the young men it destroyed. There are still those who trust to co-operative intelligence to produce a clear and freer world. But there is no lack of those, of whom Spengler is merely the most articulate, who see no hope in the future, and a possible complete collapse of that civilization that Athens, Florence and Chartres enshrine. In the fantastic hazard of modern commercial and even professional life, personal success seems largely a gamble, and, when achieved, a delusion. Nor is there any tradition immune to criticism, any fund of religious sanctions, to which one can turn for hope or sustenance or consolation. As in early Christian times, therefore, the social imagination turns to any current mystery, any faith in which by partaking, by becoming a communicant, a man may be saved. All of these traditional religions have this in common, that in the traditional sense they are not religions at all.[1] But most of the current religions have the guise and the vocabulary, if not the spirit, of science. They resemble the traditional religions in many minor

---

[1] Though there are, it must be admitted, those who in a desperate flight from things as they are, are indulging in a flight at once wistful and romantic to religions as they were; of these the Anglo-Catholic movement, or the modernistic mediaevalism of Jacques Maritain are good examples.

points; they have their rituals, their rites, their formulas, their mystic inspirations and their ecstasies of vision. They resemble them in one major point: they promise the unhappy and the discontented, the confused and the forlorn (those who would once have been called sinners, or lost souls) happiness, or, as it was once called, salvation.

24   An examination of these living systems of salvation would reveal how various is the nature of these faiths, and how not unlike mystery religions they are. They are ways of life or of a life beyond life; they have their esoteric language and their prophets or half-legendary heroes; they promise all those who are heavy laden and who come to them that they will give them rest.

25   There is one embittered or ensoured group who have indeed thought themselves beyond the traps of any new scheme of salvation. The modernists in cynicism, scepticism and despair have thought that by a complete disillusion they could at least save themselves from ever again being taken in. "We prefer" — writes Mr. Joseph Wood Krutch at the conclusion of his *The Modern Temper* — "to die as men rather than to live as animals." To the disillusionist at least one virtue remains, that of intellectual *askesis*. No trapdoor of factitious glory will delude him; no sentimental renascence of an outmoded culture or religion, no Tolstoyan revival of a simple faith in simple man will hypnotize him from the cool and amused gaze with which he faces himself, his fellows and his world. He has found the salvation in its least luxurious form, the compensation, at most bleak and austere, of seeing things without fantasy, deriving at once the satisfaction of truth and the enjoyment of its ironic recognition. To see the object itself as it really is, so the disillusionist after his fashion follows Matthew Arnold; and seeing it as it is, to smile, if a little wryly — this also is a way of saving the soul that one has ceased to believe in.

26   Not many can succeed in finding peace in the wry admission of uncharming truths. It is improbable that even the disillusionist finds it thus. There is usually no real gaiety in his laughter, and too rhetorical a courage in his facing of the truth. Most men still wish to be saved, and there are certain characteristics to be observed in current ways to peace.

27   The first of these that impresses the observer is the faith in intelligence. Francis Bacon first gave publicity to the idea (he was certainly not its discoverer nor, even among his contemporaries, the best illustration) now echoed by every liberal thinker on two continents, that intelligence may save the individual soul and rescue mankind. One must postpone consideration of the history of this notion, or its fallacies. It reduces itself most simply to the belief that that disciplined inquiry which has transformed the face of nature may transform the life of mankind. Not only may mountains be moved, but the soul may be ordered and commonwealths be organized by that same technique of exploration and experiment which has brought the comfort, the speed and the luxury of modern life. How well grounded is this

belief is also a question that need not here for the moment be settled. All that matters is that, led by writers as different as H. G. Wells and John Dewey, there has grown up the remarkable faith that what men once left to God they can now attain of their own disciplined and controlled action. Creative intelligence, scientific control, the technique of the laboratory — by whatever name they may be called — the modern man in increasing numbers has believed that by his own intelligence he might be saved. No catastrophe of war, no meeting of personal problems that at once transcend or utterly defeat intelligence counts. The faith remains, and it has its own poets as well as prophets.

28   The faith has its heretics and its obvious difficulties. Even the most romantic adherents of the possibilities of intelligent control grant that death and unrequited love cannot quite be solved by its efforts. There are those, too, who despairing of the world that the war has left us, bemoaning the change in a civilization that seems ultimately to consist in nothing but change, have tried to retreat to some indefeasible realm, as snug and sure as a protected harbour, as certain and eternal as a traditional Paradise. These have to go back to Plato or to Hindu philosophy for their salvation. Only in the passive beholding of those unchanging essences, of the forms of all being, and the eternal postures and gestures which existence may take, can salvation be found. By giving up all save the irreducible essences, by abnegating all but the eternal, sure and non-existent, these (Santayana is their most eloquent spokesman) count on being saved. Only by giving up the whole world of existence may they save their own souls, become the pure disinterested spectators of what always is and ever has been. They reduce life to the hearing of a music, pure and bodiless, in the uncaring hearing of which alone is the bliss of disinterestedness found. It is an austere enough Heaven, and only a metaphysician or a musician of the more metaphysical sort can enjoy himself therein. There are others who will not thus retreat to Platonism, but like the Platonists cannot feel happy in the contemporary world. They are homesick for what is dead, nostalgic for a Heaven of which the cultures, languages and traditions of the past are echoes and memories. They would escape, not by fleeing to eternal timelessness, but by fleeing to the equally changeless — because irrevocable — world of the past. It may be with some the revival of some ancient national culture, its literature, its modes, its language, of which the Gaelic revival in Ireland, or the to-do about Welsh or Basque may be cited. Out of the colourlessness and confusion of a vast promiscuous modern world, these homesick revivalists hope to recover the clear thread, the unconfused light of their own national traditions.

29   It may again be a retreat to an ancient faith. Much certainly of the modernistic embracing of Catholicism by hitherto sceptical and disillusioned intellectuals is the clutching at some hold, clear and definitive, in an intellectual realm where there is nothing but confusion to cling to. Thus we have the spectacle of Jews long without any belief turning to the code of their

fathers and the ethics of their prophets, and Protestants who were scarcely even that, turning with fanaticism to Rome. In these cases, unless one is very much mistaken, it is not religion in the sense of an experience or a theology by which they as believers are coerced, but some religion in the old Roman sense of something by which one may be bound, a theme in the light of which life gains some order, a tradition which gives it a dignity that cannot be corrupted and a significance that cannot be questioned. For all the parade of intellectuality that accompanies these conversions, it is clear that they are the fruits of sentimental nostalgias. It is homesickness that makes the converted intellectuals call these thin intellectual adoptions of ancient faiths a going home.

30   Not science, nor an intellectual reviving of religion, nor a nursing into flame of dead cultures, can satisfy some of the disenchanted. Their intellectual scruples will enable them to detect the weakness or the anachronisms of each of them in turn. There are two further characteristic flights to be noted. One of them is the hard-boiled escape into mere action for the sake of avoiding thought; the other may be described as the soft-boiledness of mysticism for the same evasive purpose.

31   There is a school of writers and of people who are indulging in a new kind of naïveté, so deliberate as to seem almost the last word in sophistication. It consists in avoiding articulateness, in dodging sentiment, in evading thought. The *faux naïfs,* Wyndham Lewis called them; but it is not our purpose here to call them so but simply to call attention to them. Like the heroes in a Hemingway novel, they trust only to the directness of action and of immediate animal feeling in a world where there is nothing else to be trusted, and where even these are likely to be clouded and impeded by thought or words.

32   And there are finally those who, sickening of both the futility of mere animal feeling or animal action, retreat, as some few in all ages have retreated, to a mystical absorption, an abandoning of the categories of life and nature and society for a rapture, vast, vague and indiscriminate. By refusing to be bound by compulsions of action or thought or things, these also hope to see the inerrable godhead of delight, to be caught up into a not impossible ecstasy, like St. Catherine or St. John of the Cross, to pass beyond the dark night of the soul to a rapturous alone with the Alone.

33   It is not the intention here to question the validity of each or of any of these faiths. That must be left for some other place, possibly for some other critic. They are noted here rather as illustrations of the central theme. Each of these ways of life has become a cult, a promise, a hope and a mystery. Each is a symptom of that still persisting quest by which the soul, in this as in past ages, recites a soliloquy of its own hopes and the obstacles it meets in itself and in things, in society and in nature; the ways, sublime, pitiable or ridiculous, by which it tries to find a home, an anchorage or an escape. The language changes, the quest is still the same. It remains to be

investigated, whether the soul's soliloquy can be made relevant to its conditions and whether the theme of salvation can generate a technique for life in this world rather than a fantasy of life in another, believed or imaginary.

Commentary and questions

1. *Paragraphs 1-2:* Edman takes pains to apologize for his use of the word "soul." Why? How does his contrast between the Middle Ages and the modern world suit his introduction? Does Edman alter the contrast as he develops it? What kind of support or illustration does he use in these paragraphs?

2. *Paragraphs 3-4:* What is the meaning of "belief" as Edman uses it here? Why does he suggest belief is valuable? How would you interpret the "mechanistic hypothesis"? What is Edman's main technique for developing his thesis to this point?

3. *Paragraph 5:* Edman calls behaviorism "absurd." What support does he offer for his opinion?

4. *Paragraph 6:* How and by what means does Edman characterize and identify "the contemporary"?

5. *Paragraph 7:* Edman brings the Middle Ages and the modern world together again. Is there any difference from his use of the two ages earlier? If so, what use does he make of the switch?

6. *Paragraphs 9-17:* This section details Edman's view of what is wrong with modern man. Paraphrase the main ideas in the section. By what means are these ideas presented? How specific is Edman's support for his thesis?

7. *Paragraphs 18-20:* Edman analyzes the contemporary sense of change as a traditional attitude. What does he specify as peculiarly modern?

8. *Paragraph 21:* A tentative conclusion appears here: Edman notes that he has listed what the modern world wants to be saved from. Does Edman intrude his own point of view here? If so, how would you describe it?

9. *Paragraphs 22-26:* Edman intensifies his criticism of modern attitudes. What devices does he use to explain and attack these attitudes? What is the tone of his mention of Krutch?

10. *Paragraphs 27-32:* This section lists and analyzes a series of modern "faiths." Paraphrase this list. How does Edman particularize and illustrate them? Which is most familiar to you as a general modern point of view? Which does Edman describe most clearly? Does Edman use the word "faith" in a straightforward, descriptive way, or does he evoke special connotations? Examine the tone of this section.

11. *Paragraph 33:* In his conclusion Edman says that he does not mean "to question the validity of each or of any of these faiths." Re-examine the tone of the language in which each is described. Is Edman's statement entirely consistent with this tone? What is that theme? Is Edman in sympathy with the general attitude he describes in the essay? Is he partly critical and partly sympathetic? Specify.

Topics for discussion and writing

I. Would you say that Edman's thesis is primarily negative?

II. Edman's essay can be divided into four distinct sections. Write an essay in which you paraphrase these sections and demonstrate their relationship to each other.

III. Compare Edman's four sections in their use of support. Which use it most often and what kinds of support are used?

IV. Edman stresses a contrast between an age of faith or religious belief and modern attitudes. Write a theme explaining this contrast in detail and showing how it is important to Edman's central thesis.

FREEDOM:
A FIGHTING FAITH

Arthur M. Schlesinger, Jr.

This selection from Arthur M. Schlesinger, Jr., The Vital Center, Copyright 1949, is reprinted by permission of and arrangement with Houghton Mifflin Company, the authorized publishers.

INDUSTRIALISM is the benefactor and the villain of our time: it has burned up the mortgage, but at the same time sealed us in a subtler slavery. It has created wealth and comfort in undreamed-of abundance. But in the wake of its incomparable economic achievement it has left the thin, deadly trail of anxiety. The connecting fluids of industrial society begin to dry up; the seams harden and crack; and society is transformed into a parched desert, "a heap of broken images, where the sun beats, and the dead tree gives no shelter, the cricket no relief, and the dry stone no sound of water" — that state of social purgatory which Durkheim called "anomie" and where Eliot saw fear in a handful of dust.

2   Under industrialism the social order ceases to be society in faith and brotherhood. It becomes the waste land, "asocial society," in Alex Comfort's phrase — "a society of onlookers, congested but lonely, technically advanced but utterly insecure, subject to a complicated mechanism of order but individually irresponsible." [1] We live on from day to day, persisting mechanically in the routine of a morality and a social pattern which has been switched off but which continues to run from its earlier momentum. Our lives are empty of belief. They are lives of quiet desperation.

[1] Alex Comfort, *The Novel and Our Time,* London, 1948, p. 12.

3   Who can live without desperation in a society turned asocial — in a social system which represents organized frustration instead of organized fulfillment? Freedom has lost its foundation in community and become a torment; "individualism" strips the individual of layer after layer of protective tissue. Reduced to panic, industrial man joins the lemming migration, the convulsive mass escape from freedom to totalitarianism, hurling himself from the bleak and rocky cliffs into the deep, womb-dark sea below. In free society, as at present constituted, the falcon cannot hear the falconer, the center cannot hold. Anarchy is loosed upon the world, and, as in Yeats's terrible vision, some rough beast, its hour come round at last, slouches toward Bethlehem to be born.

4   Through this century, free society has been on the defensive, demoralized by the infection of anxiety, staggering under the body blows of fascism and Communism. Free society alienates the lonely and uprooted masses; while totalitarianism, building on their frustrations and cravings, provides a structure of belief, men to worship and men to hate and rites which guarantee salvation. The crisis of free society has assumed the form of international collisions between the democracies and the totalitarian powers; but this fact should not blind us to the fact that in its essence this crisis is internal.

5   Free society will survive, in the last resort, only if enough people believe in it deeply enough to die for it. However reluctant peace-loving people are to recognize that fact, history's warning is clear and cold; civilizations which cannot man their walls in times of alarm are doomed to destruction by the barbarians. We have deeply believed only when the issue of war has reduced our future to the stark problem of self-preservation. Franklin Roosevelt read the American people with his usual uncanny accuracy when he named the Second War, not the "war for freedom," but the "war for survival." Our democracy has still to generate a living emotional content, rich enough to overcome the anxieties incited by industrialism, deep enough to rally its members to battle for freedom — not just for self-preservation. Freedom must become, in Holmes's phrase, a "fighting faith."

6   Why does not democracy believe in itself with passion? Why is freedom not a fighting faith? In part because democracy, by its nature, dissipates rather than concentrates its internal moral force. The thrust of the democratic faith is away from fanaticism; it is toward compromise, persuasion and consent in politics, toward tolerance and diversity in society; its economic foundation lies in the easily frightened middle class. Its love of variety discourages dogmatism, and its love of skepticism discourages hero-worship. In place of theology and ritual, of hierarchy and demonology, it sets up a belief in intellectual freedom and unrestricted inquiry. The advocate of free society defines himself by telling what he is against: what he is for turns out to be certain *means* and he leaves other people to charge the means with content. Today democracy is paying the price for its systematic cultivation of the peaceful and rational virtues. "Many a man will live

and die upon a dogma; no man will be a martyr for a conclusion." [2]

7   Democracy, moreover, has not worn too well as a philosophy of life in an industrial age. It seemed more solid at the high noon of success than it does in the uncertainties of falling dusk. In its traditional form, it has presupposed emotional and psychological stability in the individual. It has assumed, much too confidently, that the gnawing problems of doubt and anxiety would be banished by the advance of science or cured by a rise in the standard of living. The spectacular reopening of these problems in our time finds the democratic faith lacking in the profounder emotional resources. Democracy has no defense-in-depth against the neuroses of industrialism. When philosophies of blood and violence arise to take up the slack between democracy's thin optimism and the bitter agonies of experience, democracy by comparison appears pale and feeble.

8   Yet it seems doubtful whether democracy could itself be transformed into a political religion, like totalitarianism, without losing its characteristic belief in individual dignity and freedom. Does this mean that democracy is destined to defeat, sooner or later, by one or another of the totalitarian sects?

9   The death pallor will indeed come over free society, unless it can recharge the deepest sources of its moral energy. And we cannot make democracy a fighting faith merely by exhortation nor by self-flagellation; and certainly not by renouncing the values which distinguish free society from totalitarianism. Yet we must somehow dissolve the anxieties which drive people in free society to become traitors to freedom. We must somehow give the lonely masses a sense of individual human function, we must restore community to the industrial order.

10   There is on our side, of course, the long-run impossibility of totalitarianism. A totalitarian order offers no legitimate solution to the problem of freedom and anxiety. It does not restore basic securities; it does not create a world where men may expect lives of self-fulfillment. It enables man, not to face himself, but to flee himself by diving into the Party and the state. Only he cannot stay there; he must either come up for air or drown. Totalitarianism has scotched the snake of anxiety, but not killed it; and anxiety will be its undoing.

11   An enduring social order must base itself upon the emotional energies and needs of man. Totalitarianism thwarts and represses too much of man ever to become in any sense a "good society." Terror is the essence of totalitarianism; and normal man, in the long run, instinctively organizes himself against terror. This fact gives the champions of freedom their great opportunity. But let no one deceive himself about the short-run efficacy of totalitarian methods. Modern technology has placed in the hands of "totalitarian man" the power to accomplish most of his ends of human subjection. He may have no enduring solution, but neither, for example, did the Dark Ages.

[2] J. H. Newman, *Grammar of Assent*, London, 1930, p. 93. This neglected work remains one of the most valuable of all analyses of the way in which man gives his assent.

Yet the darkness lasted a longer time than the period which has elapsed since the discovery of America.

12 We cannot count upon totalitarian dynamism running down of its own accord in a single generation. Man is instinctively anti-totalitarian; but it is necessary for wise policies to mobilize these instincts early enough to do some good. Our problem is to make democracy the fighting faith, not of some future underground movement, but of us all here today in the middle of the twentieth century.

13 The essential strength of democracy as against totalitarianism lies in its startling insight into the value of the individual. Yet, as we have seen, this insight can become abstract and sterile; arrogant forms of individualism sometimes discredit the basic faith in the value of the individual. It is only so far as that insight can achieve a full social dimension, so far as individualism derives freely from community, that democracy will be immune to the virus of totalitarianism.

14 For all the magnificent triumphs of individualism, we survive only as we remain members of one another. The individual requires a social context, not one imposed by coercion, but one freely emerging in response to his own needs and initiatives. Industrialism has inflicted savage wounds on the human sensibility; the cuts and gashes are to be healed only by a conviction of trust and solidarity with other human beings.

15 It is in these fundamental terms that we must reconstruct our democracy. Optimism about man is not enough. The formalities of democracy are not enough. The fact that a man can cast a secret ballot or shop in Woolworth's rather than Kresge's is more important to those free from anxiety than it is to the casualties of the industrial order. And the casualties multiply: the possessors are corrupted by power, the middling undone by boredom, the dispossessed demoralized by fear. Chamber-of-commerce banalities will no longer console industrial man.

16 We require individualism which does not wall man off from community; we require community which sustains but does not suffocate the individual. The historic methods of free society are correct so far as they go; but they concentrate on the individual; they do not go far enough. It would be fatal to abandon Winston Churchill's seven tests of freedom. But these tests are inadequate to create free society because they define means, not ends. We know now that man is not sufficiently perfect to shape good means infallibly to good ends. So we no longer describe free society in terms of means alone: we must place ends as well in the forefront of our philosophy of democracy.

17 An adequate philosophy of free society would have to supplement the Churchill tests by such questions as these:

18 Do the people have a relative security against the ravages of hunger, sickness and want?

19 Do they freely unite in continuous and intimate association with likeminded people for common purposes?

20 Do they as individuals have a feeling of initiative, function and fulfillment in the social order?

21 It has become the duty of free society to answer these questions — and to answer them affirmatively if it would survive. The rise of the social-welfare state is an expression of that sense of duty. But the social welfare state is not enough. The sense of duty must be expressed specifically and passionately in the heart and will of men, in their daily decisions and their daily existence, if free men are to remain free.

22 The contemporary schism between the individual and the community has weakened the will of man. Social conditions cannot, of course, make moral decisions. But they can create conditions where moral decisions are more or less likely to be made. Some social arrangements bring out the evil in man more quickly than others. Slavery, as we knew well in America, corrupts the masters; totalitarian society, placing unbearable strains on man's self-restraint, produces the most violent reactions of fanaticism and hatred; the unchecked rule of the business community encourages greed and oppression. So the reform of institutions becomes an indispensable part of the enterprise of democracy. But the reform of institutions can never be a substitute for the reform of man.

23 The inadequacy of our institutions only intensifies the tribute that society levies from man: it but exacerbates the moral crisis. The rise of totalitarianism, in other words, signifies more than an internal crisis for democratic society. It signifies an internal crisis for democratic man. There is a Hitler, a Stalin in every breast. "Each of us has the plague within him," cries Tarrou in the Camus novel; "no one, no one on earth is free from it. And I know, too, that we must keep endless watch on ourselves lest in a careless moment we breathe in somebody's face and fasten the infection on him. What's natural is the microbe. All the rest — health, integrity, purity (if you like) — is a product of the human will, of a vigilance that must never falter." [3]

24 How to produce a vigilance that never falters? how to strengthen the human will? Walt Whitman in his later years grew obsessed with the moral indolence of democracy. Once he had hymned its possibilities with unequaled fervor. Now he looked about him and saw people "with hearts of rags and souls of chalk." As he pondered "the shallowness and miserable selfism of these crowds of men, with all their minds so blank of high humanity and aspiration," then came "the terrible query . . . Is not Democracy of human rights humbug after all?" The expansion of the powers of government provided no solution. "I have little hope of any man or any community of men, that looks to some civil or military power to defend its vital rights. — If we have it not in ourselves to defend what belongs to us, then the citadel and heart of the towns are taken."

25 Wherein lies the hope? In "the exercise of Democracy," Whitman finally answered. ". . . to work for Democracy is good, the exercise is good

[3] Albert Camus, *The Plague*, New York, 1948, p. 229.

— strength it makes and lessons it teaches." The hope for free society lies, in the last resort, in the kind of men it creates. "There is no week nor day nor hour," wrote Whitman, "when tyranny may not enter upon this country, if the people lose their supreme confidence in themselves, — and lose their roughness and spirit of defiance — Tyranny may always enter — there is no charm, no bar against it — the only bar against it is a large resolute breed of men." [4]

26 In times past, when freedom has been a fighting faith, producing a "large resolute breed of men," it has acquired its dynamism from communion in action. "The exercise of Democracy" has quickened the sense of the value of the individual; and, in that exercise, the individual has found a just and fruitful relation to the community. We require today exactly such a rededication to concrete democratic ends; so that the exercise of democracy can bring about a reconciliation between the individual and the community, a revival of the *élan* of democracy, and a resurgence of the democratic faith.

27 The expansion of the powers of government may often be an essential part of society's attack on evils of want and injustice. The industrial economy, for example, has become largely inaccessible to the control of the individual; and, even in the field of civil freedom, law is the means society has for registering its own best standards. Some of the democratic exhilaration consequently has to be revived by delegation: this is why we need the Franklin Roosevelts. Yet the expansion of the powers of government, the reliance on leadership, as Whitman perceived, have also become a means of dodging personal responsibility. This is the essential importance of the issues of civil rights and civil liberties. Every one of us has a direct, piercing and inescapable responsibility in our own lives on questions of racial discrimination, of political and intellectual freedom — not just to support legislative programs, but to extirpate the prejudices of bigotry in our environment, and, above all, in ourselves.

28 Through this joint democratic effort we can tap once again the spontaneous sources of community in our society. Industrialism has covered over the springs of social brotherhood by accelerating the speed and mobility of existence. Standardization, for example, while it has certainly raised levels not only of consumption but of culture, has at the same time cut the umbilical cord too early; it has reduced life to an anonymity of abundance which brings less personal fulfillment than people once got from labor in their own shop or garden. More people read and write; but what they read and write tends to have less connection with themselves. We have made culture available to all at the expense of making much of it the expression of a common fantasy rather than of a common experience. We desperately need a rich emotional life, reflecting actual relations between the individual and the community.

29 The cultural problem is but one aspect of the larger problem of the rôle

[4] Walt Whitman, "Notes for Lecturers on Democracy and 'Adhesiveness,' " C. J. Furness, *Walt Whitman's Workshop*, Cambridge, 1928, pp. 57, 58.

of independent groups, of voluntary associations, in free society. There is an evident thinness in the texture of political democracy, a lack of appeal to those irrational sentiments once mobilized by religion and now by totalitarianism. Democracy, we have argued, is probably inherently incapable of satisfying those emotions in the apparatus of the state without losing its own character. Yet a democratic society, based on a genuine cultural pluralism, on widespread and spontaneous group activity, could go far to supply outlets for the variegated emotions of man, and thus to restore meaning to democratic life. It is the disappearance of effective group activity which leads toward emptiness in the individual, as it also compels the enlargement of the powers of the state.

30   People deprived of any meaningful rôle in society, lacking even their own groups to give them a sense of belonging, become cannon fodder for totalitarianism. And groups themselves, once long established, suffer inevitable tendencies toward exclusiveness and bureaucratization, forget their original purpose and contribute to the downfall of freedom. If the American Medical Association, for example, had given serious attention to the problem of meeting the medical needs of America today, Doctor Fishbein would not be dunning his membership for funds to support a lobby against national health insurance. In the short run, the failure of voluntary initiative invites the spread of state power. In the long run, the disappearance of voluntary association paves the way for the pulverization of the social structure essential to totalitarianism. By the revitalization of voluntary associations, we can siphon off emotions which might otherwise be driven to the solutions of despair. We can create strong bulwarks against the totalitarianization of society.[5]

31   Democracy requires unremitting action on many fronts. It is, in other words, a process, not a conclusion. However painful the thought, it must be recognized that its commitments are unending. The belief in the millennium has dominated our social thinking too long. Our utopian prophets have always supposed that a day would come when all who had not worshiped the beast nor received his mark on their foreheads would reign for a thousand years. "And God shall wipe away all tears from their eyes; and there shall be no more death, neither sorrow, nor crying, neither shall there be any more pain: for the former things are passed away."

32   But the Christian millennium calls for a catastrophic change in human nature. Let us not sentimentalize the millennium by believing we can attain it through scientific discovery or through the revision of our economic system. We must grow up now and forsake the millennial dream. We will not arise one morning to find all problems solved, all need for further strain and struggle ended, while we work two hours a day and spend our leisure eating

[5] For the rôle of private associations, see Alexis de Tocqueville, *Democracy in America*, Part I, chap. 12, Part II, bk. i, chaps. 5-7; and the essay, "Biography of a Nation of Joiners," Arthur M. Schlesinger, *Path to the Present*, New York, 1949.

milk and honey. Given human imperfection, society will continue imperfect. Problems will always torment us, because all important problems are insoluble: that is why they are important. The good comes from the continuing struggle to try and solve them, not from the vain hope of their solution.

33 This is just as true of the problems of international society. "What men call peace," Gilson has well said, "is never anything but a space between two wars; a precarious equilibrium that lasts as long as mutual fear prevents dissension from declaring itself. This parody of true peace, this armed fear . . . may very well support a kind of order, but never can it bring mankind anything of tranquillity. Not until the social order becomes the spontaneous expression of an interior peace in men's hearts shall we have tranquillity." [6] Does it seem likely (pending the millennium) that we shall ever have an interior peace in the hearts of enough men to transform the nature of human society? The pursuit of peace, Whitehead reminds us, easily passes into its bastard substitute, anesthesia.

34 So we are forced back on the reality of struggle. So long as society stays free, so long will it continue in its state of tension, breeding contradiction, breeding strife. But we betray ourselves if we accept contradiction and strife as the total meaning of conflict. For conflict is also the guarantee of freedom; it is the instrument of change; it is, above all, the source of discovery, the source of art, the source of love. The choice we face is not between progress with conflict and progress without conflict. The choice is between conflict and stagnation. You cannot expel conflict from society any more than you can from the human mind. When you attempt it, the psychic costs in schizophrenia or torpor are the same.

35 The totalitarians regard the toleration of conflict as our central weakness. So it may appear to be in an age of anxiety. But we know it to be basically our central strength. The new radicalism derives its power from an acceptance of conflict — an acceptance combined with a determination to create a social framework where conflict issues not in excessive anxiety, but in creativity. The center is vital; the center must hold. The object of the new radicalism is to restore the center, to reunite individual and community in fruitful union. The spirit of the new radicalism is the spirit of the center — the spirit of human decency, opposing the extremes of tyranny. Yet, in a more fundamental sense, does not the center itself represent one extreme? while, at the other, are grouped the forces of corruption — men transformed by pride and power into enemies of humanity.

36 The new radicalism, drawing strength from a realistic conception of man, dedicates itself to problems as they come, attacking them in terms which best advance the humane and libertarian values, which best secure the freedom and fulfillment of the individual. It believes in attack — and out of attack will come passionate intensity.

37 Can we win the fight? We must commit ourselves to it with all our vigor

[6] Etienne Gilson, *The Spirit of Medieval Philosophy*, New York, 1936, p. 399.

in all its dimensions: the struggle within the world against Communism and fascism; the struggle within our country against oppression and stagnation; the struggle within ourselves against pride and corruption: nor can engagement in one dimension exclude responsibility for another. Economic and political action can help restore the balance between individual and community and thereby reduce one great source of anxiety. But even the most favorable social arrangements cannot guarantee individual virtue; and we are far yet from having solved the social problem.

38   The commitment is complex and rigorous. When has it not been so? If democracy cannot produce the large resolute breed of men capable of the climactic effort, it will founder. Out of the effort, out of the struggle alone, can come the high courage and faith which will preserve freedom.

Commentary and questions

1. *Paragraphs 1-4:* Schlesinger opens with a survey of the "crisis" in Free Society, its anxieties, failures, torments, and emotional sterility. The following terms are typical of the language of these paragraphs: benefactor and villain, slavery, parched desert, quiet desperation, society turned asocial, panic, lemming migration, womb-dark sea, anarchy, staggering. Which are metaphors? Which are used for their emotive impact? What concepts and emotions do they express? Together do they convey any unified impression?

This section carries frequent direct and indirect quotation and allusion. How much do you recognize? For example "womb-dark sea" is a parody of the Homeric formula "wine-dark sea," and presumably Schlesinger intends it to suggest the anti-heroic quality of modern man's search for escape from anxiety.

2. *Paragraph 5:* This paragraph completes the introductory note. How does it differ from the first four? What does it predict and what does it urge? Having now completed the essay, return to the first five paragraphs and see how closely they epitomize the structure of the whole.

3. *Paragraph 7:* What has Schlesinger established to justify the metaphor "the neuroses of industrialism?"

4. *Paragraphs 10-14:* Here Schlesinger evaluates the relative merits and disadvantages of totalitarianism and democracy. He believes that totalitarianism will not triumph because it is prey to the same anxieties as democracy, but he also fears that democracy's "insight into the value of the individual . . . can become abstract and sterile." What does he suggest is the cause of the danger? What is meant by a "full social dimension"? Describe the paradox he plays upon in this section. See especially paragraph 14.

5. *Paragraphs 15-23:* The dominant tone of this group of paragraphs is negative. Compare the criticisms here to those in paragraphs 1-4. Are the former more detailed versions of the latter? Do they add any concepts to the earlier section? What assumptions must Schlesinger accept to hold a position from which to criticize democracy as he does? Examine the phrases "optimism about man," "casualties of the industrial order," "means, not ends." Why does he emphasize "moral decisions"?

6. *Paragraphs 24-38:* Although this section of the essay continues to rehearse the inadequacies of democracy, its main point is to urge remedies. Study paragraph 27; it moves from analysis of the problem of individual action and delegated authority to exhortation. Examine paragraph 28 for analytical and hortatory statements. What is meant by the phrase "actual relations between the individual and the community"?

7. *Paragraph 30:* What is the importance of the word "voluntary"? Has it been anticipated in less direct statements?

8. *Paragraphs 31-38:* Schlesinger concludes by arguing the necessity of accepting "conflict." What precisely does he mean by the word? In what way does he establish it as a virtue? Have the criticisms of democracy focused on a lack of conflict? How would you differentiate conflict and anxiety?

Topics for discussion and writing

I. Write an essay in which you discuss Schlesinger's use of metaphor.

II. Select three key terms used throughout the essay and analyze their role in developing its main theses. You should pay attention to their suggestive value as well as to the precise meanings Schlesinger gives them.

III. "Freedom" is a word normally used in a political context. Do you think Schlesinger is primarily concerned with politics? If so, why his emphasis on the moral condition of individuals and why his frequent literary quotations?

IV. Schlesinger, Krutch, and Edman all attempt to expose the weaknesses of "the modern temper." Write an essay in which you compare their views of what is wrong.

V. From what areas of human experience do Schlesinger, Krutch, and Edman draw their material? Do they concern themselves with all areas?

OUR PRESENT DISCONTENTS Crane Brinton

Crane Brinton, Ideas and Men: The Story of Western Thought. *Copyright 1950 by Prentice-Hall, Inc., Englewood Cliffs, N. J. Reprinted by permission.*

IN THE perspective of Western intellectual history, we can see that many of the problems that seem to our alarmists so new, so demanding, so imperative of solution, are in fact very old problems that men and women of Western culture have managed to survive without solving. Notably, those prophets of doom who hold that modern Western man must agree on the Big Questions, that we must somehow escape from our present multanimity into a new Age of Faith, have against them several thousand years of Western history in which men have disagreed over these fundamental questions. But beyond this problem of agreement on the Big Questions there lies a more specific cosmological question that is concretely a problem for our times: Can we continue to hold even those modified eighteenth-century ideas of progress, of the possibility of closing here and now, or very shortly, that gap between "is" and "ought to be" which as historians we have to note Western man has never come very close to closing, and yet has never, for very long, given up trying to close?

2   There is always the possibility that the next few generations will see almost no change in Western cosmology, that we shall continue on the whole to accept as answers to the Big Questions those we accept now, in all their bewildering and mutually contradictory variety. Such a persistence of existing states of mind is, of course, possible, and to certain temperaments, even probable. We certainly do not know clinically how much variation in attitudes toward fundamental problems of value and conduct a society can stand. Yet it does not seem likely that those prophets who keep talking of crisis, crossroads, and the little time left are *wholly* wrong. Some further emendations in our inheritance from the Enlightenment we shall almost certainly have to make. For the gap between our ideals and our behavior, between the world we think desirable — indeed, morally right, necessary — and the world we have to live in has been since the Enlightenment a gap of very different psychological character from the gap the traditional Christian knew and felt.

3   The gap between what ought to be and what is probably exists in all men's minds, certainly in all civilized men's minds. But ordinary men and their leaders *must not be constantly, naggingly aware of this gap.* Most of the time, they must — though the outside observer may think their position hypocrisy — somehow persuade themselves that the gap really isn't there. There are many ways of filling it. On one's own private account, there are ritual practices, conviction of belonging to a body of the elect, mystic submission to some greater will, all of which will help close the gap. For those who have to take humanity as a whole into view, there is the more difficult way of the optimistic reformer just about to close the gap with one last law, one last sermon. There is also the Christian attitude toward the gap — that it can never be wholly closed here on earth, but that those who work honestly, justly, considerately toward closing it on earth will find it fully closed in heaven, that those who do not will find it fully closed in hell.

4   But to many of the heirs of the Enlightenment the gap is still painfully there, yawning as wide as ever. They cannot take the Christian way out, for they cannot believe in any other world than this nowadays rather un-

pleasant one. They have a firm notion of what is on the other, the ideal side of the gap — peace, plenty, happiness in all its range from lazy comfort to the leap of the heart. They believe we human beings should have what we want, and that we cannot successfully fill in the gap between what we want and what we have with words, ritual, or any other consoling illusion. This last is, from a naturalistic-historical point of view, one reason why the Victorian compromise did not hold, why the lower classes refused to stay put, why socialism preached the need for economic democracy after political democracy had been attained. Men wanted economic equality, not just spiritual equality. No ritual could satisfy the desire of the poor to be materially richer. The material ideals of the eighteenth century are deceptively simple; just because they are so simple and so material it has been very hard to pretend we have attained them when we have not.

5   Now it may be possible to lessen the gap between the real and the ideal by bringing the ideal a long way back toward reality, by setting small, modest goals all along the line — not temperance but less criminal alcoholism; not perfect sexual life on earth but fewer divorces; not the elimination of "soap operas," but better-balanced radio programs; not complete economic security but less disastrous depressions with less widespread unemployment; not a world government that will forever guarantee peace, but a United Nations that will help us stave off war and perhaps make it less barbarous when it comes. The list could be prolonged indefinitely. The moderate realist asks that democracy give up some of its eighteenth-century optimism about the natural goodness and reasonableness of man, about the magic effect of a readily changeable social and political environment (laws, constitutions, treaties, new educational institutions and curricula), about the nearness of the approaching millennium. He asks that democracy accept some of the pessimism of traditional Christianity as embodied in the doctrine of original sin, some of the tragic sense of human limitations that has inspired great literature, some of the doubts about the universal capacity of all men to think straight that come out of modern psychology, some of the practical, common-sense awareness of the impossibility of perfection that most of us have in those fields of activity where we act under the burden of responsibility.

6   Western democrats may be able to shake off the burden of excessive optimism about human perfectibility that they have inherited from the Enlightenment, and adapt their ideals to this harsh world. Many of them are increasingly aware that something must be done to close the gap between promise and performance the years have opened up in the Western democracies. They cannot go along with the self-deluded idealists who seem to think that all that is necessary is to reaffirm the promise more firmly than ever. For one thing, they begin to detect a touch of bitterness in the affirmation which shows that even the idealists can look about them. You will find the case for a democracy willing to face the facts of life very cogently put by

Mr. A. M. Schlesinger, Jr., in his *The Vital Center.* It is not at all unlikely
that in the next few years this point of view will make real gains in the West.
7   But is such a pessimistic democracy likely or even possible — a democracy that resolutely refuses to promise heaven on earth and still does not
return to the older heaven in another world? One very strong element in
the democratic cosmology, we have insisted, has been a denial of the supernatural, a denial of an afterlife. We have indeed seen that much of the
democratic cosmology has been after a fashion reconciled with formal
churchgoing Christianity; but we have also noted that, especially in the
liberal Protestant groups, very little indeed of the divine, the miraculous,
the transcendental has been left in a formal, rationalistic faith. Finally, of
course, there remain in all the Western democracies millions of men and
women who range all the way from violent positivists and anticlericals to
the completely worldly and indifferent, millions who are simply not Christians. Can these men and women find the spiritual resources needed to face
hardship, frustration, struggle, and unhappiness — all the evils they have
been taught to believe would be banished shortly from human life?
8   Though there have persisted through these last three centuries many
Christian groups who held to the spirit and the letter of the traditional faith,
there have also grown up certain surrogates for the Christian faith that many
had lost, or that had been altered into pseudo-Christian optimistic rational-
ism. These surrogates are democracy, nationalism, socialism, fascism, and
their many variant creeds and sects. Most of these surrogates have in common
a belief in the fairly rapid perfectibility of men here on earth — provided
the proper measures are taken. Most of them deny the existence of any
supernatural being capable of interfering in the affairs of this earth, though
many do indeed retain the notion of some sort of guiding principle of goodness — a kind of impersonal God — and all believe that the universe can
be made a comfortable place for man to live in. Back of them all lies the
very general attitude or cosmology of the Enlightenment, which perhaps
takes on its most representative form in the kind of liberal, democratic system of values you find in John Mill. But the actual institutional form, the
Church for this faith, has been the territorial nation-state, so that in practice
democracy and nationalism have been united in complex and varying
fashion. Socialism is originally an heretical development of earlier democratic thought — or if you prefer, a deepening of democratic aims — which
also, wherever it has been successful, has got itself tied up with the nation-
state and with nationalism.
9   Now we have deliberately used of these impersonal faiths — these
formally nontheistic religions in which abstractions like virtue or liberty,
groups like the national in-group, are hypostasized — the term *surrogate,*
with all its connotations of a somewhat synthetic and not quite adequate
substitute. The inadequacy of the impersonal faiths in comparison with
Christianity is especially evident in relation to the problems of the indi-

vidual in trouble. These impersonal faiths are weak in their cure of souls. It is true that in their fighting and crusading stages — socialism before it comes to power, for instance — they are able to enlist the full spiritual ardor of many of the faithful, give them a sense of belonging to something very great indeed, melt away their petty selfishnesses in emotional self-surrender. But once they are established, once they are faced with this routine world, these impersonal faiths have little to offer the unhappy, the maladjusted, the suffering.

10 Nationalism is probably the strongest of these faiths. It bulwarks the weak and the inadequate with their membership in the great whole, their share of the "pooled self-esteem" of patriotism. It has in times of crisis been able to rely on both human patience and human daring. But it does not take the place of a consoling God. Marianne, the symbol of the French Republic, is a heroic figure of the barricades. But it is hard to pray to Marianne, as generations have prayed to the Virgin Mary. Socialism would seem to have even less of the consoling touch. It is no doubt encouraging to the faithful Marxist to know that Dialectical Materialism is hard at work making things better for the oppressed. But the really unhappy need something more human, something more aware of *them*, not as temporary victims of the mode of production, but as important, unique, sovereign human beings deserving the immediate attention of God or his agents.

11 Moreover, there is another psychological weakness in modern surrogates for older theistic faiths. These new lay religions find it very hard to permit repentance. In the numerous trials for treason (heresy) that have gone on in Soviet Russia, though the accused have usually broken down and made most complete confessions of their errors, they were by no means forgiven and taken back into the fold. The United States government tends apparently in these days to the opinion that "once a Communist, always a Communist," especially in the case of Englishmen and other West Europeans. A French intellectual who admits to having joined the Communist party in the dark days of the thirties but has since declared his repentance is apparently still a Communist to the State Department. But the phenomenon is obvious in any study of modern social and political movements. In the great French Revolution, for instance, it was very difficult, indeed almost impossible, for a man who had voted conspicuously with the Moderates in 1790 to excuse himself in 1793 with the then triumphant Extremists by pleading his error, by claiming that he had repented and seen the light. He commonly ended on the guillotine. It is hard to repent effectively in these impersonal religions.

12 Yet the forgiving of the repentant sinner has been one of the great strengths of Christianity, one of the ways wise Christian leadership has tempered the wind to the shorn lamb. Now it may be that the rigid attitude toward repentance displayed by the newer impersonal faiths is related to the abstract and perfect ideal — *an ideal improperly separated from the*

real — that they hold for human behavior in the Utopia they were designed to achieve on earth. Those who hold these ideals desire so passionately that man be perfect that they cannot forgive him the slightest imperfection. A wholly this-worldly idealist can hardly avoid trying to eliminate those who do not behave according to his ideals. No doubt the riper democracies, like the English, are much less exacting than the Communists, much more willing to put up with human weaknesses. Still, none of them seems to offer to their leaders the chance for effective and not at all shaming compromise that the Christian requirement (note that it *is* requirement) of forgiveness to the penitent affords; nor do they offer to the faithful the spiritual security, the flexible discipline, that the Christian doctrine of sin and repentance offers.

13   Finally, these abstract faiths are a grave danger for the modern intellectual since they make easy, indeed they seem to ennoble, his ready assumption that he knows just what is wrong with the world, and how to right it. These faiths encourage the separation of the ideal from the real, as we have noted, for they oversimplify human nature. But the modern intellectual, already separated from the mass of his fellows by a rift that has surely not narrowed since it developed its modern form early in the nineteenth century, needed rather to be called back to the close and realistic study of the whole range of human behavior than to be allowed to develop in fine moral indignation his notions of "ought to be." Indeed, even when these notions take on the appearance of realism, of hard-boiled acceptance of things-as-they-are, they are a very evident form of that "inverted idealism" some writers have already found in Machiavelli. Balance, a sane resolution of the tensions between the ideal and the real, is the heart of the matter. Certainly, the balance can be tipped, as many a modern intellectual like Pareto has tipped it, much too far away from the ideal. But at this moment in history, tipping toward the ideal, the *over-simple* ideal, is a grave danger encountered by the rawness and simplicities of our surrogate faiths. The intellectual can so readily let himself go. In retrospect, this furious urge to the ideal in a man like Carlyle, for instance, is what lays him open to the otherwise unfair charge of being proto-fascist. Carlyle, like Nietzsche, would unquestionably have repudiated the flesh-and-blood Nazis; but Carlyle tossed off in complete irresponsibility so many fine and indignant ideas that many of them proved effective Nazi ideas.

14   In summary, then, these newer faiths do not have the richness and depth of awareness of what human beings are really like that the older religions have; they are therefore not as able as the older religions to cope with the problem of human relations in a time of troubles. Democracy and socialism have hitherto, in a sense, had relatively comfortable going in a world where most of the material indices really were going up in a steady curve. They have not yet had to face from too many unhappy men and women for whom this is not even remotely heaven on earth the menacing and very natural cry of "put up or shut up." Perhaps they will not. It may

be that the great masses in the West can take the attitude, hitherto confined to aristocracies like the Stoic, that this is a tough world in which nobody is always happy, in which everybody has got to keep coping with his troubles, and in which there is no reward beyond the grave. But this seems most unlikely. The mass of mankind, even in the West, have never been able to take the tragic view without the help of a personal religion, a religion hitherto always transcendental, supernatural, otherworldly. Somehow, democracy, if it is not to return wholeheartedly to Christianity (which many today would have it do), must take on the cure of souls.

15 There is still another, and more definitely intellectual, difficulty in the way of a pessimistic, realistic democracy without belief in the supernatural. This democracy would have to extend to all our activities the tentativeness, the willingness to experiment, the patience, the acceptance of slowness, the recognition of the limits set on human effort by those two words *impossible* and *insoluble* which characterizes the work of the scientist as scientist and which, in part at least, all of us attain in the specific tasks we must fulfill. In such a democracy a very large number of people indeed would have to forgo the delights of certitude, the assurance that comes from knowing in advance that certain absolutes are true, that there is something that never changes, something not part of history but still part of ourselves. But it is clear that we humans cling to certitude; those who lost Christian certitude promptly tried to find scientific certitude, historical certitude, certitude anywhere they could turn it up. And we cling to omniscience as the companion of certitude — an omniscient force, if we cannot have an omniscient God. If a thoroughgoing relativism (not of course nihilism) in values is to be asked of our new citizens of a pessimist democracy — and it would seem that only such a relativism could effectively sustain their pessimism and keep them from hoping at least for some new kind of pie in the sky — then such a democracy will be very difficult indeed to set up in our time. It would ask too much of poor human nature, more actually than optimistic democracy asked, since the average citizen of the old optimistic democracy was allowed his bit of the old consoling religion.

16 Moreover, we come in the mid-twentieth century to the same difficulty we encountered in ancient Athens: Just what is the relation between the attitudes taken toward the Big Questions by the intellectuals and the whole structure, the whole equilibrium, of a society? The slightest attention to what is going on among Western intellectuals — existentialists in France, followers of Barth and Niebuhr in Germany and America, the bright young Catholic converts in England — makes it plain that the intellectuals are tightening their spiritual belts, getting set for a long spell of hard going, growing very scornful of such cheerful democrats as Benjamin Franklin, or such shallow democrats as Thomas Jefferson. The Enlightenment may well be due for even more bitter attacks than those it received from the romanticists of Wordsworth's day. Yet one finds it very hard to imagine the average

American — or indeed the average European — in quite the mood of sensitive, high-minded, world-embracing despair that has come over the vanguard of Western intellectuals. There is a certain coarseness, like that that wells up from the *fabliaux* in the midst of the high-minded thirteenth century, that one suspects will keep the fleshpots boiling for a while even in our tragic world.

17   It will not do, then, to conclude that our Western culture is about to make some sort of *volte-face* into another Age of Faith. The democratic cosmology is almost certain in the West to receive another revision even more thorough than the revision the nineteenth century gave to its original heritage from the Enlightenment. One cannot be at all sure in 1950 what form that revision will take. A very great deal will depend on the result of the struggle between the United States and Soviet Russia, a struggle in which the whole cosmology is at stake. The very necessities of the struggle may drive the West into a much more regimented society than our tradition holds good. For it is one of the unpleasant facts of human relations — one of the kinds of facts that the new realistic democrats have got to face — that in war, cold or hot, you have to have more authority and less liberty than in quieter times.

18   Very roughly, and with all sorts of specific twistings and turnings in each that contradict the generalization, it would seem that in the United States and in Russia are temporarily embodied a number of the sets of opposites that in some kind of union have hitherto maintained that tension which is so characteristic of the West. We are not, of course, pure Liberty, and they pure Authority. We do not stand for the individualism of the great cats, nor they for the collectivism of the beehive or anthill. We are not variety, and they are not uniformity. Neither of us lives up to the extremes of our own systems of values. Still, the opposition is there, and is very real. We do, on the whole, stand for the series of values that in this book have been treated as the central values of Western culture — a feeling for the irreducible something in each human being still best suggested by that worn old word *liberty,* a feeling which, though it will pause a little and turn on itself when confronted with the very real problems suggested by such phrases as "force a man to be free" or "you are free when you do right, but a slave when you do wrong" or "liberty, not license," is nevertheless deep down defiantly unconvinced that these paradoxes are necessary. The Western tradition of which we are now the chief defenders is not dogmatically, not even idealistically, but all the more firmly *individualist.*

19   Our chances of maintaining the traditions of the West, and of preserving them in a form not unfairly described as democratic, are greater than our prophets of doom will admit. For if the anti-intellectualism of the last few decades has been corrosive of the more naive hopes of a heaven on earth through the perfecting of human nature, or simply by the release of human nature from its bad environment, it has given us reason to believe

that if our democratic way of life really is anchored in our habits, traditions, sentiments, conditioned reflexes, and super-egos it may well survive even a very harsh reality. What to our grandfathers seemed the strength of democracy, its dependence on the rationality of men, now indeed seems its weakness; but perhaps after all democracy does not depend on the rationality of men. The democratic West has now withstood two wars in which it was supposed, with its addiction to variety, indiscipline, spiritual multanimity, and even comfort, to go down before the superior discipline, toughness, and unanimity of its antidemocratic foes. It did not go down, but won through to victory in spite of, or more likely because of, what looked to certain critics like weaknesses.

20   For what looks in purely intellectual analysis like disintegration, squabbling, rank inability to agree on anything at all may well be no more than disagreement on matters we Westerners have been disagreeing on publicly and violently most of the time since Socrates played the gadfly in Athens. If you think of the full logical implications of their creeds, it is really astonishing that Catholics, Protestants, Jews, and Marxist materialists fought side by side in the American forces in the two world wars. You may say that they did not really believe as much in their respective formal faiths as in the United States, but this would be much too logical a position to be true. You may say that they "believed in" religious toleration as a positive good, and that would no doubt be true in part of many of them. But the truest thing you could say would be that they never thought at all about the general problem of religious toleration, that most of them simply accepted the existence of Catholics, Jews, Protestants, and all varieties of materialist as one of the facts of life, one of the things you take, like the weather. A very great deal of the Western way of life is thus embedded somewhere in quite ordinary Americans, not in their cerebral cortexes, probably, but in a much safer place which the physiologist hasn't quite located — we used to say, in the heart.

21   We come back, then, to the proposition that for all we yet know in terms of a cumulative social science, the relation between the strength of a given society and the degree of agreement on matters cosmological among its members cannot be determined. There seems to be excellent evidence that very considerable multanimity in matters of theology, metaphysics, art, literature, and even ethics can persist if the existence of such disagreement is taken, not as a lofty ideal of toleration, of progress through variation (though for many intellectuals it is just that) but as something given, something normal for human beings. If democracy really means anything so unnatural to Western intellectuals as intellectual agreement, then it is all up with democracy. But the whole course of our intellectual history would indicate that in some perverse, obstinate way Western intellectuals have always thrived on their differences, and that somehow these differences have not really disturbed the nonintellectuals enough to upset the social equilibrium.

Even today, there is no good evidence that the intellectual alarums of our age of philosophical worries have really gone beyond that small section of the population that possesses high verbal aptitudes. We are not even quite sure that social psychologists like Erich Fromm are right in declaring that nervous instability, even neurosis, is so far common in all parts of our society as to threaten our traditional democratic way of life. Maybe the flight from freedom has been exaggerated.

22   But even if these diagnosticians are right, even if ours really is a sick society, it seems unlikely that the earnest intellectuals who urge us to get together and believe something lofty together are on the right track. If we must have a new religion, all Western precedent suggests that the religion will not come from the intellectuals, but from a far humbler source, and that for a while at least it will be very hard on established intellectuals — even on those who prophesied its coming.

23   There is a further grave intellectual difficulty no thinking democrat can avoid facing. We have granted, in accordance with the current of modern anti-intellectualism, and probably also of common sense, that there is a deep energy and toughness in the human race no intellectual system can contain, that our culture has sources of strength not greatly affected by our philosophy — or lack of one. Yet even Pareto lists as one of his strongest residues the *residue to make derivations* — that is, to make sense. The need for satisfying our desire to understand, to have our experience hold together logically, not to be shockingly, patently, inconsistent, not to be hypocrites in our own or in others' eyes — this is a very strong need among human beings. It is safe to say that no civilization has been led by an intellectual class persuaded that their world of values, their explanation of why they were there, was pretense, hypocrisy, pure fake. In a democracy there cannot be for long an unbelieving intellectual class and a believing nonintellectual class; nor can a skeptical or cynical intellectual class devise a religion for the masses.

24   Now our intellectual classes are by no means today in such a plight. But many of them are puzzled, and they are likely to be more puzzled until they come more successfully to grips with the problem of modifying our eighteenth-century heritage from the Enlightenment. Let us make a final brief summary of that problem.

25   The democratic world-view was formulated in the eighteenth century at the end of three centuries of change that had culminated in the great triumph of natural science in the work of Newton and his fellows. Whatever may have been the philosophical and theological opinions of these working scientists as private persons — and to this day many of them are sincere Christians — as scientists they had to make use of an intellectual method of arriving at generalizations, a method that was wholly at the mercy of observed facts. These facts were ultimately, no matter how much more subtle than human senses the instruments by which they were recorded, statements about the world of sense experience, this world — and no other.

Briefly, a proposition made in accordance with the methods of natural science has to accord with the facts of this world; it may not transcend them and it may not contradict them.

26   Now two of the master generalizations of the democratic faith as it emerged in the eighteenth and nineteenth centuries, the doctrine of the natural goodness and reasonableness of men and the doctrine of inevitable unilinear progress toward human perfectibility on earth, either transcend the scientific attitude toward truth or contradict it. You have only to follow down through the ages from Thucydides to Machiavelli to the ablest of modern social scientists to note that the tradition among those who really observe carefully the behavior of human beings is one of conviction that men are born to trouble, and that in recorded time, at least, human nature has not greatly changed. If you study the recorded behavior of *homo sapiens* from the earliest times right down to the mid-twentieth century in the spirit and with the methods of the natural scientist (as far as the inadequacies of the historical record will permit such study) you will be unable to take anything like the attitude of Condorcet, for instance, or even that of Paine and Jefferson. You will be unable to accept as even rough scientific generalizations the concepts of the natural goodness and reasonableness of man and of the increasing perfection, in human terms, of our life on earth.

27   Democracy, in short, is *in part* a system of judgments inconsistent with what the scientist holds to be true. This inconsistency would not create difficulties — or at least would not create some of the difficulties it now creates — were the democrat able to say that his kingdom is not of this world, able to say that his truth is not the kind that is in the least tested by the scientist, any more than the truth of the Catholic doctrine of the Eucharist is tested by the chemical analysis of the bread and wine. Such a solution of the democrat's intellectual quandary is not a happy one, but is not altogether inconceivable. Democracy may become a genuinely transcendental faith, in which belief is not weakened by lack of correspondence between the propositions it lays down and the facts of life on this earth. There are cynics who say that when an American boasts about the lack of class distinctions in his country he never bothers his mind with the facts, the facts of our class structure, the facts about Negroes, Jews, Mexicans, Nisei. We Americans have no trouble at all in recognizing the fact that the basic principles of that democratic heresy, Marxism, are contradicted by almost every principle of the actual structure of present-day Russian social life; we recognize that Russian "democracy" is defined quite differently from ours. In short, democracy may be able to take its promised heaven out of this world, and put it in the world of ritual performed, of transcendental belief, of vicarious satisfactions of human wants, may keep it an ideal not too much sullied by the contrast with the spotted reality.

28   Or we may see the working out of a democratic attitude toward the world which accepts the limitations of ordinary human nature, which accepts

a pessimistic view of this world, a democracy with no pie in the sky and no really ineffable, no all-satisfying pie in the larder. Its enemies have long said that democracy is a fair-weather thing, that even in its incomplete realization of liberty, equality, fraternity it sets for human nature standards that can be approximated in human conduct only in times of ease and prosperity. In a time of troubles, they say, we shall need discipline, leadership, solidarity not to be achieved by letting men even in theory, even in fantasy, follow their own private wills. Such discipline men do indeed accept in times of crisis, as the Western democracies showed well in this last war. The English took with amazingly little apparent psychic damage the bombing of cities which put all civilians on no mere metaphorical battle line. Even more striking in a way was the spirit with which most Americans went into this last war. To the horror of the tender-minded idealist, they went into it with very little apparent belief that they were going to make a much better world, with very little of the crusading spirit of the war of 1914-1918. They went into it as into a disagreeable but necessary task that they were able to do very well indeed, but which they saw no reason to pretend to enjoy, or to ennoble. *They went into it as realists, not as cynics.*

29   And here we may well conclude, as far as a book of this sort can conclude. An *idealistic* democracy, a *believing* democracy (in the old transcendental sense of religious belief) is perhaps possible, though such a democracy would find it hard to accommodate its this-worldly and scientific heritage to an other-world faith. Its God would at the very least need to make some difficult compromises with the psychiatrist. A *realistic,* pessimistic democracy — a democracy in which ordinary citizens approach morals and politics with the willingness to cope with imperfection that characterizes the good farmer, the good physician, the good holder of the cure of souls, be he priest, clergyman, counselor, or psychiatrist — such a democracy would demand more of its citizens than any human culture has ever demanded. Were its demands met, it might well be the most successful of cultures. Finally, a *cynical* democracy, a democracy whose citizens profess in this world one set of beliefs and live another, is wholly impossible. No such society can long endure anywhere. The tension between the ideal and the real may be resolved in many ways in a healthy society; but it can never be taken as nonexistent.

Commentary and questions

1. *Paragraph 1:* This outlines the problem Brinton proposes to discuss and suggests the basic structure of the essay. He introduces three related topics: (a) the perspective from which contemporary problems will be treated; (b) the question of the solution of these problems or "Big Questions"; and (c) what characterizes them, or how they are to be identified. The reader should analyze this paragraph closely, studying the relationship between the three topics and spelling them out clearly for himself.

There is another order paralleling that mentioned above: each topic is spelled out as a contrast. The reader should also identify these and follow their path throughout the essay.

2. *Paragraph 2:* Note Brinton's language as he develops the contrast between mankind's attempt at solutions to its problems, topic (b), and the persistence of uncertainty. How does he describe topic (a)?

3. *Paragraph 3:* Topic (c) is restated here. Why does Brinton use italics? What solutions to the psychological problem do men devise?

4. *Paragraph 4:* How does the attitude described here contrast with that mentioned in the previous paragraph?

5. *Paragraphs 5-6:* Paraphrase the point of view outlined here. What is its relation to the two previous attitudes? How is the "moderate realist" characterized?

6. *Paragraph 7:* What phrase establishes the connection between this and the previous paragraph? Note that Brinton questions the point of view he has described in paragraph 6. What are his grounds for doubt? To what contrasting general attitude does he refer?

In general the first seven paragraphs are descriptive. What elements do you find that suggest Brinton's own point of view toward the attitudes or states of mind he describes?

7. *Paragraphs 8-14:* In this section Brinton treats "surrogate" faiths and Christianity in detail. What are the motives, advantages, and disadvantages he lists for each one? What motif informs his discussion? According to what principle are these faiths tested?

8. *Paragraph 15:* This paragraph is a re-emphasis of "pessimistic, realistic democracy" as a focus of discussion. Brinton mentions that human beings crave a sense of "certitude." Has this notion been implicit in earlier paragraphs? What relation has it to the terms "ideal" and "faith"?

9. *Paragraphs 16-20:* Three main topics dominate this section: the role of the "intellectual" in modern beliefs, the problem of political competition between the United States and Russia, and the "tensions" and advantages of the democratic way of life. Examine the bearing of each of these topics on the main general themes of the essay. How are they developments of the material that has preceded them? Are they an expansion of generalizations, detail to be included in generalizations already established, or do they merely restate the set of contrasting ideas with which Brinton has been occupied? Does Brinton continue to use historical contrast in this section?

10. *Paragraphs 21-24:* Building on ideas he has treated earlier, Brinton handles the problem of the maintenance of belief by examining possible sources for such maintenance. Describe in your own words these two sources. Which does Brinton favor and why? Does this section bring Brinton's own view more into the open than it has been? What are the premises for his opinion?

11. *Paragraph 26:* Brinton sees one general view of human nature as most valid. How would you describe it?

12. *Paragraph 27:* Why is democracy partially inconsistent with "what the scientist holds to be true"? Does this suggestion restate a contrast mentioned earlier?

13. *Paragraphs 27-28:* What solutions to the problem of belief does Brinton discuss? Which does he seem to prefer and why?

14. *Paragraph 29:* How certain and confident is this conclusion? How certain can you be of Brinton's own point of view toward the situation he has described?

Topics for discussion and writing

I. Make a list of Brinton's expository techniques. Which is the most crucial?

II. Brinton contrasts the Age of Faith and the Enlightenment. What particular attitudes and concepts are referred to by these terms? Re-examine the essay for the implicit and explicit definitions of the terms.

III. What does Brinton have to say about the ideal and the real? What concepts and problems are raised by this general contrast? How does Brinton use the contrast to develop his thesis?

IV. One of Brintons' expository techniques is to rephrase concepts two, three, and four times. What is the purpose of such restatements? Are the concepts modified or developed as they appear in new contexts?

V. Write an essay explaining how Krutch, Edman, and Brinton describe the need for belief. What is the attitude of each toward that need?

VI. Write a theme listing and comparing the criticisms each author makes of the modern state of mind.

VII. Each author may be presumed to write from a general view of what mankind is, its needs, attitudes, and moral condition. Write a theme discussing and comparing these views.

VIII. What evidences of the "modern temper" do you find from your own knowledge of prevailing contemporary attitudes? Write an essay on this topic.

IX. In paragraph 1 Brinton uses the word "alarmists." Do you think it applies to any of the other writers in this section? Defend your answer.

ONE MAN'S BELIEF

George Jean Nathan

From Living Philosophies, *copyright, 1931, by Simon and Schuster, Inc. Reprinted by permission of Simon and Schuster, Inc.*

IN THE exposition of what I myself happen to believe, it is certainly not my purpose to argue or even to hint that this personal set of beliefs is either philosophically or emotionally admirable or that its adoption by anyone else is a consummation devoutly wished on my part. I suspect that what other men believe, though it be often objectionable to me, may stand them in quite as sound service as my own beliefs stand me, and that it may contribute equally to their self-esteem, happiness, bank accounts, worldly eminence and wives' low opinion of them. A man's beliefs, after all, save he be a professional practitioner of letters and hence a racketeer of words, a self-blackmailer and a Judas unto himself, are and should be his private, personal property, as safe from vulgar public scrutiny as his love-making or his underwear. There is something indelicate, even bounderish, in exposing one's most secret articles of faith, a fact appreciated by the relatively gentlemanly among the professional carpenters of letters mentioned, as may be witnessed by the obvious posturings, evasions and mendacities they indulge in when they engage, for hire, to contribute to the public prints. There is about the "beliefs" they expound on such occasions a considerabe air of fraud; it is plain that, while they are ostensibly betraying their confidences, they are witholding much that is true of themselves and of their private philosophies, and much that, being true, would be altogether too embarrassing to set down in print. By way of subterfuge, they accordingly offer to the public a bold, forthright, cocksure and impudent front — but with their fingers carefully crossed behind their backs. If we may put any trust in the gossipy records, there never lived a bigger liar than Rousseau. And if I personally out of long association know anything of a number of writers who are in the habit of undressing their beliefs in public, you have my word for it that the ghost of Rousseau still walks.

2   While I do not desire to appear in the light of an exceptional truth-teller and while frankly confessing that I entertain certain beliefs that a delicacy inherited from an illegitimate great-uncle, together with a skepticism as to the police, forbids me indiscriminately to merchant, there are certain convictions, deeply imbued in me after forty-odd years on this earth, that seem to me legitimately communicable. The first of these is that, of all philosophies governing life and conduct, that sponsored by the Cyrenaic academy, somewhat qualified, is the only one that is eminently satisfactory, eminently workable and productive of any real happiness. In a hedonism that combines the forthrightly egoistic with a modest measure of the altruistic, that governs its pleasures partly by intellect and partly by emotion — depending upon the vagaries and humors of the occasion — and that foams effervescently in the wake of work seriously and painstakingly done, I believe above all other beliefs. To me, pleasure and my own personal happiness — only infrequently collaborating with that of others — are all I deem worth a hoot. It would make me out a much finer and nobler person, I duly appreciate, to say that the happiness and welfare of all mankind were close to my heart, that nothing gave me more soulful happiness than to make others happy and that I would gladly sacrifice every cent I have in the world, together

with maybe a leg, to bring a little joy to the impoverished and impaired survivors of the late Afridi raids in India, but I have difficulty in being a hypocrite. As a matter of fact, the happiness and welfare of mankind are not my profession; I am perfectly willing to leave them to the care of the professional missionaries of one sort or another; I have all that I can do to look out for my own happiness and welfare. And so has any other man, unless he happens to be a multi-millionaire, a failure in life who seeks to conceal his failure from himself in devoting himself to worse failures than himself, a gourmand of publicity, or a devout server of God. I happen to be exactly none of these — though, so far as the second catalogue goes, I surely do not view myself as a stunning success — and consequently regard myself as a sufficient problem without looking about me for other problems.

3   That I am selfish and to a very considerable degree possibly offensive is thus more or less regrettably obvious. All that I am able to offer in extenuation is that so are most other men if you dig down into them and, paying no attention to their altruistic pretensions, get at the hearts of them. In all my experience I have yet to find and know intimately a man worth his salt in any direction who did not think of himself first and foremost. He may drop a quarter into the hat of a beggar (when somebody is looking); he may have gracious manners; he may obey the punctilio on every occasion; he may be genial and liberal and hearty; he may buy the drinks when it comes his turn; he may be scrupulously polite, considerate and superficially lovable. But under it all his first interest, his first consideration and his first admiration are reserved for himself. The man who thinks of others before he thinks of himself may become a Grand Master of the Elks, a Socialist of parts or the star guest of honor at public banquets, but he will never become a great or successful artist, statesman or even clergyman.

4   Happiness is the goal of every normal human being. As it is given to few men to die happy, the best that man can hope and strive and pray for is momentary happiness during life, repeated as frequently as the cards allow. Pleasure, whatever its species, is the drink in the desert. It is the beautiful, transient reward of travail and pain. There is no other reward, except for those still sufficiently aboriginal to believe in an hereafter. The ambrosia of the gods, the lovely angels, eternal blue skies and peace, the music of golden harps are too far off and dubious so far as my own metaphysic goes. I prefer to trust to the more realistic and visible Grand Montrachet, pretty girls, Mediterranean coast and symphony orchestras of the here and now.

5   What makes for pleasure and consequent happiness? Each man to his own poison. In my case, a life devoted, both professionally and in leisure hours, to literature, drama, criticism, music and the arts generally, with due and careful heed paid to a moderate but satisfying alcoholic diet, guaranteed by a constantly replenished wine cellar that has complacently de-

cided never to hear of the Eighteenth Amendment, to decently prepared foods, to the society of selfish and hence interesting comrades, to the amiable company of amiable women, and to the avoidance of any and everything that might disturb my annoying equanimity. The life of a writer has always seemed to me to be about as good a one as any low human being could hope for. His office is in his hat; his tools are in his pocket; his boss is himself; he is foot-loose, free, clockless, independent. He can say what he wants to, however inexpedient, injudicious and discommodious, and get paid handsomely for what other working men would promptly get sacked for. He can keep his mind alive and kicking with controversy and enjoy himself in putting his inferiors in their places. He can, with relatively little work and with easy hours — if he has any talent at all — earn a very satisfactory livelihood. He moves in a world not of trade but of ideas. He deals in words, for which he doesn't have to lay out a cent and hence takes no financial risk, instead of in commodities that have to be paid for first out of his own funds. He is rewarded for his fun, like most artists, where other men are rewarded more often only for their misery. Serious or gay, he is a playboy in a world that other men run for him with the sweat of their brows.

6   As a very humble and lowly member of the craft and as one who still has a very considerable distance to go before he may deserve the name of artist, I can yet appreciate the tremendous advantages over other men that a real artist enjoys. In the first place, he has contempt, that most valuable of human self-wrought and self-sustained gifts. In the second place, he has liberty, freedom and autonomy — more than any other man. In the third place, he can be himself at all times and in all places. He can work when he feels like working, loaf when he feels like loafing, keep superiorly aloof from politics and all other such scurvy diversions of the rabble. He is free always to choose his friends as he will, without the usual man's often necessary regard for their business connections and influence; he may be indiscreet without damage to his work; he can tell the world to go to hell and make the world like it. If any man stands a chance for happiness on this earth, it is the artist who has the choicest position at the post.

7   Although I myself, due doubtless to defective skill, have to work pretty hard, I do not believe in too hard work. The hardest workers are and properly should be the congenital clerks, bookkeepers, mill-hands and suchlike pathetic incompetents and slaves. The superior man should be able and privileged to take life with relative ease. A life spent in constant labor is a life wasted, save a man be such a fool as to regard a fulsome obituary notice as ample reward. Show me a man who, as the phrase goes, works himself to death and I'll show you an unimaginative dolt. There is a lot of amusement in this world and a man should get his full share of it. There probably never lived but two men who gained importance and honorable celebrity in this selfsame world who did not take considerable time off in which to have some sport, and of the two exceptions one is suspect because of his

peculiar taste for communion with birds, while the other finds at least part of his story still scouted by many millions of people.

8   "Work," airily observed a character in a play of the late Haddon Chambers, "is for workmen." An Englishman, Chambers once remarked to me that he had written the line as an evangelical text for Americans. I believe about work as I believe about drink: it should be used in moderation.

9   I believe in a college training but not in a college education. The latter, I have learned from personal experience, is worth very little; the former, which imparts a knowledge of the value and uses of leisure, a somewhat superior ease and serenity, and a humorous view of indignation, whatever form the latter may take, is not without its advantages.

10   I believe in the state of bachelorhood, at the very least up to the age of fifty. Thereafter, a man may conceivably marry to his benefit, but certainly not before. The arguments in favor of earlier marriage, customarily advanced by the presumptively purer of the species, strike me as being peculiarly obscene and, where they are not obscene, hollow. The superior biological and hence inferentially superior amatory qualifications of the younger in years constitute one of the chief of these arguments. While fully conscious of the importance of sex in any contentful marital relationship, such a *plaidoyer* seems to me to be as illogical as it is indelicate, since it contends that two persons possibly ill-suited to each other in every other way — spiritually, intellectually, socially and economically — are to be recommended, endorsed and applauded as life-long companions simply on the ground of their virtuosity in anatomical arithmetic. Another favorite contention is that a man should marry while he is still malleable, that is, before he becomes set in his habits, — in other words, that the moulding of a man's character, his psyche and his future should be entrusted not to himself but to a woman. Up to the age of fifty, a man should be responsible to himself and to his work alone. A wife, however sympathetic, patient and charming, by very reason of her sympathy, patience and charm, would be a too pleasant and agreeable distraction. At fifty, a man has learned himself more or less completely, and has sounded out fully the possibilities and potentialities of his profession and his career. Then and only then should he consider matrimony. It is a rare marriage, negotiated at or after that age, that does not turn out prosperously and satisfactorily. The great majority of marriages that go on the rocks are those contracted in earlier years.

11   I am against all reforms and all reformers. The world, as I see it, is sufficiently gay, beautiful and happy as it stands. It is defective only to those who are themselves defective, who lack the sagacity, imagination, humor and wit to squeeze out its rich and jocose juices and go swimming in them. With Norman Douglas I agree: "I am not the stuff of which reformers are made; rather than indulge in that variety of meddlesomeness I would sweep a crossing. Nine-tenths of the reformers of humanity have been mischief-

makers or humbugs. I have no desire to be added to the list. A man who has reformed himself has contributed his full share towards the reformation of his neighbor."

12   While I do not care for money and own to the somewhat vainglorious boast of never having consciously written a line with any thought of its marketability in mind, I am neither poseur nor fool enough to affect an air of disdain of it. The man with money in his pocket not only enjoys a power that men without money do not; he is also in a position to do his work in the world more carefully, more independently, more truthfully and more successfully. The best artists living to-day, the men who are doing their finest work, are without exception men who have no need longer to worry about financial matters. They have looked out for that first. A destitute and miserable man may write a good book, or paint a good picture, or write a good piece of music, but the records hint that he seldom, in these days, contrives to do another.

13   It seems to me that the writers who are loudest in proclaiming their veneration of truth are most often simply vociferous admirers of their own pet fallacies. As for me, while given to an equal esteem of truth, I freely confess that I do not know what the truth, the final truth, about most things is and — like my colleagues alluded to — conceal my doubts and misgivings in self-persuading and, I hope, occasionally more publicly convincing convolutions of the English language, periodically enriched with more or less showy borrowings from the French, German, Italian and Hindu. As with most men, I believe most positively in my own ideas, right or wrong. These, to me, constitute the truth, whatever others may think of them. Once I believe a thing head and tail, no one can alter my conviction.

14   It also seems to me that the current American literary school of cynicism as to sentiment, love and romance is cheap-jack, fraudulent and silly. The American, as I have on more than one occasion observed, being generically the most sentimental of men, is ashamed of his sentiment and, like a man with thinning hair who drops miscellaneous jokes at the expense of baldheads, seeks to conceal or at least to divert uncomfortable attention from the fact by deprecating it in others. The most cynical writers in America to-day are personally so many honeydew melons, happily and sweetly sentimental husbands and fathers. It is merely that, like uncertain and unconfident men ever, they offer their public protestations of hard-boiled manliness — in the American definition — in order to hide from their womenfolk, laughing up their sleeves, their irresolution, nervousness, weakness and innate childishness. Romantic love is the privilege of emperors, kings, soldiers and artists; it is the butt of democrats, traveling salesmen, magazine poets and the writers of American novels.

15   My code of life and conduct is simply this: work hard, play to the allowable limit, disregard equally the good or bad opinion of others, never

do a friend a dirty trick, eat and drink what you feel like when you feel like, never grow indignant over anything, trust to tobacco for calm and serenity, bathe twice a day, modify the æsthetic philosophy of Croce but slightly with that of Santayana and achieve for one's self a pragmatic sufficiency in the beauty of the æsthetic surface of life, learn to play at least one musical instrument and then play it only in private, never allow one's self even a passing thought of death, never contradict anyone or seek to prove anything to anyone unless one gets paid for it in cold, hard coin, live the moment to the utmost of its possibilities, treat one's enemies with polite inconsideration, avoid persons who are chronically in need, and be satisfied with life always but never with one's self. An infinite belief in the possibilities of one's self with a coincidental critical assessment and derogation of one's achievements, self-respect combined with a measure of self-surgery, aristocracy of mind combined with democracy of heart, forthrightness with modesty or at least with good manners, dignity with a quiet laugh, honor and honesty and decency: these are the greatest qualities that man can hope to attain. And as one man, my hope is to attain them.

16   I am against snobbery in all its lovely American forms. As a born American, I suppose that I am naturally and unpleasantly infected with some of the bacteria, but I keep about me constantly a large and handy assortment of antitoxins. I am for all religions equally, as all impress me as being equally hollow. The variation is merely one either of external and superficial beauty or hideousness of spectacle. I believe that no man's life is finally complete and rounded — to quote an eminent Hungarian — without a wife, a child, a home, though I have not practiced what I preach and have neither wife nor child and live in that apologetic substitute for a home, a New York apartment. (It looks out on a building given over to shyster lawyers!) I believe, with Nietzsche, though I dislike the banality of dragging him forth on every occasion, that so long as you are praised, believe that you are not yet on your own course but on that of another. And also that it happens sometimes by an exception that a man only reaches the highest when he disclaims his ideal, for this ideal previously drove him onward too violently, so that in the middle of the track he regularly got out of breath and had to rest.

17   The observation that when a given truth survives it is no sign that anyone has cherished it over a given duration of time, but simply a sign that believers in it have succeeded one another in an unbroken succession — this observation seems to me to be one of the few truths of which a careful man may say without qualification that it is substantially true. Much of what I believed in 1910 I no longer believe, but someone else *does* believe it — some pathetic ass. Thus every truth with any merit in it whatsoever is kept alive. As one crowd of believers goes out another comes in.

18   To be thoroughly religious, one must, I believe, be sorely disappointed. One's faith in God increases as one's faith in the world decreases. The happier the man, the farther he is from God.

¹⁹   Politics impresses me as a peep-show the particular low humor of which is derived from the circumstance that the performers have their eyes glued to the other end of the same keyhole that is used by the onlooking customers.

²⁰   A Socialist, as I see it, is ideally fitted for going to jail. All his ideas are ready-made and quite solid, and so he can risk being alone. Unlike other men, solitude brings him no metaphysical and philosophical doubts, concerns and despairs. Socialism is thus a sort of insurance against insanity, like patriotism and religion. A man swallows it, gives up thinking, and is happy.

²¹   I believe that a man's tastes, in essence, change but little. His tastes at fifty are at bottom his tastes of twenty filtered through the gauze of wisdom, prudence and ennui.

²²   I hold that companionship is a matter of mutual weaknesses. We like that man or woman best who has the same faults that we have.

²³   I am always skeptical of the honesty of a man's culture if his library shelves fail to reveal at least a few grotesquely unintelligible volumes. In the heart of every genuinely cultivated man there is a peculiar fondness for certain books that, though perhaps trashy and empty to some of us, are for one reason or another close to his secret fancy.

²⁴   The true artist, I believe, has no goal, but a dozen goals: each a milestone on a road whose end is ever some miles beyond the grave into which he is finally laid. It is only the superficial artist who has a goal, and who often achieves it.

²⁵   The world, I have found, respects the man who smashes its philosophical illusions, but it despises the man who smashes its emotional ones.

²⁶   I admire J. Pierpont Morgan but not Rockefeller. Morgan is hard-fisted, hard-punching, ruthless, brave, forthrightly avaricious and lacking in all hypocrisy. Rockefeller, a moral coward, wraps himself in the seven veils of church and charity by way of concealing the true golden-yellow color of his psychical epidermis. I respect Clemenceau for his courageous errors and disrelish Wilson for his cowardly exactitudes. I have no patriotism, for patriotism, as I see it, is often an arbitrary veneration of real estate above principles. I believe that one intelligent man is worth ten parcel of beautiful women, but I would rather spend an evening with the beautiful women. I believe that intelligent men should be taken on at lunch. I believe that whiskey and gin are bad for the system and that wine and beer are more beneficial to it than all the drugstore philtres in Christendom. I owe my glowing health to wines and beers, although I occasionally drink whiskey and gin and find that, despite my belief to the contrary, they do not seem to do any particular damage. I believe that Richard Strauss is the only substantial living composer, that Sinclair Lewis is the most significant American novelist, that there is not a living statesman worth serious consideration, that Stephen Phillips is a much greater poet than many think, that the only young serious dramatist in Europe worth talking about is Franz Werfel, that the most beautiful spot in the world is a certain little inn hidden away on the bank of a stream in the Black Forest, that Lindberg, Coste, Byrd and all that crew

are absurd futilitarians, that the best place to eat on earth is, first, Madame Génot's in the Rue de la Banque, Paris, and, second, the Vieux Logis in the Rue Lepic of the same town, that Spatenbräu is the most perfect beer, that the faint cinnamon smell of a carnation is the most gratifying of all flower perfumes, that the only completely original playwright since Ibsen is Pirandello, that the only authentic gentlemen left in the world are the Austrians, that athletic sports, save in the case of young boys, are designed for idiots, that money is meant to be spent and not saved, that since we are all now duly and perfectly aware that America has its full share of Rotarians, Kiwanians and Ku Kluxers, not to mention the Anti-Saloon League, the W.C.T.U., the Y.M.C.A., the D.A.R. and the Methodist Board of Temperance, Prohibition and Public Morals, we may as well stop harping on the subject, that it is occasionally well, by way of making the world more palatable, to indulge one's self luxuriously in a remission of judgment and delude one's self momentarily with illusion, and that, when all is said and done, each and every man's philosophy of life, whatever it may be, is profoundly right so long as it makes him happy.

Commentary and questions

1. *Paragraphs 1-2:* Nathan's first paragraph argues for the privacy of personal beliefs; yet paragraph 2, and indeed the whole essay, seems to contradict that argument. Is Nathan able to reconcile the apparent contradiction and, if so, where and how?

How would you type the statements in the first two paragraphs? Are they assertions, statements of fact, opinion, hypothesis? What attitudes toward autobiographical writing and writing in general do they suggest? Are these needless digressions or do they in some way serve the main purposes of the essay?

2. *Paragraphs 3-4:* Examine the tone of these paragraphs. What effect is intended? What techniques contribute to the effect?

3. *Paragraphs 5-8:* What points outlined in the first four paragraphs are developed here? Is the method of development a movement from generality to particularity, from conclusive statement to explanatory detail? Does Nathan seek to prove the rightness or justness of his beliefs? If so, how and where?

4. *Paragraphs 8-26:* These are, in appearance at least, a list of Nathan's particular beliefs and opinions. Which would you call beliefs and which opinions? Is there any discernible order to the list: order of climax, of relative seriousness or triviality, or some other? If there is no consistent order, what purpose might Nathan have in using a haphazard structure?

Topics for discussion and writing

I. Summarize in a paragraph the general quality of Nathan's personal beliefs. What sort of individual does he seem to be? If your judgment of him is unfavorable, do you think that he wrote with an awareness that he would create such an impression? Are his opinions a pose?

II. Write a theme discussing Nathan's use of the following techniques: irony, humor, name-calling, exaggerated assertion, and slang.

III. Write a theme analyzing Nathan's attitude toward religion and religious or philosophical questions. To what extent does he exhibit the lack of faith, the disillusionment with ideals referred to by the other authors in this section?

IV. Write a theme explaining what elements in Nathan's attitude and personality do not conform to the views of modern man presented by the other authors.

V. Would Nathan's most serious attitudes equip him for the democratic faith espoused by Schlesinger? Or would he be nearer, intellectually or temperamentally, to another estimate of the modern state of mind?

VI. A good bit of Nathan's opinions reveal his contempt for a great deal that is still prevalent in modern American life. Choose two or three of the things he attacks and discuss the validity (or lack of it) of his criticisms. Can one make the same criticisms today? (Nathan was writing in the late 1920's.)

VII. On what grounds would you attempt to refute Nathan's individualism? Write a theme doing so.

The work and the critic: Corinna's going a-maying,

Robert Herrick · what does poetry communicate?, Cleanth Brooks · the open boat, Stephen Crane · style and meaning in stephen crane: *The Open Boat*, James B. Colvert

Professional literary criticism is one of the least under-stood and most flourishing kinds of prose exposition. Its legitimate purpose is to illuminate and increase our understanding of literature, but it is all too frequently damned as a form of analysis destructive of the creative spirit that informs literature and hostile to the emotional response of the reader of literature. Unintelligent or misinformed criticism can, of course, do these things, and for this reason the responsible critic is usually careful to let his reader in on his method.

The two critics reprinted here with the objects of their criticism are alike in this respect. Each tries to make plain the assumptions from which he looks at the poem or story, and each argues for his method by arguing against the methods of others. Each is reasonably scrupulous in defining his approach and those he opposes. Each is concerned with the style of the work he analyzes, and each has a fundamental conception of what style is and what it can do.

This is not to say that either critic is necessarily completely right in his interpretation, for it is in the nature of literature that it resists final, scientific proof of the rightness of any interpretation. What one critics overlooks, the next may find. And one method — that which pays close attention to style, to the details of language, in this case — may reveal what others have missed, and vice versa.

Finally, it is important to note that the strategy of the critical essay is essentially no different from that of other types of exposition. It uses logic, reference to fact, definition, and other familiar elements of rhetoric to support and develop a thesis or point of view. The footnotes are not just an academic affectation; they permit the interested reader to check the accuracy

498

of the critic and reveal the sources of whatever factual information he uses. The definition of terms, a matter with which both Brooks and Colvert are concerned, is both necessary for clarity where there might be confusion (for example, the meaning of "Naturalism" receives considerable attention in Colvert's essay) and a useful persuasive device. Notice also that both essays are organized persuasively: possible objections to what each critic is going to say are disposed of first so that he may seem, for the rest of his essay, to be in possession of the field. Whether he is or not is up to the reader, who is equal to the critic in one important respect: he has the poem and the story before him.

CORINNA'S GOING A-MAYING   Robert Herrick

First published in 1648.

> Get up, get up for shame, the Blooming Morne
> Upon her wings presents the god unshorne.
>   See how *Aurora* throws her faire
>   Fresh-quilted colours through the aire:
>   Get up, sweet-Slug-a-bed, and see
>   The Dew bespangling Herbe and Tree.
> Each Flower has wept, and bow'd toward the East,
> Above an houre since; yet you not drest,
>   Nay! not so much as out of bed?
>   When all the Birds have Mattens seyd,
>   And sung their thankfull Hymnes: 'tis sin,
>   Nay, profanation to keep in,
> When as a thousand Virgins on this day,
> Spring, sooner than the Lark, to fetch in May.

> Rise; and put on your Foliage, and be seene
> To come forth, like the Spring-time, fresh and greene;
>   And sweet as *Flora*. Take no care
>   For Jewels for your Gowne, or Haire:
>   Feare not; the leaves will strew
>   Gemms in abundance upon you:
> Besides, the childhood of the Day has kept,
> Against you come, some *Orient Pearls* unwept:
>   Come, and receive them while the light
>   Hangs on the Dew-locks of the night:
>   And *Titan* on the Eastern hill
>   Retires himselfe, or else stands still

Till you come forth. Wash, dresse, be briefe in praying:
Few Beads are best, when once we goe a-Maying.

Come, my *Corinna*, come; and comming, marke
How each field turns a street; each street a Parke
    Made green, and trimm'd with trees: see how
    Devotion gives each House a Bough,
    Or Branch: Each Porch, each doore, ere this,
    An Arke a Tabernacle is
Made up of white-thorn neatly enterwove;
As if here were those cooler shades of love.
    Can such delights be in the street,
    And open fields, and we not see't?
    Come, we'll abroad; and let's obay
    The Proclamation made for May:
And sin no more, as we have done, by staying;
But my *Corinna*, come, let's goe a-Maying.

There's not a budding Boy, or Girle, this day,
But is got up, and gone to bring in May.
    A deale of Youth, ere this, is come
    Back, and with *White-thorn* laden home,
    Some have dispatcht their Cakes and Creame,
    Before that we have left to dreame:
And some have wept, and woo'd, and plighted Troth,
And chose their Priest, ere we can cast off sloth:
    Many a green-gown has been given;
    Many a kisse, both odde and even:
    Many a glance too has been sent
    From out the eye, Loves Firmament:
Many a jest told of the Keyes betraying
This night, and Locks pickt, yet w'are not a-Maying.

Come, let us goe, while we are in our prime;
And take the harmlesse follie of the time.
    We shall grow old apace, and die
    Before we know our liberty.
    Our life is short; and our dayes run
    As fast away as do's the Sunne:
And as a vapour, or a drop of raine
Once lost, can ne'er be found againe:
    So when or you or I are made
    A fable, song, or fleeting shade;
    All love, all liking, all delight

> Lies drown'd with us in endlesse night.
> Then while time serves, and we are but decaying;
> Come, my *Corinna,* come, lets goe a-Maying.

WHAT DOES POETRY COMMUNICATE?

Cleanth Brooks

From The Well Wrought Urn, *copyright, 1947, by Cleanth Brooks. Reprinted by permission of Harcourt, Brace and Company, Inc.*

THE question of what poetry communicates, if anything, has been largely forced upon us by the advent of "modern" poetry. Some of that poetry is admittedly highly difficult — a very great deal of it is bound to *appear* difficult to the reader of conventional reading habits, even in spite of the fact — actually, in many cases, *because* of the fact — that he is a professor of literature.

2   For this reason, the difficult moderns are often represented as untraditional and generally irresponsible. (The War, incidentally, has encouraged the tendency: critics who ought to know better lend themselves to the popular plea that we should go back to the good old days when a poet meant what he said and there was no nonsense about it.)

3   The question, however, allows only one honest answer: modern poetry (if it is really poetry, and, at its best, it is really poetry) communicates whatever any other poetry communicates. The fact is that the question is badly asked. What does traditional poetry communicate? What does a poem like Herrick's "Corinna's going a-Maying" communicate? The example is a fair one: the poem has been long praised, and it is not noted for its difficulty.

4   The textbook answer is easy: the poem is a statement of the *carpe diem* theme. So it is, of course. But what does the poem do with the theme — specifically: Does the poet accept the theme? How seriously does he accept it? Within what context? etc., etc. These are questions of the first importance, a point that becomes obvious when we come to deal with such a matter as the following: after describing the joys of the May-day celebration, the poet prefaces his final invitation to Corinna to accept these joys by referring to them as "the harmlesse follie of the time." Unless we are absent-mindedly dictating a stock answer to an indifferent freshman, we shall certainly feel constrained to go further in describing what the poem "says."

5   Well, let us try again. Herrick's poem says that the celebration of nature is a beautiful but harmless folly, and his invitation to Corinna, thus, is merely playful, not serious. The Anglican parson is merely pretending for the moment that he is Catullus and that his Corinna is a pagan nymph. The poem is a pretense, a masquerade.

6   But there are the closing lines of the poem:

> Our life is short; and our dayes run
> As fast away as do's the Sunne:
> And as a vapour, or a drop of raine
> Once lost, can ne'er be found againe:
>   So when or you or I are made
>   A fable, song, or fleeting shade;
>   All love, all liking, all delight
>   Lies drown'd with us in endlesse night.
> Then while time serves, and we are but decaying;
> Come, my *Corinna*, come, let's goe a-Maying.

Obviously, there is a sense in which the invitation is thoroughly serious.

7   Confronted with this apparent contradiction, we can conclude, if we like, that Herrick is confused; or, softening the censure, we can explain that he was concerned only with providing some sort of framework for a description of the Devonshire spring. But if Herrick is confused about what he is saying in the poem, he behaves very strangely for a man in that plight. Far from being unconscious of the contradictory elements in the poem, he quite obviously has them in mind. Indeed, he actually takes pains to stress the clash between the Christian and pagan world views; or, rather, while celebrating the pagan view, he refuses to suppress references to the Christian. For instance, for all the dew-besprinkled description of the morning, he makes the ominous, unpagan word "sin" run throughout the poem. While the flowers are rejoicing and the birds are singing their hymns of praise, it is a "sin" and a "profanation" for Corinna to remain within doors. In the second stanza, the clash between paganism and Christianity becomes quite explicit: Corinna is to be "briefe in praying:/ Few Beads are best" on this morning which is dedicated to the worship of the nature god. And in the third stanza, paganism becomes frankly triumphant. Corinna is to

> . . . sin no more, as we have done, by staying. . . .

8   Moreover, a great deal that is usually glossed over as decoration or atmosphere in this poem is actually used by the poet to point up this same conflict. Herrick persists (with a shrewdness worthy of Sir James Frazer) in seeing the May-day rites as religious rites, though, of course, those of a pagan religion. The flowers, like worshipers, bow to the east; the birds sing "Mattens" and "Hymnes"; and the village itself, bedecked with greenery, becomes a cluster of pagan temples:

> Devotion gives each House a Bough,
> Or Branch: Each Porch, each doore, ere this,
> An Arke a Tabernacle is. . . .

The religious terms — "devotion," "ark," "tabernacle" — appear insistently. Corinna is actually being reproached for being late to church — the church of nature. The village itself has become a grove, subject to the laws of nature. One remembers that the original sense of "pagan" was "country-dweller" because the worship of the old gods and goddesses persisted longest there. On this May morning, the country has come into the village to claim it, at least on this one day, for its own. Symbolically, the town has disappeared and its mores are superseded.

9   I cannot see how we can avoid admitting that all this is communicated by the poem. Here it is in the poem. And its repercussions on the theme (if we still want to view the poem as a communication of a theme) are important. Among other things, they qualify the theme thus: the poem is obviously not a brief for the acceptance of the pagan ethic so much as it is a statement that the claims of the pagan ethic — however much they may be overlaid — exist, and on occasion emerge, as on this day.

10   The description of Corinna herself supplies another important qualification of the theme. The poet suggests that she properly falls under the dominion of nature as do the flowers and birds and trees. Notice the opening of the second stanza:

> Rise; and put on your Foliage. . . .

And this suggestion that she is a part of nature, like a plant, is reinforced throughout the poem. The trees drenched in dew will shake down dew-drops on her hair, accepting her as a companion and equal. Her human companions, the boys and girls of the village, likewise are plants —

> There's not a budding Boy, or Girle, this day,
> But is got up, and gone to bring in May.

Indeed, as we go through the first three stanzas of the poem, the old relationships gradually dissolve: the street itself turns into a park, and the boys and girls returning with their arms loaded with branches of white-thorn, merge into the plants themselves. Corinna, like them, is subject to nature, and to the claims of nature; and the season of springtime cannot, and ought not, to be denied. Not to respond is to "sin" against nature itself.

11   All this is "communicated" by the poem, and must be taken into account when we attempt to state what the poem "says." No theory of communication can deny that this is part of what the poem communicates, however awkwardly a theory of communication may be put to it to handle the problem.

12   We have still not attempted to resolve the conflict between the Christian and pagan attitudes in the poem, though the qualification of each of them, as Herrick qualifies each in the poem, may make it easier to discover possible resolutions which would have appealed to Herrick the Anglican parson who lived so much of his life in Devonshire and apparently took so much interest, not only in the pagan literature of Rome and Greece, but in the native English survivals of the old fertility cults.

13   Something of the nature of the poet's reconcilement of the conflicting claims of paganism and Christianity — and this, again, is part of what the

poem communicates — is foreshadowed in the fourth stanza. The paganism
with which the poem is concerned is clearly not an abstract and doctrinaire
paganism. It comes to terms with the authoritative Christian mores, casually
and without undue thought about the conflict — at least the paganism in
action does: the village boys and the girls with their grass-stained gowns,
coming to the priest to receive the blessing of the church.

> And some have wept, and woo'd, and plighted Troth,
> And chose their Priest, ere we can cast off sloth. . . .

After the poet's teasing play between attitudes in the first three stanzas, we
are apparently approaching some kind of viable relation between them in
this most realistic stanza of the poem with its

> Many a jest told of the Keyes betraying
> This night, and Locks pickt. . . .

The explicit resolution, of course, is achieved, with a change of tone, in the
last stanza, with its

> Come, let us goe, while we are in our prime;
> And take the harmlesse follie of the time.
> We shall grow old apace, and die . . .

[14]   I shall not try to indicate in detail what the resolution is. Here one must
refer the reader to the poem itself. Yet one can venture to suggest the tone.
The tone would be something like this: All right, let's be serious. Dismiss my
pagan argument as folly. Still, in a sense, we are a part of nature, and are
subject to its claims, and participate in its beauty. Whatever may be true in
reality of the life of the soul, the body does decay, and unless we make haste
to catch some part of that joy and beauty, that beauty — whatever else may
be true — is lost.

[15]   If my clumsy paraphrase possesses any part of the truth, then this is still
another thing which the poem communicates, though I shall hardly be able
to "prove" it. As a matter of fact, I do not care to insist upon this or any
other paraphrase. Indeed it is just because I am suspicious of such necessarily abstract paraphrases that I think our initial question, "What does the
poem communicate?" is badly asked. It is not that the poem communicates
nothing. Precisely the contrary. The poem communicates so much and communicates it so richly and with such delicate qualifications that the thing
communicated is mauled and distorted if we attempt to convey it by any
vehicle less subtle than that of the poem itself.

[16]   This general point is reinforced if we consider the function of particular
words and phrases within the poem. For instance, consider

> Our life is short; and our dayes run
> As fast away as do's the Sunne:
> And as a vapour, or a drop of raine
> Once lost, can ne'er be found againe. . . .

Why does the rain-drop metaphor work so powerfully? It is hardly because the metaphor is startlingly novel. Surely one important reason for its power is the fact that the poet has filled the first two stanzas of his poem with references to the dew. And the drops of dew have come to stand as a symbol of the spring and early dawn and of the youth of the lovers themselves. The dew-drops are the free gift of nature, spangling every herb and tree; they sparkle in the early light like something precious, like gems; they are the appropriate decoration for the girl; but they will not last — Corinna must hasten to enjoy them if she is to enjoy them at all. Thus, in the context of the poem they become a symbol heavily charged with meanings which no dictionary can be expected to give. When the symbol is revived at the end of the poem, even though in somewhat different guise, the effect is powerful; for the poet has made the little globule of moisture come to stand for the brief beauty of youth. And this too is part of what the poem says, though it is said indirectly, and the dull or lazy reader will not realize that it has been said at all.

17   The principle of rich indirection applies even to the individual word. Consider

> Then while time serves, and we are but decaying;
> Come, my *Corinna,* come, let's goe a-Maying.

"While time serves" means loosely "while there is yet time," but in the full context of the poem it also means "while time serves us," while time is still servant, not master — before we are mastered by time. Again, mere recourse to the dictionary will not give us this powerful second meaning. The poet is exploiting the potentialities of language — indeed, as all poets must do, he is remaking language.

18   To sum up: our examination of the poem has not resulted in our locating an idea or set of ideas which the poet has communicated with certain appropriate decorations. Rather, our examination has carried us further and further into the poem itself in a process of exploration. As we have made this exploration, it has become more and more clear that the poem is not only the linguistic vehicle which conveys the thing communicated most "poetically," but that it is also the sole linguistic vehicle which conveys the things communicated accurately. In fact, if we are to speak exactly, the poem itself is the *only* medium that communicates the particular "what" that is communicated. The conventional theories of communication offer no easy solution to our problem of meanings: we emerge with nothing more enlightening than this graceless bit of tautology: the poem says what the poem says.

19   There is a further point that comes out of our examination: our examination tends to suggest that not only our reading of the poem is a process of exploration, but that Herrick's process of making the poem was probably a process of exploration too. To say that Herrick "communicates" certain matters to the reader tends to falsify the real situation. The old description

of the poet was better and less dangerous: the poet is a maker, not a communicator. He explores, consolidates, and "forms" the total experience that is the poem. I do not mean that he fashions a replica of his particular experience of a certain May morning like a detective making a moulage of a footprint in wet clay. But rather, out of the experiences of many May mornings, and out of his experience of Catullus, and possibly out of a hundred other experiences, he fashions, probably through a process akin to exploration, the total experience which is the poem.

20   This experience is *communicable*, partially so, at least. If we are willing to use imaginative understanding, we can come to know the poem as an object — we can share in the experience. But the poet is most truthfully described as a *poietes* or maker, not as an expositor or communicator. I do not mean to split hairs. It is doubtless possible to elaborate a theory of communication which will adequately cover these points. I believe that I. A. Richards, if I understand him correctly, has attempted to qualify his theory in precisely this way. At any rate, the net effect of his criticism has been to emphasize the need of a more careful reading of poetry and to regard the poem as an organic thing.

21   But most proponents of poetry as communication have been less discerning, and have used this view of poetry to damn the modern poets. I refer to such typical critics as Max Eastman and F. L. Lucas. But perhaps the most hard-bitten and vindictive of all the adherents of the theory is a man to whom the phrase "theory of communication" may seem novel and unfamiliar: I mean the average English professor. In one form or another, whether in a conception which makes poetry a romantic raid on the absolute, or in a conception of more didactic persuasion which makes poetry an instrument of edification, some form of the theory of communication is to be found deeply embedded in the average teacher's doctrine of poetry. In many contexts it does little or no harm; but it can emerge to becloud the issues thoroughly when one confronts poetry which is unfamiliar or difficult.

22   Much modern poetry is difficult. Some of it may be difficult because the poet is snobbish and definitely wants to restrict his audience, though this is a strange vanity and much rarer than Mr. Eastman would have us think. Some modern poetry is difficult because it is bad — the total experience remains chaotic and incoherent because the poet could not master his material and give it a form. Some modern poetry is difficult because of the special problems of our civilization. But a great deal of modern poetry is difficult for the reader simply because so few people, relatively speaking, are accustomed to reading *poetry as poetry*. The theory of communication throws the burden of proof upon the poet, overwhelmingly and at once. The reader says to the poet: Here I am; it's your job to "get it across" to me — when he ought to be assuming the burden of proof himself.

23   Now the modern poet has, for better or worse, thrown the weight of the responsibility upon the reader. The reader must be on the alert for shifts of

tone, for ironic statement, for suggestion rather than direct statement. He must be prepared to accept a method of indirection. He is further expected to be reasonably well acquainted with the general tradition — literary, political, philosophical, for he is reading a poet who comes at the end of a long tradition and who can hardly be expected to write honestly and with full integrity and yet ignore this fact. But the difficulties are not insuperable, and most of them can be justified in principle as the natural results of the poet's employment of his characteristic methods. For example, surely there can be no objection to the poet's placing emphasis on methods characteristic of poetry — the use of symbol rather than abstraction, of suggestion rather than explicit pronouncement, of metaphor rather than direct statement.

24 In stressing such methods, it is true, the modern poet has not produced a poetry which easily yields manageable abstractions in the way that some of the older poetry seems to do. But this is scarcely a conclusion that is flattering to the antagonists of modern poetry. What does an "older poem" like "Corinna's going a-Maying" say? What does this poem communicate? If we are content with the answer that the poem says that we should enjoy youth before youth fades, and if we are willing to write off everything else in the poem as "decoration," then we can promptly censure Eliot or Auden or Tate for not making poems so easily tagged. But in that case we are not interested in poetry; we are interested in tags. Actually, in a few years, when time has wrought its softening changes, and familiarity has subdued the modern poet's frightful mien, and when the tags have been obligingly supplied, we may even come to terms with our difficult moderns.

Commentary and questions

1. *Paragraphs 1-3:* This section begins to establish the issues to be treated and it suggests an attitude that Brooks will argue. What is Brooks's position about poetry and the problems in reading it? How do these paragraphs establish a context for an interpretation of Herrick's poem? Do they suggest what the main thesis of his essay will be?

2. *Paragraphs 4-6:* Brooks paraphrases and argues against two possible interpretations of Herrick's poem. Does he object to these interpretations on the grounds that they are not useful for this particular poem or does he object generally to the method of reading they imply?

3. *Paragraphs 7-14:* This section comprises Brooks's account of what the poem says. Note that he mentions a conflict between pagan and Christian values. What is the nature of his evidence for this conflict? Does he seem to go outside the poem to find evidence? How does he see the conflict as resolved in the poem?

4. *Paragraphs 15-16:* Why does Brooks delay until this point his discussion of his own criteria for reading a poem? Does he deliberately cast doubt on his own reading of Herrick's poem? If so, why? If not, why does he call his own reading a "clumsy paraphrase"?

5. *Paragraphs 16-17:* What aspect of language is Brooks discussing here? Does this approach to Herrick's poem differ from the approach in paragraphs 7-14?

6. *Paragraphs 18-21:* Here Brooks argues against the concept that poetry is a means of communication, although he admits that Herrick's poem does communicate something. How does he resolve this apparent contradiction? How does he define standard theories of communication?

7. *Paragraphs 22-24:* This section returns to an issue broached at the beginning of the essay. What answer to the problem of the difficulty of reading modern poetry does Brooks offer? What types of argument has he supplied for his answer?

Topics for discussion and writing

I. Is the main purpose of Brooks's essay an analysis of Herrick's poem, an answer to the question posed in the title, the exposition of Brooks's own theory of what poetry is, or a plea for more intelligent reading of poetry? Write a theme defending your choice among these possibilities.

II. On the basis of the following phrases, write a theme explaining what Brooks's concept of poetry is:

(a) "our reading of the poem is a process of exploration . . . Herrick's process of making the poem was probably a process of exploration too." (paragraph 19)

(b) "the total experience which is the poem" (paragraph 19)

(c) "the poet is . . . a *poeites* or maker" (paragraph 20)

(d) "the poem as an organic thing" (paragraph 20)

III. The two main divisions of Brooks's essay concern an analysis of Herrick's poem and an argument against certain methods of interpreting poetry. Why does Brooks split these into several parts, beginning with an argument against the methods he dislikes, then embarking on his own analysis, then returning to the argument, and so on? Does this alternating structure have anything to do with his use of support?

IV. In paragraph 23 Brooks refers to "methods characteristic of poetry" — symbol, suggestion, and metaphor. Write a theme demonstrating Herrick's use of these methods in his poem.

V. Write a theme employing Brooks's method of close reading with "delicate qualifications" in an analysis of a poem with which you are familiar or which is supplied by your instructor.

THE OPEN BOAT

Stephen Crane

First published in 1898, as given here. Used by permission of Alfred A. Knopf, Inc. Included currently in Stephen Crane: An Omnibus, *edited by Robert Wooster Stallman,* copyright *1952 by Alfred A. Knopf, Inc.*

NONE of them knew the color of the sky. Their eyes glanced level, and were fastened upon the waves that swept toward them. These waves were of the hue of slate, save for the tops, which were of foaming white, and all of the men knew the colors of the sea. The horizon narrowed and widened, and dipped and rose, and at all times its edge was jagged with waves that seemed thrust up in points like rocks.

Many a man ought to have a bath-tub larger than the boat which here rode upon the sea. These waves were most wrongfully and barbarously abrupt and tall, and each froth-top was a problem in small-boat navigation.

The cook squatted in the bottom, and looked with both eyes at the six inches of gunwale which separated him from the ocean. His sleeves were rolled over his fat forearms, and the two flaps of his unbuttoned vest dangled as he bent to bail out the boat. Often he said, "Gawd! that was a narrow clip." As he remarked it he invariably gazed eastward over the broken sea.

The oiler, steering with one of the two oars in the boat, sometimes raised himself suddenly to keep clear of water that swirled in over the stern. It was a thin little oar, and it seemed often ready to snap.

The correspondent, pulling at the other oar, watched the waves and wondered why he was there.

The injured captain, lying in the bow, was at this time buried in that profound dejection and indifference which comes, temporarily at least, to even the bravest and most enduring when, willy-nilly, the firm fails, the army loses, the ship goes down. The mind of the master of a vessel is rooted deep in the timbers of her, though he command for a day or a decade; and this captain had on him the stern impression of a scene in the grays of dawn of seven turned faces, and later a stump of a topmast with a white ball on it, that slashed to and fro at the waves, went low and lower, and down. Thereafter there was something strange in his voice. Although steady, it was deep with mourning, and of a quality beyond oration or tears.

"Keep 'er a little more south, Billie," said he.

"A little more south, sir," said the oiler in the stern.

A seat in this boat was not unlike a seat upon a bucking broncho, and, by the same token, a broncho is not much smaller. The craft pranced and reared and plunged like an animal. As each wave came, and she rose for it, she seemed like a horse making at a fence outrageously high. The manner of her scramble over these walls of water is a mystic thing, and, moreover, at the top of them were ordinarily these problems in white water, the foam racing down from the summit of each wave, requiring a new leap, and a leap from the air. Then, after scornfully bumping a crest, she would slide and race and splash down a long incline, and arrive bobbing and nodding in front of the next menace.

A singular disadvantage of the sea lies in the fact that, after successfully surmounting one wave, you discover that there is another behind it, just as important and just as nervously anxious to do something effective in the way of swamping boats. In a ten-foot dinghy one can get an idea of the resources of the sea in the line of waves that is not probable to the average experience, which is never at sea in a dinghy. As each slaty wall of water approached, it shut all else from the view of the men in the boat, and it was not difficult to imagine that this particular wave was the final outburst of the ocean, the last effort of the grim water. There was a terrible grace in the move of the waves, and they came in silence, save for the snarling of the crests.

In the wan light the faces of the men must have been gray. Their eyes must have glinted in strange ways as they gazed steadily astern. Viewed from a balcony, the whole thing would, doubtless, have been weirdly picturesque. But the men in the boat had no time to see it, and if they had had leisure, there were other things to occupy their minds. The sun swung steadily up the sky, and they knew it was broad day because the color of the sea changed from slate to emerald-green streaked with amber lights, and the foam was like tumbling snow. The process of the breaking day was unknown to them. They were aware only of this effect upon the color of the waves that rolled toward them.

In disjointed sentences the cook and the correspondent argued as to the difference between a life-saving station and a house of refuge. The cook had said: "There's a house of refuge just north of the Mosquito Inlet Light, and as soon as they see us they'll come off in their boat and pick us up."

"As soon as who see us?" said the correspondent.

"The crew," said the cook.

"Houses of refuge don't have crews," said the correspondent. "As I understand them, they are only places where clothes and grub are stored for the benefit of shipwrecked people. They don't carry crews."

"Oh, yes, they do," said the cook.

"No, they don't," said the correspondent.

"Well, we're not there yet, anyhow," said the oiler in the stern.

"Well," said the cook, "perhaps it's not a house of refuge that I'm thinking of as being near Mosquito Inlet Light; perhaps it's a life-saving station."

"We're not there yet," said the oiler in the stern.

II

As the boat bounced from the top of each wave the wind tore through the hair of the hatless men, and as the craft plopped her stern down again the spray slashed past them. The crest of each of these waves was a hill, from the top of which the men surveyed for a moment a broad, tumultuous expanse, shining and wind-riven. It was probably splendid, it was probably glorious, this play of the free sea, wild with lights of emerald and white and amber.

"Bully good thing it's an on-shore wind," said the cook. "If not, where would we be? Wouldn't have a show."

"That's right," said the correspondent.

The busy oiler nodded his assent.

Then the captain, in the bow, chuckled in a way that expressed humor, contempt, tragedy, all in one. "Do you think we've got much of a show now, boys?" said he.

Whereupon the three were silent, save for a trifle of hemming and haw-ing. To express any particular optimism at this time they felt to be childish and stupid, but they all doubtless possessed this sense of the situation in their minds. A young man thinks doggedly at such times. On the other hand, the ethics of their condition was decidedly against any open suggestion of hopelessness. So they were silent.

"Oh, well," said the captain, soothing his children, "we'll get ashore all right."

But there was that in his tone which made them think; so the oiler quoth, "Yes! if this wind holds."

The cook was bailing. "Yes! if we don't catch hell in the surf."

Canton-flannel gulls flew near and far. Sometimes they sat down on the sea, near patches of brown seaweed that rolled over the waves with a move-ment like carpets on a line in a gale. The birds sat comfortably in groups, and they were envied by some in the dinghy, for the wrath of the sea was no more to them than it was to a covey of prairie-chickens a thousand miles inland. Often they came very close and stared at the men with black, bead-like eyes. At these times they were uncanny and sinister in their unblinking scrutiny, and the men hooted angrily at them, telling them to be gone. One came, and evidently decided to alight on the top of the captain's head. The bird flew parallel to the boat, and did not circle, but made short sidelong jumps in the air in chicken fashion. His black eyes were wistfully fixed upon the captain's head. "Ugly brute," said the oiler to the bird. "You look as if you were made with a jack-knife." The cook and the correspondent swore darkly at the creature. The captain naturally wished to knock it away with the end of the heavy painter, but he did not dare do it, because anything resembling an emphatic gesture would have capsized this freighted boat; and so, with his open hand, the captain gently and carefully waved the gull away. After it had been discouraged from the pursuit the captain breathed easier on account of his hair, and others breathed easier because the bird struck their minds at this time as being somehow gruesome and ominous.

In the meantime the oiler and the correspondent rowed; and also they rowed. They sat together in the same seat, and each rowed an oar. Then the oiler took both oars; then the correspondent took both oars; then the oiler;

then the correspondent. They rowed and they rowed. The very ticklish part of the business was when the time came for the reclining one in the stern to take his turn at the oars. By the very last star of truth, it is easier to steal eggs from under a hen than it was to change seats in the dinghy. First the man in the stern slid his hand along the thwart and moved with care, as if he were of Sèvres. Then the man in the rowing-seat slid his hand along the other thwart. It was all done with the most extraordinary care. As the two sidled past each other, the whole party kept watchful eyes on the coming wave, and the captain cried: "Look out, now! Steady, there!"

The brown mats of seaweed that appeared from time to time were like islands, bits of earth. They were traveling, apparently, neither one way nor the other. They were, to all intents, stationary. They informed the men in the boat that it was making progress slowly toward the land.

The captain, rearing cautiously in the bow after the dinghy soared on a great swell, said that he had seen the lighthouse at Mosquito Inlet. Presently the cook remarked that he had seen it. The correspondent was at the oars then, and for some reason he too wished to look at the lighthouse; but his back was toward the far shore, and the waves were important, and for some time he could not seize an opportunity to turn his head. But at last there came a wave more gentle than the others, and when at the crest of it he swiftly scoured the western horizon.

"See it?" said the captain.

"No," said the correspondent, slowly; "I didn't see anything."

"Look again," said the captain. He pointed. "It's exactly in that direction."

At the top of another wave the correspondent did as he was bid, and this time his eyes chanced on a small, still thing on the edge of the swaying horizon. It was precisely like the point of a pin. It took an anxious eye to find a lighthouse so tiny.

"Think we'll make it, Captain?"

"If this wind holds and the boat don't swamp, we can't do much else," said the captain.

The little boat, lifted by each towering sea and splashed viciously by the crests, made progress that in the absence of seaweed was not apparent to those in her. She seemed just a wee thing wallowing miraculously, top up, at the mercy of five oceans. Occasionally a great spread of water, like white flames, swarmed into her.

"Bail her, cook," said the captain, serenely.

"All right, Captain," said the cheerful cook.

III

It would be difficult to describe the subtle brotherhood of men that was here established on the seas. No one said that it was so. No one mentioned it. But it dwelt in the boat, and each man felt it warm him. They were a captain, an oiler, a cook, and a correspondent, and they were friends — friends in a more curiously iron-bound degree than may be common. The hurt captain, lying against the water-jar in the bow, spoke always in a low voice and calmly; but he could never command a more ready and swiftly obedient crew than the motley three of the dinghy. It was more than a mere recognition of what was best for the common safety. There was surely in it a quality that was personal and heartfelt. And after this devotion to the commander of the boat, there was this comradeship, that the correspondent, for instance, who had been taught to be cynical of men, knew even at the time was the best experience of his life. But no one said that it was so. No one mentioned it.

"I wish we had a sail," remarked the captain. "We might try my overcoat on the end of an oar, and give you two boys a chance to rest." So the cook and the correspondent held the mast and spread wide the overcoat; the oiler steered; and the little boat made good way with her new rig. Sometimes the oiler had to scull sharply to keep a sea from breaking into the boat, but otherwise sailing was a success.

Meanwhile the lighthouse had been growing slowly larger. It had now almost assumed color, and appeared like a little gray shadow on the sky. The man at the oars could not be prevented from turning his head rather often to try for a glimpse of this little gray shadow.

At last, from the top of each wave, the men in the tossing boat could see land. Even as the lighthouse was an upright shadow on the sky, this land seemed but a long black shadow on the sea. It certainly was thinner than paper. "We must be about opposite New Smyrna," said the cook, who had coasted this shore often in schooners. "Captain, by the way, I believe they abandoned that life-saving station there about a year ago."

"Did they?" said the captain.

The wind slowly died away. The cook and the correspondent were not now obliged to slave in order to hold high the oar; but the waves continued their old impetuous swooping at the dinghy, and the little craft, no longer under way, struggled woundily over them. The oiler or the correspondent took the oars again.

Shipwrecks are *apropos* of nothing. If men could only train for them and have them occur when the men had reached pink condition, there would be less drowning at sea. Of the four in the dinghy none had slept any time worth mentioning for two days and two nights previous to embarking in the dinghy, and in the excitement of clambering about the deck of a foundering ship they had also forgotten to eat heartily.

For these reasons, and for others, neither the oiler nor the correspondent was fond of rowing at this time. The correspondent wondered ingenuously how in the name of all that was sane could there be people who thought it amusing to row a boat. It was not an amusement; it was a diabolical punishment, and even a genius of mental aberrations could never conclude that it was anything but a horror to the muscles and a crime against the back. He mentioned to the boat in general how the amusement of rowing struck him, and the weary-faced oiler smiled in full sympathy. Previously to the foundering, by the way, the oiler had worked double watch in the engine-room of the ship.

"Take her easy now, boys," said the captain. "Don't spend yourselves. If we have to run a surf you'll need all your strength, because we'll sure have to swim for it. Take your time."

Slowly the land arose from the sea. From a black line it became a line of black and a line of white — trees and sand. Finally the captain said that he could make out a house on the shore. "That's the house of refuge, sure," said the cook. "They'll see us before long, and come out after us."

The distant lighthouse reared high. "The keeper ought to be able to make us out now, if he's looking through a glass," said the captain. "He'll notify the life-saving people."

"None of those other boats could have got ashore to give word of the wreck," said the oiler, in a low voice, "else the life-boat would be out hunting us."

Slowly and beautifully the land loomed out of the sea. The wind came again. It had veered from the northeast to the southeast. Finally a new sound struck the ears of the men in the boat. It was the low thunder of the surf on the shore. "We'll never be able to make the lighthouse now," said the captain. "Swing her head a little more north, Billie."

"A little more north, sir," said the oiler.

Whereupon the little boat turned her nose once more down the wind, and all but the oarsman watched the shore grow. Under the influence of this expansion doubt and direful apprehension were leaving the minds of the men. The management of the boat was still most absorbing, but it could not prevent a quiet cheerfulness. In an hour, perhaps, they would be ashore.

Their backbones had become thoroughly used to balancing in the boat, and they now rode this wild colt of a dinghy like circus men. The correspondent thought that he had been drenched to the skin, but happening to feel in the top pocket of his coat, he found therein eight cigars. Four of them were soaked with sea-water; four were perfectly scatheless. After a search, somebody produced three dry matches; and thereupon the four waifs rode in their little boat and, with an assurance of an impending rescue shining in their eyes, puffed at the big cigars, and judged well and ill of all men. Everybody took a drink of water.

IV

"Cook," remarked the captain, "there don't seem to be any signs of life about your house of refuge."

"No," replied the cook. "Funny they don't see us!"

A broad stretch of lowly coast lay before the eyes of the men. It was of low dunes topped with dark vegetation. The roar of the surf was plain, and sometimes they could see the white lip of a wave as it spun up the beach. A tiny house was blocked out black upon the sky. Southward, the slim light-house lifted its little gray length.

Tide, wind, and waves were swinging the dinghy northward. "Funny they don't see us," said the men.

The surf's roar was here dulled, but its tone was nevertheless thunderous and mighty. As the boat swam over the great rollers the men sat listening to this roar. "We'll swamp sure," said everybody.

It is fair to say here that there was not a life-saving station within twenty miles in either direction; but the men did not know this fact, and in consequence they made dark and opprobrious remarks concerning the eyesight of the nation's life-savers. Four scowling men sat in the dinghy, and surpassed records in the invention of epithets.

"Funny they don't see us."

The light-heartedness of a former time had completely faded. To their sharpened minds it was easy to conjure pictures of all kinds of incompetency and blindness and, indeed, cowardice. There was the shore of the populous land, and it was bitter and bitter to them that from it came no sign.

"Well," said the captain, ultimately, "I suppose we'll have to make a try for ourselves. If we stay out here too long, we'll none of us have strength left to swim after the boat swamps."

And so the oiler, who was at the oars, turned the boat straight for the shore. There was a sudden tightening of muscles. There was some thinking.

"If we don't all get ashore," said the captain, — "if we don't all get ashore, I suppose you fellows know where to send news of my finish?"

They then briefly exchanged some addresses and admonitions. As for the reflections of the men, there was a great deal of rage in them. Perchance they might be formulated thus: "If I am going to be drowned — if I am going to be drowned — if I am going to be drowned, why, in the name of the seven mad gods who rule the sea, was I allowed to come thus far and contemplate sand and trees? Was I brought here merely to have my nose dragged away as I was about to nibble the sacred cheese of life? It is preposterous! If this old ninny-woman, Fate, cannot do better than this, she should be deprived of the management of men's fortunes. She is an old hen who knows not her intention. If she has decided to drown me, why did she not do it in the beginning, and save me all this trouble? The whole affair is absurd. . . . But no; she cannot mean to drown me. She dare not drown me. She cannot drown me. Not after all this work!" Afterward the man might have had an impulse to shake his fist at the clouds. "Just you drown me, now, and then hear what I call you!"

The billows that came at this time were more formidable. They seemed always just about to break and roll over the little boat in a turmoil of foam.

There was a preparatory and long growl in the speech of them. No mind unused to the sea would have concluded that the dinghy could ascend these sheer heights in time. The shore was still afar. The oiler was a wily surfman. "Boys," he said swiftly, "she won't live three minutes more, and we're too far out to swim. Shall I take her to sea again, Captain?"

"Yes; go ahead!" said the captain.

This oiler, by a series of quick miracles and fast and steady oarsmanship, turned the boat in the middle of the surf and took her safely to sea again.

There was a considerable silence as the boat bumped over the furrowed sea to deeper water. Then somebody in gloom spoke: "Well, anyhow, they must have seen us from the shore by now."

The gulls went in slanting flight up the wind toward the gray, desolate east. A squall, marked by dingy clouds, and clouds brick-red, like smoke from a burning building, appeared from the southeast.

"What do you think of those life-saving people? Ain't they peaches?"

"Funny they haven't seen us."

"Maybe they think we're out here for sport! Maybe they think we're fishin'. Maybe they think we're damned fools."

It was a long afternoon. A changed tide tried to force them southward, but wind and wave said northward. Far ahead, where coast-line, sea, and sky formed their mighty angle, there were little dots which seemed to indicate a city on the shore.

"St. Augustine?"

The captain shook his head. "Too near Mosquito Inlet."

And the oiler rowed, and then the correspondent rowed; then the oiler rowed. It was a weary business. The human back can become the seat of more aches and pains than are registered in books for the composite anatomy of a regiment. It is a limited area, but it can become the theater of innumerable muscular conflicts, tangles, wrenches, knots, and other comforts.

"Did you ever like to row, Billie?" asked the correspondent.

"No," said the oiler; "hang it!"

When one exchanged the rowing-seat for a place in the bottom of the boat, he suffered a bodily depression that caused him to be careless of everything save an obligation to wiggle one finger. There was cold sea-water swashing to and fro in the boat, and he lay in it. His head, pillowed on a thwart, was within an inch of the swirl of a wave-crest, and sometimes a particularly obstreperous sea came inboard and drenched him once more. But these matters did not annoy him. It is almost certain that if the boat had capsized he would have tumbled comfortably out upon the ocean as if he felt sure that it was a great, soft mattress.

"Look! There's a man on the shore!"

"Where?"

"There! See 'im? See 'im?"

"Yes, sure! He's walking along."

"Now he's stopped. Look! He's facing us!"

"He's waving at us!"

"So he is! By thunder!"

"Ah, now we're all right! Now we're all right! There'll be a boat out here for us in half an hour."

"He's going on. He's running. He's going up to that house there."

The remote beach seemed lower than the sea, and it required a searching glance to discern the little black figure. The captain saw a floating stick, and they rowed to it. A bath towel was by some weird chance in the boat, and tying this on the stick, the captain waved it. The oarsman did not dare turn his head, so he was obliged to ask questions.

"What's he doing now?"

"He's standing still again. He's looking, I think. . . . There he goes again — toward the house. . . . Now he's stopped again."

"Is he waving at us?"

"No, not now; he was, though."

"Look! There comes another man!"

"He's running."

"Look at him go, would you!"

"Why, he's on a bicycle. Now he's met the other man. They're both waving at us. Look!"

"There comes something up the beach."

"What the devil is that thing?"

"Why, it looks like a boat."

"Why, certainly, it's a boat."

"No; it's on wheels."

"Yes, so it is. Well, that must be the life-boat. They drag them along shore on a wagon."

"That's the life-boat, sure."

"No, by — it's — it's an omnibus."

"I tell you it's a life-boat."

"It is not! It's an omnibus. I can see it plain. See? One of these big hotel omnibuses."

"By thunder, you're right. It's an omnibus, sure as fate. What do you suppose they are doing with an omnibus? Maybe they are going around collecting the life-crew, hey?"

"That's it, likely. Look! There's a fellow waving a little black flag. He's standing on the steps of the omnibus. There come those other two fellows. Now they're all talking together. Look at the fellow with the flag. Maybe he ain't waving it!"

"That ain't a flag, is it? That's his coat. Why, certainly, that's his coat."

"So it is; it's his coat. He's taken it off and is waving it around his head. But would you look at him swing it!"

"Oh, say, there isn't any life-saving station there. That's just a winter-resort hotel omnibus that has brought over some of the boarders to see us drown."

"What's that idiot with the coat mean? What's he signalling, anyhow?"

"It looks as if he were trying to tell us to go north. There must be a life-saving station up there."

"No; he thinks we're fishing. Just giving us a merry hand. See? Ah, there, Willie!"

"Well, I wish I could make something out of those signals. What do you suppose he means?"

"He don't mean anything; he's just playing."

"Well, if he'd just signal us to try the surf again, or to go to sea and wait, or go north, or go south, or go to hell, there would be some reason in it. But look at him! He just stands there and keeps his coat revolving like a wheel. The ass!"

"There come more people."

"Now there's quite a mob. Look! Isn't that a boat?"

"Where? Oh, I see where you mean. No, that's no boat."

"That fellow is still waving his coat."

"He must think we like to see him do that. Why don't he quit it? It don't mean anything."

"I don't know. I think he is trying to make us go north. It must be that there's a life-saving station there somewhere."

"Say, he ain't tired yet. Look at 'im wave!"

"Wonder how long he can keep that up. He's been revolving his coat ever since he caught sight of us. He's an idiot. Why aren't they getting men to bring a boat out? A fishing-boat — one of those big yawls — could come out here all right. Why don't he do something?"

"Oh, it's all right now."

"They'll have a boat out here for us in less than no time, now that they've seen us."

A faint yellow tone came into the sky over the low land. The shadows on the sea slowly deepened. The wind bore coldness with it, and the men began to shiver.

"Holy smoke!" said one, allowing his voice to express his impious mood, "if we keep on monkeying out here! If we've got to flounder out here all night!"

"Oh, we'll never have to stay here all night! Don't you worry. They've seen us now, and it won't be long before they'll come chasing out after us."

The shore grew dusky. The man waving a coat blended gradually into this gloom, and it swallowed in the same manner the omnibus and the group of people. The spray, when it dashed uproariously over the side, made the voyagers shrink and swear like men who were being branded.

"I'd like to catch the chump who waved the coat. I feel like soaking him one, just for luck."

"Why? What did he do?"

"Oh, nothing, but then he seemed so damned cheerful."

In the meantime the oiler rowed, and then the correspondent rowed, and then the oiler rowed. Gray-faced and bowed forward, they mechanically, turn by turn, plied the leaden oars. The form of the lighthouse had vanished from the southern horizon, but finally a pale star appeared, just lifting from the sea. The streaked saffron in the west passed before the all-merging darkness, and the sea to the east was black. The land had vanished, and was expressed only by the low and drear thunder of the surf.

"If I am going to be drowned — if I am going to be drowned — if I am going to be drowned, why, in the name of the seven mad gods who rule the sea, was I allowed to come thus far and contemplate sand and trees? Was I brought here merely to have my nose dragged away as I was about to nibble the sacred cheese of life?"

The patient captain, drooped over the water-jar, was sometimes obliged to speak to the oarsman.

"Keep her head up! Keep her head up!"

"Keep her head up, sir." The voices were weary and low.

This was surely a quiet evening. All save the oarsman lay heavily and listlessly in the boat's bottom. As for him, his eyes were just capable of noting the tall black waves that swept forward in a most sinister silence, save for an occasional subdued growl of a crest.

The cook's head was on a thwart, and he looked without interest at the water under his nose. He was deep in other scenes. Finally he spoke. "Billie," he murmured dreamfully, "what kind of pie do you like best?"

v

"Pie!" said the oiler and the correspondent, agitatedly. "Don't talk about those things, blast you!"

"Well," said the cook, "I was just thinking about ham sandwiches, and —"

A night on the sea in an open boat is a long night. As darkness settled finally, the shine of the light, lifting from the sea in the south, changed to full gold. On the northern horizon a new light appeared, a small bluish gleam on the edge of the waters. These two lights were the furniture of the world. Otherwise there was nothing but waves.

Two men huddled in the stern, and distances were so magnificent in the dinghy that the rower was enabled to keep his feet partly warm by thrusting them under his companions. Their legs indeed extended far under the rowing-seat until they touched the feet of the captain forward. Sometimes, despite the efforts of the tired oarsman, a wave came piling into the boat, an icy wave of the night, and the chilling water soaked them anew. They would twist their bodies for a moment and groan, and sleep the dead sleep once more, while the water in the boat gurgled about them as the craft rocked.

The plan of the oiler and the correspondent was for one to row until he lost the ability, and then arouse the other from his sea-water couch in the bottom of the boat.

The oiler plied the oars until his head drooped forward and the overpowering sleep blinded him; and he rowed yet afterward. Then he touched a man in the bottom of the boat, and called his name. "Will you spell me for a little while?" he said meekly.

"Sure, Billie," said the correspondent, awaking and dragging himself to a sitting position. They exchanged places carefully, and the oiler, cuddling down in the sea-water at the cook's side, seemed to go to sleep instantly.

The particular violence of the sea had ceased. The waves came without snarling. The obligation of the man at the oars was to keep the boat headed so that the tilt of the rollers would not capsize her, and to preserve her from filling when the crests rushed past. The black waves were silent and hard to be seen in the darkness. Often one was almost upon the boat before the oarsman was aware.

In a low voice the correspondent addressed the captain. He was not sure that the captain was awake, although this iron man seemed to be always awake. "Captain, shall I keep her making for that light north, sir?"

The same steady voice answered him. "Yes. Keep it about two points off the port bow."

The cook had tied a life-belt around himself in order to get even the warmth which this clumsy cork contrivance could donate, and he seemed almost stove-like when a rower, whose teeth invariably chattered wildly as soon as he ceased his labor, dropped down to sleep.

The correspondent, as he rowed, looked down at the two men sleeping under foot. The cook's arm was around the oiler's shoulders, and, with their fragmentary clothing and haggard faces, they were the babes of the sea — a grotesque rendering of the old babes in the wood.

Later he must have grown stupid at his work, for suddenly there was a growling of water, and a crest came with a roar and a swash into the boat, and it was a wonder that it did not set the cook afloat in his life-belt. The cook continued to sleep, but the oiler sat up, blinking his eyes and shaking with the new cold.

"Oh, I'm awful sorry, Billie," said the correspondent, contritely.

"That's all right, old boy," said the oiler, and lay down again and was asleep.

Presently it seemed that even the captain dozed, and the correspondent thought that he was the one man afloat on all the oceans. The wind had a voice as it came over the waves, and it was sadder than the end.

There was a long, loud swishing astern of the boat, and a gleaming trail of phosphorescence, like blue flame, was furrowed on the black waters. It might have been made by a monstrous knife.

Then there came a stillness, while the correspondent breathed with the open mouth and looked at the sea.

Suddenly there was another swish and another long flash of bluish light, and this time it was alongside the boat, and might almost have been reached with an oar. The correspondent saw an enormous fin speed like a shadow through the water, hurling the crystalline spray and leaving the long glowing trail.

The correspondent looked over his shoulder at the captain. His face was hidden, and he seemed to be asleep. He looked at the babes of the sea. They certainly were asleep. So, being bereft of sympathy, he leaned a little way to one side and swore softly into the sea.

But the thing did not then leave the vicinity of the boat. Ahead or astern, on one side or the other, at intervals long or short, fled the long sparkling streak, and there was to be heard the whiroo of the dark fin. The speed and power of the thing was greatly to be admired. It cut the water like a gigantic and keen projectile.

The presence of this biding thing did not affect the man with the same horror that it would if he had been a picnicker. He simply looked at the sea dully and swore in an undertone.

Nevertheless, it is true that he did not wish to be alone with the thing. He wished one of his companions to awake by chance and keep him company with it. But the captain hung motionless over the water-jar, and the oiler and the cook in the bottom of the boat were plunged in slumber.

V I

"If I am going to be drowned — if I am going to be drowned — if I am going to be drowned, why, in the name of the seven mad gods who rule the sea, was I allowed to come thus far and contemplate sand and trees?"

During this dismal night, it may be remarked that a man would conclude that it was really the intention of the seven mad gods to drown him, despite the abominable injustice of it. For it was certainly an abominable injustice to drown a man who had worked so hard, so hard. The man felt it would be a crime most unnatural. Other people had drowned at sea since galleys swarmed with painted sails, but still —

When it occurs to a man that nature does not regard him as important, and that she feels she would not maim the universe by disposing of him, he at first wishes to throw bricks at the temple, and he hates deeply the fact that there are no bricks and no temples. Any visible expression of nature would surely be pelleted with his jeers.

Then, if there be no tangible thing to hoot, he feels, perhaps, the desire to confront a personification and indulge in pleas, bowed to one knee, and with hands supplicant, saying, "Yes, but I love myself."

A high cold star on a winter's night is the word he feels that she says to him. Thereafter he knows the pathos of his situation.

The men in the dinghy had not discussed these matters, but each had, no doubt, reflected upon them in silence and according to his mind. There was seldom any expression upon their faces save the general one of complete weariness. Speech was devoted to the business of the boat.

To chime the notes of his emotion, a verse mysteriously entered the correspondent's head. He had even forgotten that he had forgotten this verse, but it suddenly was in his mind.

> A soldier of the Legion lay dying in Algiers;
> There was lack of woman's nursing, there was dearth of woman's tears;
> But a comrade stood beside him, and he took that comrade's hand,
> And he said, "I never more shall see my own, my native land."

In his childhood the correspondent had been made acquainted with the fact that a soldier of the Legion lay dying in Algiers, but he had never regarded it as important. Myriads of his school-fellows had informed him of the soldier's plight, but the dinning had naturally ended by making him perfectly indifferent. He had never considered it his affair that a soldier of the Legion lay dying in Algiers, nor had it appeared to him as a matter for sorrow. It was less to him than the breaking of a pencil's point.

Now, however, it quaintly came to him as a human, living thing. It was no longer merely a picture of a few throes in the breast of a poet, meanwhile drinking tea and warming his feet at the grate; it was an actuality — stern, mournful, and fine.

The correspondent plainly saw the soldier. He lay on the sand with his feet out straight and still. While his pale left hand was upon his chest in an attempt to thwart the going of his life, the blood came between his fingers. In the far Algerian distance, a city of low square forms was set against a sky that was faint with the last sunset hues. The correspondent, plying the oars and dreaming of the slow and slower movements of the lips of the soldier, was moved by a profound and perfectly impersonal comprehension. He was sorry for the soldier of the Legion who lay dying in Algiers.

The thing which had followed the boat and waited had evidently grown bored at the delay. There was no longer to be heard the slash of the cutwater, and there was no longer the flame of the long trail. The light in the north still glimmered, but it was apparently no nearer to the boat. Sometimes the boom of the surf rang in the correspondent's ears, and he turned the craft seaward then and rowed harder. Southward, some one had evidently built a watch-fire on the beach. It was too low and too far to be seen, but it made a shimmering, roseate reflection upon the bluff back of it, and this could be discerned from the boat. The wind came stronger, and sometimes a wave suddenly raged out like a mountain-cat, and there was to be seen the sheen and sparkle of a broken crest.

The captain, in the bow, moved on his water-jar and sat erect. "Pretty long night," he observed to the correspondent. He looked at the shore. "Those life-saving people take their time."

"Did you see that shark playing around?"

"Yes, I saw him. He was a big fellow, all right."

"Wish I had known you were awake."

Later the correspondent spoke into the bottom of the boat.

"Billie!" There was a slow and gradual disentanglement. "Billie, will you spell me?"

"Sure," said the oiler.

As soon as the correspondent touched the cold, comfortable sea-water in the bottom of the boat and had huddled close to the cook's life-belt he was deep in sleep, despite the fact that his teeth played all the popular airs. This sleep was so good to him that it was but a moment before he heard a voice call his name in a tone that demonstrated the last stages of exhaustion. "Will you spell me?"

"Sure, Billie."

The light in the north had mysteriously vanished, but the correspondent took his course from the wide-awake captain.

Later in the night they took the boat farther out to sea, and the captain directed the cook to take one oar at the stern and keep the boat facing the seas. He was to call out if he should hear the thunder of the surf. This plan enabled the oiler and the correspondent to get respite together. "We'll give those boys a chance to get into shape again," said the captain. They curled down and, after a few preliminary chatterings and trembles, slept once more the dead sleep. Neither knew they had bequeathed to the cook the company of another shark, or perhaps the same shark.

As the boat caroused on the waves, spray occasionally bumped over the side and gave them a fresh soaking, but this had no power to break their repose. The ominous slash of the wind and the water affected them as it would have affected mummies.

"Boys," said the cook, with the notes of every reluctance in his voice, "she's drifted in pretty close. I guess one of you had better take her to sea again." The correspondent, aroused, heard the crash of the toppled crests.

As he was rowing, the captain gave him some whisky and water, and this steadied the chills out of him. "If I ever get ashore and anybody shows me even a photograph of an oar —"

At last there was a short conversation.

"Billie! . . . Billie, will you spell me?"

"Sure," said the oiler.

VII

When the correspondent again opened his eyes, the sea and the sky were each of the gray hue of the dawning. Later, carmine and gold was painted upon the waters. The morning appeared finally, in its splendor, with a sky of pure blue, and the sunlight flamed on the tips of the waves.

On the distant dunes were set many little black cottages, and a tall white windmill reared above them. No man, nor dog, nor bicycle appeared on the beach. The cottages might have formed a deserted village.

The voyagers scanned the shore. A conference was held in the boat. "Well," said the captain, "if no help is coming, we might better try a run through the surf right away. If we stay out here much longer we will be too weak to do anything for ourselves at all." The others silently acquiesced in this reasoning. The boat was headed for the beach. The correspondent wondered if none ever ascended the tall wind-tower, and if then they never looked seaward. This tower was a giant, standing with its back to the plight of the ants. It represented in a degree, to the correspondent, the serenity of nature amid the struggles of the individual — nature in the wind, and nature in the vision of men. She did not seem cruel to him then, nor beneficent, nor treacherous, nor wise. But she was indifferent, flatly indifferent. It is, perhaps, plausible that a man in this situation, impressed with the unconcern of the universe, should see the innumerable flaws of his life and have them taste wickedly in his mind, and wish for another chance. A distinction between right and wrong seems absurdly clear to him, then, in this new ignorance of the grave-edge, and he understands that if he were given another opportunity he would mend his conduct and his words, and be better and brighter during an introduction or at a tea.

"Now, boys," said the captain, "she is going to swamp sure. All we can do is to work her in as far as possible, and then when she swamps, pile out and scramble for the beach. Keep cool now, and don't jump until she swamps sure."

The oiler took the oars. Over his shoulders he scanned the surf. "Captain," he said, "I think I'd better bring her about, and keep her head-on to the seas, and back her in."

"All right, Billie," said the captain. "Back her in." The oiler swung the boat then, and, seated in the stern, the cook and the correspondent were obliged to look over their shoulders to contemplate the lonely and indifferent shore.

The monstrous inshore rollers heaved the boat high until the men were again enabled to see the white sheets of water scudding up the slanted beach. "We won't get in very close," said the captain. Each time a man could wrest his attention from the rollers, he turned his glance toward the shore, and in the expression of the eyes during this contemplation there was a singular quality. The correspondent, observing the others, knew that they were not afraid, but the full meaning of their glances was shrouded.

As for himself, he was too tired to grapple fundamentally with the fact. He tried to coerce his mind into thinking of it, but the mind was dominated at this time by the muscles, and the muscles said they did not care. It merely occurred to him that if he should drown it would be a shame.

There were no hurried words, no pallor, no plain agitation. The men simply looked at the shore. "Now, remember to get well clear of the boat when you jump," said the captain.

Seaward the crest of a roller suddenly fell with a thunderous crash, and the long white comber came roaring down upon the boat.

"Steady now," said the captain. The men were silent. They turned their eyes from the shore to the comber and waited. The boat slid up the incline, leaped at the furious top, bounced over it, and swung down the long back of the wave. Some water had been shipped, and the cook bailed it out.

But the next crest crashed also. The tumbling, boiling flood of white water caught the boat and whirled it almost perpendicular. Water swarmed in from all sides. The correspondent had his hands on the gunwale at this time, and when the water entered at that place he swiftly withdrew his fingers, as if he objected to wetting them.

The little boat, drunken with this weight of water, reeled and snuggled deeper into the sea.

"Bail her out, cook! Bail her out!" said the captain.

"All right, Captain," said the cook.

"Now, boys, the next one will do for us sure," said the oiler. "Mind to jump clear of the boat."

The third wave moved forward, huge, furious, implacable. It fairly swallowed the dinghy, and almost simultaneously the men tumbled into the sea. A piece of life-belt had lain in the bottom of the boat, and as the correspondent went overboard he held this to his chest with his left hand.

The January water was icy, and he reflected immediately that it was colder than he had expected to find it off the coast of Florida. This appeared to his dazed mind as a fact important enough to be noted at the time. The coldness of the water was sad; it was tragic. This fact was somehow mixed and confused with his opinion of his own situation so that it seemed almost a proper reason for tears. The water was cold.

When he came to the surface he was conscious of little but the noisy water. Afterward he saw his companions in the sea. The oiler was ahead in the race. He was swimming strongly and rapidly. Off to the correspondent's left, the cook's great white and corked back bulged out of the water; and in the rear the captain was hanging with his one good hand to the keel of the overturned dinghy.

There is a certain immovable quality to a shore, and the correspondent wondered at it amid the confusion of the sea.

It seemed also very attractive; but the correspondent knew that it was a long journey, and he paddled leisurely. The piece of life-preserver lay under him, and sometimes he whirled down the incline of a wave as if he were on a hand-sled.

But finally he arrived at a place in the sea where travel was beset with difficulty. He did not pause swimming to inquire what manner of current had caught him, but there his progress ceased. The shore was set before him like a bit of scenery on a stage, and he looked at it, and understood with his eyes each detail of it.

As the cook passed, much farther to the left, the captain was calling to him, "Turn over on your back, cook! Turn over on your back and use the oar."

"All right, sir." The cook turned on his back, and, paddling with an oar, went ahead as if he were a canoe.

Presently the boat also passed to the left of the correspondent, with the captain clinging with one hand to the keel. He would have appeared like a man raising himself to look over a board fence if it were not for the extraordinary gymnastics of the boat. The correspondent marveled that the captain could still hold to it.

They passed on nearer to shore, — the oiler, the cook, the captain, — and following them went the water-jar, bouncing gaily over the seas.

The correspondent remained in the grip of this strange new enemy, a current. The shore, with its white slope of sand and its green bluff, topped with little silent cottages, was spread like a picture before him. It was very near to him then, but he was impressed as one who, in a gallery, looks at a scene from Brittany or Algiers.

He thought: "I am going to drown? Can it be possible? Can it be possible? Can it be possible?" Perhaps an individual must consider his own death to be the final phenomenon of nature.

But later a wave perhaps whirled him out of this small deadly current, for he found suddenly that he could again make progress toward the shore. Later still he was aware that the captain, clinging with one hand to the keel of the dinghy, had his face turned away from the shore and toward him, and was calling his name. "Come to the boat! Come to the boat!"

In his struggle to reach the captain and the boat, he reflected that when one gets properly wearied drowning must really be a comfortable arrangement — a cessation of hostilities accompanied by a large degree of relief; and he was glad of it, for the main thing in his mind for some moments had been horror of the temporary agony; he did not wish to be hurt.

Presently he saw a man running along the shore. He was undressing with most remarkable speed. Coat, trousers, shirt, everything flew magically off him.

"Come to the boat!" called the captain.

"All right, Captain." As the correspondent paddled, he saw the captain let himself down to bottom and leave the boat. Then the correspondent performed his one little marvel of the voyage. A large wave caught him and flung him with ease and supreme speed completely over the boat and far beyond it. It struck him even then as an event in gymnastics and a true miracle of the sea. An overturned boat in the surf is not a plaything to a swimming man.

The correspondent arrived in water that reached only to his waist, but his condition did not enable him to stand for more than a moment. Each wave knocked him into a heap, and the undertow pulled at him.

Then he saw the man who had been running and undressing, and undressing and running, come bounding into the water. He dragged ashore the cook, and then waded toward the captain; but the captain waved him away and sent him to the correspondent. He was naked — naked as a tree in winter; but a halo was about his head, and he shone like a saint. He gave a strong pull, and a long drag, and a bully heave at the correspondent's hand. The correspondent, schooled in the minor formulæ, said, "Thanks, old man." But suddenly the man cried, "What's that?" He pointed a swift finger. The correspondent said, "Go."

In the shallows, face downward, lay the oiler. His forehead touched sand that was periodically, between each wave, clear of the sea.

The correspondent did not know all that transpired afterward. When he achieved safe ground he fell, striking the sand with each particular part of his body. It was as if he had dropped from a roof, but the thud was grateful to him.

It seems that instantly the beach was populated with men with blankets, clothes, and flasks, and women with coffee-pots and all the remedies sacred to their minds. The welcome of the land to the men from the sea was warm and generous; but a still and dripping shape was carried slowly up the beach, and the land's welcome for it could only be the different and sinister hospitality of the grave.

When it came night, the white waves paced to and fro in the moonlight, and the wind brought the sound of the great sea's voice to the men on shore, and they felt that they could then be interpreters.

STYLE AND MEANING
IN STEPHEN CRANE:
The Open Boat

James B. Colvert

From *Texas Studies in English*, Vol. XXXVII (1958). Reprinted by permission of the author and The University of Texas Press.

As a STYLIST, Stephen Crane puzzled some of his contemporaries. One critic, reviewing *The Red Badge of Courage* in 1900, identified him as one of the worst offenders of a new school of writers who, "in their effort to be vivid and striking, have allowed themselves to be carried away into extremes. The straining after effect and the extravagant use of onomatopoeticism here become so evident as to be uncouth." [1] Another reviewer, writing in the *Literary Digest*, offered a parody:

> Nothing is easier. The method is simple. It presents no difficulties. It is distinct. It appeals to many. It is new. Therefore it pleases. For a time. But not permanently. Men of intelligence yawn. The trick is too

[1] *The Literary Digest*, XX (Feb. 10, 1900), 182.

readily seen through. It is like an infant's reader: My cat is called Tom. Do you like cats? No, I like dogs. I like both cats and dogs.[2]

2   Critics of a later generation were not so much concerned with Crane's eccentricities of style. One reason, perhaps, is that readers in the 'twenties, accustomed to the experiments of the imagists and symbolists, no longer expected writing to adhere to the prose norm of the 1890's, a compromise between the nineteenth-century grand style and the plain style of the literary realists. A more important reason is that academic criticism by this time had already firmly attached to Crane's writing a literary label which encouraged the critic to ignore, largely, the question of style. He was a Naturalist. And since the Naturalist — particularly one of the school of Zola, to which Crane was assumed to belong — is theoretically indifferent to style, critics generally gave their attention to the ethical implications of his "mechanistic" world view, reading in his work a vision of man as a helpless and driven animal at the mercy of all-powerful forces about him. Beyond a few observations about his extraordinary color imagery and his predilection for ironic understatement, critics, especially the academic critics, seldom pursued the question of his language.

3   Robert Spiller's account of "The Open Boat" in *The Literary History of the United States* excellently summarizes the established attitude. To Spiller, Crane's "masterpiece" is a "simple record of the actual wreck of a filibustering vessel off the coast of Florida," an account which "achieves its effect by understatement." The significant meaning, the meaning which strikes deepest into Crane's world view, Spiller says, is expressed in the revelation that nature is indifferent to man. "This," he remarks, "is [to Crane] the meaning of life, in so far as it has a meaning." [3]

4   The doctrine of Naturalism is, of course, supremely rational and consequently invites the test of logical coherence and consistency. The important question which the Naturalistic story raises is whether the fictional statement squares in all its implications with the demands of the doctrine it is supposed to exemplify. Charles Walcutt, who applies this test to Crane, finds this consistency to be the chief proof of his excellence:

> The meaning is always the action; there is no wandering into theory that runs counter to what happens in the action; and nowhere does a character operate as a genuinely free ethical agent in defiance of the author's intentions. Crane's success is a triumph of style: manner and meaning are one.[4]

If the reader is able to ignore the intrusion of "extraneous elements," Walcutt's phrase for certain stylistic features presumably outside the require-

[2] Jane H. Findlater, "The New Art of Description in Fiction," *The National Review* (Jan., 1900); quoted in *The Literary Digest,* XX (Feb. 10, 1900), 182.
[3] Robert E. Spiller, "Toward Naturalism in Fiction," in *The Literary History of the United States,* ed. Spiller, Canby, Thorp, *et al.* (New York, 1948), p. 1024.
[4] Charles C. Walcutt, *American Literary Naturalism, A Divided Stream* (University of Minnesota Press, 1956), p. 67.

ments of a pure Naturalistic fiction, then this seems to be a just appraisal of Crane's art. But another critic, reading Crane as a Naturalist and giving close attention to details of style, disagrees. Examining the images and metaphors of "The Open Boat," John W. Schroeder finds that they introduce non-logical elements which tend to contradict the logic of the Naturalistic attitude which he assumes to underlie the story:

> Logically, a vision of Nature's indifference should cancel out the equally powerful vision of Nature as somehow possessed by forces deadly to man. It seems somewhat curious that the same work which contains this clear and definite statement of indifference should also speak of the "wrath" of the ocean, which "growls" at least three times and whose waves rage "like a mountain cat." It is curious, too, that the prospect of drowning in this viciously animated sea should be styled "a cessation of hostilities." [5]

The "logical force" of Crane's reaction to nature as both *hostile* and *indifferent*, Schroeder thinks, "is slight," though he admits that "its poetic force is extreme." But the critic's concern is not with poetic force but with logical contradictions. Committed to his understanding of Crane as a Naturalist, he seems to conclude that "clear and definite statements" of this view should not be confused by contradictions implicit in metaphor and imagery.

[5] The fact that these critics have written on Crane in very recent years suggests how persistent these traditional assumptions about his method and themes really are. Not until after 1950, when a revival of interest in Crane began to place him in a new critical light, was the standard approach to his writing challenged. Robert W. Stallman, who has been largely responsible for this revival, has shifted the focus of attention away from Crane's Naturalism to his style, which this critic finds not at all extraneous to Crane's art, but on the contrary the most significant aspect of it. "A great stylist," Stallman writes, "Crane puts language to poetic uses, which is to use it reflexively and symbolically. *The works that employ this reflexive and symbolic language constitute what is permanent of Crane.*" [6] Applying the techniques of formal analysis, Stallman discovers Crane's fiction to be mythic, ritualistic, symbolical, and allegorical:

> Crane's language is the language of symbol and paradox: the wafer-like sun in *The Red Badge*; or in *The Open Boat* the paradox of "cold, comfortable sea-water," an image that calls to mind the poetry of Yeats, with its fusion of contradictory emotions. This single image evokes the sensation of the whole experience of the men in the dinghy.[7]

To Stallman, clearly, Crane's stories are for the consideration of practical criticism, long prose-poems; in those very elements which the "Naturalist"

---

[5] John W. Schroeder, "Stephen Crane Embattled," *University of Kansas City Review,* XVII (Winter, 1950), 127.
[6] Robert W. Stallman, "Introduction," *Stephen Crane: An Omnibus* (New York, Knopf, 1952; London, Heinneman, 1954), p. xlv.
[7] *Ibid.*

critics ignore or find so unaccountable, he discovers new dimensions of meaning.

6   Stallman's reading has been vigorously disputed by Philip Rahv, who finds it, like so much recent criticism of fiction, vitiated by a "wholesale disgorgement of shibboleths lifted from contemporary poetry criticism" with all its biases toward symbolism, allegory, paradox, and irony.[8] Protesting against a critical system derived from a widespread "superstition of the word," Rahv argues that "a novel and a lyric poem are not to be equated as works of verbal art because the relation in them between theme and composition is quite different." [9] Normally, he says,

> . . . the language of the novel does not possess the autonomous value that it has in poetry. It only intermittently lends itself to that verbal play characteristic of poetic speech, a play which uncovers the phonic texture of the word while at the same time releasing its semantic potential.[10]

And though he grants that "there is such a thing . . . as a purely formal prose, in which the elements of style and composition dominate . . ." he seems to regard this kind of "art-prose" as decadent and somewhat outside the healthy norm of fiction as a genre distinct from poetry. He condemns Stallman's approach to Crane on the grounds that it falsely identifies "style as the essential activity of imaginative prose . . . and confuses the intensive speech proper to poetry with the more openly communicative, functional, and extensive language proper to prose." [11]

7   I am not concerned here with the significance of this argument for the theory of style in fiction. But it does seem to be a timely warning for the practical critic, for certainly, as Rahv says, we need to make clearer distinctions between the forms of the poem and of the story — even, I would add, of the symbolist story, to which the concepts of modern poetry criticism would seem most applicable. Stallman's failure to make this distinction sometimes leads him, I think, into error. His reading of *The Red Badge*, for example, as a Christian allegory insists that the symbols and images in the novel function in the same way that they seem to function in the more highly organized language of poetry; clearly, as Stallman says, there is crucifixion imagery in the famous passage describing Jim Conklin's death, but to say also that "the key to the symbolism of the whole [novel is] the religious symbolism that radiates outwards from Jim Conklin" is to press for an allegorical meaning which the structure of the novel cannot express. What bearing does the religious symbolism associated with Conklin's death have upon the subsequent moral development of Henry Fleming? So far as we are told, Conklin enters Henry's thoughts only once more, when the

[8] Philip Rahv, "Fiction and the Criticism of Fiction," *The Kenyon Review*, XVIII (Spring, 1956), 282.
[9] *Ibid.*, 291-292.
[10] *Ibid.*, 293.
[11] *Ibid.*, 280.

youth, rejoining his regiment, suddenly remembers and relates almost casually the news of Conklin's death (Chapter Fourteen). And in the end, when Henry takes stock of his experience and comes to some conclusions about the meaning of all the events of his life as a soldier, it is not the image of Conklin's death, but the image of the deserted tattered man which occupies the central place in his thoughts.

8   Still, Stallman's approach to Crane is much more meaningful than the one suggested by Rahv, who insists that the language of fiction is properly nothing more than a "kind of transparent envelope or medium through which we watch the action." This, it seems to me, is doubtful. Action in fiction exists only in the language, not apart from it; if the language is changed the character and meaning of the action is changed. For it would appear that language in even the most "objective" fictional style embodies attitudes and value judgments which must be dealt with as elements in the structure of the story. Rahv's point of view seems to favor, as his remarks about Dostoevsky's style indicate, the notion that an "objective realism" in writing is a possible and desirable aesthetic:

> . . . we are able to recognize Dostoevsky's greatness as a novelist at the same time that we are not in the least impressed by his stylistic powers. He is in fact a most indifferent stylist, but that hardly bothers us in reading him, for once we are caught up by the moving current of mock-reality in his narratives we cease noticing the words as such. . . .[12]

It is just this bias, as I have tried to show, which underlies the attitudes of Crane's contemporaries, which vitiated Crane criticism for over fifty years, and which still stands behind the kind of assertions made in Gordon Haight's recent comparison of Crane's "decadent impressionism" to De Forest's "true realism":

> Everything that Crane sees looks like something else; De Forest describes things as they are. He never sees a wood as a chapel, boughs as a door, and pine needles as a carpet, nor do his corpses remind one of the exhibits in Madame Taussaud's chamber of horrors. Crane's hero sees tents spring up "like strange plants. Camp fires, like red, peculiar blossoms, dotted the night." To De Forest, who sees them from the inside, tents are canvas, usually rotten enough to let the rain through, and camp-fires are lit for warmth. That is the difference between a somewhat decadent impressionism and true realism.[13]

But this is merely an objection to style predominantly metaphorical and indirect. What these images might mean, how they might be significantly relevant to Crane's aesthetic or to his world view are questions which the method altogether discourages. Rahv's plea for a reading of *The Red Badge*

---

[12] *Ibid.*, 295.
[13] Gordon S. Haight, "Introduction," *Miss Ravenel's Conversion*, by J. W. De Forest (New York, 1955), p. xvi.

that will tell us that "the novel is actually 'about' what it seems to be, war and its impact on human beings moved by pride, bravado, fear, anxiety and sudden panic," seems implicitly to demand a similar approach.

9   But Crane cannot rightly be read in this way. His method, unlike that of the realists, is metaphorical, imagistic, and symbolic. The burden of meaning in his fiction is carried in large part by image, metaphor, recurring motifs, contrasts in tone and mood, and other suggestive devices — in other words, by style. Consider, for example, the stylistic indirection of the writing in the first chapter of "The Open Boat." The poetically heightened opening sentence ("None of them knew the color of the sky") sets the dramatic tone of the passage, suggests the condition of mental stress of the men in the boat, and establishes the point of view to be developed — the point of view of the men totally absorbed in the experience of the rushing waves. The diction and regularized rhythm of the second sentence ("Their eyes glanced level and were fastened upon the waves that swept toward them") sustains the poetic heightening (chiefly in the phrase "glanced level"), fixes more firmly the point of view, and enforces the image of the men's fearful concentration on the threatening sea. The comparatively irregular third sentence is nearer to the rhythmic norm of prose ("These waves were of the hue of slate, save for the tops, which were of foaming white"), but toward the end it is again regularized ("and all of the men knew the colors of the sea") into a rhetorical and rhythmical balance with the first sentence ("None of them knew the color of the sky"). Coming in the middle of the paragraph, this gives the paragraph something of the balance and design of a stanza of poetry, a subtle commitment carried out in the deliberate onomatopoeia of the last sentence, which imitates the movement of the waves in the first half and suggests in the buzzing, sibilant sounds and broken rhythms of the last part the cruel threat of the imagined rocks:

> The horizon narrowed and widened
> and dipped and rose,
> and at all times its edge was jagged with waves
> that seemed thrust up in points like rocks.

10   Obviously the language here is not so highly organized rhythmically as the more or less tightly metered language of poetry, but if this analysis is acceptable it should suggest that Crane's style is more consciously poetic than the prose "norm" which Rahv seems to have in mind. Crane does in this sense put language to poetic uses, and it would seem that the techniques of poetry analysis, used with discretion and with regard for the more expansive and more explicitly dramatic structure of his fiction, are valid and necessary if we are to grasp the full meaning and significance of his writing. And to get at his meaning — to search out not only the structure of his art but also the nature of the world view which it expresses — is to remove from his best writing the stigma of a naive and ingenuous philosophical naturalism and find in it, as Edward Garnet did years ago, something of the "perfect

fusion of [the] forces of passion and irony [which] creates Crane's spiritual background and raises his work, at its finest, into the higher zone of man's tragic conflict with the universe." [14]

11   No reader could find this meaning in his work without taking style into account, for it is in style that this meaning exists in Crane's fiction. To read, for instance, the image of nature's wrath in "The Open Boat" into the author's world view is to fall into the error which leads Schroeder to conclude that contradictory visions of the sea as both hostile and indifferent are proof of Crane's confused "Naturalism." But it is important to understand that these different visions of nature are aspects of Crane's perception of irreconcilable contradictions in reality. To the men, whose vision is concentrated with such fierce intensity upon the rolling sea, an intensity suggested in their exquisite perception of the violent contrast between the slate-colored waves and their crests of boiling white and suggested further in their vivid sense of the shifting, swelling motion of the sea — to these men, then, the hostile appearance of the waves *is*, at this moment, their absolute reality. "As each slaty wall of water approached, it shut all else from the view of the men in the boat, and it was not difficult to imagine that this particular wave was the final outburst of the ocean, the last effort of the grim water." But from the point of view of the narrator (and the reader), whose sense of the situation is not affected by an imprisoning wall of jagged waves, their reality might well be something else. "Viewed from a balcony," the narrator states later on, "the whole thing would, doubtless, have been weirdly picturesque. But the men in the boat had not time to see it. . . ."

12   This ironic contrast suggests a theme so central to Crane's consciousness that it can be taken as almost a definition of his world view, the vision of life governed by his profound sense of the consequences of our faulty perceptions of reality. The grand subject of his fiction is man's struggle to bring into some sort of meaningful order the confusions and contradictions of experience. His heroes, burdened with a perceptual machinery which renders them incapable of reconciling all the apparently disparate elements in their experience, stand uncertain and defenseless in a flux of imperfectly comprehended events. One of Crane's letters shows, I think, his sense of the meaning of this limitation of consciousness:

> I understand that a man is born into the world with his own pair of eyes, and he is not at all responsible for his quality of personal honesty. To keep close to this personal honesty is my supreme ambition.
>
> There is a sublime egotism in talking of honesty. I, however, do not say that I am honest. I merely say that I am as nearly honest as a weak mental machinery will allow. This aim in life struck me as being the only thing worth while. A man is sure to fail at it, but there is something in the failure.[15]

[14] Edward Garnett, "Stephen Crane and His Work," in *Friday Nights* (New York, 1922), p. 213-214.
[15] Stallman, *op. cit.*, p. 680.

Crane's heroes rarely have such a clear insight into their own limitations for seeing the world clearly and truly. More often they are compelled to maintain in their private worlds the images of themselves which their fallible consciousness demands. They must be the darlings of the gods, the central facts of creation, the aspiring masters of nature and themselves. Bound in darkness, they must be children of light — or what they think is light.

13 When we speak of Crane's ironical style we refer properly to the general relation between this attitude and the verbal forms which express it, not merely to the fact that his writing is normally couched in the language of ironic understatement. "Irony," Kierkegaard observes, "is an existential determination and nothing is more ridiculous than to suppose that it consists in the use of a certain phraseology, or when an author congratulates himself upon succeeding in expressing himself ironically. Whoever has irony has it all day long, not bound to any specific form, because it is the infinite within him." [16]

14 But our question is how irony in this sense is expressed in the structure and style of Crane's writing, and for a characteristic example we may return to the opening section of "The Open Boat," where two apparently contradictory ideas about the reality of the sea are set up not only in direct, openly communicative statement, but also — and more significantly — in the images of space, color, and motion and in the rhythm, balance, and tone of the sentences. I have mentioned how the image of the waves as threatening, pointed rocks suggests to the men that nature is hostile and how the contrary idea is introduced in the narrator's statement that the scene, "viewed from a balcony," might be merely picturesque. But before the narrator intrudes to state it openly and discursively, the idea is evoked by stylistic indirection. The tone and direction of reference of the first sentence of the second paragraph ("Many a man ought to have a bathtub larger than the boat which here rode upon the sea") seems to express not so much an opinion of the narrator as a self-conscious protest from the sailors who, overwhelmed by the pathos of their situation, cry out against the injustice of their plight. Although there are ironic overtones in the conditional *ought* and in the implicit contrast of the domestic bathtub with the nearly swamped boat, still the main expressive force of the sentence is nonironical because the cry can be taken as a just and accurate expression of the genuine pathos of their situation. But the ethical reproach expressed in the sentence which immediately follows ("These waves were most wrongfully and barbarously abrupt and tall") must be taken ironically: to a detached observer ocean waves are neither right nor wrong, barbarous nor civilized. Clearly another attitude is admissible; the sea is perhaps weirdly picturesque or, as the correspondent comes finally to believe, merely indifferent.

15 But only admissible, not necessarily true; nature is only *perhaps* in-

16 Soren Kierkegaard, *Kierkegaard's Concluding Unscientific Postscript,* trans. by David Senson and Walter Lowrie (Princeton University Press, 1941), p. 449.

different or picturesque. The reservations are important, indeed, the very essence of the ironic view; for the ironical man, though detached from the world of contradictions he perceives, does not pass final judgments upon them. "In fact," as Andrew Wright says,

> the ironist is deeply concerned with both aspects of the contradictions he perceives; and this concern leads to an ambivalence of attitude to one side and to the other — to both at once. Searching the orchards of human experience he finds the bittersweet apple of confusing appearance and ambiguous essence — and he becomes a man of the divided, the ironic, vision.
>
> This has led some to feel that "the basic feature of every irony is a contrast between a reality and an appearance." But the matter is not so simple: the ironist is not sure which is and which merely seems.[17]

The ambivalence of attitude of the true ironists bears greatly upon the structure and meaning of "The Open Boat," for in his handling of point of view and imagery, Crane always implicitly allows for errors of perception — his own as well as the men's. Though nature appears at different times in different guises, sometimes cruel, wrathful, deadly to man; sometimes wildly beautiful, picturesque; and sometimes merely indifferent — still none of these aspects, the detached narrator knows, necessarily excludes the others. The language always allows for perceptual error. To the men the waves only "*seemed* thrust up in points like rocks." Seen from a balcony the sea would *doubtless* have been picturesque. It was *probably* splendid, it was *probably* glorious. It merely *occurs* to a man that nature does not regard him as important, and the "high cold star" is the word the correspondent *feels* that nature says to him. Sometimes, as we have seen, the narrator seems to be *in* the boat, seeing and feeling as intensely as the men, sharing sympathetically their conclusions about the meaning of their plight; at other times he seems to be observing their situation from afar, seeing it then critically, dispassionately, or even mockingly.

[16] Consider how the tension between these conflicting points of view is basic to the ironic effect of the argument between the cook and the correspondent about the difference between a life-saving station and a house of refuge. The cook's assertion that they will be rescued by the life-saving crew is like a proposition in a formal debate, challenged after a brief question and answer by the correspondent's formal counter assertion. The futile impasse is moderated by the oiler's "Well, we're not there yet," and then the cook, unwilling to abandon his hopeful position, again asserts his conviction that they will finally be rescued by a crew from the shore. The passage ends with the skeptical oiler's repeated "We're not there yet." The formal design of this colloquy, with its balance and contrast of assertion and counter-assertion and the refrain-like interpolations of the oiler, gives

[17] Andrew H. Wright, "Irony and Fiction," *The Journal of Aesthetics and Art Criticism,* XII (Sept., 1953), 113.

to the men's speculations a tone of ironic presumption. The effect is powerfully reinforced when the narrator later states almost casually: "It is fair to say here that there was not a life-saving station within twenty miles in either direction; but the men did not know this fact, and in consequence they made dark and opprobrious remarks concerning the eyesight of the nation's life-savers."

17   Ironic tension is also sustained in the leitmotifs which refer to various contradictory aspects of nature. To the men, the sea gulls seem at one point to be allies of the hostile sea, for "the wrath of the sea was no more to them than it was to a covey of prairie chickens a thousand miles inland." Against the malice — if indeed it is malice — of the gull which attacks the captain's head, the men are almost helpless. The captain waves it "gently and carefully" away with the heavy painter just as the oiler gingerly and skillfully navigates the hostile sea with a "thin little oar . . . [which] seemed often ready to snap." When the gulls came close "and stared at the men with black beadlike eyes," they then seemed "uncanny and sinister" and "struck their minds at this time as being somehow gruesome and ominous." But only at this time, for later, when the birds are seen going in "slanting flight up the wind toward the gray desolate east," they seem less a symbol of an ineffable, perhaps demoniac malice, than a remote and beautiful design in nature.

18   The shark, the unnamable "thing" whose "enormous fin" cuts "like a shadow through the water" is to the correspondent both admirable and horrifying. Subjectively, it is, like the gulls, a symbol of nature's inscrutable malice; still, in his despair and exhaustion, the correspondent can also see the shark objectively. It does not affect him with "the same horror that it would if he had been a picnicker," and at the same time that he looks dully into the sea and swears in an undertone, he can reflect that "the speed and power of the thing was to be greatly admired." But later the image of this terrible "thing" seems to the narrator to suggest indifference rather than hostility. "The thing which had followed the boat and waited had evidently grown bored at the delay. There was no longer to be heard the slash of the cutwater, and there was no longer the flame of the long trail."

19   In the end the correspondent, to whom the "high cold star" and the wind-tower are the correlatives of nature's indifference, concludes that it is just this which is the significant reality of his experience:

> This tower was a giant, standing with its back to the plight of the ants.
> It represented in a degree, to the correspondent, the serenity of nature
> amid the struggles of the individual — nature in the wind, and nature in
> the vision of men. She did not seem cruel to him then, nor beneficent,
> nor treacherous, nor wise. But she was indifferent, flatly indifferent.

The passage is always read as an expression of not only the correspondent's conclusion, but of Crane's as well, as if at this point in the story the ironic contradictions are resolved in a final statement of the author's naturalistic world view. Daniel Hoffman, commenting on the meaning of the oiler's death, makes the point that the correspondent at the end of the story is still under Crane's ironic inspection, the evidence being according to Hoffman the fact that the correspondent sees not the oiler as the men's true sacrificial savior, but the "haloed and saintlike" vacationer who rushed into the surf to rescue the foundering men. The whole question of the theme of sacrificial death in Crane is, I think, debatable,[18] but Hoffman's feeling that Crane's irony extends beyond the correspondent's final conviction about the relation of man to nature is crucially significant. "The truth of the correspondent's interpretation," Mr. Hoffman says in reference to this failure of consciousness, "lies not in his last impressions but in the manner in which he recreates the entire experience in the reader's imagination." [19]

[20] The correspondent's passionate conviction that his experience has led him to the final truth, however deeply moving, is after all only a passionate conviction. The ironic overtones of other convictions, held at other times just as passionately, echo contradictions. It is suggestive that the story closes on an image of the sea as romantically and mysteriously beautiful:

> When it came night, the white waves paced to and fro in the moonlight, and the wind brought the sound of the great sea's voice to the men on shore, and they felt they could then be interpreters.

Who can say in what various ways the survivors interpret their experience or what one way could be understood to exclude the others? In the reverberating ironies of the last word, charged with the cumulative meanings evoked in the poetic indirections of Crane's style, the final meaning of the men's experience escapes at last into mystery.

[18] A heroic sacrifice would seem to involve a conscious choice on the part of the one who offers himself for immolation. The oiler's death, like Jim Conklin's in *The Red Badge,* is a matter not of choice but of fate.
[19] Daniel G. Hoffman, *The Poetry of Stephen Crane* (Columbia University Press, 1957), p. 278.

Commentary and questions

1. *Paragraphs 1-4:* Colvert summarizes the brand of criticism that places importance on matters other than Crane's style. What is Colvert's definition of "Naturalism"? What, in these paragraphs, suggests that he disagrees with the view of Crane as a "Naturalist"? Compare his summary of the Naturalist position with Brooks's remarks at the beginning of his essay. Which is the more explicit in defining a point of view he dislikes?

2. *Paragraph 5:* Some of the terms associated with Crane's style have specific technical meanings, and a handbook of literary terminology might be helpful.* Something of their meaning can be inferred from their contrast to "Naturalism." Why does Colvert apparently give only qualified approval to Stallman's views?

* See Barnet, S., et al., *The Study of Literature: A Handbook of Critical Essays and Terms.* Boston: Little, Brown, 1960.

3. *Paragraphs 6-8:* How is the conflict of opinion and critical method between Stallman and Rahv useful to Colvert? Precisely what elements in the statements of each does Colvert select for approval?

4. *Paragraphs 8-10:* Colvert wants to establish a means of reading Crane that lies between the extremes of Stallman's allegorical interpretation and Rahv's denial of the importance of style. What are Colvert's general assumptions about the nature of style, and why is it important that he mention them here? What single element in Crane's style does he emphasize in paragraphs 9-10? Find examples in "The Open Boat" other than those listed here.

5. *Paragraphs 12-20:* In one sense these are supporting paragraphs, for they illustrate in detail Colvert's thesis that Crane's central purpose is to be discovered through his style and specifically through the poetic elements in his style. But the paragraphs also develop another definition. What term is defined? Precisely how does it bear on Colvert's thesis?

6. *Paragraph 14:* What is the central distinction here?

7. *Paragraphs 15-16:* What particular elements of style does Colvert select for attention and why?

8. *Paragraphs 17-20:* Does this unit bear out Colvert's earlier statement, in paragraph 9, that "The burden of meaning in his fiction is carried in large part by image, metaphor, recurring motifs, contrasts in tone and mood, and other suggestive devices"? Return to the story to check your answer.

Topics for discussion and writing

I. What is the chief difficulty of a "Naturalistic" interpretation of "The Open Boat"?

II. How many types of support does Colvert use? Cite examples of each and rank them in order of importance.

III. Write a theme in which you support Colvert's reading of Crane's presentation of the irony of nature with examples not cited in the essay.

IV. Write a theme explaining from your own reading of "The Open Boat" precisely how and why "the final meaning of the men's experience escapes at last into mystery" is an accurate statement. If you disagree with the statement, defend your disagreement.

V. Write a theme discussing the specific similarities and differences in the critical assumptions, methods, and purposes of Colvert and Brooks.

Appendix A: SUGGESTIONS FOR EFFICIENT READING

Habit counts for a good deal in reading, and the habits a reader develops should allow him to understand the technique and organization of what he reads. Understanding is never simply an answer to the question, "What does it mean?" It also involves an awareness of an important general consideration.

This consideration, *how* particular meanings are accomplished, is most crucial for the reader when he is faced with essays and books that are more complex and difficult than he has been used to before. In such a situation his first instinct is probably to look up unfamiliar words in the dictionary, and within limits that instinct is the right one. But the dictionary definitions of new words are never enough to thoroughly establish their meanings in particular contexts. When words are fitted together in discourse, dictionary meanings are narrowed or expanded, and the writer invests them with tones and attitudes that carry over from word to word or change as the discourse moves forward.

Because writers use old words to fashion new meanings, the reader must be alert both to dictionary definitions and to the special senses, attitudes, and tones imposed by the individual author, and he must be alert to these things all at once. The reader cannot assume that he may resort to the dictionary for one paragraph and study the connotations or emotional overtones of another. To find exact meanings, a good rule to follow is to look for words that the writer seems to consider important and at the same time to ask why they seem important. Consider the following paragraph, which, though not especially difficult, makes its point indirectly:

> Most people who bother with the matter at all would admit that the English language is in a bad way, but it is generally assumed that we cannot by conscious action do anything about it. Our civilization is decadent and our language — so the argument runs — must inevitably share in the general collapse. It follows that any struggle against the abuse of language is a sentimental archaism, like preferring candles to electric light or hansom cabs to aeroplanes. Underneath this lies the half-conscious belief that language is a natural growth and not an instrument which we shape for our own purposes. (*From George Orwell, "Politics and the English Language"; see p. 41.*)

539

There are a number of words here that can be tentatively assumed to be important: "English language," "bad way," "conscious action," "decadent," "natural growth," "shape." "English language," a term that occurs in the title of Orwell's essay, conforms to the general subject of the essay; the others fall into categories which indicate that there is a condition that everyone deplores and two possible attitudes toward that condition. These two attitudes are directly opposed.

Thus far we have used a few words extracted from the paragraphs as handy references to its apparent meaning. Orwell's topic is the English language and the ways in which it is seen to grow and change. But in every sentence there are clues to a more specific and less obvious meaning. The statements Orwell makes refer to the views of others; he does not state his own but seems merely to report general opinion. The careless reader, if asked what it is Orwell has to say, might well paraphrase thus: "Orwell thinks the English language is in a bad way, and he says that nothing can be done about it." There is, of course, some excuse for this paraphrase. Orwell devotes most attention to the view that it is impossible to correct the decadence of the English language. The phrase "it is generally assumed" indicates a majority opinion. When he says "It follows," Orwell appears to adopt this argument as his own, and the analogy to "preferring candles to electric light or hansom cabs to aeroplanes" seems to annihilate by ridicule the opposing point of view about language. "Sentimental archaism" apparently works in the same direction.

A closer look at the paragraph shows that Orwell never explicitly says that *he* believes nothing can be done about the state of the English language, and there are a number of careful reservations in his reporting of that view. "So the argument runs" is a phrase that permits him to remain aloof from the difference of opinion he presents. "Most people" and "it is generally assumed" do not necessarily commit him to general opinion. Futhermore, the refutation of the view that the state of the language can be corrected is almost too easy, and the last phrase in the paragraph, "an instrument which we shape for our own purposes" may well refer to a concept on which Orwell places value. The emotional effects of the paragraph thus work in two ways, and many readers concerned with the state of the language and anxious to find a solution would hardly classify themselves as "sentimental" or their views as "archaisms." In other words, Orwell's position may well be just the opposite of the point of view to which he gives the most attention. A final judgment of Orwell's opinion must wait for further reading, and, as a matter of fact, he does believe that something can be done and suggests some remedies. But if we confine our reading to this paragraph alone we must recognize that that is only a possibility and accept the paragraph for what it is, a series of statements that present the issue to be discussed, two points of view from which it may be treated, and a preparation for the rest of the essay.

In summary, these are the steps we have taken: (1) a tentative selection of what seem to be the more important words; (2) next a grouping of those words according to the concepts they point to; (3) a decision about the type of statement Orwell is making. This is the most important step, for it involves our understanding of Orwell's own point of view and, if at first glance we are inclined to think that Orwell favors the view to which he seems to give most weight, it leads us to examine the implications of the paragraph, its emotional effect, its tone, the connotations of its language. Thus we are prompted to see that Orwell may be saying the opposite of what he seems to be saying. The fact that no certain decision is possible on the basis of this paragraph alone is likely to draw us on to what follows with more interest than if he had shown his hand at once.

Not every paragraph we read can be analyzed so closely, and the experienced reader is likely to follow a process such as this almost automatically. His attention is trained to work quickly and efficiently and accurately where the novice may have to proceed slowly and deliberately. And the reader confronted with writing that may at first seem beyond his depth will do well to analyze the words, statements, and connotations of sample paragraphs to test and exercise the accuracy of his attention. There is no need to work in the order presented here, but there is a definite value in being systematic, for then what is read will assume a greater order and clarity in the reader's mind.

Analytical reading on a larger scale requires the same sense of method. It also demands close attention to the structure of paragraphs — to the type and order of statements — and to the ways in which successive paragraphs are put together. Here again the writer's meaning is inseparable from his discoverable purpose and from the technique he uses to further the presentation of his meaning. The following paragraphs are the first three* in David Riesman's essay "Thoughts on Teachers and Schools" and are chosen to illustrate a number of things that are common to expository structure: (1) the method by which a writer particularizes his statements and illustrates them; (2) the utility of classification; (3) significant order in the presentation of detail; (4) the importance of recognizing the links between paragraphs; (5) the way assumptions operate; (6) the understanding of connotation as a clue to the author's purpose and point of view.

1   One way of looking at American society at present is to divide it into groups of people: one, a relatively small white-collar and professional group who work long hours and bear disproportionate responsibilities; and the other, a relatively large group who work short hours (even if one does not include coffee breaks) and bear few taxing responsibilities. This latter group includes the millions of forty-hour-per-week workers, of thirty-hour-per-week school children, and of retired people.

* A more complete selection from the same source, "Thoughts on Teachers and Schools," appears in this book on pp. 81-91.

2   American life is, of course, unevenly mechanized and systematized, and the first-named group must fill in for America's deficiencies—and rise to its challenges—out of their personal energies and at the frequent expense of their own budget of leisure and ease. Some in this group of people are industrial managers, well-paid in money and prestige for worrying about productivity, the meaning of which has been extended to include employee morale, health, psychological security, and general happiness; and for worrying about selling a product, a transaction which now embraces many novel private and public services (budgeted for under "good will"). Some in this group of people are high civil servants, paid neither in money nor in unambiguous prestige for worrying about the resentments of the rest of the world. Some of these people are doctors, paid with very great prestige and moderately great fees for working sixty- and seventy-hour weeks to repair the health of a nation which can increasingly afford health, and which redefines it to extend from the somatic to the psychosomatic to the psychosocial, and from the cure of acute illness to the prevention of debility and the extension and beatitude of the life span. And some of the people in this first group of overtime worriers are professors, perhaps increasingly bitter about pay and prestige, and more and more harassed in trying to make sense of their data (too much of it, and too equivocal), of each other (more conferences, committees, and projects than ever), and of their students (more of whom can now afford college and fewer of whom, for reasons we shall examine, come with elementary literacy). Even so, these professors' pay and prestige, if it appears low to them, is worlds above that of most public school teachers, and the latter also have many more compulsory classroom hours (though there are a few, in the best city and suburban systems, who will fare better financially than, for instance, a classics professor at a small non-ivy campus). Indeed, many members of this first group are "paid" for their long hours by the variety and freedom their work permits: they prefer accepting even wearisome responsibilities to enduring meaningless routines under others' supervision.

3   Public school teachers are, in all probability, the largest aggregation of those who, themselves left behind by industrial advance and the general shortening and lightening of hours, must supply much of the energy for that advance and much of the training for the work-free future of their pupils. Teachers are in fact the archetype of these white-collar functionaries, who, in helping bring about a society of greater abundance, have their own official and unofficial lives torn and complicated in the process. The teaching function, since it does involve the training or "guidance" of children for an era of abundance, has been extended to include training in group co-operation, manners, the arts, and self-understanding, as well as in large residues of the traditional curriculum. Teachers, therefore, are under growing pressure to provide a "happy and rounded atmosphere" in the classroom, while they themselves lead lives of harried desperation, not only because of the multiplying demands of the classroom, but because of the many "voluntary" activities expected of them: advising the dramatics or journalism club, consulting with parents, partici-

pating in civic and church groups. Many feel they must use their "vacations" attending summer school to acquire needed credits, or earning
extra money with summer camps. (*From "Thoughts on Teachers and
Schools" by David Riesman, The Anchor Review, No. 1. Reprinted by
permission of the author and editor.*)

One of the first things apparent about these three paragraphs is that they
move from rather broad topics to more and more particular issues: "looking
at American society" in the opening paragraph narrows to the financial problems of public school teachers in the third paragraph. Something else happens in the process. The reader might suppose that the more particular issue
exists to illustrate something about the broader one, that teachers' finances
prove some point about American society. But the reverse seems to be true;
American society is called in to serve as a context for discussion about
"teachers and schools." The general issue is the background that shows up
the particular.

Secondly there are a number of things Riesman says about American
society which govern the things he is going to say about teachers and
schools, and he here uses a method of classification dividing American society into various groups according to occupation. First there is the distinction between "a relatively small white-collar and professional group" and
"a relatively large group," that is, workers, students, and retired people. The
second paragraph discusses the white-collar group, dividing it according to
three criteria: monetary compensation, duties performed, and their difficulties. Note that Riesman's method of classification also involves distinctions,
first a large one between white-collar group and workers, and next a somewhat more precise one that allows him to discriminate between industrial
managers, civil servants, doctors, professors, and public school teachers.
Thus the method of the first two paragraphs is much more than an association of public school teachers with others of a similar kind; it also isolates
teachers from the others, suggesting that they do not enjoy the rewards that
other professionals have. In other words, as Riesman classifies, he provides
a motive for talking about teachers.

The public school teachers appear last on the list, not simply because
they can therefore be made more prominent, but also because Riesman wants
to furnish a basis on which to give his remarks on teachers a further significance. Notice what is accomplished by the order of the details in paragraph 2: members of the professional group are associated with responsibilities, prestige, and high compensation. As the paragraph proceeds, the
comparative scale of income goes down. Doctors receive "moderately great
fees"; professors are "increasingly bitter about pay and prestige"; public
school teachers are by comparison ill-paid and enjoy little prestige. The only
exception in this order are "high civil servants" but they are underpaid by
comparison to industrial managers and, perhaps, doctors. Their prestige is
ambiguous; that is, it can be desirable or not. The unspoken suggestion is

that professors and public school teachers have worries and responsibilities like those of civil servants and, like them, lack proper compensation. The industrial manager and the doctor, on the other hand, are duly paid for their hard work and heavy, important duties. Finally, Riesman lays increasing stress, throughout the paragraph, on the burdens the professional man must bear: the "wearisome responsibilities" are linked most intimately with his description of professors and teachers. The structure of the paragraph thus indicates the specific comparative position of public school teachers according to the criteria established in Riesman's system of classification.

The fourth consideration, the links between paragraphs, is fairly clear in this selection. The first and second paragraphs are tied together by continuity of phrasing: "American society" is matched by "American life," while "the first-named group" in the second paragraph proceeds directly from the division Riesman has made in the first paragraph. These are signs that he intends to work within the framework of the categories he uses (the second consideration).

When we move to the links between the second and third paragraphs we also notice verbal signs indicating continuity of discussion. "Public school teachers" are the last item of detail in paragraph 2, and although the end of the paragraph returns to a brief discussion of the entire "first group" ("white-collar workers" or "professionals"), Riesman merely has to begin the third paragraph with "Public school teachers" to maintain the focus of his emphasis. But the three paragraphs are concerned with more than just a treatment of public school teachers and other professional groups. There is, as we have noted, a wider context of discussion, involving the working conditions of American society as a whole. Thus we are drawn back to the first paragraph where Riesman has mentioned the shorter hours and "few taxing responsibilities" of the "relatively large group." This group and its circumstances are now important because Riesman thinks that school teachers are especially involved with it: they "must supply much of the energy for that advance and much of the training for the work-free future of their pupils." Thus the third paragraph serves to draw together paragraphs 1 and 2 in a new way, uniting the larger conditions of American economic life with the special conditions of the professional group, and we are to remember that the teachers illustrate the conditions of professional life in an especially sharp way. Riesman reminds us of this, for he calls teachers "the archetype" and goes on to explain precisely why. Note that we have delayed analysis of the third paragraph, because its purpose in analyzing the conditions of teachers' role in society is better understood if its connections with the other two paragraphs are clear.

In paragraph 3 Riesman is no longer classifying as he did before; rather he is making distinctions so as to illuminate a paradoxical situation. Teachers must train their pupils for a kind of life that they themselves are denied, and the latter half of paragraph 3 illustrates this assertion in some detail.

Riesman's illustrations of his basic assertions are factual, but he does not document his facts, perhaps because he assumes that no one will dispute them and perhaps also because his aim is to interpret conditions acknowledged to exist. His remarks about the pay and prestige and working conditions of various groups refer to typical situations, and most readers could confirm some of these "facts" from their own experience. It is true that Riesman's facts are not scientifically exact. They include no statistics, and the use of accurate statistics might lead a critic to modify his remarks about the pay of civil servants, for example. But generally Riesman is trying to illustrate his points by reference to conditions he believes that most readers would accept as true. A quick check with any teacher or school superintendent would no doubt confirm most of the statements in the third paragraph.

But there are other assumptions upon which Riesman's discussion rests. One of them is that American society is an affluent one and is dedicated to leisure. Without these assumptions his remarks about the plight of the white-collar group and teachers in particular would be seriously weakened. The discussions of industrial managers and doctors in paragraph 2 and of teachers in paragraph 3 most pointedly suggest an atmosphere of affluence and leisure, and we can refer to such incidental phrases as "industrial advance" or "the general shortening and lightening of hours" to confirm our impression of what Riesman assumes. Here, of course, there may be room for debate. It might be argued that Riesman takes these conditions too much for granted, that workers and the aged or retired are not so secure and unburdened by worry and responsibility as he suggests. Whatever he decides, the careful reader should recognize these assumptions and keep them in mind if he wishes to test the validity of Riesman's argument.

Our five considerations so far have pretty well established Riesman's purpose and point of view, but our awareness of it can be intensified if we attend to the connotations of some of the words he uses. "Long hours," "short hours," "responsibilities," "America's deficiencies," "challenges," "energies," "general happiness," and a number of other similar terms refer to matters that concern the lives of most of us. These are things we worry about and by which we measure our own conditions. At the very least Riesman's use of such words is likely to command our attention. Moreover, he uses them and another group of terms relating to the rewards of money and prestige to suggest that there is a basic unfairness in the make-up of American society: those who perform the most essential and difficult services are badly compensated. Riesman is appealing to our sense of justice.

One might go much further in discussing the persuasive elements of these three paragraphs, but this is enough to suggest the author's method and purpose, and together the six considerations under which this analysis has been conducted should reveal what can be discovered by systematic reading. More important, it is only close reading that allows us to say with confidence that we know what a writer means and to estimate fairly the value of his meaning.

Looked at from another angle, this process of analysis is an extension of an outline, or, perhaps, six outlines. And even though such outlines may exist only in the reader's mind, they nevertheless give him a tool with which to manage his reading efficiently. At first it is well to begin by writing down outlines for every essay read. The type may vary: it may be a paragraph outline, substituting a sentence for every paragraph. It may be a topic outline (this would be much better for the Riesman selection, for it would make clearer the ways in which he works his topics together and develops them), which organizes the main divisions of idea according to their relative importance. And the making of such an outline would give rise to various questions: Are the ideas comparatively or contrastingly related? Do they give particular explanations for general ideas? Do they develop by the addition of detail to detail according to some principle of selection (chronological, descriptive, etc.)? Do they proceed by posing a question and suggesting possible answers, some of which are rejected and others retained? The sentence outline simply covers main topics by stating them as complete sentences; it does not necessarily follow paragraph divisions. In any case, whatever type of outline is used it should be so constructed as to point to the author's technique of discussion. For example, we might use something like the following for the three paragraphs of Riesman:

    I. American society divides in two according to criteria of pay and responsibilities.
      A. White-collar group has heavy responsibilities.
      B. Workers and others have short hours, few responsibilities.
    II. White-collar group generally sacrifices leisure and ease.
      A. Industrial managers and doctors are well-paid for this sacrifice.
      B. Civil servants, professors, and especially teachers are poorly paid for sacrifice.
    III. Teachers epitomize the plight of the white-collar group.
      A. They work hard to create an affluent and leisured society for others.
      B. They themselves lead lives of harried desperation.

This outline suggests the substance of Riesman's discussion, and the process of particularizing against the background of general social and economic conditions; it points up the comparisons and distinctions Riesman makes and the order in which he makes them; and it roughly indicates Riesman's point of view. No outline can contain the subtler elements in writing: the finer points of tone and attitude need more extensive analysis. But the outline does provide a shorthand method of locating the major features of a piece of writing and isolating them for further study.

The habits of outlining and methodical analysis are the main avenues to efficient and perceptive reading, but there are other devices that may be of help from time to time. The paraphrase, in which the reader translates the author's words into his own often gives a simplified version of what is meant. But by itself the paraphrase is not enough. The analyses of the paragraphs from Orwell and Riesman make use of limited paraphrase, but they go beyond it. An inexperienced reader who contents himself with paraphrase is apt to ignore his own distortion of an author's meaning. Paraphrase should always be part of the larger process of analysis.

Finally, two suggestions should be helpful: (1) Always examine closely those words and phrases a writer tends to use more than once or twice. They usually embody concepts the writer thinks important, and they may simplify the problem of following the development of his main thesis. (2) Wherever possible it is good practice to take notes in the margin, as well as on a separate sheet of paper. Marginal notes simplify the task of rereading, and they encourage a reader in the habit of fastening his attention to what is essential.

The following essays of moderate difficulty may be used for beginning analyses:

1. George Orwell, "Paddy," pp. 198-205
2. John M. Synge, "The Vagrants of Wicklow," pp. 183-187
3. George Jean Nathan, "One Man's Belief," pp. 488-496
4. William H. Whyte, Jr., "The Organization Children," pp. 60-68
5. Winston Churchill, "Leon Trotsky, *Alias* Bronstein," pp. 110-116

Appendix B: PLANNING AND ORGANIZING A THEME

Every paper that you write will pose its own problems. Every paper is different. But the fact that makes it possible to teach composition is that most papers have similar problems, too. Every theme is about something, and although at first glance this fact might not seem concrete enough to be valuable, it actually gives a good beginning.

Every paper has some basic topic, and before you begin you should know exactly what your subject is. The best way to assure that you do is to write down in one succinct, concrete statement (a thesis sentence) just what your paper is to discuss. The more definite you are, the more likely you are to have a good paper, for a concrete thesis statement indicates a clear concept of the paper-to-be. And clarity of intention at the outset is crucial.

Although the thesis sentence is the first thing to write, it cannot be set down without important preliminaries, the first of which is an analysis of the topic itself. In your analysis, two questions should be posed: What does the topic ask for? What concepts or terms must be clarified before the topic can be clearly understood?

Here, for example, is one of the suggested topics for writing which you will find elsewhere in this book: "Write a theme comparing [Jack] London's narrative technique to that of [John M.] Synge" (p. 198). What must you know to write on this topic? You begin, of course, reading the essay by London and the essay by Synge. Next, you examine their narrative techniques. But what is "narrative technique"? What exactly does the topic ask for?

As a part of a topic for writing, the term does not occur in the same vacuum as it does here. It is examined against a background of reading, class discussion, and questions in the text. With these in mind, several statements can be made to clarify "narrative technique." Narrative technique is the author's presentation of his material by means of a chronological structure. This statement helps, but it does not get to the purpose of the question; it merely repeats the topic in different words. What is implied by a question on such a topic as narrative technique? Why does the instructor want a theme on this particular topic? In this case you know that you have been examining the uses of description and the emphasis and selection of details. You know that these readings occur in the part of the book that is devoted to such matters as statements and assumptions. You know that other questions on the two essays deal with the way these authors convey their attitudes and ideas. In short, you know that the phrase "narrative technique" should be interpreted partly in terms of the purpose of the topic, and that purpose is not isolated but fits into the context of the course itself. Thus, even if your instructor does not explain the topic, there is enough evidence to decide that "narrative technique" can be interpreted to mean an author's use of chronological structure to convey the facts of a situation as well as his own attitudes, assumptions, and interpretations. An examination of the essays of London and Synge with this concept of narrative technique in mind will show that both authors are doing a great deal more than merely narrating incidents.

What does the topic ask you to do with this information? It asks that you *compare* London and Synge. The word "compare" usually means show similarities and differences, though the word is ambiguous; some instructors may ask for a development of similarities only. Unless your instructor limits the term, let it mean both similarities and differences.

Analysis of the topic is an essential preliminary in any writing you do. The next step is to compare the techniques of London and Synge. The best policy here is to let the comparison wait and develop your ideas of the techniques of each author separately. If you start your comparison too soon, you may well distort the ideas of one man or the other. Go through the essays jotting down what you consider the main points to be made in discussing the technique of each. The excellence of your comparison will depend largely upon the validity of these separate analyses.

Now you are ready to draw your two analyses together, to begin the actual comparison itself. The misleading tendency most writers show at this point is to arrange things neatly so that one author's characteristics either contrast or show likeness to a corresponding trait in the other author. If you have made your individual analyses carefully, your evidence will probably show that most things, people, ideas, and techniques are not either exactly alike or totally different and that not all points you make about the work of one man will have corresponding points in the work of the other. A valid comparison is one that does not rely on easy, surface judgments, but searches out similarities and differences that really exist and reveal something worth knowing.

You are now dealing with the specific problem proposed by the question. But you are not yet ready for a thesis sentence because you do not yet know what your conclusions are. Writing should come after you know what you think.

For your comparison you should work with points that are in some way significant. The longer the paper you plan, the more liberal your definition of "significant" can be. Arrange your ideas in three rough groups: those that seem to be alike, those that seem to be different, and those that don't correspond at all. In other words, classify your evidence. As you reach this point you get your first methodically supported inkling of what your paper will be like. Now you examine your evidence carefully. Draw your conclusion about similarities and differences in the author's techniques. This conclusion will be the point of your paper. A selection of the evidence you used will furnish supporting illustrations.

Now you are ready to write your thesis sentence. This sentence forces you to make a definitive statement of the content of your paper. It is also influential in that it often controls the structure of the paper. Suppose, for example, your thesis sentence states that the narrative techniques of London and Synge are alike in three specified ways. The likelihood is that your paper will open with a statement of the similarity and continue with three supporting sections. Suppose your thesis states: London and Synge seem in specified ways to differ; actually they convey forcefully their own ideas and impressions. You have committed this paper to a different sort of structure. The influence of the thesis sentence is neither good nor bad; it is simply a fact that every writer ought to be aware of in order to use it to his own advantage.

After finding a thesis, organize your theme around it. If there is an organization inherent in the thesis, it is usually a good idea to follow it, for it is usually logical, representing a coherent development of the topic. If there is no inherent structure, you must arrange your points in a logical, effective order. The general principal to remember here is that your main points should either refer back, or ahead, to your thesis; or each ought to relate in a logical way to the point that precedes it and the one that follows. Of course you will often mix these forms, but you should be aware of it when you do and understand for what purpose you are doing it.

Here is a recapitulation of the steps so far taken:

(1) Analysis of the topic to see what it means and what it asks the writer to do.
(2) An analysis of the essays themselves.
(3) With the purpose of the paper in mind, coming to a conclusion about the essays.
(4) Statement of the conclusion as a thesis sentence, keeping in mind that the form of the thesis sentence may well determine the final structure of the paper.
(5) Organization of the paper from the thesis sentence.

A comparison has been used as an example so far because it requires explicit preparation and organization. Skipping any of the steps listed above may well result in failure to carry out the assigned comparison. The most common deficiency in papers of comparison is the thesis itself. These papers, as a consequence, reveal nothing. They simply record that London does this; Synge does that. Points are listed side by side, but there is little or no attempt to decide how they are different, why they are different, or why their differences are worth thinking about. Such discussions may make points, but they do not develop ideas.

Now you have decided what your thesis is, what your main points and supporting evidence are, and the order in which you will present your points. Write them down in outline form. A desirable form for papers of a thousand words or less is a two-level, sentence outline arranged topically. A two-level outline (Roman numerals and capital letters only) keeps your detail out of the outline. The sentence form requires a complete, explicit statement of the material to be covered under each head. Arranging outline heads topically allows you to see the relationship, or lack of relationship, among the parts of the paper.

The first paragraph is always the hardest for the writer who does not know exactly what his theme is to be about. If you know what you are going to write on and have planned how to do it, making a start is usually less of a problem. There is no "right" way. Some themes begin with the thesis sentence; others may open with a statement of the problem. Some writers believe that a subject ought to be introduced, though only long papers can usually afford space for this luxury. Whatever the actual opening sentence, the purpose of the paper ought to be expressed explicitly somewhere early in the paper, and it is often desirable to add how you intend to accomplish the purpose.

A theme is a series of developed ideas (main points in a certain order and supporting evidence or illustration) which relate to one another and to a central idea (thesis). The developed ideas will consist of paragraphs and groups of paragraphs. For the sake of simplicity, we will consider them here as paragraphs.

The paragraph is like the whole theme in that it should have a single, explicitly stated subject. While the topic sentence is not a necessity, it is most desirable, for it furnishes the writer an explicit idea to develop. A paragraph with an implied subject can be misleading to the writer as well as to the reader, for it allows supporting statements and instances to masquerade as the main idea.

The idea stated in the topic sentence should be developed fully, logically, and with the proper sort of supporting evidence or materials. The most common type of developmental material is instances and details. These are used either to limit or to clarify the topic. They may do both in the same paragraph. If you are writing on the rebel, for example, one of your topic sentences might very well be "Winston Churchill shows a great deal of sympathy for Boris Savinkov." This statement could be supported by citing three significant points in the essay which evince a sympathetic attitude. In order to make sure, however, that your reader does not think Churchill is wholly sympathetic, you might want to add "But Churchill has many reservations, too." You might then cite an instance illustrating Churchill's lack of approval. If you wrote such a paragraph you would have stated your ideas explicitly, but you would not have *one* topic sentence. Your idea would be contained in two sentences. Instances selected from the essay would illustrate your ideas, though you would have shown the limitations on Churchill's approval by further illustrations.

The necessity for full and intelligent use of instances, details, comparison and contrast, statement, anecdote, and other means of development is absolute. It is one mark of the good writer and careful thinker. Without such material a paper is reduced to generalizations — and the unsupported, unmodified, or sweeping generalization is the tool of the demagogue, not of the man whose interest is truth.

The final step in any plan should be reappraisal. Sometimes this is called rewriting, but the word "rewriting" suggests the mere changing of words and phrases, and this is not enough. Any paper ought to be examined to see whether it contains an explicit statement of purpose, whether the main ideas are arranged in the most effective order, whether the ideas are fully developed and whether each of them maintains a proper proportion with the others. Of course it is also important to subject sentence structure and word choice to the same careful scrutiny.

There is a good deal more to "writing" a paper than taking pen in hand. Writing is only one step, actually a late one, in thinking through the problem, coming to a conclusion, and expressing that conclusion with adequate explanation and support.

Index

References in boldface are to the introductory discussions, *e.g.*, **8-16**, or to the commentary, questions, and topics, in which case they include item numbers, *e.g.*, **18.6**.

References to rhetorical matters in the readings are illustrative and include paragraph numbers, *e.g.*, 54.1-58.18.